NEW YORK

NEW YORK

A COLLECTION FROM
HARPER'S MAGAZINE

GALLERY BOOKS
An Imprint of W. H. Smith Publishers Inc.
112 Madison Avenue
New York City 10016

This volume first published in 1991 by
Reed International Books Limited
Michelin House, 81 Fulham Road, London SW3 6RB

This edition published in 1991 by Gallery Books
an imprint of W. H. Smith Publishers Inc.
112 Madison Avenue, New York 10016

ISBN 0 - 8317 - 4257 - 7

Printed in Great Britain by The Bath Press, Avon.

CONTENTS

APPROACHES TO NEW YORK 7

THE DUTCH FOUNDING OF NEW YORK (PART 1) 15

MANHATTAN LIGHTS 28

THE NEW YORK STOCK EXCHANGE 37

A HASHISH-HOUSE IN NEW YORK....................................62

GREENWICH VILLAGE 69

NEW YORK REVISITED (PART 1) 88

NEW YORK - CITY OF ROMANCE 95

THE EVOLUTION OF NEW YORK (PART 1) 107

LONDON AND NEW YORK..124

THE STORY OF A STREET (PART 1) 133

THE PROBLEM OF LIVING IN NEW YORK.........................141

THE VOLUNTEER FIRE DEPARTMENT (PART 1)..............148

OLD NEW YORK COFFEE-HOUSES.....................................166

THE DUTCH FOUNDING OF NEW YORK (PART 2)..........185

DOWN LOVE LANE 197

THE EVOLUTION OF NEW YORK (PART 2) 211

SUPERSTITIONS OF A COSMOPOLITAN CITY 226

THE STORY OF A STREET (PART 2) 230

ITALIAN LIFE IN NEW YORK..240

LITERARY NEW YORK...249

NEW YORK REVISITED (PART 2) 261

THE BROOKLYN BRIDGE 267

THE STORY OF A STREET (PART 3) 289

EAST-SIDE CONSIDERATIONS 299

NEW YORK COLONIAL PRIVATEERS 310

THE VOLUNTEER FIRE DEPARTMENT (PART 2) 321

IN UP-TOWN NEW YORK 332

THE STORY OF A STREET (PART 4) 341

THE NEW YORK CUSTOM-HOUSE 350

CERTAIN NEW YORK HOUSES 374

NEW YORK REVISITED (PART 3) 385

LISPENARD'S MEADOWS 393

THE STORY OF A STREET (PART 5) 402

THE NEW YORK POLICE DEPARTMENT 411

RIDING IN NEW YORK 435

THE CITY TO THE NORTH OF 'TOWN' 448

SEA ROBBERS OF NEW YORK 461

THE DUTCH FOUNDING OF NEW YORK (PART 3) 476

THE ICE AGE ABOUT NEW YORK 487

THE STORY OF A STREET (PART 6) 495

THE CITY OF BROOKLYN 504

THE NEW YORK COMMON SCHOOLS 525

THE METROPOLITAN OPERA HOUSE 531

APPROACHES TO NEW YORK

Fort Lafayette.

AT THE NARROWS.

I.—BY THE SEA.

THOSE who have approached New York by the sea need not be told that the harbor of New York is exceedingly beautiful. It has also other advantages. It is not separated from the ocean by a long river like the Thames, nor by an island wall like Ireland, as Liverpool is, and while the Atlantic beats up to the very entrance, the turbulence of the sea is shut out by a circle of hills which form a basin large enough to shelter all the fleets of the world. The conformation of the estuary lends itself to a system of fortification which in the event of war could be made impregnable; the bar admits vessels of the largest draught at all seasons; the shoals are in a measure permanent, and do not harass the mariner by the gradual changes which in some harbors necessitate the discovery of new passages; the currents are not strong or treacherous, and the beacons, lights, and buoys are numerous and distinct. The many captains to whom I have spoken at various times in reference to New York Harbor have all praised it for its capacity, safety, and ease of access. If it has any disadvantages, they are such as result from the far-reaching corruption and incompetency of the municipal government.

The bluffs of the Highlands and the sandy spit of the Hook are passed; then the quiet embouchure of Raritan Bay, with fleets of fishing-boats. On one side Staten Island, hilly, and green to the water's edge, bends to meet the opposite shore, and where the distance between them is

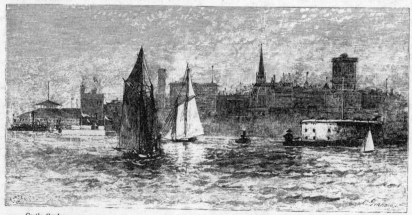

Castle Garden.

VIEW OF NEW YORK FROM BELOW GOVERNOR'S ISLAND.

EASTERN STEAMERS ROUNDING THROGG'S NECK.

least stand Fort Richmond and Fort Hamilton, which together could hurl such fire upon an invader as would cripple him at the portals of the city.

Just beyond the Narrows (as the passage between the forts is called) the two shores curve further apart, forming the upper bay, at the head of which the city lies. A blue haze wreathes itself around Staten Island, upon the heights of which are villas that, from a distance at least, appear tasteful and attractive. The Long Island shore, losing the white, barren, sandy aspect it has outside the Narrows, becomes woody and fertile. The water is a clear green, and even the vessels have a holiday cleanness novel to the emigrant, who, before he reaches Castle Garden, is charmed by the little he sees of his future home.

If we should say there are safe moorings for nearly all the navies of the world, our readers would still be unable to comprehend the vast space available in the harbor. Measurements are more explicit. The Hudson or North River washes thirteen miles of the city's shore-line, every foot of which may be made available for vessels of the greatest tonnage; the East River washes nine and a quarter miles, most of which may also be made available to vessels of all classes; and the Harlem River has an available frontage of two and a quarter miles. The area of the Hudson and East rivers immediately opposite the city which is available for anchorage is thirteen and a half square miles, the anchorage of the upper bay is fourteen square miles, and that of the lower bay eighty-eight square miles. Thus, besides twenty-four and a half miles of wharfage, we have over one hundred and fifteen square miles so safe that the gale would need to be of uncommon force which could drag a ship whose anchor had been cast upon any spot of this wide area.

II.—BY THE SOUND.

But the channels through the bays are not the only inlet from the sea to the city, though all vessels of the greatest burden select them. Another approach is by the way of Long Island Sound, which is stirred by a hurrying fleet of smaller traders, both sail and steam.

The Sound itself is wide and deep enough for any vessels, and though the waves run high after prolonged storms,

Long Island is interposed between it and the ocean. On both sides of it there are fashionable summer resorts, quiet old fishing villages with primitive inhabitants, and long expanses of prosperous farm-land. In the summer weather its banks blend the charms of the country and the shore. From a stretch of pasturage or the porch of a farm-house we look down upon a motionless schooner with brown sails, or a snowy yacht so airy and phantom-like that she appears to be hung in a mirage.

At the southwestern extremity the Sound becomes a narrow strait with low grassy banks. There are boat-houses at the water's edge, and trim little cat-boats and sloops are moored to private wharves. Straggling little canals lead off into the sedge, which ripples in the wind; and along here, toward five o'clock in the afternoon, is a sight which can not be seen anywhere else in the world. Between the low banks, and towering above them, come the steamers which connect at New London, Stonington, Providence, and Fall River with the railway for Boston, their colors streaming, and the passengers promenading to the music of their string bands. These vessels are the principal feature of travel on the Sound, and in size and luxury of appointments they are superior to all others. They rival in size and surpass in beauty ocean steamers, and their brilliant whiteness and gay flags are reflected in the water, which swells and dashes in big waves on the shore as they pass. Another fleet comes from the opposite direction in the morning; and standing at the bow of one of these as we round Throgg's Neck and Fort Schuyler, we may briefly end our survey of the second approach to New York from the sea. We pass Ward's and Randall's islands with their enormous red brick charities; the Harlem curves off to the northwest; and here, where that river and the Sound join the East River, a strong current shows the former site of Hell Gate. Now our course is almost due south down the East River, which for nearly half a mile is divided into two channels by Blackwell's Island, with its work-houses, hospitals, and prisons; then the stream widens from an eighth of a mile or less to a mile, and the view on both sides includes the half-hidden streets, the close buildings, and the roofy wilderness of the metropolis. Soon the boat passes under the wide span of the Brooklyn Bridge, and, rounding the Battery, reaches its pier on the Hudson River.

III.—BY RAIL AND FERRY FROM THE WEST.

Whoever has approached the city as a stranger must remember the experience of some emotion which is revived, in memory at least, as often as he retraces the path. The character of the emotion is determined by the object which brings the pilgrim hither; it may be hope, apprehension, or delight; and the quiet observer may see all of these at work among the passengers on a train that has come a long distance toward New York. After leaving Trenton, which, though it is some fifty miles from this city, is an outpost of it in the idea of those who have travelled a thousand miles, the stations and the villages became more and more frequent; the road widens, and has four tracks, and we are constantly meeting other trains. Big signs confront us with offers of desirable building sites, and we see gangs of workmen putting up new villas and laying open new streets. New Brunswick, Elizabeth, and Newark are left behind, and then the landscape changes. The suburban cottage with its garden and orchard and suggestiveness of tranquil domesticity, the plenteous farm-lands, the growing little towns with the chiming of the trowels, are absent, and instead we see a great flat wilderness of brownish-green marshes, stagnant but for the train, which, if we could stand away from it and watch, would appear like some long black monster hurrying through the desert. The Passaic River flows alongside the tracks for some distance, and winds off into Newark Bay; we are carried over the Hackensack on a high bridge, which gently sways under the weight upon it. At times a wonderful light dwells on the dull green sedge of the marshes, which at sunset glows with crimson fires that give it a grandeur many artists have found out. At the edge of the marshes we are whirled through another village, and thence the railway is in a deep rock cutting, with a sharp curve that suddenly brings you into Jersey City, through which we are carried between two rows of shops and dwellings, with only a low fence on each side to separate the track from the street. A quick transfer is made to the ferry-boats which are in waiting, partings are said, a gong is struck, and in ten minutes more we

West Shore Railroad.

Brooklyn Bridge.

VIEW OF NEW YORK FROM WEEHAWKEN HEIGHTS, NEW JERSEY.

Del. and Lac. R.R., Erie R.R., Pa. R.R., and Cent. R.R. of N. J.

APPROACH TO NEW YORK BY THE HUDSON.

stand in a crowd of solicitous hack-drivers and expressmen on the New York side.

The tonnage of the ferry-boats now in use varies from seven hundred and twenty-five to one thousand and twenty-two, the value of each of them is over one hundred thousand dollars, and the computed horse-power of one is seven hundred and twenty-five. Unlike the English ferry-boats, which are ocean steamers in miniature, these are a type by themselves; their hulls support a huge deck overhanging the water, and stout enough to resist all sorts of "bumps"; in the centre is a roadway divided into two parts by the narrow space required for the walking-beam which drives the side-wheels; and on either side is a long, covered cabin for foot-passengers. The deck is rounded at both ends, and as the boat reaches her landing "end on," it fits closely into the "slip." It is as though a section of roadway shuttled to and fro between the shores; and the living freight loads and unloads itself down the "bridge," or tidal float, on the one side, and up that on the other, with surprising facility. Some of these ferry-boats, as the *Maryland*, which makes the journey around New York, from the Jersey to the Harlem shore, are fitted with rails, and can take a whole railway train at a load.

The Pennsylvania is only one of a number of great roads which reach the metropolis by means of ferries from the New Jersey side of the river. The New Jersey Central crosses Newark Bay on a viaduct of pile-work nearly two miles long; the Erie Railway enters Jersey City over salt-meadows adjoining those crossed by the Pennsylvania road; the Delaware and Lackawanna comes through the sylvan valleys of the Orange Mountains, and also runs across the meadows parallel with the Pennsylvania; the new West Shore line accords with its name by following the west bank of the Hudson from Albany to its terminus at Weehawken, nearly oppo-

site Forty-second Street; and still other suburban lines make the New Jersey shore, as seen from the heights of Wee-hawken, a very gridiron of rails.

IV.—BY THE HUDSON RIVER.

But the approach most famed for its picturesqueness—famed, indeed, the world over—is that from the north by the Hudson River. The summer traveller reaching Albany from Montreal or Saratoga has choice of three routes—the New York Central and Hudson River Railroad, hugging the shore at the water level on the east side, in its day one of the greatest feats of railroad engineering; the new "West Shore" line, already referred to, which runs now inland through pleasant rural landscape, now close by the water's side, or on the edge of a height that gives fine outlook over the rolling stream below—each a part of great routes from the West; and, finest of all, by Albany "day boat" or "night boat," both of them superb specimens of river craft, not unlike the Sound steamers. The "day boat" leaves Albany about eight, and reaches New York, a hundred and fifty miles distant, before six, making landings here and there. The passage through the Highlands is reached at West Point, where, between Storm King and Anthony's Nose, the great river, narrowed and deepened, breaks its way through a spur of the Appalachian chain of mountains. Below here the river widens into the calm expanse of the Tappan Sea, and thence to New York the east-side hills are crowned with the finest villas that the metropolis can show, while villages and minor cities nestle at the river's edge or climb half-way up the hills. The Palisades come in sight at last—the long bare face of mountain-wall that seems set to confine the great river in its due course —and soon we pass the picturesque north end of Manhattan Island, and catch our first glimpse of the great city.

V.—BY THE GRAND CENTRAL SYSTEM.

The only approach to New York which avoids the ferries is that by the railways which, reaching the island by the bridge over the Harlem River, land their passengers at the Grand Central Depot.   These include the Hudson River Railroad, which leaves the banks of the river at the entrance to Spuyten Duyvil Creek, where (though a branch still borders the river down to Sixty-eighth Street) the main line diverges, and passes under High Bridge, that splendid piece of masonry by which the Croton Aqueduct is carried over the

precludes the possibility of collisions, except through the failure of the signaling machinery or the carelessness of those in charge, but also, it seems to us, embodies, with a force that can not fail to excite wonder, the highest results attained in mechanical science.   Electricity, captive and subject to an ivory disk not larger than the tip of a lady's finger, conveys by semaphore the invisible, inaudible, and unmistakable messages that need no transcription, and that control the movements of hundreds of trains rushing to and from the city in a chain which with a few connections

Hudson River Railroad.

HIGH BRIDGE.

Harlem River; the Harlem, which comes from the north over the hills of Westchester; and the New Haven, which, passing the pretty suburban towns of Connecticut, connects Boston and the rest of New England with New York.   The Hudson River, the New Haven, and the Harlem meet at a point some five miles above Forty-second Street, and enter the city on the same tracks.   From the Harlem River to One-hundred-and-sixteenth Street the tracks, four in number, are carried through a sunken cut, thence to Ninety-eighth Street they are on a viaduct; thence to Fifty-third Street they are in a tunnel, and thence they are again in a sunken cut until they emerge into the station yard.   The viaduct, tunnel, and the walls of the cuts are substantially built of masonry, and this approach is by far the most convenient of all.   All trains are operated by the block system, which in its perfection not only

would be endless—control them not merely by indicating to the engineers what it is proper to do, but more effectually by making it impossible for the engineers to do otherwise, except in the face of extreme peril.

The mainspring of the system is in an octagonal observatory, not much larger than the clock at the other end, projecting from the northern wall of the Grand Central Depot at a dizzy height from the floor—a position which commands a view of the interior and the tracks outside, and at a glance seems inaccessible, though in fact it is easily reached from the offices in the western wing of the building.

Come with us up here, reader, or if the narrow gallery which we have to trace is at an elevation greater than your nerves are equal to, picture the place from these details.   A box inconveniently small for three persons, with a glass inclosure, revealing on one side the depot partly filled with cars, and on the other side the tracks converging into the deep cutting that leads northward: the depot is very quiet, and a few knots of manikins are discussing Lilliputian affairs on the platforms, while others, quite unconscious that we are watching them, are gathering up their skirts and packages and hurrying into the cars. The furniture of our lookout consists of a chair, a desk, a table, a clock, and what an organist would call a "bank" of ivory keys about the size of the chips used in games of cards, besides which there are a few wires secured to the walls and bells. You now have an account of all the visible apparatus with which the electrician in the signal-box is provided, and by which he regulates the arrival and departure of over one hundred and fifty trains daily.

The train in the depot which the people are entering is the 2.20 P.M. to New Haven. At two o'clock the electrician depresses one of the keys, which are divided into three sets, one set, classified X, for Harlem trains, another, classified Y, for New Haven trains, and the third, classified Z, for Hudson River trains. Each key has engraved upon it a word indicating its purpose, and that just touched in the Y set opens the doors leading from the New Haven waiting-rooms to the New Haven platform. The corresponding key in the X set would open the doors of the Harlem waiting-rooms, and that in the Z set the Hudson River waiting-rooms. Only passengers holding tickets and the officials are admitted to the platforms, and even the former are excluded until twenty minutes before the departure of the train. From two o'clock, when the doors are opened, until "two-fifteen" the "two-twenty" train gradually fills without confusion, and the electrician then depresses another key in the Y set, which warns tardy passengers that they have only five minutes to spare before the departure of the train, and also intimates to the baggage men that they are to stop checking baggage. Precisely at "two-twenty," the advertised time of departure, another key is touched, which closes the door leading from the waiting-room, and thirty seconds are allowed to enable those who have just entered upon the platform to board the train. At the end of these moments of grace, during which the knots of talkers break up and the stragglers enter the cars, the dispatcher, as the electrician is technically called, puts his finger upon a fourth key, that sounds a bell attached to a pillar by which a locomotive is standing outside the depot; and at this signal the locomotive backs in, and, when it is coupled to the foremost car, glides off with the train with the extremest smoothness. Observe that during the five or six seconds spent in coupling, the locomotive is not wholly within the depot; the smoke-stack is kept outside the wall, for the managers are careful of the fresh blue and gray paint with which the interior of the building is decorated.

Trains, like ships, are cast in the feminine gender by their operators, and the moment the "two-twenty" is started, the dispatcher telegraphs by an ordinary instrument the number of cars *she* includes to the signal-man at the junction above Mott Haven, that the latter official may see that no cars have been inadvertently left behind, and at the same time he depresses another of the small ivory keys, which "blocks" the railway from the "cross-over" at Fifty-third Street to the depot. A word of explanation is necessary here. The outgoing trains leave the depot and proceed as far as the "cross-over" on the western tracks, where they are thrown over to the eastern tracks; similarly the incoming trains approach the city on the western track until they reach the "cross-over," which throws them to the eastern track, the change being necessitated by the fact that the depot must be approached from the eastern side. Now the key which the dispatcher touches as the "two-twenty" leaves the depot sets all the signals in positions and colors which forbid any train to pass the "cross-over" until she is clear of it, and a bell rings continually with great liveliness in the dispatcher's lookout; but as she clears it the bell ceases, and she touches a track instrument which automatically reverses all the signals, and shows that the line is open for other trains. A track instrument is a very simple-looking contrivance—a slender iron shaft like a small street hydrant, placed a few inches from the rail, but the momentary pressure a wire connecting with it receives from the passage of the train causes it to change the color of all the lamps used in signaling between the depot and the "cross-over" at night, and all the daylight marks used for the same purpose, by a magic which eclipses the cleverest feats of Heller.   Before our cicerone has finished his explanation a "pinging" bell is heard, announcing that the "two-twenty" has passed Seventy-second Street; and by this time another train is made up, and the electrician is repeating his previous performance on the ivory keys.   The position of the dispatcher is a most responsible one, requiring the greatest caution and an intense degree of application.   Until the "two-twenty" clears Seventy-second Street the track is blocked between that point and Fifty-third Street, but is open between Fifty-third and the depot; then the section between Seventy-second and Fifty-third is opened, and that between Seventy-second and Ninety-sixth is blocked.   Meanwhile an incoming train signals itself to the dispatcher by a track instrument at Sixty-third Street; a minute later it is at the "cross-over," and the dispatcher, by touching another of the ivory keys, gives it a flying switch into the depot; that is to say, the locomotive is uncoupled from the cars, and they are thrown on one track, while it is thrown over to another.

The depot and all the plant between Forty - second Street and the junction above Mott Haven are used in common, as we have said, by the Harlem, the Hudson River, and the New Haven companies, which are separately and proportionately assessed by a distinct corporation known as the Grand Central.   The Grand Central owns and operates the depot and all the tracks to the junction, and employs its own servants.   The depot is the finest in America, and has few equals in Europe. It covers two blocks, and is spanned by a graceful arch of iron and glass, painted with delicate shades of blue and gray; instead of being the nerve-torturing Babel that some depots are, it is clean, cheerful, and orderly, the locomotives not being admitted until the minute of departure, and all persons except passengers and officials being excluded.

Here our account must end.   The approaches to New York, as one thinks of them at his desk, seem like a heroic frieze, with multitudes of living figures coming and going in an interminable procession, the knight, the priest, the merchant, and the warrior—seekers after fortune and fortune's complement, fame ; some to win both, others neither; and as we contemplate the variety of mankind and the diversity of motive which the procession suggests, the mechanical details sink into insignificance.

THE DUTCH FOUNDING OF
NEW YORK
(PART 1)

I

ARTFUL fiction being more convincing than artless fact, it is not likely that the highly untruthful impression of the Dutch colonists of Manhattan given by Washington Irving ever will be effaced. Very subtly mendacious is Irving's delightful *History of New York from the beginning of the World to the end of the Dutch Dynasty.* Bearing in mind the time when he wrote—before Mr. Brodhead had performed the great work of collecting in Europe the documents relating to our colonial history, and while the records of the city and of the State still were in confusion—his general truth to the letter is surprising. But precisely because of his truth to the letter are his readers misled by his untruth to the spirit. Over the facts which he was at such pains to gather and to assemble, he has cast everywhere the glamour of a belittling farcical romance: with the result that his humorous conception of our ancestral Dutch colony peopled by a sleepy tobacco-loving and schnapps-loving race stands in the place of the real colony peopled by hard-headed and hard-hitting men.

Irving's fancy undoubtedly is kindlier than the plain truth. They were a rough lot, those Dutchmen who settled here in Manhattan nearly three hundred years ago; and they did not—the phrase is from our own frontier vocabulary—come here for their health. As has happened in the case of much later outpost settlements on this continent, they cheated the savages whom they found in residence, and most cruelly oppressed them. Also, on occasion, they cheated each other; out of which habit, as is shown by the verbose records of their little courts, arose much petty litigation of a snarling sort among themselves. In a larger and more impersonal fashion, they consistently cheated the revenue laws of the colony; and with a fine equanimity they broke any other laws which happened to get in their way—a line of conduct that is not to be condemned sweepingly, however, because most of the revenue laws of the colony, and many of its general laws, were unjust intrinsically, and were administered in a manner that gave to those who evaded or broke them a good deal in the way of colorable excuse. In a word, our Dutch ancestors who founded this city had the vices of their kind enlarged by the vices of their time. But, also, they had certain virtues—unmentioned by Irving—which in their time were, and in our time still are, respectable. With all their shortcomings, they were tough and they were sturdy and they were as plucky as men could be. Of the easy-going somnolent habit that Irving has fastened upon them as their dominant characteristic there is not to be found in the records the slightest trace. I am satisfied that that characteristic did not exist.

Certainly, there was no suggestion of somnolence in the promptness with which the Dutch followed up Hudson's practical discovery of the river that now bears his name. Hudson's immediate backers, to be sure, the members of the Dutch East India Company, took no action in the premises. They had sent him out to find a northerly passage to the Indies—and that he had not found. What he had found was of no use to them. The region drained by his great river was outside the limits of their charter; and trade with it did not promise—though promising much—returns at all comparable with those which were pouring in upon them from their spice-trade with the East. Therefore, his voyage having been a mere waste of their money, they charged off the cost of it to their profit-and-loss account and sent him away to sea again: on that final quest of his for the impossible passage to the East by the North that ended in his death in Hudson Bay.

But when Hudson's report of the fur-yielding country that he had found was made public in Holland certain other of the Dutch merchants pricked up their ears. These were the traders who carried European and Eastern goods to Russia and there bartered them for Muscovy furs: a commerce that had its beginning toward the end of the sixteenth century, and that was greatly stimulated by certain concessions granted by the Czar to the Dutch in the year 1604. Those concessions provided, in effect, that goods might be imported into Russia, and that goods to an equal value might be exported thence, on the payment of landing and loading duties of two and a half per cent., while on exports above the value of imports a farther duty of five per cent. was laid: a tariff system which, for those times, was at once so liberal and so simple that it drew to Archangel a fleet of from sixty to eighty Dutch ships a year.

But Hudson's exposition of the fur trade possible in America made a still better showing. In dealing with ingenuous savages, unhampered by a government of any sort whatever, there would be no duties to pay on either imports or exports; and instead of being compelled to give value for value—a custom that all traders of all times have resented—a ship-load of furs could be had for the insignificant outlay of a few jerry-made hatchets and some odds and ends of beads. (It is but just to the Netherlanders to add that they have lost nothing, in the passing of the centuries, of their acuteness in such matters: as is evidenced by their ability to get and to keep the weather-gage of the unlucky savages of the Congo Protectorate to-day.) And so, in the summer of 1610, certain merchants of Amsterdam — suffering no grass to grow under their feet—despatched to the island of Manhattan a vessel loaded with "a cargo of goods suitable for traffic with the Indians": and no doubt but it was a precious lot of rubbish that they put on board!

I am sorry to say that the name of that first trading-ship sent to this port remains unknown. But the fact of her sailing is established, as is also the fact that her crew in part was made up of men who had sailed with Hudson in the *Half Moon*. Mr. Brodhead is of the opinion

that she was commanded by Hudson's Dutch mate; and he cites the tradition that the Hollanders who came again to this island, and the Indians living here, were "much rejoiced at seeing each other": a cordiality which—however reasonable it may have been on the side of the Dutch—showed that the savages had no endowment of prophetic instinct to warn them that the stars in their courses were fighting against them, and that then was the beginning of their end.

For my present purposes it suffices to say that the briskness with which that first trading voyage was undertaken and accomplished strikes the key-note of Dutch character. Keenness and alertness — not the drowsiness upon which Irving so harps in his persistent pleasantries—were the personal and national characteristics of the people who founded this city; and who founded it, we must remember, in the very thick of their glorious fight for freedom with what then was the first sea-power of the world. Those qualities clearly were in evidence in their despatch to Manhattan—almost on the instant that Hudson's report of his discovery was made public—of that little nameless merchantman: with the coming of which into this harbor, solely as a trader, the commerce of the port of New York began.

II

There was a nice touch of prophetic fitness in the fact that the very first product of skilled labor on our island was a ship; and a still nicer touch—since the commercial supremacy of our city was assured at the outset by its combined command of salt-water and of fresh-water navigation—in the farther fact that that ship was large enough to venture out upon the ocean, and yet was small enough to work her way far into the interior of the continent: up the channels of the thirteen rivers which fall into, or which have their outlet through, New York Bay. And, also, I like to fancy that the spirit of prophecy was upon the Dutch builders of that heroically great little vessel when they named her the *Onrust*: because, assuredly, the word "Restless"—in its sense of untiring energy—at once describes the most essential characteristic of, and is the most fit motto for, the city of New York. Indeed, I wish that this early venture in ship-building had been remembered when our civic arms were granted to us; and that then—instead of our beaver and of our later-added windmill sails and flour-barrels, full of meaning though those charges are—we had been given a ship for our device, and with it for our motto the pregnant word: "Onrust."

Our little first ship—built almost in the glowing moment of the city's founding—was a child of disaster; but all the more for that reason, I think, was the making of her heroic. Following quickly in the wake of the little nameless merchantman, other ships were sent to the river Mauritius—as they were beginning to call it in honor of their Stadtholder—to win a share of the profits in the newly opened trade. From Amsterdam were sent the *Fortune,* commanded by Hendrick Christiansen, and the *Tiger,* commanded by Adriaen Block; and another ship, also called the *Fortune,* commanded by Cornelis Jacobsen, was sent out from Hoorn. By the year 1613 half a dozen voyages had been made; and by that time, also, there was some sort of a little trading-post here: a group of huts, possibly stockaded, which stood where the Fort stood later and where the irrational walls of the new Custom-house are rising now.

The disaster to which the building of the *Onrust* was due was the burning of Block's ship, the *Tiger,* just as he was making ready to return in her to Holland—in the autumn of the year 1613. Had Block and his men been of a ruminative habit—the habit that Irving has ascribed to the Dutch generally—they would have meditated the winter through, with their hands in their pockets, upon the disaster that had overtaken them. What they actually did was to set to work instantly to build another vessel. Presumably they saved from the burned *Tiger* what little iron-work they needed (ships in those days were pegged together with wooden pins, which was why they came apart so easily and leaked so prodigiously), and for ship-timber there was not need to go farther up town—as we should say nowadays—than Rector Street; very likely there was not need to go so far. And so they buckled down to their work, and by the spring-time of the year 1614 the

Onrust was finished and launched: a yacht, as she was classed, of 44 feet 6 inches keel; 11 feet 6 inches beam; and of "about eight lasts burthen"—that is to say, of about sixteen tons. The Dutch are not a demonstrative race—but I fancy that there was cheering on this island on the day that the *Onrust* slid down the ways!

There is good ground for believing that the ship-yard in which Block and his men worked was close by the present meeting-place of Pearl and Broad streets, on the bank of the creek that then flowed where Broad Street now is. It is my earnest hope that a monument may be set up there to commemorate that great building of our little first ship: the ancestor of all the ships which have been built on this island in the now nearly completed three centuries since she took the water; the ancestor of all the ships which will be built on this island in all the centuries to come. And I am the more eager to see my monument erected because at this very time precisely the site for it is being prepared. The purchase of Fraunces's Tavern, for permanent preservation, includes the purchase of a half-block of land at Pearl and Broad streets — whence the modern houses are to be removed, that in their place may be laid out a little park. Possibly the *Onrust* was built on the very piece of land thus to be vacated; almost certainly she was built not a stone's-cast from its borders. In that park, therefore, the monument to New York's first ship must stand.

As the direct result of the building of the *Onrust* the Dutch field of American discovery and possession materially was enlarged. Block sailed away in her, in the sunshine of that long-past spring-time, to explore the bays and rivers to the eastward — "into which the larger ships of the Dutch traders had not ventured." He laid his course boldly through Hell Gate—it is probable that the *Onrust* was the first sailing-vessel to make that perilous passage — and, going onward through Long Island Sound, crossed Narragansett Bay and Buzzards Bay, coasted Cape Cod, and made his highest northing in "Pye Bay, as it is called by some of our navigators, in latitude 42° 30', to which the limits of New Netherland extend." As he returned southward he

fell in with the *Fortune,* homeward bound
from Manhattan, and went back in her
to Holland to report upon the new countries which he had found—leaving the
Onrust to make farther voyages of discovery under the command of Cornelis
Hendricksen.

Block's claim that Pye Bay (in mercy to
summer residents upon the North Shore
of Massachusetts, we call it Nahant Bay
now) marked the limits of New Netherland to the northward was one of those
liberal assertions common to the explorers
of his day. That claim clashed with
claims under English grants, and while it
was asserted it was not maintained. But
the Dutch did claim resolutely, in their
subsequent wranglings with the English,
as far north as the Fresh Water—that is
to say, the Connecticut River: on the
ground that Block was the first European
to enter that river, and that the Dutch
planted the first European colony upon
its banks. On like grounds they claimed,
and for a long while held without dispute, the whole of Long Island. Broadly speaking, therefore, the building of
the *Onrust* and the voyages made in
her resulted in bringing within the
Dutch "sphere of influence," as we should
phrase it nowadays, both shores of Long
Island Sound.

The official record of what the *Onrust*
accomplished, and of what came of it, was
spread upon the minutes of the States-
General (August 18, 1616) in these
words: " Cornelis Henricxs⁵, Skipper, appears before the Assembly, assisted by
Notary Carel van Geldre, on behalf of
Gerrit Jacob Witssen, Burgomaster of
Amsterdam, Jonas Witssen, Lambrecht
van Tweenhuyzen, Paulus Pelgrom *cum
suis,* Directors of New Netherland, extending from forty to five-and-forty degrees,
situate in America between New France
and Virginia, rendering a Report of the
second Voyage, of the manner in which
the aforesaid Skipper hath found and discovered a certain country, bay, and three
rivers [the Housatonic, Connecticut, and
Pequod, or Thames] lying between the
thirty-eighth and fortieth degree of Latitude (as is more fully to be seen by the
Figurative Map) in a small yacht of
about eight Lasts, named the *Onrust.*
Which little yacht they caused to be
built in the aforesaid Country, where

they employed the said Skipper in looking for new countries, havens, bays, rivers, etc. Requesting the privilege to
trade exclusively to the aforesaid countries for the term of four years, according
to their High Mightiness's placard issued in March 1614. It is resolved, before determining herein, that the Com-
parants shall be ordered to render and to
transmit in writing the Report that they
have made."

III

" Their High Mightiness's placard,"
above cited, was an epoch-making document. It had its origin in a joint resolution of the states of Holland and West
Vriesland taken March 20, 1614, " on the
Remonstrance of divers merchants wishing to discover new unknown rivers countries and places not sought for (nor resorted to) heretofore from these parts;"
and it declared that " whoever shall resort
to and discover such new lands and
places shall alone be privileged to make
four voyages to such lands and places
from these countries, exclusive of every
other person, until the aforesaid four
voyages shall have been completed."

To make the resolution effective, it was
sent up to be confirmed by the Assembly
of the United Provinces at the Hague;
and there, evidently, it had strong backers who were in a hurry. Their High
Mightinesses were not given to acting
precipitately. Quite the contrary. But
on that occasion—as the result, we reasonably may assume, of very lively lobbying
on the part of a delegation sent to the
Hague from Amsterdam—the resolution
of the states of Holland and West Vriesland was " railroaded " at such a rate that
in a single week the Assembly had embodied it in a placard, or proclamation,
which gave it the authority of a national
law. As the making of Manhattan was
the outcome of the local resolution and
of the general proclamation which gave
it effective force, a pleasing parallel may
be drawn between this piece of brisk
legislation and other pieces of brisk legislation in later times; indeed, it is not
too much to assert that the precedent
then was established of sending lobbying
delegations from New York to Albany—
and I see no reason for doubting that the
Hague lobby was run then very much as
the Albany lobby is run now. Customs

and clothes change from one century to another; but it is well to remember that the men inside of the clothes and customs do not change much from age to age.

Without going deeper into this matter of ethics, it suffices here to state that the placard issued by the States-General gave the Amsterdam ring what it wanted—but with a commendably greater dignity of expression than usually is found in the legislative acts affecting "cities of the first class" which issue from Albany to-day. The charging points of that famous placard are as follows: "Whereas, we understand that it would be honourable serviceable and profitable to this Country, and for the promotion of its prosperity, as well as for the maintenance of sea-faring people, that the good Inhabitants should be excited and encouraged to employ and occupy themselves in seeking out and discovering Passages, Havens, Countries, and Places that have not before now been discovered nor frequented; and being informed by some Traders that they intend, with God's merciful help, by diligence labour danger and expense, to employ themselves thereat, as they expect to derive a handsome profit therefrom, if it pleased Us to privilege charter and favour them that they alone might resort and sail to and frequent the passages havens countries and places to be by them newly found and discovered for six voyages, as a compensation for their outlays trouble and risk . . . Therefore: We, having duly weighed the aforesaid matter, and finding, as hereinbefore stated, the said undertaking to be laudable honourable and serviceable for the prosperity of the United Provinces, and wishing that the experiment be free and open to all and every of the inhabitants of this country . . . do hereby grant and consent that whosoever from now henceforward shall discover any new Passages Havens Countries or Places shall alone resort to the same or cause them to be frequented for four voyages, without any other person directly or indirectly sailing frequenting or resorting from the United Netherlands to the said newly discovered and found passages havens countries or places until the first discoverer and finder shall have made, or caused to be made, the said four voyages: on pain of confiscation of the goods and ships wherewith the contrary

attempt shall be made, and a fine of fifty thousand Netherland Ducats, to the benefit of the aforesaid finder or discoverer."

It would seem from the foregoing that the Amsterdam men asked for six voyages and were granted four: even as at Albany a "strike" nowadays is so made that the Assembly may manifest a fine faithfulness to the public interests by cutting it down handsomely—and still give the "strikers" all they want. Again I may observe that in this energetic piece of legislation — obviously rushed through that older Assembly by powerful private interest—there is no very pointed manifestation of the Dutch sleepiness upon which Irving so freely descants.

Indeed, as I have already stated, and as I shall state more at length presently, the Dutch showed a most lively eagerness during the years immediately following Hudson's discovery to seize upon and to develop the trade with North America. Broadly, they sought to capture that trade before it fell into the hands of other nations. Narrowly, they sought to wrest it from each other—as may be seen in the fierce contention for trading privileges which went on among themselves. Petitions and counter-petitions for trading rights pestered the several assemblies of the states and the States-General. One large company was formed to take, and for a time did take, the whole of the American contract. There was a constant wrangling that disturbed the land. Partly to quiet that wrangling, but more to serve high national interests, measures at last were taken which put an end to all rivalries (other than with outsiders) by creating a single powerful corporation in which was vested an exclusive right to the American trade.

IV

Very great principles of religion and of state, along with other principles of a strictly commonplace selfish sort, lay at the root of the founding of the Dutch West India Company. In a grand way, that Company was intended to win freedom for the Netherlands by smashing the power of Spain. In a less grand way—but in a way that never was lost sight of—it was intended to line the pockets of the practical patriots who were its stockholders. On its larger lines, as an in-

THE "HALF MOON" ON THE HUDSON

strument of justice, and incidentally as
an instrument of personal and political
revenge, it was to a great extent a success. On its smaller lines, as a commercial investment, it was a ruinous failure.
We of New York are none the better for
its success, and we distinctly are the
worse for its failure. That failure gave
this city a bad start.

William Usselinex the originator of
the Company, and for thirty years its most
persistent promoter, was one of the half-
million or so of Protestant Belgians who
were driven to take refuge in Holland
by Spanish persecution. As an Antwerp
merchant, under Spanish rule, he had
traded to America; and so had come to
know that the colonies whence Spain
drew her main revenues were at once her
strength and her weakness. He realized
that those colonies, widely scattered and
individually ill-defended, were secure
only because they were not attacked; and
he farther realized that even a small
naval force, resolutely handled, could give
a good account of the treasure-fleets
which sailed annually from America to
Spain. His simple plan, developed from
those conditions, was to seize and to sack
the richer cities of the Spanish islands
and the Spanish Main, and to capture
such plate-ships as could be caught con-

veniently upon the sea—with the immediate result of a very satisfactory return
in cash from his sackings and capturings,
and with an ultimate result of a greater
and more far-reaching sort. On that
larger side was patriotism. His great
purpose was to cripple Spain by seizing
her revenues at their source, and still
farther to cripple her by breaking her
line of communication with that source:
both by the actual capture of her treasure-
laden ships, and by the threat of capture
that would make Spanish shipmasters
fearful of their voyage. The threat was
a potent one. In our own day, when the
Alabama was afloat, we have seen what
such a threat, backed by only a ship or
two, will do to wreck the commerce of a
nation by driving its vessels to the shelter of foreign flags. In those large days
of hard fighting refuge under a foreign
flag was a thing unknown. Spain had no
choice but to stand up and take Dutch
punishment until—and that was intended to be the glorious ending of the struggle—she should be so weakened that her
hold upon the Netherlands could be
broken for good and all.

It was in the year 1591 that Usselinex
broached his heroic project for organizing
that private military corporation which
anticipated by almost precisely three cen-

turies Mr. Stockton's "Great War Syndicate": an association of financiers who, in a strictly business way, were to expel the Spaniards from the Netherlands—and who were to net upon the transaction a profit of from fifty to one hundred per cent. Also, it was on business lines that his project was opposed—but with a mingling in the opposition of considerations of classes and of creeds. The destruction by the Spaniards of the commerce of Antwerp had thrown a large part of that commerce to Rotterdam and Amsterdam. It was asking a good deal, therefore, to ask the Dutch to take a hand in a venture that would bring them to grips with the strongest state in the world; and that would have for its outcome, if successful, the return of the Belgian refugees in triumph to their own country to re-establish—at the cost of their Dutch allies—their lost trade on the Scheldt. John of Barneveldt, as a statesman—perhaps as a somewhat narrow-minded statesman—opposed the Belgian plan. Behind him were the town aristocracies of birth and of wealth, the advocates of republicanism, the Arminians. The Belgians had for allies the lower classes in the towns of Holland, the monarchists, the strict Calvinists, and for a rallying centre the House of Orange—the head of which great House, taking a strictly personal interest in the matter, played always and only for his own hand. The two great parties then formed lasted intact until the French Revolution, and are not extinct even now. For thirty years the fight between them—broadly on the Belgian matter, but with many side-issues—was waged vigorously. In the first acute stage of the struggle, 1607-1609, the main issue was war or truce or peace with Spain—and the threat implied by Usselinex's project had much to do with compelling Spain to accept the humiliating twelve years' truce that was signed in the year 1609. In the second acute stage, 1617-1619, the main issue was theological: the fight for supremacy between the Calvinists and the Arminians. That fight ended, on May 13, 1619, with the execution of Barneveldt. Then Usselinex's plan was taken up in good earnest: with the result that things began to move forward briskly toward the founding of New York.

I confess that there is a suggestion of anticlimax in treating as mere incidents of that great struggle the wrecking of the power of Spain and the winning of freedom for the United Netherlands; and as its culmination nothing more stirring than the establishment of a fur-traders' camp on a lonely islet nooked in the waters of an almost unknown land. But I protest that, for my present purposes, the most important result which flowed from the rise of the Dutch Republic precisely was the establishment of that fur-traders' camp.

V

Just the same human nature that still is in use showed itself in the fight that went on in the Low Countries during those strenuous thirty years. That much is made clear by the records of the states of Holland and of West Vriesland—where the Belgian party was strongest—and by the records of the States-General. But the spicy personal details of the conflict, being hid in the phrases "divers merchants" and "divers traders," are lost.

On June 21, 1614, when the light sparring of the second round was beginning, a petition of "divers traders of these provinces" was presented to the States-General praying for power to form "a general company for the West Indies, the coast of Africa, and through the Straits of Magellan." The petition was ordered to lie over for four weeks, to the end that "their High Mightinesses may thoroughly examine the matter"; but its opponents—by means which were not recorded in the minutes—managed to keep it in committee for more than two months. It did come up again, however, on the 25th of August; and so vigorously that the Assembly voted "that the business of forming a general West India Company shall be undertaken to-morrow morning." Again the opposition got in some fine work—and the business was not undertaken on that "to-morrow morning" of nearly three hundred years ago. It was adjourned until September 2. On that day the two parties came to a clinch—that ended for the Belgian party in a clean fall. During the morning the Belgians clearly had the lead, and the Assembly resolved "that the affair of the

HENDRIK HUDSON

West India Company shall be continued this afternoon." But it wasn't—and before the West India Company was founded that momentary stoppage had stretched out into nine years. Very interesting would be the record—if it existed, and if we could get at it—of what happened that day at the Hague after the morning session of the Assembly stood adjourned! Having no record to go by, we can only make guesses: being guided a little in our guessing by knowledge of what has happened at Albany, between two sessions of another Assembly, in later times.

A little light is thrown on the situation by an act passed (September 27, 1614) by the states of Holland and West Vriesland: in which is the pointed suggestion that under cover of a general company "some may secretly endeavor to pursue trade to Guinea . . . in case the trade to the other countries should . . . happen to fail, to be interrupted, or to cease." Probably, then, the Dutch slave-traders had a hand in "knifing" the bill that day. Some measures in our own Congress were "knifed" by the slaveholding interest much less than three centuries ago. Also, it is fair to assume that the promoters of the New Netherland Company had much to do with the "knifing." Certainly, that Company was chartered only a little more than a month after the West India Company went by the board.

Among the members of the New Netherland Company were Hans Hongers, Paulus Pelgrom, and Lambrecht van

Tweenhuysen, owners of the ships *Tiger* and *Fortune*—and therefore the owners of the yacht *Onrust:* and the major claim on which they rested their request for special trading privileges was their right to benefit from the discoveries that had resulted from the little yacht's voyage. To that Company the States-General granted a charter (October 11, 1614) which gave the right "to resort to, or cause to be frequented, the aforesaid newly discovered countries situate in America between New France and Virginia, the sea coasts whereof lie in the Latitude of forty to forty five degrees, now named New Netherland, as is to be seen by a Figurative Map hereunto annexed; and that for four voyages within the term of three years commencing the first January XVI^c and fifteen next coming, or sooner, to the exclusion of all others."

In that document the name "New Netherland" first was used officially; and was used, to quote Mr. Brodhead, to designate the "unoccupied regions of America lying between Virginia and Canada by a name which they continued to bear for half a century—until, in the fulness of time, right gave way to power and the Dutch colony of New Netherland became the English province of New York."

The question of title that Mr. Brodhead raises in this loose statement of fact is far too large a question to be dealt with here. But it is only fair to add that his

SEAL OF NEW NETHERLAND

hot contention that the Dutch had a just right to their North-American holding is denied with equal heat by a Dutch authority. The peppery Mr. Asher—in his life of Hudson, prepared for the Hakluyt Society—disposes of the claims of his own countrymen in these words: "The [Dutch] title itself was little better than a shadow. It was entirely founded on the boldest, the most obstinate, and the most extensive act of 'squatting' recorded in colonial history. The territory called New Netherland, which the West India Company claimed on account of Hudson's discovery, belonged by the best possible right to England. It formed part of a vast tract of country, the coast of which had been first discovered by English ships, on which settlements had been formed by English colonists, and which had been publicly claimed by England, and granted to an English company, before Hudson ever set foot on American ground. But the wilds and wastes of primeval forests were thought of so little value that the Dutch were for many years allowed to encroach upon English rights, without more than passing remonstrance of the British government."

It is my duty to state the clashing opinions of these two fiery historians; but I have not the effrontery to discuss the question on which, so signally, they are at odds. Nor is discussion necessary. Most happily, that once burning question was quieted by the Treaty of Breda (1667) and has been a dead issue for more than two hundred years.

In the end, as I have written, Usselincx and the Belgians won through. When John of Barneveldt's head ceased to be associated with his body—the equities of that detachment need not here be discussed—opposition to the founding of the West India Company came to an end. The actual establishment of the Company had to be postponed until the expiration of the truce with Spain. But matters immediately were set in train for it: and, upon the renewal of hostilities, the act of incorporation (June 3, 1621) was passed.

Under the terms of the charter—which, as Mr. Brodhead puts it, "created a sort of marine principality with sovereign rights on foreign shores"—the Company was granted exclusive rights to trade on the coasts of Africa between the Tropic of Cancer and the Cape of Good Hope; to the West Indies; and to the coast of America between Newfoundland and the Strait of Magellan: with power to make treaties, to found colonies within those limits, to appoint governors over such colonies, to administer justice in them, and to raise a military force for their defence. Farther, the States-General engaged to defend the Company against every person in free navigation and traffic; to "assist" it with a grant of a million guilders; and to give it sixteen warships—that the Company was to man and to equip, and to match by raising an equal naval force of its own: the whole fleet to be under the command of an admiral whom the States-General should name. Also, the States-General reserved the right to confirm or to reject the governors nominated by the Company, and to exercise a general control of its affairs.

Thus, at last, the Dutch West India Company was launched. Had Irving touched upon its history he probably would have attributed the long delay to Dutch sleepiness; and would have given us many neatly turned pleasantries about the number of pipes smoked drowsily, and about the drowsy talk that went on for thirty years between those stolid Dutch statesmen and those stolid Dutch financiers—all of which would have been vastly amusing, but would have left something on the side of fact to be desired.

There was substantial cause for that long delay. In addition to the great problems of statecraft which had to be dealt with, the Dutch were dealing with a new great project on new great lines. Their nearest approach to a precedent was the East India Company: of which the primary purpose—as trade went and as peace was understood in those days—was peaceful trade. The primary purpose of the West India Company was war. Its main dividends were expected to come from, and eventually did come from, the capture of Spanish treasure. But provision had to be made for earning money in between whiles — during the close season for treasure-hunting—by employing its armed fleet in ordinary trade: in carrying cargoes

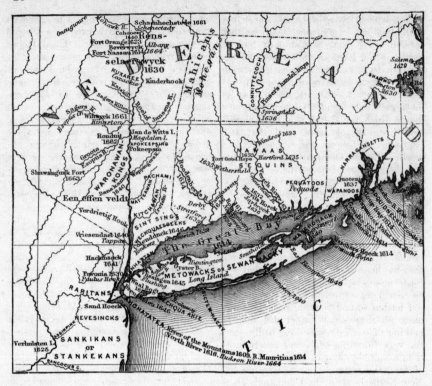

MAP OF NEW NETHERLAND ACCORDING TO THE CHARTERS GRANTED BY THE STATES-GENERAL (1614-21)

of slaves and peltries and other general merchandise of the times. And at every turn conflicting interests, political and commercial, had to be reconciled and brought into line. Nowadays a half-dozen corporation lawyers would get together and organize such a company in a fortnight, and in another fortnight—if the New Jersey Legislature happened to be in session—it would have its charter and would be established as a going concern. But we do these things quickly now—being also freed from the trammels of state policy—because we have precedents in abundance to work by, and because we have the tools to work with (I use the phrase with a broad impersonality) lying ready to our hands. To take a strictly legal parallel: any little seventeenth-century English conveyancer was able to get the weather-gage of the Statute of Uses after Orlando Bridgman had showed him how it could be done. Yet sleepiness—whatever may be said of its

slowness—never has been suggested as a distinguishing characteristic of the seventeenth-century English bar. Nor were the Dutch of that century sleepy. They were very wide-awake indeed.

One other point in the making of the West India Company I must touch upon. With the sincere immodesty that is not the least marked of our civic traits, we of New York are accustomed to believe that that Company was organized and chartered mainly for the purpose of exploiting our own New Netherland. Actually, the part that our little island (and its dependent continent) had in that large piece of statecraft was microscopic: as we realize when we consider the great elements—rival trade interests, contending factions, warring creeds—which were combined in it under the strangely blended pressure of sordid selfishness and lofty patriotism and hot revenge. Looked at in that way, there is nothing in the history of the Company to stir our vanity.

But looked at in another way, even our vanity has its consolations. Although the splendid part that the Company took in fighting to a glorious finish the glorious fight that Holland put up with Spain is not forgotten, its share of honor in a way is lost: being merged into, and almost indistinguishably blended with, the national honor which the Dutch won by a victory that instantly benefited, and that still continues to benefit, the whole civilized world. But the Company shared with no one the glory of planting the city of New Amsterdam, that in time's fulness was to be the city of New York—nor had it, I venture incidentally to assert, the least notion that out of that trifling colonial venture any glory ever would come. Yet that most minor of all its accomplishments is precisely the accomplishment that has kept green its memory; that will continue to keep green its memory as long as New York endures.

I hasten to add that we owe the Company no thanks. What it did for the making of our city was done badly—and the very founding of it was barely more than a mere by-blow of chance. In point of fact, the nearest approach to naming New Netherland in the Company's charter was the mandatory clause ordering the colonization of " fruitful and unsettled lands." At least, the description is recognizable. Manhattan was both of those then, and is one of them still.

VI

Even before the West India Company was organized the germ of the destruction of Dutch rule in North America had taken form. In November, 1620, the patent had passed the Great Seal by which King James granted to the Plymouth Company " an absolute property in all the American territory extending from the fortieth to the forty-eighth degree of latitude and from the Atlantic to the Pacific." That large-handed grant was qualified, to be sure, by the proviso that colonies might not be planted in any region " actually possessed or inhabited by any other Christian prince or state "; but as England refused to acknowledge that the Dutch had any possessions between the Virginia and the New England plantations, and as the English ambassador in Holland, Sir Dudley Carleton,

lodged (February 9, 1622) a formal protest against the planting of the New Netherland colony, that proviso was no more than a politely turned phrase. On the other hand, the States-General paid very little attention to the protest, and never formally replied to it. However, there it was on the record; and so was in readiness for use. But England went slowly in those days. Almost half a century passed before it was used. Mr. Chamberlain and Sir Alfred Milner were quicker in getting from cause to consequence a couple of years or so ago.

While the ambassadors talked—or maintained a discreet but aggravating silence —the merchants acted. In the years while the West India Company was in course of formation the foundation of the sea-wealth of New York was laid. The Dutch planted their trading-post on the island of Manhattan because the many waterways which came together there obviously made it a good place for trade with the interior of the country. As exploration continued, the fact was demonstrated that it not only was a good place but that it absolutely was the best place for trade on the coast of North America: that there was no other such great landlocked harbor, which at once was near to the sea, easily open to it, and free from the dangers of outlying reefs and shoals; that nowhere else — and this fact continued to count first with us until the time of railroads—was there any such system of interior waterways as that which made the Sandy Hook channel the inlet to the trade of a vast part, and a vastly rich part, of the continent. Therefore the Dutch shallops went and came on our thirteen rivers—and beyond the shallop service, plying in the upper reaches of those rivers and in countless minor streams, was a still farther-reaching service of canoes. And all of that trade ebbed from and flowed to this island of Manhattan: where the round-bellied Dutch ships linked it with and made it a part of the commerce of the world. Even a minor prophet, with those geographical facts in his possession, would not have hesitated to prophesy a great future for such a seaport with such a hold upon the land.

When the West India Company came into existence it therefore had among its assets—although ignored in its chartered list of assets—a little trading-post that was in the way of promotion to be the capital of a flourishing colony, had there been manifested even a very small amount of common-sense and common justice in the management of its affairs. And at the beginning—being stimulated to wise action, perhaps, by the English assertion of a counter-claim to their American possessions—the Company did go at the planting of New Netherland with a certain show of energy, and on lines of broader policy than were called for by the mere requirements of trade.

Upon the completion of the Company's organization the management of the affairs of New Netherland was confided by the Directorate, the Council of XIX., to the Chamber of Amsterdam—whence came the name that was given to the settlement on Manhattan Island—and by that Chamber the first shipload of colonists, thirty families, was despatched from the Texel in the ship *New Netherland* in March 1623. Making their course to the westward by a long reach into the south—as was the habit of the Dutch navigators, who ever were fearful of North Atlantic storms—they touched at the Canaries and at Guiana, and then beat up the coast to Sandy Hook and made their harbor early in May. (Possibly our otherwise unaccounted-for custom of May-day movings had its origin in their arrival about May-day, and the consequent running of their yearly tenures from that date.)

They were of good stuff, those colonists—mostly Walloons, very eager to get away from European religious in-

tolerance for good and all. Their coming marks the real founding of New York. They were the first Europeans who came to dwell upon this island with the intention of spending their lives here; and, in the end—though that part of their intention was understood rather than stated—of making

A PART OF THE NEW NETHERLAND CHARTER

themselves permanently a part of it by being buried in its soil.

Meantime, by way of fortifying the situation politically, the States-General erected into a province the West India Company's cometlike holding—which had a tiny material head upon the seaboard, and a vast vaporous tail that extended vaguely across the continent westward—

and gave it, as a province, the heraldic rank and bearings of a count.

Then it was that our beloved Beaver came to us: the same worthy animal who still figures gallantly in the arms of the city of New York. As we first received him, he was our civic crest. Later, when new civic arms were granted to us by the English crown—in the time of great commercial prosperity that followed upon the passage of the Bolting Act—he modestly descended from his proud eminence to join the windmill sails and the flour-barrels, and so became a mere beaver " in chief and in base " in the charges of the shield. And there he remains to this day: in lasting memorial of the fact that the foundation of the sea-wealth of this city was laid in its trade in furs.

[TO BE CONTINUED.]

MANHATTAN LIGHTS

WHEN the twenty-four-hour-day man has been evolved and perfected he will pass his summers, maybe, near the north pole, where the sun is visible and radiant half the year at a time. For by that time, no doubt, the arctic end of the world will be easily accessible, and better equipped than now to furnish steady work or entertainment to an energetic person. But his winters at least he can spend in New York—a city which darkness invades only to a limited extent, in which night as well as day has its full quota of shining hours, and human activities improve every one of them.

All American cities are comparatively well lighted nowadays. Even the quietest country villages have their rows of coal-oil lamps filled to last during the hours of darkness and to go out automatically for lack of kerosene some time about

On Riverside Drive—Grant's Tomb in the Background

dawn. Protection as well as convenience demands light, and when something happens, like the San Francisco earthquake, to put a great city's lighting apparatus out of commission, there is immediate alarm for fear of crimes that marauders and thieves may be tempted to undertake under cover of the unaccustomed darkness. Travelling at night and looking out of the car window, one notices all the degrees of nocturnal effulgence with which the various grades of towns and cities provide themselves. Arc-lights are the common sentinels of the larger towns and big suburban villages. Following them come the long stretches of street lights slanting out into the distance, and then the obstreperous combination of street lights, saloon lights, shop lights, and advertising signs joining in boisterous exuberance at the centre of evening traffic. Coming from the north or the east through Westchester County into New York, the last half-hour or more of the journey is through a succession of suburban towns whose lights merge into a continuous illumination. Miles above the Harlem River the city blocks begin, and at the river itself spring out graceful rows and stretches of lights regularly spaced on the bridges and viaducts that span the river and cross the big gully that gashes the metropolitan end of the Bronx. By whatever route you reach or leave Manhattan Island in the evening, the river lights are beautiful. On the North River the spectacle varies according to the hour and the season, for the down-town lights in Manhattan are more numerous when the days are short and the tenants of the great office-buildings have to light up to finish their day's work. Across from the lower Jersey ferries late in the afternoon of a winter day glow and sparkle the great company of tall shafts grouped against the sky, each one pierced to the top with regular rows of shining windows. A memorable sight they make, those shafts and huge blocks of gleaming holes, reaching far above

FIREWORKS ON THE NIGHT OF THE OPENING OF THE NEW BRIDGE OVER THE EAST RIVER

their neighbors that come between them and the river. There is much in that spectacle to recompense a tired man for being a commuter, and nowhere else on earth is there the like of it.

And besides the tall shafts and the intervening lower lights, and the glow of the streets that run to the river and border it, there are all the river lights—the ferry-boats, with their long rows of bright windows, hurrying on their various courses; the Sound steamers going out; other steamers coming in; all manner of lights more sober on all manner of shipping; the street glare and the ferry-house and wharf lights ashore; and higher up, here and there, the obtrusive and commercial, but none the less radiant, advertising signs.

The down-town office-building lights go out early—most of them—but up the river some of the tall up-town hotels continue, all the evening and in spite of curtained windows, to be lighthouses.

On the East River, besides the city lights and the river lights, are the high, curving bridges, very striking and beautiful, with their unobstructed outlines marked by the glow of the electric bulbs.

There is poetry in these river lights, bordered and framed by the dark shining water and reflected in it. Travellers and the winter commuters see the most of them. The hundreds of thousands of people who cross the bridges see something of them, and so may the crowds that throng the recreation piers on summer evenings. And the piers, like the bridges, are part of the spectacle. When Blackwells Island is turned into a park, as surely it will be some day, it will be, in its way, the most interesting park New York will have, and will be an admirable place wherefrom to watch the river lights. The night views from Corlears Hook Park, with both the bridges in sight, must be charming, and the far-down East-Siders doubtless profit by them; but for dwellers in mid-Manhattan, Corlears Hook is farther away than London and less often visited. When the twenty-four-hour man comes, no doubt he will go down there and see the night sights on the East River, for possibly he will have time to spare.

We sixteen-hour people, who have to go to bed for a little while even in New

LOOKING UP WALL STREET TO TRINITY CHURCH

York, travel, as a rule, on definite beats. If we live in New York, we see by daylight certain streets and by nightlight certain others; the same ones year after year and no others, except when some unwonted enterprise diverts us from our usual course. If we spend our summers, or part of them, in town, we may come to know the Claremont and the Hudson River lights as one looks north from there, and the lights on the Jersey shore opposite. Newspaper men, newsdealers, and all who are concerned with the publication or distribution of morning newspapers, know the City Hall Park, still the most important centre of newspaperdom and still one of the liveliest all-night centres in New York. Wall Street is dead at night, but it never is dark. It is always there, usually solitary except for policemen, but almost as carefully lighted as Fifth Avenue. Dark streets are not favored in the banking districts, and nowhere in New York is there a stronger contrast than Wall Street by day and Wall Street by night. Nobody sleeps there except janitors and their families. Nobody works there at night

except scrub-women, though in very busy times the clerks of the brokers and the bankers and the lawyers work until very late. Usually six o'clock finds Wall Street all but deserted, and at midnight the whole district is dead, and the lights that burn so faithfully are like so many candles burning to the better repose of Business, dead and laid out in a great narrow high-walled church.

Farther down-town, around the Battery and the ferry-houses and the Elevated Railway stations, there is activity all night long. Within easy walking distance in other directions are streets so crowded with humanity that there is no hour when all the people are abed. Any one who pictures in his mind the down-town residence and shopping streets as dismal or murky will gain a very interesting readjustment of his ideas whenever he goes to see them. The soberest and dimmest lighted streets in town are very respectable ones, like those that run east and west of Fifth Avenue, and are still uninvaded by business. They are quiet at all times, and at night are lighted just enough for protection and convenience.

THE RECREATION PIERS ARE BRILLIANT SPOTS ALONG THE SHORE

THE SHERMAN STATUE AT THE ENTRANCE TO CENTRAL PARK

To go from one of them in the evening to one of the populous thoroughfares of the East Side is like coming out of a dusky wood into daylight. The East Side and every great tenement-house district spends its evenings, in good weather, as far as possible out-of-doors. That means in the street, and the streets are lighted according to the use that is made of them. The street lights are many and bright; the shops shine, the billiard-rooms glitter, the saloons blaze. Coming back from them to the blocks where richer people live, a whole house to every family, curtains closely drawn, and no shops or saloons, is a return to twilight from noonday.

But not all up-town New York is soberly lighted of an evening. Go to the pleasure centre, and you will find a nightly illumination which, they all tell us, no other city in the world can quite hold a candle to. That is what they say about Broadway between Twenty-seventh Street and Forty-sixth. In no other city, we are assured, is there so brilliant a stretch of artificial evening radiance. It is the theatre district, as every one knows, and also the before-and-after-theatre district, much frequented by persons who dine in restaurants, and by others, or the same ones, who have the curious habit of wanting supper after the play. Resident in New York and the ter-

ON THE LEFT THE VENERABLE CITY HALL STANDS DARK AMONG ITS BRILLIANT SURROUNDINGS

ritory immediately tributary to it is a very imposing number of people who go often to the theatres. Stopping in New York there are at all times somewhere between fifty and a hundred thousand people, a large proportion of whom go to the theatre in the evening. It is this enormous money-spending crowd that has caused the theatre district in New York to become a world-famous curiosity in electrical street illumination. All day long this part of Broadway is a crowded and busy district, full of shops and restaurants, and a great thoroughfare of a great city; but at eight o'clock of an evening in the theatre season it is deluged with a crowd which quickly disappears and is lost for three hours, when it surges out again, and fills the streets, the restaurants and lobster palaces, the carriages, the motor-cars, the cabs, the Subway, the Elevated stations, and the street-cars. A part of this crowd goes home immediately when the theatres let out; part of it disperses to various hotels and restaurants on Fifth Avenue or the cross-town streets, and part of it clings to Broadway, and eats and drinks in the light of its radiance. Wherever this up-town theatre crowd pauses, there the lights are bright and the streets are lively until after midnight. It is to catch the eyes of this evening crowd that the theatre section of Broadway has been so bejewelled with all manner of electrical contrivance. Advertisement is the motive. The result is somewhat blinding, but it is undoubtedly interesting, and, softened by due distance, it stirs the imagination and becomes even beautiful.

The most dazzling part of this show is still between Thirty-fourth and Forty-sixth streets, but the centre of greatest radiance is moving up-town, and Longacre Square is on the point of being the shiningest place in Manhattan. There, besides a theatre or two and some restaurants with profuse electrical embellishments, one sees to best advantage the pretty outside electric-light decoration of two great new hotels. Up Broadway is the distant glitter of the Columbus Circle; down Broadway, bordered by high buildings, is the blazing chasm of the theatre district. Out spring the cross streets on either side with their lights.

Up and down speed automobiles with great glaring eyes, and here and there, a little way back, where a vacant roof invites, flame advertisements in white and colored lights, not especially edifying as to the wares they cry, but beautiful in their brightness, as well as, in some cases, in their color and design.

Up at the Columbus Circle there is another light centre, and looking from there, farther up Broadway, you see other centres still, and note the crimson letters flaming on the walls of theatre and hotel. All over Manhattan Island there are such light centres, all more or less party-colored and brilliant, and garish though they may be, all more or less beautiful.

For light itself is beautiful, and though indoors it is easy to have too much of it, out-of-doors it is hard to misuse it so extravagantly that it will not still please the eye. The long rows of white street lights—incandescent gas-lights and arc-lights tempered by ground-glass shades—are pretty as they stretch away; the orange globes of intense light that hang by the theatre doors and the colors of the signs and names and emblems are all pretty. But most beautiful and most stirring to the spirit are the lights to which distance lends its enchantments—the river lights, and the shore lights seen from the rivers, the bridge lights, the tall shafts of buildings with windows all aglow. The show in New York is provided every night and with profuse prodigality; the trouble is to get the perspective.

And, after all, that is a prevailing difficulty about life itself on the island of Manhattan. The show there is a lavish show in a thousand particulars, but the perspective is somewhat to seek. The people who see the Manhattan lights in which there is the greatest charm and which most inspire the mind that contemplates them are not those of the surging crowd in the theatre district, but of the army of travellers and late commuters who cross the river to go home. A degree of detachment, it seems, and of contemplative distance is favorable to full appreciation of Manhattan. Its lights are like its noises—stunning when too near, but soothing and inspiring from afar.

THE NEW YORK STOCK EXCHANGE

J. EDWARD SIMMONS, PRESIDENT OF THE NEW YORK STOCK EXCHANGE.
From a drawing by F. Dielman.

THE NEW YORK STOCK EXCHANGE.

THE New York Stock Exchange is a building, an association, an exchange of securities for currency or its representatives. Ordinarily speaking, it signifies the body of men by whom the change of securities for valuable considerations is effected in an edifice devoted to that purpose. This edifice occupies a portion of the space between Broad and New streets, has a frontage of 65 feet on the first and of 158 on the second thoroughfare, and has also an entrance on Wall Street. It

THE NEW YORK STOCK EXCHANGE.

is a solid and unpretentious but imposing structure, designed by James Renwick, the architect of Grace Church and the Roman Catholic Cathedral. Improved arrangements that will give an additional six-sevenths to the floor of the Exchange—now 53 by 140 in size—have been projected by the Governing Committee, and will doubtless be effected. The legal title to all the real estate owned and occupied by the association known as the New York Stock Exchange is vested in the New York Stock Exchange Building Company, of which Donald Mackay is president. The cost of the whole is over $1,800,000, and the amount annually expended by the Committee of Arrangements for its preservation and for the salaries of the different individuals employed therein ranges from $150,000 to $200,000.

Strangers are not admitted to the ground-floor except by courtesy. Entering from Wall Street, the Board Room, with its Babel of voices, is on the right, or New Street side. On the left, or Broad Street side, is the Long Room, devoted to telegraphic apparatus and subscribers who pay $100 per annum for the privilege of using it. A door through the partition affords direct ingress to the parlor sacred to brokers, who therein indulge

THE BOND ROOM.

in some reading, more smoking, and incessant draught and chess playing. Stockbrokerage and the latter abound in shrewd combinations. Between the Board and Long rooms are telephonic and telegraphic instruments of communication with near and distant offices. The famous Callahan "ticker," whose patent was purchased of the Gold and Stock Telegraph Company by the Western Union Telegraph Company, and which prints its electric messages on endless strips of paper, is perpetually at work during the hours of business. Its owners yearly pay $18,000 to the Stock Exchange for the privilege of giving information about transactions in the market. The Commercial Telegram Company also enjoy the same privileges on the same terms.

Inspection of the Board Room, littered with torn memoranda of executed orders, after the day's proceedings are over, discovers that the several stocks have their respective locations upon the floor. Here is St. Paul; a board informs us what the price of the last sale was and how many shares were sold on the day previous. Next comes Northwest. At the south end is Reading, also the New York Central. A row of sign pillars runs along the middle of the room from end to end. On the first we find, to the south, Lake Shore, Wabash Preferred, and Common. This stock is not in active demand; the figures show what was bid and what was asked, without any sales. On the second pillar is New Jersey Central and Denver and Rio Grande. In like manner prices and sales of the previous day are recorded of the Oregon Transcontinental and Texas Pacific on the third pillar, of the Missouri, Kansas, and Texas and the Louisville and Nashville on the fourth, of the Central Pacific and Manhattan Consolidated (Elevated) Railway on the fifth. Omaha Preferred, Western Union Telegraph, and Union Pacific also have their places on the right of the chairman's rostrum. Mining stocks are sold at the north end of the room. On the New-Street side are the Canadian Pacific, Minnesota and St. Louis, Alton and

D. C. HAYS, TREASURER OF THE NEW YORK STOCK EXCHANGE.

Terre Haute, Rome and Watertown, Erie Second Consols, Mobile and Ohio, Chesapeake and Ohio, Rock Island, Pacific Mail, Ohio and Mississippi, Missouri Pacific, Ohio Central, sundry Southern roads, the Delaware, Lackawanna, and Western, and the Michigan Central. The names and figures of all these stocks indicate the vital relation of the Stock Exchange to the commerce and development of the country.

A bulletin-board apprises the brokers that certain of their number have been allowed extended time in which to settle with their creditors, and who are proposed for re-admission or election to the board. Two annunciators also attract notice. These instruments are covered with numbered knobs, one of them running from 1 to 340. A member is wanted outside; but no voice is strong enough to outscreech that Indian hubbub of bids and offers. The messenger whistles through a tube to the boy behind the annunciator; he replies, "Well?" and receives the order, "Put up 24"—the number of the broker wanted; 24 is put up; by pulling the knob bearing that number it instantly appears under the raised section of a tes-

sellated arrangement in front of a gallery —of which there are two—allotted to spectators. The eye of the broker catches the silent announcement, which is discontinued when it has served its purpose.

On the New Street side is a corridor, railed off from the Board Room, accessible to subscribers at $100 per annum, clerks and messengers, and permitting direct contact of client with agent. Three chandeliers, filled with 198 electric lamps, diffuse clear, soft, and abundant light when needed. The arrangements for heating and cooling the room are no less admirable. The ventilating apparatus is as effective as it is necessary, and cost $30,000. Not only does it supply pure air, but perfumes it at the same time. "What bouquet have you this morning, doctor?" is not an uncommon inquiry of the superintendent. Washington and also New York time is kept at the Stock Exchange. Punctually at 10 A.M. the gong strikes for the opening of business, at 2.15 P.M. for deliveries, and at 3 P.M. for the cessation of traffic.

In the second story is the office of the Committee on the Stock List, the Bond Room, where railroad bonds and bank stocks are bought and sold, the office of the President and that of the Secretary, and last, not least in attractiveness to strangers, the galleries, from which may be witnessed scenes compared with which street fights are nothing in point of earnestness and interest. In the third story are the rooms of the several committees, the assistant secretary, the stenographer, and the Glee Club. Mammon has some music in him. The sixteen (more or less) members of the club voice it in excellent style. Their annual concerts in Chickering Hall are fashionably and largely attended, and are sometimes repeated. Truth compels the statement that they engage the best vocal and instrumental assistance. Still, on organ and piano they are amateur experts.

The vaults under the building are among the strongest in the world, and contain 1032 safes for securities. Citizens not connected with the Stock Exchange hire about 400 of them. There are also rooms for messengers and members, with lavatories, closets, and other conveniences on the same floor.

Such are the present quarters of the New York Stock Exchange. They are in startling contrast with those of the

ON NEW STREET.

twenty-four brokers who met under a buttonwood-tree in front of what is now No. 60 Wall Street in 1792, and there created what has grown into the present organization. Their association was as crude as the resources of the country. Business was chiefly done at the Tontine Coffeehouse, a favorite resort for merchants, at the corner of Wall and Water streets. The commercial revival following the war

GEORGE W. ELY, SECRETARY OF THE NEW YORK STOCK EXCHANGE.

of 1812–15 made better organization an urgent need. The character and importance of current transactions called for a precise and binding system. In 1817 the New York Stock and Exchange Board was constituted after the model of that in Philadelphia, and its meetings were held, after 1820, in the office of Samuel J. Beebe, 47 Wall Street, next in a room in the rear of Leonard Bleecker's, and subsequently in the domicile of the old *Courier and Enquirer*. In May, 1817, it removed to an upper room in the Merchants' Exchange, on Wall and William streets. Thence it was ousted by the great fire of 1835, and for some years afterward held its sessions in a hall in Jauncey Court. In 1842 it returned to a hall in the new Merchants' Exchange, now the Customhouse. The board was then a close corporation, but an eminently honorable one, and decidedly averse to any publication

of its doings. The Open Board of Brokers, gotten up in the rotunda, in or about 1837, tried to force themselves into the association, and, failing in that, cut away the beams and dug out the bricks of the regular Board Room, in order to insert their heads and learn what was being done. In 1853 the board removed to rooms on the top floor of the Corn Exchange Bank, at the corner of Beaver Street, and from thence into Dan Lord's building, on Beaver, above William, near Exchange Place, where it was located in the panic of 1857, and also at the outbreak of the great rebellion.

In 1863, a second Open Board of Brokers, the first being defunct, was established in a dismal William Street basement, denominated the "Coal Hole." This soon had several hundred members, and did an immense business. Thence it passed into a fine hall on Broad Street—within one door of the Stock Exchange, which had fixed its quarters in the edifice now occupied, and which was built for its use in December, 1865—and by 1869 had acquired fully one-half the speculative business done on "the street." Warfare between the old and the new was annoying to both. Negotiation followed, and ended in consolidation. The government department of the old board was absorbed at the same time. Since then all have enjoyed equal rights and privileges in the same structure.

The members of the New York Stock Exchange are *sui generis*. In number they are eleven hundred. This limit was reached in November, 1879. They constitute an association, not a legalized corporation. In 1871 a perfect charter was drawn up by business men for the incorporation of the Stock Exchange. Tweed was then in the zenith of his legislative power. Thinking that the application presented an opportunity for making money, he caused false names to be inserted in place of the true, had it passed by the New York Legislature, and signed by the Governor. A hundred thousand dollars, or thereabouts, was asked for this superserviceable meddling, but both demand and charter were rejected by the indignant members.

The twenty-four brokers who signed an agreement not to buy or sell stocks for less than one-fourth of one per cent. commission, and to prefer each other in negotiations, increased in number slowly. Only

JACOB LITTLE.

twenty-five adopted the constitution of 1817. Among the thirty-nine who had signed it in revised form in 1821 were Nathaniel Prime, Leonard Bleecker, and other experienced bankers of the highest reputation. Exquisitely sensitive in matters of honor, scrupulous in regard for right, dignified and urbane in manners, they were worthy of the utmost confidence and regard. J. L. Joseph, whose firm was the agent of the Rothschilds, joined them in 1824, and the celebrated Jacob Little in 1825. Large accessions were received during the civil war, at the consolidation of the boards in 1869, and again in 1879, when the present maximum was attained.

The form of government under which the Stock Exchange acted for many years was that of pure democracy. Consolidation with the "government department"

CHAIRMAN JAMES MITCHELL.
From a drawing by F. Dielman.

erning Committee. Administrative and judicial powers are intrusted to the latter, whose decision in all cases is final.

The President of the New York Stock Exchange, elected in May, 1884, and unanimously re-elected in 1885, is J. Edward Simmons, a gentleman of the highest respectability, of established reputation, solid attainments, and enviable popularity. James Mitchell, the Chairman since the consolidation in 1869; Alexander Henriques, the Vice-Chairman since 1880; D. C. Hays, the Treasurer since 1866; Commodore James D. Smith, the Vice-President; and George W. Ely, Assistant Secretary from 1874, and Secretary since 1883—all possess the same characteristics. The services of the President are gratuitous, although their importance is such as to require his constant care and attention.

The President sees to the enforcement of the rules and regulations, cares for the general interests of the Exchange, presides over it when he chooses, and is a member and the presiding officer of the Governing Committee. In his absence the Vice-President assumes the same power and functions. The Chairman presides over the board when assembled for business, calls the stocks and bonds as they are printed on the list, maintains order, and enforces the rules. In his absence the Vice-Chairman discharges these duties. Neither, while presiding, can operate in stocks. The Secretary has charge of the books, papers, and correspondence of the Exchange, keeps record of the opening and closing of the different transfer books for dividends, elections, etc., of the various corporations in which it is interested, and posts the amount and date of such dividends upon the bulletin-board. The Roll-Keeper preserves a list of the members, and of the fines imposed upon them. He

on May 1, 1869, and with the "Open Board of Stock-Brokers" on the 8th of the same month, brought with it the adoption of a republican constitution, by which the government is vested in a committee of forty—divided into four classes, of which one goes out of power every year—and in its President and Treasurer. These constitute the Governing Committee, and, with the Vice-President and Secretary, are the officers of the Exchange. The President, Secretary, Treasurer, Chairman, and Vice-Chairman are annually elected by ballot of all the members present and voting, on the second Monday in May. The Governing Committee chooses the Vice-President, and also appoints the Roll-Keeper. Vacancies are filled by election, either of the whole body or of the Gov-

INTERIOR OF NEW YORK STOCK EXCHANGE.

W. E. CONNOR.

also collects the latter, and reports semi-annually to the Exchange.

Applications for membership are publicly announced, together with the name of the member nominating, and the name of the member seconding the applicant. The nominators are asked in committee if they recommend the applicant—whom they must have known for twelve months —in all respects, and if they would accept his uncertified check for $20,000. The latter query is crucial. The nominee is requested to state his age, whether he be a citizen of the United States, what his business has been, whether he ever failed in business; if so, the cause of his failure, amount of indebtedness, and nature of settlement. He must also produce the release from his creditors. He is asked, if indebted, what judgments have been given against him; if not in debt, whether he pays for the membership and the accompanying initiation fee with his own means ; whether his health be and has been uniformly good; whether his life be insured, and if not, for what reason; what kind of business he purposes to do; alone or in partnership. A copy of his statement is forwarded to him, and is read and certified by him as correct. Any willful misstatement upon a material point subjects him to lasting ineligibility for admission, or to deprivation of membership, as the case may be. Not less than eight

hundred admitted men have been thus questioned by A. M. Cahoone, Chairman of the Committee on Admissions. "The best policy is honesty," is the cardinal maxim of the Stock Exchange. Financial morality satisfies its requirements. Further than that is beyond its chosen province.

An elected member must sign the constitution and by-laws, pledge himself to abide by the same, pay an initiation fee of $20,000, or, if admitted by transfer, of $1000 in addition to the price of his membership. All new members are now admitted through transfer. In 1792 no initiation fee was demanded; in 1823, only $25; in 1827, $100; in 1833, $150; in 1842, $350; in 1862, $3000, and for clerks, $1500. Thence it rose in 1866 to $10,000, at which figure it stood until 1879, when it was raised to $20,000. There is little hazard in predicting a future rise to $100,000. Even at that figure it would be little if any higher than such a privilege has cost at the Paris Bourse. It ought to imply corresponding guarantee of the capital and character of the broker. The semi-annual dues amount to $25. Ten dollars for the Gratuity Fund are charged to the account of each on the death of one of the members. Fines also are charged in the half-yearly bills, and are levied on the exuberant and indiscreet at the rate of from twenty-five cents to ten dollars, at the discretion of the presiding officer, for such offenses as knocking off hats, throwing paper wads, standing on chairs, smoking in the halls (five dollars), indecorous language, interrupting the presiding officer while calling stocks, or calling up a stock not on the regular list. The revenue from fines is quite large. Some New York stock-brokers compensate themselves for strict legality in one direction by breaking minor rules in others.

A single membership in the Stock Exchange has sold as high as $32,500. At an average of $30,000 the whole number of memberships is worth $33,000,000. Some of the brokers are very rich; others comparatively poor. Estimating the average capital at $100,000, and multiplying this by 1100, we have $110,000,000, which, added to the value of the memberships, gives $143,000,000 as the capital invested by the members.

Generally speaking, brokers are of three classes. The first does a regular commission business; never speculates, except on occasions, and succeeds best. The second are the scalpers, who buy and sell in the hope of making one-eighth or one-quarter of one per cent. profit. These are the physiognomists of the institution. Reading the faces of associates who have large orders, they buy with the intention of selling to them at a rise. The scalpers are busiest when there are more brokers than business. Too smart to live, they usually die of pecuniary atrophy. The guerrillas are a sub-class of the scalpers, few in number, and by making specialty of dealing in inactive stocks have formerly fixed the unsavory appellations of "Hell's Kitchen" and "Robbers' Roost" upon certain localities of the floor. The third class is com-

posed of traders in particular stocks, by whose rise and fall they strive to enrich themselves, in some instances closing contracts every day. One trader in Northwest for sixteen years is said to have accumulated a handsome fortune. The ideal broker is cool, imperturbable, unreadable, knowing or accurately guessing the movements of the great operators, able to buy the most stock with the least fluctuation, covering his tracks in the execution of a large order by purchasing in small quantities, and by shrewd selling at the same time. Washington E. Connor, partner and broker of Jay Gould, does presumably the largest brokerage business in the Exchange.

W. H. VANDERBILT.

The compensation paid to commission brokers ought to be satisfactory. It is one-eighth of one per cent. upon the purchase and upon the sale of all securities other than government bonds, estimated at par value, when made for a party who is not a member of the Exchange. No business can be done for less than this rate to non-members. The minimum rate charged to members is one-thirty-second of one per cent., except where one member merely buys or sells for another (giving up his principal on the day of the transaction), and does not receive or deliver the stock, in which case the rate must not be less than one-fiftieth of one per cent. The commission on mining stocks selling in the market at $5 per share or less is $3 12½ per 100 shares; if at more than $5 and not over $10 per share, $6 25; if more than $10 per share, $12 50. To members of the Exchange the minimum commission charged is $2 per 100 shares. Contracts for a longer period than three days carry six per

C. J. OSBORNE.

cent. interest. Any violation, direct or indirect, of these laws—even the *offering* to do business at less than these rates—is punishable by expulsion from the Exchange, and sale forthwith by the Committee on Admissions of the membership of the offender. The commission broker who carries stock for his customer and furnish-

es most of the money occasionally charges one-fourth of one per cent., or $25 per 100 shares. Ten bonds, at par of $1000 each, are reckoned equivalent to 100 shares, and are subject to the same commissions.

What compensation will these rates afford to brokers? For the year ending December 31, 1881, the transactions of the Stock Exchange are computed to have amounted to $12,816,246,600. Checks for this enormous amount were drawn and paid. The commissions thereon at one-fourth of one per cent. would be $32,040,-616; which, divided equally among 1100 brokers, would give to each the snug little sum of $29,127. This, as related to the cost of his seat, is almost or quite equal to the Israelite's "shent per shent." Not all the brokers receive this remuneration; some receive five or six times as much. Profit is proportioned to size of sales and purchases. It is impossible, without possession of an abstract of each broker's business, to accurately estimate the amount of fictitious sales, or sales on "margins," as compared with sales to *bona fide* investors. It can not, we judge, be less, and is probably much more, than one-half of the whole.

Brokers may be either principals or agents, or both. Not all the great operators, such as A. W. Morse, Jacob Little, John Tobin, L. and A. G. Jerome, Daniel Drew, W. S. Woodward, Cornelius Vanderbilt, James Fisk, Jun., W. Belden, H. M. Smith, D. P. Morgan, D. O. Mills, C. F. Woerishoffer, William H. Vanderbilt, Jay Gould, Cyrus W. Field, James Keene, and Russell Sage, have been members of the Exchange. The last-named, as also C. F. Woerishoffer and others, are distinguished illustrations of the trading and commission broker combined in one. Examples are not uncommon of operators, even of brokers, selling "short" the stocks in which they are interested as directors. The Vanderbilts are reputedly as free from this vice as any of the money magnates in the street. One of the most popular brokers and large operators—bull or bear as an excellent judgment may dictate—is C. J. Osborne.

Stock-brokers have a dialect of their own that is caviare to the crowd. Like the trade-marks and "shop" terms of merchants, it must be explained to be intelligible to the multitude. It is pithy, pungent, scintillating, and sometimes rank. It precisely characterizes every variation and aspect of the market. A broker or operator is "long of stocks" when "carrying" or holding them for a rise; "loads" himself by buying heavily, perhaps in "blocks" composed of any number of shares—say 5000 or 10,000—bought in a the price from declining; "milks the street" when he holds certain stocks so skillfully that he raises or depresses prices at pleasure, and thus absorbs some of the accessible cash in the street; buys when the

CYRUS W. FIELD.

lump, and is therefore a "bull," whose natural action is to lower his horns and give things a hoist. He "forces quotations" when he wishes to keep up the price of a stock; "balloons" it to a height above its intrinsic value by imaginative stories, fictitious sales, and kindred methods; takes "a flier," or small side venture, that does not employ his entire capital; "flies kites" when he expands his credit beyond judicious bounds; "holds the market" when he buys sufficient stock to prevent "market is sick" from over-speculation; keenly examines "points"—theories or facts—on which to base speculation; "unloads" when he sells what has been carried for some time; has a "swimming market" when all is buoyant; "spills stock" when he throws great quantities upon the market, either from necessity or to "break," i. e., lower, the price. He "saddles the market" by foisting a certain stock upon it, and is "out of" any stock when he has sold what he held of it.

Brokers and operators are "bears" when they have sold stock, and particularly stock that they did not own, contracting to deliver it at some future time.

ADDISON CAMMACK.

They are then "short of the market." The disposition of the bear is to pull things down. The Wall Street bear is often found "gunning a stock" by putting forth all his strength and craft to break down the price, and especially when aware that a certain house is heavily loaded and can not resist his attack. He "buys in" by purchasing stock to meet a "short" contract, or to return borrowed stock; "covers," or "covers his shorts," by buying stock to fulfill his contract on the day of delivery. This is a self-protective measure, and is called "covering short sales." A "drop" in the price of a stock is to a bear the next best thing to a "break." He rejoices in an "off" market when prices fall. He "sells out" a man by forcing down the price of a stock that the person is carrying so low that he is obliged to let it go, and perhaps to fail. He groans lustily when the bulls get a "twist on the shorts" by artificially raising prices, and "squeezing," or compelling the bears to settle at ruinous rates. Neither "bull" nor "bear" is an altogether safe "critter." The latter, however, is reputed to be about four times as mischievous as the former, inasmuch as he rudely sells another man's property, whereas the bull contents himself with carrying his own.

The bear occasionally finds himself in a "corner," where it is impossible to buy the stock of which he is "short," and which he must deliver at a specified time. He growls and begs, but must pay what the holders of his contracts are willing to accept. Some relief is afforded by a "let up," or the withdrawal from the market of the "clique," or "pool," or combination of operators that cornered him. A "squeal in the pool" is the revelation of its secrets by one of its members, and a "leak in the pool" is when one of the parties sells out his interest without the knowledge of the others. Either form of defection yields some mitigation to the bear's sufferings. Very popular among the members of this special zoological class is the most extensive operator of their number—one whose strength of character defies opposition—A. Cammack.

Brokers demand "ten up," or a deposit of ten per cent. on the selling value of the stock, in order to insure the fulfillment of contracts. A "wash"—one hand washing the other—is an arrangement between brokers whereby one fictitiously buys what the other fictitiously sells of a certain stock, to keep up or advance the price, and thus to lay a foundation for real sales. "To wipe out an operator" is to confuse and overreach him so that he utterly fails. Sometimes the broker or operator is caught by "traps," or worthless securities. In that event he runs the risk of classification as a "gosling," or a "lame duck," who can not meet his engagements, or a "dead duck," who is absolutely bankrupt. He may even degenerate into a "gutter snipe," or "curbstone" broker, who belongs to no regular organization, has no office where comparisons may be made and notices served (as all members of the Stock Exchange must have), does business mainly upon the sidewalk, and is supremely happy in the light and warmth of the Subscribers' Room or corridor when he can raise shekels sufficient to pay for them. Quoting the vernacular of the Board Room: "The gutter snipe carries his office in his hat. Where one buys of another in New Street, and the market goes up, the buyer is on hand immediately after breakfast, but the seller and his office are absent, and *wikey wersa*." These last words are our old friends *vice versa* in guise of Romaic pronunciation.

Brokers are nothing if not classical—extremely so.

The technology of the Stock Exchange is too large for full quotation. "Conversions" are the exchanges of bonds for equivalent shares of stock, such bonds being called "convertibles." "Collaterals" are securities of any kind pledged for borrowed money. Pledging them is termed to the Governors. "Differences" are money balances paid where stock is not transferred—which seldom happens. To lend "flat" means without interest. To "water" stock is to increase its quantity and impair its quality. To "pass a dividend" is not to pay it. There are other slang phrases used in connection with the business of stock privileges, which is not

RUSSELL SAGE.

"hypothecation." A "good delivery" is of certificates of stock or bonds legally issued, bearing satisfactory power of attorney on the back or appended, and transferred agreeably to the laws of the Exchange. A "bad delivery" is the opposite, and involves the right of appeal to the Committee on Securities, and thence "recognized" by or done publicly at the Exchange. Privileges to receive or to deliver securities are bought and sold outside the institution. Russell Sage is the king operator in these peculiar transactions. Stock privileges are "puts" and "calls," or combinations of both. A "put" is the privilege of putting or selling to the one

who sells it a certain quantity of a specified stock at a designated price within a
fixed time. A "call" is the privilege of
calling for or buying a certain stock at a
specified price within a given time. The
seller of the put must be ready to buy,
and of the call to sell, whenever called
upon. A "straddle" is the option of either buying or selling; it combines the
put and call in one, and differs from the
"spread" in that the market price at the
time of purchase is filled into the latter,
while in the "straddle" the price may
vary from that of the market, by agreement or otherwise. The cost of stock privileges varies with the length of time they
have to run, the difference between the
prices named in them from those current
on the day the privileges are sold, the activity of the market, and other conditions,
and is from one per cent. to three per cent.
of the amount involved. Experts affirm
that they have a duplex character—that
of policies of insurance and that of tickets
in a lottery. In exceptional cases only
are they means of profit to any but those
who issue them. Even the latter—with
the exception of the shrewd operator now
so conspicuous in the business, and possibly not even of him—are likely to come to
grief, as the large majority of their predecessors have done. The gain of the holder
is dependent, first, on favorable turns in
the market, and next, on his ability and
promptness in utilizing them. Keen intellect, prevision, nerve, watchfulness,
and tigerish spring at opportunity must
unite to prevent the loss of what is invested in them. "Don't," is the best advice
to those who seek advice about fooling
with them.

The activities of stock-brokerage involve exhaustive drain of vital energy.
The nervous force necessarily expended
in rapid reasoning and quick decision is
often directed into other channels to relieve the overtasked brain. The younger
section of the broker tribe indulges in an
annual regatta of its rowing association,
in base-ball contests with the callow ath-
letes of popular colleges, or in friendly
struggles among themselves, in which the
"Good Boys" are pitted against the "Bad
Boys," in go-as-you-please pedestrian
matches in the Central Park, in Bacchic
dances to the entrancing music of Italian
organ-grinders, in tremendous attempts at
Græco-Roman wrestling, and in exaspera-
ting "tug-of-war" contests at either end of

a stout rope. It also revels, in company
with the elder, in the concerts of the Glee
Club, and never fails to make the annual
song festival at Chickering Hall, or the
less frequent one in the Brooklyn Academy of Music, a grand success in respect of
enthusiasm, flowers, and numbers. At
the Christmas season it luxuriates in the
blowing of tin horns and bugles, smashing of broker hats, pelting with blown
bladders, wet towels, and surreptitious
snow-balls, and in the sly insertion of
the cooling crystals between the collars
and necks of unsuspecting brethren. Hot
pennies are sometimes substituted. If
the victim whose spinal column glows
with unwonted heat be of dynamite temperament, a fierce explosion is the inevitable result. This same juvenile section
is addicted to horse-play with unconscious
intruders into the Board Room, and with
subjects of practical jokes. The clothes
of both grow rapidly worse for wear, and
are badly marked with uncertain quotations of stocks in still more uncertain figures in chalk. This is all the more incongruous in view of the faultless and almost dudish attire of many of the members. Fashionable tailors can not crave
better advertisement, nor florists more
striking coign of vantage, from which to
display their choicest wares.

This class of gentlemen reveals remarkably affectionate interest in the advent of
a new-comer to the broker household, cir-
culates tidings of the joyful event, con-
gratulates the blushing *père*, and takes up
a collection for the purchase of some appropriate or inappropriate present to the
infantine monarch. They are also somewhat prone to the hazing of new members,
and are not always discreet in the choice
of methods. If the welcome be peculiarly
hearty, the novice may receive a free ride
around the Board Room, the transfer of
quotations from the blackboard to the back
of his coat, and see the necessity of new
orders to his hatter and tailor. In vain
does the Chairman use his gavel on such
occasions. The spirit of fun is riotous,
and does not hesitate to run off with that
symbol of authority. At other times it
may leave him alone in his glory to call
the list in awesome silence to empty
benches. These irrepressibles welcome
some visitors with profound respect.
Prince Hohenlohe is regarded in silence;
"God Save the Queen" is sung with enthusiasm in presence of Sergeant Ballan-

CHRISTMAS CARNIVAL IN THE NEW YORK STOCK EXCHANGE.

tine; and loud applause greets a brief speech from "Tom Brown." Oscar Wilde does not fare as well. The cheers are derisive, the jostling severe, and the sunflower knight finds it difficult to keep his æsthetic legs. A Manitoba insurance agent, looking like a Russian bear in his fur cap and hairy coat, enters the gallery. He is a blizzard to the brokers. They rub their hands, swing their arms, and outdo the pantomime of a half-frozen stage-driver. Eloquence affects them strangely when it springs from their own officers. Cat-calls, cheers, howls, and whistles testify to their high appreciation. The less there is of it, the better they like it. "I am sorry," is an exordium that evokes conflicting counsels, such as "Hire a hall," etc., etc. "Thank you," was the staple speech of one of the best secretaries the Exchange ever had, and never failèd to bring down the house. The hilarity and practical jocosity at rare intervals overleap due bounds, and provoke fistic encounters, in which case the impromptu Sullivans and Morrisseys are parted, and then punished by temporary suspension from all privileges of the Exchange.

Repartee is piquant, always pointed, sometimes Falstaffian. In dull times the lovers of fun amuse themselves with parodies of election tickets, railroad regulations, and corporation circulars. Of the latter, that of the Great Bric-à-brac Company is a specimen. It proposed the manufacture of antique china, bric-à-brac, and bronzes out of old fruit cans, broken crockery, old iron, tin-foil tobacco wrappers, and other refuse. Domestic discussions were possibly reflected in it.

As a rule, the stock-brokers are a self-indulgent, genial, expensive, and generous class of fellow-citizens. They dine well, dress well, bubble over with animal spirits, bear bravely the reverses of fortune, and enjoy robust health. Many of them are graduates of colleges; few are rough and uneducated. Composed of the best blood of the people, they are not, as a whole, distinguished for literary achievements. Stephen H. Thayer is a contributor to the departments of poetry and criticism in the *Christian Union*, Brayton Ives is represented by newspaper editorials and by contributions to the *North American Review*, Strong Wadsworth is one of the ablest writers in *Johnson's Cyclopædia*, and Edmund C. Stedman, the American Rogers, is accomplished and brilliant in poetry and prose.

Failures in business are not so common with brokers as with their clients. One of the more prominent is credited with the assertion that "if there were no fools, most of the members of the Stock Exchange would have to retire from business." Not two per cent. of the latter become insolvent, but as folly is a constant quantity in human nature, the percentage of its exponents is much higher.

The employés of the New York Stock Exchange merit passing notice. Of these and of paid officials there are about 178. The employés, numbering over 160, receive salaries varying from $200 upward, and include about fifty pages, called "graybacks," from the color of their uniforms. These run errands from the floor of the Exchange to the telegraph department, whence some seventy-five blue-clad messengers convey messages and packages to and from the offices of the members. The pay-roll of the financial year ending in 1884 exhibits an expenditure of $119,082 for salaries.

One sergeant of police and ten privates are constantly on duty at the Stock Exchange, except on Sundays and holidays. On the 23d of May, 1884, thirty-five police officers were on hand; and in seasons of great excitement all the force available is sent down to protect the interests of this dominant financial institution.

The securities bought and sold at the New York Stock Exchange are certificates of stock, and bonds issued under national, State, or municipal authority, or by corporations doing business as common carriers, or in banking, mining, manufacturing, or other industrial pursuits. Securities evidencing debt and contracting to pay specified sums of money on a future day are denominated bonds. Certificates of shares (stocks) in the capital stock of corporations represent the cash contributed to each particular enterprise at the risk of the investors. In Great Britain railroad bonds are termed debentures, and are rarely secured by mortgage. "Stock" means public funds or government securities representing money loaned to the nation; and also the capital stock of railroad or other companies not distributed into shares. Petroleum stocks are excluded from the Stock Exchange.

Before any issue of bonds or stock is admitted to the privileges of the Exchange, it must pass the scrutiny of the Committee on the Stock List, and receive the approval of the Governing Committee.

Certificates of stock must be indorsed with an irrevocable power of attorney, containing a full bill of sale and a power of substitution, to constitute them a good delivery. Stocks and bonds—such as those of the Illinois Central, Cleveland and Pittsburgh, Harlem, and New York and New

BRAYTON IVES.

Haven railroads—that pass into the hands of permanent investors are infrequent subjects of traffic in the Exchange. Speculative or active stocks are commonly those of corporations ruled by directors in their own interest. History shows that such directors have, in some instances, by indirect methods, awarded building contracts to themselves, built railroads by means of "rings," turned them over, in more or less finished condition, at a profit of sixty or one hundred per cent. to themselves, to the company, and then have raised or depressed the price of stock at pleasure.

Government, State, and railroad bonds, bank stocks, and other securities are called twice a day in the Bond Room—at 11 A.M. and 1.45 P.M. Chairman Mitchell, whose memory is longer than his list of over six hundred securities, usually presides in the morning, and the vice-chairman in the afternoon. Stocks are not called in the Board Room. Formerly all bonds and shares

were called in regular sequence, transactions effected in each as it was reached, and daily business closed with the exhaustion of the list. The secretary recorded all sales, and the members approved his minutes, which were final evidence of the terms of the contracts.

The cash value of the annual transactions of New York stock-brokers defies ordinary comprehension. On the 25th of February, 1881, 721,303 shares of stocks on the regular list were sold on the floor of the Exchange, 848,940 shares on November 22, 1882, and 3,022,407 in the week ending March 26, 1881. The largest single sale recorded is that of W. H. Vanderbilt to a syndicate of American and foreign bankers and railroad operators. Public sentiment being decidedly averse to the control of the New York Central Railroad by a single family, he, in deference to it, sold less than half his interest in it. But what he did sell amounted to the enormous sum of thirty million dollars. One hundred and fifty thousand shares, at 120, were sold outright, and the option of a hundred thousand more at the same price was subsequently taken up by the same purchasers. The securities daily bought and loaned are paid for by checks on city banks. The yearly business of the New York Clearinghouse exceeds fifty billion dollars, and the principal part of this is from the transactions of the New York Stock Exchange. The London system of settlements twice a month by the payment of differences has failed of adoption in our chief money mart, and is certainly neither so safe nor so judicious as that of cash payments.

The methods of business in this national monetary institution are precise, positive, and suited to its nature. At 9.50 A.M. the members may enter the Board Room; at 10 the gavel of the presiding officer announces that it is open for business; at 3 P.M., precisely, it is closed. A fine of fifty dollars is imposed for each offense in public trading before or after these hours, and any contract thus made will not be recognized or enforced by the Governing Committee.

Collected in groups, like spring chickens in a rural boarding-house keeper's hen-yard, New York Central, Northwestern, Milwaukee and St. Paul, being special points of attraction, no sooner does the gavel fall than a dozen blending thunder-storms break loose. The air is rent by explosive cries, shrieks, yells, hoots, irregularly rising and falling in gusts ungovernable, broken only by the deep bellowings of broad-chested sons of Boanerges. And thus for five long hours the tempest rages, with accompaniment of flitting forms, fierce gestures, uplifted hands, tossing heads, and other inexplicable confusions that shroud the innocent spectator in appalling mystery. Here and there are individuals cool and collected as if in church, but they only throw the anarchic uproar into more striking relief. "Mad, sirs!—mad as March hares!" But there is wondrous method in this madness. Each offers the stock he has to sell—cries it loudly, number of shares, price. Buyers name the prices and conditions they bid for desired stocks. Hundreds are vociferating at the same moment; every ear is attent to what the owner wishes to catch. The brokers take it all in, sometimes buy and sell without looking at each other, so familiar are they with each other's voices; cry out while scribbling memoranda, "Take 'em," "Sold," "I bought 500 of you at 97," and afterward report to principals who the active traffickers are, thus supplying them with data for guessing at the trend of the market. In the Bond Room comparative order reigns. All are seated. Occasionally manners are free, laughter loud, and jokes practical. The bids and offers to sell are intelligible. Between bond calls the brokers who deal in these securities transact business in one corner of the Board Room, to which they descend by an elevator, with the stockbrokers from whom they receive orders. There the voices of the traffickers are torn into tattered shreds of sound, which convey no more meaning to the uneducated ear than the gutturals of so many Choctaws. At times the noise is terrible, especially in panics.

Heard by participants in the crushing throng, the sounds are distinct enough. "Five hundred [New York Central] at 85—at $4\frac{7}{8}$." "Take 'em," shouts a buyer. "One hundred [Chicago and Northwestern] at 84, cash." "Eighty-three and three-quarters for 100," with shake of uplifted hand from buyer. "Sold," rejoins the seller. "Five thousand [Northern Pacific Preferred] at 42, buyer 30." "I'll give 41 for the lot." "Sold." "Hundred [Lake Shore] at $\frac{1}{2}$, buyer 3." "Three-eighths, seller 3, for 100." (Delaware, Lackawanna, and Western) "—any part of 1000 at $\frac{1}{2}$, cash." "One hundred at $\frac{3}{8}$."

"I will give 117 for 500" (Chicago, Burlington, and Quincy). "Sold the lot." "I'll give $\frac{3}{4}$ [$41\frac{3}{4}$] for 300" (New Jersey Central). "I'll loan 200." "I'll take 100, flat." "Fifty [Rock Island] at '$10\frac{1}{2}$." "Hundred at $\frac{5}{8}$." "I'll sell 500 more." "Take 'em." "Give it for 500 more." "Sold." "What's the price?" (Lake Shore). "Three-eighths—$\frac{1}{2}$." "What $\frac{3}{8}$?" "Why, $65\frac{3}{8}$." "I'll give $\frac{3}{8}$ for 1000." "Sold the lot." Bids are monosyllabic as possible. Names of stocks are not vocalized in the localities where the stocks are sold. Brokers waste no breath in trading. All offers made and accepted are binding. The securities on the free list are not called unless asked for.

Sales are either for *cash*, in which case delivery is made on the same day at or before 2.15 P.M., or in the *regular way*, when delivery is made on the day following, or on *time*, usually three, ten, thirty, or sixty days. More frequently option sales are for three days: when stock is cliqued they may be for thirty or sixty days. In option sales the delivery of the stock within the specified time may be at the buyer's option or at the seller's option. It must be within sixty days at the longest. In all option contracts extending over three days twenty-four hours' notice must be given, not later than 2 P.M., before securities can be delivered or demanded.

The sixty days limitation of contracts originated in one of the famous speculative ventures of Jacob Little soon after the panic of 1857. He had sold large blocks of Erie, seller's option, at six and twelve months. The "happy family," composed of the most eminent members of the board, combined against him. The day of settlement came; Erie shares had been run up to a high figure. At 2 P.M. the brokers prophesied that the Napoleon of finance would meet his Waterloo. At 1 P.M. he stepped into the Erie office, presented a mass of convertible bonds that he had quietly purchased in England, and demanded the instantaneous exchange of share equivalents for them. The requisition was met. Little returned to his office, fulfilled his contracts, broke the corner, and was Wellington and Napoleon in one. The convertibles were his Blücher and night. To prevent the repetition of such victories the present option limit was adopted by the Exchange.

Strictly legitimate use of the Stock Exchange is when the investor who buys for permanent holding pays the full price of the stock transferred to him and takes it away. Speculators who desire to find a more direct and easy way to affluence than that of patient toil, and therefore wish to buy more stock than they can pay for, are accommodated by brokers, who provide the money by means of a loan on the hypothecation of the securities. Loans are easily obtained in ordinary times to an amount within twenty per cent. of the market value of these collaterals. The speculator advances the difference between the current price and the sum borrowed. This difference is the *margin*. The margin is a magnificent instrument of stock speculation. Twenty per cent. is ample. Some brokers require much less. Ten per cent. is the rule. Traders not in the Exchange offer to do business for customers on a margin as narrow as one per cent. Just as long as the loan can be continued or renewed the broker may carry the stock until his client wishes to realize. Decline in current price decreases the margin and increases the risk of carrying. Therefore the broker calls for more margin from his principal. If it is not forth-coming, he sells out the stock to save himself from loss. If a number of brokers, similarly circumstanced, unload at the same time, the market is correspondingly depressed.

The financial institutions loaning most largely to brokers are the Farmers' Loan, Union, and United States Trust Companies, the Bank of the State of New York, the Fourth National, Union, Merchants', Mechanics', Gallatin, Leather Manufacturers', Importers' and Traders' Banks, the Bank of America, and the Bank of North America. The brokers also lend stocks and money to each other. Call loans of money on stock collaterals are commonly made at the north end of the Board Room.

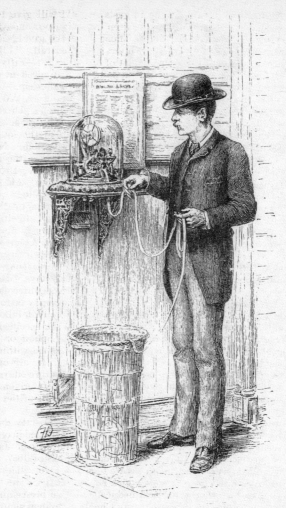

THE TICKER.

This used to be done on the sidewalk. The loan is usually about eighty or ninety per cent. of the market value of the collaterals, and bears interest at different rates, according to the condition of the money market. Statute law prohibits more than six per cent. per annum. Borrowers therefore pay commissions of one-eighth, one-quarter, one-half, of one per cent., or even one per cent., per diem—365 per cent. per annum—in panics to those who borrow for them. For weeks together the monetary stringency has been such as to command the higher rates. At other sea-

S. V. WHITE.

a large quantity of the stock, cleared about $10,000 in a few hours, and complacently retraced his steps to the City of Brotherly Love.

All securities sold are actually delivered; all securities bought are paid for on delivery; all borrowed stock is returned; all borrowed money is refunded. There are but few exceptions to these rules. In cases of default the stocks involved are publicly bought or sold, under the rule, by the Chairman, the contracts closed, and the differences paid. "You must do as you agree," is the homely iron law of the Stock Exchange. Refusal subjects to inexorable suspension or expulsion.

Notes of sales as they occur are made by twenty-four quotation clerks, who are also telegraph operators, and send the news by "sounders" to the main offices of the Western Union and Commercial Union Telegraph Companies. Thence the news of sales is sent by "transmitter" from each office over the tickers, of which there are many hundreds in and out of the city, in the offices—private, in hotels, club rooms, etc.—of their patrons. There agents, speculators, and investors watch the fluctuations as they follow, and intelligently issue orders to their brokers. Boston, Philadelphia, and other cities are thus in instantaneous communication with the New York market. Publicity is also given to the history of each day's transactions by a printer who makes it his business, and who distributes copies of his printed list to subscribers.

Stock-brokers also establish private telegraph codes between themselves and clients, codes in which certain words stand for names, phrases, numbers, etc. Thus, "Boxwood of London wants capsicum," that is, 10,000 shares of a known stock. "Sell 1000 Bouncer," "Buy 500 Zulu," "Loan Hickory Toadstool," "Take all that Godly Goodbub has to sell," "Close out Sandringham sharp," are telegrams that recipients holding the key fully understand.

Four telegraph companies—the Western Union, Baltimore and Ohio, Bankers' and Merchants', and Mutual Union—receive and deliver messages at the Stock Exchange by public wires, and also by about one hundred private ones, owned by different persons. On one day, in the space of five hours, 5727 telegrams were received from or dispatched to various parts of the country; and 1904 messages

sons, when the market is easy, the rate of call loans scarcely averages three per cent. —at present it is about one and a half per cent.—per annum. Brokers also loan stocks, either "flat," *i. e.*, without interest, or with interest, to those of their number who have made "short sales," or, in other words, have sold stocks they did not possess. The borrower pays the current price and delivers his stock; then waits for a drop in the price, buys as he can, returns an equal quantity of stock, and reclaims his money. If the lender does not call for his stock next day, the custom is to regard the loan as continued. If he does call for it, and the borrower fails to respond, then the Chairman of the Exchange may publicly purchase it under the rule, and charge the difference, if any, to the delinquent. Or the borrower may borrow the stock of another who has it to lend, and continue the process until the price falls and he can satisfactorily close his contract. The rates paid for the loan of scarce stock are sometimes extraordinary. Thus, in a recent scarcity of Northern Pacific Preferred, a Philadelphia owner hired a special train to New York, appeared at the Stock Exchange, loaned at two or three per cent. per diem, and soon returned worth several thousand dollars more than when he came. In the Lackawanna corner engineered by Deacon S. V. White, another Philadelphian loaned

sent by messengers to people in the neighborhood of the building. Such is the accuracy of the service that it is asserted mistakes have not occurred in the delivery of a million and a half of messages that would involve the loss of five hundred dollars. From one to two millions are annually paid by brokers for communications with European correspondents.

The ideal business of the New York Stock Exchange is unquestionably as legitimate as that of the Produce Exchange, or of any intermediary between the seller and the buyer. That there are grave evils incident to its operation is equally unquestionable. The war for the preservation of the national Union largely converted the American people into a nation of speculators. The rage for sudden wealth was further intensified by the discoveries of mineral oil and the precious metals. These created innumerable companies for the exploitation of mines, the construction of railroads, and other objects. Sudden and violent fluctuations in the price of stocks, and the daily report thereof in the newspapers, aggravate the speculative spirit. Considerations of morality and prudence are set at naught by those who will be rich, and who dream of opulence by other methods than the slow and steady measures of their fathers. Professional men, merchants, manufacturers, mechanics, farmers, widows, and spinsters, blinded by the glare of success, and hoping to strengthen their slender income, have adventured their savings upon the treacherous sea of Wall Street, and lost them all. To them the Exchange Building is a whited sepulchre in which fortunes lie entombed, a sea in which voracious sharks rend or swallow the little fish who dare to enter its troubled waters, a gambling saloon where deceit and desperation wait upon the players. It may have been such to them, simply because they made it such, not because they availed themselves of its real functions.

An immense amount of gambling is done in piratical relation to it, and in spite of the strenuous exertions of the stockbrokers to prevent it. The "bucket shops" situated in the large towns and cities of the country are the instruments by which it is carried on. The proprietors of these nefarious establishments surreptitiously obtain quotations from the Stock Exchange. Tickers are refused to them by the Western Union unless four members

of the board vouch for the worthiness of each applicant. The quotations desired are furnished by persons who have bound themselves to that telegraph company not to do so, and who have obtained injunctions from the courts restraining the corporation from removing their instruments. Former insolvent members of the Stock Exchange, now known as "exempt members," are among the users of the knowledge thus acquired. Because of this grievance the Chicago Board of Trade has compelled the Western Union to remove its tickers from their offices—a precedent that the New York Stock Exchange will probably follow unless this grievance be redressed.

In these bucket shops a blackboard, with list of stocks at prices quoted in New York inscribed thereon, is displayed. Speculative clerks and others are invited to bet upon these quotations, under the pretense of the put and call system. For example, one is induced to buy, on a margin of $1 per share, five shares of Missouri, Kansas, and Texas stock at 16¼. If it rises to 17¼, he gets back his margin and gains $5. If it drops to 15¼, he loses his margin or bet. The secret of ruin in thousands of instances is to be found in the gambling of bucket shops. Yet the wealthy patronize and are fleeced by them. Quirk of Knaveville keeps a bucket shop, and receives the quotations. He confidentially informs his trusting patrons that he has certain knowledge that an inactive stock is about to rise in price—say the Denver and Rio Grande, now selling at 9—and persuades them to venture $1 per share to the extent of 15,000 shares. This done, he telegraphs to a broker to "sell 3000, D. and R. G.—quick, quick," in blocks from 8¾ to 8. The selling broker, alone or with assistance, makes his offers, which are accepted by another broker to whom Quirk has telegraphed to buy the stocks offered at those prices. The last quotation, 8, fixes the price. The telegraph announces it at Knaveville. The $15,000 margin, minus the one-fourth of one per cent. brokerage on the fictitious sales, is swept into the swindler's pocket.

While the Stock Exchange has legitimate and invaluable uses, it is none the less true that it has been and is converted into a gambling arena by the great speculative operators, most of whom have sprung from the lower walks of rural life, who control the management of railroads whose stocks are active. The facts of good or bad harvests, freight or passenger traffic, rates of transportation, can not explain the fluctuations of their prices. The secret is to be found in the parlors of directors. There flaming reports of prosperity are vain," the conspirators acquire colossal wealth. The New York *Times* of July 31, 1884, devotes the whole of its first page to the history of the Union Pacific Railroad, in which it affirms that Jay Gould, after the panic of 1873, purchased

JAY GOULD.

perity are prepared, and unearned dividends declared, to "bull" the stock. There accounts are "cooked" so as to exhibit decreased earnings, needless expenses for rolling stock and improvements of permanent way incurred, floating debts swelled, acceptances issued for discount, and that will purposely be allowed to go to protest when due, earned dividends passed, evil prophecies uttered, to "bear" the stock. By "ways that are dark and tricks a controlling interest, buying, it is said, at 15 to 20, and eventually selling at 90 to par. Its securities then and for some time afterward were dividend-paying, by virtue of good management and high traffic charges. This fact he and his associates—for Jay Gould is often multitudinous—resolved to turn to their own account. He bought up the dishonored bonds of the Kansas Pacific for much less than par (40 and upward), and its almost worthless stock for next to nothing—1 to 4; and also purchased the securities of the Denver Pacific. Next he proposed the consolidation of the three roads under the title of the Union Pacific; effected the consolidation in 1880; loaded the old Union Pacific with $14,000,000 of Kansas Pacific bonds, $10,000,000 of Kansas Pacific stock, and $4,000,000 Denver Pacific stock, and received new certificates of the same quantity and face value as the old ones. Next this original genius and his fellow-directors, who knew his plans and possibly shared his profits, issued over ten millions of additional stock, and in 1879 and 1883 over seven millions of Union Pacific bonds. Such is the current report.

How was this series of feats accomplished? "Jay Gould pays for his knowledge," remarked a Wall Street veteran. He does retain the best legal talent in his service. He also employs the powers of the subtlest intellect in the market. "Matched orders" raise or depress prices without regard to intrinsic values. Brokers are intermediary agents. Orders to buy or sell stocks may come through half a dozen hands before reaching them. The fingers that pull the wires which set the puppets dancing are often enveloped in densest darkness. Cash advances from the principal owners of Kansas Pacific pay the coupons next due. Provision is made for the payment of those past due. Kansas Pacific credit rises. Its stock is dead—no demand for it at 4. Brokers receive orders to buy large blocks at 4, and those orders are "matched" by instructions to other brokers to sell equal quantities at 4. The stock is galvanized. Next come orders to buy at 5, 6, 10, 12, and orders to sell at the same figures. Again come purchases and sales at 20, 40, 60. Kansas Pacific is extremely active. It leaps up to 105—ten per cent. higher than Union Pacific—and is really worth no more than when at 5. Long before the top notch is reached other speculators buy this active stock at rising prices. The owners unload much of their burden, to the tune of shekels clinking into their coffers. Of course they are obliged to support the stock, and to buy what may be offered while prices are advancing. A consolidated mortgage for twenty-nine or thirty millions upon the Kansas Pacific is next issued, and new bonds, guaranteed by the Union Pacific, exchanged for the old ones. Money is advanced to pay the first six months' interest. This imparts to the road an appearance of

strength. Better conditions of trade do really raise its value, but by no means to the extent fictitiously indicated. Blocks of bonds and shares are transferred to confiding investors during this interesting process, and what remain in possession of the manipulators are of greater worth than the original Kansas Pacific bonds and stock.

Corners of stocks are affairs in which few except gambling speculators are injured, and in which legitimate stockholders may profit from higher prices. They occur in stocks of which the amount issuable or issued is known, and which have been oversold. Too many operators have made contracts for future delivery, or borrowed stocks which they have sold and delivered. The bulls, in clique or pool, ascertaining or estimating the extent of the "shorts," quietly buy up all the stock in the market, and when the contracts of the bears mature, drive those animals into a corner.

Excessive stock speculation causes stringency in the money market, compels brokers who carry stocks with scanty supply of clients' funds to realize quickly, and thus forces prices below the normal standard. It aggravates panics by making it the interest and habit of the bears to circulate alarming rumors of trouble in banks, and of important firms about to suspend. Suspicion is intensified by remembrance of former failures. All stocks sympathize. The bears are then "wreckers."

On the principle that charity begins at home, the New York Stock Exchange has established a gratuity fund, amounting at present to $700,000. It also makes a voluntary gift of $10,000, free from all claims, to the heirs of a deceased member. One-half is paid to the widow and one-half to the children; if there be no widow, the whole is paid to the children; if there be neither widow nor children, the whole is paid to his legal representatives. His membership is sold, and the proceeds—less any dues or balances of unfulfilled contracts against his name—paid to his heirs. Of the income of the Stock Exchange from fees, dues, fines, and rentals, amounting to $300,000, one moiety, after defraying all expenses, is appropriated to the gratuity fund, and the other in rebate to the members. The natural increase of the gratuity fund will soon render further assessments unnecessary.

A HASHISH-HOUSE IN NEW YORK

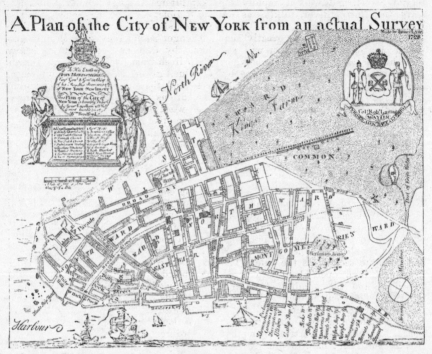

MAP OF NEW YORK, 1728.

THE CURIOUS ADVENTURES OF AN INDIVIDUAL WHO INDULGED IN A FEW PIPEFULS OF THE NARCOTIC HEMP.

"AND so you think that opium-smoking as seen in the foul cellars of Mott Street and elsewhere is the only form of narcotic indulgence of any consequence in this city, and that hashish, if used at all, is only smoked occasionally and experimentally by a few scattered individuals?"

"That certainly is my opinion, and I consider myself fairly well informed."

"Well, you are far from right, as I can prove to you if you care to inform yourself more fully on the subject. There is a large community of hashish smokers in this city, who are daily forced to indulge their morbid appetites, and I can take you to a house up-town where hemp is used in every conceivable form, and where the lights, sounds, odours, and sur-roundings are all arranged so as to intensify and enhance the effects of this wonderful narcotic."

"I must confess that I am still incredulous."

"Well, if it is agreeable to you, meet me at the Hoffman House reading-room to-morrow night at ten o'clock, and I think I shall be able to convince you."

The above is the substance of a conversation that took place in the lobby of a down-town hotel between the writer of these lines and a young man about thirty-eight years of age, known to me for some years past as an opium-smoker. It was through his kindness that I had first gained access to and had been able to study the subject of opium-smoking. Hence I really anticipated seeing some interesting phases of hemp indulgence, and was not disappointed.

The following evening, at precisely ten o'clock, I met the young man at the Hoffman House, and together we took a Broadway car up-town, left it at Forty-second Street, and walked rapidly toward the North River, talking as we went.

"You will probably be greatly surprised at many things you will see to-night," he said, "just as I was when I was first introduced into the place by a friend. I have travelled over most of Europe, and have smoked opium in every *joint* in America, but never saw anything so curious as this, nor experienced any intoxication so fascinating yet so terrible as that of hashish."

"Are the habitués of this place of the same class as those who frequent the opium-smoking dives?"

"By no means. They are about evenly divided between Americans and foreigners; indeed, the place is kept by a Greek, who has invested a great deal of money in it. All the visitors, both male and female, are of the better classes, and absolute secrecy is the rule. The house has been open about two years, I believe, and the number of regular habitués is daily on the increase."

"Are you one of the number?"

"I am, and find the intoxication far pleasanter and less hurtful than that from opium. Ah! here we are."

We paused before a gloomy-looking house, entered the gate, and passed up the steps. The windows were absolutely dark, and the entranceway looked dirty and desolate. Four pulls at the bell, a pause, and one more pull were followed by a few moments' silence, broken suddenly by the sound of falling chain, rasping bolt, and the grinding of a key in the lock. The outer door was cautiously opened, and at a word from my companion we passed into the vestibule. The outer door was carefully closed by some one whom I could not distinguish in the utter darkness. A moment later the inner door was opened, and never shall I forget the impression produced by the sudden change from total darkness to the strange scene that met my eyes. The dark vestibule was the boundary line separating the cold, dreary streets and the ordinary world from a scene of Oriental magnificence.

A volume of heavily scented air, close upon the heels of which came a deadly sickening odour, wholly unlike anything I had ever smelled, greeted my nostrils. A hall lamp of grotesque shape flooded the hall with a subdued violet light that filtered through crenated disks of some violet fabric hung below it. The walls and ceilings, if ever modern, were no longer so, for they were shut in and hung by festoons and plaits of heavy cloth fresh from Eastern looms. Tassels of blue, green, yellow, red, and tinsel here and there peeped forth, matching the curious edging of variously coloured bead-work that bordered each fold of drapery like a huge procession of luminous ants, and seemed to flow into little phosphorescent pools wherever the cloth was caught up. Queer figures and strange lettering, in the same work, were here and there disclosed upon the ceiling cloth.

Along one side of the hall, between two doors, were ranged huge tubs and pots of majolica-like ware and blue-necked Japanese vases, in which were plants, shrubs, and flowers of the most exquisite colour and odour. Green vines clambered up the walls and across the ceiling, and catching their tendrils in the balustrades of the stairs (which were also of curious design), threw down long sprays and heavy festoons of verdure.

As my companion, who had paused a moment to give me time to look about me, walked toward the far end of the hall, I followed him, and passed into a small room on the right, where, with the assistance of a coloured servant, we exchanged our coats, hats, and shoes for others more in keeping with our surroundings. First a long plush gown, quilted with silk down the front, and irregularly ornamented in bead and braid with designs of serpents, flowers, crescents, and stars, was slipped on over the head. Next a tasselled smoking-cap was donned, and the feet incased in noiseless list slippers. In any other place or under any other circumstances I should have felt ridiculous in this costume, but so in keeping was it with all I had seen, and so thoroughly had I seemed to have left my every-day self in the dark vestibule, that I felt perfectly at home in my strange dress. We next crossed the hall to a smaller room, where a young man, apparently a Frenchman, furnished us, on the payment of two dollars each, with two small pipes and a small covered bronze cup, or urn, filled with a dry green herb, which I subsequently learned was *gunjeh* (the dried tops and leaves of the hemp plant), for smoking. My friend, on the payment of a further sum, obtained a curious little box which contained some small black lozenges, consisting of the resin of hemp, henbane, crushed datura seeds, butter, and honey, and known in India as *Majoon*, amongst the Moors as *El Mogen*.

Passing from this room we ascended the richly carpeted stairs, enarboured by vines, and paused upon a landing from which three doors opened. Upon one a pink card bore Dryden's line,

"Take the good the gods provide thee."

The knob turned by my friend's hand allowed the door to swing open, and, welcomed by a spice breeze from India, we were truly in paradise.

"This," he said, in a whisper, "is the public room, where any one having pipe or lozenge, and properly attired, may enter and indulge—eat, smoke, or dream, as best suits him."

Wonder, amazement, admiration, but faintly portray my mental condition. Prepared by what I had already seen and experienced for something odd and Oriental, still the magnificence of what now met my gaze far surpassed anything I had ever dreamed of, and brought to my mind the scenes of the *Arabian Nights*, forgotten since boyhood until now. My every sense was irresistibly taken captive, and it was some moments before I could realise that I really was not the victim of some dream, for I seemed to have wholly severed my connection with the world of to-day, and to have stepped back several centuries into the times of genii, fairies, and fountains —into the very heart of Persia or Arabia.

Not an inharmonious detail marred the symmetry of the whole. Beneath, my feet sank almost ankle-deep into a velvety carpet—a sea of subdued colours. Looked at closely, I found that the design was that of a garden : beds of luxurious flowers, stars and crescents, squares and diamond-shaped plots, made up of thousands of rare exotics and richly coloured leaves. Here a brook, edged with damp verdure, from beneath which

peeped coy violets and tiny bluebells; there a serpentine gravelled walk that wound in and out amongst the exquisite plants, and everywhere a thousand shrubs in bloom or bud. Above, a magnificent chandelier, consisting of six dragons of beaten gold, from whose eyes and throats sprang flames, the light from which, striking against a series of curiously set prisms, fell shattered and scintillating into a thousand glancing beams that illuminated every corner of the room. The rows of prisms being of clear and variously coloured glass, and the dragons slowly revolving, a weird and ever-changing hue was given to every object in the room.

All about the sides of the spacious apartment, upon the floor, were mattresses covered with different-coloured cloth, and edged with heavy golden fringe. Upon them were carelessly strewn rugs and mats of Persian and Turkish handicraft, and soft pillows in heaps. Above the level of these divans there ran, all about the room, a series of huge mirrors framed with gilded serpents intercoiled, effectually shutting off the windows. The effect was magnificent. There seemed to be twenty rooms instead of one, and everywhere could be seen the flame-tongued and fiery-eyed dragons slowly revolving, giving to all the appearance of a magnificent kaleidoscope in which the harmonious colours were ever blending and constantly presenting new combinations.

Just as I had got thus far in my observations I caught sight of my friend standing at the foot of one of the divans, and beckoning to me. At the same moment I also observed that several of the occupants of other divans were eyeing me suspiciously. I crossed to where he was, esteeming it a desecration to walk on such a carpet, and, despite my knowledge to the contrary, fearing every moment to crush some beautiful rose or lily beneath my feet. Following my friend's example, I slipped off my list foot-gear, and half reclined beside him on the divan and pillows, that seemed to reach up and embrace us. Pulling a tasselled cord that hung above our heads, my friend spoke a few words to a gaudily turbaned coloured servant who came noiselessly into the room in answer to his summons, disappeared again, and in a moment returned bearing a tray, which he placed between us. Upon it was a small lamp of silver filigree-work, two globe-like bowls, of silver also, from which protruded a long silver tube, and a spoon-like instrument. The latter, I soon learned, was used to clean and fill the pipes. Placing the bronze jar of hashish on the tray, my friend bade me lay my pipe beside it, and suck up the fluid in the silver cup through the long tube. I did so, and found it delicious.

"That," said he, "is tea made from the genuine cocoa leaf. The cup is the real *mate* and the tube a real *pombilla* from Peru. Now let us smoke. The dried shrub here is known as *gunjeh*, and is the dried tops of the hemp plant. Take a little tobacco from that jar and mix with it, else it will be found difficult to keep it alight. These lozenges here are made from the finest Nepaul resin of the hemp, mixed with butter, sugar, honey, flour, pounded datura seeds, some opium, and a little henbane, or hyoscyamus. I prefer taking these to smoking, but, to keep you company, I will also smoke to-night. Have no fear. Smoke four or five pipefuls of the *gunjeh*, and enjoy the effect. I will see that no harm befalls you."

Swallowing two of the lozenges, my guide filled our pipes, and we proceeded to smoke, and watch the others. These pipes, the stems of which were about eighteen inches in length, were incrusted with designs in varicoloured beads, strung on gold wire over a ground of some light spirally twisted tinsel, marked off into diamond-shaped spaces by thin red lines. From the stem two green and yellow silken tassels depended. A small bell-shaped piece of clouded amber formed the mouth-piece, while at the other end was a small bowl of red clay scarcely larger than a thimble. As I smoked I noticed that about two-thirds of the divans were occupied by persons of both sexes, some of them masked, who were dressed in the same manner as ourselves. Some were smoking, some reclining listlessly upon the pillows, following the tangled thread of a hashish reverie or dream. A middle-aged woman sat bolt-upright, gesticulating and laughing quietly to herself; another with lack-lustre eyes and dropped jaw was swaying her head monotonously from side to side. A young man of about eighteen was on his knees, praying inaudibly; and another man, masked, paced rapidly and noiselessly up and down the room, until led away somewhere by the turbaned servant.

As I smoked, the secret of that heavy, sickening odour was made clear to me. It was the smell of burning hashish. Strangely enough, it did not seem to be unpleasant any longer, for, although it rather rasped my throat at first, I drew large volumes of it into my lungs. Lost in lazy reverie and perfect comfort, I tried to discover whence came the soft, undulating strains of music that had greeted me on entering, and which still continued. They were just perceptible above the silvery notes of a crystal fountain in the centre of the room, the falling spray from which plashed and tinkled musically as it fell from serpents' mouths into a series of the very thinnest huge pink shells held aloft by timid hares. The music seemed to creep up through the heavy carpet, to ooze from the walls, to flurry, like snow-flakes, from the ceiling, rising and falling in measured cadences unlike any music I had ever heard. It seemed to steal, now softly, now merrily, on tiptoe into the room to see whether we were awake or asleep, to brush away a tear, if tear there was, or gambol airily and merrily, if such was our humour, and then as softly, sometimes sadly, to steal out again and lose itself in the distance. It was just such music as a boatful of fairies sailing about in the clear water of the fountain might have made, or that with which an angel mother would sing its angel babe to sleep. It seemed to enter every fibre of the body, and satisfy a music-hunger that had never before been satisfied. I silently filled my second pipe, and was about to lapse again into a reverie that had become delightfully full of perfect rest and comfort, when my companion, leaning toward me, said:

"I see that you are fast approaching Hashishdom. Is there not a sense of perfect rest and strange, quiet happiness produced by it?"

"There certainly is. I feel supremely happy, at peace with myself and all the world, and all that I ask is to be let alone. But why is everything so magnificent here? Is it a whim of the proprietor, or an attempt to reproduce some such place in the East?" I asked.

"Possibly the latter; but there is another reason that you may understand better later. It is this: the colour and peculiar phases of a hashish dream are materially affected by one's surroundings just prior to the sleep. The impressions that we have been receiving ever since we entered, the lights, odours, sounds, and colours, are the strands which the deft fingers of imagination will weave into the hemp reveries and dreams, which seem as real as those of every-day life, and always more grand. Hashish eaters and smokers in the East recognised this fact, and always, prior to indulging in the drug, surrounded themselves with the most pleasing sounds, faces, forms, etc."

"I see," I answered, dreamily. "But what is there behind those curtains that I see moving now and again?" The heavy curtains just opposite where we lay seemed to shut in an alcove.

"There are several small rooms there," said my companion, "shut off from this room by the curtains you see move. Each is magnificently fitted up, I am told. They are reserved for persons, chiefly ladies, who wish to avoid every possibility of detection, and at the same time enjoy their hashish and watch the inmates of this room."

"Are there many ladies of good social standing who come here?"

"Very many. Not the cream of the *demi-monde*, understand me, but *ladies*. Why, there must be at least six hundred in this city alone who are *habituées*. Smokers from different cities, Boston, Philadelphia, Chicago, and especially New Orleans, tell me that each city has its hemp retreat, but none so elegant as this."

And my companion swallowed another lozenge and relapsed into dreamy silence. I too lay back listlessly, and was soon lost in reverie, intense and pleasant. Gradually the room and its inmates faded from view; the revolving dragons went swifter and more swiftly, until the flaming tongues and eyes were merged into a huge ball of flame, that, suddenly detaching itself with a sharp sound from its pivot, went whirling and streaming off into the air until lost to sight in the skies. Then a sudden silence, during which I heard the huge waves of an angry sea breaking with fierce monotony in my head. Then I heard the fountain;

the musical tinkle of the spray as it struck upon the glass grew louder and louder, and the notes longer and longer, until they merged into one clear, musical bugle note that woke the echoes of a spring morning, and broke sharp and clear over hill and valley, meadow-land and marsh, hill-top and forest. A gayly caparisoned horseman, bugle in hand, suddenly appeared above a hill-crest. Closely following, a straggling group of horsemen riding madly. Before them a pack of hounds came dashing down the hill-side, baying deeply. Before them I, the fox, was running with the speed of desperation, straining every nerve to distance or elude them. Thus for miles and miles I ran on until at last, almost dead with fright and fatigue, I fell panting in the forest. A moment more and the cruel hounds would have had me, when suddenly a little field-mouse appeared, caught me by the paw, and dragged me through the narrow entrance to her nest. My body lengthened and narrowed until I found myself a serpent, and in me rose the desire to devour my little preserver, when, as I was about to strike her with my fangs, she changed into a beautiful little fairy, tapped my ugly black flat head with her wand, and as my fangs fell to earth I resumed my human shape. With the parting words, "Never seek to injure those who endeavour to serve you," she disappeared.

Looking about I found myself in a huge cave, dark and noisome. Serpents hissed and glared at me from every side, and huge lizards and ugly shapes scrambled over the wet floor. In the far corner of the cave I saw piles of precious stones of wondrous value that glanced and sparkled in the dim light. Despite the horrid shapes about me, I resolved to secure some, at least, of these precious gems. I began to walk toward them, but found that I could get no nearer—just as fast as I advanced, so fast did they seem to recede. At last, after what seemed a year's weary journey, I suddenly found myself beside them, and falling on my knees, began to fill my pockets, bosom, even my hat. Then I tried to rise, but could not: the jewels weighed me down. Mortified and disappointed, I replaced them all but three, weeping bitterly. As I rose to my feet it suddenly occurred to me that this was in no way real—only a hashish dream. And, laughing, I said,

"You fool, this is all nonsense. These are not real jewels; they only exist in your imagination." My real self arguing thus with my hashish self, which I could see, tired, ragged, and weeping, set me to laughing still harder, and then we laughed together—my two selves. Suddenly my real self faded away, and a cloud of sadness and misery settled upon me, and I wept again, throwing myself hysterically upon the damp floor of the cave.

Just then I heard a voice addressing me by name, and looking up, I saw an old man with an enormous nose bending over me. His nose seemed almost as large as his whole body. "Why do you weep, my son?" he said; "are you sad because you cannot have *all* these riches? Don't, then, for some day you will learn that whoso hath more wealth than is needed to minister to his wants must suffer for it. Every farthing above a certain reasonable sum will surely bring some worry, care, anxiety, or trouble. Three diamonds are your share; be content with them. But, dear me, here I am again neglecting my work! Here it is March, and I'm not half through yet!"

"Pray what is your work, venerable patriarch?" I asked; "and why has the Lord given you such a huge proboscis?"

"Ah! I see that you don't know me," he replied. "I am the chemist of the earth's bowels, and it is my duty to prepare all the sweet and delicate odours that the flowers have. I am busy all winter making them, and early in the spring my nymphs and apprentices deliver them to the Queen of the Flowers, who in turn gives them to her subjects. My nose is a little large because I have to do so much smelling. Come and see my laboratory."

His nose a little large! I laughed until I almost cried at this, while following him.

He opened a door, and entering, my nostrils met the oddest medley of odours I had ever smelled. Everywhere workmen with huge noses were busy mixing, filtering, distilling, and the like.

"Here," said the old man, "is a batch of odour that has been spoiled. Mistakes are frequent, but I find use for even such as that. The Queen of Flowers gives it to disobedient plants or flowers. You mortals call it asafœtida. Come in here

and see my organ;" and he led the way into a large rocky room, at one end of which was a huge organ of curious construction. Mounting to the seat, he arranged the stops and began to play.

Not a sound could be heard, but a succession of odours swept past me, some slowly, some rapidly. I understood the grand idea in a moment. Here was music to which that of sound was coarse and earthly. Here was a harmony, a symphony, of odours! Clear and sharp, intense and less intense, sweet, less sweet, and again still sweeter, heavy and light, fast and slow, deep and narcotic, the odours, all in perfect harmony, rose and fell, and swept by me, to be succeeded by others.

Irresistibly I began to weep, and fast and thick fell the tears, until I found myself a little stream of water, that, rising in the rocky caverns of the mountain, dashed down its side into the plain below. Fiercely the hot sun beat upon my scanty waters, and like a thin grey mist I found myself rising slowly into the skies, no longer a stream. With other clouds I was swept away by the strong and rapid wind far across the Atlantic, over the burning sand wastes of Africa, dipping toward the Arabian Sea, and suddenly falling in hugh rain-drops into the very heart of India, blossoming with poppies. As the ground greedily sucked up the refreshing drops I again assumed my form.

Suddenly the earth was rent apart, and falling upon the edge of a deep cavern, I saw far below me a molten, hissing sea of fire, above which a dense vapour hung. Issuing from this mist, a thousand anguished faces rose toward me on scorched and broken wings, shrieking and moaning as they came.

"Who in Heaven's name are these poor things?"

"These," said a voice at my side, "are the spirits, still incarnate, of individuals who, during life, sought happiness in the various narcotics. Here, after death, far beneath, they live a life of torture most exquisite, for it is their fate, ever suffering for want of moisture, to be obliged to yield day by day their life-blood to form the juice of poppy and resin of hemp in order that their dreams, joys, hopes, pleasures, pains, and anguish of past and present may again be tasted by mortals."

As he said this I turned to see who he was, but he had disappeared. Suddenly I heard a fierce clamour, felt the scrawny arms of these foul spirits wound about my neck, in my hair, on my limbs, pulling me over into the horrible chasm, into the heart of hell, crying, shrilly, "Come! thou art one of us. Come! come! come!" I struggled fiercely, shrieked out in my agony, and suddenly awoke, with the cold sweat thick upon me.

"Are you, then, so fond of it that nothing can awaken you? Here have I been shaking and pulling you for the past five minutes. Come, rouse yourself; your dreams seem to be unpleasant."

Gradually my senses became clearer. The odours of the room, the melodies of early evening, the pipe that had fallen from my hand, the faces and forms of the hemp-smokers, were once more recognised.

My companion wished me to stay, assuring me that I would see many queer sights before morning, but I declined, and after taking, by his advice, a cup of Paraguay tea (cocoa leaf), and then a cup of sour lemonade, I passed down-stairs, exchanged my present for my former dress, returned my pipe, and left the house.

The dirty streets, the tinkling car-horse bell, the deafening "Here you are! twenty sweet oranges for a quarter!" and the drizzling rain were more grateful by far than the odours, sounds, and sights, sweet though they were, that I had just left. Truly it was the cradle of dreams rocking placidly in the very heart of a great city, translated from Bagdad to Gotham.

GREENWICH VILLAGE

I.

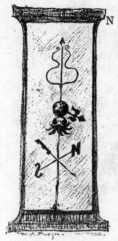

IN the resolute spirit of another Andorra, the village of Greenwich maintains its independence in the very midst of the city of New York—submitting to no more of a compromise in the matter of its autonomy than is involved in the Procrustean sort of splicing which has hitched fast the extremities of its tangled streets to the most readily available streets in the City Plan. The flippant carelessness with which this apparent union has been effected only serves to emphasize the actual separation. In almost every case these ill-advised couplings are productive of anomalous disorder, while in the case of the numbered streets they openly travesty the requirements of communal propriety and of common-sense: as may be inferred from the fact that within this disjointed region Fourth Street crosses Tenth, Eleventh and Twelfth streets very nearly at right angles—to the permanent bewilderment of nations and to the perennial confusion of mankind.

In addition to being hopelessly at odds with the surrounding city, Greenwich is handsomely at variance with itself. Its streets, so far as they can be said to be parallel at all, are parallel in four distinct groups; they have a tendency to sidle away from each other and to take sudden and unreasonable turns; some of them start out well enough, but, after running only a block or two, encounter a church or a row of houses and pull up short. Here, in a word, is the same sort of irregularity that is found in the lower part of the city between Broadway and the East River, and it comes from the same cause: neither of these crooked regions was a creation; both were growths. As streets were wanted in Greenwich they were opened—or were made by promoting existing lanes—in accordance with the notions of the owners of the land; and that the village did grow up in this loose and easy fashion is indicative of its early origin. Actually, excepting the immediate vicinity of the Battery, this is the oldest habitation of white men on the Island of New York.

But there were red men living here before the white men came. In the Dutch Records references are made to the Indian village of Sapokanican; and this name, or the Bossen Bouerie—meaning farm in the woods—was applied for more than a century to the region which came to be known as Greenwich in the later, English, times. The Indian village probably was near the site of the present Gansevoort Market; but the name seems to have been applied to the whole region lying between the North River and the stream called the Manetta Water or Bestavaar's Kill.

Although the Manetta Creek no longer is visible on the surface, it still flows in diminished volume through its ancient channel—as those living near or over it sometimes know to their cost. Its east branch rises east of Fifth Avenue between Twentieth and Twenty-first streets, whence it flows in nearly a straight line to the southwest corner of Union Square; thence in a slightly curving line to a junction with the west branch (which rises east of Sixth Avenue, between Fifteenth and Sixteenth streets) near the middle of the block bounded by Eleventh and Twelfth streets and Fifth and Sixth avenues; from this junction it flows to Fifth Avenue and Clinton Place; and thence across Washington Square, through Minetta Street, and nearly parallel with Downing Street, to the North River between Charlton and Houston streets. Notwithstanding the fact that this creek has been either culverted over or filled in throughout its entire length, it still asserts itself occasionally with a most undesirable vigor. Heavy buildings cannot be erected on or near its bed without recourse to a costly foundation of piles, nor can deep excavations be made anywhere near its channel without danger of overflow. Both of these conditions have been in evidence recently—the pile-driving, on a very large scale.

OLD HOUSES ON GREENWICH STREET.

for the Lincoln Building at the south-west corner of Union Square; the inundation, in the deep cellar lately dug on Sixth Avenue a little below Eleventh Street, and also in the cellar of the new building No. 66 Fifth Avenue.

In primitive times the land between Manetta Water and the North River was very fertile—a light loamy soil, the value of which anybody with half an eye for soils could see at a glance. Wherefore Peter Minuit, first of the Dutch Governors, with a becoming regard for the interests of his owners—this was just after he had bought the whole Island of Manhattan from the unsuspecting savages for sixty guilders, or twenty-four dollars—set apart Sapokanican as one of the four farms to be reserved to the Dutch West India Company in perpetuity. With even greater, but more personal, astuteness the second Dutch Governor, Wouter Van Twiller—having a most unbecoming regard for his own strictly individual interests—made himself at once grantor and grantee of this property, and so appropriated the Company's Farm No. 3 as his own private

tobacco plantation. He was a weak brother, this Governor Van Twiller, and his governing was of a spasmodic and feeble sort; but his talent for converting public property to private uses was so marked that it would have given him prominence at a very much later period in the history of the Ninth Ward—the whole of which section of the future city, it will be observed, with some considerable slices from the adjacent territory, he grabbed with one swoop of his big Dutch hands.

Van Twiller, coming over in the *Soutberg*, landed on this island in April, 1633. As he was dilatory only in matters of state it is reasonable to suppose that he annexed Sapokanican in time to sow his first crop of tobacco that very year. His farm-house doubtless was the first house erected on the island of Manhattan north of the settlement around Fort Amsterdam; and with the building of this house at the Bossen Bouerie, Greenwich Village was founded—only a dozen years after the formal colonization of the New Netherland, and rather more than two centuries and a half ago.

Things went so easily and gently in those placid times that a long while passed before the Bossen Bouerie suffered the smallest change. Twenty years later, in the time of Governor Stuyvesant, mention is made of "the few houses at Sappokanigan"; and nearly half a century later a passing reference to the settlement there is made in the Labadist journal so fortunately discovered by the late Henry C. Murphy during his residence at the Hague. Under date of September 7, 1679, the journal contains this entry: "We crossed over the island, which takes about three-quarters of an hour to do, and came to the North River, which we followed a little within the woods to Sapokanikee. Gerrit having a sister and friends there, we rested ourselves and drank some good beer, which refreshèd us. We continued along the shore to the city, where we arrived at an early hour in the evening, very much fatigued, having walked this day about forty miles. I must add, in passing through this island we sometimes encountered such a sweet smell in the air that we stood still because we did not know what it was we were meeting."

And so for about a century after Governor Van Twiller, in a prophetically aldermanic fashion, had boodled to himself the whole of the future Ninth Ward, the settlement at the Bossen Bouerie, otherwise Sapokanican, was but a hamlet, and a very small hamlet, tucked into the edge of the woodland a little to the northward of where the docks of the Cunard and White Star steamers were to be in the fulness of time: and the hamleters doubtless had very fine trout-fishing between the future Fifth and Sixth avenues in the Manetta Water; and, in the autumn, good duck-shooting over the marsh which later was to be Washington Square.

II.

I know not how long a time may have elapsed between the conquest of this island by the English and the discovery by the Dutch living retired at the Bossen Bouerie that, a sea-change having overswept their destinies, they had passed from the domination of the States General to the domination of the British King.

It is said that when the engineers of the West Shore Railroad, provided with guides and interpreters, penetrated into the valley of the Hackensack, a dozen

ON THE STEPS.

SIR PETER WARREN K.B.
Vice Admiral of the Red Squadron

burg and Kinderkamack, and the towns thereto adjacent, as mere idle talk. Naturally, the much more impossible story told by the engineers involved so violent a strain upon human credulity that the tellers of it were lucky in getting safely away, across the hills by Rockland Lake to the Hudson Valley, with unbroken theodolites and whole hides. The matter, I may add, is reported to have remained in uncertainty until the running of milk trains brought this region into communication with the outside world.

The case of the people dwelling at Sapokanican was different. This hamlet being less remote, and far less inaccessible, than the towns in the Hackensack Valley, being, indeed, but a trifle more than two miles northward of the Dutch stronghold, there is reason for believing that the news of the surrender of Fort Amsterdam to the English, on the 8th of September, 1664, penetrated thither within a comparatively short period after the gloomy event occurred. Indeed— while there is no speaking with absolute precision in this matter—I can assert confidently that within but a trifle more than half a century after the change of rulers had taken place the inhabitants of this settlement were acquainted with what had occurred: as is proved by an existing land conveyance, dated 1721, in which the use of the phrase "the Bossen Bouerie, alias Greenwich," shows not only that the advent of the English was known there, but that already the new-comers had so wedged themselves into prominence as to begin their mischievous obliteration of the good old Dutch names.

years or so ago, they created a great commotion among the honest Dutch folk dwelling in those sequestered parts by taking in the news that something more than eighty years previously the American Republic had been proclaimed. Some few of the more wide-awake of these retired country folk had got hold, it was found, of a rumor to the effect that the New Netherland, having been traded away for Surinam by the provisions of the Treaty of Breda, had become a dependency of the British crown; but the rumor never had been traced to an authoritative source, and was regarded by the older and more conservative of the inhabitants of Tenafly and Schraalen-

For a long while I cherished the belief that the name of Greenwich had been given to the Bossen Bouerie by a gallant sailor who for a time made that region his home: Captain Peter Warren of the Royal Navy—who died Sir Peter Warren, K.B., and a Vice-Admiral of the Red Squadron, and whose final honor was a tomb in the Abbey in the company of other heroes and of various kings. Applied by a British sailor to his home ashore, there was an absolute fitness in the name; and it had precisely a parallel in the bestowal of the name of Chelsea upon the adjoining estate by a soldier, Colonel Clarke. But a considerate survey of the facts has compelled me, though very reluctantly, to abandon this pleasingly poetical hypothesis. I am inclined to believe that the name Greenwich was in use as early as the year 1711, at which time Peter Warren was a bog-trotting Irish lad of only eight years old; and it certainly was in use, as is proved by the land conveyance cited above, as early as the year 1721, at which time my gentleman was but a sea-lieutenant, and had not (so far as I can discover) laid eyes on America at all.

Admiral Sir Peter Warren was a dashing personage in his day and generation, but his glory was won in what now are wellnigh forgotten wars. Irish by birth, and with as fine a natural disposition for fighting as ever an Irishman was blessed with, he worked his way up in the service with so handsome a rapidity that he was gazetted a post-captain, and to the command of his Majesty's ship *Grafton*, when he was only twenty-four years old—and his very first service after being posted was in the fleet with which Sir Charles Wager knocked the Rock of Gibraltar loose from the rest of the Spanish possessions, and, thereafter, with more rigor than righteousness, annexed it to the dominions of the British Crown.

This was in the year 1727. In the year 1728 Captain Warren was on the American station in the *Solebay*, frigate; probably was here again in 1737; and certainly was here from about 1741 until 1746 in the *Squirrel*, sloop, the *Launceston*, frigate, and the 60-gun ship *Superbe*. In the spring of 1744 Sir Chaloner Ogle left him for a while commodore of a squadron of sixteen sail on the Leeward Island station —where his luck so well stood by him that off Martinique, in but little more than four months (February 12–June 24) he captured no less than twenty-four prizes: one of which was a register ship whereof the lading of plate was valued at £250,000!

Most of these prizes were sent into New York to be condemned; and "Messieurs Stephen De Lancey & Company" (as appears from an advertisement in *The Weekly Post Boy* for June 30, 1744) acted as the agents of Captain Warren in the sale of

RESIDENCE OF ABRAHAM VAN NESS.

his French and Spanish swag. Naturally, the good bargains to our merchants which came of his dashing performances made him vastly popular here. After his brilliant cruise he returned to New York that the *Launceston* might "go upon the careen"; and when he had refitted and was about to get to sea again the *Post Boy* (August 27) gave him this fine send-off: "His Majesty's ship *Launceston*, commanded by the brave Commodore Warren (whose absence old Oceanus seems to

OLD HOUSE IN DOWNING STREET.

lament), being now sufficiently repaired, will sail in a few Days in order once more to pay some of his Majesty's enemies a Visit.

"The sails are spread; see the bold warrior comes
To chase the French and interloping Dons!"

III.

I have revived for a moment the personality of this gallant gentleman because the village of Greenwich, while not named by him, had its rise on one of the estates which he purchased with his winnings at sea.

Flying his flag aboard the *Launceston*, commanding on the station, and making such a brave show with his captured ships, Captain—by courtesy Commodore—Warren cut a prodigiously fine figure here in New York about the year of grace 1744; so fine, indeed, that never a man in the whole Province could be compared with him in dignity save only the Governor himself. And under these brilliant circumstances it is not at all surprising that pretty Mistress Susannah De Lancey was quite ready to complete his tale of "Irishman's luck" by giving him in her own sweet person an heiress for a wife; nor that her excellent father—who already must have made a pot of money out of this most promising son-in-law—was more than ready to give his consent to the match. It was about the time of the Commodore's marriage, probably, that he bought his Greenwich farm—a property of not far from three hundred acres; which was a little increased, later, by a gift of land voted to him by the city in recognition of his achievement at Louisburg in 1745.

Pending the building of his country-seat, and probably also as a winter residence, Captain Warren occupied the Jay house near the lower end of Broadway. One of the historians of New York, falling violently afoul of another historian of New York, has asserted hotly that Captain Warren built and lived in the house, known as the Kennedy house, which long occupied the site No. 1 Broadway. Heaven forbid that I should venture to thrust my gossiping nose (if so bold a metaphor may be tolerated) into this archæological wrangle; but, with submission, it is necessary for my present purposes to assert positively that Captain Warren had no more to do with the building of the Kennedy house than he had to do with the casting down of the walls of Jericho. In the English Records, under date of May, 1745, is this entry: "Ordered: That a straight line be drawn from the south corner of the house of Mr. Augustus Jay, now in the occupation of Peter Warren, Esquire, to the north corner of the house of Archibald Kennedy, fronting the Bowling Green in Broadway, and that Mr. William Smith, who is now about to build a house (and all other persons who shall build between the two houses) lay their foundations and build conformably to the aforesaid line." This record, I conceive, fixes definitely Captain Warren's downtown residence, and also sufficiently confirms the accepted genesis of the Kennedy house.

Concerning the country-seat at Greenwich even the historians have not very materially disagreed. It was built by Captain Warren on a scale of elegance appropriate to one who had only to drop across to the Leeward Islands and pick up a Spanish plate ship, or a few French West-Indiamen, in order to satisfy any bills which the carpenters and masons might send in; and the establishment seems to have been maintained upon a footing of liberality in keeping with this easy way of securing a revenue. The house stood about three hundred yards back from the river, on ground which fell away in a gentle slope toward the water-side. The main entrance was from the east; and at the rear—on the level of the drawing-room and a dozen feet or so above the sloping hill-side—was a broad veranda commanding the view westward to the Jersey Highlands and southward down the bay clear to the Staten Island hills. I like to fancy my round little captain

seated upon this veranda of placid sum-mer afternoons, smoking a comforting pipe after his mid-day dinner, and taking with it, perhaps, as sea-faring gentlemen often did in those days, a glass or two of substantial rum-and-water to keep every-thing down under hatches well stowed. With what approving eyes must he have regarded the trimly kept lawns and gar-dens below him, and with what eyes of affection the *Launceston*, all a-taunto, lying out in the stream! Presently, doubtless, the whiffs from his pipe came

A STAGE IN THE THIRTIES.

at longer and longer intervals, and at last entirely ceased—as the spirit which animated his plumply prosperous body, lulled by its soft and mellowing surroundings, sank gently into peaceful sleep. And then I fancy him, an hour or two later, wakened by Mistress Sue's playing upon the harpsichord; and his saying handsome things to her (in his rich Irish brogue) when she comes from the drawing-room to join him and they stand together—one of his stout little arms tucked snugly about her jimp waist—looking out across the gleaming river and the Elysian Fields, dark in shadow, at the glowing splendor of the sunset above the foot-hills of the Palisades.

The picture of the house which is here reproduced was made a hundred years after the admiral had ceased to cruise upon the waters of this planet, and when the property was in the possession of the late Abraham Van Ness, Esq.—whose home it was for more than thirty years. Great locust-trees stood guard about it, together with a few poplars; and girding the garden were thick hedges of box, whence came in the summer days of hot sunshine —as I am told by one of the delightful old gentlemen with whom of late I have been holding converse—a sweetly aromatic smell. The poplar-trees, probably, dated from the first decade of the present century, at which period they had an extraordinary vogue. It was in the year 1809 that Mr. Samuel Burling's highly injudicious offer to plant the principal street of New York—from Leonard Street northward to the Greenwich Lane—with poplar-trees was accepted gratefully by the corporation, "because it will be an additional beauty to Broadway, the pride of our city"; and the outcome of that particular piece of beautifying was to make Broadway look for a great many years afterwards like a street which had escaped from a Noah's ark.

But long before anybody had even dreamed that the Broadway ever would be extended to these remote northern regions the Warren farm had passed from the possession not only of Sir Peter, but also from the possession of his three daughters—Charlotte, Anne, and Susannah—who were his sole descendants and heirs. The admiral seems to have been but little in America during the later years of his life; and after 1747—when he was elected a member of Parliament for the borough of Westminster—I find no authentic trace of him on this side of the Atlantic. But Lady Warren, while Sir Peter was spending the most of his time at sea blazing away with his cannon at the French, very naturally continued to reside near her father and brother here in New York; not until his election to Parliament, at which time he became a householder in London, did she join him on the other side.

Doubtless, also, consideration for her daughters—in the matter of schooling, and with a look ahead toward match-making —had much to do with her Ladyship's move. So far as match-making was concerned, the change of base enabled her to make a very fair score—two, out of a possible three. Charlotte, the eldest daughter, married Willoughby, Earl of Abingdon, and Ann, the second daughter, married Charles Fitzroy, afterward Baron Southampton: whereby is seen that real estate in New York, coupled with a substantial bank account, gave as firm assurance of a coronet sevenscore years ago as it does to-day. Susannah, the youngest daughter, was indiscreet enough, I fear, to make a mere love-match. She married a paltry colonel of foot, one William Skinner—and presently died, as did also her husband, leaving behind her a baby Susannah to inherit her third of the chunky admiral's prize-moneys and lands.

The names of the husbands of all three of these ladies became attached to the property in New York. Skinner Road was the present Christopher Street; Fitzroy Road ran north, near the line of the present Eighth Avenue, from about the present Fourteenth Street to about the present Forty-second Street; and the Abingdon Road (called also Love Lane), almost on the line of the present Twenty-first Street, connected what now is Broadway with the Fitzroy Road and eventually was extended to the North River. The only survival of any of these names is in Abingdon Square.

The deeds for the property in the Greenwich region all begin by reciting— with the old-womanly loquacity of deeds —the facts in regard to Sir Peter's issue set forth above; and in addition tell how his estate was partitioned by a process in which the solemnity of legal procedure was mitigated by an agreeable dash of the dicing habits of the day: "In pursuance of the powers given in the said antenuptial deeds the trustees therein named, on March 31st, 1787, agreed upon a partition of the said lands, which agreement was with the approbation and consent of the cestui que trusts, to wit: Earl and Lady Abingdon, and Charles Fitzroy and Ann his wife, the said Susannah Skinner the second not then having arrived at age. In making the partition the premises

It was on the lines of the map made for this partition that Greenwich went along easily and peacefully until it was brought up with a round turn, in the year 1811, by the formation of the present City Plan.

IV.

The lots into which the Warren property was divided were of twelve or fifteen acres, suitable for small farms or country

A WISTARIA WALK, HORATIO STREET.

were divided into three parts on a survey made thereof and marked A, B, and C; and it was agreed that such partition should be made by each of the trustees naming a person to throw dice for and in behalf of their respective cestui que trusts, and that the person who should throw the highest number should have parcel A; the one who should throw the next highest number should have parcel B; and the one who should throw the lowest number should have parcel C—for the persons whom they respectively represented: and the premises were partitioned accordingly."

seats, and the base-line naturally adopted was the present Greenwich Avenue, then Monument Lane. By the turn of the dice, the homestead, with fifty-five acres of land round about it, fell to the share of Lady Abingdon; who united with her husband in selling it, in 1788, for $2200. A little later the property passed into the possession of Abijah Hammond; and from him the mansion-house, with the square bounded by Fourth, Bleecker, Perry, and Charles streets, was purchased by Mr. Van Ness in 1819 for $15,000. Until August, 1865, this beautiful property remained intact—save that the trees ever grew larger and that

TINY HOUSE, WEST TENTH STREET.

height to save it from being heavy in wet weather and in part under water with strong spring tides. For the greater convenience of the dwellers at Greenwich, therefore, inland communication between that region and the city was provided for by opening a lane (formally approved in 1768) from the Post Road (now the Bowery) westward across the fields. Two sections of this lane still are in existence: the bit between the Bowery and Broadway (formerly Art Street) that now is Astor Place; and the bit between Eighth and Fourteenth streets that now is Greenwich Avenue. Being prolonged on the lines thus established, the two sections met at an angle of about 45° near the northwest corner of the present Washington Square.

the house took on a mellower tone as the years went on—and then it was swept away, and the existing stupid brick houses were built in its place.

For more than a century and a quarter the Warren house was the most important dwelling on this portion of the island. It was the nucleus about which other country-seats clustered—including, before the year 1767, those of William Bayard, James Jauncey, and Oliver De Lancey, Lady Warren's brother, whose estate, later, was confiscated because of his loyalty to the Crown. Very proper and elegant people were all of these, and—their seats being at a convenient distance from the city—their elegant friends living in New York found pleasure in making Greenwich an objective point when taking the air of fine afternoons. And even when visiting was out of the question, a turn through Greenwich to the Monument was a favorite expedition among the gentle-folk of a century or so ago.

Until about the year 1767, access to this region was only by the Greenwich Road, close upon the line of the present Greenwich Street and directly upon the waterside. Where it crossed Lispenard's salt-meadows (the low region lying on each side of the present Canal Street) and the marshy valley (about Charlton Street) of the Manetta Creek, the road was raised upon a causeway—but not to a sufficient

Greenwich Lane was called also Monument Lane and Obelisk Lane: for the reason that at its northern extremity, a little north of the present Eighth Avenue and Fifteenth Street, was a monument in honor of General Wolfe. After the erection of this memorial to the hero of Quebec the drive of good society was out the Post Road to the Greenwich turning; thence across to the Obelisk; thence by the Great Kill Road (the present Gansevoort Street) over to the Hudson; and so homeward by the river-side while the sun was sinking in golden glory behind the Jersey hills. Or the drive could be extended a little by going out the Post Road as far as Love Lane, and thence south by the Southampton, Warren, or Fitzroy Road to the Great Kill Road, and so by the water-side back to town.

With the exceptions noted, all of the old roads hereabouts have disappeared under the City Plan; yet many traces of them still survive and can be found by careful searching along their ancient lines.* For instance, the Union Road—

* In determining the lines of the old roads, and the boundaries of the old estates, I have had the assistance of Mr. Richard D. Cooke, the highest authority in such matters in New York, and the use of his unique collection of maps.

which connected the Skinner and Great Kill roads—seems at the first glance to have been entirely ploughed under. But such is not the case. It began about in the rear of the frame dwelling No. 33 West Eleventh Street; and not two hundred feet from its beginning its slanting line across Twelfth Street still is defined clearly by the corner cut off and the corner projecting of the houses numbered 43 and 45. On West Thirteenth Street an old wooden house, No. 38, marks with its slanting side the line of the road: and an actual section of the road survives in the alley beside this house, leading diagonally to a very picturesque old wooden dwelling—built when all about here was open country—which is buried in the centre of the block.

As to the monument to General Wolfe, which gave a name to Monument Lane and an objective point for afternoon drives, it seems to have dissolved into thin air. It certainly was in position during the British occupation of New York in Revolutionary times, but since those times no vestige of it has been found. The theory has been advanced that the English soldiers took away with them this memorial of their gallant countryman—fearing that harm might come to it if left in a rebellious land. But an obelisk is not a handy thing for an army to carry around with it, even though, as in this case, the obelisk is a small one and the army is travelling by sea; nor is it so inconspicuous an object that it can be picked up or set down by an army without attracting a certain amount of attention on the part of the by-standers. Therefore I think that had it really been put aboard ship somebody here would have chronicled the queer fact; and that had it been landed in another country news as to its

whereabouts would have come to New York in the century and more that has slipped away since it disappeared. On the other hand, had it remained on this island, it ought still to be somewhere in sight.

On the line of the Monument Lane, or Greenwich Lane, lay the Potter's Field, a part of which now is Washington Square. In 1794 the Potter's Field was established at the junction of the Post Road and the Bloomingdale Road, on land now a part of Madison Square; but this site was abandoned three years later, partly because the United States Arsenal was

GAY STREET.

erected there and partly because reasonable exception was taken to the obtrusion of pauper funerals upon the fashionable drive. On this latter score the move, in 1797, to what now is Washington Square did not much mend matters, and very strong remonstrances were urged against it. But the move was

Arch. Unfortunately, I was out of the country when these tombstones were dug up; and, later, when I searched for them they had disappeared.

North of Greenwich Lane, extending from the Bowery across to about the easterly line of the present Fifth Avenue, was the Eliot estate, which later was owned by Captain Robert Richard Randall, and was bequeathed by him (June 1, 1801) for the founding of the Sailors' Snug Harbor. The estate, in all, comprised about twenty-one acres of good farming land, with which went the mansion-house, and also two or three lots in the First Ward. It was Captain Randall's intention that the Snug Harbor should be built upon this property—for which he had paid £5000 when he bought it, in 1790, from "Baron" Poelnitz—and that the farm would supply all the grain and vegetables which the inmates of the institution would require. The trustees, however, perceived that farming was not the most profitable use to which the property could be put; and while the suits to break the will still were pending they procured an act of the Legislature (April, 1828) which enabled them to lease it and to purchase the property on Staten Island where the asylum now stands. But it was not until the year 1831, the case having been settled definitely in favor of the trust by the decision of the United States Supreme Court in March, 1830, that this purchase was made. At the time of Captain Randall's death his estate yielded an annual income of about $4000; by 1848 the income had increased to nearly $40,000; by 1870 to a little more than $100,000; and at the present time it is about $350,000.

Plan of part of the City of NEW-YORK & Environs.
By John Montresor, Engr. 1775.

Valuable though the Snug Harbor property is, it certainly would have increased in value far more rapidly, and would be far more valuable as a whole at the present day, had it fallen into the market on its owner's death instead of becoming leasehold property in perpetuity. Leaseholds are the direct product

made, and there the graveyard remained—on the north side of the lane, about at the foot of the present Fifth Avenue—until the year 1823. It was not strictly a pauper's graveyard—a fact that was demonstrated by the unearthing of tombstones (a luxury not accorded to paupers) while excavation was in progress, in the summer of 1890, for the Washington

of the law of entail or primogeniture—under which the title to land is held only in trust by the male line in seniority, and the fee becomes simple only when the line is extinguished and a division is made among the general heirs. Holdings of this sort essentially are un-American in principle, and have the practical inconvenience of two ownerships (which conceivably may become antagonistic) in what virtually is a single possession: a house and the land on which it stands.

There is a very considerable amount of leasehold property in New York, and in almost every instance this encumbered land is less valuable—*i. e.*, brings in a smaller return—than land immediately

V.

Simultaneously with the founding of the country-seats at Greenwich, two small settlements of a humbler sort were formed on the shore of the North River in that region. One of these, known as Lower Greenwich, was at the foot of Brannan (now Spring) Street, and the other, known as Upper Greenwich, was at the foot of what now is Christopher Street and then was the Skinner Road. Of this latter an entire block still remains: the row of low wooden houses on West Street between Christopher and Tenth, of which the best view is from Weehawken Street in the rear. These houses were standing, certainly, as far back as 1796—as is shown on the Commissioners' map

WEST TENTH STREET.

adjoining it of which the fee may be transferred. In the case of the Snug Harbor estate the first leases, when the existing dwelling-houses were erected, were made to advantage; but this tied-up property was skipped over, when business moved northward, in favor of the region above Fourteenth Street where the fee can be acquired.

by the indentation to accommodate them upon the State-prison property acquired in that year. Probably they are the houses indicated on the Ratzen Map as standing at this point one hundred and twenty-six years ago.

The building of the State-prison brought to the upper village what might have been called—could the use of the word

HOME FOR AGED COUPLES, HUDSON STREET, OPPOSITE GROVE.

have been anticipated by four-fifths of a century—a boom. As passed, the act of Assembly of March 26, 1796, provided for the erection of two prisons, one in Albany and one in New York; but a subsequent modification of the act applied the entire sum appropriated—about $200,000—to the erection of a single building here. The prison stood at the foot of Amos (now Tenth) Street, on the site occupied by the existing brewery, into the structure of which (as may be seen just inside the Tenth Street entrance) have been incorporated parts of the old walls. The building—200 feet long, with wings extending from it at right angles toward the river—stood in grounds of about four acres in extent, the whole enclosed by a stone wall twenty-two feet high on the side toward the river, and fourteen feet high elsewhere. One of my aged gossips has told me that a wharf was built out into the stream, but that it did not extend far enough to be available at all stages of the tide. This particular gossip was a river-captain in his day, sixty years and more ago, and among the queer freights which he used to bring to the city there would be now and then a load of convicts. His passengers did not like it at all, he said, when, the tide not serv-

ing, he was compelled to carry them past the prison to which they were bound and to land them at the Battery, "and I must say I didn't wonder," he added. "Just think how it would be yourself— walkin' clost on to three mile of a br'ilin' summer day, with nothin' better'n gettin' jailed when you comed t' the end of it! It was only human natur' for them poor devils t' get up on their ears an' swear." Log rafts from up the river used to make fast near the State-prison wharf pending their purchase by the ship-builders and lumber-dealers down in the city. It was great fun, one of my cheery old gentlemen tells me, going in swimming off these rafts about sixty years ago.

The prison was opened November 28, 1797, when seventy prisoners were transferred thither, and it continued in use a little more than thirty years. The male prisoners were transferred to Sing Sing in 1828, and the female prisoners in the spring of 1829—when the entire property was sold into private hands. This was one of the first prisons in which convicts were taught trades; but for a long while the more conspicuous results of this benevolent system — a feature of which was the assembling together of the prisoners in large work-rooms, with consequent abundant opportunities for concocting conspiracies — were dangerous plots and mutinous outbreaks. In June 1799 fifty or sixty men revolted and seized their keepers; and not until the guards opened fire on them with ball cartridge—by which several were wounded, though none were killed—was the mutiny quelled. In April 1803 about forty men broke from the prison to the prison-yard, and, after setting fire to the building, attempted to scale the walls; and again the guards came with their muskets and compelled order—this time killing as well as wounding—while the keepers put out the fire. In May 1804 a still more dangerous revolt occurred. On this occasion the keepers were locked into the north wing of the building, which then was fired. Fortunately, according to a contemporaneous account, "one more humane than the rest released the keepers"; but the north wing was destroyed, involving a loss of $25,000, and in the confusion many of the prisoners escaped. A long sigh of thankfulness must have gone up from Greenwich when this highly volcanic institution became a thing of the past.

Yet the people of Greenwich were disposed to feel a certain pride in their penal establishment, and to treat it as one of the attractions of their town—as appears from the following advertisement of the Greenwich Hotel in *The Columbian* of September 18, 1811:

"A few gentlemen may be accommodated with board and lodging at this pleasant and healthy situation, a few doors from the State Prison. The Greenwich stage passes from this to the Federal Hall and returns five times a day."

A little later, 1816, Asa Hall's

line of stages was running, with departures from Greenwich on the even hours and from New York, at Pine Street and Broadway, on the uneven hours all day. The custom was to send to the stage office to engage a seat to town; and then the stage would call for the passenger, announcement being made of its approach—so that the passenger might be ready and no time lost—by noble blasts upon a horn. The fare each way was twenty-five cents. One of the freshest and most delightful of my old gentlemen remembers it all as clearly as though it were but yesterday—beginning with his mother's brisk, "Now, Dan, run up to Asa's and tell him to send the eight-o'clock stage here"; continuing with a faint burst of horn-blowing in the distance which grew louder and louder until it stopped with a flourish at the very door; and ending with the stage disappearing, to the accompaniment of a gallant tooting growing fainter and fainter, in a cloud of dust down the country road.

This country road was the present Greenwich Street south of Leroy. It was on Leroy Street that my old gentleman lived, seventy years and more ago, and

OLD HOUSE FACING BARROW STREET, ON WASHINGTON PLACE.

all about his home were open fields. Eastward the view was unobstructed quite across to Washington Square—as he knows positively because he remembers seeing from his own front stoop the gallows which was set up (near the present Washington Arch) for the execution of one Rose Butler, a negro wench who was hanged for murder in the year 1822. (Another of my elderly acquaintances remembers stealing away from home and going to this very hanging—and coming back so full of it that he could not keep his own secret, and so was most righteously and roundly spanked!)

South of Leroy Street was open country as far as Canal Street, "and probably farther"; but my gentleman is less certain, because there was no convenient gallows in that direction to fix a limit to his view. On this head, however, there is abundant evidence. Mr. Peter Gassner, treating of a period a little earlier—about the year 1803—writes: "Corri, another Frenchman, had a mead-garden and flying-horses on the eminence between Franklin and Leonard streets. It was at least fifty feet from [above] the road. You got to it by wooden stairs; and, when up, would overlook the space to Greenwich—nothing occupying the space until you met Borrowson's and old Tyler's, both mead-gardens and taverns." And the precise Mr. John Randel, Jun.—engineer to the Commissioners by whom was prepared, under the act of April 13, 1807, the present City Plan—writes that in 1809 he crossed the ditch at Canal Street on a wooden plank and walked thence nearly the whole distance to Christopher Street through open fields.

VI.

What tended most to develop Greenwich into a town—a cause more potent than its embryotic trade in lumber, its very small ferry, and its explosive prison, all combined—was its positive healthfulness; and the consequent security which it offered to refugees from the city when pestilence was abroad. The salubrity of this region (which is as marked now, relatively, as it was a century ago) is due to its excellent natural drainage, and to the fact that its underlying soil to a depth of at least fifty feet is a pure sand. In former times the sanitary conditions were still more favorable—when the ample space about the scattered houses assured an abundance of fresh air, and when the stretch of more than a mile of open country between the village and the city constituted a barrier which no pestilence but small-pox ever overcame.

It is in connection with small-pox that I find the first reference to Greenwich as a place of refuge. This occurs in a letter dated April 18, 1739, from Lieutenant-Governor Clarke to the Duke of Newcastle, beginning: "I beg leave to inform your Grace that, the Small Pox being in town, and one third part of the Assembly not having had it, I gave them leave to sit at Greenwich, a small village about two or three miles out of town." In this case, however, safety was not secured—for "the Small Pox" went along with the Assemblymen to Greenwich and sat there too.

It is hard to realize nowadays the deadliness of those early times in New York—before small-pox was controlled by vaccination and before yellow fever was guarded against by a tolerably effective system of quarantine. Judging from the newspaper references to it, small-pox seems to have been a regular feature of every winter; while yellow fever was so frequent a visitor that Mr. John Lambert, in his sketch of New York in the year 1807, wrote: "The malignant, or yellow, fever generally commences in the confined parts of the town, near the waterside, in the month of August or September." And to this, still in the same matter-of-course manner, Mr. Lambert added: "As soon as this dreadful scourge makes its appearance in New York the inhabitants shut up their shops and fly from their houses into the country. Those who cannot go far, on account of business, remove to Greenwich, a small village situate on the border of the Hudson River about two or three miles from town. Here the merchants and others have their offices, and carry on their concerns with little danger from the fever, which does not seem to be contagious beyond a certain distance. The banks and other public offices also remove their business to this place; and markets are regularly established for the supply of the inhabitants. Very few are left in the confined parts of the town except the poorer classes and the negroes. The latter, not being affected by the fever, are of great service at that dreadful crisis; and are the only persons who can be found to discharge the hazardous duties of attending the sick and burying the dead. Upwards of 20,000 people removed from the interior parts of the city and from the streets near the water-side in 1805."

Yellow fever seems to have been epidemic for the first time in New York in the summer of 1703. It was not recog-

But the most severe fever summers of the last century came close together in its final decade. Of these the first was 1791, in which the death rate was comparatively low; the second, 1795, was more severe, the deaths rising to upwards of 700; while in the course of the third, 1798—when more than 2000 deaths occurred, and the

WEEHAWKEN STREET.

nized as yellow fever, and is referred to in the records of the time as "the great sickness"; but from the description given of it, coupled with the fact that the infection was traced to a ship come in from St. Thomas, there is little room for doubt in regard to the nature of the disease. The mortality was so considerable that a panic seized upon the inhabitants of the city and they fled to the country for safety—thus establishing the habit to which Mr. Lambert refers as being fixed so firmly a century later on. Again, in the summer of 1742 and 1743 there was "a malignant epidemic strongly resembling the yellow fever in type," which caused upwards of two hundred deaths in the latter year.

city was forsaken by its inhabitants and commerce for a time was crushed—the fever became an overwhelming calamity. While the panic lasted, not only Greenwich but all the towns and villages roundabout were crowded with refugees.

The epidemics of fever which appeared with great frequency during the first quarter of the present century culminated in the direful summer of 1822—when, under stress of the worst panic ever caused by fever in this city, the town fairly exploded and went flying beyond its borders as though the pestilence had been a bursting mine. Hardie gives the following vivid sketch of the exodus: "Saturday, the 24th August, our city presented the appearance of a town besieged. From daybreak till night one line of carts, containing boxes, merchandise, and effects, were seen moving towards Greenwich Village and the upper parts of the city. Carriages and hacks, wagons and horsemen, were scouring the streets and filling the roads; persons with anxiety strongly marked on their countenances, and with hurried gait, were hustling through the streets. Temporary stores and offices were erecting, and even on the ensuing day (Sunday) carts were in motion, and the saw and hammer busily at work. Within a few days thereafter the Custom House, the Post Office, the Banks, the Insurance Offices, and the printers of newspapers located themselves in the village or in the upper part of Broadway, where they were free from the impending danger; and these places almost instantaneously became the seat of the immense business usually carried on in the great metropolis."

Devoe, who quotes the above in his "Market Book," adds: "The visits of yellow fever in 1798, '99, 1803 and '5, tended much to increase the formation of a village near the Spring Street Market and one also near the State Prison; but the fever of 1822 built up many streets with numerous wooden buildings for the uses of the merchants, banks (from which Bank Street took its name), offices, etc.; and the celerity of putting up these buildings is better told by the Rev'd Mr. Marcellus, who informed me that he saw corn growing on the present corner of Hammond [West Eleventh] and Fourth streets on a Saturday morning, and on the following Monday Sykes & Niblo had a house erected capable of accommodating three hundred boarders. Even the Brooklyn ferry-boats ran up here daily."

Among the more notable of the remnants of the time when the Greenwich region for the most part was open country are those at the southeast corner of Eleventh Street and Sixth Avenue: the little triangular graveyard and the two old framed dwellings which now rest on the lines of the street and the avenue, but which primitively stood—a few feet from their present site—on the now almost obliterated Milligan's Lane.

The triangular graveyard is a remnant of the second Beth Haim, or Place of Rest, owned on this island by the Jews. The first Beth Haim—purchased in 1681 and enlarged in 1729—is on the line of the elevated railway just south of Chatham Square. This was closed early in the present century, and then the Beth Haim at Greenwich was purchased—a plot of ground with a front of about fifty feet on Milligan's Lane, and thence extending, a little east of south, about one hundred and ten feet. In the year 1830, when Eleventh Street was opened on the lines of the City Plan—saving only the bit between Broadway and the Bowery on which stood the house of the stiffnecked Mr. Henry Brevoort—almost the whole of the Jewish burial-ground was swept away. The street went directly across it—leaving only the corner on its south side, and a still smaller corner on its north side.

VII.

Greenwich Village always has been to me the most attractive portion of New York. It has the positive individuality, the age, much of the picturesqueness, of that fascinating region of which the centre is Chatham Square; yet it is agreeably free from the foul odors and the foul humanity which make expeditions in the vicinity of Chatham Square, while abstractly delightful, so stingingly distressing to one's nose and soul.

Greenwich owes its picturesqueness to the protecting spirit of grace which has saved its streets from being rectangular and its houses from being all alike; and which also has preserved its many quaintnesses and beauties of age—with such resulting blessings as the view around the curve in Morton Street toward St. Luke's Church, or under the arch of trees where Grove and Christopher streets are mitred together by the little park, and the many friendly old houses which stand squarely on their right to be individual and have their own opinion of the rows of modern dwellings all made of precisely the same material cast in precisely the same mould.

The cleanliness, moral and physical, of the village is accounted for by the fact that from the very beginning it has been inhabited by a humanity of the better sort. From Fourteenth Street down to Canal Street, west of the meridian of Sixth Avenue, distinctively is the American quarter of New York. A sprinkling of French and Italians is found within these limits, together with the few Irish required for political purposes; and in the vicinity of Carmine Street are scattered some of the tents of the children of Ham. But with these exceptions the population is composed of substantial, well-to-do Americans—and it really does one's heart good, on the Fourth of July and the 22d of February, to see the way the owners of the roomy comfortable houses which here abound proclaim their nationality by setting the trim streets of Greenwich gallantly ablaze with American flags. As compared with the corresponding region on the east side—where a score of families may be found packed into a single building, and where even the bad smells have foreign names—this American quarter of New York is a liberal lesson in cleanliness, good citizenship, and self-respect.

And how interesting are the people whom one hereabouts encounters (with but the most trifling effort of the imagination) stepping along the ancient thoroughfares which once knew them in material form!—Wouter Van Twiller, chuckling over his easily won tobacco plantation; the Labadist envoys, rejoicing because of their discovery of a country permissive of liberty of conscience and productive of good beer; General Ol. De Lancey—wearing the Tory uniform which later cost him his patrimony—taking the air with his sister, Lady Warren, the stout, bewigged Sir Peter, and the three little girls; Governor Clinton, with the harried look of one upon whom an advance copy of the Declaration of Independence has been served; Senator Richard Henry Lee, of Virginia, who honored Greenwich by making it his home during the session of Congress in 1789; Master Tom Paine—escaped from Madame Bonneville and the little boys in the house in Grove Street—on his way to the Old Grapevine for a fresh jug of rum; shrewd old Jacob Barker, looking with satisfaction at the house in Jane Street bought from a butcher who had enough faith in him to take the doubtful notes of his bank at par. Only in Greenwich, or below the City Hall—a region over-noisy for wraiths—will one meet agreeable spectres such as these.

NEW YORK REVISITED
(PART 1)

THE single impression or particular vision most answering to the greatness of the subject would have been, I think, a certain hour of large circumnavigation that I found prescribed, in the fulness of the spring, as the almost immediate crown of a return from the far West. I had arrived at one of the transpontine stations of the Pennsylvania Railroad; the question was of proceeding to Boston, for the occasion, without pushing through the terrible town—why "terrible," to my sense, in many ways, I shall presently explain—and the easy and agreeable attainment of this great advantage was to embark on one of the mightiest (as appeared to me) of train-bearing barges and, descending the western waters, pass round the bottom of the city and remount the other current to Harlem; all without "losing touch" of the Pullman that had brought me from Washington. This absence of the need of losing touch, this breadth of effect, as to the whole process, involved in the prompt floating of the huge concatenated cars not only without arrest or confusion, but as for positive prodigal beguilement of the artless traveller, had doubtless much to say to the ensuing state of mind, the happily excited and amused view of the great face of New York. The extent, the ease, the energy, the quantity and number, all notes scattered about as if, in the whole business and in the splendid light, nature and science were joyously romping together, might have been taking on again, for their symbol, some collective presence of great circling and plunging, hovering and perching sea-birds, white-winged images of the spirit, of the restless freedom of the Bay. The Bay had always, on other opportunities, seemed to blow its immense character straight into one's face—coming "at" you, so to speak, bearing down on you, with the full force of a thousand prows of steamers seen exactly on the line of their longitudinal axis; but I had never before been so conscious of its boundless cool assurance or seemed to see its genius so grandly at play. This was presumably indeed because I had never before enjoyed the remarkable adventure of taking in so much of the vast bristling promontory from the water, of ascending the East River, in especial, to its upper diminishing expanses.

Something of the air of the occasion and of the mood of the moment caused the whole picture to speak with its largest suggestion; which suggestion is irresistible when once it is sounded clear. It is all, absolutely, an expression of things lately and currently *done,* done on a large impersonal stage and on the basis of inordinate gain—it is not an expression of any other matters whatever; and yet the sense of the scene (which had at several previous junctures, as well, put forth to my imagination its power), was commanding and thrilling, was in certain lights almost charming. So it befell, exactly, that an element of mystery and wonder entered into the impression—the interest of trying to make out, in the absence of features of the sort usually supposed indispensable, the reason of the beauty and the joy. It is indubitably a "great" bay, a great harbor, but no one item of the romantic, or even of the picturesque, as commonly understood, contributes to its effect. The shores are low and for the most part depressingly furnished and prosaically peopled; the islands, though numerous, have not a grace to exhibit, and one thinks of the other, the real flowers of geography in this order, of Naples, of Capetown, of Sydney, of Seattle, of San Francisco, of Rio, asking how if *they* justify a reputation, New York should seem to justify one. Then, after all, we remember that there are reputations and reputations; we remember above all that the imaginative response to the conditions here presented may just happen to proceed from the intellectual extravagance of the given observer. When this personage is open to corruption by almost any large view of an intensity of life, his vibrations tend to become a matter difficult even for *him* to explain. He may have to confess that the group of evident facts fails to account by itself for the complacency of his appreciation. Therefore it is that I find myself rather backward with a perceived sanction, of an at all proportionate kind, for the fine exhilaration with which, in this free wayfaring relation to them, the wide waters of New York inspire me. There is the beauty of light and air, the great scale of space, and, seen far away to the west, the open gates of the Hudson, majestic in their degree, even at a distance, and announcing still nobler things. But the real appeal, unmistakably, is in that note of vehemence in the local life of which I have spoken, for it is the appeal of a particular type of dauntless power.

The aspect the power wears then is indescribable; it is the power of the most extravagant of cities, rejoicing, as with the voice of the morning, in its might, its fortune, its unsurpassable conditions, and imparting to every object and element, to the motion and expression of every floating, hurrying, panting thing, to the throb of ferries and tugs, to the plash of waves and the play of winds and the glint of lights and the shrill of whistles and the quality and authority of breeze-borne cries—all, practically, a diffused, wasted clamor of *detonations*—something of its sharp free accent and, above all, of its sovereign sense of being "backed" and able to back. The universal *applied* passion struck me as shining unprecedentedly out of the composition; in the bigness and bravery and insolence, especially, of everything that rushed and shrieked, in the air as of a great intricate frenzied dance, half merry, half desperate, or at least half defiant, performed on the huge watery floor. This appearance of the bold lacing-together, across the waters, of the scattered members of the monstrous organism—lacing as by the ceaseless play of an enormous system of steam-shuttles or electric bobbins (I scarce know what to call them), commensurate in form with their infinite

work—does perhaps more than anything else to give the pitch of the vision of energy. One has the sense that the monster grows and grows, flinging abroad its loose limbs even as some unmannered young giant at his "larks," and that the binding stitches must forever fly further and faster and draw harder; the future complexity of the web, all under the sky and over the sea, becoming thus that of some colossal set of clockworks, some steel-souled machine-room of brandished arms and hammering fists and opening and closing jaws. The immeasurable bridges are but as the horizontal sheaths of pistons working at high pressure, day and night, and subject, one apprehends with perhaps inconsistent gloom, to certain, to fantastic, to merciless multiplication. In the light of this apprehension indeed the breezy brightness of the Bay puts on the semblance of the vast white page that awaits beyond any other perhaps the black overscoring of science.

Let me hasten to add that its present whiteness is precisely its charming note, the frankest of the signs you recognize and remember it by. That is the distinction I was just feeling my way to name as the main ground of its doing so well, for effect, without technical scenery. There are great imposing ports—Glasgow and Liverpool and London—that have already their page blackened almost beyond redemption from any such light of the picturesque as can hope to irradiate fog and grime, and there are others, Marseilles and Constantinople say, or, for all I know to the contrary, New Orleans, that contrive to abound before everything else in color, and so to make a rich and instant and obvious show. But memory, and the actual impression, keep investing New York with the tone, predominantly, of summer dawns and winter frosts, of sea-foam, of bleached sails and stretched awnings, of blanched hulls, of scoured decks, of new ropes, of polished brasses, of streamers clear in the blue air; and it is by this harmony, doubtless, that the projection of the individual character of the place, of the candor of its avidity and the freshness of its audacity, is most conveyed. The "tall buildings," which have so promptly usurped a glory that affects you as rather surprised, as yet, at itself, the multitudinous sky-scrapers standing up to the view, from the water, like extravagant pins in a cushion already overplanted, and stuck in as in the dark, anywhere and anyhow, have at least the felicity of carrying out the fairness of tone, of taking the sun and the shade in the manner of towers of marble. They are not all of marble, I believe, by any means, even if some may be, but they are impudently new and still more impudently "novel"—this in common with so many other terrible things in America—and they are triumphant payers of dividends; all of which uncontested and unabashed pride, with flash of innumerable windows and flicker of subordinate gilt attributions, is like the flare, up and down their long, narrow faces, of the lamps of some general permanent "celebration."

You see the pincushion in profile, so to speak, on passing between Jersey City and Twenty-third Street, but you get it broadside on, this loose nosegay of architectural flowers, if you skirt the Battery, well out, and embrace the whole plantation. Then the "American beauty," the rose of interminable stem, becomes the token of the cluster at large—to that degree that, positively, this is all that is wanted for emphasis of your final impression. Such growths, you feel, have confessedly arisen but to be "picked," in time, with a shears; nipped short off, by waiting fate, as soon as "science," applied to gain, has put upon the table, from far up its sleeve, some more winning card. Crowned not only with no history, but with no credible possibility of time for history, and consecrated by no uses save the commercial at any cost, they are simply the most piercing notes in that concert of the expensively provisional into which your supreme sense of New York resolves itself. They never begin to speak to you, in the manner of the builded majesties of the world as we have heretofore known such—towers or temples or fortresses or palaces—with the authority of things of permanence or even of things of long duration. One story is good only till another is told, and sky-scrapers are the last word of economic ingenuity only till another word be written. This shall be possibly a word of still uglier meaning, but the vocabulary of thrift at any price shows boundless resources, and the con-

sciousness of that truth, the consciousness of the finite, the menaced, the essentially *invented* state, twinkles ever, to my perception, in the thousand glassy eyes of these giants of the mere market. Such a structure as the comparatively windowless bell-tower of Giotto, in Florence, looks supremely serene in its beauty. You don't feel it to have risen by the breath of an interested passion that, restless beyond all passions, is forever seeking more pliable forms. Beauty has been the object of its creator's idea, and, having found beauty, it has found the form in which it splendidly rests.

Beauty indeed was the aim of the creator of the spire of Trinity Church, so cruelly overtopped and so barely distinguishable, from your train - bearing barge, as you stand off, in its abject helpless humility; and it may of course be asked how much of this superstition finds voice in the actual shrunken presence of that laudable effort. Where, for the eye, is the felicity of simplified Gothic, of noble preeminence, that once made of this highly pleasing edifice the pride of the town and the feature of Broadway? The answer is, as obviously, that these charming elements are still there, just where they ever were, but that they have been mercilessly deprived of their visibility. It aches and throbs, this smothered visibility, we easily feel, in its caged and dishonored condition, supported only by the consciousness that the dishonor is no fault of its own. We commune with it, in tenderness and pity, through the encumbered air; our eyes, made, however unwillingly, at home in strange vertiginous upper atmospheres, look down on it as on a poor ineffectual thing, an architectural object addressed, even in its prime aspiration, to the patient pedestrian sense and permitting thereby a relation of intimacy. It was to speak to me audibly enough on two or three other occasions—even through the thick of that frenzy of Broadway just where Broadway receives from Wall Street the fiercest application of the maddening lash; it was to put its tragic case there with irresistible lucidity. "Yes, the wretched figure I am making is as little as you see my fault—it is the fault of the buildings whose very first care is to deprive churches of their visibility.

There are but two or three—two or three outward and visible churches—left in New York 'anyway,' as you must have noticed, and even they are hideously threatened: a fact at which no one, indeed, appears to be shocked, from which no one draws the least of the inferences that stick straight out of it, which every one seems in short to take for granted either with remarkable stupidity or with remarkable cynicism." So, at any rate, they may still effectively communicate, ruddy-brown (where not browny-black) old Trinity and any pausing, any attending survivor of the clearer age— and there is yet more of the bitterness of history to be tasted in such a tacit passage, as I shall presently show.

Was it not the bitterness of history, meanwhile, that on that day of circumnavigation, that day of highest intensity of impression, of which I began by speaking, the ancient rotunda of Castle Garden, viewed from just opposite, should have lurked there as a vague nonentity? One had known it from far, far back and with the indelibility of the childish vision—from the time when it was the commodious concert-hall of New York, the firmament of long-extinguished stars; in spite of which extinction there outlives for me the image of the infant phenomenon Adelina Patti, whom (another large-eyed infant) I had been benevolently taken to hear: Adelina Patti, in a fanlike little white frock and "pantalettes" and a hussarlike red jacket, mounted on an armchair, its back supporting her, wheeled to the front of the stage and warbling like a tiny thrush even in the nest. Shabby, shrunken, barely discernible to-day, the ancient rotunda, adjusted to other uses, had afterwards, for many decades, carried on a conspicuous life— and it was the present remoteness, the repudiated barbarism of all this, foreshortened by one's own experience, that dropped the acid into the cup. The skyscrapers and the league-long bridges, present and to come, marked the point where the age—the age for which Castle Garden could have been, in its day, a "value"— had come out. That in itself was nothing—ages do come out, as a matter of course, so far from where they have gone in. But it had done so, the latter half of the nineteenth century, in one's own

more or less immediate presence; the difference, from pole to pole, was so vivid and concrete that no single shade of any one of its aspects was lost. This impact of the whole condensed past at once produced a horrible, hateful sense of personal antiquity.

Yet was it after all that those monsters of the mere market as I have called them, had more to say, on the question of "effect," than I had at first allowed?— since they are the element that looms largest for me through a particular impression, with remembered parts and pieces melting together rather richly now, of "down-town" seen and felt from the inside. "Felt"—I use that word, I dare say, all presumptuously, for a relation to matters of magnitude and mystery that I could begin neither to measure nor to penetrate, hovering about them only in magnanimous wonder, staring at them as at a world of immovably closed doors behind which immense "material" lurked, material for the artist, the painter of life, as we say, who shouldn't have begun so early and so fatally to fall away from possible initiations. This sense of a baffled curiosity, an intellectual adventure forever renounced, was surely enough a state of feeling, and indeed in presence of the different half-hours, as memory presents them, at which I gave myself up both to the thrill of Wall Street (by which I mean that of the whole wide edge of the whirlpool), and the too accepted, too irredeemable ignorance, I am at a loss to see what intensity of response was wanting. The imagination might have responded more if there had been a slightly less settled inability to understand what every one, what any one, was really doing; but the picture, as it comes back to me, is, for all this foolish subjective poverty, so crowded with its features that I rejoice, I confess, in not having more of them to handle. No open apprehension, even if it be as open as a public vehicle plying for hire, can carry more than a certain amount of life, of a kind; and there was nothing at play in the outer air, at least, of the scene, during these glimpses, that didn't scramble for admission into mine very much as I had seen the mob seeking entrance to an up-town or a down-town electric car fight for life at one of the apertures.

If it had been the final function of the Bay to make one feel one's age, so, assuredly, the mouth of Wall Street proclaimed it, for one's private ear, distinctly enough; the breath of existence being taken, wherever one turned, as that of youth on the run and with the prize of the race in sight, and the new landmarks crushing the old quite as violent children stamp on snails and caterpillars.

The hour I first recall was a morning of winter drizzle and mist, of dense fog in the Bay, one of the strangest sights of which I was on my way to enjoy; and I had stopped in the heart of the business quarter to pick up a friend who was to be my companion. The weather, such as it was, worked wonders for the upper reaches of the buildings, round which it drifted and hung very much as about the flanks and summits of emergent mountain-masses—for, to be just all round, there *was* some evidence of their having a message for the eyes. Let me parenthesize, once for all, that there are other glimpses of this message, up and down the city, frequently to be caught; lights and shades of winter and summer air, of the literally "finishing" afternoon in particular, when refinement of modelling descends from the skies and lends the white towers, all new and crude and commercial and over-windowed as they are, a fleeting distinction. The morning I speak of offered me my first chance of seeing one of them from the inside—which was an opportunity I sought again, repeatedly, in respect to others; and I became conscious of the force with which this vision of their prodigious working, and of the multitudinous life, as if each were a swarming city in itself, that they are capable of housing, may beget, on the part of the free observer, in other words of the restless analyst, the impulse to describe and present the facts and express the sense of them. Each of these huge constructed and compressed communities, throbbing, through its myriad arteries and pores, with a single passion, even as a complicated watch throbs with the one purpose of telling you the hour and the minute, testified overwhelmingly to the *character* of New York—and the passion of the restless analyst, on his side, is for the extraction of character. But there would be too much to say, just here, were

this incurable eccentric to let himself go; the impression in question, fed by however brief an experience, kept overflowing the cup and spreading in a wide waste of speculation. I must dip into these depths, if it prove possible, later on; let me content myself, for the moment, with remembering how from the first, on all such ground, my thought went straight to poor great wonder-working Émile Zola and *his* love of the human aggregation, the artificial microcosm, which had to spend itself on great shops, great businesses, great "apartment-houses," of inferior, of mere Parisian scale. His image, it seemed to me, really asked for compassion—in the presence of this material that his energy of evocation, his alone, would have been of a stature to meddle with. What if *Le Ventre de Paris,* what if *Au Bonheur des Dames,* what if *Pot-Bouille* and *L'Argent,* could but have come into being under the New York inspiration?

The answer to that, however, for the hour, was that, in all probability, New York was not going (as it turns such remarks) to produce both the maximum of "business" spectacle and the maximum of ironic reflection of it. Zola's huge reflector got itself formed, after all, in a far other air; it had hung there, in essence, awaiting the scene that was to play over it, long before the scene really approached it in scale. The reflecting surfaces, of the ironic, of the epic order, suspended in the New York atmosphere, have yet to show symptoms of shining out, and the monstrous phenomena themselves, meanwhile, strike me as having, with their immense momentum, got the start, got ahead of, in proper parlance, any possibility of poetic, of dramatic capture. That conviction came to me most perhaps while I gazed across at the special sky-scraper that overhangs poor old Trinity to the north—a south face as high and wide as the mountain-wall that drops the Alpine avalanche, from time to time, upon the village, and the village spire, at its foot; the interest of this case being above all, as I learned, to my stupefaction, in the fact that the very creators of the extinguisher are the churchwardens themselves, or at least the trustees of the church property. What was the case but magnificent for pitiless ferocity?—that inexorable law of the growing invisibility of churches, their everywhere reduced or abolished *presence,* which is nine-tenths of their virtue, receiving thus, at such hands, its supreme consecration. This consecration was positively the greater that just then, as I have said, the vast money-making structure quite horribly, quite romantically justified itself, looming through the weather with an insolent clifflike sublimity. The weather, for all that experience, mixes intimately with the fulness of my impression; speaking not least, for instance, of the way "the state of the streets" and the assault of the turbid air seemed all one with the look, the tramp, the whole quality and *allure,* the consummate monotonous commonness, of the pushing male crowd, moving in its dense mass—with the confusion carried to chaos for any intelligence, any perception; a welter of objects and sounds in which relief, detachment, dignity, meaning perished utterly and lost all rights. It appeared, the muddy medium, all one with every other element and note as well, all the signs of the heaped industrial battle-field, all the sounds and silences, grim, pushing, trudging silences too, of the universal will to move—to move, move, move, as an end in itself, an appetite at any price.

In the Bay, the rest of the morning, the dense raw fog that delayed the big boat, allowing sight but of the immediate ice-masses through which it thumped its way, was not less of the essence. Anything blander, as a medium, would have seemed a mockery of the facts of the terrible little Ellis Island, the first harbor of refuge and stage of patience for the million or so of immigrants annually knocking at our official door. Before this door, which opens to them there only with a hundred forms and ceremonies, grindings and grumblings of the key, they stand appealing and waiting, marshalled, herded, divided, subdivided, sorted, sifted, searched, fumigated, for longer or shorter periods—the effect of all which prodigious process, an intendedly "scientific" feeding of the mill, is again to give the earnest observer a thousand more things to think of than he can pretend to retail. The impression of Ellis Island, in fine, would be—as I was

to find throughout that so many of my impressions would be—a chapter by itself; and with a particular page for recognition of the degree in which the liberal hospitality of the eminent Commissioner of this wonderful service, to whom I had been introduced, helped to make the interest of the whole watched drama poignant and unforgettable. It is a drama that goes on, without a pause, day by day and year by year, this visible act of ingurgitation on the part of our body politic and social, and constituting really an appeal to amazement beyond that of any sword-swallowing or fire-swallowing of the circus. The wonder that one couldn't keep down was the thought that these two or three hours of one's own chance vision of the business were but as a tick or two of the mighty clock, the clock that never, never stops—least of all when it strikes, for a sign of so much winding-up, some louder hour of our national fate than usual. I think indeed that the simplest account of the action of Ellis Island on the spirit of any sensitive citizen who may have happened to "look in" is that he comes back from his visit not at all the same person that he went. He has eaten of the tree of knowledge, and the taste will be forever in his mouth. He had thought he knew before, thought he had the sense of the degree in which it is his American fate to share the sanctity of his American consciousness, the intimacy of his American patriotism, with the inconceivable alien; but the truth had never come home to him with any such force. In the lurid light projected upon it by those courts of dismay, it shakes him—or I like at least to imagine it shakes him—to the depths of his being; I like to think of him, I positively *have* to think of him, as going about ever afterwards with a new look, for those who can see it, in his face, the outward sign of the new chill in his heart. So is stamped, for detection, the questionably privileged person who has had an apparition, seen a ghost in his supposedly safe old house. Let not the unwary, therefore, visit Ellis Island.

The after-sense of that acute experience, however, I myself found, was by no means to be brushed away; I felt it grow and grow, on the contrary, wherever I turned:

other impressions might come and go, but this affirmed claim of the alien, however immeasurably alien, to share in one's supreme relation was everywhere the fixed element, the reminder not to be dodged. One's supreme relation, as one had always put it, was one's relation to one's country—a conception made up so largely of one's countrymen and one's countrywomen. Thus it was as if, all the while, with such a fond tradition of what these products predominantly were, the idea of the country itself underwent something of that profane overhauling through which it appears to suffer the indignity of change. Is not our instinct in this matter, in general, essentially the safe one—that of keeping the idea simple and strong and continuous, so that it shall be perfectly sound? To touch it overmuch, to pull it about, is to put it in peril of weakening; yet on this free assault upon it, this readjustment of it in *their* monstrous, presumptuous interest, the aliens, in New York, seemed perpetually to insist. The combination there of their quantity and their quality —that loud primary stage of alienism which New York most offers to sight—operates, for the native, as their note of settled possession, something they have nobody to thank for; so that *un*-settled possession is what we, on our side, seem reduced to — the implication of which, in its turn, is that, to recover confidence and regain lost ground, we, not they, must make the surrender and accept the orientation. We must go, in other words, *more* than half-way to meet them; which is all the difference, for us, between possession and dispossession. This sense of dispossession, to be brief about it, haunted me so, I was to feel, in the New York streets and in the packed trajectiles to which one clingingly appeals from the streets, just as one tumbles back into the streets in appalled reaction from *them,* that the art of beguiling or duping it became an art to be cultivated —though the fond alternative vision was never long to be obscured, the imagination, exasperated to envy, of the ideal, in the order in question; of the luxury of some such close and sweet and *whole* national consciousness as that of the Switzer and the Scot.

NEW YORK – CITY OF ROMANCE

NEW YORK—port of the sea—is, for most of us Americans, at least the gateway of Romance. Down the gay dancing waters of her incomparable bay, under her high, pale, clear sky, each day great ships bear thousands of sentimental pilgrims to an older, lovelier world. New York tosses her buildings skyward in an indifferent good-by; we speak something of the marvellous progress of steel construction, something more of the day's Wall Street news, and then fix our eyes on Romance across the tossing waves of the North Atlantic. And yet, to make romantic and transatlantic synonymous is to be lazy, blind, and stupid.

Romance is of course still, broadly speaking, a foreign commodity. It is staple there; it is organized, accessible, and well advertised. You choose your brand, and purchasing it, you settle yourself to consume and enjoy it. From the Pincian Hill you watch the sun set behind St. Peter's. Along leafy English lanes you brush the dew from the hawthorn. Or in France you see the white road rise and fall beneath your rushing motor, while across the wheat fields come into sight the gray spires of some great Gothic church.

All such experience is lovely; nothing is more to the credit of our nation than that we know its value. But here at home, as our great town grows toward maturity, New York is coming to have a character, a tone of its own, to be one of the world's capitals, and unlike any other. Unperceived by most of us a faint bloom creeps over it, there ventures forth a strange new beauty which exists by none of the old rules, but will soon insist on fresh ones revised to include it.

Beauty, labelled and docketed as such, three-starred in the red guide-book, need lose for us nothing of its old worth. He is the poorer man for that who cannot stand in the Florentine sunlight by the Cathedral's side, rapt in admiration before Giotto's Campanile. But he is also so much the richer who can get something of the same glow when, from the Staten Island ferry-boat on a quiet Sunday evening, he sees the flaming Singer Tower rise above the monstrous heaped-up black of deserted office-buildings. Here is something as romantic—that is, as bewildering, as lovely, as incredible.

Perhaps as quick and easy a definition of romance as is possible would be that it is the thing which is incredible, which seems so remote from ordinary everyday human conditions that only by a sudden effort of the imagination can we adjust ourselves to it. We all know how the sight of some old building can send fancy scampering back across the centuries. Such moments our city of New York can provide when she chooses—but what no city through the whole world's history has ever offered as does New York to the bewildered stranger is the Romance of the Future.

Daily the town is torn down and rebuilt before our very eyes. That restless, imaginative, modern genius of invention leaps so far ahead of the average power of seeing, that New York is forever a fantastic thing, the miraculous product of a single night. While our necks are lame from trying to see the top of the Flatiron Building, lo! the white tower of the Metropolitan Life pierces the sky, and the frightened Flatiron shrinks to the size of a thatched cabin, no longer able to surprise or impress us.

The caldron boils and its seething surface petrifies into dreams. Stand in Long-Acre Square as a winter night falls in flying snow, see the cream-colored sentinel that guards the crossing of Broadway and Forty-second Street soar into dim cloudy upper distances where you can already almost hear the airships scream their warnings and see them flap strange wings; watch the electric crests of huge hotels flash out, and Broadway, in a kind of intoxicated frenzy, light the innumerable dazzling signals of its illuminated signs; see all this glittering through the swirling flakes, and then dare deny that it is incredible, that it is a "brave translunary thing," that there is over it a light that never was on sea or land. Who that feels his senses tingle at this vision cares to stop long enough to inquire whether or not it is beauty in the classic sense? He knows at least that his foot is on one of the main highways of Romance.

As the great ships from Europe come up the bay, the thousands of poor ignorant immigrants who crowd at the rails have perhaps more than we homecoming Americans the vision, catch the symbolism of the long city piled between its rivers. Perhaps they only see meaning in the statue on Bedloe's Island, the gift of France, which gives France's interpretation of us, not our own. To these strangers New York beckons, promising a feature big with unknown promise of prosperity and happiness from an overflowing store — gifts romantic and incredible.

Indeed the older continent can never be forgotten here in this gateway of the New World. On the days when the people go holiday-making English is not always the language most commonly spoken, and the American observer sometimes feels caught in the eddies and whirlpools of that great stream of foreign immigration which forever pours through the Narrows. Memories of things across the Atlantic, faint hints of the fair places and the treasure spots of Europe float mistily over the face of things here. And foreign events and ceremonials, bravely and loyally carried through on an alien soil, sometimes have a kind of pathetic and romantic charm.

In June, for example, they celebrate the festival of St. Antony of Padua—in Fordham. They hang lanterns and festoon arches in a dreary little street of wooden houses, a prim and unpicturesque setting for the *festa*. Yet cannot the imaginative lounger catch a glimpse, a dim vista at the street's end, of the half-Oriental domes of the great Paduan church around which the gayer festival across the seas is happening? And in

September Our Lady has her shrine in a side street just off Second Avenue, and by night twinkling lanterns make you believe, almost, that the ugly East Side tenements are *palazzi* that have seen better days.

There are American festas too, indigenous customs that are only half recognized. The winter holidays send forth upon the streets thousands of children in the costumes of the carnival, rude masks that you could find nowadays upon the Roman Corso or the Parisian boulevards, and more spontaneous merriment. In May the parks fill each Saturday with May parties. Thousands of schoolgirls clad in the classic white muslin, and wreathed with the admirable but old-fashioned smilax, dance upon the greensward and wind the May-pole. Even in the crowded city streets, as spring comes, Robin Hood and his Merry Men make festival.

Thus in unnoticed ways New York comes into her own place as one of the world's great cities, learns to have her own idiosyncrasies, her own fancies. The face of her civilization grows richer and more romantic.

The lower end of New York is the most astonishing thing in America, perhaps in the world. Not what you saw yesterday, but to-day's New York. That tiny building, if you please, is the one you were taken to see when you first visited the town, fifteen years ago! It was there that a wonderful elevator shot you up a fabulous twelve stories! Once —do you remember?—you could tell the time for miles around by the clock on the Produce Exchange's tall tower; now it sits in a kind of pit or cup! A new city has been set upon a hill, as are the graystone eagles' nests of Europe, the fighting cities of the Old World. But here we build the hill itself; the turrets stand not upon a mountain, but on a beehive.

As the day closes in the down-town district, shadows and colors come, romance grows bolder. Come across the Brooklyn Bridge some evening, facing the sunset. The mountainside glitters with the light from ten thousand windows. And black against the western red is silhouetted a strange, romantic sky-line. There are in it hints of the Orient and of the Occident—of the cities of the moon, if you like. It is as nothing before it has ever been, picturesque, fantastic.

Some December evening, when darkness comes early, before the workers have gone home, take the ferry from the Jersey shore to Barclay Street. Beyond the river, with its bright darting boats, a huge curtain hangs across the night. Can you remember a tawdry Oriental fabric, thickly set with tiny oval pieces of looking-glass, which fascinated you as a child? Here it is, magnified and transmuted. From the darkness of midstream the great buildings lose their outline, all blend into one plane, each giving its shining windows to pick out the one great pattern. High toward the zenith runs this magic velvet of purple and blue-black, embroidered with gems that pulse with their own inner radiance. One distinguishable building only floats in the pink mist of those hidden lights which always illuminate it, the great tower proudly holding its little coronet above the spangled romantic fabric.

It is hard not to call such visions beauty. Who is to judge? Old gentlemen in England may write scathingly to the *Spectator* about the "Singer-horn." But if beauty and usefulness are still to go hand in hand, must not the code be revised to include the forty-story building? Had it been possible, would not the Greeks have scraped the sky above the Acropolis? And might not medieval piety have built a tiny chapel on the peak of some huge building, or set a great statue of the Virgin to crown some tower, so that sailors down the bay might see her and know that they were safe at home and in her care?

It is impossible for the twentieth century to know, while it builds things, their worth. Yet there is a curious compensation; never before did things age so quickly. A scant generation or two gives perspective, enables us to judge artistic merits with some detachment of mind. The Brooklyn Bridge, for example, is already ridiculously old. Go where at one glance you can see it and the Williamsburg and the new Manhattan Bridge, now building. An engineer could tell you what advances in science have brought about the structural changes which distinguish the two new

bridges. You can, however, tell for yourself that it might have been centuries ago that the river was spanned, that it might almost have been the old builders of Gothic cathedrals who spun that lovely spider's web between slender twin towers. Once we marvelled at an engineering triumph, now we enjoy a structure beautiful architecturally and charming for its atmosphere, its old-fashioned regard for tradition, its tranquil romantic atmosphere of the seventies.

"Ah, they did things better in those days!" we sigh, looking at the ugly new bridges which cross the river higher up. Ugly now, yes; but who shall say for how long?

It is an interesting speculation in the theory of æsthetics to wonder how soon the general sense of beauty will adjust itself to steel construction. Centuries of the stone arch made it impossible for a long time to see anything but ugliness in its steel substitute. Then perhaps you were in Paris and saw the Pont Alexandre III. skim across the Seine with the flattened curve of the swallow's flight, and suddenly realized that here was an airy, graceful thing impossible in stone. Steel is still plunging far ahead of us into the architectural future. When we catch up with it at last, we may think it stone's younger and worthy brother. Is there any evidence, one may ask, that the splendid flying buttresses of the great Gothic churches were at the time of their building regarded as anything but cumbrous, possibly ugly structural necessities?

To some, talk of the romance of the future may seem mere paradox. There is romance of the past as well, up and down the island of Manhattan, for such as choose to see it. But you must really not travel always by the Subway; you must take occasional Saturday afternoons to lounge through unfamiliar quarters in search of your own special kind of picturesqueness. If you will only once imagine that New York is a foreign town, the very folder that advertises the varied sights of New York will tell you of her innumerable fascinations.

Little need be said of the more obviously romantic buildings. Even the man-in-the-street has seen St. Paul's.

THE THINGS THAT TOWER
Etching by Joseph Pennell

He has noticed Trinity, standing with the real air of a cathedral church at the head of Wall Street—though it is probable he has never seen the curious monument to an early bishop in a small chapel to the right of the altar, nor known that there was precious King George and Queen Anne silver in the treasury, as also a chalice covered richly with the jewels of a pious lady who was once a parishioner.

St. John's, for a long time forgotten, has recently come into some prominence, and some hundreds of thousands who had never heard of Varick Street have seen the beautiful old church there.

From an architectural point of view it is the best we have, with its noble brown-stone porch, its light and elegant spire, its simple, well-proportioned interior, and the two admirable brick houses that flank it. And for many years it had the gently pathetic air of decay which was, for the sentimental sightseer, an added charm. Slum children played around the columns of the portico or sat on the steps in the sun. And in the vestry a pleasant, rosy-cheeked young vicar, who had fallen genuinely in love with his neglected church, would show you old engravings of the days when Hudson Square was a pretty park surrounded by the houses of the town's aristocracy, and on a summer's day you could stand at the altar and look through the open church door across the greensward and down a short street to the blue river beyond.

Of the old houses around Hudson Square there are three left, abandoned to utter squalor and dilapidation by their somewhat sinister-looking tenants. Only the richly wrought iron railings and ornamental newel-posts by the battered door-steps show their original character. The centre of the square is occupied by the freight depot of a railroad, for which purpose the muddle-headed inhabitants sold their park, even while they foolishly planned still to live on in their family mansions. The building itself is a sombre, heavy, brick structure, not notable except for the amazing sculptural ornaments of its western pediment. Here indeed is art in the making, the clumsy efforts of that earlier day. The workmanship is of the ordinary stone-cutter, who, having finished the depot, put in a few hours' overtime at sculpture to complete the job. If you can step around the corner in just the right mood, the elder Vanderbilt dispensing the blessings of transportation to a grateful country will seem somehow naïvely humorous. Crouched submissively at his right is Columbia, at his left Neptune. The freight depot stands proudly in the middle, surrounded by the various products of our fields and factories. From it a pleasant little train emerges, hauled by an engine with a comic smoke-stack. From a distance, through a deliciously wooded country, presumably Eleventh Avenue at about Fourteenth Street, another train approaches. And, above all, the elder Vanderbilt, in a fine fur coat and with a hand benignantly extended, surveys the scene. The master-

NEW YORK FROM WEEHAWKEN

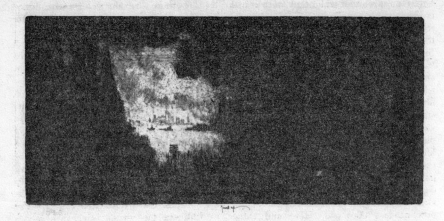

A NEW CITY HAS BEEN SET UPON A HILL

piece is dated 1868, and, in a town where we have so little architectural sculpture, deserves attention.

Already 1868 has a flavor. And the 40's and 50's in this quick-moving town of ours are genuinely romantic. They are fading quickly from us; to all intents and purposes they are now as remote as the eighteenth century. Yet we have, especially in the arts, so long kept our eyes fixed on the colonial period that the early and middle nineteenth century will pass before we have time to recapture and enjoy their charm. If the present article had any one special object, it would be to urge that the time of *Godey's Lady's Book*, and hoop-skirts and fashion in Second Avenue, is a fresh untouched field of romance. Let us worship a heroine of Manhattan by all means. But let her be not a belle of the Revolutionary days, but rather Miss Flora McFlimsey of Madison Square, and of the world of fashion of that recent, yet strangely remote, strangely unrecognized day.

In any city the progress of the fashionable world leaves a trail of romance behind it, splendid houses now abandoned. Washington Square and Fifth Avenue and its adjoining streets south of Fourteenth, aside from the dignity and beauty of their buildings—it would be hard anywhere to match the north side of the square—have already the charm that comes from crowding memories, and from the sureness that the quarter can-

not much longer resist the invading tide of shops and slums. But the greater romantic flavor is found in the districts where the tide has already receded, leaving only a few obstinate families to carry on in those spacious, distinguished old red-brick houses the tradition of early New York luxury.

At one time Stuyvesant Square and Second Avenue were established as the centre of what was probably termed the " upper ten " or the " *crème de la crème* " of New York society. But the family which controlled most of the land of the region held it at high, almost prohibitive prices. At last adventurous and poor young couples began to venture into the social wilderness of Fifth Avenue, and before the proud Knickerbocker landlords realized it the current had turned.

Below the square there are several appealing suggestions of those earlier days. By St. Mark's, so pleasantly and irregularly placed on its green plat, is a spacious old house only recently deserted by its owners. And farther south in a region of crowded flat-buildings and noisy German and Hungarian cafés are the two remotest outposts of that bygone world, houses where behind polished plate glass and beyond immaculate curtains you may perhaps catch glimpses in the afternoon of old ladies in snow-white caps, and may imagine it possible that they still dine at five-thirty or six, and have good claret and madeira in the cellar. Even the older gentlemen in the up-town clubs only remember that when they were young blades they began their New-Year's calls in the region of St. Mark's Place, and that they have rarely been there since. Most of us Americans are gipsies and vagabonds in our own towns; it is like a fairy-tale that we have among us people who even now continue to live in old houses just because their fathers did.

Here, too, south of Fourteenth Street, were until lately those two strangely desolate and forgotten cemeteries where, hidden behind swarming tenements, were the graves of so many of those who had helped to make New York in an earlier day. For a long time musty charters and old endowments preserved these, but now at last they go. Here and there over the town the law keeps poor little fragments of burying-grounds. One you may see, as you stroll, between Fifth and Sixth avenues near Washington Square.

And there is a curious legend, difficult if not impossible to authenticate now, of one small burying-ground caught in the very middle of a huge Sixth Avenue department store. It could not legally be disturbed, it was said, but access to it was denied, and there was but one window on one turn of a staircase from which could be seen this pathetic, battered, yet gallant reminder of those who slept there.

But to come back to our itinerary:

South of Stuyvesant Square the outer signs of early architectural dignity have for the most part been swept away. Ugly cornices and door-casings, sprawling iron fire-escapes, crudely painted fronts, seem to indicate the usual, fairly prosperous East Side tenements. But in many cases this unalluring exterior only masks an old house. There is, for example, a little German café, just around the corner from the avenue, where you may drink your fragrant cup of coffee and munch your spice - cake in as beautiful a drawing-room as you can find in London or New York to-day. The tables and chairs are cheap, it is true, and the floor sanded. But the proportions of the apartment remain, the fine old woodwork — cream picked out in gold— with the lotus-flower capital so characteristic of the New York of that day, the solid old mahogany doors still shining brightly, and the white marble chimneypiece (probably imported from Italy, as they did then) with graceful nymphs on either side. It is a pleasant nook; may it not be contended that it also is faintly fragrant of

AMONG THE SKY-SCRAPERS

THE QUAKER SCHOOL IN STUYVESANT SQUARE

romance—as well as of the cinnamon in excellent buns?

In Stuyvesant Square, St. George's has already the air of antiquity, and the Quaker church and school—red brick and white, and dating only to the forties— have the serenity and peace of buildings in a cathedral close. There should be rooks wheeling round the trees near by and a bishop in shorts crossing the green.

In this quarter it was that Thackeray had friends when he visited New York. And there still lives in the square a lady with whom he used to find it pleasant to drink tea. She is a faithful and loyal daughter of Manhattan; she deserts it neither winter nor summer. And it is the privilege of the inhabitants of that delightful region to see her daily, at an hour that scarcely varies by a minute, go forth and take the air in a wonderful high-swung old barouche—a privilege at once distinguished and romantic; for the old lady, erect and charming still, carries one back with her own and her family's traditions to the earliest and best days of the colonial period.

The Academy of Music with its curious fading mid-century architecture, and its already half-forgotten traditions of great days, is a perpetual delight to the sentimental traveller in Manhattan. While it stands one can never forget the days when fashion dwelt in Fourteenth Street.

And farther west the thoroughfare can still show some solid mansions of the Dutch families.

Gramercy Park, Irving Place, and lower Lexington Avenue have all the *cachet* of an aristocratic respectability which is passing. And the process goes

St. Mark's

ther from New York than the remotest Long Island or New Jersey suburb, and Greenwich Village, never the home of fashion, but rather of a prosperous shopkeeping *bourgeoisie*. In the latter are now clean quiet streets that might almost be those of some English provincial town. In fact, the whole quarter keeps a British flavor. Even in the Italian district you may find hints, in the names of public institutions, that once they called this Richmond Hill.

Greenwich has also its small surprises, its village grandiloquence. In a peaceful side street, in a pretty red - brick house of a modest size which unfortunately has gone out of fashion in New York, you will find the Catholic University of America! And some night at the opera you may catch in the boxes a glimpse of the admirable lady, in a quaint cap, who founded it. She herself with her papal title modestly employed, and her air of the early New York, would perhaps not resent being called a pleasantly romantic figure in the latter-day town.

on. Is it all imagination to think that now, when the rush is to the East Seventies, Eighties, and Nineties, there has crept over the side streets off Fifth Avenue below Thirty-fourth something of this same autumnal air? Are the houses not already a little quaint? The main current has swept by, but is it not pleasant, and a little romantic in the backwater?

There are special regions like Chelsea, which gathers around the quadrangle of the Episcopal Theological Seminary with something of the academic pride of a small college town, and is obviously far-

Proximity to the West Twenty-third Street ferries has made fairly familiar the curious houses on that street and Twenty-fourth between Ninth and Tenth avenues. The more pretentious houses on the more important thoroughfare, with their green dooryards, achieve a kind of symmetry and real dignity. And the tiny cottages back of them have an air of discreet gayety, with their small porches over-elaborate with lattices and ironwork in intricate designs that almost suggest Spain or the Orient.

So far our sentimental sightseer has only found the romance which is on the usual and daily path of each one of his readers. Undiscovered New York there is as well; even in that great uncouth crowded East Side there are pleasant promenades for any one who will carry there the holiday mood and the appreciative eye which he habitually takes abroad.

A recommended itinerary would perhaps begin under the Elevated at C h a t h a m Square, and go first by t h a t strange little fragment of the old J e w i s h burying-ground, which once lay "outside the walls," and is now forever disturbed by the clatter of trains passing over it. The saunterer would then plunge into the network of streets which extend toward the East River, into the atmosphere of the sea, and of days when there were American sailors and American clipper-ships.

It is the names of the churches of the region which more t h a n anything else sound romantically in the ear, and would lure the most wearied sightseer to their side. Here are the Mariner's Church, the Mariner's Temple, and the Presbyterian Church of the Sea and of the Land. Quaint pleasant names, the last one with a kind of haunting loveliness in the very sound of the words which it would be hard to match the world over. The Temple is of sober brownstone, and has two great pillars and a cupola. The Mariner's Church is of pale-cream brick, with broad windows of tiny panes, and a ridiculous crenelated top. The Church of the Sea and of the Land, which boasts five trees on its south side, is in a thin Gothic style,

built of gray rubble. This rubble seems a favorite material in the region. There is a synagogue built of it, as is the little Church of All Saints in Henry Street, which has a homely rectory and one desolate tree in the best manner of a London city church. All these were built

CHAPEL OF THE THEOLOGICAL SEMINARY—CHELSEA

for the salvation and the care of the souls of our mariners. But since mariners are not frequent now, wisely the churches have managed accommodation for the small Protestant congregations of the various nationalities which swarm in the region. In the Mariner's Temple, for example, there are services each Sunday in English, Italian, German, Russian, and Danish. Here in this part of the town we are indeed at the very foot of the Tower of Babel. There is one open-air pulpit where in a single evening you may hear preaching in six languages.

A Doorway in Gramercy Park

The very spreading of the gospel takes on in this town of ours strange, grotesque, and romantic forms. You may have heard it in great churches, you may have listened to it on the greensward of Hyde Park in London. Now stand an evening at Fourteenth Street and Third Avenue, watch the flashing lights of vaudeville down the street, be deafened by the clang of surface cars and the rumble of Elevated trains above, and hear the gospel from some pale missionary standing in the gutter there. The message flashes intermittently in the thunderous night as the careless, indifferent town rushes by, the preacher cracking his throat to rise above the horrid tumult in which he has planted himself.

But we were lounging on the East Side. There are beautiful old houses there, too, in Henry and Rutgers streets, with elaborate doorways and fine iron railings. But the characteristic dwellings are less pretentious. The main street, and the most interesting, of this region is East Broadway, a long, wide thoroughfare to the easternmost point of Manhattan, a far and unknown region to most of us. The street has no need to be apologetic; it has not precisely gone to seed. Its houses were never fashionable, only comfortable; and comfortable on a somewhat reduced scale many of them evidently are still. In the down-town, west-end part, where are incidentally the best architecture and the best twisted-iron rails, there is the usual invasion of business in a small, rather squalid way. But up-town—that is, in its eastern end—it is a placid, sleepy, residential street, stopping at a tiny green park. It begins near Chatham Square, but one would swear that it ended somewhere far outside New York. It is in its own mild way a strange, undreamt-of corner. A large part of the mystery of great towns for their lover lies in the endless riddle of just who it may be makes homes behind all the front doors by which he passes. It is easy to imagine who inhabits Fifth Avenue or the flats of Harlem. But who lives in the quiet streets of Greenwich, or in East Broadway?

The water-front of New York is to the eye not notably picturesque. Steam-craft have driven away much of the outward romance. Yet there by the East River they still fit out revolutions for South America and all the Indies, and there, by the waterside, gentlemen ad-venturers are forever swaggering and plotting. There they believe in hidden treasures and forlorn hopes.

One way and another, through the length and breadth of the town, the senti-mental pilgrim will be given good quar-ters of an hour. While others may stare at the silly fish in the Aquarium, he will see in his mind's eye the round audi-torium, the four slender columns by the stage blooming into quaint lily-shaped capitals, and Jenny Lind kissing her hand to some thousands of her new-found admirers.

Fordham will be for him full of mem-ories, and all through the Bronx he will pause before old wooden farmhouses and country-seats which look wistful and bewildered by these strange new streets that sprawl over everything. In Central Park he will stop idly to note how the style of the fountains, and of the great flight of steps that descends to the lake from the Mall, has grown oddly out of the mode, and to wonder how soon, in this quick-moving century, it will have the charm of quaintness. He will wander through the Park delighting in the queer old-fashioned people who still drive horses; by day watching children play and, toward the northern end, groups of old men who sit in the sun and discuss phi-losophy; by night regarding lovers come to walk, and also seeing queer derelicts and curious sinister wanderers prowl into the Park's obscurity from the flaring lights of the Plaza and the Circle.

But why should one make out his itinerary, write, star, and double-star his guide-book for him? All that need be done for the sentimental sightseer is to try to hint that New York, now one of the world's great capitals, waits only to be wooed. Few have as yet learned to know her as she can be, mys-terious and lovely, true city of romance.

THE EVOLUTION OF NEW YORK
(PART 1)

I.

THERE was no element of permanence in the settlement of New York. The traders sent here under Hendrick Christiansen, immediately upon Hudson's return to Holland in 1609, had no intention of remaining in America beyond the time that would pass while their ships crossed the sea and came again for the furs which meanwhile they were to secure. Even when Fort Manhattan was erected—the stockade that was built about the year 1614 just south of the present Bowling Green—this structure was intended only for the temporary shelter of the factors of the United New Netherland Company while engaged with the Indians in transient trade; for the life of this trading organization specifically was limited by its charter to four voyages, all to be made within the three years beginning January 1, 1615. Fort Manhattan, therefore, simply was a trading-post. If the Company's charter could be renewed, the post would be continued while it was profitable; upon the expiration of the charter, or when the post ceased to be profitable, it would be abandoned. That the temporary settlement thus made might develop, later, into a permanent town was a matter wholly aside from the interests in view. Leavenworth, Denver, a dozen of our Western cities, have been founded in precisely the same fashion within our own day.

Not until the year 1621, when the Dutch West India Company came into existence, were considerate measures taken for assuring a substantial colonial life to the Dutch settlement in America. The earlier trading association, the United New Netherland Company, expired by limitation on the last day of the year 1617; but its privileges were revived and maintained by annual grant for at least two years; probably for three. Then the larger organization was formed, with chartered rights (so far as the power to grant these lay with the States General of Holland) to the exclusive trade of all the coasts of both Americas.

Unlike the English trading companies —whose administration of their colonial establishments flowed from a central source—the Dutch West India Company was in the nature of a commercial federation. Branches of the Company were established in the several cities of Holland; which branches, while subject to the authority (whereof they themselves were part) of the organization as a whole, enjoyed distinct rights and privileges, and had assigned to them, severally, specific territories, over which they exercised all the functions of government, and with which they possessed the exclusive right to trade.

In accordance with this scheme of arrangement, the trading-post on the island of Manhattan, with its dependent territory—broadly claimed as extending along the coast from the Virginia Plantations northward to New England, and inland indefinitely—became the portion of the Amsterdam branch; wherefore the name of New Amsterdam was given to the post, even as the territory already had received the name of New Netherland.

As a commercial undertaking, the Dutch West India Company was admirably organized. Its projectors sought to establish it on so substantial a foundation that its expansion would not be subject to sudden checks, but would proceed equably and steadily from the start. To meet these requirements, mere trading-posts in foreign countries were not sufficient. Such temporary establishments were liable to be effaced in a moment, either by resident savages or by visiting savages afloat out of Europe—for in that cheerful period of the world's history all was game that could be captured at large upon or on the borders of the ocean sea. For the security of the Company, therefore, it was necessary that the New Netherland should be held not by the loose tenure of a small fort lightly garrisoned, but by the strong tenure of a colonial establishment firmly rooted in the soil. With this accomplished, the attacks of savages of any sort were not especially to be dreaded. Colonists might be killed in very considerable numbers and still (the available supply of colonists being ample) no great harm would be done to the Company's interests, for the colony would

survive. Therefore it was that with the change in ownership and in name came also a change in the nature of the Dutch hold upon this island. Fort Manhattan had been an isolated settlement established solely for purposes of trade; New Amsterdam was the nucleus of a colonial establishment, and was the seat of a colonial government which nominally controlled a region as large as all the European possessions of Holland and the German states combined.

It would be absurd, however, to take very seriously this government that was established in the year 1623. The portion of the American continent over which Director Minuit exercised absolutely undisputed authority was not quite the whole of the territory (now enclosed by the lower loop of the elevated railway) which lies south of the present Battery Place. Within that microscopic principality he ruled; outside of it he only reigned. That he was engaged in the rather magnificent work of founding what was to be the chief city of the Continent was far too monstrous a thought to blast its way to his imaginative faculty through the thickness of his substantial skull.

Yet Fort Amsterdam, begun about the year 1626—its northern wall about on the line of the existing row of houses facing the Bowling Green—really was the beginning of the present city. The engineer who planned it, Kryn Frederick, had in mind the creation of works sufficiently large to shelter in time of danger all the inhabitants of a considerable town; and when the Fort was finished, the fact that such a stronghold existed was one of the inducements extended by the West India Company to secure its needed colonists; for these, being most immediately and personally interested in the matter, could not be expected to contemplate the possibility of their own massacre by savages of the land or sea in the same large and statesmanlike manner that such accidents of colonial administration were regarded by the Company's directors. The building of the Fort, therefore, was the first step towards anchoring the colony firmly to the soil. By the time that the Fort was finished the population of this island amounted to about two hundred souls; and the island itself, for a consideration of $24, had been bought by Director Minuit for the Company, and so formally had passed to Dutch from Indian hands.

While the town of New Amsterdam thus came into existence under the protection of the guns of its Fort, the back country also was filling up rapidly with settlers. In the year 1629 the decree issued that any member of the West India Company who, under certain easy conditions, should form a settlement of not less than fifty persons, none of whom should be under fifteen years of age, should be granted a tract of land fronting sixteen miles upon the sea, or upon any navigable river (or eight miles when both shores of the river were occupied), and extending thence inland indefinitely; and that the *patroons* to whom such grants of land should be made should exercise manorial rights over their estates. In accordance with the liberal provisions of this decree, settlements quickly were made on both sides of the Hudson and on the lands about the Bay; but these settlements were founded in strict submission to the capital; and by the grant to the latter (by the Charter of Liberties and Exemptions, 1629) of staple rights—the obligation laid upon all vessels trading in the rivers or upon the coast to discharge cargo at the Fort, or, in lieu thereof, to pay compensating port charges—the absolute commercial supremacy of the capital was assured. Thus, almost contemporaneously with its founding, the town of New Amsterdam —at once the seat of government and the centre of trade—became in a very small way what later it was destined to be in a very large way: a metropolis.

II.

The tangle of crowded streets below the Bowling Green testifies even to the present day to the haphazard fashion in which the foundations of this city were laid. Each settler, apparently, was free to put his house where he pleased, and to surround it by an enclosure of any shape and, within reason, of any size. Later, streets were opened—for the most part by promoting existing foot-paths and lanes—along the confines of these arbitrarily ordered parcels of land. In this random fashion grew up the town.

Excepting Philadelphia, all of our cities on the Atlantic seaboard have started in this same careless way: in as marked contrast with the invariably orderly pre-arrangement of the cities in the lands to the south of us as is the contrast between the Saxon and the Latin minds. Yet the piece-made city has to commend it a lively personality to which the whole-made city never attains. The very defects in its putting together give it the charm of individuality; breathe into it with a subtle romance (that to certain natures is most strongly appealing) somewhat of the very essence of the long-by dead to whom its happy unreasonableness is due; preserve to it tangibly the tradition of the burning moment when the metal, now hardened, came fluent from the crucible and the casting of the city was begun.

Actually, only two roads were established when the town of New Amsterdam was founded, and these so obviously were necessary that, practically, they established themselves. One of them, on the line of the present Stone and Pearl streets —the latter then the water-front—led from the Fort to the Brooklyn ferry at about the present Peck Slip. The other, on the line of the present Broadway, led northward from the Fort, past farms and gardens falling away towards the North River, as far as the present Park Row; and along the line of that street, and of Chatham Street, and of the Bowery, went on into the wilderness. After the palisade was erected, this road was known as far as the city gate (at Wall Street) as the Heere Straat, or High Street; and beyond the wall as the Heere Wegh—for more than a century the only highway that traversed the island from end to end.

Broad Street and the Beaver's Path primarily were not streets at all. On the line of the first of these, with a roadway on each side, a canal extended as far as Beaver Street; where it narrowed to a ditch which drained the swamp that extended northward to about the present Exchange Place. On the line of the Beaver's Path, east and west from the main ditch, were lateral ditches at the lower end of the swamp. This system of surface drainage having converted the swamp into a meadow, it became known as the Sheep Pasture. That the primitive conditions have not been wholly changed was made manifest within the past two years by the very extensive system of piling which was the necessary preparation to the erection of the ten-story building on the northwest corner of Broad and Beaver streets. Down beneath the modern surface the ancient swamp remains to this present day.

Because of the homelikeness—as one

sat contentedly smoking on one's stoop in the cool of summer evenings — that there was in having a good strong-smelling canal under one's nose, and pleasant sight of round squat sailor-men aboard of boats which also were of a squat roundness, Broad Street (then called the Heere Graft) was a favorite dwelling-place with the quality of that early day; and even the Beaver's Path—which could boast only a minor, ditchlike smell, that yet was fit to bring tears of homesickness into one's eyes, such tender associations did it arouse —was well thought of by folk of the humbler sort, to whom the smell of a whole canal was too great a luxury.

Finally, one other street came into existence in that early time as the outgrowth of constraining conditions; this was the present Wall Street, which primitively was the open way, known as the Cingle, in the rear of the city wall. As to the wall, it was built under stress of danger and amidst great excitement. When the news came, March 13, 1653, of a threatened foray hither of New-Englanders—a lithe, slippery, aggressive race, for which every right-thinking Dutchman entertained a vast contempt, wherein also was a dash of fear—there was a prodigious commotion in this city: of which the immediate and most wonderful manifestation was a session of the General Council so charged with vehement purpose that it continued all day long! In the morning, the Council resolved "that the whole body of citizens shall keep watch by night, in such places as shall be designated, the City Tavern to be the temporary headquarters; that the Fort shall be repaired; that some way must be devised to raise money; that Captain Vischer shall be requested to fix his sails, to have his piece loaded, and to keep his vessel in readiness; that, because the Fort is not large enough to contain all the inhabitants, it is deemed necessary to enclose the city with breast-works and palisades." And then, in the afternoon of this same momentous day — after strenuously dining —the Council prepared a list for a forced levy by which the sum of 5000 guilders was to be raised for purposes of defence. Having thus breathlessly discharged itself of so tremendous a rush of business, it is not surprising that the Council held no sitting on the ensuing day, but devoted itself solely to recuperative rest; nor that it suffered a whole week to elapse before

it prepared specifications for the palisades —the erection of which thereafter proceeded at a temperate speed.

Fortunately for themselves, the New-Englanders staid at home. Governor Stuyvesant, being a statesman of parts, doubtless saw to it that news was conveyed across the Connecticut of the landsturm which arose in its might each night, and made its headquarters at the City Tavern—whence it was ready to rush forth, armed with curiously shaped Dutch black bottles, to pour a devastating fire of hot schnapps upon the foe. Wherefore the New-Englanders, being filled with a wholesome dread of such a valorous company—well in its cups, and otherwise fuming with patriotic rage—wisely elected to give this city a wide berth; and it is but just to add that Dominie Megapolensis claimed some share in averting the threatened direful conflict because at his instigation Governor Stuyvesant, in view of the unhappy state of affairs, appointed the ninth day of April, 1653, as a day of general fasting and prayer.

As the wall never was needed, its erection actually did more harm than good. For nearly half a century its effect was to restrain that natural expansion northward of the city which certainly would have begun earlier had it not been for the presence of this unnecessary barrier. Yet even without the wall there would have been no such quick development of the suburbs as characterizes the growth of cities in these modern times. The fact must be remembered that for a century after the wall was built—that is, until long after it was demolished—the inherited tendency to pack houses closely together still was overwhelmingly strong. For centuries and centuries every European city, even every small town, had been cramped within stone corsets until the desire for free breathing almost was lost. Long after the necessity for it had vanished the habit of constriction remained.

Excepting these five streets—Pearl (including Stone), Broadway, Broad, Beaver, and Wall; to which, perhaps, Whitehall should be added, because that thoroughfare originally was the open way left on the land side of the Fort—all of the old streets in the lower part of the city are the outcome of individual need or whim. The new streets in this region—South, Front, part of Water, Greenwich, Wash-

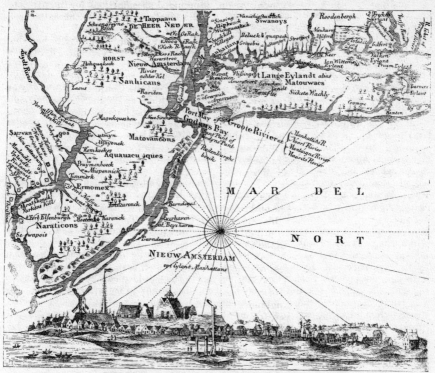

MAP OF NEW NETHERLANDS,
With a view of New Amsterdam, (now New-York.) A D. 1656.
Copied from A. Vander Donck's Map, for D.T. Valentine's Manual 1852.

ington, and West—are the considerate creations of later times, all of them having been won from the water by filling in beyond the primitive line of high tide.

Having thus contrived—by the simple process of permitting every man to make lanes and streets according to the dictates of his own fancy—to lay out as pretty a little tangle of a town as could be found just then in all Christendom, and a town which resembled in the crooks of its crookedness (to an extent that was altogether heart-moving) the intricate region just eastward of the Botermarkt in the ancient city after which it was named, the Governor in Council, about the year 1653, promulgated a decree that a map should be made of New Amsterdam, and that the town should remain from that time forward without alteration.

Doubtless Jacques Cortelyou, the official surveyor, executed the first part of this decree; but very diligent search in this country and in Holland has failed as yet to bring to light the map which he then made. The most widely known early map, therefore, is the "Duke's Plan" (as it usually is styled), which represents "the town of Mannados or New Amsterdam as it was in September, 1661," being a draft made in the year 1664, upon the capture of the town by the English, to be sent to the Duke of York. Presumably, this map differs from Cortelyou's map only in showing a few more houses, in the substitution of English for Dutch text, and in its gallant display of the English flag.*

* The earliest map of New York known to be in existence is that now in the possession of Mr. Henry Harisse, a plan of "Manatus, drawn on the spot by Joan Vingboons in 1639," to which great additional value is given by its marginal legend recording the names of the first forty-five householders on this island. This most precious document was exhibited in July, 1892, in Paris, at the Columbian exhibition of maps and globes.

The Duke's Plan is of exceeding interest, in that it exhibits the extent of the town at the moment when it passed from Dutch to English ownership: a triangle whereof the base was the present Wall Street, and the sides were on the lines of the present Water, Front, State, and Greenwich streets, which then, approximately, were the lines of high tide. Nor was even this small area closely built up —by far the larger part of it was given over to garden plots in which fair Dutch cabbages grew. The northern limit of the map is about the present Roosevelt Street, where Old Wreck Brook (as it was called later) discharged the waters of the Fresh Water pond into the East River across the region which still is known as "The Swamp." All told, there were but twelve buildings outside of the wall, of which the most important were the storehouses belonging to Isaac Allerton close by the "passageway" to Brooklyn—that is to say, the present Peck Slip. Inside the wall the only block built up solidly was that between Bridge and Stone streets—then divided by the Winckel Straat, upon which stood the five stone storehouses of the Dutch West India Company. This was the business centre of the town, because here were the landing-places. From the foot of Moor Street (which derived its name, now corrupted to Moore, from the fact that it was the mooring-place), the single wharf within the town limits extended out a little beyond the line of the present Water Street. Here, and also upon the banks of the canal in the present Broad Street, lighters discharged and received the cargoes of ships lying in the stream. Already, as is shown by the houses dotted along the East River front outside the wall, the tendency of the town was to grow toward the northeast; and this was natural, for the Perel Straat—leading along the water-side to the Brooklyn ferry—was the most travelled thoroughfare in the town. In the year 1661, when the draft was made from which the Duke's Plan was copied, New Amsterdam was a town of about one thousand souls, under the government, organized in 1652, of a schout, two burgo-masters, and five schepens. The western side of the town, from the Bowling Green northward, was a gentle wilderness of orchards and gardens and green fields. On the eastern side the farthest outlying dwelling was Wolfert Webber's tavern,

on the northern highway near the present Chatham Square—whereat travellers adventuring into the northern wilds of this island were wont to pause for a season while they put up a prayer or two for protection, and at the same time made their works conform to their faith by taking aboard a sufficient store of Dutch courage to carry them pot-valiantly onward until safe harbor was made again within the Harlem tavern's friendly walls. Save for the Indian settlement at Sappo-kanican (near the present Gansevoort Market) and the few farm-houses scattered along the highway, all this region was desert of human life. Annual round-ups were held, under the supervision of the Brand-master, of the herds which ran wild in the bush country whereof the beginning was about where the City Hall now stands.

And upon the town rested continually the dread of Indian assault. At any moment the hot-headed act of some angry colonist might easily bring on a war. In the early autumn of 1655, when peaches were ripe, an assault actually was made: being a vengeance against the whites because Hendrick Van Dyke had shot to death an Indian woman whom he found stealing peaches in his orchard (lying just south of the present Rector Street) on the North River shore. Fortunately, warning came to the townsfolk, and, crowding their women and children into the Fort, they were able to beat off the savages; whereupon the savages, being the more eager for revenge, fell upon the settlements about Pavonia and on Staten Island: where the price paid for Hendrick Van Dyke's peaches was the wasting of twenty-eight farms, the bearing away of one hundred and fifty Christians into captivity, and one hundred Christians outright slain.

III.

At eight o'clock on the morning of September 8, 1664, the flag of the Dutch West India Company fell from Fort Amsterdam, and the flag of England went up over what then became Fort James. Governor Stuyvesant—even his wooden leg sharing in his air of dejection—marched dismally his conquered forces out from the main gateway, across the Parade to the Beaver's Path, and so to the Heere Graft, where boats were lying to carry them to the ships at anchor in the stream. And at the same time the English march-

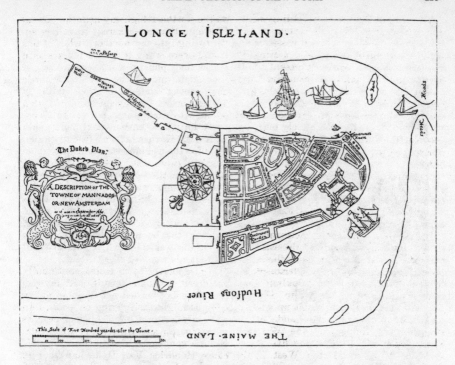

ed gallantly down Broadway—from where they had been waiting, about in front of where Aldrich Court now stands—and Governor Nicolls solemnly took possession of New Amsterdam, and of all the New Netherland, in the name of the English sovereign, and for the use of the Duke of York.

This change of ownership, with which came also a change of name, was largely and immediately beneficial to the colony. Under the government of the Dutch West India Company, the New Netherland had been managed not as a national dependency, but as a commercial venture which was expected to bring in a handsome return. Much more than the revenue necessary to maintain a government was required of the colonists; and at the same time the restrictions imposed upon private trade—to the end that the trade of the Company might be increased — were so onerous as materially to diminish the earning power of the individual, and so correspondingly to make the burden of taxation the heavier to bear. Nor could there be between the colonists and the Company—as there could have been between the colonists and even a severe

home government—a tie of loyalty. Indeed, the situation had become so strained under this commercial despotism that the inhabitants of New Amsterdam almost openly sided with the English when the formal demand for surrender was made, and the town passed into British possession and became New York without the striking of a single blow.

Virtually, this was the end of Dutch ownership hereabouts. Once again, from July 30, 1673, until November 10, 1674, the Dutch were in possession—following that "clap of thunder on a fair frosty day," as Sir William Temple called it, when England declared war against Holland in the year 1672. But this temporary reclamation had no influence beyond slightly retarding the great development of the city, and of all the colony, which came with English rule.

Although the New Netherland had been acquired, nominally, by force of arms, New York by no means was treated as a conquered province. Colonel Richard Nicolls, who commanded the English military force, and who became the first English Governor of the Province, conducted his government with such wise

ON THE RIVER FRONT.

conservatism that there was no shock whatever in the transition from the old to the new order of things, and the change was most apparent in agreeable ways. Not until three-fourths of a year had passed was the city government re-organized, in accordance with English customs, by substituting for the schout, burgomasters, and schepens, a sheriff, board of aldermen, and a mayor; and even when the change was made it was apparent rather than real, for most of the old officers simply continued to carry on the government under new names. The Governor's Commission, of June 12, 1665, by which this change was effected, is known as the Nicolls Charter. It did actually slightly enlarge the authority of the municipal government; but its chief importance was its demonstration of the intention of the English to treat New York not as a commercial investment, but as a colonial capital entitled to consideration and respect.

The most emphatic and the most far-reachingly beneficial expression of this fostering policy was the passage, in the year 1678, of what was styled the Bolting Act; in accordance with the provisions of which this city was granted a monopoly in the bolting of flour, and in the packing of flour and biscuit for export under the act. No mill outside of the city was permitted to grind flour for market, nor was any person outside of the city permitted to pack breadstuffs in any form for sale; the result of which interdict was to throw the export trade in breadstuffs, mainly with the West Indies and already very considerable, exclusively into the hands of the millers and merchants of New York. Outside of the city, and with justice, this law was regarded with extreme disfavor. From the first, strong efforts were made by the country people to secure its repeal; but the "pull" of the city members in the Provincial Assembly (the whole matter has an interestingly prophetic flavor), was strong enough to keep it in effect for sixteen years. At last, in 1694, the country members broke away from their city leaders—as has happened also in later times—and most righteously repealed this very one-sided law.

But the Bolting Act had been in force long enough to accomplish a result larger and more lasting than its promoters had contemplated, or, indeed, than they well

could comprehend; it had laid the foundation of the foreign commerce of New York.

During the sixteen years that the act remained operative the city expanded, under the stimulus of such extraordinary privileges, by leaps and bounds. Fortunately, an authoritative record has been preserved—in the petition filed by the New York millers and merchants against the repeal of the act—of precisely what the city gained in this short space of time. In the year 1678 (the petitioners state), the total number of houses in New York was 384; the total number of beef cattle slaughtered was 400; the sailing craft hailing from the port consisted of three ships, seven boats, and eight sloops; and the total annual revenues of the city were less than £2000. On the other hand, in the year 1694 the number of houses had increased to 983; the slaughter of beef cattle (largely for export), to nearly 4000; the sailing craft to 60 ships, 40 boats, and 25 sloops; and the city revenues to £5000. In conclusion, to show how intimately this prodigious expansion was associated with the milling interest, the petitioners declared that more than 600 of the 983 buildings in the city depended in one way or another upon the trade in flour. In view of these facts, very properly do the arms of New York —granted in the year 1682, in the midst of its first burst of great prosperity—exhibit, along with the beaver emblematic of the city's commercial beginning, the sails of a windmill and two flour barrels as emblems of the firm foundation upon which its foreign commerce has been reared.

By comparing the map of 1695 with the Duke's Plan of 1664, the development of the city under the influence of the Bolting Act may be seen at a glance. In 1664 fully one-third of the available street-front space remained vacant in the city proper, and only eighteen buildings had been erected outside of the wall. By 1695 the six hundred new buildings had occupied almost all the available street-front space in the city proper, and had forced the laying out of so large a group of new streets to the northward of the wall that the city had been almost doubled in size. In the annexed district few houses had been erected west of King (William) Street; and the new streets west of Broadway possibly had not even been opened—for the

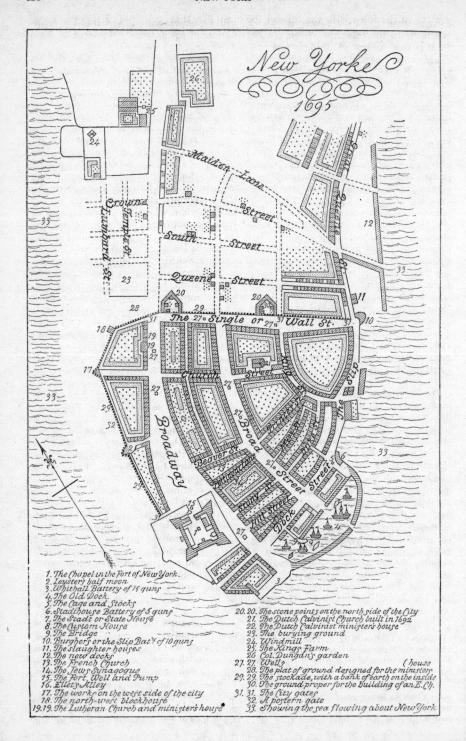

New Yorke 1695

1. The Chapel in the Fort of New York.
2. Leyster's half moon
3. Whitehall Battery of 15 guns
4. The Old Dock.
5. The Cage and Stocks
6. Stadthouse Battery of 5 guns
7. The Stadt or State House
8. The Custom House
9. The Bridge
10. Burghers or the Slip Bat'l of 10 guns
11. The slaughter houses
12. The new docks
13. The French Church
14. The Jews Synagogue
15. The Fort, Well and Pump
16. Ellet's Alley
17. The work on the west side of the city
18. The north-west blockhouse
19.19. The Lutheran Church and minister's house

20.20. The stone points on the north side of the City
21. The Dutch Calvinist Church built in 1692
22. The Dutch Calvinist minister's house
23. The burying ground
24. Windmill
25. The Kings Farm
26. Col. Dungan's garden
27.27. Wells   (house
28. The plat of ground designed for the minister
29.29. The stockade, with a bank of earth on the inside
30. The ground proper for the building of an E. Ch.
31.31. The City gates
32. A postern gate
33. Showing the sea flowing about New York.

growth of the town still was toward the northeast. But the many new buildings east of King Street, and the provision upon so large a scale of new streets, showed the alert enterprising spirit that was abroad. This was, indeed, the most active period in real estate transactions that the city so far had known. Prices were rising prodigiously. By the year 1689 fourteen lots near Coenties Slip were sold at auction for £35 each, and a lot at the foot of Broad Street actually was valued at £80. However, while affected by the rise in real estate values generally, the extraordinary rise in prices hereabouts was due to the building at the foot of Broad Street—at the same time that the canal was filled in —of the Wet Docks: two basins of a sufficient size to harbor a whole fleet of the little ships of that day while their cargoes were taken in or discharged. And about the same time, so rapidly was the commerce of the city increasing, two new wharves were built upon the East River front. Finally, in the midst of this most flourishing period, New York received, April 22, 1686, the very liberal charter—known as the Dongan Charter, because granted through the Governor of that name—which still is the basis of our civic rights.*

During this energetic and highly formative period, while wise and sound English government was doing so much to foster the welfare of the city, the English race distinctly was in a minority among the citizens. This fact is brought out clearly in the following statement made by Governor Dongan, in the year 1687, in his report to the Board of Trade: "For the past seven years there have not come over to this Province twenty English, Scotch, or Irish families. On Long Island the people increase so fast that they complain for want of land, and many remove thence to the neighboring provinces. Several French families have lately come from the West Indies and from England, and also several Dutch families from Hol-

land, so that the number of foreigners greatly exceeds the King's natural born subjects."

In point of morals, the New York of two hundred years ago seems to have been about on a par with frontier towns and outpost settlements of the present day. About the time that Governor Dongan made his report to the Board of Trade, the Rev. John Miller—for three years a resident of the colony as chaplain to the King's forces—addressed to the then Bishop of London a letter in which he reviewed the spiritual shortcomings of the colonists. Mr. Miller's strictures upon the Dissenters, naturally warped by his point of view, scarcely are to be quoted in fairness; but of the clergymen of the Establishment, towards whom his disposition would be lenient, he thus wrote: "There are here, and also in other provinces, many of them such as, being of a vicious life and conversation, have played so many vile pranks, and show such an ill light, as have been very prejudicial to religion in general and to the Church of England in particular." Continuing, he complains broadly of "the great negligence of divine things that is generally found in the people, of what sect or sort soever they pretend to be." And, in conclusion, he declares: "In a soil so rank as this no marvel if the Evil One finds a ready entertainment for the seed he is ready to cast in; and from a people so inconstant and regardless of heaven and holy things no wonder if God withdraw His grace, and give them up a prey to those temptations which they so industriously seek to embrace."

These cheering remarks relate to the Province at large. Touching the citizens of New York in particular, the reverend gentleman briefly but forcibly describes them as drunkards and gamblers, and adds: "This, joined to their profane, atheistical, and scoffing method of discourse, makes their company extremely uneasy to sober and religious men."

IV.

On the turn from the seventeenth to the eighteenth century, the population of New York was about 5000 souls: Dutch and English nearly equal in numbers; a few French, Swedes, and Jews; about 800 negroes, nearly all of whom were slaves. It was a driving, prosperous, commercial community; nor is there much cause for wonder—in view of the

* The Dongan Charter, granted by James II., was amended by Queen Anne in 1708, and was further enlarged by George II. in 1730 into what is known as the Montgomery Charter. This last, confirmed by the General Assembly of the Province in 1732, made New York virtually a free city. The Mayor was appointed by the Governor in Council until the Revolution, by the State Governor and four members of the Council of Appointment until 1821, by the Common Council of the city until 1834, and since this last date (in theory) by the people.

Rev. Mr. Miller's pointed lament over its ungodliness — that a great deal of its prosperity came through channels which now would be regarded as intolerably foul. But in those brave days natures were strong, and squeamishness was a weakling virtue still hidden in the womb of time.

Slave-dealing then was an important and well-thought-of industry—or, in the more elegant phrase of one of the gravest of New York historians, "a species of maritime adventure then engaged in by several of our most respectable merchants." The Dutch are credited with having brought the first cargo of slaves to the northern part of America—from their possessions on the Guinea Coast to the Virginia plantations—and a regular part of the business of the Dutch West India Company was providing African slaves for use in its American colonies. The profits of the business—even allowing for the bad luck of a high death rate on the western passage — were so alluringly great that it was not one to be slighted by the eminently go-ahead merchants of this town ; and the fact must be remembered that, as a business, slave-dealing was quite as legitimate then as is the emigrant traffic of the present day. Young Mr. John Cruger has left on record a most edifying account of a voyage which he made out of New York in the years 1698–1700, in the ship *Prophet Daniel*, to Madagascar for the purchase of live freight; and the sentiment of the community in the premises is exhibited by the fact that the slave-dealing Mr. Cruger was elected an alderman from the Dock Ward continuously from the year 1712 until the year 1733, and that subsequently he served four consecutive terms as mayor. In addition to the negro slaves, there were many Indian slaves held in the colony. For convenience in hiring, the law was passed, November 30, 1711, that "all negro and Indian slaves that are let out to hire within the city do take up their standing in order to be hired at the market-house at the Wall Street Slip."

Probably the alarm bred of the so-called Negro Plot of 1741 was most effective in checking the growth of slavery in this city. Certainly, the manner in which the negroes charged with fomenting this problematical conspiracy were dealt with affords food for curious reflection upon

the social conditions of the times. After a trial that would have been a farce had it not been a tragedy, Clause was condemned to be "broke upon a wheel"; Robin to be hung in chains alive, "and so to continue without any sustenance until he be dead"; Tom to be "burned with a slow fire until he be dead and consumed to ashes," and so on. However, everything depends upon the point of view. In that strong-stomached time judicial cruelty to criminals met with universal approval; and as to slavery, the worshipful Sir Edward Coke, but a very few years earlier, had laid down the doctrine that pagans properly could be held in bondage by Christians, because the former were the bond-slaves of Satan, while the latter were the servants of God.

When it came to piracy, public opinion in New York was not keyed up to a pitch that could be called severe; and it is a fact that the foundations of some highly respectable fortunes still extant in this community were laid in successful ventures—to use the euphuistic phrase of the day—"on the account." Under the generously liberal rule of Governor Fletcher (1692–8), any pirate, or any New York merchant taking a flyer in piracy, was entirely secure in his business provided he was willing to pay a fair percentage of its profits to that high functionary (even as the modern city contractor is secure if he will "stand in" with the right city officials); because of which cordial leniency matters here became such a hissing and reproach that the home government was compelled to recall Fletcher and to send out in his place Lord Bellamont—who specifically was charged with the duty of breaking up what elegantly was styled "the Red Sea trade."

Much of this piracy was carried on under cover of privateering; and from genuine privateering—which was held to be an entirely honest and legitimate business —the city derived a large amount of wealth. During almost the whole of the century of warfare that began in the year 1688—when war was declared by Spain against France, and when England joined in on the Spanish side—there were fine chances for private armed ventures against England's enemies on the high seas. From this port, most notably in the fourth decade of the last century, a dashing fleet of privateers went forth; and the *Weekly Post Boy* of that period blazes

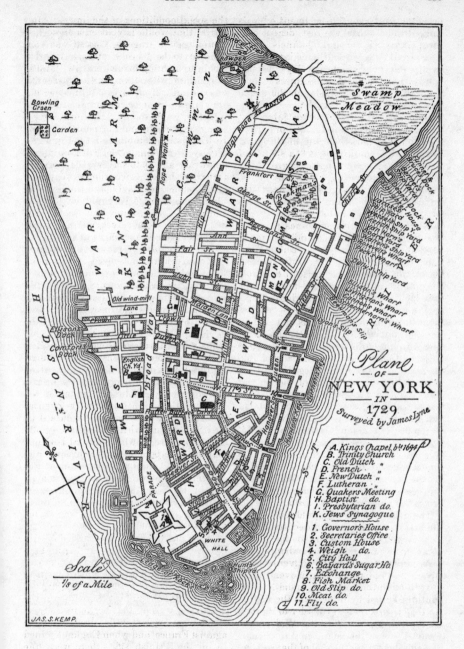

Plan of NEW YORK IN 1729 Surveyed by James Lyne

A. Kings Chapel b.t 1694.
B. Trinity Church
C. Old Dutch "
D. French "
E. New Dutch "
F. Lutheran "
G. Quakers Meeting
H. Baptist do.
I. Presbyterian do.
K. Jews Synagogue

1. Governor's House
2. Secretaries Office
3. Custom House
4. Weigh do.
5. City Hall
6. Bayard's Sugar Ho.
7. Exchange
8. Fish Market
9. Old Slip do.
10. Meat do.
11. Fly do.

Scale
1/8 of a Mile

JAS. S. KEMP.

with calls " to all Gentlemen Sailors, and others, who have a mind to try their Fortunes on a Cruizing Voyage against the enemy," to enter on one or another of the private armed vessels about to put to sea. In addition to the many prizes taken by the privateers, many prizes taken by King's ships—about this time the dashing Captain Warren commanded on this station—were sent into New York to be condemned; and it is not impossible that these last netted almost as much to the ingenuous merchants who had the handling of them as did the out-and-out captures on private account.

And all the while that money thus easily was coming in over the bar at Sandy Hook with almost every tide, substantial business interests of a quieter sort, yet in the long-run more solidly profitable, were in the course of development. Especially did the West India trade—so firmly established by the Bolting Act that the repeal of that act did not do it any lasting injury—become constantly of increasing importance. It did not, of course, bring in the great profits which came from it while the city held the monopoly of milling; but it was conducted so intelligently—provisions shipped hence being exchanged for West Indian products; these in turn being shipped to England and exchanged for manufactured goods and wares; and these last being brought to this city for sale or trade—that each round of transactions left three profits in the merchants' hands. At the same time a considerable coastwise trade was maintained, and a large business was done in ship-building—ships even being built in this city to be sent to England for sale.

According to figures preserved in the chance letter of a German traveller, Professor Kalm, 211 vessels entered and 222 vessels cleared from this port between December 1, 1729, and December 5, 1730. By the year 1732 the population of the city had increased to 8624 souls; and in this same year the advance in the value of real estate was made manifest by the sale of seven lots on Whitehall Street at prices varying from £150 to £200.

The extent of New York at the end of the first quarter of the eighteenth century is shown by the map drawn by James Lyne from a survey made in the year 1729; and the fact which this map most strongly emphasizes is the continued growth of the city northeastward and the continued unimportance of Broadway. At that period several causes were united to discourage the development of the western side of the island and to encourage the development of the eastern side: as has been the case again in our own times, when we have seen the most desirable part of New York—the Riverside region north of Seventy-second Street—suddenly spring into popular favor after years of entire neglect. At the begin-

ning of the last century practically all the business interests of the city were centred on or near the East River front. Here, from the docks at Whitehall Street northward to Roosevelt's wharf, all the shipping of the port was harbored—for the practical reason that the salt water did not freeze, and that consequently the shipping was safe in winter from ice; here, for the same reason, were the yards of the ship-builders; here were the warehouses of the merchants; and here, along Great Queen (Pearl) Street—the street leading to the Brooklyn ferry—all the considerable shops were situated in order to make sure of catching the Long Island trade.

Broadway actually was in a remote and obscure part of the town. Below Crown (Liberty) Street dwelling-houses had been erected, of which a few near the Bowling Green were prodigiously fine; but north of Crown Street all the west side of Broadway was open fields. This unimproved region, beginning at the present Fulton Street and thence extending northward, was the Church Farm.*

The farm-house pertaining to this farm—standing very nearly upon the site of the present Astor House—is shown on Lyne's map, immediately to the south of the Broadway rope-walk. Later it became a tavern of some celebrity—the Drover's Inn, kept by Adam Vanderberg. Undoubtedly, the church ownership of this large parcel of land tended to delay its utilization for building purposes, and so helped to retard the extension of the city on the line of Broadway. Even in those early days the strongly American desire to build on land owned in fee oper-

---

* The estate known as the Company's Farm, set aside by the Dutch to be tilled for the benefit of the Company's servants, civil and military, lay between the present Fulton and Duane streets and Broadway and the North River. Upon the English conquest this estate became the private property of the Duke of York. Subsequently, in the year 1671, by purchase from seven of the eight heirs of Annetje Jans, the boundary of the Duke's Farm was carried northward (but not continuously) as far as the present Christopher Street. When the Duke of York ascended the throne the property became known as the King's Farm, and as the Queen's Farm upon the accession of Queen Anne. In this last reign, in the year 1705, reserving a quit-rent of three shillings, the then Governor, Lord Cornbury, granted the entire estate to Trinity Church. The litigation that has arisen over a portion of this property has been instituted by the heirs of the eighth heir of Annetje Jans, who was unconsenting to the sale in the year 1671.

ated against the use of leasehold property. Not until the need for the Church Farm became pressing was it taken for improvement on the only terms upon which it could be acquired.

Maerschalck's map (1755) shows that by the middle of the last century the growth of the city, creating this pressing need, had warranted the laying out of streets through the southern portion of the church property, and that five-and-twenty buildings had been erected between the present Liberty Street and the palisade. But the stronger tendency of growth, it will be observed, still was toward the northeast. This was, in fact, the line of least resistance. Advance up the middle of the island was blocked by the Fresh Water pond, and up the western side it

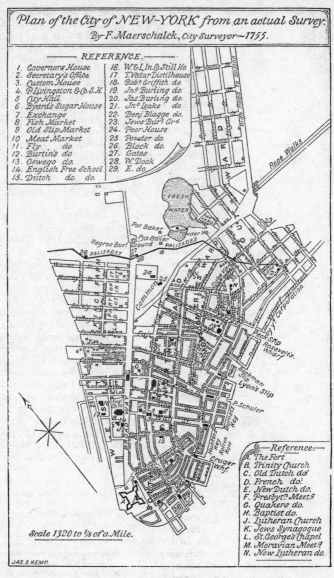

was impeded by the marshy valley, known as Lispenard's meadows, through the midst of which, on the line of the present Canal Street, was the artificial drain from the Fresh Water to the North River. Before this low-lying region was reached, the obstacle caused by the leaseholds was encountered. Finally, the base-line of west-side development, an extension of Broadway, was but a lane leading to cow pastures, and stopping frankly, not far

from the present Leonard Street, at a set of bars. Not until the road, now Greenwich Street, leading to Greenwich Village was opened (at an uncertain date, anterior to 1760) was there any thoroughfare on the western side of the island. The only life in this isolated suburb, therefore, was that of its few inhabitants: who dwelt here for economy's sake, far removed from the agreeable activities of the town.

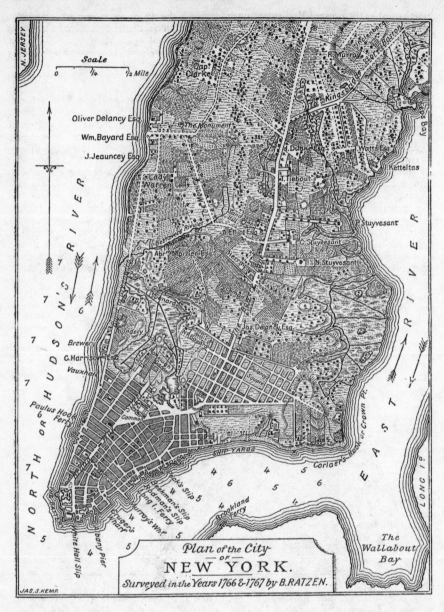

Plan of the City
—OF—
NEW YORK.
Surveyed in the Years 1766 & 1767 by B. RATZEN.

—On the eastern side of the island all was energy and go. Here were centred all the important business interests, and the base-line for further development was the Boston Post Road—a blithe and bustling highway, along which ebbed and flowed constantly a strong tide of travel between the city and its dependent villages and the populous region lying in-land from Long Island Sound. Upon this highway—called in its lower reaches the Bowery Lane, because of the farms or *boweries* thereabouts—settlements had been made very early in colonial times, and by the third quarter of the eighteenth century—as is shown on Ratzen's larger map (1767)—there was an almost continuous line of country-seats extending as far northward as the present Madison Square. At the intersection of the highway with Monument Lane (of which lane two sections survive, in the present Astor Place and Greenwich Avenue) was the nucleus of a village; and Greenwich, to which the lane led, was a village of some importance. In a word, the growth of the city on this line was inevitable, for here, to the thrust of the expanding community was added the attraction of the settlements already established beyond the city's bounds.

On the smaller of Ratzen's maps, also of 1767, here reproduced, the great extension of the city in the twelve years following 1755 is strikingly exhibited; but the scheme of drafting—showing projected streets as though they actually were in existence, and not showing individual houses—is such that no precise concept can be formed of the actual gain. Most of this map is mere prophecy, of which the fulfilment did not come for more than a score and a half of years; and the very best of its prophecies, the Great Square, never was fulfilled at all. This liberal project for establishing a public park on the line of Grand Street—in a part of the city now most urgently in need of precisely such a breathing-space —had its origin in a speculative desire to provide an agreeable spot for suburban homes. That it was alive nine years later is shown by the fact that the square —then called De Lancey Square—appears on Major Holland's map, drawn from surveys made in 1776. But that was the last of it. On Hill's map, 1782, close upon the present line of Grand Street, the British earth-works grimly traverse the very place where the park should be. In common with every other phase or promise of the city's prosperity, the Great Square was ploughed under by the Revolutionary war.

LONDON AND NEW YORK

BUILT BY TITANS, LAID OUT BY EUCLID, FURNISHED BY EDISON

COMING from Bow Bells to Trinity chimes, the course of an Englishman's experience in New York runs on zigzag lines. He begins in rhapsodies; he ends as often as not in gnashing of teeth, and it is not till he gets back to London and turns an Anglo-American eye upon English ways of doing things that he partly reverts to his first opinion. The two cities should really only be written of in the way of comparison or contrast by those who have spent five years in each, and passed from one to the other and back again without a break. No one ever knows his own city or his own country till he has been abroad and returned, and the opinions of an Englishman on New York only begin to be valuable when he has had a chance of studying London through American spectacles. At first everything finds approval. The thousand and one mechanical conveniences, undreamed-of in London—the cable and electric cars, the

elevated railroads, the telephones, the numbered streets, the elevators—become themes for lyrical congratulation. Here, one exclaims, is a city where everything that machinery can do to make life easy and comfortable is done, and done thoroughly. The latest invention comes redhot from the Patent Office and spreads over the city while you sleep. In London one draws up the blind in the morning to see if it has stopped raining; in New York, to find out whether a service of flying-machines has not been organized overnight. Put on one side the stuffy, top-heavy, lumbering, bone-breaking London omnibuses, and on the other the swift, trim electric cars that are forever flashing past you, and you epitomize the outward aspects of the two cities. The abashed Englishman, as he looks on the contrast, can only wonder what sort of a prehistoric country he hails from; and in the first flush he will argue that no town that has not New York's system of transportation, that cannot take hold of a man and shoot him up a twenty-story building like a torpedo from its tube, or whirl him along an elevated railroad on a line with somebody's second-floor parlor, can possibly be worth living in. And these things are only symptoms of what in truth is the very atmosphere of Manhattan Island. Activity is as assuredly the note of New York as that of London is repose. The rush and swing of the city act on the effete European as a sting and challenge. New York is the living gospel of work, the consecrated city of labor, and leaves on its devotees an ineffaceable stamp. One stands on Broadway, amid the jar and clatter of it all, and watches with something like awe the sliding procession of sallow, hurried faces, the tense lips tight drawn as though to repress a cry, the gestures abrupt, decisive. And yet it is an awe that links, not separates. New York summons to toil as Monte Carlo to idleness, with irresistible imperiousness. One is ashamed to be caught doing nothing. Business which in London is business merely, in New York is everything. A

stress, universal and compelling, is put upon one to "get out and hustle"; and work, so far from being, as in England one is apt to think it is, an unpalatable interruption, becomes suddenly the alpha and omega of life. Thackeray used to say it was an excellent thing for Englishmen, and especially young Englishmen, to visit the United States; it knocked the conceit and self-sufficiency out of them. It is no less fatal to their conventional view of work. England is democratic only politically, in forms and institutions, hardly at all in spirit, and the number of employments not considered "respectable" enough for the young Englishman of decent family and upbringing is still appalling. It is therefore good and wholesome for him to come to New York and see Americans of his own station not in the least afraid to take off their coats and begin at the beginning. Where all are workers, there is no question of the precise degree of respectability attaching to this or that trade or profession. So long as it is honest, clean, and promising, any chance that comes along is good enough for the young American. The social conventions, so far from limiting his choice, merely insist that he shall not be idle; and it is this view of things that makes up the first of the atmospheric differences between London and New York. It is the Englishman's introduction to democracy, and he takes readily to the stimulus of the new acquaintance.

Nor is it only the exhilaration of the place and the evidences all round him of bustling vitality that hold the Englishman captive. The first time I walked up Fifth Avenue I thought I was in another Paris. The strenuousness of Broadway shows there its social side, and to one just fresh from the dreary drab and studied

CLOSE TO BOW BELLS, LONDON

languor of London the result is exceedingly happy. Given a bright May morning, a Sunday by choice, and from the mixture of crystalline air, white houses, the long clean stretch of street, and the radiant prima-donna effects of American women, you extract a combination hard to equal, and in its way impossible to beat. It is the Bois without the trees; not quite Parisian, for the last touch of perfect naturalness is wanting, but still less English, for it is at once light-hearted and elegant and bubbling over with sheer *joie de vivre*. New York throws into all its pleasures an infectiousness and relish distinctively its own. An Englishman has to quicken his mental pace somewhat to keep in touch. Work or play, it is just the same. Into whatever he takes up, the New-Yorker imports a new and 'invigorating zest. Wherever he turns, the Londoner finds himself urged to more exertion than he is altogether used to, if he would hold his own. The competition is not very fierce, but the competitors are of a higher average. The best foot has constantly to be put and kept forward, to make money or conversation; and so stimulating may be the clash of the struggle that we have even known Englishmen who, after six months in New York, have actually learned how to tell a tale as it should be told. He must, indeed, be singularly surly or unambitious who can hold back. The reception given one is so genial, and the reward so wholly tempting, that the new-comer plunges into business and society with an enthusiasm that surprises himself. The Englishman who does not succumb to New York in the first three months is a lost soul.

But all things have their ebb, and slowly the Englishman feels his enthusiasm on the wane. Catch him after a two years' residence, and he is more likely to be full of anathemas than praise. He has reached the attitude and state of mind

which are the proverbial offspring of familiarity. Even the handiest invention, once accepted, becomes no invention at all, but part of the ordinary routine of life, for which any special gratitude is superfluous. When the novelty has worn

UNDER TRINITY CHIMES. NEW YORK

off, the hundred and one ways in which New York ministers to one's comfort—and it is surprising how quickly it does wear off, how easily one takes it all as a matter of course—there comes the sense of having sacrificed to false gods. and the city resolves itself into nothing more than a triumph of mechanics, of iron, steel, bricks, and electricity, built by the Titans, laid out by Euclid, and furnished by Edison. Behind it there lies little or nothing to satisfy—no surprises, no hidden nooks, no glimpse of the past, nothing but the whir and glitter of a vast machine. And busily idealizing his own country as the exile always does, the Englishman begins to feel as though in coming to New York he had laid down Matthew Arnold's poems to enter a powerhouse. There comes a time when he can think of himself as nothing but a bundle of freight in the grip of an exaggerated express company. New York stretches out before him as a gigantic counter, split up into little squares to make business easy of despatch, and scaled down to the dull prose of buying and selling, of doing things at the swiftest possible speed, of saving at any cost an inch of space and a second of time.

It is this undisguised triumph of mechanics over æsthetics, of the new and useful over the old, that after a time makes New York for an Englishman rather a deadening city to live in. The iron enters into one's soul, and comfort, one feels, can be bought at too high a price. If only Americans could learn to do things a little more clumsily, their metropolis would have many more charms for the English exile. He misses the hundred and one lacunæ and inconveniences which at home can be damned, and as a matter of fact are damned with such hygienic heartiness. He never has a chance to grumble. In the long-run mechanical perfection becomes almost as difficult as moral perfection to live with at ease. One turns a screw, and in twenty minutes one's room is warmer than two fires could make it in half a day. It is demoralizing, sybaritish. In England, if the same system were introduced, one could always rely on its being entertainingly out of order. But nothing seems to get out of order in New York, not even that great stand-by of English cemeteries and conversation, the drains. There is a dull and deadly unerringness about the way people go through life and carry on their business in New York. If only the express companies knew how to lose things, or would condescend to deliver them at the wrong houses; if only the New York storekeepers would allow one time just to get home before one's purchases arrive; if only the ice-man would forget to call once or twice a decade—what a spice would be given to life on Manhattan Island!

It seems, then, to come to this, that there is too much machinery in New York, and it is too inhumanly good of its kind. After the first few months of

envious admiration at the ingenuity of it all, one asks what lies behind, and the reluctant answer of New York, as of all cities that have been built and have not grown, is, nothing. The past is so overlayed that not the most picturesque imagination can recall it. Dutch New York, English New York, for all the most pertinacious search can discover, are as though they had never been. A view of the city less than fifty years old seems incredibly remote. Some small tangle of streets "downtown," here and there an incongruous wooden shanty holding its own between palatial restaurants and clubs of dazzling marble, are the only visible proofs that New York was not hit off at a stroke and dumped down on the island by contract. As a place to dine and do business in, New York is admirable; financially, indeed, it is always charming, but its stony lack of suggestiveness makes up an atmosphere difficult after a while for an Englishman to breathe in freely. One feels, too, singularly cut off from the rest of the world, and especially from the rest of America. The eyes of New York are turned eastward, and of its own hinterland it knows as little as the average Londoner of Scotland. I never really felt myself in America till I was free of New York and its concentrated self-sufficiency. The city is a little world in itself, immensely wrapped up in its own concerns, and in far closer touch with London or Paris than with Chicago or Denver. It finds it easier to look across the Atlantic than beyond the Palisades. It is, indeed, a most serviceable watch-tower from which to spy out on the two continents, being on the main stream of neither European nor American life, but in a backwater of its own making. Therein possibly lies its chief educational value for the Englishman; it gives him a new perspective, the invaluable outside point of view. But unless of a heroic complacency one cannot live in a backwater forever, not at least without some loss of vitality. One gets too much at second hand, and one criticises too eagerly and mistakenly the echoes and pale reflections and half-lights that reach one. Is it carrying honesty to the point of social criminality to confess that foreigners sometimes detect in New York a grandi-

CHURCH OF ST. MARY-LE-STRAND

ose provincialism? After all, the fact that a number of people of different nationalities make it their home without too much friction does not stamp a city as cosmopolitan. Otherwise we should have Chicago putting in a claim for the title. Cosmopolitanism, of course, is not a matter of statistics, but a mellow something in the social air. What that something exactly is, and what qualities go to its make-up, it is not easy to say. Repose, perhaps, is one of them; the tolerance that comes of a wide experience is another; the habit of taking things for granted without question and without surprise is a third. Possibly the essence of it all is the "nothing too much" of the Greek sect, the calm outlook, the tempered enjoyment, interest without enthusiasm, pleasure without passion. This is hardly the note of New York, where everything is apt to run to extremes, and moderation alone is voted commonplace. I have known the city shaken to its depths by a fancy-dress ball, and talk of nothing else for three weeks and more. New York, in fact, is never bored. It has—all America has—the secret of perpetual enjoyment. It gossips with real relish, not, as London does, more from a sense of social duty. Nowhere is an attractive novelty—it must be attractive

THE SWIFT, TRIM ELECTRIC CARS

as well as novel, for New York's taste is only one degree less refined than the Parisian—surer of being caught up, passed round, adopted, and laughed over in a nine days' carnival. Society in New York reflects more precisely than elsewhere the average man, and it has been said of the American that if he is never quite young, he is certainly never old. To the last he is elemental, fresh in his enthusiasms, ready to be interested, ready to enjoy himself. Nothing seems to impair his zest for life, and his determination to get as much out of it as possible. And if this is true of the men, it is doubly so of the women. The consequence is that, side by side with an electrifying "go" and swing, there runs through social New York a curious strain of naïveté, a sort of fundamental artlessness, which separates it from London by more than the breadth of the Atlantic. New York is always "wanting to know," and does not hesitate to ask, if necessary; it revels in the small points of life; it is as free and frank with its emotions as with its introductions or its compliments. It even allows stories to be told as a form of social entertainment. In no city is so much anxious thought

spent on the externals of hospitality, and nowhere are the results so ingenuously striking. Allowing for a certain difference in the degree of barbarism, Rome in its decline could alone furnish a parallel to New York's "Four Hundred." The American "aristocracy" has no equal in Europe for ability to turn the simplest sort of diversion into a function, and every function into a ceremony. It is not of them I write, though their passion for incongruous artificialities and the glare in which they live have infected all strata. An exasperated Englishman once described the social atmosphere of Manhattan Island as "rather fussy," but that was only in comparison with the English ways of doing things. The charm of London hospitality is that there is never the slightest strain put upon either host or guest. The American hostess, like the French hostess, feels that she must be continually "entertaining" her guest; she considers it a reflection on her hospitality if the guest is left a moment alone; she looks upon it as her duty to be continually providing fresh amusements, and is constantly troubled by doubts as to whether the visitor is really "enjoying" himself. That is one of the reasons why Americans, after the pampering they get at home, are apt to feel themselves neglected in London, and left out in the cold. The difference between the two styles of hospitality is the difference between a man who thrusts a handful of bank-notes upon you, telling you to spend them any way you like, and a man who makes you a multitude of small gifts, each costing him an infinity of thought, and yourself a repeated embarrassment of thanks. A foreigner is more often oppressed in New York than in London with a sense of effort in the host and hostess, an anxiety lest something should go wrong rather than a taking for granted that everything will go right. The immaculately "correct thing," I imagine, finds more stringent devotees in New York than in London, and produces at times an atmosphere of formalism and restraint that is really altogether at war with the instincts of the people. The New York clubs, for instance, are far more magnificent, inside and out, than any we have in London. All the appointments and furnishings are, generally speaking, as tasteful as they are luxurious; and yet somehow the club spirit does not take hold of a man as it does in London. Whatever be the reason — and probably the nearness of the clubs to the members' homes is at the root of it — one misses, or thinks he misses, something of the easy unconventionality, the sense of comfortable *camaraderie*, that make club life in London so particularly pleasant. There is a stricter atmosphere, fewer relaxations, and a more insistent code of etiquette. My first instinct on entering a New York club was always the last one would be likely to be prompted by in London—to take off my hat.

New York can damn or boom a play, sell a novel, and settle to the satisfaction of the rest of America what is the right thing to do and wear, but therewith its influence comes abruptly to an end. It is not a literary centre, nor a scientific nor an artistic centre, still less is it the pivot of American politics. Literature, science, and art all flourish in New York, but they flourish equally well in Boston and Chicago. New York has none of the compelling power that drew

A LUMBERING LONDON OMNIBUS

Daudet to Paris, or Dr. Johnson to London, and a writer or an artist who settles down on Manhattan Island does so more to satisfy his pocket than his soul. The elements do not blend as they used to in France before democracy destroyed the *salon,* and as they still do in London.

All Americans who have lived in London will have noticed the curious facility with which Englishmen contrive to neutralize Americans by only adopting them in part. I remember the architect of a building who evidently was infected by American ideas. He had heard of elevators and dumb-waiters and speaking - tubes, and he had obviously made up his mind to lead all London by including these conveniences in his block of flats. But instead of connecting the speaking - tube with the kitchen, he put it outside the drawing-room, so that, had it been used at all, the entire household would have been obliged to overhear the struggles of the servants with the tradesmen; and instead of running up the dumb-waiter alongside the kitchen or pantry, he had placed it outside the flat altogether, in the hall, opposite the elevator. The consequence was, of course, that neither dumb-waiter nor speaking-tube could be

THEY RUN TO EXTREMES IN NEW YORK

utilized, and two very happy American inventions were discredited in English eyes for lack of simple attention to the necessary details. That, in itself, is a small thing, but it stands for a good deal.

House-hunting in London is not the simple business it is in New York. You cannot inspect the house or flat without an " order to view " from the agent, who may live round the next corner or at the other end of the city. Moreover, when all the formalities are complete, fresh surprises await one. Ordinarily no house or flat in London can be taken for less than three years! In New York a fully appointed flat would include, as a matter of course, steam heat, electric light, and all the necessary fixtures, a gas and coal range, a constant supply of hot water, a built - in refrigerator, picture-mouldings, day and night elevators, store - rooms, dumb - waiters, and a bewildering variety of cupboards. In London most of these accessories are still undreamed - of. Steam - heating is almost unknown. If a flat is wired for electric light or piped for gas, the incoming tenant has to provide the brackets and fittings at his own expense—taking them away with him when he moves. As every flat has to produce its own supply of hot water from the kitchen boiler, gas-ranges are useless. I really believe the shock of finding himself expected to provide a refrigerator would kill the average English landlord. Picture-mouldings, too, the tenant has to pay for himself, the landlord, with true English stupidity, preferring to have his walls knocked about with nails. I have visited some score of the best flat-houses in London, and not one had a store-room for the reception of trunks and boxes, not one had an elevator that ran after midnight, and not one but was abominably deficient in cupboards and every kind of storage facilities.

I cannot resist quoting the opinion of an American lady who has had a good deal of housekeeping experience both in London and New York. " Wages," she writes, " are less in London; but the amount of work done by the domestic servant is as nothing compared with what is accomplished in America. A sort of inchoate trades-unionism penetrates even into the kitchen. The list of things which are 'not expected' of the English cook or the English house-maid or the English parlor-maid is appalling. An English cook cooks—if she does even that. Certainly she does nothing else, and would feel insulted if you told her to, and that is one of the reasons why house-keeping is much easier in New York than in London."

To get hold of a retail dealer of whatever kind in London — butcher, baker, grocer, or fruiterer—who will not overcharge you, who will not give you false weights, and who will not smuggle into his monthly accounts items never ordered or delivered, is so nearly impossible that Londoners are gravitating more and more towards the big-store system, where you are served by men who are the employees of other men, and therefore under less personal temptation to get the better of you. The charges of the ordinary tradesman are regulated simply by his estimate of the precise amount of extortion you are likely to stand.

It is a most expensive luxury to be "a gentleman" in England. In London, especially, you pay for the title through a fixed tariff on the accessories that New York, with its big way of doing business, throws in gratis. You dine, let us say, at a restaurant. There is a charge of from 2d. to 6d. for guarding your hat and coat in the cloak-room, and, being "a gentleman," a tip in addition is expected. You want to wash your hands—another 2d. or another 6d., and, of course, another tip. You take up the menu, and, behold, there is an intimation that a charge of 3d. each person will be made under the guise of "table-money." This charge varies according to the nature of the place; 3d. is the lowest, 6d. perhaps the average, though at a good many restaurants it is 1s., and in at least two that

could be named, 1s. 6d. The only difference is that in the lower-priced restaurants it is called "table-money," and in the higher-priced ones placed under the alluring head of *couvert*. An entrance fee frankly demanded at the door would be much less offensive, and I felt a good deal of sympathy with the American who, on running over his bill, and finding himself called upon to pay for the privilege of dining at the place at all, as well as for such obnoxious items as bread and butter, called up the waiter, and said: "Look here; I've breathed one hundred and ninety-two times. How much?" But this sort of thing is typical of a kind of paltry, underhand spirit which runs through London enterprise—the spirit that charges 6d. for theatre programmes, and adds 1s. 6d. to your hotel bill for "service." Londoners, however, being for the most part blissfully ignorant of New York methods, do not in the least object to these exactions. They seem almost to relish them. There is a huge store in London which charges a sum of 5s. a year for permission to buy its goods, and on every package delivered beyond a radius of a quarter of a mile makes a further levy of 2d. And yet this concern turns over more than $15,000,000 a year. The spirit that can tolerate such things is obviously something it takes a New-Yorker time to grow into. Yet in some things — clothing, for example— they run to extremes in New York.

The conclusion of the matter seems to be that New York and London were meant to be complementary to each other, and that the ideal city is only to be constructed by mingling the best points of both. Whether this would not involve the preliminary banishment of most London women and most New York men is a point one might debate forever.

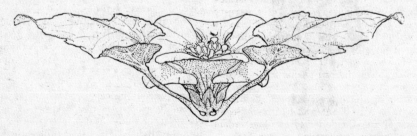

THE STORY OF A STREET
(PART 1)

O N the morning of March 31, 1644, a man of clerkly appearance might have been seen standing at the entrance to the dilapidated fortress of New Amsterdam, with a sheaf of official papers in his hand. It was not an inviting prospect which confronted the observer that raw spring morning, for the roughly built, wooden houses scattered about the fort looked sadly weatherbeaten, and the straggling, ill made roads and paths which served as streets were littered with refuse and rubbish of every sort and ankle deep in mud. Even the new stone tavern on the East River and the still newer stone church, whose stanch construction had recently earned John and Richard Ogden a goodly builder's premium, appeared decidedly bedraggled. Grimy mounds of melting snow encumbered each step of their stairlike gables, and the dirty water which trickled from them like muddy tears gave a finishing touch to their melancholy aspect. Nowhere was there a sign of cheer or comfort, and the unpaved streets were wellnigh deserted, save for a few disconsolate individuals who idled about the doorways, silently watching the hungry hogs rooting among the road refuse or exploring the muddy ramparts in search of food. To the north of the fort a badly placed windmill made a brave show of activity, groaning and whirring under the gusty winds from the bay, but its wild twistings to the capricious gyrations of the rusty weathercocks gave an air of futility to its exertions that was far from relieving the depressing desolation of the scene.

The man at the fort did not, however, waste much time in gazing at these discouraging surroundings. They were familiar to him in every dreary detail, for Cornelis Van Tienhoven had been Secretary of the Council at New Amsterdam for many years, and if he had ever been disturbed by the prevailing wretchedness of the town, it had long since ceased to afford him the slightest concern. Slowly turning his back to the view, he tacked one of his official documents to the wall of the fort, and then swinging about and picking his way across the miry ground to a convenient tree, affixed another paper. The few spectators of this proceeding viewed it with undisguised chagrin, for communications from the government were not apt to increase the happiness of the little Dutch settlement. On the contrary, they usually portended the imposition of some new burden or the curtailment of some coveted privilege at the hands of his High Mightiness, Governor Wilhelmus Kieft, whose six years of misrule had taught New Amsterdam to regard his proclamations with unmitigated dread. Unwelcome as they were, however, experience had taught the inhabitants that it was not prudent to ignore them, and the Secretary had scarcely posted his notices before people began to saunter from their houses and gather about the improvised bulletin boards, the scholar in each group deciphering the script.

Van Tienhoven's handwriting was easily read. Indeed, good penmanship was the only qualification he had ever displayed for his office, and that virtue had wholly failed to endear him to the populace, who hated the very sight of his clerical fist. The particular notice he had transcribed that morning, however, was singularly free of offence. It merely recited a resolution of the Director and Council of New Netherland* that a barrier be erected at the north of the settlement, sufficiently strong to prevent the straying of cattle and to protect

* New York Colonial MSS. 4: 186. State Library, Albany.

WALL STREET IN 1644

The early records indicate that Kieft's cattle guard was built a little to the north of the present Wall Street. De Heerewegh (Broadway) practically terminated a short distance to the north of the cattle guard, but existed as a path or trail beyond that point

them from the Indians, and "warned" all interested persons to appear on "next Monday, the 4th of April, at 7 o'clock," for the prosecution of this work. A more reasonable demand probably never emanated from the Director General, and yet it unquestionably suggested the belated closing of a stable door. During the administration of his predecessor, Van Twiller, almost all the cattle of the colony had mysteriously disappeared, and as the ex-Governor's recently acquired bouwerie was found surprisingly well supplied with live stock, there were grounds for suspecting that some of the missing herds might have strayed in his direction. Kieft, however, was the last man in the world to investigate a trail of this sort, for there was honor among Governors in those days, and William the Testy, though philosophic in no other

respect, thoroughly believed in taking things as he found them. Indeed, rumor had it that his adherence to this belief was responsible for his migration from Holland, with his portrait adorning the public gallows to evidence his bankruptcy, and a charge of embezzling trust funds hanging over his head. These stories may have been the invention of enemies, but there certainly had been nothing in his conduct as Governor to discredit them, and for dastardly cowardice and wanton cruelty his record had been unsurpassed. Indeed, it was a close question whether the Indians or the Dutch had the best cause for hating this representative of the Chartered West India Company in 1644; but, however that may have been, both feared him equally and lost no time in obeying his decrees.

It was not long, therefore, before the

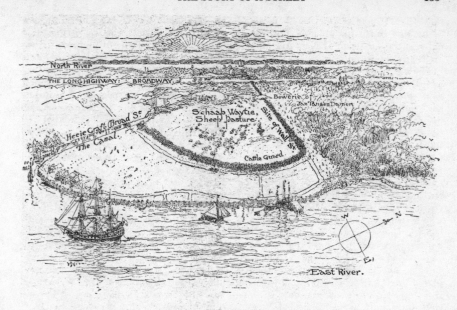

BIRD'S-EYE VIEW OF NEW AMSTERDAM
Based upon original records and maps in New York Historical Society and Lenox
Library, showing line of the cattle guard of 1644 which located Wall Street

colonists were hard at work at the projected cattle guard, and within a few days it stood completed. There is no authoritative information as to how it was constructed, but there is evidence that it consisted mainly of untrimmed trees felled at the edge of the adjoining forest and piled together to form a sort of barricade, and that its northern line, running certainly from the present William Street, New York city, to what is now Broadway, and possibly from shore to shore, marked the farthest limits of New Amsterdam, as it then existed, and practically determined the location of Wall Street.

Such was the origin of the best known thoroughfare of the Western Hemisphere, and the same forest which supplied material for its earliest landmark doubtless furnished Adrian Block, the discoverer of Block Island, with timber for the good ship *Restless*—an appropriate name for the first vessel launched from Manhattan Island, and prophetically suggestive of its most historic highway.

Director General Kieft did not survive his clumsy cattle pen, for some three years after its completion the colony was relieved of his presence by the arrival of a new Governor, whose advent was attended with truly royal ceremonies, and whose bearing and person suggested the very height of majesty. But the residents of New Amsterdam soon discovered that this kingly personage who had descended upon them, splendidly attired in a velvet jacket with slashed sleeves, a broad, drooping white collar, magnificently slashed hose secured at the knee by a rich scarf tied in a knot, and a shoe adorned by a large, bravely colored rosette, had little of the aloofness characteristic of the wearers of imperial purple. Indeed, he had not been long upon the shores of his new domain before he was stumping over it on his silver-banded wooden leg, sticking his nose into all sorts of odd corners, and rendering a general housecleaning in no uncertain tones. Tyrannical he undoubtedly was, but the sway of Petrus Stuyvesant was that of a benevolent despot, confident that he knew what his subjects needed better than they did themselves, and determined that they should have it whether they would or no, and under his domineering, paternal rule the condition of New Amsterdam gradually improved.

The southern end of Manhattan Island was then much narrower than it is to-day. Pearl Street was its eastern boundary, and only a few hundred feet of meadow land separated Broadway from the North River. Within these slender limits, and south of the so-called fence, there were, less than ten years after Stuyvesant landed, nearly two hundred houses, peopled by almost a thousand tenants, while seventeen well defined streets were already plainly traceable, which, thanks to the energy of the choleric Governor, were fairly clean. The houses were for the most part crudely constructed of wood, but some of the more substantial boasted variously colored glazed brick laid in checker, and wrought iron numerals to mark the date of construction, and even the humblest roof supported an ornamental weathercock. Moreover, nearly every house had a bright bit of garden, and if the general appearance of the little town was not as tidy as it has sometimes been pictured, it was not the fault of the tireless potentate who, from the moment of his arrival, ceaselessly harangued, scolded, bullied, and prayed for his people. Meanwhile the commerce of the community, which had been practically annihilated by Kieft's disastrous Indian wars, gradually revived, and for six peaceful years the wharf on the water front witnessed an increasingly brisk business, wherein the natural instincts of the Dutch trader appeared to good advantage. Then news of hostilities between the United Provinces and England turned Stuyvesant's attention from civic affairs and brought into play his martial talents, concerning which authorities differ. But whether he was a hero or not at St. Martin, his wooden leg proves that he was at least at the post of danger, and he certainly rose to the occasion in 1653, when his country's possessions were threatened by the enemy. Indeed, he

WALL STREET IN 1653

Drawn from the original plans and specifications for the palisade, published by the Committee acting for the Director General, Council, and Magistrates of New Amsterdam, March 15, 1653. The line of the stockade was a little to the north of the north side of the present street. The southern side of the parade ground marks the southerly line of the street as it is to-day, and the width of the parade ground shows what a broad highway Wall Street really ought to have been

"GOOD WAMPUM"
The contract for building Wall Street's wall provided
for this grade of "devil's currency," the value of which
depended upon quality and was regulated by law
Ordinance of May 30, 1650

of this city will receive proposals for a certain piece of work to set off the city with palisades twelve to thirteen feet long, by the rod. Any one who wishes to undertake this work may come to the City Hall next Tuesday afternoon, hear the conditions, and look over the work. Done, &c., Mch. 15, 1653. Let one tell it to another!

displayed such a bold front and such indomitable energy that he actually succeeded in inspiring the not too patriotic burghers of New Amsterdam with a little of his own spirit, and induced them to rush through some preparations for defence with really extraordinary speed. On the 13th of March, 1653, the assembled Burgomasters and Schepens organized night and day patrols for guarding the approaches to the city; directed the skipper of the vessel representing the navy to bend his sails, load his pieces, and prepare for every emergency; recommended the repair of the fort, and resolved "to surround the greater part of the city with a high stockade and small breastwork to draw in time of need all the inhabitants behind it and defend as much as possible their persons and goods from attacks."

All this was accomplished at the morning session, and by the afternoon a goodly defence fund had been subscribed. Indeed, before two days had passed, a committee of three was duly empowered to supervise the construction of the new works, and the members of this committee entered upon their duties with such energy that the following notice* was posted and cried within a few hours of their election:

The committee appointed by the Director General, Council, and Magistrates

* *Records of New Amsterdam.* Vol. I., p. 69.

Meanwhile, Stuyvesant was stumping along the line of Kieft's old cattle guard, seeking an advantageous location for the palisade, and a brave picture the old war dog must have presented as, splendidly attired, with sword at thigh and hand on hilt, he surveyed the ground and advised his bustling committee to erect the new defences some forty or fifty feet south of the old barrier and practically parallel to it—which advice, being accepted, determined the southerly line of Wall Street.

Active as Committeemen La Montagne, Beeckman, and Wolfersen (van Couwenhoven) were, they could not immediately publish their plans, but before the day appointed for receiving bids, the competitors for the contract were supplied with detailed specifications whose minuteness left nothing to be desired. The contemplated palisade was to be 180 rods, or 2340 feet, in length, extending from the East River (Pearl Street) straight across the island, skirting De Heere Graft (the ominously named canal which became Broad Street), and passing directly through what is now Trinity Church to a rise in the ground near the North River which afforded a natural breastwork. It was to be constructed of round wooden posts, twelve feet in length and eighteen inches in girth, sharpened to a point at the top, and placed in a line interrupted at intervals by larger posts, to which split rails were to be nailed two feet below the top. A sloping breastwork, a ditch, and a parade ground were also contemplated, and lest all the minute particulars which the careful committeemen set forth should not suffice, they drew a plan of the whole work and spread it upon the records of the Burgomasters and Schepens, where it remains to-day, an abiding memorial of their thoroughness and zeal.*

The bidding on these proposals was most encouragingly brisk, no less than four competitors entering the lists, the successful candidate being Tomas Bacxter, whose subsequent career as a pirate may, as has been suggested, have originated in his securing this award. But however that may have been, we know from the official records that he was paid in good wampum—then coin of the realm—and that the cost was divided as follows:

```
1404 planks at 1½ florins......2106 florins
340 posts.....................  304   "
Nails ........................  100   "
Transport ....................  120   "
For setting them up and car-
    penters' wages............  500   "
```

or a total of about $1300, from which it would appear that "setting them up" was even then an important item in the estimates of municipal contractors. Bacxter completed his work in about six weeks, but no enemy having appeared to test its powers of resistance, the enthusiasm of the Burgomasters and Schepens speedily waned, and in spite of Stuyvesant's urgent remonstrances the repairs to the fort remained wholly neglected. Indeed, when the question of paying for the palisade, breastwork, and ditch was presented to their Worships they stoutly declared that the West India Company was bound to defend its own property without expense to the citizens, and from this position they would not recede until Stuyvesant abandoned the excise duties imposed upon the inhabitants and surrendered to the civic treasury the moneys received from that source. This masterly stroke of business was undoubtedly Wall Street's first financial triumph.

About two years after this event another war scare caused the city fathers to look again to their defences. It was then discovered that some sixty-five of the palisades had been chopped down for firewood, and that the whole work was otherwise in such a sad state of repair that extensive renovations were imperative. Probably it was at this date that the five bastions shown on what is known as the "Duke's Plan" were constructed. These were small, two-gun artillery mounts, one of which pro-

jected from the wooden bulwark at what is now the head of Hanover Street; another covered the present site of No. 44 Wall Street, just west of William Street; a third stood on part of the ground now occupied by the Sub-Treasury; a fourth dominated No. 4 Wall Street; and the last commanded what was to become Trinity Churchyard, from a point a little to the rear of the existing church. In addition to these formidable batteries, the defences were further strengthened by nailing boards to the height of ten or twelve feet above the sharpened ends of the palisades, forming a sort of screen calculated to prevent the Indians from scaling the barricade; but as no enemy appeared, the warlike energies of the burghers again subsided, and before long two gateways were constructed to facilitate communication between the townspeople and the farmers of the outlying bouweries. One of these openings, known as the Land Gate, was situated at Broadway, and the other, called the Water Poort, pierced the stockade at what was then the river road (now Pearl Street),* and for nine more or less peaceful years a steadily increasing stream of commerce poured through these narrow apertures. Then rumors of war once more caused them to be closed and barricaded.

Again, as in 1653, it was the English who threatened, although no war had been declared, and again Stuyvesant succeeded in diverting the inhabitants from the joys of successful trading to the less profitable duties of patriotism. From August 29, 1664, to September 2, the vigorous Governor, then seventy-two years of age, hopped and hobbled anxiously up and down the length of the palisade, encouraging and berating the workers tinkering at the defences under a hot summer sun; but patriotism was sadly lacking, and most of the labor was performed by negro slaves whose masters begrudged their services.

* About this time (1655–6) the residents of Pearl Street, inconvenienced by the high tides, caused a sea wall to be erected, and the space between this barrier and their houses to be filled in, making a roadway known as De Waal, or Lang de Waal. Incautious investigators have confused this with Wall Street, and their error has resulted in some astonishing "history."

* *Records of New Amsterdam.* Vol. I. p. 72.

Unsupported as he was, however, Stuyvesant managed to keep his unwilling workers at their task, until news reached the city that the Duke of York's war vessels were in the harbor and that their commanders offered liberal terms for immediate surrender. Then the intrenching tools were thrown aside, and despite the Governor's prayers and remonstrances the populace virtually welcomed the invaders. Doubtless resistance would have been futile, and submission to the semi-piratical attack was the part of prudence, but the lonely figure of the grim Dutch warrior, standing gamely by his guns, will always contrast gratefully with the crowd of discreet traders gaping at the enemy from Battery Park, and make one doubt the maxim defining the better part of valor.

The town which thus easily fell into the hands of that royal buccaneer, the Duke of York, had grown during Stuyvesant's administration. In it the new Governor, Colonel Richard Nicolls, found no less than two hundred and twenty houses and over fourteen hundred people, while facing the parade ground designed for the manœuvring of troops, behind the palisade, there were at least ten dwellings, occupied by a merchant trader, a wool spinner, a chimney sweep, a tapster, a miller, and other estimable citizens of a similar class. Indeed, the house of the merchant trader — one Moesman — had been erected as early as 1656 on a portion of the site lately abandoned by the Custom House, and was undoubtedly the first residence known to Wall Street.

Nicolls attempted no disturbing innovations in the administration of the city which then became New York, and it is doubtful if he was responsible for the alterations in the palisade which were made in the year of the surrender. However, four of its five original bastions disappeared about that time, the one on the present site of No. 44 Wall Street alone remaining as first placed, and the so-called fortification continued in practically this condition for nine years, when the city passed, without a struggle, into the possession of its former owners.

This time the capture was effected in time of war, Admirals Evertsen and Benckes quietly sailing into the harbor during the absence of Governor Lovelace, and landing Captain Anthony Colvé at about the foot of the present Park Place to take possession of the city and establish martial law. Almost the first act of this military governor was to demolish some buildings which had been erected just outside the palisade, the western line of which he then proceeded to rebuild, turning it to the south almost along the present site of Rector Street. He also forbade all entrance to or exit from the city except through the gates under penalty of death, and those avenues of communication were rigidly closed after nightfall. All this occurred before the spring of 1674, and within a twelvemonth the city once more reverted to England under the terms of peace with Holland.

The returning Englishmen found the city obviously larger than they left it, and steadily pressing upon the northern barrier. Fully seventeen houses now faced the parade ground lying parallel to and immediately behind the palisade, its width of a hundred feet affording an inviting frontage, and promising a generously broad thoroughfare—a promise destined to remain unfulfilled.

Meanwhile the palisade, which had long outlived its usefulness, was repeatedly repaired, and it was not until 1685 that the land immediately north of it became the subject of a notorious speculation which inflicted irreparable injury upon the future highway. His Excellency Thomas Dongan was the royal Governor at that time, and his sharp eyes, which rarely wandered from the main chance, quickly detected a business possibility in this property. Indeed, he was in a position where he could materially influence its value, and if he did not make the most of his opportunity it will have to be conceded that he did the best he knew. Through the agency of a " dummy " purchaser—one Captain John Knight of his official staff—he secretly acquired from the Damen Estate a strip of land a thousand feet long and eighty feet deep fronting upon the wall,[*] together with all the right, title, and interest which the sellers had in the parade ground behind the wall, which they and every one else supposed would become the public thoroughfare.

[*] L. 13, pp. 124–150. December 14, 1685. New York Register's Office.

The day after this deal had been safely consummated, however, Dongan ordered one Leonard Beckwith to survey the wall* and officially establish the new street, and so promptly did the surveyor set about his task that he returned a report within twenty-four hours, laying out a street not one hundred, but thirty - six, feet in breadth, and presto! Dongan's eighty-foot lots became one hundred and twenty-four feet deep. By this financial coup the royal Governor achieved the distinction of being the first insider to make something out of nothing on the narrow, if not straight, path which resulted from his acquisitiveness.

Three years later Dongan again turned his attention to Wall Street, appointing commissioners to make an official inspection of the palisade and inform him as to its condition, the upshot of which was a report showing the Water Gate and the artillery mounts in ruins, the Land Gate tottering, the curtain palisades either prostrate or falling, and the land actually staked out for building purposes. Of this last fact, however, Dongan must have been even better informed than his commissioners, for he was then actively marketing some of his queerly acquired property, and by as strange a chain of circumstances as was ever unearthed from the records one of his lots passed into the hands of a gentleman whose exploits have been recounted in verse and prose for more than two hundred years.

This historic parcel of land (part of which is now known as No. 56 Wall Street) lies opposite the head of the present Hanover Street, and one Browne was the original purchaser. Browne almost immediately transferred his bargain to a well known citizen named William Cox, whose wife Sarah (*née* Bradley) was destined to greater fame than he. Shortly after acquiring this plot, Cox is said to have built a house upon it, and if this be so, the building was the first erected on the north side of Wall Street. In 1689, however, he succumbed to what has since proved fatal to many dwellers on that highway, for the report of his demise says that " he took too much water in," and his widow, to whom he left his property, straightway consoled herself by marrying

one John Oort. This gentleman fell a victim to her charms so speedily that she took out letters of administration on his estate, May 15, 1691, and the next day married no less a person than Captain William Kidd, the future pirate, who thus became one of the earliest proprietors of Wall Street—a locality in which people have been treasure hunting for over a century.

But Captain Kidd was not the only pirate known to New York at the latter end of the seventeenth century. Indeed, the little city with its rascally governors and its mixed population, many of whom were adventurous traders ready to turn almost any kind of penny, was for years a favorite stamping ground of the sea rovers, and their gorgeous persons became very familiar not only to Wall Street, but throughout the whole town, where their confidential transactions with certain enterprising citizens laid the foundation of more than one existing fortune.

Meanwhile the palisades still survived, and if it be true that the English laughed when they first inspected it, they kept up the joke a long time, for in 1692—seven years after Dongan had the street surveyed—it was once more repaired, substantial stone bastions being erected on the site of the artillery mounts at William Street and at Broadway, and three years later, just after the street had been partially paved, more renovations were attempted. Indeed, a contemporary historian remarked that the maintenance of this wall cost the community some £8000, and described it as " a monument to our Folly." Nevertheless, it was not until 1699 that a committee of citizens petitioned His Excellency through the Common Council to remove it as an obstructing nuisance and utilize the stones of its bastions for the new City Hall.

Then the end came, and with the passing of this ancient landmark New York ceased to be a walled city, and its new highway almost immediately became the resort of so many noted men and the scene of such dramatic events that for wellnigh a hundred years its story supplies a unique footnote to American history.

THE PROBLEM OF LIVING
IN NEW YORK

IN no considerable, thoroughly settled city on the civilized globe is material living attended with so many difficulties as in New York. Even in London, to which alone we are second in commercial importance, it is not hard to find a house or rooms within the municipal limits at any season. The same may be said of Paris, Berlin, Vienna, St. Petersburg—of any of the Old World capitals, or of any social centre in the Western Hemisphere. But one of the greatest troubles of the average New-Yorker is to secure a roof to shelter him and his. He has no expectation of a home—anything like a home is reserved for the very prosperous few; the most he dares to hope for is a sojourning place for six months, or a year or two at furthest. The effort he makes to this end, the anxiety he suffers, are incalculable. Where and how he is to live is an ever-present, carking thought. He never passes a dwelling marked To Let, in whole or in part, without wanting, even in his busiest moments, to stop to inquire when, how long, and for how much it may be had. He is seldom settled anywhere; he is simply staying in such a street, at such a number, until he may discover another street and number where he may stay. Moving from place to place is his custom and his curse: he is a kind of Aristeas, for whom there is no rest, on whom the inexorable spirit of Manhattan has inflicted the doom of disquietude. Years and years he has been waiting for a better, or less bad, order of things: there have been promises of such periodically, but the promises have never yet been redeemed. He tries to become resigned to what seems the inevitable; he buys a lot in Greenwood or Woodlawn, and comforts himself with the reflection that, once a tenant there, he need not move—that he has at last secured a home.

The difficulty of living here is due, of course, to the fact that the bulk of the city is built on an island, and that the island is long and narrow, causing land, from its numerous occupation, to be so dear that every square foot is naturally turned to the utmost profit. Small houses or reasonable rents are, as a consequence, unattainable; there is, indeed, no such thing. There have been but two ways of living here, presuming one does not board—either in a tenement or in an expensive dwelling. Americans will not,

and can not, as a rule, occupy tenements. They who are poor, therefore, are forced out of town. Formerly, persons of ordinary means who felt constrained to stay here had recourse to leasing large houses, often at double or treble their own incomes, and to taking lodgers in order to make up the sum for which they were liable. This was a desperate shift, for lodgers were uncertain; they, after having been got, might vacate their premises any day, leaving the lessee, who had counted on them, irretrievably in arrears. Still, many persons, by force of circumstance, including no little luck, contrived to rub along in this manner; but many more fell into every sort of financial perplexity, and were rendered doubly wretched in their struggle for existence.

This species of household tragedy continued for many years, when a break was seen in the darkness, the break coming from the erection of flats, or apartment-houses, so universal in Paris, and so common in most cities of continental Europe. The first of these, a reconstructed club-house at Fifteenth Street and Fifth Avenue, was small, inconvenient, and very expensive; but it was all leased long before completion by persons delighted with the novelty. Others were built, also in fashionable quarters, and were so dear as to be beyond the reach of moderate incomes. They who owned them said they must get high rents while they could, for in a short while there would be so many apartments that rents would be reduced beyond a point of satisfactory profit. That time was eagerly looked for and longed for, but it has not yet arrived. It ought to have arrived, it would seem, years since, for many apartment houses have been erected on ground not very valuable, notably in the region of upper Broadway, above Forty-second Street, and in the Nineteenth Ward. Such neighborhoods were not thought desirable for private residences, and single-family houses of the better kind could not have been leased there at all. But by the putting up of comfortable and elegant flats high rents were obtained.

A number of families will live under the same roof where one family will not, because, no doubt, if there be any objection to the quarter, the objection is believed to be less, if not wholly removed.

by a numerous sharing of it. This peculiar though common feeling of human nature has been repeatedly exemplified in the construction of flats of an ambitious order. Scores of them in different parts of the city, near stables, rum-shops, tenement-houses, rookeries, are occupied by refined, fastidious people, and with entire content, who would no more have thought of living there as a single family than they would of living in the Fourth or Seventh Ward.

The land on which those houses are was comparatively cheap, but the rents are the reverse of cheap. There is no prospect, in fact, of desirable flats—that is, apartments of any size, convenient, light, and airy—being other than expensive in this city. It is twelve years since the first apartment-houses were built; hundreds of them of divers grades have been put up all over town; but those capable of accommodating a small family, with an elevator, and pleasant, well-ventilated rooms, can not be had for less than from $1500 to $2000. There are flats in poor quarters that rent for from $600 to $800; but they usually have dark chambers, they are ill arranged, and are seldom really wholesome. As a generalization, it may be said that reasonable apartments are not good, and that good apartments are not reasonable. The fond anticipations cherished eight or ten years ago that a nice, healthful apartment might be procured for from $500 to $600 annually have long been dispelled. They who have no more than that to spend for a home, so called, are obliged to put up with sundry discomforts, and to jeopard their health more or less by sleeping in dark, close chambers.

It would seem as if economy of any kind were impracticable in this the costliest of capitals. The mere decencies of life are well-nigh beyond the reach of men dependent on salaries or ordinary incomes. The average earnings here of men even of education and taste are not, it is alleged, in excess of $1500 to $1600, and as the majority of them have families (the unwritten law of Manhattan demands that no couple, unless financially independent, shall have more than two children), they are forced into a ceaseless contest for self-sustainment. They toil through life, endure vexation, disappointment, tribulation, pain, and quit the world leaving no provision for their families, but generally in debt. Comparatively few men who can command credit die, it is said, with all their liabilities discharged. The proportion of New-Yorkers of whom this is true must be larger than of other citizens, for credit here is easily got, and the cost of living is far greater than elsewhere.

What can be expected of a husband and a father who can earn no more than $1500 or $1600 ? How is it possible for him to stem the current always running so strong against him, especially against the refined and sensitive poor of Anglo-Saxon strain ? It is clear that he can not live in the city proper; he must pitch his tent, as it may justly be styled, in the rear of Brooklyn, along the lines of the New Jersey railroads, among the sand knolls of Long Island, or amid the pastures of Westchester. He must come and go daily to and from his business in every sort of weather, keeping mind and nerves on the stretch lest he miss the boat or train. His wistful life is regulated by schedule time; he is ever hurried, planning to save a few minutes, and yet wasting, from the perpetual stress of circumstance, his entire years. He has no leisure, no repose; he is absorbed in town, feverish in the country; he sees little of his family, nothing of his friends; he is engrossed with his petty affairs, which he may despise, but which he can not afford for an hour to neglect. His life is a dull, wearisome round, his most serious thought how he shall get on, and while still thinking of it, the cord snaps and the end comes. He has done his work. True; but was it worth doing ? After years of grinding labor, what has he achieved ? where is his recompense ? He has been striving faithfully for his family, and at the close he leaves them the discouragement of his example, and probably a legacy of debt. Such is the inspiring destiny of the average New-Yorker. Verily is honesty its own and only reward!

Although flats have proved a partial failure in solving the problem for the mass of Americans, they have been warmly welcomed by people of liberal incomes. They have become the fashion, and in a certain way are very convenient. Some of those that are very elegant bring from $2500 to $4000, and are readily taken. One might not believe that an apartment could be leased at such a price, when whole houses, and handsome ones, may be had at those figures. But it should be remembered that very expensive apartments are a saving, in that they require less furniture and fewer servants, a smaller outlay of every kind, than an entire house, and at the same time enable their tenants to present an equally fair appearance in the eyes of the world. This last point is one of grave consideration with New-Yorkers, who will, as a rule, keep up appearances at almost any sacrifice. They save, too, by the new method of living, much trouble, much friction. A flat simplifies house-keeping greatly, and they feel that they can safely leave it and go to the country, or abroad, for an indefinite period. If they had a house they would continually be afraid, and with reason, of its being enter-ed by burglars; and to people who travel so frequently as New-Yorkers do, freedom from such fear is not to be disesteemed. Thus, socially and practically, there are arguments in favor of flats, and arguments of weight. As respects the mass of the native population, likewise, apartments have been a gain, notwithstanding the financial disappointment they have caused. They have enabled those to have some-thing akin to a home of their own; they have largely done away with the hazard-ous experiment of leasing houses in the hope of covering the rent by sub-letting; they have materially reduced the number of boarding-houses.

The cheaper flats are far from what they should be, but they are a marked advance on what preceded them. The poorest flat, provided it be not unhealthful, is prefer-able to the best boarding-house, which is as necessarily hostile to true comfort as it is to domesticity. A decent flat may be procured for from $400 to $500, and however unattractive it may be to persons of dainty or exacting disposition, it will furnish a very small family with a wholly separate habitation and a certain kind of independence. That such a shelter and retreat may be had to-day—it was impos-sible ten years ago—is testimony that the city is slowly advancing. If an apart-ment is not strictly a home (perhaps it de-serves the name of a genteel tenement) it is an approach to a home, which the board-ing-house is not, and never will be.

When the elevated railroads had been constructed they were greeted with wide ap-proval, despite their manifest invasion of private rights, their obnoxiousness in the vicinity of their lines, and their serious disfigurement of the streets, because, in addition to their rapid transit, they pro-mised to be the forerunner of small dwell-ings in the upper part of the island. Small houses have been wanted for a generation, but were not built, for the obvious reason that large ones were more remunerative. The elevated roads, it was argued, would make them remunerative, and would bring back to town thousands of its citizens who had been expelled by lack of city roofs at moderate rents. Numbers of small houses were built, countless citizens were brought back, but the old trouble was encounter-ed. Rents were nearly double what had been anticipated, and many citizens who had moved in moved out again. The roads that had hurt real estate down town helped it up town, making it so valuable that landlords declared they must get cer-tain rents in order to meet increased tax-ation and the like. Once more the lower middle class were disappointed. Reason-able rents, they said, will never be; and who shall contradict them? Year after year New York seems to justify the pain-ful, dispiriting averment that it is a city of paupers and millionaires. Are not the rich growing richer and the poor poorer as time moves on? Will there ever be a period when the distance between them will be less? Hope answers, "Yes;" Reason answers, "No."

The latest—let us trust it will not be the last—attempt to secure moderate rents was made some three years ago by the pro-mulgation of a plan to build co-operative apartment-houses. The plan was for six or eight or more persons, the number to be regulated by the size of the house, to form a club or association, and for each member to contribute a given and equal amount for the purpose. It was maintain-ed that many of the dearer apartments had been made superfluously expensive by gar-niture and decoration in order to recom-mend them to well-to-do Americans, who might naturally have a prejudice against them by association with common tene-ments, and who would therefore wish to see a marked outward distinction between the two. The assertion was well based. The costliness of the earliest apartments was often deliberate, measurably attribu-table to excess of ornamentation for the sake of show and effect, with a view to incurring the favor of appearance-loving New-Yorkers. At the same time actually important things, such as plumbing, venti-lation, and drainage, which could be kept out of sight, were inferior or slighted.

An intelligent economy, a substantial

improvement, was proposed by the architect who had broached the co-operative scheme. Gilding, glitter, all redundancies, were to be avoided, and convenience, comfort, and health were to be substituted therefor. The circulars and pamphlets issued by the architect declared that a man might be certain of a refined, every way desirable home by adopting his plan, at less than half, possibly at a third, of what he would be obliged to pay otherwise. The promise was very tempting, the statements were plausible, and in a few months eight citizens of less income than culture, who wanted a roof of their own, and to be independent of the whims and exactions of landlords, were found ready to enter into the enterprise. The house was to be, and is, built in Fifty-seventh Street, and has now been occupied about a twelve-month. The estimated cost to each of the owners was to be about $5000, some $60,000 to be raised on mortgage, making the value of the house, including real estate, $100,000. Estimates are never correct; they are always below the actuality. When completed, the house cost about $130,000, or some $9000 to each owner. In it were studios and apartments, common property, whose rents go toward defraying the current expenses of the building, such as coal, gas, engineer, janitor, elevator boys, taxes, interest on mortgage, etc. After appropriating such rents, the eight partners, each of whom owns an apartment in the building plus one-eighth of the common property, have reason to believe that $500 each, independent of the money invested, will suffice to meet the annual running expenses.

The house was contracted for when mechanics' wages were much lower than now; the ground was bought to great advantage—it would bring at present nearly double the price paid; and consequently, despite various drawbacks in one way or another, the house is decidedly cheap. It stands on two lots, 25 by 100 feet each; contains ten apartments and eight studios, the larger apartments having eleven rooms, counting the bath-room, and the smaller apartments, with the bath, eight and nine rooms. The owners consider the house worth $200,000 easily, and that their rent is not, at most, more than sixty per cent. of what they would have to pay were they not their own landlords. Some of them say that their rent, considering the present high figures, is not above for-ty-five per cent. of the rents generally charged. All of them agree that if they wished to rent their apartments, their investment would yield them in all probability from twelve to fifteen per cent. per annum. It must be borne in mind, however, that their building is exceptionally cheap, owing, as I have said, to the lower prices of wages and real estate some three years ago. The same building, put up now, would cost fully forty per cent. more.

Various other co-operative apartment-houses, in Fifty-eighth Street, Fifty-ninth Street, Fifth Avenue, Seventh Avenue, and Madison Avenue, have been built, and are building, since the initial one in Fifty-seventh Street; but only two or three are as yet occupied. Most of them are far more expensive and more pretentious than the first. Some of them have apartments owned by the partners together, aside from the apartments owned by the individual partners—these are less expensive to the owners—and other houses have no common property at all. It is computed that original owners (there has naturally been a good deal of speculation in these enterprises, men going into them and selling out for a premium) have generally secured an investment paying from ten to twelve per cent. per annum, and that their apartments, when occupied by themselves, save them at least thirty to forty per cent. in rent. It is impossible to be exact, since the houses are so different in size, cost, and arrangement, and the rules governing the co-operative associations are so dissimilar.

All these associations are stock companies, made such for more convenient handling, the owners holding all the stock, and declaring dividends to one another—the dividends go toward the general expenses—and paying nominal rent, merely for form's sake, in order to comply with the requirements of a corporation. Each owner is a trustee. A president, secretary, treasurer, and a house committee consisting of three are elected annually. No owner is privileged to rent or sell his apartment without the concurrence of his associates, and such rules and regulations are binding upon each and all as serve for the protection alike of the association and its members. An apartment may be held, transferred, or sold—an act of the State Legislature has been passed to this effect —precisely as a whole house may be held, transferred, or sold, so that there is small danger of legal complication or financial loss through partnership in the co-operative houses. Many sales have been made already, and without the slightest trouble or hinderance. It is desirable, of course, that parties entering into such a scheme should be well acquainted with one another personally and professionally, and in nearly all cases they have been so acquainted. The opinion that many difficulties would be encountered in carrying out the plan has deterred not a few from sharing in it, but as none of the anticipated difficulties has as yet occurred, nor is likely to occur, fears on this score are passing away.

The objection to co-operative houses in many minds is not legal but personal. He who participates in such a project can not tell how long his associates will remain with him, or who will succeed them. Men, particularly New-Yorkers, are forever changing their investments and mode of living. A certain proportion of any number who would co-operate to secure a home would be likely at the end of three or four years to withdraw from the company. Their successors might be inharmonious with the others, thus marring if not subverting the primary condition which had been the inducement to enter into the enterprise. Satisfaction with the scheme, if not its success, must depend on the reciprocal relations of the owners. The very moment they should become antagonistic, or even very uncongenial, to one another, co-operation would virtually cease to co-operate. While many of these companies will prosper, and the members be delighted with their connection therewith, other companies may have trouble, and the members express regret at the imprudence of their action. Everything must hang on the individuals, and their disposition to one another. That there is a degree of risk from the causes named in the co-operative project is evident, and it is not strange, therefore, that many persons who believe in the theory are skeptical of its desirableness. The whole matter is thus far tentative. It will be ten years at least before any correct general conclusion can be reached on the subject.

If $2000, or $3000, or even $4000, were sufficient for ownership in a co-operative house—and there is no reason why it should not be—a large number of very small families in humble circumstances could be provided with far more comfort-

able abiding-places than they have had hitherto. It is this class that need domiciliary benefit and relief in New York. Those who can readily put $10,000 and upward into a habitation may manage for themselves; they are beyond the range of philanthropic sympathies.

But apartments at best are not and can not be, in any accurate import, homes. They are abodes where persons stay until they can find an opportunity or the means to go somewhere else. There is no idea or association of permanence with them. How can there be in any place that has no cellar, no nursery, no storeroom, no closets worthy the name ? An apartment is simply a suite of rooms, seldom more than eight, where a man and his wife may live with tolerable convenience and comfort, and where one or two children may, if absolutely unavoidable, be squeezed in. An apartment is not intended for children; but if they will insist on being born, they must take their chances, as they are forced to do everywhere in this city. Home means the habitation of a family; family means a married couple and their offspring, who, if capable of understanding the adverse conditions of Manhattan Island, might feel tempted to spring off it into the water with which it is so suggestively surrounded. There has never been a city whose situation and construction are more unfavorable, not to say inimical, to progeny. They seem to be regarded here as interlopers, certainly as impertinences. They do not belong, as everybody knows, in hotels or boarding-houses, and parents always experience difficulty in having them received there. In leasing houses, apartments, or rooms, the landlord or agent invariably asks the applicant, "Have you any children ?" very much in the tone and manner that he would ask, "Have you committed murder ?" or, "Are you afflicted with leprosy ?" If obliged to plead guilty to one or two children, even though they be very small, he obviously does not regard smallness either of number or size as any mitigation of your offense: he insults you with a glance of hatred or contempt, and if he fails to reject you altogether, accepts you with an air of protest, but only at an advanced rate.

New York is a Malthusian city. It almost constrains the conditions which the English political economist considered essential to repressing population. His positive and preventive checks are ever in action here—the former, by shortening human life among adopted citizens in the hideous tenement-houses; the latter, by hindering marriage and increase of family among native citizens. Food is abundant here, but places to live are for Anglo-Saxons totally inadequate. In Manhattan there enters into the theme of propagation a factor which Malthus had not taken into account. Who would suppose that the shape of a city would seriously interfere with natural laws? The New-Yorker looks upon wedlock and its usual accompaniments at a financial angle, and very naturally, under the circumstances. Why should a perfectly sane man assume connubial or paternal responsibilites when he is conscious that there is no room for them? New York may be an Elysium for bachelors, but for a husband and a father with an ordinary income it is next door to Hades. Every street, every house, every provision, says to him: "If you would tarry here, remain single! Transgress celibacy, and we cast you out! This island is reserved for the very rich and the very poor, for the heedless and the homeless. Being none of these, go elsewhere!

Every way of living, except in a home proper, is amply furnished here. There are innumerable hotels of all grades, and countless boarding-houses; there are apartments of every sort, from the finest to the shabbiest; there are rooms in private residences and over shops; rooms with meals and without meals; but there are no quiet, comfortable, attractive places for a family except at prices which the average New-Yorker may not afford. Within a few years nice family hotels, as they are called, have been opened, and they are admirably kept. But besides being very dear, they are not desirable for children. A suite of rooms, furnished or unfurnished, may be hired there for a length of time, generally not less than a year, meals being served in the restaurant at a fixed rate, generally fifteen dollars a week per person. A man and his wife may be delightfully accommodated for from $100 to $200 a week; but with an income to justify such expenditure, they could, perhaps, afford babies and a real home. There are six or eight such hotels in Fifth Avenue now, and there are others elsewhere. They are increasing, though they do not meet the urgent want; they do not aid in the solution of the problem of living.

Rooms are frequently rented, and meals sent in from the outside by professional caterers at prices ranging from five to fifteen dollars a week per head. Not less than twenty caterers make this either their entire business or a feature of it. They serve customers at considerable distances, having wagons especially designed for the purpose, and serve them well. This is plainly anti-domestic, a gypsy method of living, a rather genteel form of Bohemian existence in no wise suggestive of home. Introduce children into any of these novel devices, and the objections to them become insuperable.

New York, doubtless, grows steadily away from the Lares and Penates, for which, indeed, there is no room in our narrow homes. If set up, however often, they would be continually knocked down with the rush and drive of our feverish life, and so disfigured as to be unrecognizable. In truth, they have not been recognizable for years. The present generation has no acquaintance with them; could not even tell how they look. Our fathers and grandfathers were familiar with and honored them, for they had a place to keep them in their spacious, delightful, old-fashioned homes—homes in fact as well as name—happily destitute of household artifice and all the modern improvements. We have no reverence for those deities; we fancy we have outgrown them because we have grown away from them. They have nearly ceased to be a memory. If we should discover them among any dusty remnants of ancestral possessions, we should be pretty sure to exchange them for broken china and Japanese idols. The Lares and Penates do not belong to the period of rampant bric-à-brac. Imagine them in a house of eighteen to twenty feet front, or, worse still, in an apartment! They would be as incongruous with the surroundings as the early Dutch settlers would be with the stock-brokers and speculators of Broad Street.

Why is it, may naturally be asked, that people should continually pour into New York when there is not room enough for half of those already here? Why should they persistently seek to live in a city where, with hosts on hosts of houses, there are no homes save for the prosperous? There is abundant space in most of the towns a hundred miles distant. Why do not people swell the census there instead of crowding into an overcrowded capital where the chance of success, of competence even, are ten thousand to one against them? They come in such numbers because so many have come before them, because New York is the commercial centre of the republic, because it is immensely rich and strong, because, in short, it does not need or want them. Great cities, like all great bodies, attract by the fact of their greatness. There is something here for everybody—everything, indeed, except a home, with what befits it, independence, freedom, and a fair chance, which most men are thought to value supremely. Having every reason to be deterred, they refuse to be deterred; they obstinately swell the hordes of the homeless, and pit themselves, sanguine with expectation, against fearfully overwhelming odds.

A great city always exercises a strange, well-nigh inexplicable fascination on the multitude not less than on individuals. The former like it for its bigness, its bustle, its movement, its variety, its fluctuations. Where there is so much of everything, they are likely, they believe, to get their share. At any rate, they want to be in the tumble and the tide. Having no inward resources, they hunger for tumultuous externals. What will they not endure to be zeros among the high figures they can never hope to touch? They will strive and toil and agonize, they will pinch and starve, will bear every degree of privation, to whirl in the maelstrom of the metropolis.

Thousands and thousands of men who have no regular employment, and no special prospects, who are materially and mentally out at elbows, whose whole life has been a spiritual tragedy, could not be persuaded to-day to leave the city where they have been so constantly baffled and tormented, where they have suffered so intensely, were they assured of a regular and respectable livelihood in some quiet town of the interior. Myriads of inmates of the squalid, distressing tenement-houses, in which morality is as impossible as happiness, would not give them up, despite their horrors, for clean, orderly, wholesome habitations in the suburbs, could they be transported there and back free of charge. They are in some unaccountable way terribly in love with their own wretchedness.

As to the individuals—the educated, thoughtful, self-disciplined—New York has its allurements for them also, its libraries, its pictures, its parks, its architecture, its cultured society, its delightful haunts. They may be poor, they may be even shifting from pillar to post, they may be in endless worry. But there is a reverse side to the painting, and in its contemplation they find recompense. For the money-getting and the pleasure-loving, Manhattan is full of seductions—no city more so. It furnishes commercial and sensuous stimulants all the year round. Whatever may fall upon them, there are still schemes and joys untried and enticing. Who has not heard hundreds of well-balanced, intelligent men and women declare, after living elsewhere, that they would rather be crowded into rear fourth-story rooms here than own a handsome home beyond the smell of the sea?

It is estimated that a man and his wife, with one or two children, can not possibly live here in any degree of comfort on less than $5000 a year. As $1500 is the limit of the average citizen's earning, what an amount of friction the mass must endure—and they endure it silently in the main—for the incomprehensible privilege of staying in New York! No wonder there is such a ceaseless struggle for betterment of condition! Homilists call it the haste to get rich. Observers know that it is merely the dread of debt and dependence, the tendency manifest throughout the universe of every particle of matter to place itself in a state of rest. It is the desire, intense though vague, and rarely fulfilled, to secure some time the possession of a home. New York is a great, a most opulent city, a marvel of enterprise and progress, in all likelihood the future capital of the world. When it has achieved its highest destiny, let us hope that amid its splendors and its blessings may be included a few more homes.

THE VOLUNTEER FIRE DEPARTMENT (PART 1)

THE OLD NEW YORK VOLUNTEER FIRE DEPARTMENT.

I.

THE romance of the earlier days of the city of New York is largely and closely associated with the heroism and hilarity of the members of its old Volunteer Fire Department, and is precisely the material for a stirring chapter of American folk-lore. Although that illustrious organization has been disbanded only fifteen years, its deeds of gallantry are already fast passing into the realm of fable. It was but yesterday that I heard a story of an old fireman who, when asked to "step up and take a drink," would accept the invitation, walk straight to the bar, call for two glasses of liquor, and empty them into his boots. The inference, of course, was that he belonged to a species of teetotaler that disdained to put ardent spirits where most men who use them put them. But a little investigation disclosed the fact that it was once very common for New York firemen in

ZOPHAR MILLS.

ing. It would be easy to enumerate other signs of the advent of the myth period, and any person who proposes to write the history of the old Volunteer Fire Department of the city of New York—and few histories are better worth the writing — must needs bestir himself if he wishes to tell the facts, especially since, if he is at all familiar with his subject, he will recognize in it several explicit reasons why the charming story of the old firemen's exploits has a natural affinity for the fabulist.

II.

A sufficiently convenient way of obtaining a bird's-eye view of the subject is to listen to two short recitals from the lips of living firemen who were winter to keep their feet from freezing by pouring rum, brandy, or whiskey into their boots. Many a member of the old Volunteer Fire Department had his feet frozen repeatedly in the discharge of his duties. Mr. Zophar Mills, for example, foreman of Engine No. 13, went home several times with frozen feet, ears, and hands; on one occasion he was unable to turn the knob of his front door, and was compelled to ask the help of a passer-by. At the great fire in 1835, which began at nine o'clock on the night of the 16th of December, and continued until four o'clock of the next afternoon, destroying property of the value of $20,000,000, the thermometer indicated seven degrees below zero, and the sight-seers walked about muffled with blankets that had been dragged in bales from the dry-goods stores. Mr. Charles Forrester, foreman of Engine No. 33, asserts that the winters nowadays are unquestionably much less severe than they were thirty years ago: so that putting liquor in one's boots turns out to be an old recipe for keeping the feet from freez-

prominent during the good old days of the department. Let them speak without preface. "The pride and ambition of each fire company," says Mr. Zophar Mills, "were to be the first to reach a fire, and the most efficient in putting it out. We had as much love for that as we possibly could have for anything else. We would leave our business, our dinner, our anything, and rush for the engine. The night I was getting married there was a fire. I could see it, and I wanted to go immediately. But the next morning early, before breakfast, there was another fire, and I went to that. So you may judge how we liked it. If we had a parade, we paid the expenses ourselves. We always paid for the painting, repairing, and decorating of our engines. Engine No. 13, to which I belonged, was silver-plated—the first that was so—at a cost of perhaps $2000. We didn't ask the corporation to foot the bill. I kept an account of my expenses in connection with the Fire Department, and I found that in seven years I had paid, in charity, in clothing, and in incidentals, $3000. Mr. W. L. Jenkins, president of the Bank of America, was a member of Engine Company No. 13. Many of its other members were Quakers. There were few 'roughs' then, as in modern times. Nor were there any salaries, except in the case of the Chief

Pearl Street, near Fulton, on the 1st of July, 1834, I had a narrow escape. The building was high, and all of it above the second story was consumed, leaving only the gable walls standing. Several firemen, after the flames had been extinguished, were ordered to take their hose

GREAT FIRE, DECEMBER 16 AND 17, 1835.

Engineer, and temporarily of the assistant engineers. Firemen now are liberally compensated; they get $1200 a year each, and are retired on half-pay, if infirm, after ten years' service. Many and many a time have I worked my breath out while pumping old Thirteen, and lain in the street, and jumped up again and seized the brakes, because there was no one to take my place. The city was not then divided into districts. I once went from this very building [in Front Street, near Wall] to Astoria, in 1841, and saved four frame buildings whose roofs were already burned off. When the alarm sounded I thought the fire was somewhere up the Bowery. I ran nearly all the way to the Hell Gate Ferry at Eighty-sixth Street, and then crossed the river.

"At a fire in Haydock's drug store, in

up to the second story, and play upon the débris, in order to prevent sparks from flying about, and fire from smouldering. As I stood there, at six o'clock in the morning, with two or three of my men, I suddenly saw one of the high gable walls spread out like a blanket, and coming down upon us. My only chance was to turn my back and take it; there was no time to run. I was knocked flat, of course, by the falling mass of brick, and was forced through the second-story floor, and also through the first-story floor, into the cellar. I remember raising myself on my elbows, and then getting up and walking out, after having gone through two floors with that wall on top of me. Why didn't it kill me? I don't know. It was Providence—a miracle. Eugene Underhill and Frederick A. Ward, who

THE RUINS.—"TAKE UP: MAN YOUR ROPE."—[AFTER LITHOGRAPH PUBLISHED BY CURRIER AND IVES, 1854.]

stood a few feet from me, and were holding the hose-pipe, were instantly killed. John T. Hall and William Phillips, two other firemen on the same floor, jumped out of a window, and one of them landed upon a fence, and was badly injured. I wore a tin trumpet swung across my back, and my flesh in consequence was black and blue for six months. My cap was not dug out of the cellar until evening. The former foreman of Thirteen, who was on the second story, advising us, was buried standing up to his neck in hot bricks—so hot as to burn off some of his toes, and a brick's length off the calf of his leg. In consideration of his misfortune he was made the first fire-bell ringer of the City Hall. He lived for thirty years after that. Chief Engineer Gulick displayed great presence of mind in the emergency. His first order was to Engine No. 17, which was working near the fire, to take off the tail-screw, let the water out of the box, and then pump air into the ruins. The men were digging all day for their buried comrades, and for the bodies of poor Underhill and Ward, who stood not fifteen feet away from me when the wall fell without warning. We were playing 'washing down,' as we called it, the object being thoroughly to put out the fire that lingered in the straw, cotton, and

so on. We considered that the fire was pretty much out, and were only giving a few finishing touches. 'Thirteen' afterward erected a marble monument to Underhill and Ward in the cemetery in Carmine Street, opposite Varick. On one side is the inscription [Mr. Mills brought out his manuscript copy, and read]:

'Here are interred
the Bodies of
EUGENE UNDERHILL,
aged 20 years, 7 months, and 9 days,
and
FREDERICK A. WARD,
aged 22 years, 1 month, and 16 days,
who lost their lives by the falling of a building
while engaged
in the discharge of their duty as Firemen,
on the first day of July,
MDCCCXXXIV.'

On another side are the words:

'This Monument is Erected
By the Members of
Eagle Fire Engine Company,
No. 13,
in connection with the Friends of the
Deceased,
to commemorate the sad event
connected with their Death,
and the Loss
which they deplore.'

This monument can be seen there now.

"At a fire at Nos. 142 and 144 Front Street, in 1833, where my office is now, the building was burned, the walls being left standing. On the De Peyster Street side there was a stairway leading up to the rear of the second story. A fireman stood at the head of these stairs, and held a pipe that played upon the smoking ruins. Suddenly the wall began to fall over into De Peyster Street. The fireman ran down the stairs and under the wall, and was crushed to death. But, wonderful to relate, another fireman, a member of Thirteen, Charles Miller by name, who was standing with his back against the wall, and who kept his position, was saved. The falling wall broke off at about fifteen feet above him, and dashed into the street in front of him, leaving him unhurt. He was standing there to keep warm: it was about three o'clock in the morning, drizzling and cold. People generally would not believe such a story as this, but it is as true as gospel. The shock affected Miller for months. It completely unnerved him. He was in a constant tremor. I knew him well, but haven't seen or heard of him these twenty years. He was in the leather business in 'the Swamp.' Our foreman then was William S. Moore, a grocer in Front Street, near Peck Slip—a very nice man of Quaker parentage. He is dead now.

"Still another time," continued Mr. Mills, "I was carried under. At the Jennings's clothing-store fire on Broadway, near Barclay Street, in the year 1854, where eleven firemen were killed, I was on the roof of an extension to the main building. I was not a fireman then, but an exempt, and had gone there to help the men get the hose up. As I was returning to the street, and had got half way down the ladder between the roof and the second story, the rear wall of the main building fell over upon the extension, carrying down perhaps twenty-five by forty feet of it. I went down with it, ladder and all, into the cellar, through two floors. You wouldn't think it possible for a man to live after going through such an experience as that. While clambering to get out I felt a man's thigh as distinctly as possible; the poor fellow was dead, I suppose. Finally I succeeded in climbing to the level of the first floor, and walked through the store into the street by the front door. The first man I saw was Matsell, Chief of Police. I had lost my cap, and the foreman of No. 42 said, 'Come around with me and I will get you a cap.' While I was gone more of the wall fell, and killed several firemen who were trying to rescue the others from the ruins. I shouldn't want to go through that again."

<h3 style="text-align:center">III.</h3>

This experience is typical, and every old fireman will recognize it as such. Typical also is the experience of Mr. Charles Forrester:

"I never lost a day in my business. Often I was out with my engine four nights in the week, yet I was at work as usual in the morning. In those earlier times—say previous to 1836—the city was not districted, and whenever there was a fire anywhere all the engines were out in a jiffy. The excitement kept us up, I suppose. One night my company went up as far as Fifty-third Street and Fourth Avenue. Another night I was sitting at home with a bad cold, and taking a vapor bath. The fire-bell rang; I threw off my blankets, and though in a dripping perspiration, ran with the engine up to Forty-second Street and Tenth Avenue. The next morning I never felt better. I was fit to run for my life. What was the inducement? Well, the love of excitement, and of excelling the rival companies. We were fully repaid when we could brag about our exploits, and make our neighbors feel jealous. The only compensation that the law allowed us was release from military and jury duty. But how cold the winters were! Six or seven feet of snow in Beekman Street in 1836, at the fire in the cabinet-maker's shop! Outside, the building was coated with ice and icicles; inside, it was a raging furnace. We ran our engine on runners—simple runners made of planking six inches wide and sixteen feet long, with the ends turned up. We had steamed the ends and turned them up ourselves. On these runners, planed smooth on the bottom, we placed the engine, wheels and all, screwing the wheels down to them by the aid of simple clamps over the rims. Four men could pull the engine easily on these runners, though it weighed three thousand pounds. We would roll her out from the engine-house across the pavement to the street on broomsticks. Everything was cheap and effectual in those days. I suppose that now hundreds of dollars would be expended to do what we did with so many cents then. In front of the house of Jonathan Thompson (late Collector of the Port of New York), at No. 83 Beek-

CHARLES FORRESTER.

drop their hose and run. No. 33 did so, but No. 13 were too proud to lose their hose, and attempted to take it with them. The wall fell, and three of them were crushed, not twenty-five feet from where I stood. A wall of a burning building will totter for a little while, but when it comes, it comes like distress. I always regretted that fire, because I felt that I was the cause of those men's death. Well, if they had obeyed orders, like 33, they wouldn't, any of them, have been caught.

"At a fire in Orange Street, now Baxter Street, Chief Anderson ordered one of his engineers to get a stream upon the burning building from the rear in Mulberry Street. To do so it was necessary to take the hose through the house behind, through a room in which two men were sleeping on two beds. The engineer thought that they were negroes, they looked so tawny. Presently one of his assistants cried out that the sleepers had 'the black small-pox.' The pipe was dropped, the firemen decamped, followed in hot haste by the engineer. They hauled their hose out after them, and they weren't reported for disobeying orders either.

"At the large fire in 1835 a number of engines were present from the neighboring cities, among them the Northern Liberties, of Philadelphia, which reached the scene of the disaster on the second night. The railroad communication was not complete; there was a stretch of six miles in New Jersey, over two sand-hills, where the rails had not been laid. Passengers were accustomed to cover the distance in stage-coaches, but the Philadelphia boys dragged their engine across those sand-hills with unflagging energy. They arrived too late to be of service, but their New York brothers handsomely dined and wined them for their pains.

"At No. 231 Water Street, near Beekman, in 1842, a stove store caught fire on the third floor. I had two streams on the

man Street, there was a tunnel through the snow. Oh, we don't have any such winters now! The charm of it all lay in the excitement of the running, in the victory over rivals, and in the daring feats in and about burning buildings. Many men lost their lives. There, for instance, was the great fire in West Street, near the Battery, in 1841 or 1842, the worst I ever knew. I was an engineer at that time, and had two streams, one from Engine 33, and the other from Hose 13, playing up the hatchway of the building; but the water came back upon us so scalding hot that it was like cards of needles in our backs every time it struck us. At length Chief Anderson ordered me to back the men out, and go to the rear of the building, to prevent the fire from getting into Washington Street. His plan always was, 'If the fire is in its infancy, go into the building; if it is well under way, go to the rear, and protect that, for the front will protect itself,' since there are always engines arriving that will help it. When we reached the rear, the floors fell in, and I saw the walls tottering. I ordered my men to

THE NIGHT ALARM.—"START HER LIVELY, BOYS."—[AFTER LITHOGRAPH PUBLISHED BY CURRIER AND IVES, 1854.]

second floor, and was throwing them up the hatchway. The floor above suddenly gave way, and the weight of the stoves on it carried every staircase down into the cellar. We looked around for means of escape, and found an old sign-board covered with a preparation of smalts—small pieces of broken glass. We put one end of the board on a window-sill, and the other down on a small out-house below, forming a very steep inclination. Then we slid down. Each of us lost the seat of his trousers, and I parted with some flesh besides, so that I didn't sit down for some time afterward.

"At the Buck's Horn Tavern fire, in 1842 or 1843, at the junction of the Boston Post-road and the Bloomingdale Road, near where the Fifth Avenue Hotel now stands, the engines were ordered to form 'a hose line' in order to save the barn. I opened the nearest hydrant, and the next, and the next, but there was no water. They had been building a fountain in Union Square, and had shut the water off. I couldn't get a drop till I got to Fourth Street. Then we began to pump from one engine into another, and so on to the end of the line; but the hose was so leaky that all the water escaped before it reached the fire, all because the Common Council had refused to make an appropriation for new hose. Finally we found a cistern near the barn, and used that.

"At the famous Crystal Palace fire, in 1858, some statuary—figures of the Twelve Apostles, which had been sent from France in the hope that they would be bought for the adornment of a Catholic church in the city—was destroyed. The commissioners of the exhibition had notified the owners to remove them before the fire started, but the latter had neglected to do so. Horace Greeley was one of the commissioners, and not long afterward, while on a visit to Paris, was thrown into Clichy Prison by the owners, who were trying to make him indemnify them for their loss. They never got any money from him, though. I remember Horace well. He used to come down to the post-office to get his newspaper exchanges, and carried them home himself. He was then editor of the *Log-Cabin*, a General Harrison campaign sheet. His shoes had no strings; his trousers caught in them behind; he wore the old white coat which James Gordon Bennett made famous; his hat was on the back of his head; and his neckcloth, when he wore one, showed its knot under his ear. Was it affectation? No; it was carelessness or recklessness. After he got married his wife rather improved him.

"At a fire in Ann Street in 1836, one morning at about sunrise, old Mr. Bennett, who had just opened an office in Clinton Hall, next door to the corner of Beekman and Nassau streets, where the

Nassau Bank now stands, came out upon the front steps, and presented each one of a crowd of two thousand persons or more with a copy of that day's *Morning Herald*. He stood in the open air, and gave a paper to everybody that came. It was a curious sight to see the entire company, seated on curb-stones and stoops, reading the *Morning Herald*. It was the best advertisement he ever had.

"At a fire in Broad Street in 1845, which burned through to Broadway and down almost to Bowling Green, there was an explosion, said to be of several tons of saltpetre, although afterward it was a popular conundrum whether saltpetre would explode at all. Some of Five's men were on the roof of the building. The roof went down, and they walked off unhurt to the pavement. One of them said that the sensation was 'as if the roof had been hoisted up and then squatted down.'

"At a fire in 1812 in Chatham Street hundreds of houses were burned to the ground. A sailor climbed up the steeple of Dr. Spring's Brick Church, which occupied the site of the *Times* Building, went out upon the roof, and extinguished the flames that had just started there. A reward was offered for his feat of valor, but he could never be found. This was considered the greatest fire in New York city up to the conflagration of 1835.

"At a fire which broke out at three o'clock one Sunday morning in March, 1824, in the ship-yard of Adam and Noah Brown, bounded by Stanton, Houston, and Goerck streets and the East River, my engine itself, known as Black Joke, No. 33, was so burned that nothing remained of it but a blackened scrap heap. This engine was the first on the ground. Its odd name was the name of an Albany sloop which, during the Revolutionary war, was transformed into a privateer, and distinguished itself by capturing a number of prizes off the coast of Nova Scotia. In the yard were two steamboats nearly finished, and two ships on the stocks, one of them under cover of the ship-house. Although Black Joke, 33, got to work very expeditiously, the flames spread so rapidly that the firemen were soon driven away from the engine, some of them being compelled to jump into the river in order to save their lives, while others were rescued in a row-boat. An unsuccessful attempt had been made to launch the ships that were on the stocks. Every vessel and all

the property in the yard were totally destroyed. This is one of the few instances where a New York fire-engine, taken out to extinguish a fire, was itself extinguished.

"The thermometer stood at more than 100° Fahrenheit one Sunday in July, 1824, when a fire broke out in a rope-walk on Orchard Street, extending into the fields. So intense was the heat that seven firemen died from the effects of it. Mr. Thomas Franklin, then Chief Engineer, father of Mr. Morris Franklin, now president of the New York Life-insurance Company, was seriously affected by the same cause.

"The Bowery Theatre has been burned three times; the first time was in 1828, when it was the finest theatre in New York city, and when Mlle. Celeste, Monsieur and Madame Achilles, Monsieur and Madame Hutin, the first importation of French dancers into this country, were drawing immense houses, and creating extraordinary excitement. Some stables south of the theatre, near Bayard Street, took fire, and the neighboring houses served as a bridge for the flames, which soon attacked the eaves of the theatre, then the roof, and in a short time the interior. For hours the conflagration was beyond the control of the firemen, notwithstanding the presence and activity of every one of the forty-seven engines and nine trucks belonging to the Department, each engine representing forty men. The difficulty of obtaining water was very great. A line was formed of not less than seventeen engines, stretching from the foot of Catherine Street to the burning building, and engaging the services of six hundred and eighty men. The water was pumped from the East River by the first engine in the line, and thence into the second engine, which pumped it into the third, and thence into the fourth, which pumped it into the fifth, and so on. The law then, and until 1835, required each householder to keep in the hall of his house two leather buckets, and to throw them into the street when an alarm of fire was heard in his neighborhood. They were picked up for use by citizens, who put themselves in lines between the fire and the nearest cisterns and pumps, and proceeded to fill the engines as rapidly as possible, passing the buckets from hand to hand. Each bucket was marked with the name and address of its owner, and was returned to him after the fire. When the

THE RACE.—"JUMP HER, BOYS; JUMP HER."—[AFTER LITHOGRAPH PUBLISHED BY CURRIER AND IVES, 1854.]

third fire had burned out the Bowery Theatre, the walls were found to be so fused from successive bakings that each wall seemed to be one immense brick."

IV.

Though the recollections of these old firemen go back fifty or sixty years, they do not reach the epoch when the Volunteer Fire Department was incorporated, much less the more distant period of its origins. The act of incorporation was passed eighty-two years ago, in 1798; and at least as long ago as two hundred and three years there were regular firemen in the city of New York. From certain manuscript and unpublished documents that have come into my possession it appears that the earliest municipal records on the subject are that in January, 1677, "overseers of chimneys and fires were appointed" by the corporation. Six years later, in March, 1683, the first law with respect to the prevention of fires was enacted by the city authorities. This law provided for the appointment of "viewers and searchers of chimneys and fire-hearths," and inflicted a penalty of twenty shillings for every defect found in the construction of those modest conveniences. It went further. "No person," it said, "shall lay hay or straw or other combustible matter within their dwelling-houses." "A fine of fifteen shillings," it added, shall be imposed "upon every person who shall suffer his chimney to be on fire." It arranged also for the purchase of "hooks, ladders, and buckets." The business of the citizen was to diminish the necessity for firemen. If his chimney caught fire, no matter how, he was fined. He should have had it properly built, and kept it cleaned. A trial of three years showed that these simple and rigorous regulations were insufficient. In 1686, "by reason of great damage done by fire," it was ordered, first, "that every person having two chimneys to his house provide one bucket"; secondly, "that every house having more than two hearths provide two buckets"; and thirdly, "that all brewers shall have six buckets, and all bakers six buckets, under penalty of six shillings for every bucket wanting." The former provision for hooks and ladders seems to have been futile, for in February, 1689, the records show that "fire ladders, with sufficient hooks thereto," were "ordered to be made"; and having gone so far, the city fathers proceeded to appoint "Brandt Meisters," or fire masters, to take charge of the property—another name for the "overseers of chimneys and fires" of the year 1677, with increased scope of operation. When the buckets got lost at a fire, the law-making power was equal to the emergency. "There was complaint," says the town-clerk's book, "of several buckets that were lost at the late fire in the ffly [a market at the foot of Maiden Lane], and it was ordered that the cryer give notice round the city that such buckets be brought to the Mayor." This was in 1692, and the law is known to have been in force for at least a hundred years afterward. When a fire had been put out, the buckets were taken to the front of the City Hall, and were there claimed by the respective owners.

The chimneys in those days bore a bad character. In December, 1697, it is recorded that "this Court, taking into consideration the danger that may happen by fire for want of a due inspection made to cleaning of chimneys and mending of hearths within the city, ordered that two sufficient persons in every ward of this city be appointed as viewers of chimneys and hearths, to view the same once a week; upon finding a defect, to give notice that such be repaired; if a person refuse, he to forfeit the sum of three shillings, one half to the city, the other half to the viewers." Still further we read that "if any person's chimney be on fire after such notice, he shall forfeit the sum of forty shillings; if the viewers neglect to perform their duty, they forfeit the sum of six shillings, and others shall be appointed in their place." This is the first record of a paid Fire Department in the city of New York. "Viewers" and "overseers" there were already; but now arrangement is made for paying, for fining, and for discharging them; and also a systematic performance of duty is required: they are to view the chimneys and hearths once a week. Five years later the constables were pressed into the inspective service: "Constables are ordered to inspect every house, to see whether they have the number of buckets required by law." As the city increased, more hooks and ladders were provided. Twenty-two years after their first appearance it is recorded that in February, 1705, Alderman Vandenburgh was ordered to "be paid nine pounds five shillings for hooks and ladders by him provided"; while in October, 1706, it was "ordered that eight ladders and two fire-hooks and poles be provided, to cost £19 2s. 0d."; and in Oc-

tober, 1716, that "a committee be appointed to provide a sufficient number of ladders and hooks for public use"; but no fire-engine seems to have been in operation until fifteen years later, when the Department was fifty-four years old.

On the 6th of May, 1731, it was that the city authorities adopted the following resolution: "Resolved, With all convenient speed to procure two complete fire-engines, with suctions and materials thereunto belonging, for the public service; that the sizes thereof be of the fourth and sixth sizes of Mr. Newsham's fire-engines; and that Mr. Mayor, Alderman Cruger, Alderman Rutgers, and Alderman Roosevelt, or any three of them, be a committee to agree with some proper merchant or merchants to send to London for the same by the first conveniency, and report upon what terms the said fire-engines, &c., will be delivered to this corporation." By December of the same year preparations were made for receiving the new apparatus; it was "ordered that workmen be employed to fit up a room in the City Hall [then located where the United States Treasury Building, formerly the Custom-house, now stands] of this city for securing the fire-engines of this corporation, with all expedition." Probably in the same month the engines arrived, for we find it further "ordered that Alderman Hardenbroeck and Mr. Beekman be a committee to have the fire-engines cleaned, and the leathers oiled and put into boxes, that the same may be fit for immediate use." The next month, January, 1733, it was "ordered that a committee employ a person or persons forthwith to put the fire-engines in good order, and also to look after the same, that they may be always in good plight and condition, and fit for present use." Mr. Engs, an old fireman, writes that he distinctly remembers to have seen one of Mr. Newsham's engines, with the maker's name on a brass plate, accompanied by a date, indicating that it was eighty years old. "It had a short oblong square box, with the condenser case in the centre, and was played by short arms at each end, and mounted on four block wheels, made of thick plank. There was no traveller forward for the wheels to play under the box; so that when you turned a corner, the machine must have been lifted around, unless there was a large sweep to move in." Suction pipes were unknown at that

THE FIRE.—"SHAKE HER UP, BOYS."—[AFTER LITHOGRAPH PUBLISHED BY CURRIER AND IVES, 1854.]

time, notwithstanding the fact that the committee had been ordered to obtain, with the engines, "suctions, leather pipes, and caps." The suctions were probably what was known afterward as "pump hose," which led the water from the pump to the engine box; the "leather pipes" were for the same purpose as the ones subsequently made of brass or other metal, and the "caps" were the nozzles.

V.

Such were the origins of the old Volunteer Fire Department. The "room in the City Hall" where the first engine was kept soon became the forerunner of a series of engine-houses; and old firemen tell how, from about the year 1820 until about the year 1836, these buildings were places of orderly rendezvous in the evenings. Tweedism was not rampant in those days. Except on Saturday nights, the boys went home as early as 10 P.M., and went to bed. They did not "bunk" with the "machine." Singing and storytelling were the chief entertainments. There was no drinking, no eating, no sleeping, no misbehavior. Even smoking and "chewing" seem to have been finable offenses in some houses; for a few days ago, while consulting the minutes of En-gine Company No. 13—an organization, however, exceptionally select and efficient —I found these curious entries:

"*December* 1, 1829.—Charles J. Hubbs reports D. T. Williams for chewing tobacco in the engine-house."

"*December* 3, 1829.—William M. Haydock reports Washington Van Wyck for smoking in the engine-house."

Liquor, however, was allowed at fires, when the men were in actual service, provision for a regular supply of it having been made by the same engine company as early as the year 1801, when the following *naïve* minute was entered on the books:

"*Berkley's Tavern, November* 12, 1801. —It being thought by the company that a steward to the company be necessary, whose business it shall be to furnish the company with liquor, &c., at the times of fire, and when it will be paid for by the company; any other member than the person above appointed finding liquors, &c., at time of fire, will do it at his own expense, as the company will not pay the same."

This provision obviated the necessity for the repetition of such entries as these:

"*November* 9, 1792.—Eighteen shillings paid to Elias Stillwell for gin at the time of the fire at the Fly Market."

"*November* 17, 1795.—Paid six shillings for Geneva had at fires, and carting sled."

"*December* 3, 1795.—This morning, between eight and nine o'clock, a most dreadful fire happened in William Street, between John Street and the North Church, in which six or seven houses were consumed......Paid six shillings for gin."

As time wore on it became the custom to use the engine-houses as dormitories, and demoralization went hand in hand with it. The law, however, still forbade the practice, and Mr. "Joe" Hoxie one night signified his accession to the office of alderman by making a general raid upon the buildings and ordering all hands out. Engine Company No. 33 thereupon made friends with the sexton of All Saints' Episcopal Chapel (now used as a machine shop), in Grand Street, near Pitt, the members lying in the pews, and using the ends of the cushions for bolsters. When turned out of this comfortable nest, they hired the second story of a house in Scammel Street, near by, only a hundred and fifty feet from their engine-house, and paid for it themselves, disdaining to modernize themselves by calling upon the city to meet the expense. They had two rooms, and these they fitted up with three rows of berths, or "bunks," along the walls, one row above another. "I was so long," says an old fireman, "that my feet hung over the end of my bunk, and the fellow who slept below me used to amuse himself by sticking pins into my bare soles." Often a member who happened to be wakeful would go to the signal lantern, which was a part of the fixtures of the establishment, scrape out of it a handful of lamp-black, and proceed to paint mustaches on the upper lips of the smooth-faced slumberers, who, when they awoke—it might have been a fire-alarm that roused them—would try to wipe the nasty stuff off, thereby making their appearance considerably worse, for the lamp-black would stick like a brother. "I have worn such mustaches many a time," continued the speaker. "All such harmless little performances made fun enough then, though they look rather silly now." There were thirty "bunks" in the Scammel Street lodging-house.

By-and-by the tastes of the firemen became less simple, and brown-stone houses were not uncommon. Harry Howard was the first Chief Engineer who openly encouraged the men to sleep in these buildings. Among the finest houses in earlier days were those of No. 13, in Duane Street; No. 6, in Henry Street, near Gouverneur (which is still standing, and is used by a steam-engine company; No. 44, in Houston Street, near Columbia, now occupied by a steam-engine; and No. 32, in Hester Street. About the year 1849 the late Mr. Tweed became foreman of Engine No. 6, most of whose members were ship-carpenters and calkers in the Seventh Ward. He was instrumental in erecting for them a fine three-story building, large enough for a ward meeting, and practically the political head-quarters of that part of the city, which excited the envy of other companies less sumptuously provided for by the corporation. Mr. Mills relates that when he belonged to Engine No. 13 there was not room enough in her house for the men to sit down. "We used to drag our engine out when we wanted to hold a meeting of the company."

VI.

It was at "a convivial party," on a winter evening in 1792, at a small tavern in Nassau Street, near Fair (now Fulton) Street, that some members of the Volunteer Fire Department first bestirred themselves with reference to the creation of a fund for the benefit of indigent and disabled firemen and their families. The building was long ago torn down, and on its site is a magnificent marble structure owned by ex-Mayor Wood; its frequenters also have long since disappeared, but their good deed has built for them a name. Six years afterward matters had taken very definite shape and finish; and when, on the 20th of March, 1798, an act "to incorporate the firemen of the city of New York" was passed by the Legislature, one of its provisions was, "that the funds of the said corporation which shall arise from chimney fires, certificates, and donations, and from such other objects as may have been heretofore or may be hereafter agreed on by the respective fire-companies, shall be appropriated to the relief of such indigent or disabled firemen, or their families, as may be interested therein, and who may, in the opinion of a majority of the trustees, be worthy of assistance; but if they shall amount to a greater sum than the trustees may think necessary to apply to the said purposes, then the said representatives shall have power to apply such surplus to the purpose of extinguishing fires, under such limitations and restrictions as they may, with the sanction of the corporation of the city of New York, deem proper." For thirty-seven years the course of the charity ran smooth. The recipients of the fund were few, and the disbursements small. What better use of the principal than to invest it in fire-insurance stock? The idea found favor, and the investment was made. Whenever thereafter the firemen put out a fire, or prevented the destruction of property, they added to the value of their charitable stock. The better they worked, the more money they had for their widows and orphans. Every dollar saved to the fire-insurance companies was a gain for the fund. But the disastrous conflagration of the year 1835 nearly swept the insurance companies from existence, and in their fall the fund also declined. It became, indeed, scarcely a fund at all. With admirable promptness and energy the trustees set themselves to the task of soliciting subscriptions for the purpose of putting the charity on its feet again, and so successful were they and their friends that in a few weeks the sum of $24,000 was secured. Tradition has not failed to embalm with especial care the names of Adam W. Spies, of Engine No. 12, and James Russell, of Hose No. 4, who distinguished themselves by their zeal in the work. Once started again, the fund moved without apparent friction. "In those days," says Mr. Giles, its present treasurer, "it was a rare occurrence for a fireman to ask relief from the fund. It seemed as if they felt unwilling, however great were their necessities, to seek assistance from a source which they thought should be reserved as a sacred trust for the benefit of widows and orphans only." Thirteen years afterward, however, in 1848, another crisis was reached. The trustees, in their annual report, regretted to state that "for three years past they have not only been unable to add anything to the permanent fund, but have experienced great difficulty in raising sufficient money to meet their actual and necessary expenditures." The principal causes of the deficiency were the great increase in the number of the widows, orphans, and other beneficiaries; the decreased sums collected from chimney and gunpowder fines, and from penalties for violating the fire laws; and the neglect or inability of the city

fire-insurance companies, which had suffered terrible losses, to contribute as liberally as had been their custom. The first-mentioned cause was the chief. The city had been growing rapidly, and the number of firemen had in consequence increased from five or six hundred to about two thousand. The condition of affairs was earnestly considered at a special meeting convened for the purpose, and each member promised "to use his best efforts to find some new source of revenue to sustain the sinking fortunes of the fund." It did not take long to discover that not less than twenty-one foreign insurance agencies were neglecting to pay to the Comptroller of the State, as required by law, two per cent. of the premiums received on policies of insurance issued by them. The law was clear; the neglect was inexcusable. Why not get the Legislature to make over to the fund this levy of two per cent.? asked the trustees one of another, and the reply being in favor of such a course, a bill was forthwith drawn, "praying the Legislature to transfer the two per cent. tax from the coffers of the State to the charitable fund of the Fire Department." A delegation of the board, accompanied by other of its friends, proceeded at once to Albany, and the bill was introduced, but on account of the lateness of the season it was not reached before the Legislature adjourned. The next winter the bill was again presented —this time early. Its friends "were met by a powerful lobby of foreign insurance agents and their friends, to defeat, if possible, its passage. Finding that we were determined to have the bill passed," continues Mr. Giles, "they proposed a conference, and offered, if we would withdraw our bill, or would not press its passage, to give to the Fire Department Fund annually $1500 so long as the Volunteer Fire Department existed. We informed them that we could not comply with their request, as our instructions were to get the bill passed; and that if we were unsuccessful we would return to the representatives of the Fire Department with the proud assurance that we had done our duty and obeyed our instructions. But by means of great exertions we were successful, the bill was passed, and we returned to our constituents, the representatives of the Fire Department, with a certified copy of the law in our pockets." The books show that during the next fifteen years the passage of this law benefited the fund to the amount of more than $200,000.

When the volunteer system was succeeded by a paid Fire Department, the opponents of the former, having gained, says Mr. Giles, the object for which they went to Albany, "turned their attention to this charitable fund; and so anxious were they to blot out and destroy every nucleus that the Volunteer Department might rally around that they were disposed to make the trustees of the paid Department the sole arbiters of this charity, with power to fill vacancies in their board." But at length the Legislature enacted that to the Exempt Firemen should be confided the trust, with the proviso that no money should be taken from the permanent fund without the consent of the Legislature. This fund at that time was $90,000. Last year it had increased to $129,307 89.

"The present paid Fire Department," however, says Mr. Zophar Mills, "have a fund of their own of about $400,000, obtained from fines and penalties for violating the building laws, through licenses for selling petroleum, fire-works, etc. The interest on this sum is twice as much as the Department spends for its widows, orphans, and infirm members. We were eighty years in collecting our fund, they only fifteen years. Five years ago we received one-third of our revenues, three years ago one-half, but about a year ago the law was changed so as to give the whole back to us. They didn't need the money, but they knew that we did; yet it is a wonder that they consented to give it up." The fund of the old Volunteer Department now yields yearly the sum of $40,000. It is one of the most modest, efficient, and praiseworthy charities in the world.

VII.

A principal source of its revenue was the "Annual Ball for the Benefit of the New York Fire Department Fund." Almost every engine company had an annual ball, but the ball of the season was the general ball for the fund. It occupied for many years a position corresponding to that of the Charity Ball in the Academy of Music, and enlisted the sympathy and support of the fashion and wealth of the metropolis. The first ball of the series was held in the Bowery Theatre in the year 1828, not long before the burning of that building. The price of tickets was two dollars; afterward it was never less than five dollars. Great care was taken in the distribution of tickets, that the entertainment should be as select as possible. The places of assembly in succeeding years were the Park Theatre, on Park Row, the Opera-house (Clinton Hall), Niblo's, and the Academy of Music, and the success was perfect, until the disbandment of the Department in 1865, when the interest began to diminish, and the difficulty of paying expenses to begin. The last entertainment given by the "Firemen's Ball Committee of the Old Volunteer Fire Department" was not a ball, but a concert, in aid of the yellow-fever sufferers, held in the Academy of Music on the 2d of October, 1878, and resulting in the collection of the handsome net sum of $5462. In the palmy period of the Department immense preparations were made for the decoration of the building in which the ball was to take place. For several days previous to the event wagons laden with trumpets, torches, hooks, ladders, axes, tormentors, and other implements of the craft might be seen driving up to the head-quarters of the Chief Engineer, at No. 21 Elizabeth Street, and depositing their treasures, so that as soon as the theatre was available all the material for ornamenting it might be within reach for expeditious use. When the curtain dropped on the stage the night before the ball, the firemen took possession of the building, and their labors in equipping its interior continued through the night and the next day. Enthusiasm, diligence, and quick intelligence presided over the task of preparation. The tickets were handsomely engraved on steel.

The preparations for the balls given by the several companies were scarcely less notable. Fine "fancy" paper with ornamented cut margins was not considered too choice, nor gilt ink too costly, nor "politest" phrases too precious.

It is almost needless to add that at a firemen's ball the dancing ceased only with the break of day.

VIII.

On one memorable occasion the labors of the New York firemen were exerted with triumphant success in Brooklyn also. In the latter city, a few blocks west of Fulton Street, near Fulton Ferry, in 1842, a fire started, burned through to Fulton

Street, crossed that street, and destroyed the houses on each side of it for a considerable distance. The Chief Engineer, in view of the extent and ferocity of the flames, was about to dispatch a messenger to the Navy-yard requesting the authorities to detail an officer for the purpose of blowing up a row of brick buildings as the only means of staying the progress of the fire. It so happened that near the Brooklyn Chief Engineer was Chief Engineer Anderson, of the New York Fire Department, and Engineer Charles Forrester. These officers urged the Brooklyn Chief to withhold the request to the Navy Department, and promised to bring over from New York a force sufficient to save the doomed buildings and extinguish the fire. The offer was gladly accepted, and Engineer Charles Forrester started for New York, bearing an order from Chief Anderson to have the City Hall bell strike five— the signal for calling out the engines in the district southeast of the City Hall Park. With characteristic forethought, Mr. Forrester got the ferry-master on the New York side to promise to keep the boat in the slip until it could be packed with engines and firemen from New York. The ferry-boats then ran less often than now. He started the Fulton Market bell, and next the City Hall bell was heard. This was responded to successively by the bells in the North Dutch tower and the old Brick Church tower. In an incredibly short time the ferry was a rendezvous of engines and firemen, the river was crossed, and a line of engines was formed from the Brooklyn side of the river, Engine No. 15 being at the dock, Engine No. 22 next, Engine No. 42 next, and Engine No. 38 next. The fire was conquered, and the row of brick buildings saved.

The Exempt Engine Company was composed of firemen who had served their time and been honorably discharged. It was called out only in extraordinary emergencies. During the war riots in 1863 many of its members staid in the *Tribune* Building for several days and nights, ready to perform duty at a moment's notice; and perilous duty it was,

when the rioters, who had set fire to private houses and orphan asylums, determined that these should be consumed. At the burning of Barnum's Museum, on Broadway, where the *Herald* Building now stands, the Exempt Engine Company is believed to have saved a quarter of a million of dollars. It had three engines —one of them a hand-engine known as the "Hay-Wagon," and the others steam-engines, which were self-propellers, each manned by ten Exempts, who did the

CORNELIUS V. ANDERSON.

work of five hundred firemen and an ordinary engine. These, with the exception of the one used by Engine Company No. 8, were the first efficient steam-engines in New York city. The "Hay-Wagon" was sold to the United States government about the year 1862, and taken to Fortress Monroe for the protection of that important place when the rebels were thought to be meditating the capture and burning of it. Mr. John Baulch, an assistant engineer of the New York Fire Department, went with the "Hay-Wagon" to Fortress Monroe, entered the service of the government, and staid there, performing "fire duty." The "Hay-Wagon," an engraving of which accompanies this article, was originally the engine of Empire Company, No. 42, but being extremely heavy and lumbersome, was abandoned by that organization for a new one. The Exempts think-

THE "HAY-WAGON."—EMPIRE ENGINE, NO. 42.

ing that she was too good a servant to be discharged, resolved to form a company of their own, and take her into their service. A good specimen of a "double-decker" engine is seen in the reproduction of the Southwark Engine, No. 38, which was the first machine of the kind in use in New York city.

IX.

A few months ago—or, to be precise, on the 18th of June, 1880—there appeared in the New York *Evening Post* a short letter, signed "C. J.," which began as follows: "Over in Greenwood there is a stately monument to the New York fireman who lost his life in saving a child. It is the only one in that city of the dead before which I take off my hat." I do not know the name of the writer, but his sentiments

are chivalrous. The occasion of the first purchase of lots in Greenwood Cemetery for the burial of firemen was the gallant deaths of Engineer George Kerr and Assistant-Foreman Henry Fargis, of the Southwark Engine Company, No. 38, at the fire in Duane Street, New York, on the 2d of April, 1848. These sad events made a deep impression upon the hearts of New York firemen, and led them to a resolution to honor in an especial manner the memory of their brave associates. A committee, consisting of Cornelius V. Anderson, George A. Buckingham, Lawrence Turnure, George W. Littell, John K. Bowen, Warren Bliven, James W. Barker, Furman Neefus, John A. Cregier, and Charles McDougall, was intrusted with the business on the 2d of May, 1848.

SOUTHWARK ENGINE, NO. 38.

These old firemen entered (to quote their own words) upon "the performance of the duties assigned them with a melancholy pleasure—melancholy in the recollection of the events which prompted this movement on your [the Fire Department's] part, but, at the same time, pleasant in the reflection that though dead in body, the virtues and excellency of character of your late associates still live in your memory, and that the remembrance of them will thus be perpetuated to your now well known to so many thousands of Americans and foreigners—"which for its natural scenery, commanding view of the bay and surrounding country, can not be surpassed." So, at all events, they reported to the Fire Department, and probably their judgment will not be questioned by anybody who has seen the beautiful place on Summit Avenue, in the southern part of that fair city of the dead.

The ground being secured, a magnificent monument, designed and built by

MONUMENT AT GREENWOOD.

posterity." They proceeded at once to visit Greenwood Cemetery, in order to select a suitable site for the erection of a monument. The comptroller of the Cemetery Association, Mr. J. A. Perry, lent them his help, and, after a careful inspection of the grounds, they chose a spot— Mr. Robert E. Launitz, was erected, at an expense of $2500. Who does not recall the leading features of this splendid memorial and this enchanting spot? The white marble shaft with its pedestal is twenty-three feet ten inches high, and is surmounted by a statue four feet eight inches high—the statue of a fireman in the act of saving a child from the flames. The shaft consists of three plain blocks, relieved by festoons of oak leaves—the emblem of strength and endurance. The pedestal is of notable design. Its base block bears the coat of arms of the city of New York, whose firemen are to be commemorated; its pilasters are adorned with tastefully grouped hydrants, hose, hooks, and ladders, the hose companies as well as the engine companies having a share in the memorial work. Above the cornice a fireman's cap and two speaking-trumpets repose on a cushion. The wreath of oak leaves that surrounds the cap is the historic emblem that the wearer has saved a citizen's life. Firemen's torches, ornamented with leaves of water plants, rise from each corner of the cornice. The general effect of the structure is exceedingly impressive.

This is the Firemen's Monument, and on its right the engineers of the Department have erected a special memorial in honor of their late associate George Kerr, while on its left rises a similar tribute to the memory of Henry Fargis, reared by the company of which he was a member. With characteristic generosity the deed of the lot on which the Kerr monument stands was made out in the name of a representative of his family, a similar course being pursued in the case of the Fargis monument. The entire ground is inclosed by a substantial and choice iron railing, the pedestals for which represent hydrants surmounted by an urn. The gate, also of iron, is composed of hose-pipes crossed by a hook, a ladder, a torch, an axe, a trumpet, and a tormentor—all of them firemen's instruments—bound together by a length of hose, and encircled by a laurel wreath. Over the gate is a scroll inscribed with the words, "New York Fire Department, incorporated A.D. 1798," and above the scroll is a bell. The cost of the railing and gate was $982 75. The entire cost of the monument and its inclosure was $4316 46, every cent of which was paid by New York volunteer firemen.

Peaceful and honored has been the sleep of the brave men who lie beneath the sward of that lovely place. On the 12th of June, 1849, the bodies of Engineer Kerr and Assistant Foreman Fargis were laid there, and it was the intention to do

the same with the bodies of all New York firemen who had been killed in the discharge of their duties; but it is a curious fact that when search was made for their graves in various burial-grounds, it was found impossible to identify them, except in two instances, namely, those of Messrs. Underhill and Ward (the story of their death has already been told), whose friends were unwilling to have the removal made unless the monuments already erected over their graves were transferred to the plot in Greenwood. This the committee could not consent to do, and the whole plan was abandoned.

Messrs. Kerr and Fargis, it may be added, were killed by the falling of a wall. Chief Engineer Anderson, in a communication to the Common Council of the city of New York a few days after the fire, eulogized his dead associates in the warmest terms.

Several attempts, in addition to the first one, were made to have the bodies of Underhill and Ward removed to Greenwood Cemetery, but the disinclination of the Trustees of the Exempt Firemen's Benevolent Fund, who have control of the firemen's plot and monument, to allow the erection of any obstruction to the view, or any unsightliness, prevented the success of the efforts. The trustees persisted in their refusal to permit the monuments now standing in the Carmine Street cemetery to be transferred to the plot in Greenwood. It is not improbable, however, that when in the course of time the former cemetery shall be converted into building lots, the dust of those two brave men will be brought away and deposited near that of their fellows who died in the same cause. After the erection of the Firemen's Monument in Greenwood it was the custom to bury at its feet the bodies of firemen who fell in the discharge of their duty. For sixteen years, or until the disbandment of the Volunteer Fire Department, the custom continued, broken only occasionally by the desire of friends to bury their dead in the family lot. The slumbers of the sleepers are not disturbed now by the advent of new-comers. Nor will they be. The beautiful spot has received its consecration of human dust, and has entered into history. Its area has never been enlarged, its tenants remain in undisturbed possession, and its turf smiles.

OLD NEW YORK COFFEE-HOUSES

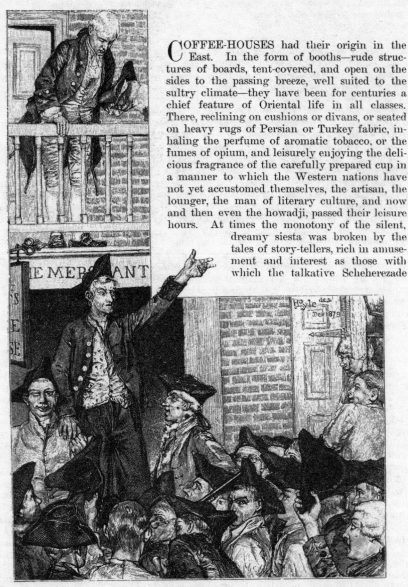

COFFEE-HOUSES had their origin in the East. In the form of booths—rude structures of boards, tent-covered, and open on the sides to the passing breeze, well suited to the sultry climate—they have been for centuries a chief feature of Oriental life in all classes. There, reclining on cushions or divans, or seated on heavy rugs of Persian or Turkey fabric, inhaling the perfume of aromatic tobacco, or the fumes of opium, and leisurely enjoying the delicious fragrance of the carefully prepared cup in a manner to which the Western nations have not yet accustomed themselves, the artisan, the lounger, the man of literary culture, and now and then even the howadji, passed their leisure hours. At times the monotony of the silent, dreamy siesta was broken by the tales of story-tellers, rich in amusement and interest as those with which the talkative Scheherezade

ISAAC SEARS ADDRESSING THE MOB.

A LONDON COFFEE-HOUSE OF THE SEVENTEENTH CENTURY.

"jolly good ale and old," was the favorite place of carousal of the Wildrakes of the day. The *Harleian Miscellany* contains two extremely curious tracts on this subject. One published in 1673, called "The Character of a Coffee-House, with the Symptoms of a Town Wit," charges that "the coffee-house is a lay conventicle, good-fellowship turned Puritan, ill husbandry in masquerade, whither people come after toping all day to purchase at the expense of their last penny the repute of sober companions; he that comes often saves twopence a week in *Gazettes*, and has his news and his coffee for the same charge."

beguiled for a thousand nights her caliph lord.

The fashion of public gathering followed the introduction of the coffee-house into Europe, with the change which climate and national characteristics required.

In 1650, as Anthony Wood relates in his Diary, "coffee was publicly sold at or neare the Angel" (a tavern sign), at Oxford. The keeper was an "Outlander, or Jew," Jacob by name. The Angel Tavern was in the parish of St. Peter, near the east gate of the old university town. He also sold "chocolate and thee"; both these new beverages, as is quaintly remarked, "were by some who delighted in novelties drunk." Accepted at Oxford, coffee soon found its way to London, and in 1652 one Bowman, coachman to Mr. Hodges, a Turkey merchant, was set up by his master in what Aubrey calls "the first coffee-house in London."

In 1663 coffee-houses were placed on the footing of taverns, and a statute of Charles II. of that year required that they should be licensed. Strangely enough, the old Eastern controversy was revived in London, with the difference that the coffee-houses became the resort of the sober, religious Puritan, while the tavern, with its

The year of the publication of this diatribe it was proposed in Parliament that coffee-houses should be suppressed, and in 1675 a proclamation of the King ordered that they should all be closed, as "seminaries of sedition"; but reflection brought wiser counsel, and the order was rescinded a few days later. Popular habits are not safely interfered with.

The second of the tracts in the *Harleian Miscellany* alluded to, printed in 1675, under the title, "The Coffee-Houses Vindicated," bears witness to the rapid increase of these establishments. "The dull planet Saturn has not finished one revolution through his orb since coffee-houses were first known among us, yet it is worth our wonder to observe how numerous they are already grown. Nor indeed have we any places of entertainment of more use or general conveniency in several respects."

At the period when Hatton wrote (1708) the "nuisances" complained of in 1652 had reached the number of 3000. In 1768, when the signs of London were taken down to allow of free circulation of air through the dingy, murky city, and the old-fashioned taverns decreased, coffee-houses multiplied in number, "the College of Physicians recommending coffee as a wholesome beverage," until in the beginning of the present century they exceeded 9000 in the city of London and its suburbs.

The customs of the English coffee-house were simple. The guest paid a penny on entering, for which he was entitled to a cup of coffee and a comfortable nap over the dull journals of the day. Sometimes there were open tables, as nowadays in France, but the exclusive Englishman generally preferred a box of his own, and the coffee-rooms were partitioned after the fashion of the old oyster boxes with which the passing generation was once familiar.

The English coffee-house was at its zenith in the beginning of this century; since then it has gradually declined; but in all of the sea-board and many of the inland towns a coffee-room is to be found in all the hostelries. The gentry occasionally frequented them even in this century; but the commercial class who drove their own traps had, with their continued custom and more liberal pay, usurped all the best places, the warmest nooks, the choicest waiters, the most careful hostlers, and even the prettiest chamber-maids. This led to a division of these accommodations into coffee-rooms and commercial rooms. There is a sad complaint on this subject by a contributor to *Notes and Queries*, none the less amusing for the vanity the writer betrays in the contentment he expresses that, though he wore a "tourist suit," he was still taken for something better than a commercial traveller, and was shown into the coffee-room. He preferred the second-class fare in this aristocratic quarter to all the luxuries with which the "commercial gents" were favored.

From England the use of coffee-houses soon passed to her American colonies. Drake, in his *History of Boston*, makes mention of the "London Coffee-House," at which books were sold in 1689. Watson, in his *Annals of Philadelphia*, locates a coffee-house in the neighborhood of Front and Walnut streets, at which a Common Council of the city was held in 1704. The first coffee-house in New York was probably established as early as either of these, as there is mention made in the report of the trial of Colonel Bayard—charged with high treason, for his participation in the Leister troubles—of a meeting of a number of citizens at the Coffee-House. This was in 1701. It appears by the evidence that a petition was signed in "the upper room," and that Colonel Bayard was present, "smoaking a Pipe of Tobacco." The Journal of the General Assembly of the Colony of New York for the following year contains a notice that the conference committee of the Council and Assembly will meet at the Coffee-House October 4, 1705; and it appears from an examination of this document that all such committees were there held until June, 1709, after which they are recorded at different taverns until 1732, when the Coffee-House again appears on the minutes as their place of meeting.

From the journals of the Council and Assembly until the printing of the newspapers, the first of which, *The New-York Gazette*, was begun in 1725, there is no intermediate field for research. Unfortunately there were but few advertisements in the earlier years. The world had not yet learned the lesson which newspapers have since taught us to consider a cardinal faith, that the only road to success (their own included) is through advertising. This as it may be. The earliest notice of a coffee-house in the newspapers appears in *The New-York Gazette* of July 28 to August 11, 1729, as the spot "where a competent book-keeper may be heard of." The first which by its context offers a clew to the location of the building is an advertisement in this same journal, March 1, 1730, of a sale of land by public vendue at the Exchange Coffee-House. Lyne's map of the city in 1728 shows that the Exchange was then at the foot of Broad Street. The increase of the city, and the natural attractions of the river-side for a population who were with few exceptions engaged in trade, had caused a gradual movement in an easterly direction, and the centre of business had passed from the Whitehall slip to the Great Dock and the market-house near by. This building, constructed in 1690-1, and for many years used as a shambles, had been repaired, and becoming the resort of traders in commodities as well as sellers of food, gradually acquired the name of the Exchange. This was the first, or Old Exchange. The building stood in the middle of the street, as was the custom of the period.' It would be difficult to find an example of any public building otherwise located. The few views of the city which remain agree in exhibiting it as an

OLD BRIDGE AND DOCK AT THE WHITEHALL SLIP.

open structure, probably only a roof erected upon pillars as a shelter from the elements. Its front foundation rested on the sea-wall. Before it was a wooden projection extending over the water in a straight line, which took the name of the Long Bridge, and divided the Great Dock into two sections, which were known as the East and West docks. The Great Dock was a wharf front extending from the Whitehall to Countess Slip (Coenties Slip), and facing a large basin, which was protected from the sea by a semicircular exterior breakwater. This great basin was the favorite anchorage for vessels, which were less exposed here than at the older wharf by the Whitehall. The buildings on the water-front rapidly grew in favor with the maritime portion of the community, and petty taverns for the accommodation of captains and sailors sprung up along the wharf—a delightful spot, with its southern exposure overlooking the beautiful surface of the bay, spotted with the islands of green, and fanned by the soft breezes which drew in from the sea. The Exchange Coffee-House was no doubt in this neighborhood, but the habits of New York innkeepers were too migratory to warrant an assumption that it was in the precise spot where it will be found a few years later. In 1732 the call for the meeting of the conference committee of the Council and Assembly at "the Coffee-House" seems to imply that there was but

one establishment of the kind in the city. In 1733 an advertisement in *The New-York Gazette* requests the return of "lost sleeve buttons to Mr. Todd, next door to the Coffee-House." Robert Todd was a vintner and popular tavern-keeper of the day. He kept the famous Black Horse Tavern, where the great ball in honor of the birthday of Frederick, Prince of Wales, was given in January, 1736. This tavern was that year in Smith (now William) Street, near the Old Dutch Church, but it seems more probable that he had removed his sign from next door to the Coffee-House to this then remote quarter of the city, than that the Coffee-House should have been so far distant from the business centre. In the early part of the last century all the principal inhabitants, with the exception of the Governor of the Province, his suite, and the officers of the navy and army, were in some manner connected with trade, and many of these were glad to find brides and fortunes in the ranks of the solid merchant families of Dutch or English stock. The professions afforded a narrow field of employment, and their members could hardly have maintained a home of their own. With these suggestions the balance of probabilities must now be left.

Wherever located, the Coffee-House was the favorite resort of the magnates of the time; not, as in England a few years previously, "a lay conventicle," or hot-bed of sedition, but the gathering-place of the friends of church and state, and of the ruling administration of the colony—the "courtiers," as they were termed by their dispute, I really was not only surprised but shocked to hear men of good sense talk after the manner they did; and one of their great men expressed himself in

Numb. 425

THE
New-York Gazette,

From *December* 10, to Monday *December* 17. 1733.

Copenhagen. October 3.
COURIER arrived this Morning from Paris with Dispatches from the Ambassador of France, and for also Margoulyel...

If there be Wind enough to blow out a double Watch Candle, it will raise 40, 50 or 60 Hogsheads of Water in an Hour, and continues this constantly to act by Day and Night...

FAC-SIMILE OF HEADING OF "THE NEW-YORK GAZETTE" FOR DECEMBER 17, 1733.

adversaries, the Dissenters and republicans. The journals of 1734, Bradford's *New-York Gazette*, the government organ, and Zenger's *New-York Weekly Journal*, the mouth-piece of the opposition, are full of this strife. A correspondent of Zenger, one Andrew Merrill, reciting his experience in public places, writes on the 15th of March of this year that the "next company he got into were all courtiers; the first evening or two passed agreeably enough, but when they entered into party the following manner: 'What! shall a parcel of mob and canaille, and especially a Dutch mob, pretend to censure the actions of those his Excellency has intrusted with power?'" To this, a few days later, a correspondent replies through *The New-York Gazette*, under the *nom de plume* of Peter Scheme: "If you please, Mr. Bradford, and you may publish it to the world, and then Mr. Zenger will know, that I also frequent the Coffee-House, to take a hitt at Back-Gammon, when I have

Numb. VII.

THE
New-York Weekly JOURNAL.

Containing the freshest Advices, Foreign, and Domestick.

MUNDAY December 17, 1733.

Mr. Zenger;

AM told your Encouragement much, far exceeded your...

WILLIAM LIGGET late of Boston, Mariner, aged about 22 Years...
on
eth. That...

FAC-SIMILE OF HEADING OF "THE NEW-YORK WEEKLY JOURNAL" FOR DECEMBER 17, 1733.

the opportunity of hearing the curious sentiments of the Courtiers (since he is pleased to call the gentlemen who frequent that place so) concerning his journal," and continues in defense of his friends and heavy satire of the opposition. Party spirit ran high, and the court party was driven to madness by the squibs, ballads, and serious charges of the democratic journal, which by no means confined itself within the bounds of polite polemics. Colonel Harrison, the Recorder, who had felt the lash of the independent journal, threatened to "lay his cane over the back" of Mr. Zenger, who replied, with that courage for which New York editors have always been celebrated, "that he wore his sword at his side." Intimidation failing, an Order of Council commanded that certain numbers of the obnoxious journal, which included the scurrilous articles, should "be burned by the hands of the common hangman or whipper, near the pillory," as seditious and libellous. But the court refused to grant the order to the sheriff (an officer under their control) to carry out this command, and even forbade his underling, the whipper, to obey it, and his place was supplied by a negro slave of the sheriff. A few days later, Zenger, the obnoxious printer, was thrown into jail.

In the spring of 1735, Zenger was tried, when Mr. Andrew Hamilton, of Philadelphia, a lawyer of repute and of great eloquence, surprised the court and the city by appearing in his defense. The case was carried on with brilliancy and vigor, and the jury brought in a verdict of not guilty, which was greeted with a storm of applause. The judge from the bench threatened the leader of the tumult with imprisonment, when Captain Norris, of the Royal Navy, declared himself the leader, and invited a new round of approbation. Captain Norris was a son-in-law of Colonel Lewis Morris, then in England. Mr. Hamilton was entertained in great state at dinner after the trial, and followed the next morning, on his departure for Philadelphia, by the whole population of the city. A short time later he was presented with the freedom of the city, by the corporation, in a gold box. The old race struggle between the descendants of the old Dutch families and those of the English usurpers, allayed by the accession of William of Orange and the establishment of the Protestant succession, had been re-

vived by the insolent arrogance of the English Governor, and popular sympathy was all with Van Dam in his struggle with Cosby. Van Dam, as senior Councillor of the Province, had become the President of the Council and acting Governor of the Province on the death of Governor Montgomerie in 1731, and had been recently displaced by the appointment, in 1732, of Governor Cosby, whom historians of all parties agree in considering an indiscreet and unsafe magistrate. Religious antipathies slumbered in embers, ready to break into blaze at the slightest breeze, and continued a perpetual element in party divisions, although the Church of England had remained quiet since the accession of George II., and the government, under Walpole's wise administration, had held both Jacobites and Dissenters in check with temperate balance.

To these causes of discord was added the struggle for power between rival families, which for a century contended for the control of the colony and the patronage of its administration. On the one hand, the thoroughly English High-Church party, led by the young, accomplished, and versatile James De Lancey, whose sympathies, notwithstanding his half-French, half-Dutch parentage (his father was a Huguenot emigrant, and his mother a Van Cortlandt), were wholly with the crown, and under his leadership the families of Walton, Cruger, Watts, Phillipse, Barclay, with their intermarriages and English alliances. On the other, the Presbyterians and dissenting element were marshalled under the veteran Colonel Lewis Morris, a man of uncommon vigor of mind and tenacity of purpose, skilled in the art of government and the management of mankind. In his support were William Livingston and James Alexander, both, like himself, large landed proprietors, representing the "country party," and William Smith, an active and adroit politician, and behind them the great republican element.

At this period the Church party and the De Lanceys had the upper hand. Morris, who had been made Chief Justice of the Province in 1702, had been displaced to make room for De Lancey. His own personal grievances he redressed by a visit to England, where, through his own personal abilities, and the influence of his family connections, his wife being a Graham, nearly allied with the Earl of Montrose,

THE EXCHANGE, FOOT OF BROAD STREET, 1752.

and his daughter married to a son of Admiral Sir John Norris, he obtained the separation of the government of New Jersey from New York, and secured for himself the appointment of Governor of the former colony, in which he was largely interested. He had inherited a large landed estate, covering the county of Monmouth, and was at this time the president of the Council of Proprietors. The republicans did not fare as well. Alexander and Smith were driven from their seats as judges, and the liberal party lost all power. From this time until the separation from the mother country the Church party ruled the city, and divided all the patronage of the government—of little advantage to them in the end, as gratitude for these benefits naturally attached them to the crown, and secured their loyalty or neutrality during the Revolutionary struggle. At the close, loyalty brought confiscation of their estates, and neutrality involved distrust and a long deprivation of political influence and honors, while the Livingstons and the Morrises enjoyed the highest positions of trust and power.

In 1737 the Exchange Coffee-House was next door to the Fighting Cocks—a tavern which appears, from the evidence in the trial at the time of that popular delusion and frenzy known as the Negro Plot, to have been kept by John Croker in 1740, by the Long Bridge. The advertisement in 1737 of Broadway lands for sale at public vendue or outcry shows that the Coffee-House was the public place of congregation. Till the close of the last, and indeed during the first quarter of the present, century, nearly all the auctions were held at the Coffee-House; the finer fabrics and articles of delicate texture were sold within, heavier merchandise from the adjoining pavement. The Coffee-House now disappears from the newspapers for several years, coming to view again in 1748, in a notice of Cheshire cheese to be sold at the Great Dock, next door to the Exchange Coffee-House. This is the first distinct location. In 1749 Andrew Ramsay opened it next door to where Mr. Cox lately kept it, and promises the old patrons of the house the best entertainment. In 1750 it was known as the Gentlemen's and Exchange Coffee-House and Tavern, "continued to be kept at the sign of the King's Arms, in the same house

FOOT OF WALL STREET AND FERRY-HOUSE, 1679.

which was kept by Andrew Ramsay, near the Long Bridge." The next year the sign was altered, and removed to Broadway, where Benjamin Pain, an old tavern-keeper from "Cruger's Wharf," at the Old Slip, announced it as the Gentlemen's Coffee-House and Tavern. In 1753 the Gentlemen's Coffee-House had migrated to Hunter's Quay, the waterline, now Front Street, between the Old Slip and Wall Street, and Mr. Payne, as he then styled himself, was selling choice Madeira, Geneva, arrack, tea, and sugars from his house opposite the Old Slip Market, at the sign of Admiral Warren.

In those primitive days, before cities were as plenty as taverns in this young country, the highest compliment that could be paid to a hero was to put his head on a tavern sign. An intermediate step, perhaps, was the naming of streets in honor of the favorite. Sir Peter Warren, whose famous exploit in the capture of Louisburg was still fresh in the memory of New-Yorkers who took part in the action, was twice favored—his head hung on a tavern sign, and his name is perpetuated in a well-known street of the city. After this period we hear no more of the Gentlemen's Coffee-House.

The Old Exchange has been described as thoroughly as the brief casual notices which the newspapers supply admitted. Fortunately there is more abundant material for an account of the building which was erected on its site in 1752. This edifice, known as the New Exchange, or Royal Exchange, was raised upon arches, above which was a large hall sixty feet by thirty, with walls fourteen feet high,

which arched to an elevation of twenty feet. The building was surmounted by a cupola. The room above was at first used as a store by Oliver De Lancey, a merchant of the city, who hired it on its completion in 1753, but in 1754 it passed into the hands of Keen and Lightfoot, who opened it on the 4th of February as a coffee-room, with a ball-room annexed. It is not certain, but probable, that a part of the open space below, which served as an exchange and thoroughfare, was at this time inclosed. In 1756 the partnership of William Keen and Alexander Lightfoot was broken up, and Lightfoot continued the coffee-room in his own name. Upon his death in 1757, his widow, Sarah, obtained a renewal of the lease of the building from the corporation of the city upon the old terms—£40 per annum—but the next year the rent was raised to £54, and it passed to the hands of Mr. Roper Dawson for a term of three years, and was restored by him to its original use—a mercantile house.

Meanwhile a rival had risen in the Merchants' Coffee-House, the history of which covers a long period full of incident and interest. Before passing to it, mention may be made of the Whitehall Coffee-House, opened by Rogers and Humphreys in 1762, whose first advertisement is of value as showing the true purposes of public-houses of this kind. They announce that "a correspondence is settled in London and Bristol to remit by every opportunity all the public prints and pamphlets as soon as published; and there will be a weekly supply of New York, Boston, and other American papers."

The Merchants' Coffee-House is first named in a notice of the 7th of November, 1743, of a house for sale, which appears (the preceding numbers of the journal being missing), in Parker's *Weekly Post Boy* of the 16th of January, 1744. The files of newspapers before this period are so incomplete that no mention remains of the opening of this house in the scattered numbers to be found in our public libraries. Its location, however, is beyond question. It stood on the southeast corner of Wall and Queen (now Water) streets, on a site familiar to New-Yorkers as that for many years occupied by the *Journal of Commerce*. The original site, with additional land on Water and Wall streets, is now covered by a five-story building of brick with granite facings, known as Nos. 91 and 93 Wall Street.

An interesting description of the style of building at this period remains in the sketch of New York by Professor Peter Kalm, a Swede, who travelled through the colonies in 1748. "Most of the houses," he says, "are of brick, and several stories high. Some had, according to old architecture, the gable end toward the street, but the new were altered in this respect. Many of the houses had a balcony on the roof, in which the people used to sit in the evenings in the summer season; these

cordance with the few remains of old architecture now existing, and no doubt accurately describes the Merchants' Coffee-House. In an advertisement of lease in 1775 it appears as a building three stories in height, and of depth enough to allow of a large store on the lower story, as well as a long-room—an indispensable part of a great public-house—on the second floor. Adjoining it was a small tenement, the lower part of which was probably used as a kitchen, and the upper as one of the noted insurance offices of the city. On the front of the house was a piazza, and on the side a platform, which served as a stand for the auctioneers, who held their sales on the bridge close by. Over the piazza a balcony.

THE PRESS-GANG IN NEW YORK.

roofs were covered with tiles or shingles of wood of the white-fir tree. The walls were covered with all sorts of drawings and pictures in small frames. On each side of the chimney they had usually an alcove, and the wall under the windows wainscoted, and had benches placed under it. The alcoves and all wood-work painted a bluish-gray." Such luxuries as hangings were unknown. This is in ac-

At the time when the coffee-house first appears, New York was in a thriving condition. Party rage, which had distracted the province to such an extent that Governor Clarke wrote to the Board of Trade of "an almost total suspension of ship-building, of houses empty for want of tenants," and of an exodus of the inhabitants, was now assuaged, and the war with France gave new life to the city.

The trade of New York in 1747 was chiefly with England and the West India Islands. England supplied the colonies with European and India goods and silk manufactures, receiving in return provisions, hides, snuff; Ireland sent over linens and canvas, and carried back flax and staves; the West Indies took flour and staves, for which they returned rum, sugar, and molasses. And there was a brisk trade with Madeira and the Canary Islands in wines and grain, while an occasional venture to the African coast brought in a cargo of negroes. These various branches of commerce employed in 1746 ninety-nine vessels of 4513 tons, and were manned by 755 seamen. The population at the same date was 9253, of which 2464 were negroes.

It is pleasant to record that even at this early day New York displayed the large and liberal spirit which has since distinguished her history. The Jews, maltreated in all parts of Europe, here enjoyed all the privileges common to other inhabitants. In 1748 Kalm reports that they had "houses and great country-seats of their own, and owned ships, in which they freighted and sent out their own goods." And he adds the more curious statement, that both the men and women dressed after the English fashion. The bonnets and long fur-trimmed cloaks which may still be seen on the streets of Frankfort and other German cities had given way to cocked hats, long waistcoats, and gartered hose, and in outward garb at least the Jews were no longer a "peculiar people." Many of them had been identified from an early period with the history of the colony. Some had emigrated from Holland, others from the Mediterranean. The names of Seixas, Hendricks, Judah, Gomez—all honored then as now—are evidence of their varied origin. They seem to have been among the larger merchants of the day.

But war, not commerce, was the business of the last century, and it must be admitted that a declaration of hostilities against France and Spain, and the royal command "to harass and annoy his Majesty's enemies," were always welcome to New York ears.

Then the coffee-houses were busy places, and the taverns on the docks did a thriving business. The adventurous merchants fitted out numbers of privateers on these occasions. Between 1743 and 1748 the names of no less than thirty-one vessels, ranging from ten to twenty-four guns, appear in the newspapers, which make record also of the numerous prizes brought in—cargoes of sugar from the Spanish islands, wines and brandies taken on the way from Bordeaux and Rochelle to the French colonies. These vessels were commanded and manned by the bloods of the city, who left off cock-fighting and horse-racing for the new and venturesome career. Captain John Jauncey opens the articles of the ship *Lincoln*, fourteen guns, at the Jamaica Arms. Jacobus Kierstede, who has just brought in a prize, calls on the young gentlemen to man the *Prince Charles*, which carries twenty-four guns. Samuel Bayard in the *Polly*, Abraham Kip in the *Don Carlos*, Peter Keteltas in the *Bachelors* (no doubt he had the cream of the fashion), John Lawrence in the *Rainbow*, and Thomas Seymour, of Hartford, in the *Clinton* and *Dragon* by turns, vie with one another in their inducements. Their profitable career, broken up by the peace of Aix-la-Chapelle in 1748, was resumed with fresh vigor on the renewal of hostilities by France in 1755. During the seven years' war which ensued, and is known in the history of the colonies as "the French war," which began with the disastrous defeat of Braddock, and closed with the surrender of the Canadas in 1763, the privateers were even more active than before. In 1757 there were already thirty-nine ships, carrying 128 guns, and manned by 1050 men, scouring the seas, and before January, 1758, they had brought into New York fifty-nine prizes, besides sending twenty into other ports for adjudicature. So popular was this employment that Lieutenant-Governor De Lancey wrote to the London Board of Trade, in 1758, "that men would no longer enlist in the army," and "that the country was drained of many able-bodied men by almost a kind of madness to go a-privateering." In addition to the old captains, who again hoisted their favorite flags, the names of Winthrop, Phœnix and Amory appear as commanders of vessels. Alexander McDougall and Isaac Sears, whose names are famous in the later history of the city, commanded the *Tyger* and *Decoy;* and Thomas Doran, who kept a tavern at the Fly Market, made rapid and successful ventures on the famous Sandy Hook pilot-boat the *Flying Harlequin*, which was armed to the teeth with fourteen guns, and won a fame for

FOOT OF WALL STREET AND FERRY-HOUSE, 1746.

speed as great as that of the *Wanderer* of our own day. There were other risks in privateering than those of death and capture by the enemy. Much more dreaded was the grip of the men-of-war, which spared neither friend nor foe when they wanted sailors, and pressed the privateersmen with peculiar satisfaction.

The merchants were not free from anxiety at home, and it appears that it was a matter of serious discussion at the Coffee-House in 1755 as to " whether the channel should not be made shallower for defense of the city against large ships." With the close of the war, commerce returned to its normal channels, and a period of remarkable activity began.

Now we find constant mention of men whose fame has come down to us not only as merchant princes, but as the leading spirits of this exciting period. John Alsop, Philip Livingston, and Isaac Low, all delegates to the First Continental Congress, were in the general importing business. Alsop had his store on Hanover Square, Livingston on Burnet's Quay, near the ferry stairs, Low near the Exchange. The brothers Cruger, Henry and John, were in the Bristol trade, and lived on the new wharf by the Old Slip, which bore

their name. Henry was later member of Parliament for Bristol, colleague and " Ditto" to Mr. Burke. John was the manly patriotic mayor who took the obnoxious stamps—symbols of exaction—from Lieutenant-Governor Colden; while a third brother, Nicholas, was settled at the little island of Nevis, in the West Indies. The three brothers bore the sobriquets of the Old Nick, the Old Harry, and the Old Boy. John, the Old Boy, was a bachelor. Gerard William Beekman confined himself to dry-goods in Dock Street, while James imported European and India goods, and sold them at his store in Queen Street. Walter and Thomas Buchanan, also a great importing house, were in Queen Street, near the Fly Market. Elias Desbrosses, of Huguenot descent, whose father was a famous confectioner, lived near the Merchants' Coffee-House, toward the Fly Market, and was also in general trade. Henry Remsen, Jun., later the patriotic chairman of the Committee of Safety, carried on the dry-goods trade in Hanover Square, and near him were the brothers McEvers, in the same line of business. Sampson and Solomon Simson, the leading Jewish merchants of the city, were in the general shipping and grocery trade in

Stone Street. The vendue masters clustered about the Coffee-House. Moore and Lynsen, Patrick McDavitt, and Daniel McCormick were in Wall Street. Hoffman and Ludlow in Dock Street (Pearl Street). Insurances were made in a primitive way at the Coffee-House at fixed hours, or at the new office established next door in 1759. The Waltons had their extensive ship-yards on the East River, and their residence in the well-known house on St. George's Square (now Franklin Square). Gerardus Duyckinck introduced displayed advertisements of "the universal store" at the sign of the Looking-Glass and Druggist Pot, in Dock Street, at the corner of the Old Slip Market, where he sold drugs, medicines, and stationery; and William Brownejohn, from London, who later purchased the Merchants' Coffee-House, was selling medicines next door, and by careful investment accumulating a large landed estate. The Bayards, who had introduced the "mystery of sugar refining," as they termed it, in 1730, had their refinery in Wall Street; Isaac Roosevelt, another, in Skinners Street, near Franklin Square, and his sale office in Wall Street. The Lispenards had a large brewery on the North River, and the Rutgers a similar establishment on the East River.

The year 1765 was a memorable one in the history of the city. In spite of the earnest remonstrances of the colonies, Parliament passed the Stamp Act. At the call of New York a Congress met in the city, and the colonies united in a resolve to resist its execution; and adding action to resolve, the merchants solemnly entered into an agreement on the 31st of October not to make any importations from Great Britain until the act should be repealed. This agreement was signed at the house kept by George Burns—the Province, or New York, Arms. The De Lancey House, converted into a tavern by Edward Willet in 1754, was taken by George Burns in 1763, and at this time occupied by him. The house stood on the site later known as that of the City Hotel. The next day was one of great popular excitement. The citizens gathered in mass, paraded through the streets, and burned the effigy of Governor Colden under the guns of the fort, then turning, marched to the Vauxhall, the residence of Major James, of the Royal Army, and sacked it of its furniture, which they destroyed. "The

next day a paper was read from the balcony of the Coffee-House, calling upon the inhabitants to suppress riots; but Isaac Sears, the old privateersman—a popular favorite and leader—addressed the people, and told them that this call upon them was only to prevent their gaining possession of the stamps." A few days later the stamps were surrendered to the mayor, and quiet was restored. By whom the Merchants' Coffee-House was kept during the twenty-five years that have come under notice it has not been possible to ascertain. Incidentally the name of Alexander Smith appears "in from the Coffee-House." He opened a tavern in the Fields (near the Park) in 1766. A widow Smith lived in the small building in the rear of the Coffee-House in 1759, and Anthony Van Dam had his insurance office there, but there is no connecting link between herself and the Alexander mentioned. One Richard Smith bought the Coffee-House of John Theobalds, the son of the old captain, on April 2, 1761; but as he sold it on the 8th of this same month to Samuel Stillwell, there seems no probability that it was more than a speculative purchase. He appears, moreover, as a merchant, which innkeepers were never called.

In January, 1770, the great subject of public interest was whether the ballot should be open or secret, a matter discussed by the independent freeholders and freemen of the city at a mid-day meeting at the Coffee-House on the 5th. The opponents of the secret ballot adroitly put their opinions in their call. They propose to "convince their Representatives in the Assembly, when the subject was under debate, that they are not to be diverted by any motives whatever from daring and choosing to speak their minds freely and openly, to do which at all times is their birthright as Englishmen and their glory as freemen." Macchiavelli himself could not have stated the case more cleverly.

This year, again, is noted for the excitement in the colonies with regard to the non-importation agreement. Ever since 1768 there had been an effort by the colonies to retaliate upon Great Britain by a refusal to receive any of the goods upon which the bill introduced by Townshend in 1766 had imposed duties, chief among which was tea. New York was warm in adhesion to the scheme, but it appearing in 1770 that the agreement had only been observed partially in the other colonies, her merchants became restive, and refused any longer to be bound by it, and called upon the colonies to send delegates to meet her own in general Congress.

These debates were generally held in the Coffee-House, and the newspapers are full of calls for committees and minutes of their sessions.

In 1771, Dr. William Brownejohn, who was then the owner of the building, which he had purchased from Samuel Stillwell in 1762, offered it for sale, with the "small adjoining tenement" which has been alluded to. It is described as occupied by Mrs. Mary Ferrara, widow. Mary Ferrara, or Ferrari, was the widow of Francis Ferrari, merchant and ship-owner, who died at St. Eustatia in 1753. From his will there is a reasonable presumption that he was from Geneva, though the name is Italian. In 1776 she was living in Maiden Lane, so that her stay in the Merchants' Coffee-House had not been of very long duration. The proposal to sell the Coffee-House did not meet with success. The next year (1772) Mrs. Ferrari leaves the old house, and opens a new coffee-house on the opposite cross corner, where a new building had been erected on the site now occupied by the Tontine Building. As she announces that the gentlemen of the two insurance offices are likewise removed from the old to the new Coffee House, it is probable the attraction of the old hostess and the new house were too strong for the mercurial New-Yorkers, always ready for novelties of every kind. Tavern-keeping was too favored a profession for a house to be long without a tenant, and Mr. Brownejohn was not a man to let his house lie unoccupied. When Madame Ferrari went out, Elizabeth Wragg came in. The house is said to be "now fitted up in the most neat and commodious manner." Breakfast was promised, and relishes at all hours, and coffee as usual. In 1773, Nesbitt Deane, a hatter from Dublin, was in possession of the house, and advertises lodgings suitable for gentlemen either of divinity, law, or physic, and fit for a notary public or insurance office, as well as a part of the lower part of the house for a large store. Deane was an eccentric creature, if any judgment can be formed of him from his puffs. "His hats," he says, "are manufactured to exceed in fineness, cut, color, and cock, and

by a method peculiar to himself to turn rain, and prevent the sweat of the head damaging the crown." If Mrs. Wragg remained in the house, as is somewhat uncertain, the coffee-room was evidently restricted in proportions. This year the noted Major James, of Stamp Act memory, sold out his house in Wall Street by public vendue at the Merchants' Coffee-House, and his stylish black coach-horses changed hands at the same place. This is mentioned to show that this remained the preferred locality for auctions, even when the Coffee-House had lost its prestige. Yet the old house was still the daily resort, and now became the scene of grave and important events.

The political crisis averted in 1766 by the influence of Pitt and the yielding of the Ministry was again, through the dogged obstinacy of the King and the weak subserviency of Lord North, rapidly drawing to a head. The East India Company's ships, with their cargoes of tea, were announced as on the way, and there were rumors that merchants would be found ready to accept the shipments. This was contrary to the agreement of non-importation, which, relaxed in other respects, was continued as to tea. The 11th November, 1773, written notices were posted at the Coffee-House, menacing destruction to any one who should "accept of the commission, or be in any way accessory thereto." On the 16th December, at a great meeting called at the City Hall, resolutions were passed not to permit the landing of the tea. A few days later, news came from Boston that the tea vessels arrived there had been boarded, and their contents thrown into the sea. Throughout the winter the citizens of New York were anxiously awaiting the arrival of the *Nancy*, Captain Lockyer, with the cargo destined to try their constancy. This vessel, which sailed in company with those for Boston, Philadelphia, and Charleston, had met with adverse winds, and been driven off the coast as far south as Antigua. She reached the Hook on the 18th of April, 1774, but was not permitted to come up to the city, the pilots being instructed not to take her in hand. The Sons of Liberty, who had organized in November, 1773, to meet every Thursday evening at the house of Mr. Jasper Drake, now kept a watch on the vessel, but permitted Captain Lockyer to come up to the city to obtain supplies.

Although Captain Lockyer was treated with entire courtesy, it was determined that he should witness the feeling which existed in the city, and public notice was given that the people would meet in convention to witness his departure. · Accordingly, on Saturday, the 30th April, at eight o'clock, all the bells in the city were rung. "About nine the greatest number of people were collected at or near the Coffee-House that was ever known in this city. At a quarter past nine the committee of the Sons of Liberty who had Captain Lockyer in charge came out of the Coffee-House. He was taken to the end of Murray's Wharf, at the foot of Wall Street, near by, and put on board the pilot-boat, amid the music of bands, the huzzas of the people, and the firing of guns. He joined his ship at the Hook, and put to sea next morning, carrying with him Captain Chambers, of the *London*, who had attempted to smuggle eighteen chests of the forbidden article. His ship had been boarded the evening previous and the tea destroyed. Fortunately Captain Chambers, whose conduct seems to have been marked by great duplicity, prudently concealed himself. Had he been found, in the excited state of public feeling, his life would have been in danger.

On the 12th of June the packet-ship *Samson* brought out copies of the bill closing the port of Boston, and a few days later the resolutions of the Bostonians urging the colonies to renew their old non-importation agreement. A public meeting was called at Francis' Tavern on the evening of the 16th. The attendance being too large for the rooms of Mr. Francis, the meeting adjourned to the Exchange. There was a sharp struggle for leadership between the mechanics and radicals, led by Isaac Sears, and the more staid and orderly merchants. The merchants prevailed, and their influence predominated in the Committee of Correspondence which was then appointed. That there might be no doubt of the distinct settlement of this disputed point of control, a subsequent meeting was called at the Coffee-House the 19th instant, at which the choice of the 16th was confirmed by a large majority. Gouverneur Morris describes this meeting as a "grand division of the city." He writes to his friend Penn: "I stood in the balcony, and on my right hand were ranged all the people of property, with some few very

poor dependents, and on the other all the tradesmen, etc., who thought it worth their while to leave daily labor for the good of the country." Fortunately for the colonies, the committee was composed of men of sense, decision, and courage. Reviewing the history of the non-importation agreements, which, except in the beginning, had failed, because unequally observed, they insisted upon a Congress which should have power not only to recommend measures, but to enforce compliance. Boston resisted until necessity compelled her to accept the plan of a Congress, and New York is justly entitled to the credit of having laid the corner-stone of the American Union.

Events now hurried on in quick succession. Wednesday, the 15th June, being the day on which the port of Boston was closed and the harbor shut, a "very great number of the friends of American liberty in the city procured the effigies" of Hutchinson, Lord North, and Wedderburn, whom they considered "most unfriendly to the rights of America in general," and raising them upon a gallows, with an effigy of the devil on their right hand, carried them through the principal streets of the city (from the Fields through Broadway, Queen, and Wall streets), and thence to the Coffee-House, where they were attended in the evening of that day, "it is thought, by the greatest concourse of spectators ever seen on a similar occasion, and there destroyed by sulphureous flames," after which the multitude dispersed in the most orderly manner. In this the citizens showed their sympathy for Massachusetts and Pennsylvania. Hutchinson had been the unpopular Governor of the one colony, and Pennsylvania had been insulted by the insolent Solicitor Wedderburn in the person of the venerable Franklin, who had sought to expostulate with the Ministry and avert the calamity of war.

The Committee of Correspondence held its sessions at the Coffee-House during the summer, and nominated the delegates to the proposed Congress. The delegates hesitated to accept the trust until the sentiments of the city were definitely ascertained. The New England party, who were set upon non-importation (at this time Massachusetts did not dream of a political union), required a pledge from the candidates that they would support such an agreement in the Congress. To

THEOPHYLACT BACHE SAVING GRAYDON FROM THE MOB IN 1776.

this, Livingston, Alsop, Low, and Jay replied "that they favored a general non-importation agreement *faithfully observed*," and carefully avoided pledging themselves further than "to support every measure in the proposed Congress that may then be thought conducive to the general interest of the colonies." This seems to have satisfied the radicals, and the delegates received the unanimous vote of the city, taken by poll lists in each ward. So New York entered with one accord into the preliminary struggle.

In 1775 Mr. Nesbitt Deane again advertises the two upper stories of the old Coffee-House as to let. He describes the premises "as being so pleasantly situated that a person can see at once the river, shipping, Long Island, and all the gentlemen resorting to the Coffee-House on business from the most distant climes." But so far as the latter part of the puff is concerned, there was more fancy than fact. The non-importation agreement or association recommended by Congress had been carefully enforced by the Committee of Inspection, and the commerce of the city was wholly suspended. The Coffee-House seems to have been almost deserted. "A Friend to the City" publishes an ad-

dress to the inhabitants of New York on the 19th October, urging them to support at least one coffee-house. He says that he is concerned, "in this time of difficulty and danger, to find that there is no place of daily general meeting." He observes with surprise that so good and comfortable a house, extremely well tended and accommodated, should be frequented but by an inconsiderable number of people, and, what was more to the purpose, that but a small part of those who do frequent it contribute anything at all to the expense of it, but come in and go out without calling for or paying anything to the house. He adds that in all the coffee-houses in London it is customary for every one that comes in to call for at least a dish of coffee, or leave the price of one. He then pleads the cause of the worthy woman who keeps the house, and after saying that the fires and candles are not lighted as usual, predicts that unless some change take place, the house must be shut. No better evidence could be given of the distress brought upon the city by the entire suspension of trade, which was its sole life and occupation.

In the winter and spring of 1776 the American army occupied the city, and some of the patriots seem to have indulged the hope that it might be permanently held. Such must have been the opinion of Cornelius Bradford, who engaged the Merchants' Coffee-House in May, and announced his intention "of keeping it in a manner to give satisfaction, and to give the greatest attention to the arrival of vessels when trade and navigation should resume their former channels." Cornelius Bradford was a warm patriot, and appears to have been the confidential express messenger between the Sons of Liberty in New York and the association in Philadelphia, as Paul Revere was between Boston and New York. His tenure of the house was of short duration, and he left with the troops when Washington evacuated the city in September. The presence of the British army gave a new life to taverns and other public-houses. Such of the merchants as were either distinctly loyal or neutral in feeling—and there were many whose close alliance with English families, or imperious considerations of personal interest, brought within the latter class—continued to frequent the Coffee-House. There remains on record a pleasing incident, of the kindly feeling which governed some of their number, in the account given by Captain Alexander Graydon, of the patriot army, who was taken prisoner at the battle of Harlem Heights. Passing the Coffee-House, he was insulted by some of the royalist mob, when Mr. Theophylact Bache and other gentlemen who happened to be sitting there came out and interfered for his protection.

In 1779, at the request of the military commandant, such of the members of the Chamber of Commerce as had remained in the city resumed their sessions, which had been suspended since 1775, and their old room over the Exchange being used for other purposes, engaged the Long Room of the Coffee-House, where they continued to meet until the close of the war. From 1779 to 1781 one Mrs. Smith was their hostess. In 1781 James Strachan, who had kept the Queen's Head Tavern on the dock, which seems to have been a favorite resort of the gentlemen of the navy and army, tries his fortune in the old building, where he promises "to pay attention not only as a coffee-house, but as a tavern in the truest sense, and to distinguish the same as the City Tavern and Coffee-House, with constant and best attendance. Breakfasts from seven to eleven. Soups and relishes from eleven to half past one. Tea, coffee, etc., in the afternoon, as in England." He hung up little bags for the correspondence with England by the British men-of-war, and levied a tax of sixpence sterling for each letter, which brought such a storm about his ears that he was compelled to apologize in the public prints, and to refund the sums received, which the captains of his Majesty's ships the *Robust* and *Janus* announce as amounting to £19. Although he had a fair share of patronage, the Chamber of Commerce taking the Long Room by the year, and the societies meeting here, the Loyal Sons of St. Andrew celebrating their anniversaries, and the Ancient York Masons holding the great festival of St. John the Baptist at his rooms, Strachan was not successful in his venture, and in 1783 made a piteous appeal to those who were in his debt to settle their accounts. A few months later the exiled patriots returned to the city, and Cornelius Bradford, who had lived near Rhinebeck during the occupation, again took possession of the house, which he announces as the New York Coffee-House. He seems to have been a man of vigorous and original mind, and by the various attractions he devised soon made the old stand the centre of business. He opened a book in which he entered the names of all vessels on their arrival and departure from the port, with such extracts from their logs as were of interest or value, which was the first marine list ever undertaken in the city. He also opened a city register, in which the merchants and others were requested to enter their names and residences—the first approach to a city directory ever made. The Exchange at the foot of Broad Street having fallen from its high estate as a meeting-place of merchants to an ordinary market-house, the Coffee-House became the rendezvous of merchants and traders, while the bridge at the side of the building in Wall Street was the daily scene of vendues of all kinds, from sheriffs' sales of houses and lands to the disposal by licensed auctioneers of cargoes of merchandise, invoices of dry-goods, and even horses and carriages. The neighborhood resumed its importance. Daniel Phœnix returned to his old residence in Water Street, opposite the lower end of the Coffee-house Bridge on the Wall Street corner, and opened an auction-room, the insurance office occupying the second floor. Below as well as above Water Street both sides of Wall were occupied by auction stores, and took the name of "the Merchants' Promenade, or the Auctioneers' Row." The brick building in Wall Street, No. 34, next door to the Coffee-House, was used on the first floor as a store by Richard Platt, and above as a notary public, conveyancing, and attorney's office by James M. Hughes. Next door to the Coffee-House, in Water Street, John Simnet, the watch-maker, who came to New York from Clerkenwell, near London, in 1764, and had been driven "by the

THE TONTINE COFFEE-HOUSE.

temper of war" to Albany, again hung out the sign of the dial from the elegant projecting window. In his window he exposed a regulator to view—a curious dial-plate twenty inches in diameter. On the opposite corner of Water Street, Shepard Kollock published the New York *Gazetteer and Country Journal*.

The Bank of New York, the first institution of the kind in the city, was projected in the Merchants' Coffee-House (the old name clung to it, notwithstanding the attempted changes of proprietors) on the 24th February, 1784, and here also it was formally organized the March following. The societies of various kinds all reorganized under State charters after the peace, and almost without exception made the Coffee-House their head-quarters. The Chamber of Commerce and Marine Society met here regularly, the governors of the New York Hospital held their annual elections, and the societies for "promoting useful knowledge" and "for the manumission of slaves" their business meetings in some one of the rooms of the old house. The sessions of the Cincinnati were held here, and the army men patronized the old patriot on all occasions when their interest or pleasure brought them together. The Grand Lodge of the Master-Masons was also here. The national societies of St. Andrew and St. Patrick followed the universal example, and held their merry anniversaries at Brad-

ford's bountiful board. The newspapers are full of notices of these festivities. In 1784 the Masons gathered here on St. John's Day, and marched in procession to St. Paul's Chapel, where the Rev. Mr. Provost preached to them a sermon. The Marine Society entertained Congress here on the 19th January, 1785, and the Chamber of Commerce received the same distinguished guests at a formal entertainment, officially accepted by the President and Congress, the 3d February following. The toasts, thirteen in number, are full of interest as showing the sentiments then entertained. Among them appear "Free trade with all nations!" "May persecuted liberty in every quarter of the world forever find an asylum in America!" In 1785 the Governor of the State, the Chancellor, Hon. Judge Jay, and other distinguished citizens dined with the Irish citizens on the anniversary of St. Patrick, "the tutelar saint of Ireland." Evacuation-day was also celebrated at the Coffee-House, when an elegant turtle supper was given to a select party of ladies and gentlemen, the day and a number of patriotic toasts were drunk, and the evening concluded with a ball for the ladies, Isaac Gouverneur, Sen., Esq., in the chair. On the morning of the 3d November the St. Andrew's Society of the State held their anniversary assembly at Mr. Bradford's. The Scottish flag was displayed on the Coffee-House at sunrise. At twelve the election of officers was had, and the Hon. R. R. Livingston, Chancellor of the State, chosen president, Robert Lenox, secretary. The business concluded, the society, honored with the company of the Governor of the State, the Mayor and Recorder of the city, sat down to dinner. Some of the toasts are too broad to bear repetition in our day. Besides the "Land o' Cakes" and the "Land we live in," mention may be made of "All the Bonnie Lassies that kiss amang the Heather," "Robert Gib's Contract," "The Tocher of Cramond," which some antiquarian Scot must interpret to modern generations.

The next year Cornelius Bradford took final leave of his many friends. He died at the age of fifty-seven years. The New York *Packet*, in an obituary notice, explains the secret of his success. It says of him not only that he "was distinguished as a steady patriot during the arduous contest for American liberty, but that he always discovered a charitable disposition toward those who differed from him in sentiment," and adds "that the Coffee-House, under his management, was kept with great dignity both before and since the war and he revived its credit from the contempt into which it had fallen during the war."

Bradford's widow continued to keep the house until 1792, and enjoyed the patronage of the societies as usual. This was a period of unusual interest in New York. The ratification of the Federal Constitution by the State Convention of Massachusetts on the 8th February, 1788, was celebrated with great joy in New York. At sunrise a standard of the United States was "joined on the Coffee-House," on which was inscribed, "The Constitution, September 17, 1787," and at noon the old flag of Massachusetts, with the figure of a pine-tree, was hung out, with the date of her adhesion. There was a large gathering of respectable citizens, including members of Congress and the Mayor, and a repast was partaken of, which, "in the true republican style," as the report says, consisted of two articles, beef and salt fish. After dinner the usual thirteen toasts were drunk, under the fire of six guns to each toast, in honor of the States which had adopted the Constitution. Delaware, Pennsylvania, New Jersey, Connecticut, Georgia, Massachusetts, were honored in turn, and "New York, may it

soon become an additional pillar to the new roof!" It was not till July, 1788, that the ringing of bells and salutes from the fort and shipping announced the joyful news of the erection of the eleventh pillar in the adoption of the new Constitution at Poughkeepsie. The merchants at the Coffee-House, who, more than all other members of the community, felt the need of stronger protection from the national arm, "testified their joy by repeated huzzas!"

The anniversary of the surrender of Cornwallis was celebrated by the army officers with great state on the 19th October, 1788, the thirteen toasts commemorating as many interesting events in the history of the country. As an expression of general sentiment, they are worthy of reproduction.

1. The memorable 5th September, 1774. Meeting of the First Congress.
2. The memorable 17th June, 1775. Battle of Bunker Hill.
3. The memorable 4th July, 1776. Declaration of Independence.
4. The memorable 26th December, 1776. Battle of Trenton.
5. The memorable 17th October, 1777. Capture of Burgoyne.
6. The memorable 6th February, 1778. Alliance with France.
7. The memorable 16th July, 1779. Stony Point taken by General Wayne.
8. The memorable 17th January, 1781. General Morgan defeats Tarleton at Cowpens.
9. The memorable 19th October, 1781. Capture of Lord Cornwallis.
10. The memorable 3d September, 1783. Definitive treaty of peace.
11. The memorable 25th November, 1783. Final evacuation of the United States by the British.
12. The memorable 17th September, 1787. New Constitution.
13. General Washington.

In 1789, under a call headed the "Test of Patriotism," the friends of a plan for the encouragement of American manufactures met in the Long Room. Out of the meeting grew an ephemeral society, which disappeared a few years later. At the Coffee-House also met a great number of citizens on the 21st February of the same year to nominate a *merchant* to represent the State in Congress. Even before the Revolution the merchants had chafed against the interference of the lawyers, who were their stipendiaries in their affairs, and the Chamber of Commerce had been compelled to pass a resolution excluding all lawyers from membership and interference in that with which they had no concern. It is quite impossible in any reasonable limits to enter into explanation of all the incidents which occurred at this period of which the Coffee-House was the scene. Enough to pass to the crowning glory of its history. On the 23d April, 1789, a Federal salute from the Battery announced that President Washington had arrived, and was coming up the East River to the landing at Murray's Wharf. He was received at the City Coffee-House, as it is termed in the newspapers, by the Governor and the principal officers of the State, the Mayor and the principal officers of the corporation, and thence accompanied to the house prepared for his reception, with an escort of military and citizens. It is an interesting thought to imagine the feelings of the chief, who had taken the simple farewell of his officers in December, 1783, at the Whitehall slip, as he received the welcome of the nation on his landing, not far distant, as the constitutional President of a united republic. This may be held as the culminating point in the history of the Merchants' Coffee-House.

In 1792 the Tontine Coffee-House was built on the opposite cross corner, and, in almost cruel mockery to the old house, the meetings of its subscribers were held in the old and famous Long Room. Indeed, the purpose of the Tontine Building was to afford new and more ample accommodations for the merchants, and particularly for the Chamber of Commerce. In 1793 Mrs. Bradford retired. She lived in Cortlandt Street until May, 1822, when she died. She was succeeded in the old house, then 200 Water Street, by John Byrne, who opened the house as the New York Hotel, and remained there until 1798, when he crossed over to the Tontine.

The story of the Coffee-House is now closed; "old times were changed, old manners gone." The Freemasons still clung to their old rendezvous, and the Friary—a social club—held its meetings here by order of the "Father."

In 1799 the veteran Edward Bardin (a famous tavern-keeper from 1764, when he first appeared as keeping the King's Arms Tavern in the Fields, and later in various public-houses, the history of which does not belong to this sketch) endeavored to revive the flickering celebrity of the famous house. He was in possession in 1804, when the old building was destroyed in one of the most distressing calamities that had ever visited New York. A fire commenced in Front Street, No. 104, and a high wind blowing, with little assistance at hand, swept away all the houses on both sides of Front Street, and the west side of Water Street as far as Wall. Among other houses, the old Coffee-House, occupied by Edward Bardin, was totally consumed. The building was of brick, and valued at $7500.

The next year (1805) the city was visited by the yellow fever, and the house, slowly rebuilt, was only re-opened as a hotel in 1806, as the Phœnix Coffee-House, Edward Bardin resuming its control. In 1816 it was turned into the Phœnix Stores. As late as 1823 the Shades, a retail liquor store, was kept on the ground-floor, at the corner of Wall and Water. John Byrne, of whom mention has been made, died while keeper of the Tontine, in 1780, and was buried from St. Peter's Church; and old Bardin, who had witnessed all the vicissitudes of tavern-keeping from 1764 till 1816, when he retired from the Tontine, which he had kept from 1812—a period including the history of New York from the beginning of the French war to the close of the war of 1812—died, at the ripe age of eighty-nine, in 1823.

The old house is gone and forgotten, yet its record may challenge that of any building on this continent for the extent and variety of the interesting historic scenes which its walls witnessed, from the day when it was opened, with the water edge close upon its rear piazza, until its destruction, when two new blocks had been filled in to the East River, and the house by the water-side had lost its original riparian charm.

THE DUTCH FOUNDING OF
NEW YORK
(PART 2)

I

AT the outset, the venture undertaken by the West India Company was a profitable one: not on the side of trade, but on the side of war. Three great successes marked the first ten years of the Company's existence: the taking of Bahia (1624), the capture of the treasure fleet (1628), and the reduction of Pernambuco (1630). Of those three events, although the Brazilian conquests counted for more in the long-run, the capture of the plate-ships naturally made the strongest impression upon the popular mind. Indeed, that magnificent cash return upon invested patriotism is talked about relishingly in Holland even until this present day. And it is not surprising. Never has there been such a bag of treasure in modern times! Admiral Peter Heyn, leaving out of the account the vessels which he sunk with their treasure in them, brought home to Holland seventeen galleons laden with bullion and merchandise valued, according to Mr. Asher, at more than fourteen—or, according to the more conservative Mr. Brodhead, at more than twelve—millions of guilders; and the Dutch guilder of that period, it must be remembered, had a purchasing value not much less than that of our dollar of to-day. Either estimate is prodigious—and on the strength of those huge winnings the Company declared upon its paid-up capital a dividend variously estimated by the same authorities at fifty and at seventy-five per cent.

But it was not a wholesome sort of money-making. "Successful war thus poured infatuating wealth into the treasury of the West India Company," is the view that Mr. Brodhead takes of it; and he adds that when, in the ensuing year, the King of Spain made overtures to renew the truce, "the pride, the avarice, and the religious sentiment of Holland were united in continuing the war." Against the truce the Company address-

EARLIEST VIEW OF NEW AMSTERDAM, 1664

From a copperplate made by Augustyn Heermanns, who came to New Amsterdam in 1633. On the left are seen the fort, inclosing the double-roofed church built by Kieft, the prison, and the Governor's house; at the river-side are seen the gallows and whipping-post; on the extreme right is seen the hill over which Fulton Street now passes.

ed to the States-General (November 16, 1629) a formal remonstrance.

The battlings of the Dutch and the Spaniards have a distinct place in our commercial annals, because one of their

direct results was to check our commercial growth at the start. The "infatuating wealth" that poured in upon the West India Company tended to make it careless of the little colony of New Netherland, and also to make it resentful of the small return which that colony yielded upon the relatively large outlay required to keep it in running order: and so led to the adoption of the "squeezing" policy which handicapped the trade of the colonists, and in the end destroyed

their loyalty and made them welcome the change to English rule.

In a report presented to the States-General (October 23, 1629) the feeling of the Company in regard to its colony is made plain. "The people conveyed by us thither have . . . found but scanty means of livelihood up to the present time; and have not been any profit, but a drawback, to this Company. The trade carried on there in peltries is right advantageous; but, one year with another, we can at most bring home 50,000 guilders."

Yet with that return, at that time, the Company should have been well satisfied. In *The Planter's Plea,* published in London in the year 1630, the English author wrote that the colonists of New Netherland "appeared to subsist in a comfortable manner, and to promise fairly both to the state and to the undertakers." The trouble was that "the undertakers" wanted too much and wanted it too soon. In the year 1629 the population of the colony could not have exceeded 350 souls; and 350 people very well might "subsist in comfort" on an export trade of 50,000 guilders a year. The Company, in short, then and always, was greedy. By holding New Netherland as an investment rather than as a trust, by laying heavy imposts upon commerce in order to raise dividends, it throttled the trade that a less selfish policy would have left free to expand.

The one sort of private ownership in the colony that was encouraged—by the granting of little principalities to patroons, who were free within certain limitations to trade on their own account— told directly against the welfare of the mass of the colonists by creating unfair distinctions of class. It was a transplanting of feudalism to America—and feudalism did not thrive in American soil. Actually, the patroonships were bagged by an inside ring of the Company's directors—the practical value of being on the ground-floor was understood in those days quite as well as we understand it now—and the outcome of that intrinsically bad policy bred evil in two ways. It created dissension in the management of the Company's affairs at home by arraying inside private interests against the common interests of the shareholders at large; and in the colony the same private interests were arrayed against the common interests of the less favored colonists. Later, the supply of arms which the savages obtained from the patroon trading-posts—but by no means only from those sources: trading guns for peltries was so profitable an illegal transaction that everybody was keen to have a hand in it —led on directly to the horrors of the Indian wars.

II

In a word, atrociously bad government was the rule almost from the beginning until quite the end of the Dutch domination of New Netherland. Execrable administration in Holland led to execrable executive management in the colony. Excepting May (1624) and Verhulst (1625), who were little more than factors, the men sent out as governors (the official title was Director-General) wretchedly neglected or absolutely betrayed the interests which they were sworn to serve.

Kieft (1638-1646) was an easy first in that bad lot. He was an ex-bankrupt, whose bankruptcy had been of such sort that his portrait had been hung up on the town gallows. Against him, unrefuted, stood the pleasing charge of having embezzled ransom - money intrusted to him to rescue Christian captives held by the Turks. His evil work in New Netherland culminated in his provocation—by a horrid and utterly inexcusable massacre of savages—of the terrible Indian war of 1643: which brought the colony to the very verge of ruin, and which aroused so violent an outcry against him on the part of the colonists that he was recalled. In a way, justice was served out to him: he went

THE STONE CHURCH AND FORT AT THE BATTERY

NIAGARA FALLS
From an old copperplate engraving—one of the earliest known

down, his sins with him, in the wreck of the ship in which he took passage for home.

The saving salt of those days was found in the few men who stood resolutely for good government and for honest ways. They would have been called mugwumps, had that word then been available for use; and no doubt they did receive some equivalent derogatory Dutch name. The most exemplary of that small but honorable company was David Pietersz de Vries: who strove hard to avert the Indian war waged by the outrageous Kieft, and who stood as distinctly for all that was good in the colony as Kieft stood for all that was bad. Had De Vries been appointed Director, instead of Kieft, we should have been saved from the blackest crime recorded in our colonial history; and had he been continued in office, in Stuyvesant's place, the colony would not have fallen into such disorder as to give the English a mere walk-over when their time for absorbing it came. No governor could have prevented that absorption. It was inevitable. But the community

taken over from De Vries would have been far sounder morally than was that which was taken over from Stuyvesant; and therefore would have been less likely to degenerate into a nest of pirates and smugglers, as it did degenerate, during the first thirty years of English rule.

Actually, in spite of bad laws badly administered, the colony of New Netherland did make headway. This country was a rich country, and its exploitation—even under heavy handicaps—yielded a good return.

The profitable trade that was developed between New Netherland and the plantations in New England and Virginia —while immediately profitable to the Dutch—was one of the most active of the several causes which led to the wresting from the Dutch of their holding in North America. The matter is too broad in its scope to be dealt with fully here; yet am I loath to relinquish it because of the many very human touches in which it abounds.

With one scrap of ancient history

wherein the humanity still is fresh and strong I am justified in dealing: the famous case of the ship *Eendracht*—driven by stress of weather into Plymouth in the year 1632, and there seized by the English port authorities (I quote the Dutch version of the matter) "on an untrue representation that the Peltries were bought within the jurisdiction or district belonging to his majesty of Great Britain." Over that seizure there was a diplomatic squabble between Holland and England that went on for years—and the whole of it, I am persuaded, was the outcome of a love-affair! According to a letter sent by the States-General to their ambassador in England, the *Eendracht* was "seized on false information of the Provost of said ship . . . and of the Pilot who, in opposition to the Director and Skipper, being on shore got married." There is the crux of it, I am sure. But for the pilot's impetuously inopportune determination to wed the widow (I am quite certain that she was a widow, because of the eagerness of it all) he very probably could have taken the *Eendracht* out of Plymouth harbor and safe away to sea. Being ordered, no doubt, to do that very thing—and the widow ashore waiting for him!—he and his friend the provost laid the "untrue representation" which led on to those years of diplomatic blustering: but which also led to the detention of the ship at Plymouth until he was safe wed to his bouncing bride!

After all, what mattered it if Holland and England were embroiled by that brave pilot's hot-hearted indiscretion? Every man thinks first of his own happiness; and in love-affairs—it has been so from the world's beginning—he thinks of nothing else. I wish that we had the end of the story. Let us hope that his widow repaid him for his gallant defiance, for her sweet sake, of the orders of captains and directors, and that it turned out well — that sailor wedding which shook two great states to their foundations nearly three centuries ago! In all seriousness, I am justified in recalling here that only half-told and long-forgotten idyl. It had its place, the love-making of that precipitate pilot, among the causes which in time's fulness changed New Netherland and New Amsterdam into the State and city of New York.

III

Under the spur of the "remonstrances" —there were many of them—sent home by the colonists, the States-General did make some effort to deal with New Netherland on lines of equity. An official inquiry was made into the affairs of the West India Company in the year 1638 that resulted in checking some of the worst of the colonial abuses; and that also led to the promulgation (1640) of a new charter of Liberties and Exemptions which materially added to the welfare of the colony, and increased the comfort of the colonists, by relaxing the regulations under which trade was conducted and by easing the conditions under which the people lived.

Kieft, be it said to his credit, gave effect to this liberal policy in so liberal a spirit that the three ensuing years—until almost ruin came with the Indian war— probably were the most prosperous in the time of Dutch rule. Notably, he encouraged English refugees, fleeing from religious persecution in New England, to settle in New Netherland; and those settlers—maintaining relations with their friends and kinsfolk—did much to develop intercolonial trade. By the year 1642 the English were so numerous in New Amsterdam that the appointment of an official interpreter became necessary; and that officer also was required to serve as an intermediary between the Dutch merchants and the English shipmasters who broke the voyage between New England and the Virginia plantations by stopping here for a bit of trade.

It was for the accommodation of such wayfarers that the City Tavern—which later became the Stadt Huys—was built in the year 1642; and it seems to have been built badly, as it manifested such a decided disposition to tumble to pieces in little more than half a century that it was torn down. It faced Coenties Slip: where its memory — in the admirable building of Dutch design belonging to the Fire Department—in a way still is preserved. I should be glad to believe that hospitality was the corner-stone of that nominally hospitable edifice; but I fancy that in building it some thought may have been taken of the fact that trade in a tavern is apt to turn in favor of the trader who has the hardest head—and it

VIEW OF ALBANY

From an old copperplate engraving

is an incontestable fact that our Dutch ancestors had heads upon which they could rely. Possibly some of those visiting English traders cherished unkindly memories of our City Tavern—as they beat down the harbor and out through the Narrows on their way to Virginia, or as they affronted the dangers of Hell Gate on their way eastward up the Sound!

The encouragement that Kieft gave to the incoming of the English, and to the trade with the neighboring English colonies, tended to the immediate good of New Netherland; but in the end, of course, the influx of those settlers, and the straining of relations with the government to which they owed allegiance, were the chief factors in hastening the downfall here of Dutch rule. George Baxter, the official interpreter—he seems to have been a fuming sort of person—was one of the leaders of the rebellion that broke out among the English on Long Island in the year 1655; a rebellion that Stuyvesant's temporizing policy did not check, and that helped to give a valuable part of New Netherland to the English nine years before they grabbed it all.

In another way Kieft's liberal administration of more liberal laws led on to catastrophe. The increased freedom in trading tended to facilitate the supply of arms—in exchange for good bargains in peltries—to the savages; and so enabled the savages to make their winning fight when, by Kieft's own abominable act, the time for fighting came. From the very beginning the trade in arms with the Indians offered temptations too strong to be resisted by the money-seeking Dutch—just as it has offered temptations too strong to be resisted by the money-seekers of our own time on our Western frontier. Under Kieft it went on swimmingly. In those days a musket sold for twenty beaver-skins, and a pound of gunpowder was worth in furs from ten to twelve guilders: and so the "boschlopers," or "runners in the woods," made their account with the savages—and gave no thought to the reaping of the whirlwind that was to come in sequence to that sowing of the wind.

IV

When Peter Stuyvesant, the last of those incompetent Directors, took over the government of New Netherland (May 27, 1647) things were in a hopelessly bad way. Mr. Brodhead, whose disposition is to make the best of Dutch shortcomings, thus summarizes the situation: "Excepting the Long Island settlements, scarcely fifty bouweries could be counted; and the whole province could not furnish, at the utmost, more than three hundred men capable of bearing arms. The savages still were brooding over the loss of sixteen hundred of their people. Disorder and discontent prevailed among the commonalty; the public revenue was in arrear, and smuggling had almost ruined legitimate trade; conflicting claims of jurisdiction were to be settled with the colonial patroons; and jealous neighbors all around threatened the actual dismemberment of the province. Protests had been of no avail; and the decimated population, which had hardly been able to protect itself against the irritated savages, could offer but a feeble resistance to the progress of European encroachment. Under such embarrassing circumstances the last Director-General of New Netherland began his eventful government." And to this Mr. Brodhead might have added in set terms what he does add virtually by his subsequent presentment of facts: that Peter Stuyvesant, so far from being the man to set a wrong-going colony right, was precisely the man to set a right-going colony wrong.

Irving, with his accustomed genial warping of the truth, has created so kindly a caricature of the last of the Dutch governors that our disposition is to link him with, almost to exalt him to the level of, the blessed Saint Nicholas—our city's patron. Such association is not justified by the facts, and our good saint—notwithstanding his notable charity and humility — most reasonably might take exception to it. In truth, Stuyvesant had little in common with any respectable saint in the calendar; and to come upon the real man—as he is revealed in the official records of his time—is to experience the shock of painful discovery.

The remonstrance presented by the colonists to the States - General in the year 1649, while dealing generally with the manifold misfortunes brought upon the colonists by bad government, deals particularly with the misdoings of the last Director: who then had been in office for only two years and a half, and who in that time had succeeded in setting the whole colony by the ears. "His arrival," declared the remonstrants, "was peacocklike, with great state and pomposity";

and the burden of their complaint, constantly recurred to, is of his brutally dictatorial methods and of his coarsely arrogant pride. "His manner in court," they declare, "has been . . . to browbeat, dispute with, and harass one of the parties; not as beseemeth a judge, but as a zealous advocate. This has caused great discontent everywhere, and has gone so far that many dare not bring any suits before the court if they do not stand well, or passably so, with the Director; for whom he opposeth hath both sun and moon against him. . . He likewise frequently submits his opinion in writing . . . and then his word is: 'Gentlemen, this is my opinion, if any one have ought to object to it, let him express it.' If any one then, on the instant, offer objection . . . his Honor bursts forth, incontinently, into a rage and makes such a to-do that it is dreadful; yea, he frequently abuses the Councillors as this and as that, in foul language better befitting the fishmarket than the Council board; and if all this be tolerated, he will not be satisfied until he have his way." In regard to the right of appeal to the home government his declaration is cited that "People may think of appealing in my time—should any one do so, I would have him made a foot shorter, pack the pieces off to Holland, and let him appeal in that way." And to this the remonstrants added by way of comment: "Oh cruel words! What more could a sovereign do?"

As the tone of the complainings shows, there was another side to all this. According to his lights (which were few) and within his limitations (which were many) Stuyvesant was in the way of being a reformer: and reformers ever have been painted blackest by those whom they sought to reform. That outrageous little colony needed a deal of reforming when he took over its government; and had his mandatory proclamations stopped with the one that forbade "Sabbath-breaking, brawling, and drunkenness," he still would have had a hornets' nest about his ears. Fancy what would have been the consensus of opinion on the part of the leading citizens of Fort Leavenworth had any reforming person fired off at them a proclamation of that sort in the old days of the Santa Fe Trail! But Stuyvesant's reforms cut deeper. Not content with trying to reduce to decency the energetic social customs of the colonists, he tried also to bring them up to the line of honest dealing: and so struck at their pockets as well as at their hearts. He forbade the sale of liquor to the savages: a most profitable business in itself, and of much indirect advantage to those engaged in it —because an intoxicated savage obviously was more desirable than a sober savage to bargain with for furs. He made stringent regulations which checked the profitable industry of smuggling peltries into New England, and European goods thence into New Netherland. He issued revolutionary commands that the frowsy and draggletailed little town should be set in order and cleansed. And on top of all this, farther to replenish the exhausted treasury of the colony, he levied a tax upon liquors and wines. That was the climax of his offending. As the outraged and indignant colonists themselves declared—becomingly falling back upon Holy Writ for a strong enough simile— the wine and liquor tax was "like the crowning of Rehoboam!"

Under such a government as Stuyvesant gave to that unfortunate colony there could be no real improvement in its affairs. Even when his attempted reforms were sound—and for the most part they were sound—the effect of them was weakened, and their realization was made difficult or impossible, by the manner in which they were applied.

V

But a better man than Stuyvesant— while he might have lost it with more dignity—could not have saved to Holland the colony of New Netherland. Forces from within and forces from without were working for its destruction. Internally, its affairs were administered with incompetence tempered with injustice— and it owed its bad government to the fact that it was but a by-venture in a great scheme of combined money-making and statecraft; and to the farther fact that it was more and more neglected, or remembered only to be more tightly squeezed, as the ruinous end of the West India Company drew near. Externally, the English constantly were pressing more closely upon its borders: strong in their determination to have the whole of

it; and in the mean time taking possession of such scraps of it—as the eastern end of Long Island — as dropped loose of their own accord. Such conditions led inevitably to the loss of that which never had been well held.

The evil star of the West India Company was the most conspicuous among the several stars in their courses which fought against the Dutch in their struggle to hold fast to their American colonies. The condition of the Company never was sound financially. By heroic marauding it did acquire a vast sum of money—which went as quickly as it came. But the Company absolutely failed to build up in any part of its dominions a substantial legitimate trade from which it could draw securely a stable revenue. From the year 1630 onward the Company's finances showed, as Mr. Asher puts it, "a terribly constant downward tendency." Only a year after it had paid its famous dividend upon its treasure-ship winnings, and out of its remaining surplus had lent 600,000 guilders to the Dutch government, it was unable to meet its running expenses. Under its charter it was entitled to a subsidy; but the government—partly because of lack of funds, but more because of the adverse action taken by the dominant political ring—was slack in making the promised payments and the subsidy fell badly into arrear. Money from other sources was not forthcoming. No colonial trade of importance had been developed; and the plan for breaking Spain's line of communication with her colonial treasure - houses had been executed so effectively that it had reacted upon its projectors after the manner of a boomerang; that is to say, although the Company had to carry the load of an armed fleet created mainly to bag Spanish plate-ships, the seas were empty of plate-ships to be bagged.

Bad luck had something to do with the Company's misfortunes, but at the root of them was bad management. The same stupidity, or worse, that was shown in the conduct of the affairs of our own little New Netherland was shown on a larger scale in the conduct of the far more important affairs in Brazil. At the end of a long series of quarrels with the Council, Count John Maurice resigned his commission in disgust in the year 1644. His successors for the most part were incompetents. When they happened to possess wits they used them in betraying the Company's interests—for a consideration — to the Portuguese. It took just ten years of that sort of thing to bring matters to their logical climax. In the year 1654 the Company's troops evacuated the Brazils.

Ten years more brought the end of everything. Mr. Asher puts the record of those ten calamitous years into a few words. "We cannot here attempt," he writes, "to describe the Company's last agony: its vain attempts to combine with the East India Company; its painful efforts to obtain from the government either armed assistance or payment of its arrears. The symptoms of bankruptcy became saddening and more threatening from year to year. At last its creditors began to seize the Company's property. The death-blow was struck in 1664—when New Netherland, the Company's last valuable possession, was conquered by the English." And so that rather grandly conceived, but consistently ill-executed enterprise, came to a miserable end. As a warning, the history of its few triumphs and of its many failures has a permanent value. And especially does its history point the moral that it is unwise, to say the least, to try to get from invested patriotism a dividend in cash.

Conceivably, by the exercise of a small amount of common-sense, the Dutch might have retained their holdings in Brazil; but from their holdings in North America—New Netherland, and the colony on the Delaware—the common-sense of all the ages could not have saved them from being squeezed out. There they were at grips with a race stronger than their own in numbers, and not less strong in sheer grit. For thirty years before the end came, the English were pressing

A DUTCH COTTAGE

in upon their territory from the east and from the south; while across-seas, with a large statesmanship, the English government was taking a hand in putting on the screws.

The most effective twist of the English screw was the passage by the Commonwealth Parliament (October 9, 1651) of the Navigation Act: which decreed that goods imported into England must come in English ships or in ships belonging to the country in which the goods were produced. As the Dutch at that time had the carrying trade of the world pretty well in their hands, the English law was in the nature of some of our own highly impersonal legislation affecting "cities of the first class." No names were mentioned—but it hit where it was meant to hit, and it hit hard. A loud buzzing of ambassadors followed that shot at Dutch commerce. But the propositions made by Holland—that there should be free trade to the West Indies and to Virginia, and that "a just, certain, and immovable boundary-line" should be fixed between the English and the Dutch territories in America—came to nothing; and so, presently, there was the louder buzzing of guns. In the handsome little war that followed (1652-54), the English experienced the unusual sensation of being soundly whipped at sea. Blake fairly was driven to take shelter in the Thames: after which Tromp went sailing up and down the Channel with a chip on his shoulder—indicated by that aggravating broom at his masthead, to which reference is inexpedient in talking with the average Englishman even now.

Here in Manhattan there was a great show of bellicosity while that waspish little war went on. It was then—under orders from Holland to put the town in a state of defence—that our famous wall was built along the line of what now is Wall Street. Thomas Baxter (who proved himself a very bad lot, a little later) had the contract for supplying the palisades which were intended to stand off his own countrymen; but which, in point of fact, never stood off anything more dangerously aggressive than wandering cows. Also, the city watch was strengthened; and preparations for a naval demonstration (in the event of a hostile fleet appearing before the city) were made by ordering Schipper Visscher "to keep his sails always ready, and to have his gun loaded day and night." In a word, we all were full of fight in that strenuous time—but, mercifully, carnage was averted. It takes two armies to make a battle: and the English army, for which we were waiting in so bloodthirsty a mood, discreetly remained at a safe distance from our pugnacious little fume of a town.

VI

Stuyvesant showed both manliness and good common-sense in dealing with the most threatening feature of that really volcanic situation: the charge made by the New-Englanders that he had endeavored to stir up against them an Indian revolt. He met the charge promptly by inviting the Commissioners* to send delegates to New Amsterdam to investigate it—and when they came he refuted it. More than that, he submitted to the delegates very reasonable and just propositions for the regulation of intercolonial affairs. In substance those propositions were: 1. Neighborly friendship, without regard to the hostilities in Europe. 2. Continuance of trade as before. 3. Mutual justice against fraudulent debtors. 4. A defensive and offensive alliance against common enemies. But the delegates refused to entertain his propositions, and went back to Boston in an unexplained but quite unmistakable huff. Very likely they had an instinctive feeling that treaties were unnecessary—since, without treaties, things were coming their way.

Moreover, the desire of the New-Englanders to fight the Dutch was strong.

* The colonies of New Plymouth, Massachusetts, Connecticut and New Haven became confederated, May 19, 1643, as "The United Colonies of New England." The administration of the affairs of the confederacy was intrusted to a board consisting of two commissioners from each colony.

Patriotism may have been at the root of that desire, but its more obvious motive was a mere commonplace human longing to lay hands on valuable Dutch property. Rhode Island—in those years, and for many succeeding years, the abode of notoriously hard characters—even made a start at a little war of spoliation on its own account. Two loose fish of thievish proclivities, Dyer and Underhill, were granted a license by that disreputable colony (June 3, 1653) to "take all Dutch ships and vessels as shall come into their power"; and the energetic Thomas Baxter—fresh from his palisading operation in Wall Street, and very likely using the profits of that operation in fitting out his expedition—also got a predatory license from Rhode Island ("turned pirate," is the way that Mr. Brodhead puts it), and made a spirited looting cruise along the Sound: that was ended by his being "run in" not by the Dutch, but by the authorities of New Haven.

Only the action of Massachusetts at that juncture averted what would have been a most horrid little war between the Dutch and the English colonies; and, as it was, the war was escaped by a very close shave. Between Massachusetts and New Netherland there was no such sharp conflict of interest as there was between New Netherland and the nearer-lying English colonies; on the contrary, there was even a certain friendliness between the two because of the trade that went on, to their common advantage, between Boston and New Amsterdam. But I think that what really prevented the war was Stuyvesant's promptness and frankness in dealing with the charge that he had sought to stir up an Indian revolt. The clearness of his defence, and his straightforward way in making it, constituted an appeal to the sense of right which then and always was characteristic of the Massachusetts colonists.

The fact is to be noted that Stuyvesant uniformly showed in what may be termed his foreign policy a far greater wisdom than he usually showed in his domestic policy. His one important aggressive act—his reduction (1655) of the Swedish colony on the Delaware, in dealing with which Irving has quite outdone himself in a passage of mingled non-

CITY TAVERN, AFTERWARDS THE STADT HUYS

sense and falsehood — was admirably planned and most successfully executed. He gained his end, without any fighting whatever, by the menacing display of an effective superior force: a method, it will be observed, that accords precisely with the rules laid down by the highest modern authorities on the art of war. It is true that in the Treaty of Hartford (1650) he yielded too much to the English; but his concessions materially lessed the dangerous border troubles, and the treaty certainly was beneficial for a time. His dealings with Virginia were to still better purpose. Even while the war between Holland and England was in progress — in accordance with his desire, scouted by the New - Englanders, for "neighborly friendship, without regard to the hostilities in Europe"—he made two attempts to conclude a commercial treaty with the Virginia authorities; and he succeeded in effecting with them a favorable working arrangement in the year 1653 that led on to the more formal and equally favorable convention of the year 1660.

The Virginia trade began to be of importance in the year 1652, when the export tax on tobacco shipped from New Netherland was removed; a concession on the part of the Amsterdam Chamber with which were united a reduction of the price of passage from Holland outward, and permission—here was the beginning of our slave trade—for the colonists to import negroes from Africa. A hint of trade direct with the Spanish colonies is found, also, in a list of charges brought (1653) by the West India Company against the proprietors of Rensselaerwyck; one of those charges being that "licenses have been granted to private individuals to sail to the coast of Florida."

Stuyvesant certainly endeavored—according to his lights — to foster the foreign trade of New Netherland. His voyage to the West Indies in the year 1655 was made expressly to that end; and his consistent effort seems to have been to make New Amsterdam a little metropolis in which should centre the American colonial trade. Possibly I am going too far in crediting him with the deliberate formulation and pursuit of a policy in which was such large statesmanship; but it is, at least, an interesting and a suggestive fact that most of his plans touching the exterior affairs of the colony do wear the look of having been conceived in the spirit of one who had that great end in view.

Unfortunately, Stuyvesant did not show in dealing with home matters the excellent qualities which he showed in dealing with intercolonial matters. Had he done so his record would have been a very different one, and his governorship—while ending in the always-inevitable loss of his province—would have ended without disgrace. The shame of the taking of New Netherland by the English was not that it was conquered; it was that its people—in their eagerness to escape from a government that had become intolerable — almost welcomed their conquerors.

VII

In the thick of that troublous time, while Holland and England were at open war and while the threat of war hung over their dependent colonies, the long-cherished desire of New Amsterdam to become a city was realized. As a matter of course, it was not realized in a satisfactory way—nothing was satisfactory to anybody, to state the case broadly, in which the West India Company had a hand; but, at least, on February 2, 1653, the civic government was established which, in one form or another, has been maintained on this island until this present day.

By the terms of the grant, from the Amsterdam Chamber, the municipal organization of New Amsterdam was to resemble " as much as possible " that of the parent city in Holland; but, as the matter worked out in practice, the possibilities proved to be so limited that the resemblance was in the nature of a caricature. Stuyvesant set up and maintained his right to appoint the members of the city government—the burgomasters, schepens, secretary, and schout —with the natural result that his authority continued to be paramount in civic matters; and in general he contrived to make the new order of things very much the same as the old order so far as any real increase of liberties was concerned. In a word, as Mr. Brodhead puts it: " the ungraceful concessions of the grudging Chamber were hampered by the most illiberal interpretation which their provincial representative could devise." For Mr. Brodhead — whose disposition toward the Director uniformly is kindly —those are very strong words. But they are amply justified by the facts.

With a modernity of method that our citizens of that period resented more keenly (being unaccustomed to it) than we resent it now, Stuyvesant made out his " slate "; and then put in his own men by the simple process of issuing a proclamation in which they were assigned to their several offices. Save in our spasmodic lucid intervals of civic reform, we still get by ways only a trifle more round-about to just the same practical results— and philologists, with these early facts available for their study, will perceive with pleasure the nice linguistic propriety that there is in our present use of the Dutch word " boss." On the very instant that this city became a city the political meaning of that word, in effect, was established and defined.

Some of the men named on Stuyvesant's " slate," as is the custom nowadays, were respectable citizens. More of them, still in accordance with modern custom, were not. And the most important office was given to the worst of them all. For Schout — an official who, in addition to presiding over the Board of Burgomasters and Schepens, performed duties which in a way combined those of our modern sheriff and district attorney—Stuyvesant appointed Cornelis van Tienhoven, the Company's fiscal: and had he searched through the whole colony he probably could not have found a man more outrageously unfit for any office at all.

There was, indeed, a popular outcry against Van Tienhoven's appointment; but it seems to have been based mainly on the ground that he was unfit to be Schout because he still continued to be an officer, the fiscal, of the Company—not on the broader and very tenable ground that he was an unfit person to hold any public office at all. And, also, the outcry came in part from citizens whose right to object to anybody on the score of immorals was of a highly attenuated sort. In the end, to be sure, he was turned out of his office in disgrace by order of the West India Company; and Stuyvesant was forbidden again to employ him—or to employ his brother, Adriaen, who had been detected in fraud as receiver-general—in the public service. But that order was a lashing of Stuyvesant over Van Tienhoven's shoulders, and it was not issued until Van Tienhoven had been Schout of the city for three years. Even Tammany has not beaten this record in civic immorality which our city scored at its very start.

DOWN LOVE LANE

FEDERAL HALL, WALL STREET.

I.

CERTAINLY all the world knows—barring, of course, that small portion of the world which is not familiar with old New York — the Kissing Bridge of a century ago was on the line of the Boston Post Road (almost precisely at the intersection of the Third Avenue and Seventy-seventh Street of the present day) about four miles out of town. And all the world, without any exception whatever, must know that after crossing a kissing-bridge the ridiculously short distance of four miles is no distance at all. Fortunately for the lovers of that period, it was possible to go round about from the Kissing Bridge to New York by a route which very agreeably prolonged the oscupontine situation: that is to say, by the Abingdon Road, close on the line of the present Twenty-first Street, to the Fitz-

roy Road, nearly parallel from Fifteenth Street to Forty-second Street with the present Eighth Avenue; thence down to the Great Kills Road, on the line of the present Gansevoort Street, thence to the Greenwich Road, on the line of the present Greenwich Street—and so, along the riverside, comfortably slowly back to town.

It is a theory of my own that the Abingdon Road received a more romantic name because it was the first section of this devious departure from the strait path leading townward into the broad way which certainly led quite around Robin Hood's barn, and may also have led to destruction, but which bloomed with the potentiality of a great many extra kisses wherewith the Kissing Bridge (save as a point of departure) had nothing in the world to do. I do not insist upon my theory; but I state as an undeniable fact that in the latter half of the last century the Abingdon Road was known generally—and, I infer from contemporary allusions to it, favorably—as Love Lane.

To avoid confusion, and also to show

OLD HOUSES IN TWENTY-SECOND STREET.

how necessary were such amatory appurtenances to the gentle-natured inhabitants
of this island in earlier times, I must here
state that the primitive Kissing Bridge
was in that section of the Post Road which
now is Chatham Street, and that in this
same vicinity—on the Rutgers estate—
was the primitive Love Lane. It was of
the older institution that an astute and
observant traveller in this country, the
Rev. Mr. Burnaby, wrote in his journal a
century and a half ago: "Just before you
enter the town there is a little bridge,
commonly called 'the kissing-bridge,'
where it is customary, before passing beyond, to salute the lady who is your companion"—to which custom the reverend
gentleman seems to have taken with a very
tolerable relish, and to have found "curious, yet not displeasing."

The later Love Lane, the one with which
I am now concerned, was but little travelled — being, primarily, the approach
from the highway to Captain Clarke's
estate known as Chelsea—and for a good
many years lovers had the chief use of
it; yet was it used also a little by polite
society taking the air of fine summer afternoons: up the Bloomingdale Road to

this turning, thence across to the river-
side, and so homeward to New York,
being one of the longest of the ordinary
afternoon drives.

To the south of the lane lay the estate
—extending from the present Broadway
to the present Eighth Avenue—that was
presented by the Corporation to Captain
Warren, afterwards Admiral Sir Peter
Warren, in the year 1745, in grateful recognition, ostensibly, of his capture of
Louisburg; but really, I fancy, because a
good many of the leading citizens were
under obligations to him of one sort or
another for benefits derived from the
many prizes which he had sent into this
port to be condemned. Later, when the
whole of the Warren estate was partitioned,
two roads were opened out from the Abingdon Road across this northern portion
of the property. The first of these, known
as the Southampton Road—Sir Peter's second daughter, Ann, married Charles Fitzroy, who later became the Baron of Southampton; his eldest daughter, Charlotte,
married the Earl of Abingdon—was a
continuation of the Great Kills Road from
(to use existing designations) the Seventh
Avenue and Fifteenth Street to Eighteenth

Street just east of the Sixth Avenue, and thence parallel with the Sixth Avenue to the northern side of Twenty-first Street. The second, known as the Warren Road, left the Southampton Road at Sixteenth Street and ran parallel with, and a little to the east of, the Seventh Avenue, also to Twenty-first Street.

At Twenty-first Street and Broadway there is nothing now to suggest that ever a Love Lane was thereabouts; and the Fifth Avenue crossing of Twenty - first Street—with a huge nine-story building on one side and the traditionally respectable Union Club on the other—presents so forbidding an appearance that the searcher after traces of these old-time byways very well may be led to abandon at the very outset, all untimely, his gentle quest. But he who hunts for ancient landmarks must not be discouraged easily; and this particular hunt, in the happy end, reveals so astonishingly large a sur-

vival that the sadness of the beginning is swept away and lost in a flood of genuine antiquarian joy. The fact, indeed, really is extraordinary that this part of the city —which has the appearance to the ordinary observer of being essentially modern and uninteresting—should so teem with signs and relics of a truly interesting past.

II.

The first traces of the Abingdon Road, otherwise Love Lane, found in West Twenty-first Street are the little two-story brick houses, Nos. 25, 27, which stand back from the street and affect a rural and cottage-like air on an insufficient capital of narrow veranda. These houses certainly were built after the present City Plan had been adopted (1811); and probably were built not much more than forty years ago —a little after the creation of London Terrace had sent into this bit of country-side a premature thrill of speculative activity.

OLD HOUSES IN EIGHTEENTH STREET.

LONDON TERRACE, CHELSEA.

Yet while thus essentially modern, they cling affectionately—using their meagre verandas and villagelike front yards as tentacles—to the traditions of a really rural past.

Only a little farther westward is a row of three houses, Nos. 51, 53, 55, which very obviously belong to the period to which the others only aspire. They are built of brick, are very small, and are only two stories and a half high: and seem still lower because the grade of the present street actually is two or three inches above the level of the ground-floor. Even yet in the rear of the little houses are deep gardens in which are genuine vines and, as a theatrical person would style them, practicable trees. They are the delight, these gardens, of the present French inhabitants of the tiny dwellings: as any passer-by about noon-time of a fine summer's day may see for himself with no more trouble than is involved in looking through one of the open front doors, down a tunnel-like passage, to the sunny open space in the rear—where he will behold (surrounded by conspicuous evidences of clear-starching) a gay Gallic company breakfasting under its own vine and ailantus-tree with such honest light-heartedness as can be manifested only by French folk eating something—eating almost anything—out-of-doors.

At first these houses were a bit of a mystery to me. I could not understand why, especially, they should be just there. But a reference to the Commissioners' map explained that they had been built upon what once was an eligible corner lot—at the very point, in fact, where the South-ampton Road came into Love Lane. It has occurred to me that the three little houses may have been, originally, a single house which served as a road-side tavern. Here would have been almost precisely the half-way point in the long drive out from town and back again of an after-noon; and at this particular corner—the Southampton Road being a short-cut down to Greenwich and across to the Great Kills Road—would have been intercepted the whole procession of thirsty wayfarers. Possibly, the tavern prospering, the tav-ern-keeper may have built out of his profits the large house, with quaint windows in the gable of its weather-boarded side, which still stands at the northeast corner of Twenty-first Street and the Sixth Avenue; and thereto may have retired, when sufficiently enriched by his genial trade, to spend in luxurious idleness the Indian summer of his alcoholic life.

West of the Sixth Avenue is a large open space which testifies silently yet strongly to the time when all this part of the island was quiet country-side and the city still was very far away. It is the Jewish graveyard—the Beth Haim, or Place of Rest. Sixty years and more ago the Beth Haim at Greenwich was swept away (save the little corner which still remains east of the Sixth Avenue) by the opening of Eleventh Street. Then it was that the Beth Haim was established here—on a lot which possessed the advantages of lying within one of the blocks of the new City Plan and therefore was safe against the opening of new streets, and

which also could be reached by an already opened country road. Although long since superseded by the Beth Haim on Long Island, this graveyard still is cared for zealously—as may be seen by looking from the back windows of the big dry-goods shop on the Sixth Avenue upon its rows of seemly monuments, whereon are legends in Hebrew characters telling of " Rest " and " Peace." And, truly, looking out from the bustle and clamor of the shop upon the grassy quiet place, with its ivy-clad dead-house and its long lines of marble gravestones whereof the whiteness has become gray as the years have gone on and on, there is a most pleasant sense of rest and peacefulness amidst this calm serenity of ancient death.

Save for the graveyard, there is no sign—at least, I have not found any sign —between the Sixth and Seventh avenues of the old country road. In this block Love Lane seems to have been ploughed under completely. The houses on both sides of the street, having still about them an air of decayed smugness, date from the period, thirty years or so ago, when West Twenty-third Street was pluming itself (vastly to the amusement of Second Avenue and Gramercy Park and Stuyvesant and Washington squares) upon being quite the smartest street of the town; and when Twenty - first and Twenty - second streets, catching a little reflected glory from this near-by glitter of fashion, exalted their horns above horns in general and gave audible thanks that they were not at all as were the other streets over on that part of the west side. It is not sur-

LITTLE HOUSES ON TWENTY-FOURTH STREET.

prising, therefore, that from
this section of Twenty-first
Street the modest memory of
Love Lane should have disappeared.

The trail shows again in
the middle of the next block.
between the Seventh and
Eighth avenues, in the little
houses standing far back from
the present street in deep
yards. But the most con-
spicuous house in the block—
the large dwelling standing
in its own grounds and having so quaint and so agreeably dignified an air that one
instantly is disposed to clas-
sify it as a survival from the
beginning of the present century—is not an antique at all.
Actually, it was built but
twenty-five or thirty years
ago; and its owner, being a
boss-mason — the builder of
the Fourth Avenue tunnel—
built it for himself according
to his own notions and in his
own way. Though a large
house, it is not at all a grand
one; but there is not a house
in New York that excels it in
the matter of positive individuality. It is delightful to
see how much meaning and
character its builder contrived
to put into it while yet employing only simple means.
He is dead, this excellent boss-
mason; but in the long stable
beside the mansion-house still
is preserved his original kit of
mason's tools. Never in his
lifetime would he permit them
to be disturbed, and his wishes concerning them have survived his death.

For many years the Abingdon Road—
to give it at parting its more dignified
name—ended at the line where now is the
Eighth Avenue and where then was the
Fitzroy Road. Later, certainly before the
year 1811, it was carried westward to the
shore of the Hudson. But the weather-
boarded, hip-roofed house still extant on
the southwestern corner of this ancient
crossway is to be classed less as a survival of Love Lane than of Chelsea Village: that ambitious suburb which, sixty
years or so ago, made its somewhat pre-

A SIDE GATE IN CHELSEA.

mature start in life on the lines of the
City Plan.

III.

"Dead as Chelsea!" is a phrase which
has been current in the British army
since the battle of Fontenoy—when a
British grenadier, of unknown name but
epigrammatic habit, first used it in apos-
trophizing himself when a round-shot
took off his right leg, and so gave him
his billet to the Royal Hospital. That he
rammed an oath down on top of this observation was no more than natural. A
military authority of the highest, the late
Captain Shandy, of Leven's regiment of

A TENNIS-COURT IN CHELSEA.

foot, who served in those very parts but a half-century earlier, has left on record his testimony to the exceeding profanity of the British troops in the Low Countries.

Almost contemporaneously with this lasting utterance of the Fontenoy grenadier, an American soldier, Captain Thomas Clarke, a veteran officer of the provincial service who had done some very pretty fighting in the old French war, gave the name of Chelsea to his country-seat—a modest estate on the shores of the Hudson, between two and three miles north of the town of New York. And he chose this name, he said, because the home to which he gave it was to be the retreat of an old soldier in the evening of his days. So nice a touch was there of the fanciful and the poetic in the selection of such a name at a period—'twas in the year 1750—when neither poetry nor fancy had become rooted in American soil, that one's heart warms toward this gentle warrior in the certainty that he must have possessed a subtler and a finer nature than fell to the lot of most men of his country and his time.

There is yet another touch of pathos in the fact that the Captain, after all, did not die in this retreat which he had hoped would shelter him until the end. While his last illness was upon him his home was burned to the ground, and he himself was but barely saved from burning with it by rescuing neighbors, who carried him to a near-by farm-house—where he and Death came presently to terms.

When all was over, Mistress Molly Clarke, the Captain's widow, being a capable and energetic woman still in her prime, set herself to the work of rebuilding; and found, no doubt, some measure of comfort and solace in being thus busily employed. The house then built was a large square structure of two stories, standing upon the crest of a little hill which sloped gently to the river-side, a hundred yards or so away. In relation to the present City Plan, the house stood two hundred feet or thereabouts west of the present Ninth Avenue, with its northern corner on the southern line of Twenty-third Street.

Mistress Molly, I fancy, had a fair allowance of peppery energy. When the Revolutionary war came on she had the pluck to remain—with her two pretty daughters—in her country house, although the house was at no great distance from the American fortified camp. To her sore vexation, a squad of Continentals was billeted upon her; and her distress was so reasonable that the officer in command—who, likely enough, had daughters of his own at home, and so was tenderly considerate of her proper motherly alarm—made a report of the matter to the commanding General. A good deal was going on just then to engross this General's attention; but, being a Virginian and a gentleman, he found time to ride over to Chelsea—on that famous white horse which curvets so dashingly in the background of Trumbull's picture—that he might express to Madam Clarke his regret that she had been troubled, and at the same time assure her that her trouble was at an end. Truly, it was very handsomely done!

While the American forces still were in possession of the island, and before the billet on Chelsea had been raised, an English frigate stood up the river one day to give her crew practical exercise at the guns, and in the course of her firing pitched a shot fairly into Mrs. Clarke's dwelling; which shot hurt nobody, but made necessary some patch-work carpentering that ever afterward showed where the ball had come cracking along. Mistress Molly happened to be abroad when this bit of military incivility occurred; and her first news of it was from one of her billet of soldiers whom she met as she was driving home, and who hailed her briskly with the announcement: "The British have fired a shot into your house, Mrs. Clarke!" To which her ladyship replied instantly, and with a not unreasonable bitterness: "Thank *you* for that!" and so drove homeward in a fine temper in her chaise.

Mistress Molly was near half a century behind her Captain in the eternal march. She died in the year 1802. At her death the dwelling, together with a part of the estate, passed to Bishop Moore and his wife; and by them, in the year 1813, was

THE CHAPEL DOOR, CHELSEA SQUARE.

A CHELSEA DOORWAY.

IV.

It was to Mr. Clement C. Moore that Chelsea owed its existence as a village a long while in advance of the period when it became a part of the city of New York. His estate, by inheritance and by purchase, extended from the north side of the present Nineteenth Street to the south side of the present Twenty-fourth Street, and from the west side of the present Eighth Avenue to the river. Sixty years or so ago he began opening through his property the existing streets and avenues on the lines of the City Plan; and thereafter he gave his energies to founding and to fostering his town—to which access from New York was easy, either by way of Love Lane from the Bloomingdale Road, or by either of the roads from New York to Greenwich and thence by the Fitzroy Road for the final three-quarters of a mile.

The most notable dwellings erected in that early time were those which comprise the still existing rows on Twenty-third and Twenty-fourth streets: London Terrace and Chelsea Cottages, as they respectively were, and continue to be, called. The first of these is the row, between the Ninth and Tenth avenues, of tall pilastered houses which gives one the impression of an Institution not very firmly fixed in its own mind and liable to become something else, yet having an air both gracious and friendly because of its deep gardens and many tall old trees; and the second is in part a reproduction of the pilastered houses upon a smaller scale, and in part chunky little two-story houses with little pudgy bay-windows and with ornate little porches over their little doors. All of these dwellings, small and large, are at odds with their present city surroundings because of their affectation of a countrified air; yet must they have been far more at odds with their surroundings when they were erected—being then remote in the country, yet presumptuously aping the manners of the town.

conveyed to the late Clement C. Moore, their son. Upon coming into possession of this last-named gentleman another story was added to the house, and cellars were built beneath the old foundation: in which reconstructed form the mansion remained standing—within its terraced and beautiful grounds, at a considerable elevation above the street level—until about forty years ago. Possibly this old house was more picturesque than it was comfortable. Certainly its owner did not seem greatly to regret its loss. To his brief history of the property, from which the facts given above are extracted, he added the curt statement that when "the corporation of the city ordered a bulkhead to be built along the river-front it was thought advisable, if not absolutely necessary, to dig down the whole place and throw it into the river; when, of course, the old house was destroyed."

Both Terrace and Cottages date from almost half a century ago. The block on which they stand was leased by Mr.

Moore to William Torrey on May 1, 1845; and Torrey thereafter built and sold the houses subject to the lease—the owner of the estate wisely retaining the fee. To a slightly more remote period belongs the large square brick house on the Ninth Avenue between Twentieth and Twenty-first streets; a house so citylike that passing strangers must have regarded it as some trick in optics when first it sprang up in that open country-side near sixty years ago. And now, the city pressing close around it, it also has somewhat

sort, still may be seen here and there: standing back shyly from the street in deep yards, and having somewhat the abashed look of aged rustics confronted suddenly with city ways. But many more of these timber-toed veterans—true Chelsea pensioners—lie hidden away in the centres of the blocks, and may be found only by burrowing through alleyways beneath the outer line of prim brick houses of a modern time. Notably, on both sides of Twentieth Street, between the Seventh and Eighth avenues, these

CHELSEA SQUARE—MODERN COLLEGE BUILDINGS.

of a country air: yet this is due mainly to the ample reaches of land about it—a lawn with a tennis-court at one side, and a sweet-smelling old-fashioned garden in the rear.

These conspicuous features of what once was Chelsea Village assert themselves—not offensively, yet with insistence born of a proper respect for their own dignity—upon the merest loiterer through the ancient roadways of the little town; and even a few of the more modest remnants of that earlier period, the little wooden houses wherein dwelt folk of a humbler

inner rows of houses may be found, and west of the Eighth Avenue on the northern side of the way. But one may rest assured that wherever, in any of the blocks hereabouts, an alleyway opens there will be found an old wooden house or a whole row of old wooden houses at its inner end.

Geographically, and in all other ways, the central feature of Chelsea—from before its ambitiously early essay at being a village on its own account even until this present day when it is in the city but not exactly of it—is the General Theological Seminary of the Protestant Episcopal

CHELSEA SQUARE—ONE OF THE OLD COLLEGE BUILDINGS.

Church. To this institution was given rent free by Clement C. Moore—the good Bishop, his father, no doubt having a share in the prompting of the gift—the whole of the block between Twentieth and Twenty-first streets and the Ninth and Tenth avenues; which lot, being for many years only in small part built upon, long was known as Chelsea Square. Here was laid the corner-stone of the East Building of the Seminary on the 28th of July, 1825; and of the West Building ten years later—both structures, with the minor edifices erected later, being of a dark gray stone which made an admirable color composition with the green of the grass and trees, and of the ivy when it began to grow later on. Only one of the original stone buildings still is standing, and the larger part of what was Chelsea Square now is covered with the great brick halls, and the brick chapel, erected within the past ten years.

Even with all this growth of new buildings there still remains a wide extent of trimly kept lawns dotted with flower beds and shaded by wide-branching trees; and there is no more delightful bit in all New York than the deeply recessed space in the east front, where the yellow-green lawn has for background the ivy-clad red brick walls of the chapel, far above which rises stately the gravely graceful square brick tower. Especially pleasing and Old-Worldly is this same place of a bright spring afternoon during the last five minutes' ringing of the chapel bell—when the seemly young Seminarists (every one of whom reasonably may hope to be a bishop before he dies) come trooping along the paths or across the grass to the chapel entrance, all properly clad in caps and gowns; while at the same time come up the pathway from the street to that same entrance (for their souls' comforting) some of the most charming and most charmingly dressed young gentlewomen to be found within a radius of a mile around. Truly, looking at this pretty sight, it is not difficult to fancy one's self a whole Atlantic away from New York in one of the English university towns.

Just across the Ninth Avenue, eastward from the Seminary, on Twentieth Street, is another picturesque bit: St. Peter's Church—a large structure of dark gray stone with a tall and massive and very well proportioned tower. Seen in broad daylight, the church is a good deal the worse for its Perpendicular porch built of pine planks, and for its absurd wooden crenellation. But these incongruous qualities disappear when dusk is falling, and in moonlight they become glorified into realities instead of cheap shams. At such times this church is beautiful with a grave beauty that fitly is its own.

V.

The Fitzroy Road, leading from Greenwich to Chelsea and thence onward to the Bloomingdale Road, was closed as the streets of the City Plan were opened; but it has by no means disappeared. It may be traced more or less clearly from its beginning, south of Fifteenth Street, to its ending, at Forty-second Street, being throughout its entire length close upon the Eighth Avenue line. Principally is its former course marked—and this is true of all the old roads hereabouts—by open spaces in the rows of houses, or by houses of only a story or two stories in height, and usually of wood—as though some doubt as to the title to land which for so long a period had been surrendered to the public use had prevented the building upon it of anything, or had prompted the building of houses of small cost. These signs are not certain. At Twentieth, Nineteenth, and Sixteenth streets there are no traces of the road at all. On the other streets south of Twenty-first its crossing is clearly marked. At Twentieth Street it passed through the opening yet remaining between the wooden houses Nos. 250, 252; at Eighteenth Street an actual section of it remains in use in the driveway to a brewery; at Seventeenth Street another section remains, west of the wooden house No. 246, in the court running into the centre of the block; at Fifteenth Street it passed beside the old gambrel-roofed house still standing, across the space now occupied by the one-story buildings Nos. 231, 233. Its union with the Great Kills Road was made a little south of the present Fifteenth Street, in the heart of the existing block; the Fifteenth Street crossing, therefore, virtually is its southern end.

There was also, I am inclined to believe—although it is not marked on the Commissioners' map—a road which ran parallel with the Fitzroy Road a little east of the present Ninth Avenue. What I take to be a trace of it on Twenty-first Street is the two-story stable, No. 341, beside a large frame house; on Twentieth and Nineteenth streets no sign of it appears; on Eighteenth Street the one-story shop, No. 368, seems to be another trace; on Seventeenth Street, between the wooden houses Nos. 352, 354, there still is a driveway into the middle of the block, where more wooden houses of ancient date are found; on Sixteenth Street the trace is a modern two-story dwelling, No. 352, in the rear of which is a small wooden house with old-fashioned outside stair; and on Fifteenth Street the traces are the one-story buildings on each side of the way, Nos. 366, 367; on Fourteenth Street, naturally, no trace survives, for here it would have been merged into the Great Kills Road.

But the most substantial evidence in favor of this vanished and unrecorded roadway is found in the two delightfully picturesque old wooden houses which stand in the rear of No. 112 Ninth Avenue —up an alluring alley and in a little court of their own. They are of the same type as those on Eighteenth Street of which a picture is given on page 584; but the outside stairs leading to the second story are not roofed over. Houses of this sort were common in New York half a century and more ago, and many of them, hidden away inside the blocks as these are, still survive. They possessed the very positive merit of giving the privacy of an entirely separate dwelling to the tenants of each floor. These houses, which certainly were built long before the Ninth Avenue was opened, must have faced directly upon the old road; and, in additional proof of this conjecture, is the fact that they stand precisely in line with the opening on Eighteenth Street where the road presumably crossed. Possibly the road never was opened officially. It may have been only a short-cut from the end of the Greenwich Road (of which, another point in its favor, it would have been a direct continuation) to Chelsea across the fields.

Of the Warren Road there is no trace on either Twenty-first or Twentieth Street; but its track is marked on Nineteenth Street by the wooden house No. 148; on Eighteenth Street by the houses Nos. 155, 157; and on Seventeenth Street by the house No. 154.

VI.

Of all these old roads the Southampton was the most thickly settled, and has left behind it the strongest surviving traces. Excepting Twentieth Street, there is not one of the modern streets throughout its length but exhibits distinct marks of its ancient course; while the line of the Great Kills Road, of which it was a continuation, is shown clearly by the oblique side wall of the house at the northwest corner of Fifteenth Street and the Seventh Avenue. Its most marked and most interesting remnant, however, is the group of wooden houses—buried in the heart of the block between Sixteenth and Seventeenth streets and the Sixth and Seventh avenues—built seventy years back, and long known as Paisley Place, or "the Weavers' Row."

This cluster of dwellings, once outlying upon Greenwich Village, came by both of its names honestly. Hand-weaving was a New York industry of some magnitude, relatively speaking, in the early years of the present century, and was carried on mainly by weavers emigrant from Scotland; and it was by some of these Scotch weavers that Paisley Place was settled and named, about the year 1822. The date is well determined, inasmuch as the settlement stands in direct relation with the yellow-fever epidemic of that year; but whether the weavers came to Paisley in order to escape the fever, or came after the fever had passed away in order to get the benefit of low rents, is not so clear.

Mr. P. M. Wetmore, in a note upon Paisley, held to the former view. "At a little distance from where the larger merchants had made their temporary homes," he wrote, referring to Greenwich Village, "ran a secluded country lane which bore the somewhat pretentious name of Southampton Road. A convenient nook by the side of this quiet lane was chosen by a considerable number of the Scotch weavers as their place of refuge from the impending danger. They erected their modest dwellings in a row, set up their frames, spread their webs, and the shuttles flew merrily from willing fingers. With the love of Scotland strong in their hearts, and the old town from which they had wandered far away warm in their memories, they gave their new home the name of Paisley Place."

On the other hand, Mr. Devoe—who lived for many years in the immediate vicinity of Paisley, and whose knowledge in the premises was personal—wrote in his Market Book: "Many of the wooden buildings in the neighborhood [of the Jefferson Market] were suddenly put up in 1822 to accommodate the bankers, insurance and other companies, merchants, etc., who left them tenantless after the dreaded yellow fever had subsided, which were at this period [1832] filled with weavers, laborers, and others, who sought low rents."

But whether the Scotch weavers came before or after the fever is immaterial to the point of present interest, which is that the little wooden houses on the line of the extinguished Southampton Road still stand where they were built more than seventy years ago—a fact that any person of antiquarian tendencies, sufficiently resolute not to be dashed by a bad smell or two, may verify personally by making an expedition up one of the several alleyways on the south side of Seventeenth Street west of the Sixth Avenue. And—without rising to such heights of dare-odor adventure as the search for the Weavers' Row up dubious alleyways—a house of the same period may be seen, No. 107, still standing or Seventeenth Street at the point where the Southampton Road left Paisley Place and bore away across country by the east and north.

Having, at first, Paisley as its nucleus, but being centred, later, upon the factory that was built at the northeast corner of Nineteenth Street and the Eighth Avenue, a scattered village grew up between Greenwich and Chelsea half a century ago—partly on the lines of the old roads and partly on the lines of the City Plan. Many scraps of this broadcast settlement still survive, and nearly every scrap has an interesting individuality. Best of all are the two delightfully picturesque wooden houses Nos. 251, 253 West Eighteenth Street, standing far back in what once very likely were gardens, but which certainly are not gardens now, and each having ascending to its second story a roofed-in stair. At the northwest corner of Seventeenth Street and the Eighth Avenue is a remnant of what, in its prime, was life of a higher caste: the brick-front wooden dwelling with a quaint little colonial porch having an iron railing which would be quite perfect were the graceful newel-posts wrought instead of cast—a house that has an air about it, and that manages to preserve even in the bedrag-glement of its now sadly fallen fortunes something of the bearing of its better days. It is far from being in as good condition as is the row of large comfort-able-looking frame dwellings a little west of it on Seventeenth Street, and yet even the tradition of its former rating suffices to throw the present undoubted well-to-do-ness of these latter entirely in the shade—in much the way that a battered and out-at-elbows gentleman still rises superior to the commonplace sort of hu-manity that is prosperous but has not in all its blood a single drop of blue. Scat-tered along the Seventh Avenue are half a dozen more of these trig and seemly but not aristocratic frame houses; and at the Eighteenth Street crossing, on the southwest corner, is a large outcrop of now shabby wooden dwellings which very likely had their genesis in the fac-tory that stood two blocks away to the west and north. In all this collection of remnants the oldest and the shabbiest are the most attractive—for on these is found that exalting touch of the picturesque or the romantic which is nature's gift in compensation for ruin and infirmity and broken age.

From Paisley Place the Southampton Road went northeastward by a way which still, save on Twentieth Street, is well defined. It crossed Eighteenth Street a few feet to the east of the Sixth Ave-nue, and there its line is recorded on the oblique western wall of the house No. 63; at Nineteenth Street it crossed where now are the small houses Nos. 52, 54; and on Twenty-first Street its trace is very clear in the little houses where now dwell French clear-starchers, and where once dwelt—I insist upon it—the genial land-lord of Love Lane.

Being come to these old houses again, we are back very nearly to the point at which our walk began.

THE EVOLUTION OF NEW YORK
(PART 2)

In 1776
The Conflagration.

H.P.

V

NEW YORK suffered greater hardships during the fight for Independence than fell to the lot of any other American city. It lost more than half of its population; it lost the whole of its commerce; the great fire of 1776, followed by the fire of 1778, laid a full fourth of it in ashes; it was occupied by the enemy uninterruptedly from almost the beginning of hostilities until after peace was declared.

When the issue was joined between the colonies and the mother-country, the dominant sentiment here was that of loyalty. This was natural. In New York, as in the Virginia and Carolina plantations, the early establishment of large landed estates had created a class of rich gentlefolk with whom loyalty

was a logical instinct. The abstract convictions, as well as the material interests, of this class were in favor of the maintenance of royal authority. It is not surprising, therefore—even in view of the vast stupidities of administration on the part of the home government which made colonial life almost unendurable—that many an honest gentleman of that period found himself awkwardly tangled in the ethics of honor while deciding between his duty to his country and his duty to his King. Rather is it surprising that the verdict of the gentle class was given with so little reservation for the patriotic side. Naturally, also, the commercial class—having vested interests to defend against the perils incident to revolution—was disposed toward loyalty. At that time about one-tenth of all the foreign commerce of the British American colonies was centred at this port; the trade inward and outward was increasing steadily and largely; even though the colonies should be in the end successful, a war with England meant an immediate collapse of business and a great money loss. And yet, with all this daunting loom of disaster—whereof the foreboding was more than justified by the event—no other American city espoused the cause of independence with a blither energy than did New York.

Until the actual outbreak of hostilities, the prosperous expansion of trade and the growth of the city continued without interruption; and then, as suddenly as the coming of tropical night—with the arrival of the British army of occupation, September 15, 1776—a blight settled over everything and was not lifted for more than seven years. Only four days after General Howe's entry came the calamity of the great fire: which swept over the region between Whitehall and Broad streets as far north as Beaver; thence, sparing the western side of the Bowling Green, over both sides of Broadway to and including Trinity Church; and thence, sparing the western side of Broadway but burning down to the river, to and including the southern side of Vesey Street —leaving behind it a broad furrow of desolation three-quarters of a mile long. Two years later, another fire reduced to wreck almost the whole of the block south of Pearl Street between Coenties and Old slips. Through all the dreary time of the English occupation these many blocks of ruins remained as the fire had left them. No reason existed for rebuilding; and, no matter how strong a reason there might have been, no money for rebuilding was obtainable. This visible material wreck fittingly represented the wreck which had overtaken the city's most vital interests. Trade with the interior and coastwise practically was cut off; and, with the destruction of these its natural feeders, the foreign commerce of the port was dead.

When New York was evacuated by the British troops, November 25, 1783, the condition of the city was miserable to the last degree. Streets which had been opened and partly graded before the war began had been suffered to lapse again to idle wastes; the wharves, to which for so long a while no ships had come, had

crumbled through neglect; public and private buildings, taken possession of by the military and used as barracks, as hospitals and as prisons, had fallen into semi-ruin; along all the western side of the town was the wreck left by the fire. In this dismal period the population had dwindled from upwards of 20,000 to less than 10,000 souls; the revenues of the city, long uncollected, had shrunk almost to the vanishing-point; the machinery of civil government had been practically destroyed. In a word, without the consoling glory of having suffered in honorable battle, the city was left a wreck by war.

The brilliant rapidity with which New York revived from what seemed to be its dying condition affords a striking proof of its inherent strong vitality. Within three years from the date of the evacuation the former population had been regained, and within five years more a farther increase of 10,000 had made the total 30,000 souls. Commerce, likewise, had returned to and then had passed its former highest limit. Public and private enterprise once more had been fully aroused. In every way the energetic life and the material prosperity of the city had been more than regained.

Before the Revolution, the filling in of the East River front had been carried forward as far as Front Street. Immediately upon the revival of commerce this work was taken in hand again—the more readily because the increasing size of ships called for deeper water at the wharves—and South Street was created. At the same time, new streets were laid out east and west of the Bowery; even Broadway, at last, began to show some signs of becoming an important thoroughfare; the streets leading out of Broadway to the North River were graded, and some of them were paved— but this region, then and for a long while afterward, was the worst quarter of the town. What tended, however, most of all to give to the city an air of fully restored vitality was the erection of new buildings on the sites so long covered by the desolate wreckage of the two fires.

Yet, for all its real prosperity—indeed, because of its prosperity—the draggled, transitional New York of that flourishing time must have been a vastly disagreeable place of residence. Not only was it ugly because of its crudeness and its harsh contrasts; it was a dangerous town to live in because of the frequent presence of epidemic disease. The prevalence of smallpox—Dr. Jenner's discovery still being a little below the surface—was not chargeable to any defect in the crudely organized system for protecting the public health; yellow fever, however, was a practically preventable disease which partly through ignorance and partly through carelessness was suffered to work great havoc here. When "a large and respectable committee of the citizens, of the physicians, and of the corporation," investigated the cause of one of the yellow-fever epidemics, about this time, they reported that the spread of the fever was encouraged (as well it might be!) by "deep damp cellars, sunken yards, unfinished water lots, public slips containing filth and stagnant water, burials in the city, narrow and filthy streets, the inducement to intemperance offered by more than a thousand tippling-houses, and the want of an adequate supply of pure and wholesome water."

But the New-Yorkers of that day—having great faith in the glorious future of their city, and being blessed with strong noses and stout hearts—rose superior to rawness and ugliness and (excepting when they died of them) to pestilence-breeding bad smells. Mangin's map, 1803, shows the extent to which—under the stimulus of a vigorously reviving commerce and a rapidly increasing population—they were disposed to discount their future. Actually, three-fourths of the impressive-looking city plotted on this map is pure prophecy: whereof there was but little fulfilment for near a score of years, and some of it never was fulfilled at all! In this brave showing of projected streets almost the only real streets—above Anthony and Hester—are those of the little group in the northwest corner, about the State prison, comprising Greenwich Village. Brannan and Bullock streets (the last-named blessedly changed to Broome, later) were laid out; the present Stuyvesant Street, Astor Place, and Greenwich Avenue were in existence as a continuous system of lanes; the Amity Street of the map (not the existing Amity Street) was another lane—of which a trace still may be seen in the oblique court leading off from the east side of South Fifth Avenue below Third Street; and Greenwich Street—from Duane northward—

was in existence as the main road to Greenwich, and was in great vogue as a fashionable drive. All the rest of these fine-looking streets were but enthusiastic projects of what was expected to be in the fulness of time.

Meanwhile, the tendency of development still was along the eastern side of the island. The seat of the foreign trade was the East River front; of the wholesale domestic trade, in Pearl and Broad streets and about Hanover Square; of the retail trade, in William, between Fulton and Wall. Nassau Street and upper Pearl Street were places of fashionable residence; as were also lower Broadway and the Battery. Upper Broadway, paved as far as Warren Street, no longer was looked upon as remote and inaccessible; and people with exceptionally long heads were beginning, even, to talk of it as a street with a future—being thereto moved, no doubt, by consideration of its magnificent appearance as the great central thoroughfare of the city upon Mangin's prophetic map.

The substantial facts of this hopeful period justified a good deal of spread-eagle prophecy. Between the years 1789 and 1801 the duties on foreign goods imported into New York increased from less than $150,000 to more than $500,000; the exports increased in value from $2,500,000 to almost $20,000,000; the tonnage of American vessels in the foreign trade ran from 18,000 to 146,000, and in the coasting trade from below 5000 to above 34,000 tons. In the same period the population had doubled—increasing from 30,000 to 60,000 souls. While its commerce thus constantly augmented, and while its borders constantly expanded to accommodate its quickly increasing population, New York buzzed with the activity of a vast hive of exceptionally enterprising and successful bees.

VI.

By far the most important improvement belonging to the last decade of the eighteenth century—though one of such magnitude that more than a decade of the nineteenth century had passed before it was completed—was the filling in of the Collect,* or Fresh Water pond.

Primitively, a marshy valley extended

---

* The name Collect was a corruption of the Dutch Kalch-hook, meaning lime-shell point, given to a shell-covered promontory, and later transferred to the pond itself.

A PRIVATEERSMAN ASHORE.

across the island from about the present Roosevelt Slip to where now is the western end of Canal Street. Nearly midway in this valley was the Collect: whereof the original outlet was a stream flowing into the East River across the low-lying region which still is called "the Swamp." As the city advanced up the shore of the East River, the Swamp was drained; and, before the Revolution, the radical improvement was effected of drawing off the overflow of the Collect in the other direction—that is to say, by a drain cut through the salt marshes to the North River. Later, this drain, on the line of the present Canal Street, was deepened sufficiently to drain the salt marsh and so to convert the western end of the valley into meadow-land. But the pond, a barrier in the way of the uniform expansion of the city northward, still remained.

Three principal plans for dealing with the Collect were held under advisement at different times. One was to make a dock of it by cutting navigable canals east and west to the rivers; another was to use it as a source of water supply for the city; and still another was to fill it in by cutting down and casting into it the nearby hills. The very great depth of the pond —so great that in early times it was reputed to be bottomless—caused some delay in deciding upon the heroic plan of filling it in; but eventually, about the end of the last century, this plan was adopted, and practically was completed in the course of the ensuing ten years.

A good deal of sentiment has been wasted, at one time and another, over the extinction of this little lake. Actually, filling in the Collect was the only possible thing to do with it. To have left it under any conditions—even in the midst of a considerable park and with underground communication with tide-water, which was one of the several suggestions made in the premises—would have resulted in the creation of a fever-trap altogether intolerable: precisely such another abiding-place of malaria and bad smells as was the Basin in the city of Providence. But, while the filling in was inevitable, a very great error was committed in using the made land for building sites. Had this unwholesome region been set aside as a public park—abundantly planted with trees which would have sucked up the moisture out of the sodden soil—the city would have made a sub-

stantial gain on the double score of beauty and of health. Even yet, a great improvement in the sanitary condition of this low-lying part of the town could be effected by planting the water-loving eucalyptus thickly along its streets.

Before the drainage of the Collect was completed, not only had the seers of that period foreseen the modern city, but a staid and practical commission—doing for New York precisely what we are laughing at the people of Chicago for causing to be done for their city now—had plotted it, as far north as 155th Street, almost as it exists to-day. Indeed, the prophecies of Mangin's map seemed quite sober realities when compared with the prophecies of the map which the Commissioners produced eight years later, 1811; and it is a fact that some parts of the Commissioners' plan still remain unrealized, although more than eighty years have slipped away since the plan was made.

As is shown on Mangin's map, the crookedness of the lower part of the city, south of the Fresh Water, was repeated north of the Fresh Water on a grander scale. In this new region the streets were straight in their several groups, but the groups were so defiantly at variance with each other that wherever their edges came together there was a tangle fit to make a loadstone lose its way; which picturesque confusion was due to the fact that each group had started from a separate base—the shore lines of various parts of the island, different angles of the line of the Bowery, and the lines of Broadway and Christopher Street—and thence had extended until, quite at hazard, they had come together, but had not joined. However, some part of this tangle still was only on paper—many of the plotted streets remaining unopened—and therefore could be corrected before it became a reality; and all of the island north of the present Fourteenth Street practically was virgin territory which could be treated in whatever way seemed most conducive to the public good. These facts being considered, the wise conclusion was reached very early in the present century to correct (so far as this was possible) the existing City Plan, which had been created by a mere patching together of scattered parts for the benefit of private interests, and to make a larger plan —so comprehensive that the growth of the city for a century or more would be provided for—in the interest of the community as a whole.

To make this rational project operative, an act of Assembly was passed, April 13, 1807, in accordance with the provisions of which Gouverneur Morris, Simeon De Witt, and John Rutherford were appointed "Commissioners of Streets and Roads in the City of New York," with instructions "to lay out streets, roads, and public squares, of such width [saving that no street should be less than fifty feet wide] and extent as to them should seem most conducive to the public good"; to establish upon the ground the City Plan thus created by the fixing of stone posts at suitable points; and to file maps of the plan with the Secretary of State, the County Clerk, and the Mayor; and the act further provided that no compensation could be had for buildings destroyed by the opening of streets when it should be shown that such buildings had been erected after the maps had been filed.

The Commissioners, who were allowed four years in which to prepare their plan and to establish it upon the ground, completed their work in outline within that period: in the year 1811 their report was made and their maps were filed which created the city, north of Houston Street, excepting in the matter of public parks, substantially as it exists to-day. The work of exact location — involving the survey of all the streets, and the placing of "1549 marble monumental stones and 98 iron bolts," as is recorded by the minutely accurate Mr. John Randel, Jun., the engineer in charge of the work—was not completed until about the year 1821.

Unfortunately, the promise of this far-sighted undertaking was far from being fulfilled in its performance. The magnificent opportunity which was given to the Commissioners to create a beautiful city simply was wasted and thrown away. Having to deal with a region well wooded, broken by hills, and diversified by watercourses—where the very contours of the land suggested curving roads, and its unequal surface reservations for beauty's sake alone—these worthy men decided that the forests should be cut away, the hills levelled, the hollows filled in, the streams buried; and upon the flat surface thus created they clapped down a ruler and completed their Bœotian programme by creating a city in which all was right angles and straight lines.

These deplorable results were not reached lightly. The Commissioners, in their stolid way, unquestionably gave their very best thought to the work confided to their indiscretion; they even, by their own showing, rose to the height of considering the claims of what they believed to be the beautiful before they decided upon giving place to the useful alone. Appended to their map are what they modestly style "remarks," in the course of which—after stating that they had "personally reconnoitred" the region with which they were dealing—they declare "that one of the first objects which claimed the attention of the Commissioners was the form and manner in which the business should be conducted; that is to say, whether they should confine themselves to rectilinear and rectangular streets, or whether they should adopt some of those supposed improvements by circles, ovals, and stars which certainly embellish a plan, whatever may be their effect as to convenience and utility. In considering that subject they could not but bear in mind that a city is to be composed principally of the habitations of men, and that straight-sided and right-angled houses are the most cheap to build and the most convenient to live in. The effect of these plain and simple reflections was decisive"—that is to say, the rectangles and straight lines carried the day.

In regard to parks, these excellently dull gentlemen had equally common-sensible views. "It may be a matter of surprise," they write, "that so few vacant spaces have been left, and those so small, for the benefit of fresh air and consequent preservation of health. Certainly if the city of New York was destined to stand on the side of a small stream, such as the Seine or Thames, a great number of ample places might be needful. But those large arms of the sea which embrace Manhattan Island render its situation, in regard to health and pleasure, as well as to the convenience of commerce, peculiarly felicitous. When, therefore, from the same causes, the prices of land are so uncommonly great, it seems proper to admit the principles of economy to greater influence than might, under circumstances of a different kind, have consisted with the dictates of prudence and the sense of duty." Holding these views the Commissioners explained that "it ap-

PLAN OF THE CITY OF NEW YORK.
Drawn from Actual Survey
By Casimir Th. Goerck and
Joseph Fr. Mangin, City Surveyor.

NEW YORK, Nov. 1803.

References

1. Government House........at the Battery
2. Trinity Church.............Broad Wy
3. St. Pauls....
4. St. Georges Ch..............Beekman St.
5. St. Marks.............Stuyvesant St.
6. Christ.....................Ann St.
7. Old Dutch................Garden St.
8. New......................Liberty St.
9. North...................William St.
10. Calvinist Reformed Ch....Nassau St.
11. German Lutheran........Frankfort St.
12. English Ch. Magazine St....Gold St.
13. Moravian Ch. Fair St. 14, Anabaptist Ch.
14. Scotch Presbyterian Ch.....Cedar St.
16. Seceder Ch...............Nassau St.
17. Presbyterian Ch............Wall St.
18.......................Beekman St.
19.......................Rutgers St.
20. Methodist Ch.............John St.
21.......................Second St.
22.......................Duane St.
23.......................Magazine St.
24. Franch.................Pine St.
25. St. Peters..............Barclay St.
26. Independent Ch..........Broad W.
27. Friends old Meeting House, Liberty St.
28........new.............Pearl St.
29. Jews Syn. Mill St. 30, City Hall. Wall St.
31. Jail........32, Bridewell, opp. the Park
33. Alms House.............Chamber. St.
34. State Prison...........Greenwich St.
35. College................Robinson St.
36. Hospital, B'way...37, Library, Nassau St.
38. Arsenal, Tryon Row 39, Theatre, Chatham St.
40. Exchange Market......41 Fly Market
42. Oswego Market........43 Bear Market
44. Catherine Slip Market
45. New Court House.....opposite the Park

JAS. S. KEMP.

pears proper, nevertheless, to select and
set apart on an elevated position a space
sufficient for a large reservoir when it
shall be found needful to furnish the
city, by means of aqueducts or by the
aid of hydraulic machinery, with a copious supply of pure and wholesome water";
and that "it was felt to be indispensable
that a much larger space should be set
apart for military exercise, as also to
assemble, in case of need, the force destined to defend the city"—out of which
secondary series of considerations came
the really magnificent Parade, extending
from Twenty-third to Thirty-fourth Street,
and from Fourth to Seventh Avenue, that
eventually shrunk away into the existing
Madison Square. The third large reservation made by the Commissioners, the
space for a great market, never got beyond the paper plan; which is the more
to be regretted because this particular
project, being quite within the range of
their capabilities, was admirably well conceived. Union Place—now called, very
unreasonably, Union Square—was a sort
of geographical accident, which in later
times has suffered a great reduction in
size. "This Place," wrote the Commissioners, "becomes necessary from various
considerations. Its central position requires an opening for the benefit of fresh
air; the union of so many large roads
demands space for security and convenience, and the morsels into which it would
be cut by continuing across it the several
streets and avenues would be of very little use or value."

The Commissioners, finally, sum up the
result of their labors in these words: "To
some it may be a matter of surprise that
the whole island has not been laid out as
a city. To others it may be a subject of
merriment that the Commissioners have
provided space for a greater population
than is collected at any spot on this side
of China. They have in this respect been
governed by the shape of the ground. It
is not improbable that considerable numbers may be collected at Harlem before
the high hills to the southward of it shall
be built upon as a city; and it is improbable that (for centuries to come) the grounds
north of Harlem Flat will be covered
with houses. To have come short of the
extent laid out might therefore have de-
feated just expectations; and to have gone
further might have furnished materials
for the pernicious spirit of speculation."

Excepting in the laying out of the city
upon so large a scale—in which there was
a touch of uncommon sense that bordered
upon imagination—common-sense of the
plainest sort was the dominant characteristic of the Commissioners' plan. Thinking only of utility and economy, they
solved their problem—which admitted of
so magnificent a solution—in the simplest
and dullest way. Yet it is not just to
blame them personally because their plan
fell so far short of what might have been
accomplished by men of genius governed
by artistic taste. All that fairly can be
said in the premises—and this quite as
much in their justification as to their reproach—is that they were surcharged with
the dulness and intense utilitarianism of
the people and the period whereof they
were a part. Assuredly, the work would
have been done with more dash and spirit
a whole century earlier—in the slave-dealing and piratical days of New York, when
life here had a flavor of romance in it,
and was not a mere grind of money-making in stupid commonplace ways.

Even on the score of utility, however,
the Commissioners fell into one very
grave error, for which, the requirements
of the case being entirely clear and obvious, there was absolutely no excuse. They
were dealing with a long and narrow
island, whereon the strong pressure of
traffic necessarily would be longitudinal
always. Yet, in the face of this most obvious fact, their provision of longitudinal
streets was one-third less to the square
mile than was their provision of latitudi-
nal streets; and their case is only made
worse by the existing proof—the greater
width of the avenues—that they did dim-
ly recognize the conditions for which they
failed to provide. The city has not yet
expanded to the point where the inconvenience arising from this blunder has
become sufficiently marked to attract attention. It will begin to be felt very soon
after the building of the bridge connecting New York and New Jersey shall have
brought the principal railway lines of the
country into direct connection, on the left
shore of the Hudson, with the principal
lines of foreign steamers, with the resulting transfer to that region of the commercial centre of the town.

VII.

While this project of a city, magnificent at least in the matter of size, was in

The Commissioners Map
of
THE CITY OF NEW YORK
1807

Randell's Id.

Great Barn Island

Marsh

Blackwells Id.

L O N G   I S L A N D

E A S T   R I V E R

H U D S O N   R I V E R

MARKET PLACE

THE PARADE

Banks St.
Christopher St.
Clarkson St.
Charlton St.
Canal St. Basin
Vestry
Beach
Duane St. Slip
Murray
Corporation Dock
Powles Hook Ferry
Albany Basin
Rector
Beaver

Scale
0 ¼ ½ ¾ 1 MILE
JAS. S. KEMP.

W E S T C H E S T E R   C O U N T Y

Spuyten Duyvil Cr. Crossing

AVENUE

Road

Fort Tryon Bridge
Fort Washington
Kings Bridge
Tenth
Fort George
155 ST.

course of elaboration by the serious Commissioners — in the very year, in fact, in which they began their work —the actually existing city of that period had the life temporarily knocked out of it by President Jefferson's Embargo Act: that curious weapon of self-offence which both surprised and annoyed its inventor by going off with such unnecessary violence at the wrong end.

The condition of New York while the deadening effect of the Embargo rested upon its commerce was trist to the last degree — as is shown vividly in the following extract, under date of April 13, 1808, from the journal of the shrewdly observant Mr. John Lambert: "Everything wore a dismal aspect at New York. The embargo had now continued upwards of three months, and the salutary check which Congress imagined it would have upon the conduct of the belligerent powers was extremely doubtful, while the ruination of the commerce of the United States appeared certain if such destructive measures were persisted in. Already had 120 failures taken place among the merchants and traders, to the amount of more than 5,000,000 dollars; and there were above 500 vessels in the harbor which were lying up useless, and rotting for want of employment. Thousands of sailors were either destitute of bread wandering about the country, or had entered the British service. The merchants had shut up their counting-houses and discharged their clerks; and the farmers refrained from cultivating their land—for if they brought their produce to market they could not sell at all, or were obliged to dispose of it for only a fourth of its value."

In another part of his journal, Lambert wrote: "The amount of tonnage belonging to the port of New York in 1806 was 183,671 tons, and the number of vessels in the harbor on the 25th of December, 1807, when the embargo took place, was 537. The moneys collected in New York for the national Treasury, on the imports and tonnage, have for several years amounted to one-fourth of the public revenue. In 1806 the sum collected was 6,500,000 dollars, which, after deducting the drawbacks, left a nett revenue of 4,500,-000 dollars, which was paid into the Treasury of the United States as the proceeds of one year. In the year 1808 the whole of this immense sum had vanished!"

Fortunately, it had vanished for only a little while. Even under the stress of the Non-intercourse Act, and of the constantly augmenting political ferment, the commerce of New York revived with such energetic celerity that by the time war was declared against England, in the year 1812, the registered tonnage of the port amounted to 266,548 tons—being equal to that of Boston and Philadelphia combined, and nearly double that of any other port in the United States. Under these circumstances, naturally, the war bore more heavily upon New York than upon any other American city; indeed, the reimposition of the Embargo scarcely would have produced here a more calamitous result.

The one redeeming feature of the situation, in a business way, was the chance that the war offered for privateering. But even success in this line of spirited endeavor did not yield unalloyed happiness; for privateering had suffered a de-

cided sea-change in the course of the years which had passed since it had been so much the vogue in these parts. It is true that a good many private armed vessels were fitted out from this port during the war of 1812, and it also is true that—to the great profit of their owners—they mowed a fairly broad swath through the English merchant marine. But public sentiment did not unanimously, as in an earlier time, endorse this energetic method of picking up a living on the high seas. Indeed, not very many years later —the more honest view of the matter, meanwhile, having increasingly prevailed—one of our local historians wrote of these very ventures of 1812-15 in the following vigorous terms: "By this legalized piracy a great amount of property belonging to British subjects was plundered at sea and brought into New York; where for a while the enriched freebooters glittered in their ill-gotten splendor, and exerted a most corrupting influence upon society"!

But the enrichment by sea-theft, even to the extent of glittering splendor, of a few freebooting New-Yorkers did not take the place of the more moderate enrichment of all the merchants of the city by legitimate trade. While the war lasted, New York languished miserably. The projects for new streets, the plans for new buildings, were abandoned. So far from increasing, the population actually was lessened by more than two thousand between the years 1810 and 1813. In 1814 the revenues of the port dropped down to but little more than half a million. This was the low-water mark, and in the very next year—peace having been concluded —the revenues shot up to fourteen millions, as foreign goods were poured into the country to make good the long drain. But so violent a revival of business did more harm than good. The vast importations glutted the market, and for six years there was great uncertainty and fluctuation in the state of trade. Not until the third decade of the century was fairly started did commercial balances adjust themselves and a new era of prosperity begin.

During this fluctuating period the growth of the city was spasmodic; but by the year 1820 substantial advances northward had been made. The most important single piece of work in the scheme of development was the completion of the deep canal on the line of Canal Street; with the consequent effective drainage of the whole valley lying between the choked Collect and the North River, and the regulation of the streets, previously laid out, on the reclaimed land. Even before this obstacle had been removed, however, the city had passed beyond it. Soon after the return of peace, building began on Broadway north of "the Meadows," and also near Broadway on Spring and Broome streets—being the beginning of the movement that twenty years or so later was to make of this region a highly fashionable quarter of the town. Even the yellow fever of 1822—the last of the serious epidemics of this disease—tended to accelerate the growth of the city northward, for many of the exiles from the lower part of the island retained their suburban homes after the fever had passed. By the year 1824—in which year "more than 1600 new houses were erected, nearly all of them of brick or stone," as is proudly stated by a contemporary chronicler—the lines of the city blocks were advancing close upon Greenwich Village, and Greenwich itself was becoming a populous suburban ward. At the same time a considerable settlement was asserting itself westward of the Bowery. Between these extremes the building of handsome villas was giving a vastly aristocratical air to the heretofore desert reaches of upper Broadway; and in order to invite the farther expansion of this fashionable quarter the old Potter's Field was reclaimed from a wilderness, and then —with the paupers still *in situ*—was transformed into the present Washington Square. By the year 1820 the population of the city had increased to 123,706 souls.

VIII.

New York's destiny as a commercial centre was settled from the start by the fact that the city—therein possessing what all other cities on the Atlantic seaboard lacked—had ample channels of communication with the interior by water.

Without examining closely a large map, it is not easy to estimate how great an extent of territory—down the whole range of coast from the Connecticut to the Shrewsbury River, and remotely inland— can be reached in perfect safety from this city in a sloop of 20 tons. And in our days of railroads it is even less easy to realize that some of these waterways—the Hackensack, for instance—ever could have

been of any serious value to the commerce of New York. But before cheap and speedy means of land carriage had been established every one of these small streams —down to those on which even a 10-ton sloop would float—was a channel of trade which appreciably added to the revenues of this town. It was, therefore, as the direct result of the advantages possessed by New York as a centre of domestic distribution that the city gained the leading place in the foreign trade of North America and acquired a registered tonnage of more than 260,000 tons by the beginning of the war of 1812.

But not until after this war was ended did the business conditions here justify the establishment of regular transatlantic lines with fixed dates of sailing—the famous lines of Liverpool packets, for which some few people of old-fashioned tendencies sigh a little as they take passage nowadays in a record-breaking "greyhound," with the full knowledge that that nondescript but spirited animal actually is a frightfully overcrowded and badly kept summer-resort hotel got away to sea.

The pioneer establishment in the Liverpool service was the Black Ball Line, started in the year 1817 by Isaac Wright and Son, Francis Thompson, Benjamin Marshal, and Jeremiah Thompson, with four large ships—as ships went, in those days; that is to say, vessels of between 400 and 500 tons — named the *Pacific*, *Amity*, *William Thompson*, and *James Cropper*, with sailing dates fixed for the first day of each month throughout the year. Four years later, when the business of the country was in an unusually flourishing condition, a second line, the Red Star, was established; also with four ships making monthly departures, but sailing on the 24th of the month. In the same year the Black Ball Line put on four more vessels, sailing on the 16th of the month; and a little later the Swallow-tail Line was started, with four ships, making monthly departures on the 8th. Thus communication was established between New York and Liverpool by a fleet of sixteen vessels, making from each end of the line weekly departures the year round.* Later, regular lines were established to London, Havre, Green-

* For a fuller description of this phase of the development of New York, see "The Old Packet and Clipper Service," by G. W. Sheldon, in HARPER'S MAGAZINE for January, 1884.

ock and other European ports; while the increase in the coastwise service naturally kept pace with that of the foreign trade.

The point to be here observed is that the weekly service to and from Liverpool —significant of a very great commercial pressure for that period—was established before the natural advantages possessed by New York as a distributing centre had received any substantial improvement; before, indeed, any improvement at all had been effected beyond the opening inland from the various watercourses of ways more or less practicable for freight-wagons and pack-trains. It was, therefore, the demand for the extension of a great business already soundly established which led to the creation of what frequently has been styled the foundation-stone of New York's commercial supremacy—the Erie Canal. In view of the natural geographical advantages possessed by this city, of the intelligent fostering of trade in the early times by the grants of staple right and of the monopoly of flour, it seems a fair inference that this so-called foundation-stone was set in when the building had got up to about the third or fourth floor. But as to the vast importance of the canal to the well-being of New York—without regard to the structural period at which its benefits became operative—there can be no question at all. Again it is necessary to examine carefully a large map in order to arrive at an adequate comprehension of what was done for this city when a waterway was cut from the Hudson River to the Great Lakes.

This large project was not conceived in its entirety: it was an evolution. In the year 1792, under the presidency of General Philip Schuyler, the Western Inland Lock Navigation Company was incorporated for the purpose of opening a communication by canal to Seneca Lake and Lake Ontario and of improving the Mohawk River. Later, at the suggestion of Gouverneur Morris—who in this matter worked for the welfare of the city with an intelligent zeal which he certainly did not manifest when he was helping to lay it out as a checker-board—the grander plan was taken into consideration of opening a canal from the Hudson River to Lake Erie. In the same year that this statesmanlike suggestion was made, 1808, the project was brought before the Assembly by Joshua

Forman; an appropriation was granted for a preliminary survey, and the survey was made by James Geddes. The matter then dropped for a year, but was revived energetically in March, 1810—at which time Senator, afterward Governor, De Witt Clinton became associated with it, and thereafter remained its most efficient promoter until the successful end.

For several years the war then going on with England prevented the prosecution of the work; and even after this military matter had been satisfactorily disposed of—it was rather a brilliant little war, so far as we were concerned, with some beautiful fighting in it—the disordered finances of the country caused still longer delay. Not until April 17, 1817, was the whole plan solidified into a legislative act—by which funds were provided for the construction of a canal 363 miles in length, with a surface width of 40 feet, a bottom width of 18 feet, and a water channel four feet in depth. But when the start fairly had been made the work went ahead rapidly. Ground was broken that same year, on July 4th, at Rome, on the middle section; and the excavation and structural work were pushed with such diligence that the canal was opened for traffic in but little more than eight years.

A picturesque celebration of "the wedding of the waters" followed the completion of the work. On the morning of October 26, 1825, the first flotilla of canal-boats bound for the seaboard left Buffalo, starting at the signal of a cannon fired at the Erie in-take. This shot straightway was echoed—guns having been stationed at regular intervals—down the whole length of the new waterway, and thence onward down the Hudson to New York: where, precisely one hour and twenty-five minutes after the first gun had been fired beside the lake, the last gun was fired beside the sea. During another hour and twenty-five minutes the answer from the ocean to the inland waters went thundering onward into the northwest.

And then, at this end of the line, the enthusiasm aroused in so thrilling a fashion had a whole fortnight in which to cool while the boats were crawling eastward. Yet crawling is a dull word to apply to what really was a triumphal progress. It would be more in harmony with the oratorical spirit of the occasion to say that the boats came eastward on

OPENING OF THE ERIE CANAL.

the crest of a wave of popular rejoicing: while all the canal towns burst forth into speeches of glorification by the lips of their local dignitaries, and listened to like speeches from Governor Clinton and Gouverneur Morris and the other migrant statesmen aboard the flotilla; while flags were flying everywhere by day and bonfires were blazing everywhere by night; and while all central New York was vibrant with the uncontrolled violence of countless brass bands.

At five o'clock on the morning of November 4th this fresh-water cyclone completed the last stage of its eventful progress, the run down the Hudson in tow of the *Chancellor Livingston*, and halted off the State prison (at the foot of the present West Tenth Street), while all the bells went off into joy-peals and there was a noble bellowing of guns. Off the State prison (a trysting-place which aroused no disagreeable doubts and dreads in the breasts of the aldermen of that earlier, non-boodling day) the flotilla was met by a deputation of the civic authorities charged with the duty of "congratulating the company on their arrival from Lake Erie," and of conducting them down stream, around the Battery, and up the East River to the Navy-yard; where a thunderous official salute was fired, and the officers of the corporation welcomed the distinguished guests in form. And then, from the Navy-yard, "a grand procession, consisting of nearly all the vessels in port gayly decked with colors of all nations," went down to the lower bay—where Governor Clinton, from the deck of the United States schooner *Dolphin*, about which all the other vessels were grouped in a great circle, poured a libation of the fresh water brought from Lake Erie into the salt water of the Atlantic Ocean—and so typified the joining together of the inland and the outland seas.

Either in dramatic effect or in commercial importance, the only other event in our national history that can be compared with this is the meeting—just forty-four years later—of the locomotives at Promontory Point: and the comparison is the more seemly because the building of the waterway from the Hudson to the lakes was one of the most important of the many acts of preparation which in the fulness of time made the building of the railway from ocean to ocean possible.

IX.

Practically, the building of the Erie Canal completed the material evolution of New York. That is to say, by the year 1825 the essential elements were assembled—a large and mixed population, transportation facilities into the heart of the continent, a foreign trade diffused over the whole globe—which constitute the New York of to-day.

This is far from saying that the city then entered upon, and ever since has continued in the possession of, unalloyed prosperity. Being essentially human, New York has a handsome potentiality of error and a fair average liability to misfortune—both of which attributes have been manifested repeatedly during the past threescore and eight years. In the way of misfortunes, for instance, a most serious one came only ten years after the canal was opened: "the great fire" of December, 1835, which began near the foot of Maiden Lane, burned upwards of six hundred buildings, including the Custom-house and the Merchants' Exchange, and caused a money loss of about twenty millions of dollars: some of which painful facts may be seen recorded to this day on a marble tablet displayed upon the building No. 80 Pearl Street. And in the way of errors, one of great magnitude was committed in this same fourth decade of the century—being an error in which the whole country had a share—when the naïve attempt was made to create unlimited credit on the alchemistic basis of paper declared to be transmuted into gold. The fire of 1835, with its vast consumption of substantial wealth, had its share in precipitating the financial panic of 1836-7; but this same panic surely would have come, and only a little later, even had there been no fire at all. Unfortunately, the lesson of 1837 was utterly wasted; and so also have been wasted the similar lessons of later date—for the disposition to dabble in that form of occult chemistry which seeks to create something out of nothing is so profoundly rooted in the human race that it needs must keep on sprouting until the very end of time.

But while on broad lines the material evolution of New York was completed in 1825, the practical development of the existing city dates from that very year. At that time the population numbered only 166,000, and the utmost stretch of fancy could not carry the limits of the city proper above Fourteenth Street. Since then the whole of the dwelling portion of New York—excepting comparatively small areas on the east and west sides of the island—has been created anew; and within the same period the region below Fourteenth Street, with the exceptions noted, has been turned over to business purposes, and a great part of it has been rebuilt—notably that portion lying south of where once was the wall—in a fashion that would make the sometime owners of the cabbage patches thereabouts use strong Dutch language expressive of awe! In this period, too, almost everything has been added to New York which distinguishes a city from an overgrown town: an adequate and wholesome water supply; an effective system of lighting; a provision of public parks so ample and so magnificently costly that 'tis fit to make the bones of the economical Commissioners of 1807 rattle a protest in their graves. And also—though these be sore and delicate points to touch upon—something has been done toward providing local transportation, toward properly paving the streets, and even toward keeping the streets clean. All of these improvements, with the others like in kind but less in degree which subsequently came to pass, were in embryo in the year 1825, and needed for their development only favoring conditions and time.

Equally existent in embryo were the developments which were to take place outside of New York but which were to be the very corner-stones of the city's later prosperity: the land and sea transportation service by steam. The ocean service came naturally, in sequence to that which had been expanded to great proportions before the new motive power had been reduced to practical working shape. Being established, the steamship lines had only to grow with the always growing trade. The existing railway service, which makes New York the seaboard terminus of all east-and-west lines, also is the necessary outgrowth of the earlier conditions when this port alone provided ample facilities for ocean carriage to all parts of the world. Possessing this advantage, the opening of the Erie Canal—a clear ten years before railways began seriously to modify the conditions of trade—gave this city a hold upon the business of the interior of the country that never afterwards was lost. And, consequently, when the railway building began in good earnest there was no question as to which of the seaboard cities should be the objective point of the traffic by rail. Whether the lines ended nominally at Baltimore or Philadelphia or Boston, their actual end—to which most of the goods for export must be brought, and from which almost all foreign goods must be received—was New York.

SUPERSTITIONS OF A COSMOPOLITAN CITY

THE incongruity is the fascination of it all. In New York, the most modern of all large cities, the very embodiment of twentieth-century youth, thrives superstition, gray with countless centuries of age.

When the night wind wails through the gorgelike streets of the great East Side, thousands tremble, for the restless cry is from the souls of children unbaptized. Where thick-packed multitudes mass, many a charm is said over the sick, many a spell is mystically woven, even as spells were whispered and charms woven in the forests of Northern Europe, centuries ago. Black art has not been banished by the electric light. Myths hold their own in spite of the railroad and the telegraph. Faith is desperately pinned to necromancy. There are, in New York, beliefs and weird practices which were old when the earliest scribe began to write upon rock.

Not long ago a quadroon was taken into court for preying upon the negroes of the Eighth Avenue colony. He claimed magic power, and in the power of his supposed magic a multitude believed. His arrest was brought about by a woman whose son remained ill despite the virtue of three green seals and a magic belt. Recently the will of a German woman, a dweller in Stanton Street, was disputed because she had profoundly dreaded the influence of witches and because, at her death, it had been found that little bags were hidden throughout her clothing, and that in them were incantations to drive the witches away. Attention was drawn, two years ago, to a woman in Ridge Street, who had many clients, and whose specialty was the bringing together of married folk who had drifted apart. She charged twenty dollars to each who invoked her aid, and for that sum she exorcised the evil spirit through whose malignancy the separation had come.

But it is seldom that the black art of Manhattan attracts the attention of the law. To find the terrible Hun who is in league with the devil, to find the seer who makes a child proof against poison by writing magic words, in blood, upon its forehead, to find the man who in consternation discovered skull and crossbones sewed upon his garment, to find where love-philters may be bought, with full instructions as to their administration, one must patiently come to know the mankind of the tenements.

Ghosts are told of in the crowded region north of Grand Street. There are tales of demonology in Chinatown. Almshouse dwellers, sitting in the sun, watching the surging tide and the glistening water, tell of spirits and banshees and fays. Italians dread the evil eye, but have faith in amulets.

Diedrich Knickerbocker narrates that at one time the witchcraft of New England threatened to spread into these Netherlands, and that certain broomstick apparitions actually appeared, but that the worthy dwellers within the gates of Manhattan kept the witches away by dint of the time-honored device of nailed-up horseshoes. It is quite evident, however, that since then witchcraft has stolen in.

Curious it is to find, in Essex or Ludlow Street or East Broadway, a belief in Lilith, the legendary first wife of Adam; but among these East Side women who pronounce incantations against her she is not Lilith as we know her in Rossetti, marvellously beautiful and eternally young, snaring the souls of men in the meshes of her enchanted hair, but a malicious personification of evil, forever watching to steal away or injure the new-born child.

Races that never heard of the predecessor of Eve share in the fear that new-born children are liable to be stolen away; they hold that fairies are the thieves, and that in the stead of infants taken away there are changelings, children deformed, the progeny of gnomes. Sometimes the fairy filching is interrupted in the very act. A Rutgers Street woman, impelled by a sudden fear, hurried back to her child, and found that in another moment there would have been a changeling substitution; for the fairy, interrupted by her return, had tucked the infant hastily back, but with its head toward the foot of the crib.

There are women who, following the dictates of ancient superstition, cruelly beat or torture the changelings that have been foisted upon them, for they hope thus to induce the child-pilferers, from very pity for the gnomish offspring, to make restitution. At least one such case, in which the child died from the severity of the burns received, has come to the definite attention of the New York police, and there is no doubt that some of the apparently inexplicable cases of fierce wrath toward children, on the part of sullenly reticent parents, obscurely root their motives in this grim belief. Especially is this likely to be the explanation when one child of a family is singled out from his brothers and sisters for savagery.

Superstition is seen, luminous in its ineradicability, in a little book of necromancy, especially for the sick, which is widely studied in Teutonic tenements. So absurd is its substance that it would only cause a smile did we not know that it is implicitly believed in by a great number of people.

It tells how to make oneself invisible, how to become impervious to shot, how to cure diseases. That many of its rules demand incantations which it is imperative properly to pronounce, or that there is designated some strange substance for medicine, often makes necessary the services of a Wise Woman.

Magic words and letters play their part in these dogmas of demonology, which dip far down into the glooming depths of human credulity. The blood of a basilisk, a black tick taken from the left ear of a cat, a stone bitten by a mad dog, the right eye of a live serpent, —such are some of the charms or medicines. One is taught, too, how to discover a witch and how to banish her. And for people who put faith in sorcery and charms, it is easy enough to believe a woman to be a witch, if she be meagre and decrepit, stunted and squeakvoiced, and if she look with a malevolent eye upon a world which has treated her malevolently.

" Take a new but useless nail. Pick the teeth well with it. Then drive the nail into a rafter, toward the rising sun, where no sun nor moon shines, and speak, at the first stroke, ' Toothache, vanish!' on the second, ' Toothache, banish!' on the third stroke, ' Toothache, thither fly!' "

Such is one of the cures, and of an amusing rather than impressive sound, in spite of impressive intent.

If one would be secure against shot, the following is infallible; but one sees why the interpretative Wise Woman must needs be called in:

" O Josophat; O Tomosath; O Plasorath! These words pronounce Jarot backwards three times."

It was through the case of a girl who was suffering in a shabby little room in a shabby tenement that I came to know of this school of necromancy and of the crass strength with which it holds sway. The girl's foot had been painfully crushed, yet all that the mother was doing for her was to have a Wise Woman come three times a day and drone over her, in German, with periodic interpolations of " the highest name of God," the following conjuration:

" Christ the Lord went through the field, and met a person who was sick of palsy. Christ the Lord spake: ' Whither art thou going, thou cold face?' The face thus addressed replied: ' I will enter into that man!' Christ the Lord said: ' Thou palsied face, thou shalt not do so. Pebble-stones thou must devour, bitter herbs thou shalt pluck. From a well thou must drink, and therein thou must sink.' "

One must grope far back among the misty shadows to find the origin of beliefs so ineradicable, so menacingly sinister. In centuries past many an old woman came to an unfelicitous end for conjurations identical with these. Yet the Wise Woman who droned the grisly jargon over the poor child's foot was far from witchlike in appearance. Of middle age, shrewd, impassive, slow, rather short, clean, clad in a plain black gown and knitted shoulder - cape — the very commonplaceness of her appearance gave an additional tang of disquiet.

It would be a mistake to think the superstitions of New York obtain among the ignorant only. The rich and the well-to-do dread thirteen at table—the result of a superstition which goes back to the Last Supper, where one was a traitor. In his great painting of the Supper, Da Vinci illustrates a prognostic in which many in Manhattan have faith —for Judas has just upset the salt! Educated men ward off rheumatism with horse-chestnuts. The Easter-egg custom comes· from rites and beliefs of unknown antiquity. Many, in moving, will not carry away a broom. Many count it unlucky to take the family cat with them to a new home. Many still put horseshoes over their doors—thus recognizing a superstition which apparently arose from the warding away of evil by the horseshoe - shaped bloodsplash of the Passover. There is a Wall Street broker who must have his right cheek shaved first, and the initial stroke must be upward. A certain horse-owner is confident of success if, on the morning of a race - day, he accidentally meets a cross-eyed man. Many a New York matron will under no circumstances remove the wedding - ring from her finger, for dire ill luck would come. A New York financier whose name is known throughout the world holds active superstitions in regard to cats. People watch the placing of valuables in a cornerstone, without suspecting that the custom is thought to have a far-distant necromantic origin in the use of human beings to strengthen buildings and bridges. The original belief still holds in out-of-theway corners of the world, and many of the Chinese believed the absurd report that the Czar of Russia was to safeguard the Manchurian railway by means of this ancient form of black art.

It is mainly among the undigested foreign element that the mightier superstitions lurk, and it is not always with the grimness which the beliefs themselves would seem to indicate.

The Italians, crowding into the city by tens of thousands, bring with them the superstitions of Italy, and belief in demon possession and in the evil eye is wellnigh universal among them. A leading churchman was believed, by a host of devout Italians, to have the power of the evil eye, though none believed that he ever wrongfully used it; and there are men and women in Roosevelt and Elizabeth streets, about Mulberry Bend and in the Little Italy of Harlem, who are held to be the possessors of this attribute.

But with the Italians magic is not of necessity a serious danger. The very commonness of it has rendered imperative and customary a multitude of counterbalancing charms, beginning with the stringing of certain shapes of coral about the necks of children, and in many cases continuing with the wearing of coral as a safeguard throughout life. Then, too, there is a way of so holding the fingers as to neutralize the evil, the method being to fold the two middle fingers into the palm, leaving the others projectively pronglike.

Properly considered, there is considerable amusement obtainable from the pervasiveness of Italian superstition and the rather practical ways of meeting and offsetting it. For example, a few years ago an Italian vice-consul went from New York to a neighboring town to investigate the murder of an Italian there. The slain man, it appeared, had sold his soul to the devil, and could at any time call that personage to do his bidding. This, not unnaturally, had the effect of minimizing the popularity of the man, and, in fact, of raising up enemies against him. The devil, it was learned, had made his life secure from steel, poison, or bullets; whereupon certain hard-headed compatriots fell upon him with clubs and tossed him into a pond to drown.

A curious epidemic of " devil frights," which followed each other in the schools of the East Side a few years ago, showed a readiness on the part of others than Italians to believe in the personal presence of the being that old Peter Stuyvesant legendarily shot with a silver bullet at Hell Gate. Time and again, while the epidemic lasted, schoolrooms were emptied by a panic following the cry that the devil was at the window.

Among the more ignorant there is a strange readiness of belief that Christians, especially those of certain settlement schools, strive by spells and branding-marks to win the children of Hebrews from their faith.

It had seemed remarkable that a fear of that particular kind should exist; but one evening I met a Hebrew, excited and eager, who told me that he had seen with his own eyes the branding on a child who attended one of these schools, and he offered to take me to see it.

He led the way to a decrepit rear tenement in Orchard Street. Men and women were agitatedly huddled in the hallway and upon the shaky stair, and others were crowded into an ill-lit room where a tall man, broom-bearded and gauntly gaberdined, was bending over a little girl, upon whose arm had been burned the letters "I O D E."

"Iesus Omnium Dominus Est— Jesus is the Lord of all," interpreted the old man, gutturally grim.

The little child, not too little to be proud of the attention it was exciting, again told the story of how a "black man" had met her in the hallway of the settlement school, and had seared the marks with a hot iron; and at that the room was filled anew with querulous Yiddish.

Yet the explanation was in the adjoining room, where a hot fire burned in a cooking-stove; for the door of the stove, upon which was the word "M O D E L," was the branding-iron. All of the word had been burned upon the child's arm except the "L" and the first three strokes of the "M." The girl's brother had pushed her against the stove, and had so frightened her with threats that she had feared to tell. With the stoicism of the poor, she had suffered in silence for a while; and then the mother, discovering the burn, had leaped at once to the conclusion that this was the dreaded branding of which she had often heard, and the neighborhood had been thrown into profound excitement.

To understand how remarkably it came about, print the letters "I O D E" on a piece of paper; lay the paper, with the ink wet, against another, and you will see the four letters reversed; turn

the slip around, as the brand would appear looking down upon it on the arm, and you will read the letters in their order, "I O D E."

Where all the continents pour their mingling human tides—in those thick-populated parts where silent Greeks smoke their long-tubed water-pipes, where turbaned Hindus bend above their rugs, where Lithuanian and Pole, Armenian and Swiss, Austrian, Scandinavian, and Hun, throng together—there are many strange beliefs. And far down along the East River, where great bowsprits stretch far over South Street, where there are casks and bales and endless rope and chain, you may hear, in ancient taverns nodding dreamily toward the water, marvellous tales from them that go down to the sea in ships, for these weather-beaten men retain belief in ancient sailors' lore.

Science cannot dispel superstition. From the view-point of the superstitious man, a wagon moving without horses, a message sent without wires, or a train propelled by an unseen current, adds to the miracle of it all.

When the wind drifts drearily in from the bay, when the storm shouts over the roofs of Poverty Hollow, when the calling wind echoes dismally in the hallways of Sunken Village and Battle Row and creeps disquietingly in and out of dusky corners, when the mist clings in ghostly folds about ships and houses, the heart of the superstitious man responds as it did when the wind roared through great forests, and the snow fell and the mist gathered and the glimmering moon shone white before the dawn of civilization.

Down in Mott Street, where gleaming lanterns swing from balconies, where the smell of incense is in the air, where joss-sticks burn and sallow-faced men bow before the figured idol, there is unquestioned belief in fiends and devils, in magic and in spells. The silent, watchful men seldom speak to you; those who know English are apt to shake their heads, and to do business in abbreviations, backed up by signs; but now and then one is found who, if his Eastern soul opens, will tell you strange tales of things unseen.

THE STORY OF A STREET
(PART 2)

HAD Captain Kidd revisited Wall Street some three-and-forty years after he had become one of its pioneer proprietors, he would have found himself in strange surroundings, and it is not at all probable that he would have realized the dignity or importance of the thoroughfare from any external evidence. Indeed, the street presented in 1734 a decidedly ragged and unattractive aspect. At its eastern end or slip, in front of the Long Island Ferry, stood the flimsily constructed Meal Market, whose transactions in corn and similar merchandise had been supplemented by a more profitable traffic in negro slaves, who were daily displayed in its stands for the benefit of those desiring to buy, sell, or hire such commodities, and on either side of this unsavory mart stretched a broken line of mean little wooden buildings extending as far west as William Street. From this point the prospect gradually improved, the Broadway end boasting some dwellings of neat and attractive appearance, but the north side remained entirely vacant save for four wholly dissimilar structures. The first of these, on the northwest between William and Nassau streets, was the property of Gabriel Thompson, a tavernkeeper, beyond which loomed a huge barnlike affair erected by the Bayards, in 1729, for what they termed "the mystery of sugar refining"—a mystery which Wall Street has not wholly fathomed to the present day; and adjoining this crude factory stood the most pretentious building on Manhattan Island—the City Hall, whose foundations had been laid in 1699 with the stones taken from the bastions of the old palisade. Beyond this, and almost adjoining it, lay the Presbyterian church, a substantial brick edifice; and at the head of the street on Broadway squatted the ugly, square little wooden building with a disproportionately tall steeple which had sheltered the congregation of Trinity Church since 1696.

Such was the condition of the street which had in less than half a century acquired political if not social ascendency over all other thoroughfares of the city, which now boasted a population of nearly ten thousand souls. The most potent influence effecting this result had, of course, been the selection of the street as the site of the City Hall, for that building was not only the seat of government, but the social centre, New York in those days being ruled by an aristocracy whose nod made the laws and set the fashions. The presence of Trinity Church had likewise given the street a certain social prestige, for it had almost immediately become the semi-official place of worship, with a pew reserved for the Mayor, Recorder, Aldermen, and other dignitaries, and its list of parishioners included many of the most notable people in the community. In fact, when Messrs. De Peyster and Bayard, who had purchased most of Governor Dongan's queerly acquired holdings of the northern frontage, enabled the Presbyterian Church to obtain a broad foothold, practically all the spiritual and temporal power of the city lay concentrated on the narrow, unlovely highway. Under these circumstances it is not at all surprising that well to do families soon began to establish comfortable residences in proximity to the churches, that the mercantile and financial exchanges clustered along the site of the old canal to the very steps of the City Hall, and that that building became the scene of almost every event associated with the early history of the rising city.

There was very little evidence of Wall Street's prosperity or popularity, however, at high noon on the 6th of November,

1734. Indeed, a more silent and deserted highway could scarcely be imagined. Not a coach rumbled up or down its cobbled roadbed, no pedestrians were astir, and its houses showed no sign of life. In fact, the whole street from the water's edge to Trinity appeared to be in the possession of two men, who stood near the pillory, whipping post, stocks, and cage at the head of Broad Street, opposite the City Hall. One of these lonely individuals, however, was a person of some consequence in the community, whose presence betokened a public function of no ordinary importance; for Jeremiah Dunbar, the Recorder, was a dignified gentleman whose offices could be required only for affairs of state, and the paper which he proceeded to read in stentorian tones demonstrated that he was attending in his official capacity. For a time it seemed as though the worthy Recorder would have no auditor except the negro slave who stood at his elbow, but, before he concluded, a little group of officers sauntered up Broad Street from the direction of Fort George and paused to learn the occasion of this proclamation to an empty street. Solemn indeed was the occasion as disclosed by the Recorder, who with due form and ceremony recited an order of the Council, dated October 17, 1734, wherein and whereby it appeared that one John Peter Zenger had set up, printed, and published divers and sundry nefarious matters defamatory of the government and his Excellency Governor Cosby, in a news sheet or paper known as the *New York Weekly Journal:* wherefore it was decreed that certain issues of said paper, numbered 7, 47, 48, and 49,* should be burned near the pillory at the hands of the Common Hangman or Whipper as a public warning to the writer and other evil minded persons, and that the printer should be duly prosecuted for the injurious statements contained in his sheet. Very little of all this was sufficient to put the Recorder's slim audience in touch with the situation, for Governor Cosby's recent encounter with the local authorities over the case

* These and subsequent details are derived from a rare publication in possession of the New York Bar Association, entitled *Narrative of the Case and Trial of John Peter Zenger,* issued in London in 1752.

of the *Weekly Journal* was unpleasantly familiar to all the powers that were. Indeed, every one in town knew that his Excellency had overreached himself by ordering the Mayor and city magistrates to attend the destruction of Zenger's paper, and that those functionaries, quick to resent any infringement of their liberties, had instantly denied his right to impose any such duty upon them, and flatly refused to lend their presence to the scene. This angry clash of authority had been followed by a petition from the sheriff praying that the public whipper be designated as the person to apply the torch, and when his request had been denied, the coerced official had appointed a negro slave to act as his deputy, and the public had decided by common consent to support the local authorities by shunning the scene of action at the appointed hour.

Such was the explanation of Wall Street's deserted aspect; but Recorder Dunbar was equal to the occasion, and the four offending papers were duly burned by the sheriff's humble substitute, to the thorough satisfaction of the spectators, who gravely watched the flames until the last scrap was reduced to ashes, and then turned on their heels with an exchange of formal salutes, Dunbar retiring to the City Hall and the officers to their local barracks.

It would be difficult to imagine a more childish performance than this whole proceeding, and even from a childish standpoint it was far from a success, for the fire was not a good one, and its flames were poorly fed. Yet of this tiny blaze started in Wall Street in the fall of 1734 came a mighty conflagration which well-nigh lit a world.

John Peter Zenger, whose editorial pages were thus cleansed with fire, was not the ablest journalist of New York, and Governor Cosby, whose administration he attacked, was not its worst Executive. The whole history of the city, however, had long been an inglorious recital of greed, corruption, incompetence, and arrogance, the royal governors having included a gentleman who made the seaport the most desirable of all piratical resorts; a noble personage who took pleasure in masquerading in women's clothing and exhibiting himself in this

Drawn by Harry Fenn

BURNING OF ZENGER'S "WEEKLY JOURNAL" IN WALL STREET, NOVEMBER 6, 1734

Based on original records and prints in Lenox Library and New York Historical Society. The building to the right are the City Hall and the Presbyterian Church. The original Trinity Church is indicated in the distance. The stocks, whipping-post, cage, and pillory are shown at the head of Broad Street

guise, with the pleasing delusion that he might be mistaken for Queen Anne; and a solemn nonentity who took himself so seriously that he exacted more deference and reverence than would have been accorded to his royal master. In fact, all the powers that were, including the landed gentry and the personal and political favorites of the provincial court, displayed an undisguised contempt for the masses, affecting an elegance of attire in which dress swords, ruffled shirts, silk stockings, and short clothes served to emphasize the class distinctions. Not all the members of this little aristocracy, however, were Englishmen, for no more proud or exclusive dignitaries ever strutted than the Dutch patroons, and when the ponderous travelling coach of one of those lords of the manor lumbered down Wall Street's cobbled roadway, on official business bent, there were few who disdained to court recognition, while the populace frankly stared with admiring wonder, many of them cap in hand.

It was this condition of affairs that had brought Zenger to the front as the nominal editor and publisher of the *Weekly Journal*, which had really been established and was mainly supported by James Alexander and William Smith, two able lawyers, under whose active leadership a popular party was rapidly forming.

Zenger himself was a young man of more courage than education, whose boldest utterances read very mildly in these days of unbridled denunciation, but any criticism of official actions was then regarded as presumptuous, and his shafts evidently hit the mark, for the destruction of his pages had been planned as a most impressive ceremony, and the humiliating fiasco which resulted, virtually forced the government to take further proceedings in defence of its dignity. Within ten days, therefore, Zenger was arrested at the instance of Governor Cosby and lodged in jail, where he remained for many months in default of excessive bail. Meanwhile the public began to take an unprecedented interest in the affair, and under the energetic leadership of Alexander and Smith such a strong sentiment was aroused in favor of the accused that the Grand Jury refused to find an indictment against him, and the Attorney-General was compelled to resort to extraordinary measures to prevent his release. This merely intensified the popular feeling, however, and before long all the scattered opponents of the government rallied to the slogan, "Freedom of the Press!" and united in supporting the imprisoned editor, whose cause immediately became a politica' issue of far reaching effect.

Never before had the general public been identified with any determined effort to secure freedom of the press in America, and far seeing men throughout the country, including Benjamin Franklin and other aspiring journalists, watched the struggle with keen interest, while in New York the opening moves of Zenger's counsel resulted in such sensational developments that the public excitement was kept at the highest pitch.

The City Hall, where Zenger had been confined, was far from a triumph of architecture, but it was dignified and spacious, affording accommodations for a court room, a jury room, a Council chamber, a common jail, a library,* and a debtor's prison, to say nothing of space reserved for the fire department, whose water supply was partially obtained from two Wall Street wells; and it was here that the lawyers for the defence began the proceedings which were destined to assume historic importance. These public spirited advocates were no other than Messrs. Alexander and Smith, under whose covert patronage the *Weekly Journal* had been established, and their appearance in the cause was particularly obnoxious to the government, which rightly suspected them of having personally contributed some of its most offensive material. Moreover, only a few years earlier they had virtually abolished the Court of Exchequer expressly convened by Governor Cosby for the destruction of Rip Van Dam, a popular official, and to punish Chief Justice Morris for his decision in that case the angry Executive had removed him and appointed James De Lancey in his place.

* Wall Street was never a literary centre, but it housed the first collection of books known to the city. This library subsequently became the Corporation Library, and eventually the New York Society Library, which exists to-day.

De Lancey was a jurist of exceptional ability, but a thorough partisan of the government, and Zenger's counsel had good reason to know that their client would receive very little consideration at his hands. Their first move therefore was to challenge his and the associate justice's* right to sit upon the bench, and regardless of consequences the petition for their removal was presented to the very men they were seeking to depose. Both the Chief Justice and his associate had been appointed during the pleasure of the Governor and not during good behavior, and this illegality, it was claimed, absolutely disqualified t h e m from holding court. There was no little shrewdness in thus appealing directly to De Lancey's sense of propriety, but it was too much to expect that a man of his character would scruple to judge his own case, and if the audacious attorneys entertained any such hope they were speedily undeceived. Indeed, they had no sooner filed their application than the indignant jurist met their defiance by significantly offering them an opportunity to withdraw it, and upon their refusal he made short work of them and their attack.

"You thought to have gained a great deal of applause and popularity by opposing this court as you did the Court of Exchequer," he exclaimed to the presumptuous counsel, "but you have brought it to this point, that either we must go from the bench or you from the bar!" Whereupon he struck the names of both offenders from the rolls of practising attorneys, and the prisoner was thus left unrepresented at the very outset

* Frederick Philipse.

of his cause. This sensational development, however, merely served to intensify the popular feeling, and John Chambers, another attorney, was almost immediately retained for the defence, and at the last moment Andrew Hamilton, of Philadelphia, the most distinguished advocate

BIRD'S-EYE VIEW OF WALL STREET ABOUT 1735

of his day, volunteered his services in behalf of the accused.

Such was the situation on the 4th of August, 1735, when the greatest crowd which Wall Street had ever harbored gathered at the City Hall clamoring for admission, and before it dispersed a long step had been taken toward American independence.

The little court room, to which only a small percentage of the crowd gained admittance, presented a brilliant picture when the prisoner was called to the dock, for the judges wore the rich robes and long judicial wigs familiar to English courts, the lawyers were arrayed in the picturesque wigs and gowns officially prescribed for barristers, and all the functions and ceremonies of English legal procedure were carefully observed.* Moreover, the audience included almost all the prominent government officials, appropriately attired for an affair of state, and many army officers, whose smart uniforms contrasted sharply with the sombre but effective dress of the popular party. Never before had Wall Street witnessed a similar gathering, and it was never to see its like again, for a new era was dawning when the people opposed their rulers in that crowded court of law.

Hamilton opened the proceedings by admitting his client's authorship of the papers in question, and announcing that he would rest his defence on the truth of the statements they contained. Thereupon an extraordinary legal battle ensued, the Attorney-General and the Chief Justice joining in an attack upon the eminent Pennsylvanian and endeavoring to ride roughshod over his contentions. But Hamilton, though enfeebled by old age and ill health, more than held his own, and when he at last acquired the right to address the jury he rose to the occasion with the most powerful plea for freedom of the press that the New World had ever heard. So masterful indeed was his argument that the Chief Justice felt constrained to counteract its influence by virtually directing the jury to convict. Nevertheless, the twelve good men and true† promptly returned a verdict of acquittal; and the moment the foreman announced this result the audience leaped to its feet and burst into a storm of cheering which De Lancey was powerless to suppress. Again and again he attempted to restore order, but one of the popular leaders practically defied his authority, and with renewed cheers the exultant victors poured into Wall Street, where the roaring crowd instantly surrounded Hamilton and attempted to carry him off in triumph on

its shoulders. That night the whole city was ablaze with enthusiasm, a grand banquet was given in Hamilton's honor, and all the popular leaders were cheered to the echo. Indeed, the public rejoicing continued throughout the following day, and when the successful advocate started for Philadelphia his barge was accompanied by an enormous throng and his departure honored by a salute of cannon. Nor was this the end, for some weeks later the Common Council awarded him the freedom of the city in recognition of his disinterested services to the people, and the address conferring this distinction was conveyed to him* in a gold box ornamented with the arms of the city. Thus ended an event which Gouverneur Morris called the dawn of American liberty, and many of the scenes which Wall Street witnessed in later years can be clearly traced to the influence of this *cause célèbre*.

Indeed, from 1735 to 1770 the history of the city is a record of constant collisions between the popular party and the royal Executive, and he was a strong man indeed who more than held his own. Governor Clark proved unequal to the task, Clinton fought fiercely for ten years and then retired exhausted, Osborn killed himself on the eve of conflict, Sir Charles Hardy virtually surrendered all authority into the hands of Lieutenant - Governor De Lancey, Major-General Monckton practically abdicated in favor of Cadwallader Colden, and Sir Henry Moore was far from the ruling power. Thus in thirty-five years the representative of the King was transformed from an autocrat into a figurehead, and further changes were already in prospect.

Meanwhile Wall Street, which had acclaimed the gorgeous inaugural processions of the incoming governors and speeded most of the retiring officials with jeers, had been altering its appearance for the better by abolishing the old slave market, which vanished in 1762, and in the same year street lamps were introduced. These public betterments were soon followed by the complete renovation of the City Hall and the removal of the whipping post, pillory, stocks, and cage, and with its house thus put

---

* This is probably the first case in New York ever tried before a "struck" jury. Order of July 29, 1735. Judge Smith states in his *History of New York* (Vol. I., p. 316) that the New York judges and lawyers never wore gowns in colonial days, but there is evidence to the contrary at the date of Zenger's trial.

† Several well known New York families were evidently represented on this jury, which included such names as Rutgers, Holmes, Man, Bell, Keteltas, Hildreth, and Goelet.

* By Alderman Stephen Bayard.

in order Wall Street welcomed the first and perhaps the most notable assemblage recorded in the history of the United States.

It was with no blare of trumpets or any official ceremonies that this distinguished company convened in the City Hall on the 7th of October, 1765, but on that day and in that building the American Revolution may fairly be said to have started, for the Stamp Congress was the first representative body organized for the common protection of all the colonies, and in it the Continental Congress was plainly foreshadowed. No less than nine colonies were represented at this famous Congress, and among the delegates who journeyed to Wall Street were Robert and Philip Livingston, James Otis, William Samuel Johnson, John Rutledge, Thomas McKean, and

others,* whose names were to become household words and whose deeds were to enroll them among the founders of the nation. These men of unsuspected powers conducted their proceedings behind closed doors, but during their deliberations, which lasted three weeks, the interest of the whole country was centred on the narrow highway, and the address to the King and the memorials to the Houses of Parliament—the first of those remarkable state papers which won the admiration of Europe—were composed almost within shadow of Trinity Church.

This dignified assemblage was still in session when the first ship bearing the obnoxious stamps arrived in the harbor,

* Full list of the delegates is to be found in New York *Mercury* issue of October 14, 1765.

ANDREW HAMILTON DEPARTING FROM THE CITY HALL, AUGUST 4, 1735

BIRD'S-EYE VIEW OF WALL STREET ABOUT 1774

and from that moment the calm deliberations of the visiting statesmen ceased to interest the excited city. Action and not argument now seemed imperative, and for several days turbulent crowds thronged the streets, and notices advocating violence were posted at every public meeting place. Finally on the evening of November 1 the storm broke, and the residents of Wall Street, aroused by the sound of a tumult in the direction of the Fields,* rushed from their houses, and then hastily retreated to bar their

* Now the City Hall Park.

doors against the strangest mob which ever invaded a peaceful thoroughfare. Down Pearl (Queen) Street a torchlight procession was advancing with shouts and shots and other alarming demonstrations, and at its head rumbled a gallows on wheels bearing an effigy of Lieutenant-Governor Colden, followed by another similar figure carried in a chair on the head of a stalwart negro. Hooting, jeering, and occasionally shooting at these effigies, several hundred sailors and rough waterside characters bearing torches and lanterns swung into Wall Street, and on their heels followed a great throng of boisterous men. Suddenly, to the dismay of the householders, anxiously watching the wild scene from behind their shuttered windows, the paraders halted before the house of one James McEvers; but their leaders immediately called for three cheers for this gentleman, who, through prudence or patriotism, had resigned his position as stamp distributor, and the crowd, responding with an approving roar and a flourish of lanterns and torches, swept on toward the City Hall.* Brief as this delay was, it had enabled the panic-stricken authorities to organize some slight resistance, and by the time the mob reached Broad Street its progress was opposed by the Mayor, Aldermen, and a squad of constables, who boldly attacked the bearers of the effigies and actually succeeded in tumbling their burdens into the street. Surprised by this vigorous assault, the rioters halted in confusion; but the moment they perceived that only a handful of men stood before them they pressed forward, carrying the officials off their feet, and in another moment they had gained the City Hall and were swarming up the narrow incline leading past the Presbyterian church to Trinity. Here the leaders swung to the left, and with an exultant roar the mob followed, heading straight for Fort George, where the hated stamps had been deposited, and in a few minutes it was massed before the entrance, clamoring for admission. No response being given to this angry demonstration, some of the more adventurous spirits broke into the Lieutenant-Governor's carriage house, and seizing one of the coaches, bundled the effigies into it and dragged it off in triumph, the others following with shouts of exultation.

Again Wall Street was invaded, but this time the crowd assembled at the Merchants' Coffee House received the crude pageant with cheers as it passed on to the Fields, where a junction was formed with another mob, and the whole force again headed for the Battery. Once more a half-hearted attempt was made to gain admittance to the fort, but after hammering on the gate with

* New York *Weekly Gazette* and the *Weekly Post Boy*, November 7, 1765.

their cudgels the ringleaders again turned their attention to the coach house, and dragging out the Lieutenant-Governor's sleighs and carriages, heaped them together on Bowling Green, threw the effigies on top, and quickly turned the whole mass into a roaring bonfire, around which hundreds of men capered in a wild and sinister dance.

Thus ended this night of terror, but for the next two days the city remained in comparative quiet. Then anonymous placards and notices began to reappear warning the authorities of further trouble if the stamps were not surrendered, and hasty conferences were held between the Mayor, the acting Governor, and the leading citizens to concert measures for maintaining order. At first Colden was for meeting force with force, but finding little support for this policy, he finally compromised by sanctioning a semi-official promise that no use should be made of the stamps until further orders from England. But the "Sons of Liberty," who had undoubtedly organized the hostile demonstrations, were in no mood to accept such empty concessions, and the only response to the Governor's proclamation was a notice calling another meeting in the Fields for the night of November 5.

At this juncture the city magistrates hurriedly convened in the City Hall, and an enormous throng gathered outside the building to learn the result of their deliberations. Finally a committee was appointed to urge that the stamps be surrendered into the custody of the local authorities, and the moment the men entrusted with this mission appeared on the street the crowd closed in and escorted them to the threshold of Fort George, where they halted in a silent but menacing mass. Very little would have sufficed at that critical moment to precipitate a violent conflict. Behind the feeble ramparts were gathered a few hundred armed but not overreliable troops, and facing them an overwhelming army of determined and not too orderly citizens. Had either side provoked the other, or even had the parley between the Executive and the committee been unduly prolonged, the first bloodshed in the cause of independence would undoubtedly have occurred near Bowling

Green. It was not long, however, before the committee reappeared and announced, amid a scene of wild rejoicing, that the acting Governor had yielded and would surrender the stamps to the Mayor. Welcome as this news was, the crowd did not disperse, but hung about the fort waiting the fulfilment of the official promise, and before long the gates opened and a strong guard marched out escorting the hated documents.

Then followed a triumphant return to Wall Street, the victorious populace surrounding the bearers of the captured papers and accompanying them to the very steps of the City Hall, where the Mayor receipted for them, their surrender being the signal for an outburst which recalled the demonstrations accorded Hamilton's first victory for the people, on the same spot, thirty years before.

Some four months later the Stamp Act was repealed, largely through the efforts of William Pitt, in whose honor a marble statue was erected in Wall Street, which was rapidly becoming the centre of fashion and was soon to be the scene of many memorable events in the founding of the nation.

ITALIAN LIFE IN NEW YORK

TRUANTS FROM SCHOOL.

ITALIAN LIFE IN NEW YORK.

THE fact that Italian immigration is constantly on the increase in New York makes it expedient to consider both the condition and status of these future citizens of the republic. The higher walks of American life, in art, science, commerce, literature, and society, have, as is well known, long included many talented and charming Italians; but an article under the above title must necessarily deal with the subject in its lower and more recent aspect. During the year 1879 seven thousand two hundred Italian immigrants were landed at this port, one-third of which number remained in the city, and there are now over twenty thousand Italians scattered among the population of New York. The more recently arrived herd together in colonies, such as those in Baxter and Mott streets, in Eleventh Street, in Yorkville, and in Hoboken. Many of the most important industries of the city are in the hands of Italians as employers and employed, such as the manufacture of macaroni, of objects of art, confectionery, artificial flowers; and Italian workmen may be found everywhere mingled with those of other nationalities. It is no uncommon thing to see at noon some swarthy Italian, engaged on a building in process of erection, resting and dining from his tin kettle, while his brown-skinned wife sits by his side, brave in her gold earrings and beads, with a red flower in her hair, all of which at home were kept for feast days. But here in America increased wages make every day a feast day in the matter of food and raiment;

and why, indeed, should not the architectural principle of beauty supplementing necessity be applied even to the daily round of hod-carrying? Teresa from the Ligurian mountains is certainly a more picturesque object than Bridget from Cork, and quite as worthy of incorporation in our new civilization. She is a better wife and mother, and under equal circumstances far outstrips the latter in that improvement of her condition evoked by the activity of the New World. Her children attend the public schools, and develop very early an amount of energy and initiative which, added to the quick intuition of Italian blood, makes them valuable factors in the population. That the Italians are an idle and thriftless people is a superstition which time will remove from the American mind. A little kindly guidance and teaching can mould them into almost any form. But capital is the first necessity of the individual. Is it to be wondered at, therefore, that the poor untried souls that wander from their village or mountain homes, with no advice but that of the parish priest, no knowledge of the country to which they are going but the vague though dazzling remembrance that somebody's uncle or brother once went to Buenos Ayres and returned with a fortune, no pecuniary resource but that which results from the sale of their little farms or the wife's heritage of gold beads, and no intellectual capital but the primitive methods of farming handed down by their ancestors, should drift into listless and hopeless poverty? Their emigration is frequently in the hands of shrewd compatriots, who manage to land them on our shores in a robbed and plundered condition.

On the other hand, the thrifty *bourgeois* who brings with him the knowledge of a trade, and some little capital to aid him in getting a footing, very soon begins to prosper, and lay by money with which to return and dazzle the eyes of his poorer neighbors, demoralizing his native town by filling its inhabitants with yearnings toward the El Dorado of "Nuova York." Such a man, confectioner, hairdresser, or grocer, purchases a villa, sets

hand struggle for bread of an overcrowded city. Hence the papers of the peninsula teem with protests and warnings from the pens of intelligent Italians in America against the thoughtless abandonment of home and country on the uncertain prospect of success across the ocean.

The fruit trade is in the hands of Italians in all its branches, from the Broadway shop with its inclined plane of glowing color, to the stand at a street corner. Among the last the well-to-do fruit-merchant has a substantial wooden booth.

A STREET-LIFE SCENE.

up his carriage, and to all appearance purposes spending his life in elegant leisure; but the greed of money-getting which he has brought back from the New World surges restlessly within him, and he breaks up his establishment, and returns to New York to live behind his shop in some damp, unwholesome den, that he may add a few more dollars to his store, and too often his avarice is rewarded by the contraction of a disease which presently gives his hard-earned American dollars into the hands of his relatives in Italy. There is an element of chance in the success of Italians which makes emigration with them a matter of more risk than with other nationalities of more prudence and foresight. The idyllic life of an Italian hill-side or of a dreaming mediæval town is but poor preparation for the hand-to-

which he locks up in dull times, removing his stock. In winter he also roasts chestnuts and pea-nuts, and in summer dispenses slices of water-melon and *aqua cedrata* to the *gamins* of the New York thoroughfares, just as he once did to the small lazzaroni of Naples or the fisherboys of Venice. With the poorer members of the guild the little table which holds the stock in trade is the family hearth-stone, about which the children play all day, the women gossip over their lace pillows, and the men lounge in the lazy, happy ways of the peninsula. At night the flaring lamps make the dusky faces and the masses of fruit glow in a way that adds much to the picturesqueness of our streets. These fruit-merchants are from all parts of Italy, and always converse cheerfully with any one who can speak their language, with the exception of an occasional sulky youth who declines to tell where he came from, thereby inviting the suspicion that he has fled to escape the conscription. That they suffer much during our long cold winters is not to be doubted, but the patience of their characters and the deprivations to which they have always been accustomed make them philosophic and stolid. As soon as they begin to prosper, the fatalism of poverty gives place to the elastic independence of success, and their faces soon lose their characteristic mournfulness. I have seen young Italian peasants walking about the city, evidently just landed, and clad in their Sunday best—Giovanni in his broad hat, dark blue jacket, and leggings, and Lisa with her massive braids and gay shawl, open-eyed and wide-mouthed in the face of the wonderful civilization they are to belong to in the future. The elevated railroad especially seems to offer them much food for speculation—a kind of type of the headlong recklessness of Nuova York, so unlike the sleepy old ways of the market-town which has hitherto bounded their vision.

There are two Italian newspapers in New York—*L' Eco d' Italia* and *Il Republicano*. There are also three societies for mutual assistance—the "Fratellanza Italiana," the "Ticinese," and the "Bersaglieri." When a member of the Fratellanza dies, his wife receives a hundred dollars; when a wife dies, the husband receives fifty dollars; and a physician is provided for sick members of the society. It gives a ball every winter and a picnic in summer, which are made the occasion of patriotic demonstrations that serve to keep alive the love of Italy in the hearts of her expatriated children. Many of the heroes of '48 are to be found leading quiet, humble lives in New York. Many a one who was with Garibaldi and the Thousand in Sicily, or entered freed Venice with Victor Emanuel, now earns bread for wife and child in modest by-ways of life here in the great city. Now and then one of the king's soldiers, after serving all through the wars, drops down in his shop or work-room, and is buried by his former comrades, awaiting their turn to rejoin King Galantuomo.

There is something pathetically noble in this quiet heroism of work-day life after the glory and action of the past. I met the other day in a flower factory,

stamping patterns for artificial flowers, an old Carbonaro who had left his country twenty-two years before—one of the old conspirators against the Austrians who followed in the footsteps of Silvio Pellico and the Ruffinis. He was gray-haired and gray-bearded, but his eyes flashed with the fire of youth when we talked of Italy, and grew humid and bright when he told me of his constant longing for his country, and his feeling that he should never see it again. It was a suggestive picture, this fine old Italian head, framed by the scarlet and yellow of the flowers about him, while the sunlight and the brilliant American air streamed over it from the open window, and two young Italians, dark-eyed and stalwart, paused in their work and came near to listen. It was the Italy of Europe twenty years back brought face to face with the Italy of America to-day. In another room, pretty, low-browed Italian girls were at work making leaves—girls from Genoa, Pavia, and other cities of the north, who replied shyly when addressed in their native tongue. Italians are especially fitted for this department of industry; indeed, their quick instinct for beauty shows itself in every form of delicate handiwork.

In the second generation many Italians easily pass for Americans, and prefer to do so, since a most unjust and unwarranted prejudice against Italians exists in many quarters, and interferes with their success in their trades and callings. It is much to be regretted that the sins of a few turbulent and quarrelsome Neapolitans and Calabrians should be visited upon the heads of their quiet, gentle, and hard-working compatriots. All Italians are proud and high-spirited, but yield easily to kindness, and are only defiant and revengeful when ill-treated.

There are two Italian Protestant churches in the city, various Sunday-schools, mission and industrial schools, into which the Italian element enters largely, established and carried on by Protestant Americans, chiefly under the auspices of the Children's Aid Society. The most noteworthy of these, as being attended exclusively by Italians, adults and children, is the one in Leonard Street.

Some four hundred boys and girls are under instruction in the afternoon and night schools, most of them being engaged in home or industrial occupations during

AN ITALIAN FÊTE DAY IN NEW YORK.

the day. The building is large and airy, containing school-rooms, bath-rooms, a reading-room, and printing-offices, where work is furnished to Italians at the usual wages, and those seeking instruction are taught. There is a class of twenty-

THE DUET.

four girls who are taught plain sewing and ornamental needle-work, including lace-making. I visited this class, and found a number of little girls employed with lace cushions, and the manufacture of simple artificial flowers. With these last they were allowed to trim the new straw hats that had just been given them. They were plump, cleanly little creatures, much better off in the matter of food and raiment than their contemporaries of the peninsula. The lace class has been in existence but a short time, and the specimens are still somewhat coarse and irregular, but there is no reason why it should not become as important a branch of industry among the Italian women of America as among those of Europe. The only wonder is that instruction in a calling which exists by inheritance in Italy should be needed here, as these girls are mostly from the villages of Liguria, of which Genoa is the sea-port, and might fairly be supposed to know something of the craft which has made Rapallo and Santa Margherita famous. Shirts for outside orders are also made in the school, and the girls receive the same wages for their labor as are offered by the shops. The attendants upon the school are mostly Ligurians, and repudiate indig-nantly all kinship with the Neapolitans or Calabrians, whom they refuse to recognize as Italians, thereby showing how little the sectional sentiment of Italy has been affected by the union of its parts under one ruler.

Under the guidance of a lady connected with the school, I explored Baxter and contiguous streets, nominally in search of dilatory pupils. Here and there a small girl would be discovered sitting on the curb-stone or in a doorway, playing jack-stones, with her hair in tight crimps, preparatory to participation in some church ceremony. An Italian feminine creature of whatever age, or in whatever clime, stakes her hopes of heaven on the dressing of her hair. Her excuse for remaining away from school was that she had to "mind the stand," or tend the baby, while her mother was occupied elsewhere, and her countenance fell when she was reminded that she could have brought the baby to school. It was noticeable that all these children, who had left Italy early or were born here, had clear red and white complexions, the result of the American climate. We passed through courts and alleys where swarthy Neapolitans were carting bales of rags, and up dark stairs where women and children were sorting them. Some of their homes were low, dark rooms, neglected and squalid; others were clean and picturesque, with bright patchwork counterpanes on the beds, rows of gay plates on shelves against the walls, mantels and shelves fringed with colored paper, red and blue prints of the saints against the white plaster, and a big nosegay of lilacs on the dresser among the earthen pots. Dogs and children were

ing his way from one watering-place to another, accompanied perhaps by his family, or at least a child or two. In answer to an inquiry concerning monkeys, we were directed to a large double house opposite, said to be inhabited entirely by Neapolitans, who were swarming about the windows in all their brown shapeliness. In the hallway, above the rickety outer stairs, lounged several men with

THE MONKEYS' TRAINING-SCHOOL.

tumbling together on the thresholds just as they do in the cool corridors of Italian towns. On the first floor of one of the houses I found an establishment for the repairing of hand-organs, where a youth was hammering at the barrel of one, and a swarthy black-bearded man, to whom it belonged, was lounging on a bench near by. Against the smoke-blackened wall an armful of lilacs stood in a corner, filling the room with sweetness, and leading naturally to the thought that with the spring and the flowers the organ-grinder prepares for a trip into the country, play-

red shirts and unkempt heads and faces. One of them was the proprietor of the monkey establishment, and his *farouche* manner disappeared with our first words of interest in his pets. He led us into the little room adjoining, where some six or eight half-grown monkeys were peering through the bars of their cages, evidently pleading to be let out. The most creditably schooled monkey was released first, handed his cap, made to doff and don it, and shake hands, orders being issued both in Italian and English. Some of the others—small brown things with bright eyes, and "not yet quite trained," said the Neapolitan—were allowed a moment's respite from captivity, at which they screamed with joy, and made for the dish of soaked bread, dipping their paws into it with great greediness, while the *padrone* laughed indulgently. A properly trained organ-monkey is worth from twenty to thirty dollars.

In the great house known to Baxter Street as the "Bee-hive," we found the handsome *padrona* whose husband rents organs and sells clocks, which latter articles appear to be essentials to Italian housekeeping, in default of the many bells of the old country. The *padrona* was at first by no means eager to give information, as she supposed, in good broad American (she was born in New York), that it "would be put in the papers, like it was before." It would appear that the advantages of communication with the outer world are not appreciated by the inhabitants of Baxter Street. The *padrona* finally informed me that the rent of an organ was four dollars a month, and that they had hard work getting it out of the people who hired them, "for they always told you they had been sick, or times were bad, or their children had been sick; and when the Italians came over they expected you to give them a room with a carpet and a clock, else they said you had no kindness." I saw in the cluster of eight houses that form the "Bee-hive" various humble homes, from the neat and graceful poverty adorned with bright colors, and sweet with the bunch of lilacs brought from the morning's marketing (the favorite flower of the neighborhood), to the dens of one room, in which three or four families live, and take boarders and lodgers into the bargain. They told me that the building contained a thousand souls, and that cases of malarial fever were frequent. It is true that the odors of Baxter Street are unhealthy and unpleasant, arguing defective drainage; but those of Venice are equally so, and exist for the prince no less than the beggar. As for overcrowding, no one who, for example, has spent a summer in Genoa, and has seen the stream of pallid, languid humanity pour out of the tall old houses of the Carignano district, can find food for sensationalism in the manner of life common to Baxter Street. It must be remembered that the standard of prosperity in America is not that of Italy, and

that a man is not necessarily destitute nor a pauper because he prefers organ-grinding or rag-picking to shoemaking or hod-carrying, and likes macaroni cooked in oil better than bakers' bread and tough meat.

I fail to find that Italians here retain their national habits of enjoyment or their love of feast-day finery. True, I have seen *contadine* in gold beads and ear-rings sitting on their door-steps on Sunday afternoons, and I have watched a large family making merry over a handful of boiled corn, just as they did at home, and I have seen the Genoese matrons dress one another's hair of a Sunday morning in the old fashion. But the indifferentism and stolidity of the country react upon them. There seems to be little of the open-air cooking, the polenta and fish stalls, the soup and macaroni booths, that breed conviviality in the Italian streets. They apparently eat in their own homes, after the New World fashion.

Undoubtedly much of the recklessness with which Italians are charged in New York is the result of the sudden removal of religious influences from their lives. At home there is a church always open and at hand, and the bells constantly remind them of the near resting-place for soul and body. When their homes are noisy and uncomfortable, they can find peace and quiet in the cool dark churches; and when they are on the verge of quarrel or crime, and the hand involuntarily seeks the knife, the twilight angelus or the evening bell for the dead softens the angry heart and silences the quick tongue. Here the only escape from the crowded rooms is in the equally crowded yard, or the door-step, or the rum-shop. The only entirely Italian Catholic church in New York, I believe, is that of San Antonio di Padova, in Sullivan Street, attended by a superior class of Italians, all apparently prosperous and at peace with their surroundings.

In the days of political persecution and struggle in Italy, America was the republican ideal and Utopia toward which the longing eyes of all agitators and revolutionists turned. When self-banished or exiled by government, they were apt to seek their fortunes in America, often concealing their identity and possible rank, and taking their places among the workers of the republic. Among these was Garibaldi, who passed some time here in the suburbs of New York, earning his living like many another honest toiler, and awaiting the right moment to strike the death-blow at tyranny. To study the Italian character in its finer *nuances*, the analyst should not limit his investigations to the broad generalizations of the Italian quarters, but should prosecute his researches in out-of-the-way down-town thoroughfares, where isolated shops with Italian names over their doors stimulate curiosity. In these dingy places, among dusty crimping-pins, pomatum-pots, and ghastly heads of human hair, half-worn clothing, the refuse of pawnbrokers' shops, you may meet characters that would not have been unworthy the attention of Balzac, and would eagerly have been numbered by Champfleury among his "Excentriques." I have one in my mind whose short round person, tall dilapidated hat, profuse jewelry, red face, keen gray eyes, and ready tongue fully qualify him for the title of the Figaro of Canal Street.

Another interesting class of Italians is found in the people attached to the opera — the chorus-singers and ballet-dancers, engaged also for spectacular dramas. It is in a measure a migratory population, crossing the ocean in the season, and recrossing when the demand for its labor ceases. Many chorus-singers who remain in New York follow different trades out of the opera season, and sing sometimes in the theatres when incidental music is required. By singers New York is regarded chiefly as a market in which they can dispose of their talents to greater pecuniary advantage than in Europe, and they endure the peculiar contingencies of American life simply in order to lay

by capital with which to enjoy life in Italy. A season in America is always looked forward to as the means of accumulating a fortune, and not for any artistic value. I have heard of more than one Italian who, after a successful engagement in New York, has invited sundry compatriots to a supper at Moretti's, and announced his intention of shaking the dust of America from his shoes for evermore, being satisfied to retire on his gains, or to sing only for love of art and the applause of artists in the dingy opera-houses of Italy. The climate of America with its sudden changes kills the Italian bodies, and the moral atmosphere chills their souls— notably among artists. The "Caffè Moretti" has for years been the *foyer* of operatic artists, and no review of Italian life in New York would be complete without a mention of it. For many years they

OLD HOUSES IN THE ITALIAN QUARTER.

have dined, and supped, and drank their native wines in this dingy, smoke-blackened place, forgetting for the nonce that they were in America, and, coming away, have left their portraits behind them,

pite from homesickness over Signor Moretti's Lachryma Christi and macaroni cooked in the good Milanese fashion. In view of the general assimilation of Italians with their American surroundings, it is surprising and delightful to find a place that retains so picturesque and Italian a flavor.

Since the abolishment of the *padrone* system one sees few child-musicians, and the wandering minstrels are chiefly half-grown boys and young men, who pass their summers playing on steamboats and at watering-places.

OLD CLOTHES DEALERS.

large and small, fresh and new, or old and smoke-dried, hanging side by side on the wall to cheer the hearts of the brother artists who should follow after them to the New World, and find a moment's res-

It is gratifying to feel that one of the disgraces of modern and enlightened Italy has been wiped from the national record by the strong hand of governmental authority.

LITERARY NEW YORK

THE LIBRARY.

I.

IT was by boat that I arrived from Boston, on an August morning of 1860, which was probably of the same quality as an August morning of 1894. I used not to mind the weather much in those days; it was hot or it was cold, it was wet or it was dry, but it was not my affair; and I suppose that I sweltered about the strange city, with no sense of anything very personal in the temperature, until nightfall. What I remember is being high up in a hotel long since laid low, listening in the summer dark, after the long day was done, to the Niagara roar of the omnibuses whose tide then swept Broadway from curb to curb, for all the miles of its length. At that hour the other city noises were stilled, or lost in this vaster volume of sound, which seemed to fill the whole night. It had a solemnity which the modern comer to New York will hardly imagine, for that tide of omnibuses has long since ebbed away, and has left the air to the strident discords of the elevated trains, the ear-slitting bells of the horse-cars, and the irregular alarum of the grip-car gongs, which blend to no such harmonious thunder as rose from

the procession of those ponderous and innumerable vans. There was a sort of inner quiet in the sound, and when I chose I slept off to it, and woke to it in the morning refreshed and strengthened to explore the literary situation in the metropolis.

II.

Not that I think I left this to the second day. Very probably I lost no time in going to the office of the Saturday Press, as soon as I had my breakfast after arriving, and I have a dim impression of anticipating the earliest of the Bohemians, whose gay theory of life obliged them to a good many hardships in lying down early in the morning, and rising up late in the day. If it was the office-boy who bore me company during the first hour of my visit, by-and-by the editors and contributors actually began to come in. I would not be very specific about them if I could, for since that Bohemia has faded from the map of the republic of letters, it has grown more and more difficult to trace its citizenship to any certain writer. There are some living who knew the Bohemians and even loved them, but there are increasingly few who were of them, even in the fond retrospect of youthful follies and errors. It was in fact but a sickly colony, transplanted from the mother asphalt of Paris, and never really striking root in the pavements of New York; it was a colony of ideas, of theories, which had perhaps never had any deep root anywhere. What these ideas, these theories, were in art and in life, it would not be very easy to say; but in the Saturday Press they came to violent expression, not to say explosion, against all existing forms of respectability. If respectability was your *bête noire*, then you were a Bohemian; and if you were in the habit of rendering yourself in prose, then you necessarily shredded your prose into very fine paragraphs of a sentence each, or of a very few words, or even of one word. I believe this fashion still prevails with some of the dramatic critics, who think that it gives a quality of epigram to the style; and I suppose it was borrowed from the more spasmodic moments of Victor Hugo, by the editor of the Press. He brought it back with him when he came home from one of those sojourns in Paris which possess one of the French accent rather than the French language; I long desired to write in that fashion myself, but I had not the courage.

This editor was a man of such open and avowed cynicism that he may have been, for all I know, a kindly optimist at heart; some say, however, that he had really talked himself into being what he seemed. I only know that his talk, the first day I saw him, was of such a quality that if he was half as bad, he would have been too bad to be. He walked up and down his room saying what lurid things he would directly do if any one accused him of respectability, so that he might disabuse the minds of all witnesses. There were four or five of his assistants and contributors listening to the dreadful threats, which did not deceive even so great innocence as mine, but I do not know whether they found it the sorry farce that I did. They probably felt the fascination for him which I could not disown, in spite of my inner disgust; and were watchful at the same time for the effect of his words with one who was confessedly fresh from Boston, and was full of delight in the people he had seen there. It appeared, with him, to be proof of the inferiority of Boston that if you passed down Wash-

ington Street, half a dozen men in the crowd would know you were Holmes, or Lowell, or Longfellow, or Wendell Phillips; but in Broadway no one would know who you were, or care to the measure of his smallest blasphemy. I have since heard this more than once urged as a signal advantage of New York for the æsthetic inhabitant, but I am not sure, yet, that it is so. The unrecognized celebrity probably has his mind quite as much upon himself as if some one pointed him out, and otherwise I cannot think that the sense of neighborhood is such a bad thing for the artist in any sort. It involves the sense of responsibility, which cannot be too constant or too keen. If it narrows, it deepens; and this may be the secret of Boston.

III.

It would not be easy to say just why the Bohemian group represented New York literature to my imagination, for I certainly associated other names with its best work, but perhaps it was because I had written for the Saturday Press myself, and had my pride in it, and perhaps it was because that paper really embodied the new literary life of the city. It was clever, and full of the wit that tries its teeth upon everything. It attacked all literary shams but its own, and it made itself felt and feared. The young writers throughout the country were ambitious to be seen in it, and they gave their best to it; they gave literally, for the Saturday Press never paid in anything but hopes of paying, vaguer even than promises. It is not too much to say that it was very nearly as well for one to be accepted by the Press as to be accepted by the Atlantic, and for the time there was no other literary comparison. To be in it was to be in the company of Fitz James O'Brien, Fitzhugh Ludlow, Mr. Aldrich, Mr. Stedman, and whoever else was liveliest in prose or loveliest in verse at that day in New York. It was a power, and although it is true that, as Henry Giles said of it, "Man cannot live by snapping-turtle alone," the Press was very good snapping-turtle. Or, it seemed so then; I should be almost afraid to test it now, for I do not like snapping-turtle so much as I once did, and I have grown nicer in my taste, and want my snapping-turtle of the very best. What is certain is that I went to the office of the Saturday Press in New York with much the same sort of feeling I had in going to the office of the Atlantic Monthly in Boston, but I came away with a very different feeling. I had found there a bitterness against Boston as great as the bitterness against respectability, and as Boston was then rapidly becoming my second country, I could not join in the scorn thought of her and said of her by the Bohemians. I fancied a conspiracy among them to shock the literary pilgrim, and to minify the precious emotions he had experienced in visiting other shrines; but I found no harm in that, for I knew just how much to be shocked, and I thought I knew better how to value certain things of the soul than they. Yet when their chief asked me how I got on with Hawthorne, and I began to say that he was very shy and I was rather shy, and the king of Bohemia took his pipe out to break in upon me with "Oh, a couple of shysters!" and the rest laughed, I was abashed all they could have wished, and was not restored to myself till one of them said that the thought of Boston made him as ugly as sin: then I began to hope again that men who took themselves so seriously as that need not be taken very seriously by me.

In fact I had heard things almost as desperately cynical in other newspaper offices before that, and I could not see what was so distinctively Bohemian in these *anime prave*, these souls so baleful by their own showing. But apparently Bohemia was not a state that you could well imagine from one encounter, and since my stay in New York was to be very short, I lost no time in acquainting myself farther with it. That very night I went to the beer-cellar, once very far up Broadway, where I was given to know that the Bohemian nights were smoked and quaffed away. It was said, so far West as Ohio, that the queen of Bohemia sometimes came to Pfaff's: a young girl of a sprightly gift in letters, whose name or pseudonym had made itself pretty well known at that day, and whose fate, pathetic at all times, out-tragedies almost any other in the history of letters. She was seized with hydrophobia from the bite of her dog, on a railroad train; and made a long journey home in the paroxysms of that agonizing disease, which ended in her death after she reached New York. But this was after her reign had ended, and no such black shadow was cast backward upon Pfaff's, whose name often figured in the verse and the epigrammatically paragraphed prose of the Saturday Press. I felt that as a contributor and at least a brevet Bohemian I ought not to go home without visiting the famous place, and witnessing if I could not share the revels of my comrades. As I neither drank beer nor smoked, my part in the carousal was limited to a German pancake, which I found they had very good at Pfaff's, and to listening to the whirling words of my commensals, at the long board spread for the Bohemians in a cavernous space under the pavement. There were writers for the Saturday Press and for Vanity Fair (a hopefully comic paper of that day), and some of the artists who drew for the illustrated periodicals. Nothing of their talk remains with me, but the impression remains that it was not so good talk as I had heard in Boston. At one moment of the orgy, which went but slowly for an orgy, we were joined by some belated Bohemians whom the others made a great clamor over; I was given to understand they were just recovered from a fearful debauch; their locks were still damp from the wet towels used to restore them, and their eyes were very frenzied. I was presented to these types, who neither said nor did anything worthy of their awful appearance, but dropped into seats at the table, and ate of the supper with an appetite that seemed poor. I staid hoping vainly for worse things till eleven o'clock, and then I rose and took my leave of a literary condition that had distinctly disappointed me. I do not say that it may not have been wickeder and wittier than I found it; I only report what I saw and heard in Bohemia on my first visit to New York, and I know that my acquaintance with it was not exhaustive. When I came the next year the Saturday Press was no more, and the editor and his contributors had no longer a common centre. The best of the young fellows whom I met there confessed, in a pleasant exchange of letters which we had afterwards, that he thought the pose a vain and unprofitable one; and when the Press was revived, after the war, it was without any of the old Bohemian characteristics except that of not paying for material. It could not last long upon these terms, and again it passed away, and still waits its second palingenesis.

The editor passed away too, not long

after, and the thing that he had inspired altogether ceased to be. He was a man of a certain sardonic power, and used it rather fiercely and freely, with a joy probably more apparent than real in the pain it gave. In my last knowledge of him he was much milder than when I first knew him, and I have the feeling that he too came to own before he died that man cannot live by snapping-turtle alone. He was kind to some neglected talents, and befriended them with a vigor and a zeal which he would have been the last to let you call generous. The chief of these was Walt Whitman, who, when the Saturday Press took it up, had as hopeless a cause with the critics on either side of the ocean as any man could have. It was not till long afterward that his English admirers began to discover him, and to make his countrymen some noisy reproaches for ignoring him; they were wholly in the dark concerning him when the Saturday Press, which first stood his friend, and the young men whom the Press gathered about it, made him their cult. No doubt he was more valued because he was so offensive in some ways than he would have been if he had been in no way offensive, but it remains a fact that they celebrated him quite as much as was good for them. He was often at Pfaff's with them, and the night of my visit he was the chief fact of my experience. I did not know he was there till I was on my way out, for he did not sit at the table under the pavement, but at the head of one further into the room. There, as I passed, some friendly fellow stopped me and named me to him, and I remember how he leaned back in his chair, and reached out his great hand to me, as if he were going to give it me for good and all. He had a fine head, with a cloud of Jovian hair upon it, and a branching beard and mustache, and gentle eyes that looked most kindly into mine, and seemed to wish the liking which I instantly gave him, though we hardly passed a word, and our acquaintance was summed up in that glance and the grasp of his mighty fist upon my hand. I doubt if he had any notion who or what I was beyond the fact that I was a young poet of some sort, but he may possibly have remembered seeing my name printed after some very Heinesque verses in the Press. I did not meet him again for twenty years, and then I had only a moment with him when

he was reading the proofs of his poems in Boston. Some years later I saw him for the last time, one day after his lecture on Lincoln, in that city, when he came down from the platform to speak with some hand-shaking friends who gathered about him. Then and always he gave me the sense of a sweet and true soul, and I felt in him a spiritual dignity which I will not try to reconcile with his printing in the forefront of his book a passage from a private letter of Emerson's, though I believe he would not have seen such a thing as most other men would, or thought ill of it in another. The spiritual purity which I felt in him no less than the dignity is something that I will no more try to reconcile with what denies it in his page; but such things we may well leave to the adjustment of finer balances than we have at hand. I will make sure only of the greatest benignity in the presence of the man. The apostle of the rough, the uncouth, was the gentlest person; his barbaric yawp, translated into the terms of social encounter, was an address of singular quiet, delivered in a voice of winning and endearing friendliness.

As to his work itself, I suppose that I do not think it so valuable in effect as in intention. He was a liberating force, a very "imperial anarch" in literature; but liberty is never anything but a means, and what Whitman achieved was a means and not an end, in what must be called his verse. I like his prose, if there is a difference, much better; there he is of a genial and comforting quality, very rich and cordial, such as I felt him to be when I met him in person. His verse seems to me not poetry, but the materials of poetry, like one's emotions; yet I would not misprize it, and I am glad to own that I have had moments of great pleasure in it. Some French critic quoted in the Saturday Press (I cannot think of his name) said the best thing of him when he said that he made you a partner of the enterprise, for that is precisely what he does, and that is what alienates and what endears in him, as you like or dislike the partnership. It is still something neighborly, brotherly, fatherly, and so I felt him to be when the benign old man looked on me and spoke to me.

IV.

That night at Pfaff's must have been the last of the Bohemians for me, and it was the last of New York authorship too, for the time. I do not know why I should not have imagined trying to see Curtis, whom I knew so much by heart, and whom I adored, but I may not have had the courage, or I may have heard that he was out of town; Bryant, I believe, was then out of the country; but at any rate I did not attempt him either. The Bohemians were the beginning and the end of the story for me, and to tell the truth I did not like the story. I remember that as I sat at that table under the pavement, in Pfaff's beer-cellar, and listened to the wit that did not seem very funny, I thought of the dinner with Lowell, the breakfast with Fields, the supper at the Autocrat's, and felt that I had fallen very far. In fact it can do no harm at this distance of time to confess that it seemed to me then, and for a good while afterward, that a person who had seen the men and had the things said before him that I had in Boston, could not keep himself too carefully in cotton; and this was what I did all the following winter, though of course it was a secret between me and me. I dare say it was not the worst thing I could have done, in some respects.

My sojourn in New York could not have been very long, and the rest of it was mainly given to viewing the monuments of the city from the windows of omnibuses and the platforms of horse-cars. The world was so simple then that there were perhaps only a half-dozen cities that had horse-cars in them, and I travelled in those conveyances at New York with an unfaded zest, even after my journeys back and forth between Boston and Cambridge. I have not the least notion where I went or what I saw, but I suppose that it was up and down the ugly east and west avenues, then lying open to the eye in all the hideousness now partly concealed by the elevated roads, and that I found them very stately and handsome. Indeed, New York was really handsomer then than it is now, when it has so many more pieces of beautiful architecture, for at that day the sky-scrapers were not yet, and there was a fine regularity in the streets that these brute bulks have robbed of all shapeless. Dirt and squalor there were aplenty, but not so much dirt, not so much squalor, and there was infinitely more comfort. The long succession of cross streets was yet mostly secure from business, after you

passed Clinton Place; commerce was just beginning to show itself in Union Square, and Madison Square was still the home of the McFlimsies, whose kin and kind dwelt unmolested in the brownstone stretches of Fifth Avenue. I tried hard to imagine them from the acquaintance Mr. Butler's poem had given me, and from the knowledge the gentle satire of the Potiphar Papers had spread broadcast through a community shocked by the excesses of our best society; it was not half so bad then as the best now, probably. But I do not think I made very much of it, perhaps because most of the people who ought to have been in those fine mansions were away at the sea-side and the mountains.

The mountains I had seen on my way down from Canada, but the sea-side not, and it would never do to go home without visiting some famous summer resort. I must have fixed upon Long Branch because I must have heard of it as then the most fashionable; and one afternoon I took the boat for that place. By this means I not only saw sea-bathing for the first time, but I saw a storm at sea: a squall struck us so suddenly that it blew away all the camp-stools of the forward promenade; it was very exciting, and I long meant to use in literature the black wall of cloud that settled on the water before us like a sort of portable midnight; I now throw it away upon the reader, as it were; it never would come in anywhere. I staid all night at Long Branch, and I had a bath the next morning before breakfast: an extremely cold one, with a life-line to keep me against the undertow. In this rite I had the company of a young New-Yorker, whom I had met on the boat coming down, and who was of the light, hopeful, adventurous business type which seems peculiar to the city, and which has always attracted me. He told me much about his life, and how he lived, and what it cost him to live. He had a large room at a fashionable boarding-house, and he paid fourteen dollars a week. In Columbus I had such a room at such a house, and paid three and a half, and I thought it a good deal. But those were the days before the war, when America was the cheapest country in the world, and the West was incredibly inexpensive.

After a day of lonely splendor at this scene of fashion and gayety, I went back

JOHN J. PIATT.

to New York, and took the boat for Albany on my way home. I noted that I had no longer the vivid interest in nature and human nature which I had felt in setting out upon my travels, and I said to myself that this was from having a mind so crowded with experiences and impressions that it could receive no more; and I really suppose that if the happiest phrase had offered itself to me at some moments, I should scarcely have looked about me for a landscape or a figure to fit it to. I was very glad to get back to my dear little city in the West (I found it seething in an August sun that was hot enough to have calcined the limestone State House), and to all the friends I was so fond of.

V.

I did what I could to prove myself unworthy of them by refusing their invitations, and giving myself wholly to literature, during the early part of the winter that followed; and I did not realize my error till the invitations ceased to come, and I found myself in an unbroken intellectual solitude. The worst of it was that an ungrateful Muse did little in return for the sacrifices I made her, and the things I now wrote were not liked by the editors I sent them to. The editorial taste is not always the test of merit, but it is the only

one we have, and I am not saying the editors were wrong in my case. There were then such a very few places where you could market your work: the Atlantic in Boston and Harper's in New York were the magazines that paid, though the Independent newspaper bought literary material; the Saturday Press printed it without buying, and so did the old Knickerbocker Magazine, though there was pecuniary good-will in both these cases. I toiled much that winter over a story I had long been writing, and at last sent it to the Atlantic, which had published five poems for me the year before. After some weeks, or it may have been months, I got it back with a note saying that the editors had the less regret in returning it because they saw that in the May number of the Knickerbocker the first chapter of the story had appeared. Then I remembered that, years before, I had sent this chapter to that magazine, as a sketch to be printed by itself, and afterwards had continued the story from it. I had never heard of its acceptance, and supposed of course that it was rejected; but on my second visit to New York I called at the Knickerbocker office, and a new editor, of those that the magazine was always having in the days of its failing fortunes, told me that he had found my sketch in rummaging about in a barrel of his predecessors' manuscripts, and had liked it, and printed it. He said that there were fifteen dollars coming to me for that sketch, and might he send the money to me? I said that he might, though I do not see, to this day, why he did not give it me on the spot; and he made a very small minute in a very large sheet of paper (really like Dick Swiveller), and promised I should have it that night; but I sailed the next day for Liverpool without it. I sailed without the money for some verses that Vanity Fair bought of me, but I hardly expected that, for the editor, who was then Artemus Ward, had frankly told me in taking my address that ducats were few at that moment with Vanity Fair.

I was then on my way to be consul at Venice, where I spent the next four years in a vigilance for Confederate privateers which none of them ever surprised. I had asked for the consulate at Munich, where I hoped to steep myself yet longer in German poetry, but when my appointment came, I found it was for Rome. I was very glad to get Rome even; but the income of the office was in fees, and I thought I had better go on to Washington and find out how much the fees amounted to. People in Columbus who had been abroad said that on five hundred dollars you could live in Rome like a prince, but I doubted this; and when I learned at the State Department that the fees of the Roman consulate came to only three hundred, I perceived that I could not live better than a baron, probably, and I despaired. The kindly chief of the consular bureau said that the President's secretaries, Mr. John Nicolay and Mr. John Hay, were interested in my appointment, and he advised my going over to the White House and seeing them. I lost no time in doing that, and I learned that as young Western men they were interested in me because I was a young Western man who had done something in literature, and they were willing to help me for that reason, and for no other that I ever knew. They proposed my going to Venice; the salary was then seven hundred and fifty, but they thought they could get it put up to a thousand. In the end they got it put up to fifteen hundred, and so I went to Venice, where if I did not live like a prince on that income, I lived a good deal more like a prince than I could have done at Rome on a third of it.

If the appointment was not present fortune, it was the beginning of the best luck I have had in the world, and I am glad to owe it all to those friends of my verse, who could have been no otherwise friends of me. They were then beginning very early careers of distinction which have not been wholly divided. Mr. Nicolay could have been about twenty-five, and Mr. Hay nineteen or twenty. No one dreamed as yet of the opportunity opening to them in being so constantly near the man whose life they have written, and with whose fame they have imperishably interwrought their names. I remember the sobered dignity of the one, and the humorous gayety of the other, and how we had some young men's joking and laughing together, in the anteroom where they received me, with the great soul entering upon its travail beyond the closed

door. They asked me if I had ever seen the President, and I said that I had seen him at Columbus, the year before; but I could not say how much I should like to see him again, and thank him for the favor which I had no claim to at his hands, except such as the slight campaign biography I had written could be thought to have given me. That day or another, as I left my friends, I met him in the corridor without, and he looked at the space I was part of with his ineffably melancholy eyes, without knowing that I was the indistinguishable person in whose "in-

MRS. JOHN J. PIATT.

tegrity and abilities he had reposed such special confidence" as to have appointed him consul for Venice and the ports of the Lombardo-Venetian Kingdom, though he might have recognized the terms of my commission if I had reminded him of them. I faltered a moment in my longing to address him, and then I decided that every one who forebore to speak needlessly to him, or to shake his hand, did him a kindness; and I wish I could be as sure of the wisdom of all my past behavior as I am of that piece of it. He walked up to the water-cooler that stood in the corner, and drew himself a full goblet from it, which he poured down his throat with a backward tilt of his head, and then went wearily within doors. The whole affair, so simple, has always remained one of a certain pathos in my memory, and I would rather have seen Lincoln in that unconscious moment than on some statelier occasion.

VI.

I went home to Ohio, and sent on the bond I was to file in the Treasury Department; but it was mislaid there, and to prevent another chance of that kind I carried on the duplicate myself. It was on my second visit that I met the generous young Irishman William D. O'Connor, at the house of my friend Piatt, and heard his ardent talk. He was one of the promising men of that day, and he had written an antislavery novel in the heroic mood of Victor Hugo, which greatly took my fancy; and I believe he wrote poems too. He had not yet risen to be the chief of Walt Whitman's champions outside of the Saturday Press, but he had already espoused the theory of Bacon's authorship of Shakespeare, then newly exploited by the poor lady of Bacon's name, who died constant to it in an insane asylum. He used to speak of the reputed dramatist as "the fat peasant of Stratford," and he was otherwise picturesque of speech in a measure that consoled, if it did not convince. The great war was then full upon us, and when in the silences of our literary talk its awful breath was heard, and its shadow fell upon the hearth where we gathered round the first fires of autumn, O'Connor would lift his beautiful head with a fine effect of prophecy, and say, "Friends, I feel a sense of victory in the air." He was not wrong; only the victory was for the other side.

Who beside O'Connor shared in these saddened symposiums I cannot tell now; but probably other young journalists and office-holders, intending littérateurs, since more or less extinct. I make certain only of the young Boston publisher who issued a very handsome edition of Leaves of Grass, and then failed promptly if not consequently. But I had already met, in my first sojourn at the capital, a young journalist who had given hostages to poetry, and whom I was very glad to see and proud to know. Mr. Stedman and I were talking over that meeting the other day, and I can be surer than I might have been without his memory, that I found him at a friend's house, where he was nursing himself for some slight sickness, and that I sat by his bed while our souls launched together into the joyful realms of hope and praise. In him I found the quality of Boston, the honor and passion of literature, and not a mere pose of the literary life; and the world knows without my telling how true he has been to his ideal of it. His earthly mission then was to write letters from Washington for the New York World, which started in

WILLIAM ALLEN BUTLER.

life as a good young evening paper, with a decided religious tone, so that the Saturday Press could call it the Night-blooming Serious. I think Mr. Stedman wrote for its editorial page at times, and his relation to it as a Washington correspondent had an authority which is wanting to the function in these days of perfected telegraphing. He had not yet achieved that seat in the Stock Exchange whose possession has justified his recourse to business, and has helped him to mean something, more single in literature than many more singly devoted to it. I used sometimes to speak about that with another eager young author in certain middle years when we were chafing in editorial harness, and we always decided that Stedman had the best of it in being able to earn his living in a sort so alien to literature that he could come to it unjaded, and with a gust unspoiled by kindred savors.

CHARLES F. BROWNE ("ARTEMUS WARD").

But no man shapes his own life, and I dare say Stedman may have been all the time envying us our tripods from his high place in the Stock Exchange. What is certain is that he has come to stand for literature and to embody New York in it as no one else does. In a community which seems never to have had a conscious relation to letters, he has kept the faith with dignity and fought the fight with constant courage. Scholar and poet at once, he has spoken to his generation with authority which we can forget only in the charm which makes us forget everything else.

But his large fame was still before him when we met, and I could bring to him an admiration for work which had not yet made itself known to so many but any admirer was welcome. We talked of what we had done, and each said how much he liked certain things of the other's; I even seized my advantage of his helplessness to read him a poem of mine which I had in my pocket; he advised me where to place it; and if the reader will not think it an unfair digression, I will tell here what became of that poem, for I think its varied fortunes were amusing, and I hope my own sufferings and final triumph with it will not be without encouragement to the young literary endeavorer. It was a poem called, with no prophetic sense of fitness, Forlorn, and I tried it first with the Atlantic Monthly, which would not have it. Then I offered it in person to a former editor of this Magazine, but he could not see his advantage in it, and I carried it overseas to Venice with me. From that point I sent it to all the English magazines as steadily as the post could carry it away and bring it back. On my way home, four years later, I took it to London with me, where a friend who knew Lewes, then just beginning with the Fortnightly Review, sent it to him for me. It was promptly returned, with a letter wholly reserved as to its quality, but full of a poetic gratitude for my wish to contribute to the Fortnightly. Then I heard that a certain Mr. Lucas was about to start a magazine, and I offered the poem to him. The kindest

MRS. R. H. STODDARD.

letter of acceptance followed me to America, and I counted upon fame and fortune as usual, when the news of Mr. Lucas's death came. I will not poorly joke an effect from my poem in the fact; but the fact remains. By this time I was a writer in the office of the Nation newspaper, and after I left this place to be Mr. Fields's assistant on the Atlantic, I sent my poem to the Nation, where it was printed at last. In such scant measure as my verses have pleased it has found rather unusual favor, and I need not say that its misfortunes endeared it to its author.

But all this is rather far away from my first meeting with Stedman in Washington. Of course I liked him, and I thought him very handsome and fine, with a full beard cut in the fashion he has always worn it, and with poet's

eyes lighting an aquiline profile. Afterwards, when I saw him afoot, I found him of a worldly splendor in dress, and envied him, as much as I could envy him anything, the New York tailor whose art had clothed him: I had a New York tailor too, but with a difference. He had a worldly dash along with his supermundane gifts, which took me almost as much, and all the more because I could see that he valued himself nothing upon it. He was all for literature, and for literary men as the superiors of every one. I must have opened my heart to him a good deal, for when I told him how the newspaper I had written for from Canada and New England had ceased to print my letters, he said, "Think of a man like —— sitting in judgment on a man like *you!*" I thought of it, and was avenged if not comforted ; and at any rate I liked Stedman's standing up so stiffly for the honor of a craft that is rather too limp in some of its votaries.

I suppose it was he who introduced me to the Stoddards, whom I met in New York just before I sailed, and who were then in the glow of their early fame as poets. They knew about my poor beginnings, and they were very, very good to me. Stoddard went with me to Franklin Square, and gave the sanction of his presence to the ineffectual offer of my poem there. But what I relished most was the long talk I had with them both about authorship in all its phases, and the exchange of delight in this poem and that, this novel and that, with gay, wilful runs away to make some wholly irrelevant joke, or fire puns into the air at no mark whatever. Stoddard had then a fame, with the sweetness of personal affection in it, from the lyrics and the odes that will perhaps best keep him known, and Mrs. Stoddard was beginning to make her distinct and special quality felt in the magazines, in verse and fiction. In both it seems to me that she has failed of the recognition which her work merits, and which will be hers when Time begins to look about him for work worth remembering. Her tales and novels have in them a foretaste of realism, which was too strange for the palate of their day, and is now too familiar, perhaps. It is a peculiar fate, and would form the scheme of a pretty study in the history of literature. But in whatever she did she left the stamp of a talent like no other, and of a personality disdainful of literary environment. In a time when most of us had to write like Tennyson, or Longfellow, or Browning, she never would write like any one but herself.

I remember very well the lodging over a corner of Fourth Avenue and some downtown street where I visited these winning and gifted people, and tasted the pleasure of their racy talk, and the hospitality of their good - will toward all literature, which certainly did not leave me out. We sat before their grate in the chill of the last October days, and they set each other on to one wild flight of wit after another, and again I bathed my delighted spirit in the atmosphere of a realm where for the time at least no

"rumor of oppression or defeat,
Of unsuccessful or successful war,"

could penetrate. I liked the Stoddards because they were, frankly not of that Bohemia which I disliked so much, and thought it of no promise or validity; and because I was fond of their poetry and found them in it. I liked the absolutely

R. H. STODDARD.

literary keeping of their lives. He had then, and for long after, a place in the Custom-house, but he was no more of that than Lamb was of India House. He belonged to that better world where there is no interest but letters, and which was as much like heaven for me as anything I could think of.

The meetings with the Stoddards repeated themselves when I came back to sail from New York, early in November. Mixed up with the cordial pleasure of them in my memory is a sense of the cold and wet outdoors, and the misery of being in those infamous New York streets, then as now the squalidest in the world. The last night I saw my friends they told me of the tragedy which had just happened at the camp in the City Hall Park. Fitz James O'Brien, the brilliant young Irishman who had dazzled us with his story of The Diamond Lens, and frozen our blood with his ingenious tale of a ghost— What was It?—a ghost that could be felt and heard, but not seen—had enlisted for the war, and risen to be an officer with the swift process of the first days of it. In that camp he had just then shot and killed a man for some infraction of discipline, and it was uncertain what the end would be. He was acquitted, however, and it is known how he afterwards died of lockjaw from a wound received in battle.

VII.

Before this last visit in New York there was a second visit to Boston, which I need not dwell upon, because it was chiefly a

EDMUND CLARENCE STEDMAN.

revival of the impressions of the first. Again I saw the Fieldses in their home; again the Autocrat in his, and Lowell now beneath his own roof, beside the study fire where I was so often to sit with him in coming years. At dinner (which we had at two o'clock) the talk turned upon my appointment, and he said of me to his wife: "Think of his having got Stillman's place! We ought to put poison in his wine," and he told me of the wish the painter had to go to Venice and follow up Ruskin's work there in a book of his own. But he would not let me feel very guilty, and I will not pretend that I had any personal regret for my good fortune.

The place was given me perhaps because I had not nearly so many other gifts as he who lost it, and who was at once artist, critic, journalist, traveller, and eminently each. I met him afterwards in Rome, which the powers bestowed upon him instead of Venice, and he forgave me, though I do not know whether he forgave the powers. We walked far and long over the Campagna, and I felt the charm of a most uncommon mind in talk which came out richest and fullest in the presence of the wild nature which he loved and knew so much better than most other men. I think that the book he would have written about Venice is forever to be regretted, and I do not at all console myself for its loss with the book I have written myself.

At Lowell's table that day they spoke of what sort of winter I should find in Venice, and he inclined to the belief that I should want a fire there. On his study hearth a very brisk one burned when we went back to it, and kept out the chill of a cold easterly storm. We looked through one of the windows at the rain, and he said he could remember standing and looking out of that window at such a storm when he was a child; for he was born in that house, and his life had kept coming back to it. He died in it, at last.

In a lifting of the rain he walked with me down to the village, as he always called the denser part of the town about Harvard Square, and saw me aboard a horse-car for Boston. Before we parted he gave me two charges: to open my mouth when I began to speak Italian, and to think well of women. He said that our race spoke its own tongue with its teeth shut, and so failed to master the languages that wanted freer utterance. As to women, he said there were unworthy ones, but a good woman was the best thing in the world, and a man was always the better for honoring women.

NEW YORK REVISITED
(PART 2)

MY recovery of impressions, after a short interval, yet with their flush a little faded, may have been judged to involve itself with excursions of memory—memory directed to the antecedent time—reckless almost to extravagance. But I recall them to-day, none the less, for that value in them which ministered, at happy moments, to an artful evasion of the actual. There was no escape from the ubiquitous alien into the future, or even into the present; there was an escape but into the past. I count as quite a triumph in this interest an unbroken ease of frequentation of that ancient end of Fifth Avenue to the whole neighborhood of which one's earlier vibrations, a very far-away matter now, were attuned. The precious stretch of space between Washington Square and Fourteenth Street had a value, had even a charm, for the revisiting spirit—a mild and melancholy glamour which I am conscious of the difficulty of "rendering" for new and heedless generations. Here again the assault of suggestion is too great; too large, I mean, the number of hares started, before the pursuing imagination, the quickened memory, by this fact of the felt moral and social value of this comparatively unimpaired morsel of the Fifth Avenue heritage. Its reference to a pleasanter, easier, hazier past is absolutely comparative, just as the past in question itself enjoys as such the merest courtesy-title. It is all recent history enough, by the measure of the whole, and there are flaws and defacements enough, surely, even in its appearance of decency of duration. The tall building, grossly tall and grossly ugly, has failed of an admirable chance of distinguished consideration for it, and the dignity of many of its peaceful fronts has succumbed to the presence of those industries whose foremost need is to make "a good thing" of them. The good thing is doubtless being made, and yet this lower end of the once agreeable street still just escapes being a wholly bad thing. What held the fancy in thrall, however, as I say, was the admonition, proceeding from all the facts, that values of this romantic order are at best, anywhere, strangely relative. It was an extraordinary statement on the subject of New York that the space between Fourteenth Street and Washington Square *should* count for "tone," figure as the old ivory of an overscored tablet.

True wisdom, I found, was to let it, to make it, so count and figure as much as it would, and charming assistance came for this, I also found, from the young good-nature of May and June. There had been neither assistance nor good-nature during the grim weeks of midwinter; there had been but the meagre fact of a discomfort and an ugliness less formidable here than elsewhere. When, toward the top of the town, circulation, alimentation, recreation, every art of existence, gave way before the full onset of winter, when the upper avenues had become as so many congested bottle-necks, through which the wine of life simply refused to be decanted, getting back to these latitudes resembled really a return from the North Pole to the Temperate Zone: it was as if the wine of life had been poured for you, in advance, into some pleasant old punch-bowl that would support you through the temporary stress. Your condition was not reduced to the endless vista of a clogged tube, of a thoroughfare occupied as but the narrow central ridge with trolley-cars stuffed to suffocation, and as to the mere margin, on either side, with snow-banks resulting from the cleared rails and offering themselves as a field for all remaining action. Free existence and good manners, in New York, are too much brought down to a bare rigor of marginal relation to the endless electric coil, the monstrous chain that winds round the general neck and body, the general middle and legs, very much as the boa-constrictor winds round the group of the Laocoon. It struck me that when these folds are tightened in the terrible stricture of the snow-smothered months of the year, the New York predicament leaves far behind the anguish represented in the Vatican figures. To come and go where East Eleventh Street, where West Tenth, opened their kind short arms was at least to keep clear of the awful hug of the serpent. And this was a grace that grew large, as I have hinted, with the approach of summer and that made in the afternoons of May and of the first half of June, above all, an insidious appeal. There, I repeat, was the delicacy, there the mystery, there the wonder, in especial, of the unquenchable intensity of the impressions received in childhood. They are made then once for all, be their intrinsic beauty, interest, importance, small or great; the stamp is indelible and never wholly fades. This in fact gives it an importance, when a lifetime has intervened. I found myself intimately recognizing every house my officious tenth year had, in the way of imagined adventure, introduced to me—incomparable master of ceremonies after all; the privilege had been offered, since, to millions of other objects that had made nothing of it, that had gone as they came; so that here were Fifth Avenue corners with which one's connection was fairly exquisite. The lowered light of the days' ends of early summer became them, moreover, exceedingly, and they fell, for the quiet northward perspective, into a dozen delicacies of composition and tone.

One could talk of "quietness" now, for the shrinkage of life so marked, in the higher latitudes of the town, after Easter, the visible early flight of that "society" which, by the old custom, used never to budge before June or July, had almost the effect of clearing some of the streets, and indeed of suggesting that a truly clear New York might have an unsuspected charm or two to put forth. An approach to peace and harmony might have been, in a manner, promised, and the sense of other days took advantage of it to steal abroad with a ghostly tread. It kept meeting, half the time, to its

discomfiture, the lamentable little Arch of Triumph which bestrides these beginnings of Washington Square—lamentable because of its poor and lonely and unsupported and unaffiliated state. With this melancholy monument it could make no terms at all, but turned its back to the strange sight as often as possible, helping itself thereby, moreover, to do a little of the pretending required, no doubt, by the fond theory that nothing hereabouts was changed. Nothing *was,* it could occasionally appear to me—there was no new note in the picture, not one, for instance, when I paused before a low house in a small row on the south side of Waverley Place and lived again into the queer medieval costume (preserved by the daguerreotypist's art) of the very little boy for whom the scene had once embodied the pangs and pleasures of a Dame's small school. The Dame must have been Irish, by her name, and the Irish tradition, only intensified and coarsened, seemed still to possess the place, the fact of the survival, the sturdy sameness, of which arrested me, again and again, to fascination. The shabby red house, with its mere two stories, its lowly "stoop," its dislocated ironwork of the forties, the early fifties, the record, in its face, of blistering summers and of the long stages of the loss of self-respect, made it as consummate a morsel of the old liquor-scented, heated-looking city, the city of no pavements, but of such a plenty of politics, as I could have desired. And neighboring Sixth Avenue, overstraddled though it might be with feats of engineering unknown to the primitive age that otherwise so persisted, wanted only, to carry off the illusion, the warm smell of the bakery on the corner of Eighth Street, a blessed repository of doughnuts, cookies, cream-cakes and pies, the slow passing by which, on returns from school, must have had much in common with the experience of the shipmen of old who came, in long voyages, while they tacked and hung back, upon those belts of ocean that are haunted with the balm and spice of tropic islands.

These were the felicities of the backward reach, which, however, had also its melancholy checks and snubs; nowhere quite so sharp as in presence, so to speak, of the rudely, the ruthlessly suppressed birth-house on the other side of the Square. That was where the pretence that nearly nothing was changed had most to come in; for a high, square impersonal structure, proclaiming its lack of interest with a crudity all its own, so blocks, at the right moment for its own success, the view of the past, that the effect for me, in Washington Place, was of having been amputated of half my history. The gray and more or less "hallowed" University building—wasn't it somehow, with a desperate bravery, both castellated and gabled?—has vanished from the earth, and vanished with it the two or three adjacent houses, of which the birthplace was one. This was the snub, for the complacency of retrospect, that, whereas the inner sense had positively erected there for its private contemplation a commemorative mural tablet, the very wall that should have borne this inscription had been smashed as for demonstration that tablets, in New York, are unthinkable. And I have had indeed to permit myself this free fantasy of the hypothetic rescued identity of a given house—taking the vanished number in Washington Place as most pertinent—in order to invite the reader to gasp properly with me before the fact that we not only fail to remember, in the whole length of the city, one of these frontal records of birth, sojourn or death, under a celebrated name, but that we have only to reflect an instant to see any such form of civic piety inevitably and forever absent. The form is cultivated, to the greatly quickened interest of street-scenery, in many of the cities of Europe; and is it not verily bitter, for those who feel a poetry in the noted passage, longer or shorter, here and there, of great lost spirits, that the institution, the profit, the glory of any such association is denied in advance to communities tending, as the phrase is, to "run" preponderantly to the sky-scraper? Where, in fact, is the point of inserting a mural tablet, at any legible height, in a building certain to be destroyed to make room for a sky-scraper? And from where, on the other hand, in a façade of fifty floors, does one "see" the pious plate recording the honor attached to one of the apartments look down on a responsive

people? We have but to ask the question to recognize our necessary failure to answer it as a supremely characteristic local note—a note in the light of which the great city is projected into its future as, practically, a huge continuous fifty-floored conspiracy against the very idea of the ancient graces, those that strike us as having flourished just in proportion as the parts of life and the signs of character have *not* been lumped together, not been indistinguishably sunk in the common fund of mere economic convenience. So interesting, as object-lessons, may the developments of the American gregarious ideal become; so traceable, at every turn, to the restless analyst at least, are the heavy footprints, in the finer texture of life, of a great commercial democracy seeking to abound supremely in its own sense and having none to gainsay it.

Let me not, however, forget, amid such contemplations, what may serve here as a much more relevant instance of the operation of values, the price of the as yet undiminished dignity of the two most southward of the Fifth Avenue churches. Half the charm of the prospect, at that extremity, is in their still being there, and being as they are; this charm, this serenity of escape and survival positively works as a blind on the side of the question of their architectural importance. The last shade of pedantry or priggishness drops from your view of that element; they illustrate again supremely your grasped truth of the *comparative* character, in such conditions, of beauty and of interest. The special standard they may or may not square with signifies, you feel, not a jot: all you know, and want to know, is that they are probably menaced — some horrible voice of the air has murmured it—and that with them will go, if fate overtakes them, the last cases worth mentioning (with a single exception,) of the modest felicity that sometimes used to be. Remarkable certainly the state of things in which mere exemption from the "squashed" condition can shed such a glamour; but we may accept the state of things if only we can keep the glamour undispelled. It reached its maximum for me, I hasten to add, on my penetrating

into the Ascension, at chosen noon, and
standing for the first time in presence
of that noble work of John La Farge,
the representation, on the west wall, in
the grand manner, of the theological
event from which the church takes its
title. Wonderful enough, in New York,
to find oneself, in a charming and considerably dim "old" church, hushed to
admiration before a great religious picture; the sensation, for the moment, upset
so all the facts. The hot light, outside,
might have been that of an Italian
piazzetta; the cool shade, within, with
the important work of art shining through
it, seemed part of some other-world
pilgrimage—all the more that the important work of art itself, a thing of the
highest distinction, spoke, as soon as one
had taken it in, with that authority
which makes the difference, ever afterwards, between the remembered and the
forgotten quest. A rich note of interference came, I admit, through the splendid window-glass, the finest of which,
unsurpassably fine, to my sense, is the
work of the same artist; so that the
church, as it stands, is very nearly as
commemorative a monument as a great
reputation need wish. The deeply pictorial windows, in which clearness of
picture and fulness of expression consort
so successfully with a tone as of magnified gems, did not strike one as looking
into a yellow little square of the south—
they put forth a different implication;
but the flaw in the harmony was, more
than anything else, that sinister voice of
the air of which I have spoken, the fact
that one *could* stand there, vibrating to
such impressions, only to remember the
suspended danger, the possibility of the
doom. Here was the loveliest cluster of
images, begotten on the spot, that the
preoccupied city had ever taken thought
to offer itself; and here, to match them,
like some black shadow they had been
condemned to cast, was this particular
prepared honor of "removal" that appeared to hover about them.

One's fear, I repeat, was perhaps misplaced—but what an air to live in, the
shuddering pilgrim mused, the air in
which such fears are not misplaced only
when we are conscious of very special re-
assurances! The vision of the doom that
does descend, that had descended all

round, was at all events, for the half-
hour, all that was wanted to charge with
the last tenderness one's memory of the
transfigured interior. Afterwards, outside,
again and again, the powers of removal
struck me as looming, awfully, in the
newest mass of multiplied floors and windows visible at this point. *They,* ranged
in this terrible recent erection, were going to bring in money—and was not
money the only thing a self-respecting
structure could be thought of as bringing in? Hadn't one heard, just before,
in Boston, that the security, that the
sweet serenity of the Park Street Church,
charmingest, there, of aboriginal notes,
the very light, with its perfect position
and its dear old delightful Wren-like
spire, of the starved city's eyes, had been
artfully practised against, and that the
question of saving it might become, in
the near future, acute? Nothing, fortunately, I think, is so much the
"making" of New York, at its central
point, for the visual, almost for the romantic, sense, as the Park Street Church
is the making, by its happy coming-in, of
Boston; and, therefore, if it were think-
able that the peculiar rectitude of Boston
might be laid in the dust, what mightn't
easily come about for the reputedly
less austere conscience of New York?
Once such questions had obtained lodg-
ment, to take one's walks was verily to
look at almost everything in their light;
and to commune with the sky-scraper
under this influence was really to feel
worsted, more and more, in any magnanimous attempt to adopt the æsthetic
view of it. I may appear to make too
much of these invidious presences, but
it must be remembered that they represent, for our time, the only claim to any
consideration other than merely statistical established by the resounding growth
of New York. The attempt to take the
æsthetic view is invariably blighted
sooner or later by their most salient
characteristic, *the* feature that speaks
loudest for the economic idea. Window
upon window, at any cost, is a condition
never to be reconciled with any grace
of building, and the logic of the matter
here happens to put on a particularly
fatal front. If quiet interspaces, always
half the architectural battle, exist no
more in such a structural scheme than

quiet tones, blest breathing-spaces, occur, for the most part, in New York conversation, so the reason is, demonstrably, that the building can't afford them. (It is by very much the same law, one supposes, that New York conversation cannot afford stops.) The building can only afford lights, each light having a superlative value as an aid to the transaction of business and the conclusion of sharp bargains. Doesn't it take in fact acres of window-glass to help even an expert New-Yorker to get the better of another expert one, or to see that the other expert one doesn't get the better of *him?* It is easy to conceive that, after all, with this origin and nature stamped upon their foreheads, the last word of the mercenary monsters should not be their address to our sense of formal beauty.

Still, as I have already hinted, there was always the case of the one other rescued identity and preserved felicity, the happy accident of the elder day still ungrudged and finally legitimated. When I say ungrudged, indeed, I seem to remember how I had heard that the divine little City Hall had *been* grudged, at a critical moment, to within an inch of its life; had but just escaped, in the event, the extremity of grudging. It lives on securely, by the mercy of fate—lives on in the delicacy of its beauty, speaking volumes again (more volumes distinctly, than are anywhere else spoken) for the exquisite truth of the *conferred* value of interesting objects, the value derived from the social, the civilizing function for which they have happened to find their opportunity. It is the opportunity that gives them their price, and the luck of there being, round about them, nothing greater than themselves to steal it away from them. They strike thus, practically, the supreme note, and—such is the mysterious play of our finer sensibility!—one takes this note, one is glad to work it, as the phrase goes, for all it is worth. I so work the note of the City Hall, no doubt, in speaking of the spectacle there constituted as "divine"; but I do it precisely by reason of the spectacle taken *with* the delightful small facts of the building: largely by reason, in other words, of the elegant, the gallant little structure's sit-

uation and history, the way it has played, artistically, ornamentally, its part, has held out for the good cause, through the long years, alone and unprotected. The fact is it has been the very centre of that assault of vulgarity of which the innumerable mementos rise within view of it and tower, at a certain distance, over it; and yet it has never parted with a square inch of its character, it has forced them, in a manner, to stand off. I hasten to add that in expressing thus its uncompromised state I speak of its outward, its æsthetic character only. So, at all events, it has discharged the civilizing function I just named as inherent in such cases—that of representing, to the community possessed of it, all the Style the community is likely to get, and of making itself responsible for the same.

The consistency of this effort, under difficulties, has been the story that brings tears to the eyes of the hovering kindly critic, and it is through his tears, no doubt, that such a personage reads the best passages of the tale and makes out the proportions of the object. Mine, I recognize, didn't prevent my seeing that the pale yellow marble (or whatever it may be) of the City Hall has lost, by some late excoriation, the remembered charm of its old surface, the pleasant promiscuous patina of time; but the perfect taste and finish, the reduced yet ample scale, the harmony of parts, the just proportions, the modest classic grace, the living look of the type aimed at, these things, with gayety of detail undiminished and "quaintness" of effect augmented, are all there; and I see them, as I write, in that glow of appreciation which made it necessary, of a fine June morning, that I should somehow pay the whole place my respects. The simplest, in fact the only way, was, obviously, to pass under the charming portico and brave the consequences: this impunity of such audacities being, in America, one of the last of the lessons the repatriated absentee finds himself learning. The crushed spirit he brings back from European discipline never quite rises to the height of the native argument, the brave sense that the public, the civic building is his very own, for any honest use, so that he may tread even its most expensive pavements and staircases (and very expensive, for the American citizen, these have lately become,) without a question asked. This further and further unchallenged penetration begets in the perverted person I speak of a really romantic thrill: it is like some assault of the dim seraglio, with the guards bribed, the eunuchs drugged and one's life carried in one's hand. The only drawback to such freedom is that penetralia it is so easy to penetrate fail a little of a due impressiveness, and that if stationed sentinels are bad for the temper of the freeman they are good for the "prestige" of the building.

Never, in any case, it seemed to me, had any freeman made so free with the majesty of things as I was to make on this occasion with the mysteries of the City Hall—even to the point of coming out into the presence of the Representative of the highest office with which City Halls are associated, and whose thoroughly gracious condonation of my act set the seal of success upon the whole adventure. Its dizziest intensity, in fact, sprang precisely from the unexpected view opened into the old official, the old so thick-peopled local, municipal world: upper chambers of council and state, delightfully of their nineteenth-century time, as to design and ornament, in spite of rank restoration; but replete, above all, with portraits of past worthies, past celebrities and city fathers, Mayors, Bosses, Presidents, Governors, Statesmen at large, Generals and Commodores at

large, florid ghosts, looking so un sophisticated now, of years not remarkable, municipally, for the absence of sophistication. Here were types, running mainly to ugliness and all bristling with the taste of their day and the quite touching provincialism of their conditions, as to many of which nothing would be more interesting than a study of New York annals in the light of their personal look, their very noses and mouths and complexions and heads of hair—to say nothing of their waistcoats and neckties; with such color, such sound and movement would the thick stream of local history then be interfused. Wouldn't its thickness fairly become transparent? since to walk through the collection was not only to see and feel so much that had happened, but to understand, with the truth again and again inimitably pointed, why nothing could have happened otherwise; the whole array thus presenting itself as an unsurpassed demonstration of the real reasons of things. The florid ghosts look out from their exceedingly gilded frames—all that *that* can do is bravely done for them—with the frankest responsibility for everything; their collective presence becomes a kind of copious telltale document signed with a hundred names. There are few of these that at this hour, I think, we particularly desire to repeat; but the place where they may be read is, all the way from river to river and from the Battery to Harlem, the place in which there is most of the terrible town.

THE BROOKLYN BRIDGE

JOHN A. ROEBLING.

PEOPLE who seventeen years ago divided an amphibious existence between New York and Brooklyn will long remember their arctic voyages in the East River during the severe winter of 1866–7. There were days in that season when passengers from New York to Albany arrived earlier than those who set out the same morning from their breakfast tables in Brooklyn for their desks in New York. The newspapers were filled for weeks with reports of the ice gorges, and with vehement demand for and discussion of the bridge, which all agreed must be built at once from New York to Brooklyn.

Public feeling was soon highly gratified by the announcement that leading citizens of Brooklyn were moving in the matter, and that a bill for chartering the New York Bridge Company had been introduced into the Legislature then in session at Albany. The popular excitement gave but a timely lift to a movement already ripe, and to a charter already placed before members of the Legislature and government of the State, months in advance of the session, while the waters of the East River were sparkling in the warm sunshine as if ice gorges were never to be known. As early as 1865 Mr. William C. Kingsley, of Brooklyn, of whom the public has since heard much in connection with this enterprise, had employed an eminent engineer to draw a plan and make estimates for a suspension-bridge very nearly in the location ultimately fixed for the present work.

The charter originally and provisionally fixed the capital at $5,000,000 (with power of increase), and gave the cities of New York and Brooklyn authority to subscribe to the capital stock of the company such amount as their Common Councils respectively should determine. This latter was in effect a sort of "caution money," or a guarantee of the sound interest which those who were to govern the work ought to take in it, for it was wisely judged that neither private capital nor municipal management could be relied on to carry such a work successfully to completion. Public credit must be joined with private enter-

WASHINGTON A. ROEBLING.

prise, in the hands of men who had too much at stake in the work to permit it to be perverted to political purposes.

But by the time the foundations of the towers—the chief difficulty to be overcome —had been successfully completed, popular jealousy of a company enjoying the control of so much public expenditure began to make itself felt in various ways, and to serve as the instrument of various personal and political rivalries and enmities. At the same time, the work was so well advanced, and its plans and methods so firmly fixed by what had already been done, that its friends now felt prepared to resign the great enterprise entirely to the two cities (acting through a commission or board of trustees, appointed half by the

Mayor and Comptroller of each city, and including those officials), and prepared a bill to that effect, which was approved by the Legislature and accepted by the city governments. Under the charter thus amended the bridge is public property, 66⅔ per cent. to be paid for and owned by the city of Brooklyn and 33⅓ per cent. by the city of New York, the actual payments by the private stockholders having been reimbursed and their title extinguished. The engineers, etc., as well as the principal working members of the directory, retained their places as from the first, so that the work is, after all, a unit from beginning to end.

On the organization of the company, in May, 1867, one month after the passage of the incorporating act, John A. Roebling was appointed engineer (May 23, 1867), and he made his report of surveys, plans, and estimates on the 1st of the following September. In March, 1869, a board of consulting engineers was convened at the request of Mr. Roebling to examine his plans, and also to report upon the feasibility of the work. In the following May a commission of three United States engineers was appointed by the War Department to report upon the general feasibility of the project, and particularly as to whether or not the bridge would be an obstruction to navigation. The plans of Mr. Roebling were fully indorsed by both boards of engineers, the government commission recommending, however, an increase of five feet in height. The work of preparing the site of the foundation of the Brooklyn tower was commenced January 3, 1870, but Mr. Roebling did not live to see the first stone laid in the magnificent structure that was to crown his illustrious career. In the summer of 1869, while engaged in fixing the location of the Brooklyn tower, a ferry-boat entering the slip thrust the timbers on which he stood in such a manner as to catch and crush his foot. The injury resulted in lock-jaw, from which he died sixteen days after.

A fit successor was found in his son, Washington A. Roebling, who had not only been the accomplished associate of his father in some of his principal works, but had aided him most efficiently in the preparation of the designs and plans of the bridge. We say a fit successor was found, for at this time, when the grandest monument of engineering skill the world has ever seen is practically completed, certainly no other testimony is needed as to the great engineering ability and pre-eminent fitness of the younger Roebling to direct such a great undertaking. During the fire in the Brooklyn caisson in December, 1871, Mr. Roebling became himself a victim to the "caisson disease," but even from his sick-room his oversight of the work has not flagged.

Before the actual work of construction had commenced, however, it became apparent that in order to more perfectly adapt the structure to its intended uses, and to make ample provision for the rapidly increasing volume of inter-urban commerce consequent upon the development and growth of the cities, considerable modification must be made in the original design. The changes were, of course, in the direction of not only a larger and more capacious structure, but also of increased solidity and strength throughout. Such changes involved a very considerable addition to the cost. Mr. John A. Roebling originally estimated the cost of the bridge at $7,000,000, exclusive of the land required, which has cost about $3,800,000, and the time of building at about five years. The actual cost of the bridge, when completed, will be about $15,500,000, which, as compared with the original estimate of $10,800,000, shows an increase in cost of nearly $5,000,000. The items of additional cost are as follows: First, the United States government required an increase of five feet in height, making the clearance under the centre of the bridge 135 feet. At the same time it was decided to widen the bridge from 80 to 85 feet. These changes involved an increase of 8 per cent. in the cost of the entire bridge, including superstructure, towers, foundations, and anchorages. Second, the amount set apart for building the foundations of the towers in the original estimate was found to be entirely inadequate. For the New York tower a pile foundation was originally intended, whereas it was found necessary to go down 78 feet to the bed-rock, and the cost of labor in compressed air at such unprecedented depths proved to be four and a half times as much as was anticipated, as was also that of excavating the hard

conglomerate under the Brooklyn tower. Third, steel was substituted for iron as the material to be used in the construction of both the cables and the suspended superstructure, thereby vastly increasing the strength of all the parts. The items thus far enumerated foot up nearly two millions, which covers the excess in cost on the bridge proper. In his original plan and estimate, Mr. John A. Roebling contemplated approaches constructed of light iron girders, or trestle-work, supported by pillars of brick or stone, but it was concluded to build entirely of granite and brick—a change that has resulted in one of the finest masonry viaducts in the world. This involved an increased expenditure of about one and a half millions. The archways have been constructed with a view to their utilization as warehouses, and $400,000 has been set apart by the trustees for the placing of fronts and floors in them. As Mr. Roebling in his original report says, the cost of these improvements should not be charged in that of the bridge, and it was accordingly omitted by him. Then there are the station buildings and the elevated railway structures that are now building on the approaches, making a connection of the system of rapid transit of New York with that of Brooklyn when it shall have been built. Of course this was not originally contemplated, and it has swelled the cost of bridge by nearly half a million. Finally, there is a comprehensive item which could not have been anticipated, but which would be underestimated at half a million, namely, the preliminary expenditures, general superintendence, interest and discount on city bonds, and expenses legal, medical, funereal, and prandial. These additions to the cost, however, would never have swelled to so large an amount if it had not been for the needless and costly delays caused by the failure of the city of New York to promptly provide its proportion of the necessary funds. That this has caused an enormous increase in the cost of the bridge is well known, but it would be difficult to name an amount. The land expenses will be largely redeemed by the rentals the cities will receive from the warehouses under the approaches.

The principal ferry to Brooklyn takes a diagonal course up stream to a point determined by the abrupt falling off of the heights near Fulton Street. The bridge takes its Brooklyn departure in obedience

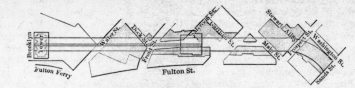

SITUATION PLAN OF BROOKLYN APPROACH.

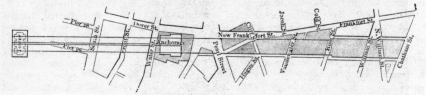

SITUATION PLAN OF NEW YORK APPROACH.

to the same topographical consideration. Its course is a straight line drawn from near the junction of Fulton and Main streets, Brooklyn, to the terminus fixed upon in New York, on Chatham Street, opposite the City Hall. This line and terminus were fixed upon as the result of Mr. Roebling's exhaustive examination and discussion of the question in his first report, of September 1, 1867, and no reason has been found to modify or to question the wisdom of his conclusions.

This line strikes the river at its eastern or Brooklyn shore close alongside of the north slip of Fulton Ferry. Its course across the river is not exactly at right angles to the shore, but makes a little down stream, striking the New York side at the foot of Roosevelt Street—four blocks further up stream, however, than the still more oblique ferry route. Here, then, are four points defined in a straight line: the two ends, and the two points at the water line, 1595½ feet apart, to be connected by the bridge proper with a single span. Three points in the air line of the bridge are also determined: the central

altitude of 135 feet above mean high water required by the United States government, and the two terminal elevations, in New York and Brooklyn respectively, of 38.27 and 61.32 feet above high-water mark. The rise from these two to the central altitude gives the line of the bridge a gentle upward curve from either end to the centre, where it will be fifteen feet higher than at the towers, and forty-six feet higher than at the anchorages.

The adoption of a suspended span of 1595½ feet, at a height of 135 feet, also determined (in combination with other mathematical and mechanical considerations) the height of the towers (276⅔ feet) from which the span must be suspended, and two other points in the air line of the bridge, at which the ends of the suspension cables are secured—in other words, the anchorages—for the cables are not to pull on the tops of the tall towers, but to rest on them with nearly a simple vertical pressure, being not even fastened; and thus, so far from tending to pull the towers over, the suspended weight tends only to hold them in position. The cables are

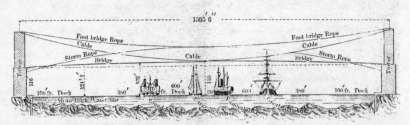

ELEVATION OF BRIDGE, SHOWING TEMPORARY ROPES USED IN CABLE-MAKING.

VIEW OF THE BRIDGE FROM NEW YORK.—After a photograph by Theodore Gubelman.

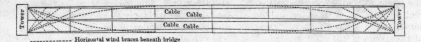

HORIZONTAL PROJECTION OF CABLE SYSTEM.

therefore anchored inland, at a distance of 930 feet back from the towers on each side.

The anchorages are solid cubical structures of stone masonry, measuring 119 by 132 feet at the base, and rising some 90 feet above high-water mark. Their weight is about 60,000 tons each, which is utilized to resist the pull of the cables. The mode of anchoring the cables will be described in its proper place. Suffice it for the present to conceive them thus anchored by their extremities on each side the river 930 feet back from the towers, and at the water-line on each side lifted up with a long, lofty, and graceful sweep over the top of a tower 276 feet high, and drooping between the two towers in a majestic curve which one can liken to nothing else for grandeur but the inverted arch of the rainbow.

Rising from the towers at an elevation of 118 feet above high-water mark in gentle but graceful curve to the centre of the river span, where it meets the cables at an elevation of 135 feet above high-water mark, is the bridge floor, an immense steel frame-work bewildering in its complexity. The frame-work consists essentially of two systems of girders at right angles to each other. The principal cross-beams or girders supporting the floor proper are light trusses thirty-three inches deep, placed seven feet six inches apart, and to these are attached the four steel rope suspenders from the cables. Half-way between these principal floor beams are lighter ones, to give additional support to the planking. To unite these cross-beams together, and to give the proper amount of stiffness and strength to the floor, there are six parallel trusses extending along the entire length of the bridge. The floor beams are further united together by small longitudinal trusses extending from one to the other, which, together with a complete system of diagonal braces or stays, form a longitudinal truss of eighty-six feet in breadth. It will be seen, thus, that this combination has immense strength, weight, and stiffness, laterally, vertically, and in every direction. To relieve the cables in a great measure of this enormous burden, and at the same time effectually prevent any vertical oscillations in the bridge floor, there is a multitude of suspensory stays of steel wire ropes diverging from the tops of the towers to points about fifteen feet apart along the bottom of four of the vertical trusses. These stays extend out for a distance of 400 feet from the towers, and are of themselves capable of sustaining unaided that portion of the great frame and its load in position. At the towers the frame-work is firmly anchored down, and again confined against the lifting or pushing force of the wind by a system of under-stays lying in the plane of the floor, so that no conceivable cause can ever disturb its rigid fixity of position and form. At and near the centre of the span, however, where these stays do not act so efficiently against any tendency to distortion, and to still further unite and stiffen the whole system, the two outside cables are drawn inward toward each other at the bottom of their curves. By this means each of them presents its weight in the form of an arch against an oblique pressure from below and the opposite side, and resists more or less in

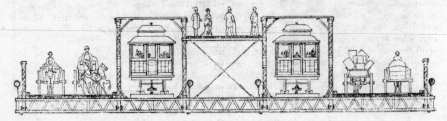

SECTION OF BRIDGE, SHOWING FOOT, RAIL, AND CARRIAGE WAYS.

the same way any force from the like directions. The two inner cables at the same time are drawn apart at the bottom of their curves, thus approaching each its outside neighbor, and pairing with it, so as to combine their opposing arches against lateral forces from either direction. The weight of the whole suspended structure (central span), cables and all, is 6740 tons, and the maximum weight with which the bridge can be crowded by freely moving passengers, vehicles, and cars is estimated at 1380 tons, making a total weight borne the river. The vertical trussing forms outside parapets eight feet high above the common bridge floor, for the security of vehicles, etc., while the inner lines of the same will form inner parapets to the cars and footways, supplemented by wire netting which will break the force of the wind. The intermediate avenues, one on each side of the footway, will be occupied by cars, constantly and rapidly moving back and forth from terminus to terminus by means of a stationary engine and endless wire rope.

THE BROOKLYN ANCHORAGE.

by the cables and stays of 8120 tons, in the proportion of 6920 tons by the cables and 1190 tons by the stays. The stress (or lengthwise pull) in the cables due to the load becomes about 11,700 tons, and their ultimate strength is 49,200 tons.

The great frame, as above described, presents on its upper side five parallel avenues of an average breadth of sixteen feet, separated by the six vertical lines of trussing, which project upward like so many steel fences. The outside avenues, devoted to vehicles, are each nearly nineteen feet wide. The central avenue has a width of fifteen and a half feet, and is elevated twelve feet above all the others, for a footway, thus giving to the pedestrians crossing the bridge an unobstructed view of

The great steel cables, fifteen and three-quarter inches in diameter, are not, however, limited to supporting the main span, but are prolonged over the tops of the towers, and descend thence to the anchorages on the shores, at distances, as before stated, of 930 feet. The portions of the cables suspended from the towers to the anchorages support the shore spans of the bridge, which are constructed precisely like the central span already described. The anchorages are therefore the next feature of the work to be noticed. They are structures at once exceedingly simple and satisfactory to the mind. There is little more to imagine than a great four-square mass of masonry, with a pair of broad arched passages through it, partly to exclude superfluous

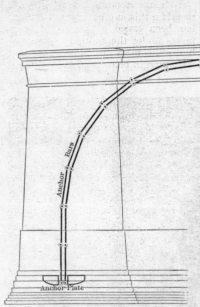

SECTION OF TOP AND BACK OF ANCHORAGE—SIDE VIEW.

cost, and partly to afford convenient avenues for locomotion. The dimensions of this mass are 90 by 119 by 132 feet, and its weight, which is its chief importance, the inconceivable amount of 120 million pounds. At the bottom of the structure, and near its rear side from the bridge, are imbedded four massive anchor plates of cast iron, one for each of the cables. These plates measure $16\frac{1}{2}$ by $17\frac{1}{2}$ feet on the face, and are $2\frac{1}{2}$ feet thick at the centre. The weight of each plate is over 46,000 pounds. And yet it is far from being a solid mass, which would waste perhaps half its material in perfectly ineffective positions. On the contrary, it is formed like a star, with many rays stretching from a massive centre, and tapering to their extremities, where greatly reduced strength and narrowed bearings are quite sufficient for the simple purpose of uniting the resistance of the superincumbent masonry upon the point of pull at the centre. This point is made by two rows of nine parallel oblong apertures through the two and a half feet of solid iron, and through these apertures pass eighteen forged bars of iron, with an eye at each end. Through each of the nine eyes, matched in position as one, below the under side of the anchor plate,

passes a round iron bolt or key, which is drawn up against the plate, fitting in a semi-cylindrical groove, and thus the first link in the anchor chain is constructed and made fast. The link bars average twelve and a half feet long; and in the first three links, where the pull from the cables is least felt, they are seven inches wide and three inches thick, being swelled at the ends sufficiently to preserve their full strength with eye-holes five to six inches in diameter. The bars of the fourth, fifth, and sixth links are increased in size to eight by three inches, and after these the size is nine by three, with the exception of the last link, in which the number of bars is doubled, and the thickness halved. The pins or bolts connecting link to link are turned shafts of wrought iron five feet long and five to seven inches in diameter.

The four great anchor plates being set in position at the bottom of the masonry, each with the first double ninefold link of its anchor chain made fast through its centre, and standing erect above it, the masonry is next built over the anchor plates, and close around the chain bars, to the height of the latter, and extended over the whole area of the structure to the same height. Then the second link or set of chain bars is set, the eyes of the new nine fitting between those of the former nine, and the heavy bolt passing through all the eighteen eyes at once, and uniting each of the two ninefold links with a joint like that of a hinge. Each new link after the first two is now made to incline forward to the bridge a little more than its predecessor, forming a regular curve, so adjusted as to bring the chain out near the opposite (upper) corner of the structure to that from which it started. Here the cables enter the face of the anchor wall for about twenty-five feet, and meet the ends of the chains. The bars of the last link number thirty-eight, arranged in four tiers. There are nineteen strands in each cable, and the end of each strand is here separately bent and fastened in a loop around an eye-piece of cast iron, called a "shoe," having a groove in its periphery to fit the strand. The ends of the strands are thus "eyed" like the link bars, and fraternize with the last set of the latter, fitting between them eye to eye, and keyed together with them by the eye-bolt. The ends of the great cables are now anchored fast with what seems to the imagination an enormous superfluity of weight and strength. It seems as if the cables would be torn apart ten times over by a force that was sufficient to pluck out their monstrous spread

TESTING STEEL.

of iron roots from the foundations of that solid cemented mass of rock. Undoubtedly this is true; but the intention of the engineer is not merely to equal the strength of the cables with that of their anchorage, but also to give the anchorage a solidity to be absolutely unaffected in the slightest degree by the incessant pull of loads and tug of storms for a hundred years, so that no loosening or vibration can ever be initiated.

To make assurance fourfold sure, the metal for this, as for every part of the work, has been tested by means of specimen pieces under the enormous power of the hydraulic press to its breaking point, a wide margin being always required above the highest possible strain that it is estimated can ever come upon it.

All this is plain work. The anchorages are far within-land. But the great suspension towers to be connected by the central span of the bridge must be pushed out to the extreme wharf line in deep water, for even then the breadth of water to

RELICS FROM THE FOUNDATION.

be bridged at one spring is such as no engineer ever attempted before—nearly 1600 feet—and not only the difficulty but the cost of the work is increased in an enormous ratio by every foot of added length in a single span. We have therefore before us here one of the most interesting problems and one of the most brilliant triumphs of engineering: to build great works of masonry up from beneath the bed and through the rushing tides of a deep arm of the ocean, with all the precision and cemented solidity of the dry-land anchorages we have just been viewing. This part of the work, therefore, was first in order: this achieved left nothing problematical, whether as to availability or cost, in the remainder of the work.

Probably to the end of time thoughtful spectators unversed in the mysteries of engineering will pause, as they now do, before these gigantic towers, more wonderful than the Pyramids, with the everlasting sea beating their mighty bases, and will perplex themselves in vain to imagine by what means the granite masonry could have been laid so solid and true beneath not forty feet depth of rushing tides alone, but eighty feet below their surface, on the rock which those tides had not touched for untold ages.

To explain this mystery in one word, the submarine portion of the tower was really built above-water, in the open air, and thence sunk toward its bed as soon as built. But this is to put a new mystery in place of the first, for how could such a mass of masonry be set firmly to a hair's-breadth in its bed against the mighty current, or how could its bed be excavated to this enormous depth to receive it?

The principle of the diving-bell, supplemented by the air force-pump, or compressor, is the solution of the difficulty. Only the diving-bell must be a peculiar one, made to carry on its back the giant tower as it dives to the bottom, as it delves into the bowels of the earth, and as it reposes at length and forever on the rock. It is technically called a *caisson* (having been first used in France), from its resemblance to an inverted chest. Imagine your diving-bell, or caisson, made of an oblong form, corresponding to the shape and size of its burden, with a margin of eleven feet excess on all sides. You must, of course, also have it built with sufficient durability of material and strength of mass both to carry down the masonry entire, without flinching, and to rest under it forever without yielding or decay. It will be best to have the sides of our oblong diving-bell flare a little, and on the inner side to taper them to a sort of edge (well shod with heavy iron), so as to make room for the laborers within to excavate conveniently to the very extremity of the dimensions of their diving-bell. To obtain sufficient strength and rigidity in the

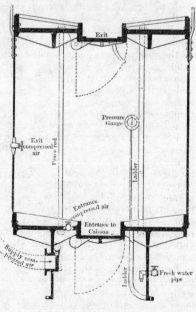

AIR LOCK.

THE CAISSON.

structure for its tremendous back-load, let its entire top, 102 feet by **172**, be built to a thickness of 22 feet of dense Southern pitch-pine in timbers twelve inches square, laid in solid courses crossing each other, fastened with powerful through-bolts, and all the joints and seams filled with pitch. (The bolts and angle-irons of this caisson at New York aggregated 250 tons.) Let the sides be eight feet thick at their junction with the top, built in the same manner, but tapered on the inside, as already suggested, down to an iron-shod edge only eight inches thick, and let the iron bolts and angle-irons, of course, be so strong and numerous that nothing can loosen timber from timber save by tearing each stick into splinters. Further, let the back or platform that is to carry down the great tower in its descent to the bed-rock be supported at intervals by six cross partitions of solid timber four feet thick, with a door in each for communication between the compartments thus formed. These partitions, like the four sides, will ultimately rest on the bed-rock, and bear their part of the monstrous and everlasting load. Finally, let the whole cavernous interior be lined with boiler iron, seamed air-tight, for its perfection as a diving-bell, and for protection against the danger of fire, which experience in building the first or Brooklyn tower of this bridge has shown to be im-

minent at all times while working by gas-light and with blasting explosives in compressed air.

Of course there must be means of ingress and egress for men and materials. There must be a well-hole through the top, and an iron well leading to it from the open air above-water for the men to go in and out. It must be lined with iron, continuous and air-tight with the lining of the interior, and must have an air-tight iron door, or rather two successive doors with an air-tight chamber between them large enough for a gang of men to enter, that the outer door may be closed on him while the inner door is opened to admit them to the artificial submarine cavern. This chamber is called an air lock, and its principle is like that of a canal lock, or still more exactly that of a pump. In going out, the men enter the air lock while its outer door is closed tight, and after the inner door through which they entered is closed behind them the outer door may be opened for their egress. Thus the loss of compressed air by the entrance and exit of a gang of men is simply what the air lock will contain and no more.

This would be too tedious a process, however, for the removal of the excavated earth. For this purpose water locks are used. The iron wells for the removal of material descend through the caisson into open pits in the ground below the level at which the water is held down by the compressed air. The water of course rises in the pits and wells to that level, and thus the compressed air is "locked" out of them, while the earth and stones dumped into the pits by the miners in the caisson tumble to the bottom of the wells, where they can be got at by simply reaching under water. In each of these wells operates a Morris and Cummings dredging-machine (either of the grapnel or "clamshell" pattern, as each was required), like those constantly seen at work at one point or another in this and most other harbors where slips and channels have to be made or deepened, or cleared of deposits, the difference being that these are of the second class in size and power, adapted to the capacity of the caisson and workmen for supplying them with materials. While the harbor machines of forty horse-power remove 2000 cubic yards of mud per day, the caisson machines of twenty-five horse-power can raise 1500 yards; and without working their full capacity, clear the pits of earth as fast as it is practicable to mine it in the caisson. The iron "clam-shell" scoop of the machine descends by its chain to the bottom of the well with its jaws open, plunging into the mud, where the jaws are drawn together by the action of the machinery through another chain. This action operates like the pull of a ship's cable on the anchor, dragging its fluke downward into the bottom. In like manner the flukes of the dredging scoop are forced down into the mud as they are drawn together, and grasp a giant handful, exactly imitating, to use Mr. Roebling's expression, the action of the human hand in picking up handfuls. The force of this grasp is illustrated by the fact that large rocks are picked up as well as earth and small stones, even when only a corner of the rock is seized between the valves of the scoop. All the rock blasted out in Hell Gate by the vast submarine excavations was picked up from the bottom and raised in this way.

While the caisson with its entrances and appurtenances approaches completion in the ship-yard, arrangements must next be made for placing it in position on the bottom of the stream. First a slip or dock must be built to fix it in the exact position of the intended tower. The "water lot" marked for occupation is levelled as well as possible by dredging, and a row of piles is driven as deep as possible

along the landward line, a length of 172 feet. At right angles with this a row of piles is driven out 102 feet into the river from each end, making three sides of an oblong inclosure or stockade. Into this inclosure the caisson is towed. The exact lines of the pier foundation are mathematically fixed by the engineers, and the caisson is placed in the proper position to a hair by blocking and wedging on all three sides. It now rises and falls with the tide, however, and is therefore not yet capable of being exactly and finally placed. The next business, accordingly, is to commence the foundations of the pier on the massive platform or raft of solid timber 22 feet thick and 102 by 172 feet square, which we have figuratively called the back of the submarine monster which is to carry the whole burden down to its final bed. The huge squared blocks of granite are now laid at leisure in hydraulic cement in uniform courses, and soon their weight overcomes the buoyancy of the caisson, and settles it to the bottom, with its top still visible above-water. The compressed air is now let into the diving-bell interior, forcing the water out beneath the iron-shod edges of the sides where they rest on the bottom. This done, the workmen can go down into the very wet cellar, and complete the levelling of the earth under the supporting edges of the structure. Now, while the caisson barely touches bottom by its weight, but does not rest too heavily, the engineers can, with their mathematical instruments and wedges, finally adjust the mass in exact position, and by easing away the bottom under it wherever required, with much patience, they at length get it level, and uniformly supported by blocking placed under its cross partitions. A few more blocks of granite laid on will make it immovable. All is now ready for the dredges to begin lifting out the mud and stones which the men of pick, shovel, and wheelbarrow pour into the water locks or wells beneath the dredging shafts.

Many formidable difficulties have thus been surmounted, and the curious observer now sees how everything so far can be done by the puny hand of man when guided by his mighty mind. But with our thoughts fixed on the mountain-like mass of rock descending full built, we are staggered still by the difficulty of letting it down eighty feet into the submarine earth, with its position as plumb and level and unchangeable at every moment of descent as that of the cornerstone at rest in its bed under any great building on land. If it should sway from its position ever so little, the mathematical accuracy and beauty of the whole after-work would be marred, and what power on earth could move it back a hair's-breadth toward its place? If a side or a corner should be hindered or hastened in its descent a little more than the rest, the mass would be wrenched and disjointed by its own irresistible weight, and the disintegrating force thus initiated within the structure could never be eradicated or counteracted. But the mode of achieving this miracle of descent—not only moving mountains, but moving them to a hair, through the earth, as the piston descends in the cylinder of a steam-engine—is so commonplace and simple that it seems almost childish. No machinery of

vast and imperceptibly slow leverage or screw-power, and of admirably scientific adjustment, is here called to our aid. Nothing but pine blocking under the six cross partitions of timber on which, as on so many legs or feet, the monstrous burden-carrier stands. As fast as the earth is dug away to make room for the descending tower, the blocking is knocked away to let it down. Impossible? Let us see. Suppose a blocking at every two or four feet beneath the supporting partitions, can not we knock out alternate blockings all round? True; but how shall we knock out the rest, and what would become of the structure deprived of support now at this point and now at that, and pitching downward this way and that with rock-rending force? Not so fast. By knocking out the alternate blockings we have just doubled the weight and compression on their fellows. By such increased com-

WRAPPING THE CABLES.

pression of its supports the tower has settled in some measure, of course, and in the most uniform measure possible. Now we just drive in again the blockings we have removed, as tightly as possible, after levelling away the earth under them. But it is evident that we can not drive them as tight as they were before under the actual weight of the tower. Besides, the new ground they now rest on is susceptible of fresh compression. Therefore, if we next knock out the blockings before undisturbed, the tower will settle down on the replaced blockings as far as its weight can compress them and the new ground under them. The fact proves to be that one complete process of this kind lets the tower down about one inch by the compression alternately of the two sets of blockings and the subjacent earth.

But what if our blockings should be driven tighter or prove harder, themselves or their foundations, at some points than at others: will not this produce an unequal settling, and strain the integrity of the masonry? No; for both the weight and strength of the mass are so predominant as to make nothing of such minor resistances, and the only result is that the presumptuous block is crushed. This mode of equalizing the pressure by its own irresistible weight was frequently observed. Again, if it be asked how we are to restrain so uncontrollable a mass from veering in one direction or another from its true position as it descends, the answer to this difficulty also is given by that same uncontrollable weight. Since it can not be influenced in position a hair's-breadth by all the power that man could bring to bear upon it, it will be equally insensible to all the fortuitous forces that would bias the direction of a more limited mass in descending, such as bowlders temporarily encountered by the under edges of the caisson at particular points, or the pressure of the tides. The mass and its movement are too majestic to suffer any influence whatever from such casual obstructions. Only if an obstruction were permanently left in the way at one point, while the caisson was lowered at other points, could such causes act against the plumb descent of the structure.

The last operation, after laying bare the bed-rock, and testing its soundness and solidity at all points, is to fill up the caisson with a solid hydraulic concrete, which will harden into rock and unite itself immovably with the rock on which it rests, becoming to the caisson what a tenon is in a mortise. This concrete is rammed as tightly as possible under the roof of the caisson; but if it be impossible to drive it as tight as if the weight of the tower actually rested on it, this is not amiss. For the continued and increasing weight on the wooden supports will certainly compress them further in time, and will eventually, in all probability, bring the weight of the tower firmly, if not altogether, upon the incompressible concrete with which the caisson is filled.

With regard to the danger of decay in wood, which presents itself to most minds in this connection, experience has long since shown that, when buried beyond reach of air and changes of temperature, wood is perfectly incorruptible, and will endure, so far as we can judge, as long as stone. Oxygen, chemically free as it is in air, is the agent of decomposition, and in its absence all substances are alike incorruptible. The sea-worms make no trouble at the depth below the bottom where we have left our timber platform. It may safely be trusted to support the bridge between New York and Brooklyn as long as there shall be need of it.

The caisson for the Brooklyn tower was towed into its berth on the 2d of May, 1870. Ten of the fifteen feet thickness of timber in its roof were built on after this, *in situ*. On the 15th of June the first granite blocks were laid on the timber. They are of from four to seven tons weight. The masonry, faced throughout with granite, is partly built of the less expensive blue limestone from Kingston, New York. The compressed air was let in, the water driven out, and excavation commenced on the 10th of July. The bed being a tenacious conglomerate of clay, sand, and bowlders, extending to a great depth, it was not necessary on this side to sink the pier to the bed-rock, and at forty-five and a half feet beneath the bottom of the river the caisson was filled up with concrete and left in its final position. The latter operation was completed on the 11th of March, 1871. Two months had been lost by the accident of a fire in the caisson, requiring the interior to be flooded with water to extinguish it. This accident cost $15,000, and its recurrence in the New York caisson was guarded against by a lining of boiler iron throughout, at an expense of $20,000.

The New York foundation was a work of much greater magnitude and difficulty. From the sandy nature of the ground it became necessary to sink the pier to the bed-rock, seventy-eight feet below high-water mark. The process was not different in method, but was much more trying to the workmen, from the greater pressure of air required in the caisson to keep out the water. The caisson was placed in its berth in October, 1871, and rested on the rock in May, 1872, after less than one year's work in sinking it to its bed.

The construction of the towers above the water line was, of course, a simple though enormous piece of mason-work. The Brooklyn tower was completed in May, 1875, and the New York tower in July, 1876. Everything was now ready for the work of cable-making, into which, having already anticipated the construction of the great floor or bridge proper, we must enter somewhat minutely, to give the reader a clear idea of its curious and interesting processes.

THE DRUMS—SPLICING THE WIRES.

Let us first imagine the cable as constructed—simply a bunch of wires, not twisted, but laid parallel, and bound together by a continuous wrapping of wire. The wires are of size No. 7, or a little over one-eighth inch in thickness; they number over 5000 in each cable, and make a bundle 15¾ inches thick. To lay and bind this prodigious bunch of wires straight and parallel would be impossible except by subdividing the mass into skeins or strands, which are first laid and bound separately, and afterward united. Each cable contains nineteen strands of 278 wires each. They are formed precisely like skeins of yarn or thread. Each skein is a continuous wire almost exactly one million feet, or nearly 200 miles, in length, passing from anchorage to anchorage, back and forth, 278 times. The turns of the wire at each

extremity of the skein pass around a solid block of iron shaped externally like a horseshoe, with a groove in its periphery, in which the bend or bight of the skein lies as a skein of yarn is held on one's thumbs for winding. Each shoe or eye-piece is fixed (after the strand is finished) between the ends of two anchor bars, a seven-inch iron bolt passing through the three, and so connecting the strand with the great anchor chain at either end. After a skein is fully laid in position (passing, of course, over the tops of the towers) it is compressed to a cylindrical form at every point by large clamp tongs, and tightly bound with wire at intervals of about fifteen inches throughout its length. The men who do this work go out for the purpose on the strand in a "buggy," so called, which is a board seat slung by ropes from the axis of a grooved wheel fitting and travelling on the strand as bound together. When the

FARRINGTON CROSSING THE SPAN.

strands are thus completed and duly regulated, the final work of wrapping the cable is accomplished in a similar manner, as hereafter described.

But to follow the process of construction, we return to the day when the towers and anchorages stood complete, but disconnected, with the intermediate spaces occupied only by the trackless air, and the question was how to initiate a connection between them all. To this end a three-quarter-inch wire rope, long enough to reach from anchorage to anchorage over the tops of the towers, was coiled on board a scow by the Brooklyn shore. First, its end was hoisted up the water face of the Brooklyn tower, and passed over the top, let down the land face, and then carried back to the top of the anchorage, and made fast. Next—waiting until an opportunity when the river was clear of vessels at that point, and stationing boats to warn coming vessels to halt—the scow was towed across to the New York tower,

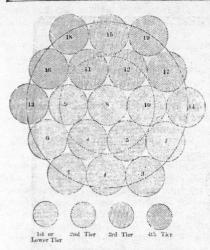

1st or 2nd Tier 3rd Tier 4th Tier
Lower Tier

SECTION OF CABLE, SHOWING STRANDS.

paying out the wire rope into the water as it went. The end remaining on board was then hoisted up the water face of the New York tower, passed over, and lowered again on the landward side. Then it was made fast to a drum connected with a powerful steam-engine, which wound up the rope from the bed of the river and over the tower, until it swung clear from side to side in mid-air, and the first connection between the shores was made. It remained only to carry the New York end back to the anchorage, hoist it up, and secure it in position there.

A second span of three-quarter-inch rope was carried over in substantially the same manner, and the ends of the two were then joined at the anchorages around grooved driving-wheels or pulleys, making an endless belt or "traveller" revolving by steam-power throughout the whole distance from anchorage to anchorage.

To accomplish the succeeding operations would require men to work hanging on this slender cord all the way from tower to tower. Mr. E. F. Farrington, the master-mechanic who superintended this part of the work on the bridge, and who had previously been engaged on the suspension-bridges at Cincinnati and Niagara Falls, now took the resolution to make the first passage of the line, and to give his men as good an example of courage and confidence as they would ever have occasion to copy.

On Friday afternoon, August 25, 1876,

the running gear for the endless traveller rope was in readiness. A boatswain's chair, consisting of a bit of board for a seat, slung by the four corners, with as many short ropes uniting in a ring overhead, was secured to the traveller rope at the Brooklyn anchorage, and Mr. Farrington took his seat on the slung bit of board for a private trip over the line of the future bridge in sight of his men. Having made his preparations so quietly, and being so quiet a man, his surprise was great, on looking down from his high starting-point, to see the house-tops beneath him black with spectators, the streets far below paved, as it were, with upturned faces, the ferry-boats conveying like stacks of humanity, and the New York shore crowded in a similar manner. As he gave the signal to start the wheels and swung out, with the rushing rope hissing and undulating like a flying serpent through the air, the boom of cannon far below announced to the modest and unsuspecting aeronaut that his intended private trip for the encouragement of his men was a public triumph. Away went the whirring rope, invisible or like a spider's thread to the eyes below, bending and swaying with the human weight that rode its cantering waves, to all appearance self-impelled, like some strange creature of serpentine flight, sweeping first downward toward the house-tops till the deepest curve his weight could give the slender rope was passed, and thence soaring sharply upward to the top of the first tower in his course. Here he gave a signal to slow the rope nearly to a stop, while the men on the tower, with excited cheering, lifted the rope and its slung rider over the parapet, supported both across to the other side, and launched them off the dizzy height again. Again the cannon roared, and the myriads of spectators swung their hats and cheered with wild excitement, while all the steam-whistles on land and water shrieked their uttermost discordance. The trip occupied twenty-two minutes, and at the end the explorer was glad to hide from the pursuing crowds that would fain have caught him as a trophy and carried him through the streets in triumph.

It was after this an easy matter to carry across the other carrier ropes; the ropes from which the "cradles," or hanging platforms, for regulating the wires, were suspended; those which supported the foot bridge for the workmen, over which sight-seers were sometimes allowed to pass ; and the "storm cables," which, stretching upward from the towers below the roadway, steadied the temporary structure against the wind.

Meanwhile all was ready in the large sheds that covered the Brooklyn anchorage for the regular and long-to-be-protracted machine-work of cable-making. Thirty-two drums, eight feet in diameter, were rigged in the position of carriage-wheels just clear of the floor, eight drums behind the destined position of each of the four cables. Hundreds of coils of wire, already delivered in the yard below, had been dipped in linseed-oil and dried again and again. A screw thread had been cut on every end of wire by a convenient machine constantly at work for this purpose (opposite ends being cut with right and left screws respectively), and the little steel coupling tubes, with inside screw-threads to match, had united fifty-two coils, or nearly ten continuous miles of wire, upon each of the thirty-two drums.

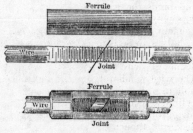

Ferrule

Wire

Joint

Ferrule

Wire

Joint

THE WIRE SPLICE.

Now the shoe, or eye-piece, around which the skein of wire to form a strand of the cable is to be turned at each extremity, is secured in a temporary position on the anchorage, and the work of winding the skein is begun. A wire is fastened to the shoe, and passed around a sheave or grooved pulley fixed and suspended to the traveller rope by iron arms reaching up from its axle. The traveller rope is set in motion, and bears forth the sheave, carrying the bight or turn of wire before it, thus taking across two spans, or a complete circuit, of the wire at once. On reaching the New York side (which takes about eight minutes) the bight of wire is passed around the shoe, completing once the circuit of the skein. The sheave, released, returns empty to the Brooklyn side.

Next the circuit of wire that has been carried across must be "regulated," that is, adjusted to the exact length and height required by its place in the strand. On the top of the Brooklyn tower, first, a clamp is fastened on the first span of wire —i. e., that directly reaching from the end fastened at the Brooklyn anchorage—a small tackle-block is hooked on, and two men haul up the slack between the tower and anchorage until the regulator men in the cradle signal that the position is accurately adjusted at their respective points. A similar regulation is made on the New York tower to adjust the curve of the wire between the towers, and the same process is likewise repeated on the New York anchorage, until the fall of the wire off that point is also accurately located. The return span is then adjusted in the same manner, in reverse order, beginning at the New York tower. On the Brooklyn side, when the last span of this circuit of wire is adjusted in position, it is passed around the shoe, held fast, and the bight is again placed on a sheave, and the traveller starts again to carry over a second circuit of the skein. Thus the skein is wound round and round its eye-pieces at either anchorage with unbroken continuity, with uniform tension, and with exact parallelism between all its threads, until the full number of 139 circuits has been made, and 278 wires are ready to be bound together in a round and solid cord three inches thick. On either side the eye-piece, of course, the cord is parted, and for a few inches is bound in two separate strands of 139 wires each, but it is shortly brought into one, leaving a loop at each end of the strand, inclosing the eye-piece or shoe, which, as before stated, is pinned between and together with two of the eighteen anchor bars in which the great anchor chains unite with each cable. Strands for each of the four great cables are made and placed simultaneously. A circuit of wire is laid and regulated in about thirty minutes, including ordinary delays. Two travellers are running, so that four circuits, or eight full lengths, of wire might be laid per hour. If weather never interfered, the 21,000 wires of which the four cables are composed could have been laid in less than a year. In point of fact, however, as it was useless to make the strands faster than the engineers could locate and adjust them in the cables—which is the grand difficulty of the work—it was doing well to lay forty wires on an average each working day.

On the commencement of impracticable weather in winter, such as incrusts the wires with snow and ice, it becomes impossible to regulate the wires properly. Then the work is necessarily suspended for the time being.

But the chief delay, as before remarked, arose from the difficulty of regulating the strands from two causes—sun and wind. Obviously the unity and strength of the cable depend on getting each strand into its exact and peculiar place. As the locations of the individual strands vary in height, the strands must vary in length. Each must hang in its own peculiar length and curve to a mathematical nicety; for if left but half an inch too long or too short for its true position, it will be too slack or too taut for its fellows, and it will be impossible to bind them solidly in one mass, and make them pull equally together. In the abstract this is a matter of exact mathematical science. But in practical engineering the actualization of the calculations is interfered with by variable forces which can not be resisted, evaded, or calculated. The chief of these in cable-making is temperature, which fluctuates so irregularly and unceasingly that the length of the strand is rarely the same for an hour together; and what is far more baffling to the engineer, the different spans are unequally acted on by the sun. One curve is in shadow while another is in full sunshine; one is exposed vertically to the sun, while another is struck by its rays at an extremely dull angle. In short, when the sun shines the several curves of each strand are all "at sixes and sevens," too unstable in position to be adjusted. The same is true of them in another sense when they are kept swaying and undulating by the wind. Hence the engineers can do nothing with them except at hours when two conditions concur—freedom from the influences of wind and direct sunshine. The hours from daylight to sunrise (when calm), and occasionally a few hours of calm and cloudy weather, are the only times available to the engineer for adjusting the length of his strands. This is done by changing the position of the "shoe." The figures of the engineer show that the deflection of the cables from the tops of the towers is 127.64 feet at 50° F., while at 90° it is 128.64 feet—a variation of nearly one-third of an inch for every degree of temperature, so that the engineer is likely to find his cables varying as much as half a foot in height in the course of a day. In short, the ponderous thing, though neither small nor agile, has a trick in common with the minute and lively insect which, when you put your finger on him, isn't there.

The running and regulating of the cable wires commenced June 11, 1877, and the last wire was run over October 15, 1878. The nineteen strands for each of the four cables having been thus made and located, the final operation is to unite and wrap them with wire. This is done by a little machine. An iron clamp is provided, the interior of which is of the size and cylindrical shape of the cable before wrapping. The temporary fastenings of wire around each strand are removed as fast as this work proceeds, and the clamp, screwed tightly, compresses the nineteen strands together, symmetrically arranged in a true cylinder, with the odd strand in the centre, and the other eighteen filling two circles around it. The wrapping machine follows up the clamp, and binds the cable with a close spiral wrapping of wire. This machine or implement consists of an iron cylinder cast in halves, to be bolted together about the cable, compressing it firmly. A reel or drum of wire encircles the cylinder. The wire winds off the drum through a hole in a steel disk on the rear end of the cylinder, whence it passes with a single turn around a small roller attached to the disk, and thence to the cable. The disk is turned by hand by a lever attached to it, and thus the wire, being held in severe tension by its turn around the roller, is tightly wound on the cable, and as it advances in its spiral or screw travel pushes forward the cylinder from which it is reeled.

The cables, thus completed, were ready for their load, the floor or bridge proper, already described. The suspender bands were next put on the cables; to these are attached the wire rope suspenders, and these in turn hold the steel floor beams of the roadway. The suspender bands are made of wrought iron five inches wide and five-eighths of an inch thick. The bands are cut at one point, and the two ends turned outward, so that they may be opened (by heating), and placed over the cables. The two ends, or ears, which hang vertically down when the bands are in

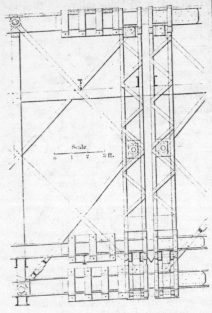

Scale

0   1   2   3 ft.

EXPANSION JOINT IN CENTRE TRUSS.

place, have holes through them for a screw-bolt one and three-quarter inches in diameter, which serves as the support of the suspenders, and also for tightening the bands and the cable. By the aid of these suspenders at short intervals all the way, it was easy to place, first, the cross-beams of the bridge floor, beginning with those nearest each anchorage and each face of the towers. The nearest suspenders hanging ready to receive the first iron beam had only to be drawn in and attached thereto by their clamps or stirrups, and the beam was swung out in position, ready to support planks for the workmen to stand on and launch the second beam, and so on. The cross beams being laid and braced together, forming the horizontal truss, the vertical truss-work is also put in, with the diagonal bracing below the floor, and the stays from the towers both above and below, and the bridge is at last ready for the planking.

The suspenders are for the most part at equal distances from each other. But it will be noticed that at the centre two suspenders from each of the four cables hang close together, sometimes but a few inches, sometimes more than a foot, apart. These give the clew to that problem of en-gineering and puzzle to the public as to how the expansion and contraction, by heat and cold, of the floor or bridge proper, are to be provided for. The great span may be said to be in two pieces or half-lengths, connected at the centre by an "expansion joint." Each half of a truss is attached to one of the two suspenders mentioned, and the two halves are connected by plates attached to one, and sliding in channels or ways in the other. No weight comes upon these guide-plates, as the two suspenders support the halves of the truss independently of each other. The planking is so arranged as to be always continuous, and the iron rails for the cars are at this point split in half lengthwise, so that one half plays upon the other, guide-rails on either side protecting the cars.

At 118 feet above high-water mark each of the towers of the bridge is divided into three masses by the two broad openings, $31\frac{1}{2}$ feet wide, which here commence. The six lines of the great steel trusses or frame-work forming the bridge pass, unbroken in their continuity, through these openings of the piers, resting on the masonry underneath, and firmly anchored down to it by huge bolts and ties of wire rope. An idea of the strength of these trusses may be obtained when it is considered that for over one hundred feet out from each side of the tower they are of themselves, without any support whatever from the cables or stays, sufficiently strong to carry all the load that may ever come upon them. The openings continue to the height of $120\frac{1}{2}$ feet, where they are closed by pointed arches. Above these arches the reunited tower rises thirty feet higher, where it receives a set of iron bed-plates, on which rest the "saddles" in which the great suspension cables ride. These are iron castings in the form of a segment of a circle, with a groove to receive the cable on the upper and convex side. The under and plane side lies on a layer of small iron rollers held in place by flanges on the surface of the bed-plate. The object of these is to give sufficient play to the bearings on which the cables rest to prevent the cables themselves slipping and chafing in the saddles if affected by the force of storms or variations of load, or when lengthening and contracting under changes of temperature. From the saddles each way the cables sweep downward in a graceful curve, the landward ends entering the an-

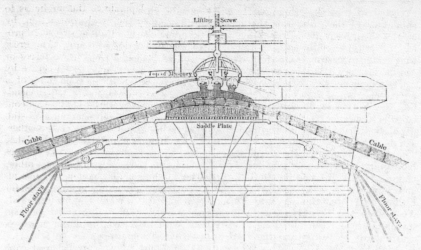

SECTION OF TOWER, SHOWING SADDLE-PLATE AND LOWERING OF STRAND INTO POSITION.

chor walls, as already described, and supporting the shore ends of the bridge, while the main bow, or inverted arch, hanging between the towers, holds up the central truss of nearly 1600 feet span.

A great work of engineering is a battle with nature, in which, as in other wars, Death must take his toll. There have been employed upon the works at one time as many as six hundred men, a small army in themselves, and in the fourteen years since the master-mind, John A. Roebling himself, became the first sacrifice, more than twenty men have been fatally hurt. Several more have been victims to the "caisson disease,"* resulting from working in compressed air; but, despite the dizzy height, no one has fallen from the main span into the water below. Besides the fire in the Brooklyn caisson, which cost no lives, and the fall of the derricks on the Brooklyn tower, which had more serious results, there has been

* The "caisson disease" is the result of living under atmospheric pressure greatly above that to which the human system is normally adapted. The blood is driven in from the exterior and soft parts of the body to the central organs, especially the brain and spinal cord. On emerging into the open air, violent neuralgic pains and sometimes paralysis follow. Advanced consumption is, on the other hand, stayed, and sometimes remedied, by compressed air. Dr. Andrew H. Smith, surgeon to the Bridge Company, reported one hundred and ten cases of the "caisson disease," of which three were presently, and probably more finally, fatal.

one great accident only; but the imagination can scarcely picture anything more dreadful. On June 19, 1878, one of the great strands broke loose from the New York anchorage, carrying with it the "shoe" and its ponderous attachments. As the end swept from the anchorage it dashed off several of the men at work, and then, with a frightful leap, grazing the houses and peopled streets below, it landed for the instant in the bridge yard close under the New York tower. The great weight mid-stream whizzed it over the tower with frightful and increasing rapidity, and the whole span plunged madly into the river, narrowly missing the ferry-boats that ply, crowded with human freight, below the line of the bridge. In these years the enterprise has lost also its president, Henry C. Murphy, and its first treasurer, J. H. Prentice, as well as its chief engineer. But, in strange and happy contrast, there has not been a single break in the engineering staff, Engineers Martin, Paine, Collingwood, McNulty, Probasco, and Hildenbrand having served continuously, most of them from the very first. And now all the extraordinary engineering difficulties are overcome, and with them the vexatious delays from unfriendly opposition, political feuds, the stoppage of financial supplies, and the adoption of a new structural material. In a few years these will have been forgotten, and the forty million passengers who are expected to cross the bridge yearly will think only of the great boon that emancipates them from the delays of fog and ice, the possible collisions, and the old-time delays in waiting for the ferry-boats. Yet the ferries will still have plenty to do.

The summer of 1883 will be memorable for the opening of the great bridge, uniting New York and Brooklyn into a metropolis of nearly two million people—a population that will soon outgrow Paris, and have only London left to vie with. The bridge is practically a new street, belonging jointly to the two cities, and making with Third Avenue, the Bowery, and Chatham Street, New York, and Fulton Street continuing into Fulton Avenue on the Brooklyn side, a great thoroughfare fourteen miles long, already continuously built up, from the Harlem River to East New York. This is longer than the great street which stretches east to west across London, under its various names, from Bow to Uxbridge Road, spanning the valley where was once the Fleet brook by that other fine work of engineering, the Holborn Viaduct. The bridge roadway from its New York terminus opposite the City Hall to Sands Street, Brooklyn, is a little over a mile long (5989 feet), and it will take the pace of a smart walker to make the aerial journey, with its arched ascent, in twenty minutes. The cities will probably decide, confining the tolls to vehicular traffic, not to charge him the one cent first proposed for the privilege of taking this trip on "foot's horse." But for five cents he can jump at either end into fine cars, built on the pattern of the newest Manhattan elevated cars, which move apparently of their own volition, until one finds the secret in the endless wire rope underneath that is worked by stationary engines on the shore and makes continual circuit, across under one roadway and back under the other. These will take him across in a little less than five minutes, and it is not improbable that through trains will ultimately convey passengers from the northernmost end of New York over the Brooklyn Elevated that is to be, bringing them nearer to the health-giving beaches of Long Island by nearly half an hour's time.

But the wise man will not cross the bridge in five minutes, nor in twenty. He will linger to get the good of the splendid sweep of view about him, which his æsthetic self will admit pays wonderful interest on his investment of nothing. The bridge itself will be a remarkable sight, as he looks from his central path of vantage down upon the broad outer roadways, each with its tide of weighted waggons and carriages of his wealthier but not wiser brethren, and nearer the centre the two iron paths upon which the trains move silently and swiftly. Under him is the busy river, the two great cities now made one, and beyond, completing the circuit, villa-dotted Staten Island; the marshes, rivers, and cities of New Jersey stretching to Orange Mountain and the further heights; the Palisades walling the mighty Hudson; the fair Westchester country; the thoroughfare of the Sound opening out from Hell Gate; Long Island, "fish-shaped Paumanok," with its beaches; the Narrows, with their frowning forts; the Bay, where the colossal Liberty will rise; at last the ocean, with its bridging ships. And when he takes his walks about New York he can scarcely lose sight of what is now the great landmark which characterises and dominates the city as St. Peter's from across the Campagna dominates Rome, and the Arc de Triomphe the approach to Paris, and the Capitol on its height our own Washington—the double-towered bridge, whose massive masonry finds no parallel since the Pyramids. Those higher masses were the work of brutal force, piling stone upon stone. The wonder and the triumph of this work of our own day is in the weaving of the aerial span that carries such burden of usefulness, by human thought and skill, from the delicate threads of wire that a child could almost sever.

THE STORY OF A STREET
(PART 3)

A TRAVEL - STAINED horseman journeying down Broadway on Tuesday, May 17, 1774, turned his jaded mount to the left on reaching Trinity Church and passed into Wall Street unrecognized and scarcely noticed. The man was evidently a stranger, but cosmopolitan New York, with a population of nearly twenty-five thousand, was accustomed to the presence of strangers, and there was nothing in the appearance of this one to attract attention beyond the fact that his clothes, saddlebags, and horse were encrusted with mud, and that his tired animal suggested a long trip over difficult country. The rider himself, scarcely less exhausted than his horse, was a sturdily built fellow about forty years of age, with a clean-shaven, rather commonplace face, and the undistinguished bearing of a farmer or petty merchant. Certainly no one would have supposed him to be a man of artistic temperament or heroic mould, and yet he was an artist of no mean calibre, and his crudest sketches were destined to be cherished by future generations of hero-worshippers, for within a year he was to win undying fame and provide a stirring theme for song and story. Wall Street, however, saw no shadow of the coming event, and Paul Revere, illustrator and engraver, dentist, merchant, goldsmith, soldier, and "Constitutional Post-rider," passed quietly on his way, staring curiously at the busy scene unfolded to his gaze.

There must have been much that was strange and diverting to the provincial in the passing throngs—the venders of tea water from the pump near the Collect pond, with their crude hogsheads carried in carts or set on wheels, the clumsy travelling coaches, the sedan chairs, the gorgeously uniformed officers and officials, the groups of sombrely attired merchants—all the life and movement of the bustling commercial and official centre must have afforded a novel contrast to quiet Boston, with her port practically closed and her commerce almost dead. Yet, unfamiliar as his surroundings were, this was not Revere's first visit to New York. Less than six months before he had carried the news of the Boston Tea Party to the local Sons of Liberty, but their headquarters were then near the Fields,* and this was possibly his first view of the street which was now almost without a rival in the fashionable quarter of the town.

Before him stretched a neat and attractive thoroughfare lined with stately shade trees and handsome houses, whose dignified appearance demonstrated that their owners were men of substance, if not of fashion. At his left the Presbyterian Church still maintained its commanding position, and just beyond it lay the reconstructed City Hall, its upper stories, supported by arches, forming an arcade through which the pedestrians passed; but the hideous sugar refinery which had disfigured the neighborhood for many years had at last disappeared, and the Verplanck mansion and other handsome private dwellings now occupied its site. Beyond these on the same side of the street lay the McEvers mansion, before which the Stamp Tax rioters had paused in their wild march some nine years earlier, and in front of which now stood Pitt's marble statue, the work of Wilton, a famous sculptor, while in its immediate vicinity ranged the comfortable residences of the Thurmans, Banckers, Ludlows, Startins, Winthrops, Whites, Janeways, and other citizens of credit and more or less renown.

Riding by these attractive homelike houses, Revere must have passed that

* Present City Hall Park.

WALL STREET IN 1774

To the right is the arcade of the City Hall; at the left the head of Broad Street;
in the foreground a vender of tea water from the pump near the Collect pond

of his friend and correspondent, John Lamb,* one of the most active members in the Sons of Liberty, whose ceaseless agitation of popular rights had for some years been forcing the hands alike of friends and foes. Indeed, if any one individual could have been held accountable for the exciting scenes which Wall Street had recently experienced, the responsibility would probably have been laid at Lamb's well-appointed door. In fact, on the very day when Revere and his fellow masqueraders were destroying the cargoes of the East India Company in Boston Harbor, John Lamb was rousing the merchants of New York to similar violence in the City Hall; and had a tea ship arrived in the port at that juncture there is no doubt that his Wall Street audience would have quickly organized a Tea Party without paint or feathers. Fortunately or unfortunately, however, no vessel had appeared at that crisis; but about four months later, when the *London* sailed into the harbor, a vigilance committee promptly boarded her without the least effort at disguise and bundled her objectionable merchandise into the sea. This had occurred on Friday, April 22, 1774, and the very next day Wall Street witnessed an exhibition

* Griswold, in his *American Court*, claims that Whigs like Lamb obtained no foothold in Wall Street till after the Revolution, but there is evidence that Lamb was an exception to this rule.

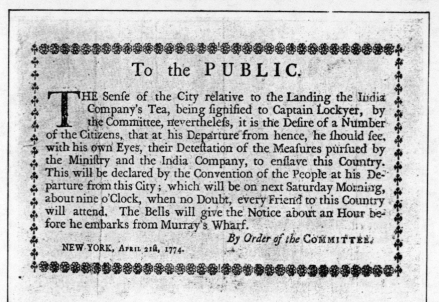

To the PUBLIC.

THE Senfe of the City relative to the Landing the India Company's Tea, being fignified to Captain Lockyer, by the Committee, neverthelefs, it is the Defire of a Number of the Citizens, that at his Departure from hence, he fhould fee, with his own Eyes, their Deteftation of the Meafures purfued by the Miniftry and the India Company, to enflave this Country. This will be declared by the Convention of the People at his Departure from this City; which will be on next Saturday Morning, about nine o'Clock, when no Doubt, every Friend to this Country will attend. The Bells will give the Notice about an Hour before he embarks from Murray's Wharf.

By Order of the COMMITTEE.

NEW-YORK, April 21ft, 1774.

BROADSIDE ANNOUNCING CAPTAIN LOCKYER'S DEPARTURE AND SUMMONING CITIZENS TO MURRAY'S WHARF ON WALL STREET

From Original in possession of the New York Historical Society

of the popular temper as unique as it was significant.

About the same time that the *London* came to anchor in the lower bay another vessel, known as the *Nancy*, arrived with a cargo of tea, imported expressly for the purpose of testing the strength of the non-importation agreement. Her commander, Captain Lockyer, made no secret of his mission, and the vigilance committee finally permitted him to visit the city for the purpose of consulting his consignees; but when those gentlemen prudently refused to receive his cargo the worthy captain was ordered to sail for England at the earliest possible moment.

Meanwhile notices had been posted throughout the city summoning all friends of the country to assemble on Murray's Wharf at the foot of Wall Street on the day of Lockyer's departure and give him a send-off which he would be likely to remember and report to his friends across the sea. Accordingly at eight o'clock on Saturday morning, April 23, bells began ringing all over the city, more and more joining in the chorus, until every clapper in town was swinging

save those of the loyal City Hall and King's College, and at this prearranged signal all sorts and conditions of men began streaming toward the rendezvous, some of them accompanied by brass bands, and all the shipping on the river front displayed its brightest bunting. For an hour the crowds continued to pour into Wall Street, massing in front of the Merchants Coffee House on the southeast corner of Wall and Water streets, where the offending mariner had taken up his abode, and when he showed himself on the balcony in the custody of a committee of citizens a deafening roar of cheers and a bedlam of bells greeted his appearance. No disorder of any sort was attempted, however, and when quiet was restored the committee solemnly introduced their victim to the crowd and signalled the bands, which burst into "God Save the King." During this demonstration of loyalty the captain was escorted with great ceremony into the street, where a lane was forced for him through the cheering multitude to the wharf, where he boarded a pilot boat, accompanied by a deputation charged

To the PUBLICK.

NEW-YORK, October 5, 1774.

BY Mr. Rivere, who left Boston on Friday laſt, and arrived here laſt night, in his way to the General Congreſs, we have certain intelligence that the Carpenters and Maſons who had inadvertently undertaken to erect barracks for the ſoldiers in that town, upon being informed that it was contrary to the ſentiments of their countrymen, unanimouſly broke up, and returned to their reſpective homes, on the 26th of laſt month; which, it is hoped, will convince the Mechanicks of this city, how diſagreeable it will be to the inhabitants of that place, for them to afford any manner of aſſiſtance to thoſe, who are made ſubſervient to the deſtruction of our American brethren.

Printed by JOHN HOLT, near the COFFEE HOUSE.

BROADSIDE ANNOUNCING AN ARRIVAL OF PAUL REVERE'S IN NEW YORK
From Original in possession of the New York Historical Society

with the duty of seeing him safely off Sandy Hook, and amid the booming of cannon and other wild demonstrations of rejoicing he sailed away to carry the news of his significant reception to ears that would not hear.

These events must have been known to Paul Revere, and possibly they were in his mind as he jogged through Wall Street,* for he was the accredited messenger not only of the Sons of Liberty, but also of the Committee of Correspondence, and it was at their unofficial headquarters, the Merchants Coffee House, that he undoubtedly alighted.

Of all the historic buildings which figure in Wall Street's story, this unpretentious tavern is fairly entitled to a place apart. Erected about 1740,* on what was then practically the water's edge, at a time when privateersmen and other adventurous sons of the sea frequented the port to compare notes and transact business of a kind best consummated over a glass of grog, behind walls devoid of ears, it had immediately become a sort of maritime exchange whose secrets never leaked and whose rear doors were exceedingly convenient for customers who preferred to be within hail of their small boats. With the passing of the privateersmen and other less admirable waterside characters, however, it gradually developed from a sailor's snug harbor into a place of general resort whose patrons were so fastidious that the adjoining slave market had to be removed for their benefit,† and from

* The exact route followed by Revere cannot now be positively identified. He left Boston May 14, 1774; was almost three days on the road; entered the city by the Bowery, or Boston Post Road; and his despatch was for the Committee of Correspondence, some of whose members were usually to be found at the Merchants Coffee House.

* The first reference to this historic building appears to be in the *Weekly Post Boy*, January 16, 1744 (No. 52, page 4), where it is mentioned in an advertisement dated November, 1743.

† "Said Meal (Slave) Markett greatly Obstructs the agreeable prospect of the East

that time onward its popularity steadily increased, until its guests included all the best people in the community and its influence was that of a civic forum.

There was nothing imposing either in the exterior or the interior of this celebrated inn. All that is known of its outward appearance is that it was a three-storied structure, with a large room on the first floor, another on the second, a piazza or balcony on the front, and a platform or porch on the side, and its interior appointments were in keeping with this very modest architectural plan. The two "long rooms," however, witnessed many a famous meeting and consultation, and their part in the prelude to the Revolution was of the first importance. Here it was that the demonstrations against the military occupation and rule of Boston had taken place in 1769; here some of the most interesting conferences of the Friends of Liberty and Trade were held; here Isaac Sears and other radicals urged the seizure of the stamps; here Lockyer was accorded his mock reception; here began the demonstration against the closing of the port of Boston which ended in the burning of Lord North in effigy before a crowded balcony; here all the political leaders foregathered; and here, on the 17th of May, 1774, Paul Revere arrived with his despatch to the Committee of Correspondence, just reorganized into the Committee of Fifty.

On its face the message which Revere delivered at this famous tavern was not of extraordinary interest, for it merely reported the resolutions adopted at Faneuil Hall, requesting New York's coöperation in suspending trade with England until the ministry should reopen the port of Boston; but the reply to this communication was epoch-making, for it undoubtedly gave the first impulse to the founding of a national government.

Before the famous post-rider was fairly on the road again, headed for Philadelphia,* a meeting of merchants and

other citizens was called at the Coffee House to nominate a committee to respond to the proposals contained in his despatch, and the existing Committee of Fifty was reappointed with one additional member. Of the assemblage gathered on this occasion Gouverneur Morris wrote: "I stood on the balcony [of the Coffee House], and on my right hand were ranged all the people of property, with some poor dependents, and on the other all the tradesmen, etc., who thought it worth their while to leave their daily labor for the good of the country." It is characteristic of the man that Morris, then in his twenty-third year, should have made himself the centre of this eventful scene, but he was undoubtedly a leader; for in New York, as in other States, the Revolution was the work of youth tempered by almost precocious maturity of judgment. Among those who, with Morris, were moulding history in Wall Street at this critical period were John Jay, aged twenty-eight; Alexander Hamilton, seventeen; Robert Livingston, twenty-seven; Marinus Willett, thirty-three; Alexander McDougall, forty-three; Isaac Low, thirty-nine; and Isaac Sears, the fire-eating veteran, forty-five. Some of these men were on the committee entrusted with the duty of answering the Massachusetts proposals, and it is doubtful if any other body of citizens ever afforded as rare a combination of youth and intellectual maturity. There were, of course, a few hotheads among them, and Alexander McDougall, disgusted with his associates' conservatism, angrily withdrew and attempted to force their hands. In this he was not successful, but the response which was finally adopted by the majority on the 23d of May, 1774, was certainly not the utterance of timorous senility. Indeed, it was nothing less than the first proposal for a convention of delegates from all the colonies, and when Paul Revere received it on his return from Philadelphia, Wall Street had won historic honors; for of this paper formulated in her famous Coffee House came the Continental Congress.

Less than one year* later Israel Bessel, another post-rider, came spurring into the Bowery road from Boston, breaking the quiet of a Sabbath morning by roar-

River which those that live in Wall St. would otherwise enjoy: that it Occasions a Dirty Street Offensive to the Inhabitants on each side and Disagreeable to those that Pass and Repass to and from the Coffee House a place of Great Resort." (Min. of Com. Coun. Vol. 6. p. 283. N. Y. City Hall.)
* May 19. 1774.

* April 23. 1775.

ing startling news at every passing group of citizens; and as the congregations of Trinity and the Presbyterian Church issued from their noonday services he burst upon them with tidings that the battle of Lexington had been fought and won four days before. In an instant he was surrounded by an anxious throng eagerly clamoring for details, and Wall Street was soon in a state of wild commotion, loyalists and patriots scattering to protect their families and property, each man suspecting and fearing the other, and all almost equally dismayed by the news. The patriots were the first to recover from the shock, however, and, headed by Isaac Sears and some of the boldest Sons of Liberty, a band of citizens hastily assembled, and taking possession of the City Hall, seized five hundred stand of arms deposited there for the troops, demanded and received the keys of the Custom House, closed the building, and virtually deposed the royal government.

From that moment all business was suspended in the city, and between April 24 and May 1, 1775, confusion reigned supreme. Then the ablest men in the community assumed control, and calling a mass meeting at the Merchants Coffee House, which had practically become the seat of government, organized a provisional Committee of One Hundred to administer the public business. By the orders of this committee the city was virtually placed under martial law, the shops and factories were closed, the streets were patrolled by improvised bands of militia, all available arms and ammunition were seized, crude preparations were made for resisting an attack, and many timorous loyalists closed their houses and sought safety at their country seats. Meanwhile some of the King's troops had been allowed to enter the city, the loyalist members of the committee feeling that their presence would insure order; but when they made an attempt to appropriate the spare arms deposited in their barracks, Marinus Willett forced an armed guard to surrender this booty, and the carts containing the weapons were triumphantly escorted by a great throng of citizens up Broadway, past the head of Wall Street, to Abraham Van Dyck's ball alley at John Street, where they were placed under lock and key.

Up to this time the leading patriots and loyalists of the city had worked together for the maintenance of order, but anything more than a temporary truce was impossible, and before long the Committee of One Hundred was split into warring factions and party feeling began to run high. Numerically the patriots were in a vast majority, but many men of property and influence were loud in their expressions of loyalty and bitter in their denunciations of the provisional government, whose legality they stoutly denied. Under such circumstances more or less disorder was inevitable, and residence in the city was made extremely uncomfortable for many of the outspoken loyalists. Indeed, some of the more obnoxious were stripped to the skin and ridden on rails through Wall Street, greatly to the scandal of the highly respectable denizens of that most decorous neighborhood.

Such was the condition of affairs in April, 1776, when Washington arrived to oppose the British forces dislodged from Boston, and under his energetic leadership the active preparations for defence which had already been begun were pushed, until the whole appearance of the town was practically transformed. Fortifications were hastily erected on the water front; batteries were planted at various posts of vantage; breastworks and barricades were thrown across the streets; bullets were cast out of lead taken from the roofs of the houses, and some of the buildings were loopholed for street fighting and a house-to-house resistance. Of these crude defences Wall Street boasted a battery masked in the cellar of a house on the East River, a breastwork near the Coffee House, and McDougall's battery, which was stationed a little to the west of Trinity, which continued to conduct its services as though nothing whatever had happened. Indeed, the clergy and congregation of that church did not seem to realize that the Revolution was a fact even when Washington arrived upon the scene, but within a few weeks the war was brought home to them in most extraordinary fashion.

The Rev. Charles Inglis was then assistant rector of the parish, and Washington had not been long in the city before an officious member of his staff called upon the clergyman and requested him to omit the customary prayers for the King, which had been loyally read at all services without the least regard for the existing political conditions. But Mr. Inglis, though a non-combatant, was evidently a believer in the church militant and a most ardent supporter of the crown, for he promptly refused the request, which Washington disavowed as soon as it was brought to his attention. Certainly the King never so needed the prayers of his faithful subjects as he did at that moment, when peace negotiations were impending, but this was not the popular view. Nevertheless the services were conducted for some weeks without alteration or interruption, while the contending forces prepared for what promised to be the bitterest struggle of the war.

One Sunday morning in May, however, a motley crew of about one hundred and fifty armed men, preceded by a fife and drum corps, invaded Wall Street and headed straight for Trinity. Whether they were soldiers or not is uncertain, but they carried bayonets on their guns and were apparently under some sort of military control. Marching to the brisk tap of drums, they passed through the street, crossed Broadway, entered the church, and swept up the aisle, drums beating and fifes shrilling in deafening uproar. Appalled by this desecrating intrusion, the congregation sat aghast, not knowing what to expect, but the white-robed clergyman calmly stood his ground, confronted the invaders, and outfaced them. Indeed, the moment the drums and fifes ceased he proceeded with the services as though nothing had happened, and conducting it with admirable dignity to the very end without the omission of a single word, drove the armed rabble into ignominious retreat.

This was the last, or one of the last, services ever held in the church, however, for its authorities soon thought best to close its doors, and within four months it was totally destroyed by fire. Meanwhile Wall Street listened to the Declaration of Independence, which was read from the steps of the City Hall on the 16th of July, 1776, to a small band of patriots, whose enthusiasm prompted them to invade the court room and tear down

the royal coat of arms, which they then proceeded to burn on the spot where Zenger's *Journal* had been consigned to the flames, thus affording a precedent for wanton destruction that was to cost the city dear before many months had passed. In fact, when the British troops entered the town two months later they looted the City Hall library without mercy, bartering the valuable books for drink, and completely scattering what would now be a unique collection. The statue of Pitt was also wrecked almost beyond recognition, but there were few who regretted its fate, for Pitt had alienated many Americans by his apparent hostility to their independence, and the statue had already been somewhat defaced before the loyalists completed the work of destruction.

With these acts of vandalism Wall Street began a long and bitter experience. Indeed, before the British troops had fairly established themselves in New York the great fire of September 21, 1776, which obliterated a large part of the city, laid Trinity in ruins, and this disaster, wrongly attributed to rebel sympathizers, resulted in such harsh measures against the American residents that many of them fled, abandoning their houses to the enemy.

It did not take long for the army of occupation to appropriate all the available property in the street to its own purposes. The City Hall was immediately transformed into a guard-house and prison, and fortunate indeed were those who were incarcerated there, for they received humane treatment and escaped the horrors which were daily enacted in the sugar-houses and hulks where the majority of American prisoners were confined. One of the earliest inmates of this Wall Street prison was General Charles Lee, and it would have been well for him had he been detained there until the end of the war. He was, however, soon set at liberty, and his subsequent conduct not only led to his disgrace, but came perilously close to wrecking the American cause.

Another famous Wall Street building was likewise utilized for the purposes of the army, for the Presbyterian Church was soon pressed into service as a hospital for the British sick and wounded, and to adapt it to this use it was practically dismantled. These changes, however, merely marked the beginning of the end, for every house vacated by the Americans was immediately placed at the disposal of a British general or official;

sumed a military air. General Knyphausen, the German commander of the Hessians, took possession of the McEvers mansion; General Robertson, the Royal Governor, established himself in the Verplanck mansion between William and Nassau streets,* and this same dwelling also sheltered Benedict Arnold for a short time after he turned traitor. General Riedesel, the Hessian, was another commander who resided in the once fashionable highway, and the famous Coffee House quickly became the favorite resort of all the army and navy officers quartered in the town.

Under these conditions the whole aspect of the street gradually changed, its buildings steadily deteriorated, and before long very little remained of its former glory. In the summer of 1779 a feeble attempt was made to turn the grounds surrounding the blackened ruins of Trinity into a place of fashionable promenade, and with this idea they were enclosed with wooden railings painted green, lamps were hung in the trees, under which benches were placed, and concerts were given by the garrison bands, to which only people of quality were admitted. This was the only effort, however, which was made to restore Wall Street's prestige, and the following winter destroyed its last claim to beauty; for during the unprecedentedly cold weather, which permitted the transport of cannon to Staten Island over the ice-covered bay, all its stately shade trees were sacrificed

New-York, Nov. 24, 1783.

The Committee appointed to conduct the Order of receiving their Excellencies Governor CLINTON and General WASHINGTON,

BEG Leave to inform their Fellow-Citizens, that the Troops, under the Command of Major-General KNOX, will take Poſſeſſion of the City at the Hour agreed on, Tueſday next ; as ſoon as this may be performed, he will requeſt the Citizens who may be aſſembled on Horſeback, at the Bowling-Green, the lower End of the Broad-Way, to accompany him to meet their Excellencies GovernorCLINTON and General WASHINGTON, at the Bull's Head, in the Bowery---the Citizens on Foot to aſſemble at or near the Tea-water-Pump at Freſh-water.

ORDER of PROCESSION.

A Party of Horſe will precede their Excellencies and be on their flanks---after the General and Governor, will follow the Lieutenant-Governor and Members of the Council for the temporary Government of the Southern Parts of the State---The Gentlemen on Horſe-back, eight in Front---thoſe on Foot, in the Rear of the Horſe, in like Manner. Their Excellencies, after paſſing down Queen-Street, and the Line of Troops up the Broadway, will a-light at CAPE's Tavern.

The Committee hope to ſee their Fellow-Citizens, conduct themſelves with Decency and Decorum on this joyful Occaſion.

CITIZENS TAKE CARE!!!

THE Inhabitants are hereby informed, that Permiſſion has been obtained from the Commandant, to form themſelves in patroles this night, and that every order requiſite will be given to the guards, as well to aid and aſſiſt, as to give protection to the patroles : And that the counterſign will be given to THOMAS TUCKER, No. 51, Water Street ; from whom it can be obtained, if neceſſary.

BROADSIDE ANNOUNCING WASHINGTON'S ENTRY INTO NEW YORK
From Original in Possession of the New York Historical Society

and so great was the demand for residential property for the housing of these gentlemen that the dwellings of all rebels were marked with a broad R to subject them to confiscation.

Wall Street thus practically became the headquarters of the army of occupation, and the entire neighborhood as-

Street's prestige, and the following winter destroyed its last claim to beauty; for during the unprecedentedly cold weather, which permitted the transport of cannon to Staten Island over the ice-covered bay, all its stately shade trees were sacrificed

* Almost on the site of the present Assay Office.

to provide fuel for the families of Generals Knyphausen, Riedesel, and other officers. From this time onward desolation and decay marked the highway for their own, and as the war drew to a close its condition passed from bad to worse; for the British naturally took no pains to preserve the property which they were soon to restore to its former owners, and dirt and débris were allowed to accumulate, until every street was a rubbish heap lined with wrecked, dismantled, or dilapidated buildings.

Such was the condition of Wall Street on the 25th of November, 1783, when Brigadier-General Henry Jackson, in command of about eight hundred men, stationed at McGowan's Pass, set his troops in motion for the Collect, or Fresh Water Pond, on the outskirts of the town, where he halted about noon under the orders of General Henry Knox, deputed by Washington to take possession of New York. At the same hour the rear guard of the British army of 6500 was marching down Broadway to embark for Staten Island, their brilliant uniforms and perfect equipment affording a brave sight for all beholders, and a little later in the afternoon one of Sir Guy Carleton's staff reported to the American commander that the last of his troops were on the transports at the Battery. This was the word which General Knox had been eagerly awaiting, and within a few minutes of its receipt the American column, composed of detachments of Massachusetts infantry, New York artillery, a militia company, and a troop of horse under Captain Stakes, was swinging toward the heart of the city. Down the Bowery road they swept with the stride of seasoned veterans, their motley uniforms encrusted with mud and showing signs of rough campaigning; their tarnished arms and torn colors present-

ing a sharp contrast to the display of the evacuating host. There was every evidence of discipline and training, however, in the movements and carriage of these weather-beaten soldiers, and as they passed through Chatham Square to Pearl (Queen) Street great crowds of enthusiastic citizens welcomed them with cheers, and falling in on either side of the conquering column, accompanied its march.

Then came the great moment for which Wall Street had waited and suffered for over seven years, and up the devastated highway, thronged with a joyous multitude, swung the tattered but stalwart ranks to the businesslike tap of drums and the music of exultant cheers. Onward they swept past the headless statue of Pitt, past shabby dwellings which their exiled owners would scarcely have recognized, past the head of Broad Street where the whipping-post had stood, past the dilapidated City Hall where the Stamp Congress had assembled, up the slight incline down which many a royal governor had paraded and along which countless throngs jostle and hurry to-day, past the dismantled Presbyterian Church where Whitfield and Jonathan Edwards had preached, to the mournful ruins of Trinity. Then, wheeling to the right, these representatives of the victorious armies lined up in Broadway near Cape's Tavern,* bravely displaying the arms of New York State upon its sign, and on that historic spot where Etienne De Lancey had built his home they halted and stood at parade rest till a salute of thirteen guns announced that the American flag floated over Fort George, and that the Revolution was ended.

On the evening of that day of days Washington attended a banquet in Wall Street. Its golden age was dawning.

* About 115 Broadway.

EAST-SIDE CONSIDERATIONS

THE BOY WHO KNEW WHERE THERE WAS A TREE.

AN enlightened official of New York said, the other day, "The happiest people in town live on the East Side." He did not speak officially, and not without knowledge that a great many very wretched people also live there, but very likely what he said was the truth, though not, of course, the whole truth. The ordinary impression of people who don't live on the East Side and who don't go there is that it is a painful quarter of the city, where all the people are poor, and live huddled up together, and nearly die every summer, and have a pretty bad time all the year round. The East Side is associated with misery; is looked upon as a consequence of the imperfect apparatus now in use for distributing money. To sink layer by layer down the strata of society and finally to bring up in an East Side tenement is the conventional, well-to-do New-Yorker's conception of an awful fate. Persons who might live in a good part of town, and who, from pious motives or because they are tired of conventional society and manners, go over and take up with the East Side, and live in tenements there, are looked upon as people who have made an enormous sacrifice. No doubt it is true that the majority of East-Siders don't live on the East Side absolutely from choice, but because life there best suits their incomes and occupations. Most of the people who live east of Broadway and south of Houston Street are poor, and live where they do not so much from any special prejudice against the Fifth Avenue side of Central Park as to be near their work, or because in the tenement-house streets they get more for their money. They are not all poor, by any means. Some East-Siders stick to the East Side because they are used to it and belong to it—yes, and because a good deal of it belongs to them, as is the case of that East Side woman whom report which seems veracious credits with owning (last year) no less than sixty-four double tenement-houses, the rents of which are said to run up to sixty thousand dollars a year. Their owner manages her own property, collects her rents, bosses her tenants, and personally postpones repairs on her property; and it suits her convenience as well as her taste to be a resident landlady, and to live where she has her own under her eye, and can better appreciate the blessings of means.

There is misery on the East Side, of course, because there are a great many more people there than should be, and because there are sickness and extreme poverty there, as well as evil passions and sin, and all the painful things one finds wherever human beings are gathered in considerable groups. But there is unquestionably unhappiness also on Fifth Avenue. Among all the wretched people in New York it would be hard to match the apparent wretchedness of some persons whom one sees driving in closed carriages in Central Park in winter. They look as if they never had had any fun, or known any emotion of real happiness. They look stunted and comatose. No doubt many of them are sick people; but many of them, too, are overfed and overcoddled citizens who have missed the joy of living from too great solicitude to retain the comforts of life.

Whatever pangs a thorough knowledge of the East Side may involve, the superficial observer does not find it sad to look upon. It happened once in April to a visitor to New York to have to make a call at the University Settlement in Delancey Street. He started early in the evening from one of the respectable residence streets on Murray Hill, and being about to penetrate he knew not how desperate and lawless a quarter, he took along a stout stick as a means of self-protection against marauders. When he got there he found a quarter where clean streets paved with asphalt were brilliantly lighted and swarmed with people. It was one of the first mild evenings of spring, and a large part of Delan-

THE BEGINNING OF A MERCANTILE CAREER.

cey Street was sitting out of-
doors. Mothers were sitting
on door-steps gossiping with
one another and watching
children who ought doubtless
to have been abed. There were
life, action, and social activity
everywhere. Saloons and billiard-rooms seemed crowded
—indeed everything seemed
crowded—and to all appearances an immense amount of
entertainment was in process
of distribution among a great
number of people. When the
visitor got back to his respectable Murray Hill street it was
uncommonly like returning
from the land of the living
to the abode of the departed.
Murray Hill was ditch-water
after Delancey Street. Nobody in the side streets; nothing going on. Not so much
light; not so good a pavement; nowhere near so much
fun in sight.

He smiled when he put
his heavy cane in the corner,
and then he sighed at the
realization that there are
losses for all our gains, as
well as gains for all our losses,
and that people who have
their choice, and families who
have whole houses to themselves, and live in-doors even
on pleasant evenings, do not
enjoy all those advantages
without paying for them to
some extent in the loss of easy fellowship, and also of many pleasant social opportunities.

Mankind is not only the noblest study
of man, but the most entertaining. People are more interesting than things or
books, or even newspapers. The East
Side is especially convenient for the observation of people because there are such
shoals of them always in sight, and because their habits of life and manners
are frank, and favorable to a certain degree of intimacy at sight. Where each
family has a whole house to itself and
lives inside of it, and the members never
sally out except in full street dress—hats,
gloves, and manners—it is hopeless to become intimately acquainted with them as
you pass on the sidewalk. You may

AN ORIENTAL TYPE.

walk up and down Fifth Avenue for ten
years and never see a Fifth Avenue mother nursing her latest born on the door-
step, but in Mott or Mulberry or Cherry
Street that is a common sight, and always
interesting to the respectful observer.
When the little Fifth Avenue children are
let out, if they don't drive off in a carriage, at least they go with a nurse, and
are clothed like field daisies, and under
such restraint as good clothes and even
the kindest of nurses involve. But the
East Side children tumble about on the
sidewalk and pavement hour after hour,
under slight restraint and without any
severe amount of oversight, hatless usually, barehanded and barefooted when
the weather suffers it. It is the children
that constitute the East Side's greatest

charm, and no doubt it is especially due
to them that a veracious man who often
walks northward or eastward from Mulberry Bend late in the afternoon is able

A LITTLE FATHER.

to testify that he invariably reaches
Bleecker Street with modified and softened sentiments toward his fellows, and
increased tolerance for creation and its
perplexing incidents. It cannot be said
that the East Side children are clean.
Some of them are clean sometimes. It is
stamped upon an observer's memory that
on a Saturday early in April he passed a
little girl in Hester Street who had one of
the cleanest heads of sunshiny hair he
ever saw. Some East Side children are
cleaner than others, but as a rule they
are pretty dirty. The streets are clean for
streets, and the children are clean for
children who play in the streets.

To be very clean indeed is a luxury of
high price. People are apt to look upon
it as a mere virtue, but that is a modern
notion born of hot and cold running water and a bath-room on every floor. Saints
in old times usually went very dirty from
religious conviction. East-Siders don't do
that, but they put up with a moderate
amount of dirt because it is one of the unavoidable conditions of their existence.
Their children are usually dirty, but only

moderately dirty, as any normal child will
be after playing in the street or anywhere
out-of-doors. Dirt or no dirt, in good
weather the children of the East Side
are very interesting to watch.
Some of them look sick, and a
sick child is a pathetic sight
wherever seen, but except in
midsummer the great majority
of them seem to be in good
health and well nourished and
lively. They play together
very much as children do everywhere, and if they are more
amusing than a lot of Fifth Avenue children, it is doubtless
because they are under less supervision and are more natural. The most natural behavior we are used to see obtains
in a cage of monkeys. The
East Side children are nearly
as untrammelled as the monkeys, but they are a great deal
kinder to one another. Little
girls tending babies and carrying them from door-step to
door-step are a common sight.
The little mothers are famous,
but it seems to be in the nature
of little girls to love babies and
be good to them. What is more
remarkable, and yet not uncommon on the
East Side, is kind and responsible little
boys who look after still smaller children, and drag them around in ram-
shackle carts or amuse them and keep
them out of harm's way. Of course one
sees something of the other side of human
nature too. There are crying children,
and mothers whose patience is worn out,
and bullying older boys, but the East
Side would not soften the heart of the
sympathetic passer-by, and make him hap-
pier for passing through it, if the evidences of human kindness were not more
plenty than the signs of the other side of
human nature. It is what you see in
people's faces that affects your spirits, not
what they wear on their backs, or even on
their heads. Fine birds in fine feathers
are a gladdening sight. Really fine people with proper souls, whose faces show
really superior qualities, and whose
clothes and cleanliness and gentility are
becoming to them, adorn creation in their
way, and are folks that observers looking
on at life are thankful for. You do not
see people of that sort on the East Side;

but, on the other hand, you are not shocked there by the contrast between the individual and his circumstances. There are no "chappies" there; there is nothing to be seen there quite so astonishing and amusing and queer and pathetic as such chappies as one may sometimes see sipping green mint and smoking cigarettes in the purlieus of the Waldorf Hotel. The East Side is thoroughly disciplined. Faces there show rarely dejection, except what comes from illness, but endurance, patience, the practical education that comes of daily labor. In front of an uptown club is a cab loaded with travelling-bags. Inside are two young fellows just starting for some railroad station. A servant stands bareheaded at the cab door. One of the young men inside is dissatisfied with something. His arrogant face, as he makes complaint, is the face of a youth who has never earned his salt; who has been overfed, over-stimulated, overamused; who has always had all material luxuries within his reach, has accepted all as his due, is grateful for nothing, is appreciative of nothing, and whose conception of his obligations in life is pretty well fulfilled if he does what he considers his part in keeping club servants thoroughly well up to his notion of their duties. Faces of the type of his face are not prevalent on the East Side. Persons whose business in life is to be carried, and to kick at their carriers when they stumble, do not abound down there. There are coarse people there, but they wear cheap clothes and work hard. There is no such disconcerting contrast between their outside and what one reads in their faces as afflicts the observer in more opulent parts of the town. If their looks are often enough commonplace and sometimes disagreeable, their environment and their clothes modify instead of aggravating them. Beggars may be pic-

turesque, but beggars on horseback are grotesque.

It may be true that fleas have still smaller fleas to bite 'em, and even on the East Side there may be a tyranny of things and a constant effort to maintain a scale of living that is uncomfortably high. But certainly it is not noticeable. The scale of living on Mulberry and Mott and the other tenement-house streets seems simple and easy. One is not perplexed and oppressed as he walks through that quarter of the city with constant recurrence of the query, where do the people who live in all these houses get the money to maintain them? The imagination which is stumped by the problem of the maintenance of miles of dwellings at from ten to fifty thousand dollars a year apiece, easily copes with the problems of paying rent for a tenement-house apartment and buying bread and simple food

FEATHER-BED DAY.

for a working-man's family. It is easy to see how East-Siders manage. The eternal servant problem never troubles them. Their social duties seem not to be exacting. Lo! on the fire-escapes and balconies, on Mondays or any of the various wash-days that race or creed or custom prescribes, their garments flap in the wind, and, on some streets, lend human interest to continuous frontages as far as the eye reaches. Food is convenient at every turn. Mott Street market-men sell Chinese roast pig already roasted, and Heaven knows what curious Oriental dainties that look as though they had crossed the sea. Mulberry Street abounds in sidewalk venders of bread which seems to have no remarkable quality (except, maybe, its cheapness), and strange white Italian cheeses, made evidently in America for the Italian market, encased in skins and shaped like tenpins. The great Jewish quarter has its butcher shops with Hebrew signs, and, in the spring, its provision of unleavened bread for the Passover. Hebrew housekeeping has other peculiarities. The street-cleaning men will tell you that after Easter it rains straw from mattresses in that part of the town, and that beds by the thousand change their stuffing.

A remarkable neighborhood is that Jewish quarter lying south of Houston Street and between the elevated railroads and the East River. On week-days parts of it swarm with push-carts. On Saturdays there are none to be seen, but thousands of orderly people in their Sabbath-day clothes meet in the streets and in the synagogues. There are synagogues of all grades and sizes, from the little room over a shop to the erstwhile church which has lost its Christian congregation and been sold to new worshippers, who have adorned it with just enough Hebrew architecture to make its change of owners and uses apparent. Religion receives profound attention in the Jewish quarter, and its interests and consolations seem to be thoroughly appreciated. One sees remarkable faces in the synagogues—rabbis with robes and stove-pipe hats manipulating ancient scrolls, and rows of men with hats on finding apparent satisfaction in ceremonies that seem curiously antiquated and perfunctory. The Jews of that quarter are usually not of the hook-nosed type familiar and accepted, but the marks of their race appear rather in the formation of the jaw and mouth and in the general facial aspect. No doubt they are largely recruited from Russia and southeastern Europe. Occasionally one sees the old familiar type—venerable, most respectable in dress and aspect,

clean, neat, bearded, and curved as to the nose. This seems like an old friend or a character out of a story-book.

And then there are the Jewish women, with lines of profound patience in their faces, and invariably false fronts of brown hair smoothed above their foreheads. They go to the synagogues too, but sit by themselves, screened off out of sight from their husbands and masters. The brown wigs abound everywhere, and are doubtless a religious requirement which the air of America has not yet availed to modify.

Life on the lower East Side is even more transitory than most life in New York. Most of the population there is of comparatively recent acquisition. Habits of life are more often brought there than formed there. It is not like the East End of London, where the people who live there now were born and have always lived. Signs abound of customs born elsewhere. The May-day parties of the East Side children are reminiscent of village life. If you see a troop of children in May, far downtown, following some leader and marching off with a definite purpose, the chances are it is a May party. A lover of the East Side, who had followed one of the parties a block or two, audaciously accosted the leader, a bright-eyed Jewish youngster, who evidently knew perfectly what he was about.

"Where are you bound for, Johnny? You can't get up to Central Park, can you?"

"Park! No; but I guess I know where there's a tree."

He did. He led his young troop through street after street, and by devious turns and twists, to the tree, a poor stunted wreck of a tree, slanting out of the sidewalk with that list away from the house fronts which city trees are wont to have. It was not much of a tree, but it answered the purposes of a May party, and what it lacked was made up by childish imaginations.

There are evidences all through the East Side of thought taken and money spent for the welfare of the dwellers there. No part of the town needs clean streets and smooth pavements so much, and no part of the town shares more fully in those blessings. Wagon traffic does not abound excessively in the streets

THE SABBATH—A SYNAGOGUE THAT WAS ONCE A CHURCH.

where the population is most dense. Most of these streets have been asphalted; all of them will be in time; and children play over their whole width. When a horse passes through, the driver picks er, big enough to hold 2500 visitors—a ministration to need by authority which it does the heart good to witness.

There are conscientious democrats who find comfort in maintaining, in the face

THE SACRED SCROLL IN THE SYNAGOGUE.

his way. The two new parks at Mulberry Bend and Corlears Hook are admirable breathing-places. In both of them the walks are lined with seats from end to end, so as to afford resting-places for the greatest possible number. Corlears Hook Park, at the bend in the East River and opposite the Brooklyn Navy-Yard, has a most interesting water-front and view. All the water traffic between the Bay and the Sound passes there. The Grand Street Ferry is close by, and all day long the river provides its entertainment for the park population. Newer still and near by is the Dock Commissioners' Recreation Pier at the foot of Third Street, with its great upper story, covered play-ground, reaching far out into the riv- of indications to the contrary, that there are no classes in this country. The contention is praiseworthy, and persistence in it is praiseworthy too, for it helps, like Jefferson's declaration of the equality of men, to keep alive an idea that needs to be sustained. But even if there are not classes in the republic, disparity of estate and training have begotten varieties, and the tendency of each variety to herd with its own sort is always in sight. It is a tendency that is based on convenience; but it has its drawbacks. It narrows our experience and impoverishes our view of life. People who live and work in big cities fall into the way of following a little daily round, which takes men down town at a certain hour and by a certain route, and back at another hour, and which confines most women to rounds of the shopping and residence streets, where they see the same sights and the same sort of people every day, month after month and year after year. It is so much easier to follow a rut than to make a track for one's self that of course most people follow ruts. But for those who appreciate the wholesomeness of variety and the value of new sensations and suggestions, the East Side is an amazingly rich field. Not only is the contemplation of the poor a relief after the contemplation of the rich, but to get our minds off

world we live in. It is only a matter of three miles or so from Madison Square to Hester Street, but who would dream, who had not seen it, that the same town held within so short a distance scenes and people so contrasted as the shops and shoppers of Twenty-third Street and the hucksters of Hester and Ludlow? Not to have seen those hucksters, and their carts, and their merchandise, and their extraordinary zest for bargaining, is to have missed a sight that once seen declines to be forgotten. If there is the like of it anywhere in Europe, there is a better chance that the uptown New-Yorkers will see it

THE ENVIRONMENT OF SCHOLARSHIP.

ourselves and our ways, and those of our immediate neighbors, gives us a wholesome jolt, and helps to adjust them to a realization of the characteristics of the

there than in their own town. The locksmiths and jobbing tinkers and plumbers, with their keys and their tools strung on a wire hoop that rests on one shoulder;

the itinerant skirt-peddlers, with their stock in trade strung along on a pole, parading along the street and searching the faces of women for the signs that bespeak the possibility of a sale—how queer they are, and how inspiring to the observer who sees them for the first time!

son can see them often enough to keep them in mind without taking thought about the social and municipal problems that they suggest. What needs to be done for the East Side? What can be done? What is being done? The observer ponders all these questions, and if

A TINKERS' EXCHANGE, HESTER STREET.

There is much more than mere entertainment to be got out of sights like these. Familiarity with them breeds neither contempt nor indifference, but rather increased interest. No thoughtful person can see them often enough to keep

he goes far enough into them they lead him into acquaintance with a net-work of enterprises in which public officers and private charity work together. Everywhere he goes the signs of this co-operation appear. The public schools, big, substantial, and often handsome, still insufficient but all the time increasing; the churches, parish-houses, libraries, kindergartens, vacation schools, dispensaries, college settlements, hospitals, fresh-air funds, and scores of other enterprises and establishments attest the persistence of the East Side in the public memory. Thousands of well-to-do New-Yorkers rarely give it a thought; but there are hundreds, not themselves members of its family, who brood over it and plan and act in its behalf. Not that it cannot help itself. The East Side, stretching from Franklin Square to the Harlem River, harbors the greater part of the manual workers of New York, and the bulk of its great population is thrifty, industrious, self - respectful, and self-sustaining. But because Manhattan Island is narrow it is crowded, and because Europe is constantly pouring needy emigrants into it who cannot speak our language, and are used to a very low scale of living, it needs an exceptional amount of help from outside. There are great areas of it, indeed, which are more justly to be

A SKIRT-VENDER.

regarded as training-schools for American citizens than as mere residence quarters for working-people. It is the crop that the East Side raises that makes it important—the great crop of American voters, from the reaping of which there is no evasion or escape.

NEW YORK COLONIAL PRIVATEERS

OF all the lines along which the sea-wealth of New York was won in colonial times I am disposed to give the first place to privateering. Piracy—being hampered by no fine-drawn distinctions as to flags, and by no over-nice requirements of prize courts—was better while it lasted; but it lasted (openly, at least) for less than a decade. Slave-trading also was profitable, and was the basis of many respectable New York fortunes; but the profits were by no means certain, and as a business—aside from the bad smells of it—'twas too dull to hit the fancy of our hot-headed young sparks. As for ordinary commerce, a round dozen of long voyages might yield a less return than a single dash of six weeks to the s'uth'ard among the fleets of the Mossoos and Dons. And so, as an all-around industry—with plenty of fighting in it, and plenty of cash flowing out of it—privateering ranked first of all.

Concerning the very beginning of our privateering, the sea-ventures out of this port in the last third of the seventeenth century, it is well to be discreetly reticent. As we all know, things went but loosely in those easy days, and mistakes were quite as likely to occur at sea as they were on land. That some of our fighting sea-dogs of that time—yielding to a professional zeal in itself not discreditable—did now and then inconsiderately capture ships sailing under a friendly flag, or even under the English flag, is not impossible. But, when all is said, 'twas a small matter: only a few stray Dutch or English merchantmen, or, of still less importance, a heathenish Arabian trader or two, snapped up half by accident in the far-off Indian Ocean or in the southern reaches of the Red Sea. Obviously it would be unfair to rouse out from the kindly obscurity of long-past years such trifling indiscretions; and as for the lawful captures of that period, they were but odds and ends of sugar-laden Spaniards and little chance Frenchmen laden with cod. Therefore, either as pirates or as privateers, the achievements of the projectors of New York privateering are not to be mentioned in the same morning with the doings of the dashing fellows who presently came upon the stage.

Yet before wholly dismissing these seventeenth-century founders of the sea-wealth of New York, these pioneers in a business which during the eighteenth century so greatly enriched our city, it is but just to credit them—and, still more, the genuine pirates who immediately succeeded them, in Governor Fletcher's time—with having prepared the ground for the harvest which was garnered later on. In other words (and without the nautical application of an agricultural simile), there was assembled here in New York, between the year 1685 and the year 1700, such a swarm of fighting sailor-men, and such strong stimulus was given to the marine industries of ship-building, rope-making, and the putting up of sea-stores, that when the opportunity came for privateering on a large scale there was not a city in America, and only a few cities in Europe, which could compare in completeness of equipment as a privateering base with New York. As to situation—ready accessibility to both West-Indian and Canadian waters—there was nothing to be desired. In a word, the conditions under which privateering could be carried on out of this port were nothing less than ideal.

II.

The war of the Spanish Succession, beginning in the year 1702, was the match that touched off the New York privateering mine. Under the circumstances, the explosion was unavoidable. It was said of the Duke of Parma, in regard to that same conflict, that "his geography made it impossible for him to be a man of honour"; and New York had an endowment of geography that made neutrality quite out of the question.

But nobody hereabouts wanted to be neutral. After the dull and unprofitable quiet of Lord Bellomont's too-moral rule—when an honest sailor-man could not take a quiet turn off soundings without having the Governor hot upon him with a whole string of impertinent questions on the very moment of his return—the joy of going cruising with the openly avowed intention of hunting prizes was exceedingly keen. Therefore it was with all the good-will in the world that our people made the most of their lucky geography by getting quickly away to sea; and presently a fleet of more than twenty sail had cleared the Hook and had stood away to the s'uth'ard with the first favoring slant of wind—for there was little worth fighting for afloat in the St. Lawrence region, while the French and Spanish craft to be had for the taking in West-Indian waters were of a sort, usually, to set a man's mouth to watering merely to think about as made prize.

It all is so long ago, almost two centuries, since these our fellow-townsmen went sailing out through the Narrows to fight for the good of their pockets and their King that of most of them survives in the way of tradition no more than their names. Yet of two or three have we with the record of their names a record also of some portion of their deeds—so that, despite the haze of years overhanging them, we almost may see their dare-devil figures, clad in antique sea-gear, and greatly beswordled and bepistolled, swaggering before us, and almost may hear their rumbling bass voices as they talk (in the frank fashion of sailor-men of all periods) about their long-past victories, and here and there clinch fast some especially strong assertion with the large and comforting oaths which seafarers of their time and kidney were wont to use.

Quite the most distinct of these half-real, half-imaginary figures which rise up from the depths of our sea-fighting past is Captain Regnier Tongrelow, of the

New York Galley—who probably was a great scamp in his day and generation, with all the making of a pirate inside his privateering veneer, but whose fighting qualities truly were of a sort to warm one's heart. His name is spelled all around the compass in the news-letters of the day—Tongrelow, Tongerlou, Tongerlow—and probably should have been spelled, though I have not found it in this form, Tangrelot. But there is no variety in the record of his fighting, his method having been invariably to fight everything—preferably beginning with the biggest, when there was any choice in the matter—that he could get within range of his guns.

The first record that I have come across of my gentleman's doings is in a news-letter of September 11, 1704, which tells: "Last week came in a Sloop from Sandy-hook, and by her not coming up we were jealous of her being a French Privateer, and, by direction of the Council, Capt. Rogers Commander of the *Jersey* put 100 able men on board a Briganteen which was bound for Suranum, with hay on her quarter for a decoy; but she coming near the Sloop most of the men run ashore. The Sloop is a Prize of Capt. Tongerlows, she has nothing on board but about 600 of Cocoa, 40 barrels of Flower, and a few Hides": from all of which it would appear that Captain Tongrelow must have taken advantage betimes of the war to go a-privateering; and that he and his men —the conduct of his prize-crew bearing a suspiciously close resemblance to the flight of professional thieves on sight of the police—very possibly were engaged in a less reputable line of sea-adventure before the war began. It is interesting to note, by-the-way, that H. M. S. *Jersey*, then on this station, was the identical vessel which was to achieve a most dismal notoriety fourscore years later as the British prison-ship for American patriots in Wallabout Bay.

Five months later, under date of February 17, 1704-5, the news-letter records that "Capt. Tongrelou is in Virginia, his Sloop was cast away about ten leagues to the Southward of the Capes of Virginia; the Master and two or three more of her Men drowned. We hear he saved the Money, and about 6 or 700*l.* in Goods, and that he designs hither." By this calamity my Captain seems to have been for a while cast on his beam-ends; yet

eventually, as became a man of courage, to have turned misfortune to his advantage by making his loss of a little ship a valid reason why he should get a big one. Under date of September 24th, following, the fact is stated that "Capt. Renier Tongrelow and others have bought the Cole and Been Galley, a Ship of 200 tons, and 18 Guns, and is now fitting of her for a Privateer and intends to carry 160 Men. Capt. Penniston is also about to fit his Ship, and designs out with her in Consort, they will sail before Winter."

I am at a loss to make sense of the name of Captain Tongrelow's purchase. Possibly he felt that way about it too. At any rate, he promptly changed it to the *New York Galley*—which latter name, in due time, he made most offensively notorious down in the southern seas. And Captain Tom Penniston, to do him justice, did some very pretty fighting down in that region too.

It was on December 24, 1705, that the two Captains got away in company; but more than half a year passed before anything of importance came of their cruising. Captain Tom, to be sure, sent in a few little prizes; but preserved a low balance in his fortunes by being "over set at Bermuda, whereby he lost 5 Guns and damnified his Powder." Captain Tongrelow sent in nothing at all. But at last, in a news-letter of June 17th, came better news of them: "On the 16th Inst. a small Prize Ship about 60 or 70 Tons loaden with Sugar arrived here in 15 Days from the Windward Passage near Cape Franswa, she was taken by Capt. Penistone, and was one of Six Sail, that come out of Petitguavus, bound for France, who were met by Captain Tongerlow and his Consort (a Curacoa Privateer) upon which the French men seperated, and Tongerlow gave chase to the biggest, which they say is a Ship of 36 Guns and 150 Men, his Consort in the pursuit broke his Boom, and left off the Chase, and afterwards met with Penistone (who had taken this Prize) and gave him this information." The report adds: "'Tis said Tongerlow has taken a Briganteen with 400 Hogsheads of Sugar on board, and also a Prize from France with Claret": good news which was proved to be true a fortnight later by the arrival of the brigantine, with a good lading of sugar and indigo, and with the captured claret also on board. The brief

" BARBAROUSLY MURDERED THE FIRST AND GRIEVOUSLY WOUNDED THE LATTER."

history given of this vessel—"taken by Capt. Tongerlow bound from Hispaniola to France, built at Brazil, and taken from the Portugese by the French on the Coast of Guinea"—is not a bad syllabus of the uncertainties of seafaring in those happy-go-lucky days.

From this time onward the luck was all in favor of Captain Tongrelow, and his prizes were many and fat. But what I most like about him is not his mere talent for prize-taking, but his zest—as in the case cited, where he "gave chase to the biggest"—for fighting against any odds. In September, 1706, being "off Cape Franswa, in company with two Jamaica Privateers and one of Curacoa, they espyed 5 Sail and gave Chase;" and again my Captain "took the biggest." In April, 1707, "arrived here a Sloop from Curacoa by whom we have advice that Captain Tongrelow, a Privateer from hence, met a French Ship of 30 or 36 Guns and 160 Men near Hispaniola, which they fought 4 hours till he had 2 men killed and 17 wounded, and finding her too strong for him he left her"—a move for prudence' sake that would have been made after much less than four hours of fighting by a captain cool enough to remember that his own armament was only twenty guns. And in July of this same year, from the French prisoners aboard the *Generous Ginney*, a recapture sent in by H.M.S. *Triton's Prize*, the writer of the news-letter got the delightful bit "that Captain Tongrelow Cruises off the Havana; and that the Governor thereof sent out 2 Privateer Sloops to take him; but that Tongrelow had taken them both."

This exploit seems to have been the climax of the Captain's performances in West-Indian waters—and the cause of his abruptly leaving them: for the Spanish Governor (who must have been in a fine temper over such an exemplary display of impudence) started instantly in pursuit of him a little fleet that even this fire-eater had not the effrontery to assail. Indeed, for once in his life, he ran away. "On the 30th last," says a news-letter of August 4, 1707, "arrived here Capt. Tongrelow, who was chased from the Havanna by a Ship, a Brigt. and a Sloop, who were fitted out from thence to take him; his Sloop was missing several Days from the place of Rendezvouz, and 'tis feared she's taken."

Being thus come safe home again, and with well-lined pockets, it would seem that my Captain sailed no more. No farther record of him appears in the news-letters, and when the *New York Galley* is mentioned—well maintaining her traditions—a hard-hitting Captain Hardy is in command. But that Tongrelow, like his ship, continued his career in a masterful fashion I am confident. 'Tis my fancy that, having won for himself a fortune, he went on in the same resistless way and won for himself a wife: "taking the biggest," as usual, by cutting out valiantly from under the guns of a dozen rivals some stout buxom widow suited to his estate and to his medium years—one of those plumply mellow quadrigenarious bodies who especially appeal to the vigorous and well-salted emotion which with sailor-men stands for love—and thereafter permitted the soft delights of Venus to fill in his manly breast the place so long given to the stern delights of Mars. It is a pleasure to think of him thus snugly harbored after all his dare-deviltries afloat—whereof he must have vapored finely when in his cups; and even of more prodigious fighting wonders as his youth loomed larger through the haze of his declining years.

III.

I have been able thus to dilate upon Captain Tongrelow because there has survived in the ancient records a more intimate suggestion of his personality than is given of any other captain of his times. But his fellows, so far as the Past surrenders them to us, seem to have been of precisely the same stripe: rash-tempered scamps, with a bellicose strut in their gait, and a stand-and-deliver air that was emphasized by their trick of constantly fingering their pistols and hangers, and by their extreme readiness in using those handy weapons to let the life out of a Frenchman or a Don.

Captain Tom Penniston, for instance, shared so fully in his consort's fancy for "taking the biggest" that, seemingly, 'twas the death of him. He is but a hazy figure—touched upon now and again in a news-letter when one of his captures is reported—until at the very last he stands for a single thrilling moment illumined in the blaze of his own glory, and then instantly and forever disappears. His apotheosis is thus presented in a news-letter of August 5, 1706: "On the 30th of July arrived Captain Basset in a month from Jamaica, who says Capt. Pennistone (a Privateer of this Port) boarded two Ships together, one of 18 and the other of 24 Guns, but was beat off with the loss of his Arm, and 9 Men kill'd, and as many wounded, and obliged to bear away to Jamaica "—into which curt statement is crowded the history of as brilliant a little sea-fight as ever was fought to a losing end.

That it was Captain Penniston's last fight seems pretty certain. In the news-letters I find no later mention of him; and this is a negation very ominous in the case of a gentleman whom we leave with his arm just shot away, with his ship in a tropical sea in blazing June weather, who at the best would have but a rough-and-ready surgeon to attend to his wound, and whose disposition under these trying circumstances to die quickly and violently of a raging fever would be largely augmented by what we reasonably may assume to have been his habits in regard to the use of strong drink. Therefore it is but too likely that Captain Tom (sewed up in a hammock, with three six-pound shot at his heels) followed his arm overboard within forty-eight hours. But we need not greatly grieve for him. No doubt this hasty yet gallant exit from life on salt water was far more to his fancy than would have been a slow stewing to death through age or infirmity on land.

Captain Gincks, of the brigantine *Dragon*—who, being off Porto Rico, "fell in with and Engaged both together two French Privateers, the *Trampoose* and another Sloop, and had taken them had they not run, and having received damage in his Rigging and Sails could not follow them "; and Captain Zacharias—who cut out a sugar-laden barque lying in Cartagena Roads in plain sight of the French fleet commanded by M. Deberville—were both of them tolerably well equipped with effrontery; but for downright insolent daring a bit of work done by Captain Nat Burches fairly takes the lead.

Burches commanded Tongrelow's tender, a little sloop of 6 guns and 27 men, which in the charge of a reasonably prudent person would have done her fighting with cockboats of somewhere near her own size. But Burches—bless his

honest heart!—had not a scrap of prudence in his whole composition: being one of those cutting and slashing captains whose whole scheme of happiness was summed in his burning longing to get at the enemy, and be d——d to him and the number of his guns! That he lived up to his convictions is testified to by the following short narrative, from a news-letter of August 5, 1706:

"On the 30th of July arrived here a Privateer Sloop of 6 Guns and 27 Men, Nath. Burches, Commander, being the Tender of Capt. Tongrelou, which a few weeks ago met with a Spanish Ship (bound from Canaries to New Spain) of 600 Tuns 24 Guns and 250 Men, near to Cuba, this Sloop fired 6 Shot at her, two whereof hull'd her, one blew up the Round House, kill'd the Captain and 5 Men, and another disabled her Main Mast which afterwards fell over board, the Sloop finding the Ship too strong for her left her, and carried notice of her to Capt. Tongrelou, who immediately thereupon went in search of her, but could not find her; the Sloop soon after she parted with Capt. Tongrelou found the Spanish Ship a Shoar about a league from Barricoe upon Cuba, the Spanyards defended her from the Shoar, and at last capitulated with the Sloop for her lading of Wines and Brandy, provided they would not burn the rest, nor the Ship; and accordingly she has brought hither 50 pipes of Canary and Brandy which they took out of her, but have not seen Tongrelou for seven nor his Consort for nine weeks past." And then, as a sort of after-thought, the writer adds: "The Spanish Ship was obliged to run a Shoar, having 8 foot water in her Hold before they knew of it, and upon her striking Ground her Main Mast tumbled over board being wounded by a shot from the Sloop, but the Sloop knew not what execution they had done till they found her a Shoar."

That Captain Burches seems to have ended by falling into the hands of the enemy—as would appear from the reference to his failure to come to the "rendezvous" already cited—is not surprising: for I do verily believe that he was quite capable of laying his absurd sloop abreast of a King's ship, and of blazing away at her with his deadly little pop-gun broadside, and of winding up by boarding her at the head of his twenty-seven men!

IV.

Considering what a terror they were afloat to their enemies, it is no great wonder that these privateersmen of ours should have been also a bit of a terror to their friends ashore. New York seems to have gloried in their deeds and to have stood in awe of their persons—as well it might, in view of their broadly impartial tendency to get drunk on anybody's premises, and thereafter to fight everybody who came along.

Probably the worst of these riots (certainly I have found no record of another equalling it) occurred in September, 1705; and the news-letter of September 24th in which it is chronicled begins with the statement that "on the 18th Instant arrived here a small Prize Sloop taken by Capt. Penniston, loaden with Wine and Brandy." The writer of the letter, who does not seem to perceive any connection between the arrival of this sloop-load of potential drunkenness and the disturbance which within twenty-four hours followed it, continues in these terms:

"On the 19th Instant, about 10 at night, some of the Privateers began a Riot before the Sheriff's House of this City, assaulted the Sheriff at his door without any provocation, and beat and wounded several persons that came to his assistance, and in a few minutes the Privateers tumultuously met together in great numbers, upon which Forces were sent out of the Fort to suppress them, and the Sheriff, Officers, and some men belonging to Her Majesties Ships made a Body to do the same, but before these Forces could meet with them, the Privateers unhappily met Lieut. Wharton Featherstone Hough, and Ensign Alcock (two Gentlemen of the Hon. Col. Livesay's Regiment that came in the Jamaica Fleet, who were peaceably going home to their Lodgings) and barbarously murdered the first and grievously wounded the latter, in several places in the head, and bruised his Body; and after they had knocked him down several times, and got his Sword, some of them run Lieut. Featherstone Hough in at the left side through his heart (as is supposed with Ensign Alcock's Sword) of which he immediately dyed. Just as the Fact was done, the Privateers were attacked by the Sheriff, Officers, and Seamen of Her Majesties Ships, and some of the Town, and in a short time were obliged to fly; several of both sides were wounded;

some of the Privateers were then taken Prisoners, and several since, who are committed, and do believe will suffer according to Law; the Soldiers killed one of the Privateers that was flying from them." The writer concludes with the indignant comment upon privateersmen in general: "It would be tedious to relate the particulars, but their insolence is beyond expression."

In the end, what was believed to be justice was served out to the murderer; that is to say, he was hanged. In a newsletter of October 29th is the statement: "On the 26th Instant, Erasmus Wilkins the Privateer was Executed for the Murder of Lieut. Featherstone Hough. He confess'd that he took a Sword from a Gentleman, and run it into another, which he believed was the Gentleman that was kill'd, and that he afterwards broke the Sword;" and the edifying information is added that he "cautioned his comrades against Drunkenness, Swearing, Wantonness, Sabbath-breaking &c and dyed very penitent and like a man."

V.

It is hard to dismiss these delightful fellows with the summary statement that they continued on the lines indicated to fight with great gusto at sea, where they killed, and on land, where they murdered, until the war came to an end. Yet in this fashion, or in some other equally curt, I must dismiss them if I am to get down through the years to their successors; who, as it seems to me, less valorously, and certainly less dashingly, took up the privateering parable when the profitless peace at last ended and honest men had a chance again legitimately to cut each other's throats and to pick each other's pockets on the high seas.

There was, to be sure, a weary time of waiting before this happy opportunity came: all the long while between the Peace of Utrecht, signed in 1713, and the war with Spain, which began in a halfhearted fashion in 1739, and was merged into the war of the Austrian Succession in 1740, but really was not worth talking about—from a privateersman's stand point—until France threw over her queer notion of fighting as a limited liability company and regularly went into the ring with England in the year 1744. This uselessly peaceful period of near a third of a century must have embittered the declining years of many a worthy privateers-man; and in the end have landed him in a most unsatisfactorily peaceful grave.

Very little attention seems to have been paid here to Governor Clarke's proclamation, of June 17, 1739, granting "letters of marqz" and "commissions of reprizal" against the Spaniards; for the reason, possibly, that such an amount of marine red tape in the case of mere Spaniards seemed superciliously absurd; but Governor Clinton's proclamation of the war against the French was the spark to a train which set off this whole town into a joyful explosion of profitable war. "I have had the honour," wrote the Governor, under date of October 9, 1744, to the Lords of Trade, "of his Grace the Duke of New-castle's letter of 31 March, with His Majesty's Declaration of War against the French King, as also His Declaration for the encouragement of His Majesty's ships of War and Privateers, together with a copy of the French King's Declaration, which overtook me at Soapus on my way to Albany, where I proclaimed His Majesty's Declaration at the Head of a Militia Regiment I was then reviewing:" a juxtaposition of defiant belligerent circumstances so apposite, and to the enemy so terrifying—for well might the King of France tremble for his Canadian possessions when the militia regiment of Esopus was up and armed!—that I am half tempted to suspect this salt-water Governor of a tendency to romance.

But of the effect of the news upon our New-Yorkers there can be no doubt. In the same letter in which he tells about his Hannibal-like proclamation of the war at the head of the Esopus legion, the Governor adds: "The merchants of this city have been extreamly alert in fitting out Privateers, at a very great expense, and have brought in several prizes:" a moderate assertion that is more than made good by the public prints of the day. The news that war had been declared could not well have been received in this country before the first week in May, yet in the Post-Boy of June 4th is the statement: "By a Sloop arrived here last Saturday Night in 8 days from Cape Fear, we hear that the two New York Privateers, with their Prize lately taken, were to sail in 4 or 5 days for this Place;" and in the issue of the week following is chronicled the arrival of "our two Privateers, the Brig Hester, Capt. Bayard, and

Sloop Polly, Capt. Jefferies, with their Prize so much talk'd of, from Cape Fare: she is a beautiful Ship, almost new, of near 200 Tons, and loaden chiefly with Cocoa; but we don't hear that the Pieces of Eight have been found, as was reported."

In keeping with this "extreamly alert" beginning, the Post-Boy thereafter bristles with announcements of the fitting of brigs and sloops "for a cruizing Voyage against His Majesty's Enemies," and with calls to "Gentlemen Sailors, and others" to join their crews; while the eager temper of our citizens thus at once to line their pockets and to serve their King is shown, presently, in the jubilant declaration that "'tis impossible to express with what Alacrity the Voluntiers enter on board." In the first year of the war thirteen privateers were afloat out of this port; a number that was increased to twenty-nine before the war came to an end. With the exception of the Prince Charles—a ship of 380 tons, mounting "24 Carriage Guns, most of them Nine-Pounders, and 34 Swivels," and carrying a crew of 200 men—our fighting-boats were little sloops and brigs and brigantines and snows of from 125 to 200 tons; with batteries of from twelve to sixteen little six-pounders and about as many swivels (that is, small pieces pivoted on the rail: in the fashion seen of late in the reanimate Santa Maria, caravel); and manned with crews rarely exceeding 100 men.

Vessel for vessel, and as a whole, this fleet was superior in strength to the fleet that had sailed hence thirty years earlier; but it seems to me that there was lighter metal in the crews. Certainly there were no such rakish heroes again afloat as Penniston and Tongrelow. Thus "the Snow Dragon, Captain Seymour, and the Brig Greyhound, Captain Jefferies, and with them the Grand Diable Sloop, a Spanish Privateer which they had taken and made a consort of ... as they were cruizing in the Bay of Mexico ... fell in with a large Spanish Ship of 36 Guns, and upwards of 300 Men, with whom they all engaged for the greatest part of two Days." But instead of taking her—it was just such another ship that Captain Burches captured with his sloop of six guns and 27 men—our people were very handsomely beaten off.

Yet while it would seem—in this and

in some other cases—that the privateers-men of this later war were not animated by the same temerarious spirit which so constantly flashed forth in the doings of their predecessors, 'twould be an injustice to give the impression that they had no spirit at all. Every now and then in the *Post-Boy* of that war-time, testifying to the blazing up again of the old fire, is a bit like the following: "On Thursday last came in here a large French Prize Ship call'd the *St. Joseph*, taken on the 29th of August last by the Privateer Brig *William*, Capt. Arnold, of this Place, after two smart Engagements, the first in the Evening before, of about an Hour, where-in the Privateer had one of her Swivel Guns burst, which Kill'd 'em 3 Men and wounded 4; and the other in the Morning of about 5 Hours, wherein they had one man Kill'd and 5 wounded; the Prize is about 350 Tons, mounts 12 Guns four-pounders, and had 57 stout Men on board; their Second Lieutenant was Kill'd, and 5 Men wounded, some of which mortal-ly."

But if lacking a little in true battle-spirit, the privateersmen of this period were nearly normal in their taste for cruel pleasantry and in their readiness to fight with a vicious ferocity ashore. When the crews of the *Castor* and *Pol-lux* "found that a Person who had en-tered on board them two or three Days before was a woman "—'twas a case of true love, no doubt, fit to make a ballad of — "they seiz'd upon the unhappy Wretch and duck'd her Three Times from the Yard-Arm, and afterwards made their negroes tarr her all over from Head to Foot, by which cruel Treatment, and the Rope that let her into the Water having been indiscreetly fastened, the poor Woman was very much hurt and continues now ill." And in the course of a fight aboard the *Hester* — a fight which seems to have begun amicably enough in mere fisticuffs—"a poor Sail-or had a large Piece of his Ear bit off in a very unfair and barbarous manner." And so it would seem that the spots upon my privateersmen remained practically unchanged: save that with their less im-petuous doings at sea seems to have come a disposition to rage less furiously upon land — little turbulencies like these just cited taking the place of heroic mutinies against the public peace under and in collision with the Sheriff's very nose.

VI.

Without being able to account for it, I can only state the fact that in the short interval between the signing of the Peace of Aix-la-Chapelle, in 1748, and the fresh outbreak of hostilities, in 1756, the sea-going population of this city experienced so marked a change of heart that 'tis a warm pleasure to any one fond of stories of good fighting afloat to read the record in the *Mercury* of the part taken by our privateersmen in the Seven Years' War.

As everybody knew, the Peace signed at Aix was but a truce; a mere provision of breathing-space while the combatants retired to their respective corners to rest a little and to be sponged off. Here in New York it was regarded, no doubt, as a sheer waste of time; a painful period of en-forced abstention from an exhilarating business in which prodigious profits were to be gained. Especially severe was the strain upon New York patience during the last few months of waiting for the war that very obviously was close at hand. In its issue of July 19th the *Mer-cury* gives a list of vessels fitting for pri-vateers or "nominated for a like pur-pose, . . . all of which we expect," it adds blithely, "will be ready to push off in a very few Days after War is declared." In-deed, all the city seems to have been straining at its collar — like a rampant bull-dog eager to get teeth into a sighted foe—in its passionate longing for the word to come from England that killing and robbing Frenchmen afloat had become a patriotic duty and had ceased to be a hang-ing crime.

When this happy news did come—in His Majesty's Proclamation dated at Ken-sington May 17th, and published here in the *Mercury* of July 26th following — crews were completed with a rush, am-munition was hustled in, stores and water were scampered aboard; and with the whir and scurry of a covey of partridges the waiting ships shot away to sea. In the *Mercury* of August 9th four privateers are reported as "fell down to the water-ing-place," four more as almost ready to sail, and "two fitting out with all Expedi-tion"; in the issue of the 30th the sailing of the brig *Johnson* is reported, with the note that "this is the eighth Privateer sent out since War was declared"; in the issue of September 6th five more vessels are reported as cleared; and in the issue of October 4th a list is given of the New

York privateer fleet, which includes 20 craft of all classes — ships, snows, brigs, and sloops—carrying 246 guns and 1900 men.

Nor did this ardor cool quickly. Half a year later, under date of March 17, 1758, Lieutenant-Governor De Lancey, writing to Secretary Pitt, declares that "the Country is drain'd of many able-bodied Men by almost a Madness to go a Privateering"; and his statement is made good by the publication in the *Mercury* of June 27, 1757, of an additional list of 23 vessels, carrying more than 300 guns and upwards of 2500 men. And, finally, according to the list compiled for Mr. Shannon, 130 privateers were commissioned here between the opening and the close of the war.

As the result of the foraging of this fleet seaward a merry lot of money came into New York across the harbor bar. Mr. Shannon quotes from a letter written hence, in June, 1757, to a London merchant: "There are now 30 Privateers out of the Place, and ten more on the Stocks and launched. They have had hitherto good Success, having brought in fourteen Prizes, Value 100,000*l*." This figuring up of the winnings is to be taken, no doubt, with several grains of salt. But if only the half of it were true there still remains £50,000, nearly equal in purchasing power to a half-million of our present-day dollars: a truly prodigious amount of wealth to be created practically from nothing within half a year in a town of only 11,000 souls. A twelvemonth later, January 9, 1758, the *Mercury* gives a list of all the captures made by the New York fleet from the beginning of the war until that date. The total is upwards of 80 vessels, which—at the rate of valuation just suggested—would represent more than five millions of dollars of the present day. Under these conditions it is not surprising that there was hereabouts "almost a madness to go a Privateering." Looking at the matter from the stand-point of that period it would have been not almost, but quite, a madness to have staid at home.

VII.

But this wholesale sea-robbery was to a great extent freed from the taint of mere sordidness by the magnificent fashion in which the sea-robbers carried it on. In them the resolute fighting spirit of the sailors of half a century earlier lived again. No enemy was too big to be attacked, and the enemy too big to be taken had to be very big indeed. In truth, the way in which our smallest craft bustled up to the assault of ships which almost might have rove tackle and hoisted them on board bodily, and the way in which our larger vessels singly attacked whole fleets, made up as pretty a spectacle of salt-water impudence as heart could desire.

Almost the first prize brought in was "a large French schooner," captured by the *Harlequin*, Captain Fenton, a sloop of 10 guns and 45 men; and to the announcement of this achievement, in the *Mercury* of September 20th, was appended the airy statement: "On the 28th of August Capt. Fenton Engaged a French ship of 18 Guns, and would have carried her, but one of his Guns bursting obliged him to draw off." In these actions the little *Harlequin* took the pace that she kept, under her seven successive commanders, throughout the war; but her captain, after he had left her and had taken command of the *Weesel* (I am spelling the name of his vessel in his own way,) managed still farther to accelerate his speed. "On the 10th Instant," reports the *Mercury* in October, 1757, "the Privateer Sloop *Weesel*, Capt. Fenton, returned here almost an entire wrack, having lost his Mast, 27 Feet of his Boom, his best Anchor, and 4 of his Guns in a violent Gale of Wind." While he was in this dismantled condition, the report continues, "he fell in with . . . a Ship and Snow, St Domingo Men, whereupon Capt. Fenton made all the Sail he could, and about 7 o'clock, came up with the Ship, when he engaged her and the Snow with only 6 Guns, and without a Mast, for three Glasses, and would have boarded one of them, but his sloop would not turn to Windward, having 75 stout Men on board; and finding it impracticable to attempt any Thing of the kind, as his Consort could not come up to his Assistance, he sheer'd off to mend his Rigging, the little he had left being almost all shot away." Yet it would seem, from the lack of comment upon this spitfire performance, that for a half-wrecked sloop to fight a ship and snow together was nothing much out of the common in that most gallant time. And as for Captain Pell of the sloop *Mary*, mounting 12 guns and carrying a crew of 100 men, one has only to read the

Mercury's short and dry account of his three days' fight with a fleet of five Frenchmen, together carrying 42 guns and 138 men, to recognize in him one of those old-fashioned captains prone to declaring that if they'd give him the odds of the weather-gage he'd double-shot his guns and fight all hell!

It is but just to add, also, that some of the very prettiest fighting done in all the war was done by ships' companies which in the end were compelled to strike their flags. There was the case of the snow *Cicero*, of 14 guns and 120 men, "taken and carried into Port Louis by a Frigate of 24 nine Pounders and 170 Men, after an obstinate Resistance of two Hours within Pistol Shot." In this breezy little fight, notwithstanding the great disproportion of the vessels in size, crews, and armament—the last the more marked because the *Cicero's* battery, presumably, consisted of six-pounders—'twas touch and go which side won. In the early part of the engagement the sloop "hull'd the Frigate so often that both Pumps were kept going, and were in such Confusion on board that they ceased Firing several Minutes"; and then, by a turn of bad luck, "Captain Smith having Mr Saltur, his Doctor, blown up, and 15 Men wounded, was obliged to Strike, his Rigging being almost all shot away." In addition to the wounded at least one of the fighting force was killed, as in the list of casualties is the entry: "Alex. Mitchell, blown up with the Doctor, and is since dead." But what a lovely bit of fighting it was!

Captain Spelling, of the snow *Hornet*, of 14 guns and 120 men, made even a better record when he was taken, in October, 1758, "by two French Frigates, being part of a Convoy to fourteen Martinico men bound to Old France." Our Captain, no doubt, made a dash for the merchantship, and then found that he was in for it with the ships of war. At any rate, he played handsomely his losing game. "Captain Spelling engaged one of the Frigates," reports the *Mercury*, "three-quarters of an hour, and Killed her nine Men; but she being joined by the other, after engaging both half an Hour, and Killing the latter 6 Men, he was obliged to Strike, having John Banning Kill'd, his Fore-Mast, Traysail Mast, and Boltsprit shot away, his Sails and Rigging almost tore to Pieces, and the Vessel so disabled that the Frenchmen, after taking out her Guns, and a few other necessaries, blew her up next Day."

VIII.

According to their lights, my old-time sailors did their whole duty. For morals were simple in their day, and their entire creed, I fancy, was summed in the conviction that Right was fighting the king's enemies to the uttermost, and that Wrong was running away. It is true that these heroes of mine, judged by the over-dainty canons of what at present is held to be propriety, were not much better than so many Turpins: ranging less for glory than for plunder the highways of the sea. Yet for myself, leaving aside the fact that in their own time their calling had no smirch upon it, 'tis impossible for me thus harshly to regard them; or, indeed, to have for them any other feeling than a warm kindliness that flows in part from envy of their doings, and in part from downright gladness that such audacious rashlings had the chance to fight their lives out in their own strong way.

THE VOLUNTEER FIRE
DEPARTMENT
(PART 2)

FIRE AT JENNINGS'S CLOTHING STORE, BROADWAY, APRIL 25, 1854.

I.

THE symbol of the old Volunteer Fire Department of the city of New York was the figure of a fireman holding in his brawny arms a child whom he had rescued from the flames. It was an emblem not less true than beautiful, yet many an old fireman does not recall a single instance of a comrade's saving anybody's life. Mr. Carlisle Norwood remembers but one case. Mr. Theodore Keeler remembers none at all. Nor does Mr. Peter R. Warner, who adds, however, that "any human being would exert himself to save a fellow-creature's life, and I am sure that if I had gone into a house and saved a woman or child, I should have dismissed the subject from my mind in a month. If a fireman could save life he would do so, and not think much about it afterward." Mr. Michael Eichell, once an engineer in the Department, and for twenty-four years in actual service there,

does not remember a single case in which a fireman saved a human life. Mr. Harry Howard, ex-Chief Engineer, says that "firemen often saved lives, but they are too modest to talk about it," yet he remembers only two instances: "J. R. Mount, recently a messenger in the Department of Public Buildings, saved the lives of a woman and child at a fire at No. 89 Bowery, a furniture establishment. The Common Council voted him a silver pitcher as a testimonial. I don't care to speak of myself, but I remember that at the fire in Jennings's clothing store, No. 231 Broadway, after the roof had fallen in and killed thirteen firemen, I heard a boy shouting from the second story, 'Save me! save me!' I went up and found him wedged in, surrounded by a part of the fallen roof, an iron safe, and a wall. Many years afterward, when a rich merchant of San Francisco—his name was S. A. Van Praag—he called at my house, and, as I was out, left his card, inscribed with the words, 'The boy that you saved from Jennings's fire.'" Mr. John A. Cregier describes Mount's performance as a most heroic act—the most remarkable instance he remembers of a fireman's saving life. The ladder being too short, it was put upon a hogshead, Mount ascended to the fourth floor, helped a woman cut of the window and down the ladder—a most difficult feat—and fainted when at last he saw her safe. Another old fireman, who is unwilling to have his name mentioned, says that on the Fourth of July, 1831, he saved a child from a burning building. "Soon after we reached the place with the engine, a mother came rushing down stairs, shrieking that her baby was left behind. I immediately hurried up stairs, took the infant from its cradle on the second floor, descended with it amid considerable smoke, and handed it to her." This old fireman never told the deed to any one but the members of his own family; and he is unwilling at this late day to set up as a hero. His many friends would be surprised if they heard his name. He is one of the most prominent capitalists in the city of New York. In the voluminous manuscript minutes of Engine No. 13, in five large folio volumes, dating back as far as the 9th of November, 1791, and continuing until the 8th of June, 1847, there is not a solitary record of a fireman's saving anybody's life. Of the almost as voluminous manuscript records of Engine No. 21 the same observation is true. After a careful reading of both series of minutes I have failed to find even the mention of such heroism. The minutes of Engine No. 5 and of Engine No. 42 tell the same story so far as I have been able to discover them. Yet the well-known

symbol of the fireman with a saved child in his arms which stands in white marble upon the top of the Firemen's Monument in Greenwood Cemetery, which formerly stood over the façade of Firemen's Hall in Mercer Street, and above the entrance

FIREMEN'S HALL.

to Engine No. 2's house in Eldridge Street, and which in varied forms graces the engraved pictures on firemen's certificates and ball tickets, is appropriate in the highest degree. It represents the readiness of brave men to become the saviors of their fellows, and the modesty which in song and story has so often been the accompaniment of valor.

II.

New-Yorkers who recall the many street fights in which firemen were the participants about the time of the disbandment of the old Volunteer Fire Department need not therefore suppose that the firemen were notoriously disorderly in earlier years. The minutes of the companies previous to the year 1830 are remarkably free from reports of pugilistic encounters. Indeed, the first entry of the kind

that has come to the observation of the present writer is dated July 9, 1830, in the books of Engine No. 21, and reads as follows: "A complaint against the riotous conduct of boys from the neighboring engine-houses after alarms of fire, and request that a stop might be put to it," the boys, of course, being not members of the companies, but only "runners" with the engines. The well-kept minutes of Engine No. 13 contain not a line of record of firemen coming to blows with each other until the 12th of June, 1831, when that company was probably at least forty years old. The occasion of the disturbance was a fire in a brick building in Dutch Street, occupied as a bakery by J. and A. Wilson. "We were on the ground in good season," writes the secretary, "and played the first water on the fire from the head of a line from a plug, then from a cistern in the rear, and finally from the river in the watch line, No. 11 at the dock into No. 13, at which place we were *overrun*, and as usual shamefully abused by the members of Engine No. 12, several of our men being struck by them." The words "as usu-

al" do not point, of course, to a notable previous condition of amity between companies Twelve and Thirteen, but this was the first time that anything worth writing down seems to have occurred.

The two companies were necessarily rivals, No. 13 keeping its engine in Duane Street near William Street, and No. 12 its engine in William Street near Duane, so that whenever a fire alarm sounded, the struggle for precedence on the way to the scene of the conflagration was hot and vigorous. On their way to a fire up town the two engines usually met at the corner of Roosevelt and Pearl streets, and when, as

ENGINE AND HOSE LAMP AND LANTERNS.

was often the case, the arrival at the hydrant or cistern was almost simultaneous, a conflict was the natural result. These rivals thus came to hate each other most cordially, and a single blow was enough to produce the explosion of a good deal of combustible matter. In like manner Engines Nos. 14 and 5 were rivals, and on their way to an uptown fire would encounter each other in front of the *Tribune* building, and begin the contest for superiority in speed, and for the possession of the desired hydrant, fire-plug, cistern, or dock, as the case might be. Engines 1, 23, and 6, on the

TWEED'S FIRE HAT.

way from their respective houses, would often meet at the corner of Chatham and Pearl streets, and begin their contest, and Engines 40 and 15 at the junction of Centre and Chatham streets, in front of the site now occupied by the *Staats-Zeitung* building. Engines 6 and 8 had many a lusty struggle. "Tweed was foreman of Six Engine then," says an old fireman, "and crowds and crowds of people would congregate at Chatham Square to see 'Big Six' and Eight Engine coming down town. Eight lay in Ludlow Street, and came down Grand, through the

the earlier days. There were no pistols, no knives, no maimings, no deaths, as in the period subsequent, say, to the year 1850, when the decline of the Department began.

III.

The old volunteer fireman had a real affection for the "machine," and was fond of recording with pride the instances in which she behaved herself with distinction. "Our engine worked unusually well this morning," wrote the secretary of company Forty-one, on December 15, 1825, "and the members were in fine glee.

FIRE DEPARTMENT BANNER.

Bowery; Six lay in Gouverneur Street, and came through East Broadway, and thence into Chatham Square; and when they met, the excitement was intense and the cheering furious as one or the other engine gained in speed." Engines 41 and 8 also were hearty rivals. All old firemen will recall the contests in which these companies were chronic participants, and will remember, too, how often and how naturally the struggles led to blows. "When did fighting begin, do you ask?" said an old fireman: "it began at the time the Department was organized, in 1798, and earlier, and continued till its disbandment. Two companies would reach simultaneously the same hydrant, for example, and would fight for the possession of it." It was only fighting with fists, though, in

Forty-one sucked on Twenty-five during the whole time of the Fire, tho' she, Twenty-five, was almost continually overrunning. We gave Twenty-eight a very good supply." On that occasion the fire was in Thompson Street near Broome, and the water was drawn from the North River by means of fourteen engines in line, one engine pumping into another, through two hundred feet of hose. Forty-one Engine pumped out her water faster than Twenty-five Engine could pump it into her, consequently, as the slang was, Forty-one Engine "sucked on" Twenty-five Engine—a result which was considered a grand trophy to the prowess of the men who were pumping Forty-one Engine, and a corresponding disgrace to the men who were pumping Twenty-five Engine. Moreover, the engine next below Twenty-five Engine was pumped so vigorously as to give Twenty-five Engine more water than the latter could pump out. Consequently the latter "was almost continually overrunning" her sides, and was still further disgraced thereby.

It is easy to understand the readiness of the volunteer fireman to spend his money on the decoration of his engine. He liked to see her look well. He always spoke of her in the feminine gender. Engine Thirteen was silver-plated at a very great expense, and many minor charges for her ornamentation are entered in the minutes of her company. As early as the year 1825, Forty-one Engine was regularly "washed with fresh water" after doing service at a fire. On December 14, 1829, "a Motion Was made and Carried that the Painting Committee have power to settle with Mr. Effy, the Dutchman, for his design"—probably of a picture painted on the back of the engine, behind her condenser case. It was usual to decorate the backs handsomely. So fond were the firemen of painting their own engines to suit themselves, that the city was in the habit of painting a new engine a temporary dull lead or a gray, and leaving to the company the function of choosing the permanent color, and of paying for putting it on. Not only so, but a "building committee" was often appointed by and from a company to superintend the construction of a new engine. Such a committee appointed by company Thirteen reported on the 8th of November, 1820, how "they have thought it expedient to adopt several improvements which alone can be tested by experience, and hope that time will manifest their utility. For that of the Roller arms—a plan promising great advantage—they must credit their associate Mr. Delano for suggesting. They likewise feel themselves indebted to Mr. G. C. Aycrigg for the piece of ornamental Brass which supports the leader, being a piece of his own device and ingenious workmanship. It eminently contributes to ornament the machine, and they trust the Company will duly appreciate its value." And on the 4th of June, 1823, this company passed a resolution as follows:

"That the body of the Engine be painted Black [with the $90 raised by subscription for the purpose], and the strip of gilding to remain as before, with the addition of a Leaf border."

Six years afterward another engine was obtained from the city by the same company, and decorated, as usual, by themselves, as witness the following entry:

"*Dec.* 2, 1829.—This morning most of the members met at the Corporation Yard for the purpose of taking our new Engine to the House. We rec'd her about 11 o'Clock, & from that time until dark we received visitors at the Engine House. Hundreds of persons called in the course of the day, & appeared much pleased with their visit—indeed, for splendor & magnificence, both as regards her Painting, Gilding, Plating, & Carving, she never will probably be equalled."

Who could have doubted it?

Not the engine only, but the enginehouse as well, was the object of a pride which recked little of expense.

The funds necessary to meet these constantly recurring expenses of repairing and decorating the engines and enginehouses were provided for in two ways: first, by special subscriptions from the members; and secondly, by fines incurred through violations of the by-laws and constitutions.

A foreigner present at the regular or special business meetings of almost any one of the old volunteer fire companies might have been excused for supposing that a principal function of those organizations was the imposition of fines. The word "fined" occurs on well-nigh every page of the not always very legible documents that describe the festivities of those occasions, the proceeds of the fining being used also to "defray the expenses" of the annual supper, and to provide for the widows and orphans of former members. The by-laws of Clinton Fire Company, No. 41, adopted November 7, 1823, provided that the foreman and assistant foreman should be fined one dollar for each neglect "impartially to enforce all laws that shall be adopted by the company," and that the treasurer should be fined one dollar for each neglect to "render a true statement of the funds when requested by the FOREMAN or ASSISTANT." They established a fine of seventy-five cents for every neglect of a member "to repair after the engine to the fire," when, on arriving at the enginehouse in obedience to an alarm, he found that the engine had already gone. Twenty-five cents was the fine for coming "direct from home without his FIRE-CAP," and for not coming to order "when called to order from the Chair." Fifty cents was the fine for absence from a regular or special meeting of the company, and twelve and a half cents for not answering to his name at roll-call, "except he be within sight of the Engine House during the call," though "sickness or death in the FAMILY is a sufficient excuse to clear him of the above fines." If he left the meeting without first obtaining leave of the chairman, he was fined fifty cents. "No POLITICS," reads Article 12, "shall be introduced at any meeting of this Company. Any member being found guilty of the same, or of improper behavior, using indecent language, profane swearing, or being intoxicated with liquor during business, or at any time when the COMPANY is together, shall pay a fine of ONE DOLLAR." Article 18 enjoins that "when the engine is under way each man shall drag at the rope, and not shove at the ENGINE unells [*sic*] absolutely necessary, under the penalty of TWENTY-FIVE cents, the Foreman and Assistant excepted"; and Article 20 makes it "the duty of every member of this COMPANY to report such Chimney as he knows to have been on fire within forty-eight hours after his knowledge of the same to the FOREMAN or one of the persons appointed to receive the same under the penalty of ONE DOLLAR." As early as the 6th of November, 1794, the fines collected at the annual meeting of company Thirteen, at Hunter's Hotel, amounted to £3 1s., there being twenty-three members present.

IV

The first Chief Engineer of the old Volunteer Fire Department was Thomas Franklin. He was a fireman forty-one years, and a Chief Engineer thirteen years, having been appointed to that office in 1799. He was known among the firemen by the affectionate sobriquet of "Uncle Tommy," and had the reputation of being careful of their lives and health, never giving them an order to enter into danger where he did not lead them. At the time of the great fire in Chatham Street, while attempting to pass from one street to another, both sides of which were swept by flames, he was overcome by the heat, and his clothes took fire. It was necessary to drench them at once by a discharge of water from one of the engines, and the chief was taken home in an exhausted condition. When the Common Council had resolved to issue fractional currency, during the war of 1812, Mr. Franklin

was appointed to sign the notes. Millions of dollars' worth received his signature. Having been nominated to the office of Register of the City and County of New York, he was supported by the firemen,

THOMAS FRANKLIN.

and triumphantly elected. During the last visit of General Lafayette to this country, Mr. Franklin was the Chief Marshal at the grand review of the Fire Department in honor of the city's illustrious guest, and received from him the most hearty congratulations.

Among certain manuscripts left by the late Mr. Philip W. Engs, an old fireman, who about twenty years ago was in the habit of reading occasionally before the Association of Exempt Firemen some reminiscences of the old Volunteer Fire Department, I find a quaintly told story of the famous Chief Engineer and one Johnny Ling:

"About this period [1817] there was a personage who chose to identify himself with the Fire Department, familiarly known as Johnny Ling. He was rather weak in intellect, had one blear eye, carried his head one-sided, and walked with a peculiar shack gait. Johnny believed that we were deficient in our appointments in the Department, and so appointed himself 'captain of the leaders.' The firemen in the neighborhood of Broad Street encouraged the whim, and procured him a fire hat with his title painted thereon, and a constable's staff painted in like manner. Thus prepared, you might see him trotting up and down the lines, ordering every one off the leaders [or hose]. He had a fondness for something

CARLISLE NORWOOD.

stronger than water, and often by the time the fire was well under he would be in a trim for sport, and the boys would excite him by treading on the hose, when he would apply his staff to them, and a general *mêlée* was produced, in which Johnny would be moved about with rather uncomfortable rapidity. On one occasion our venerable Chief, Thomas Franklin, who loved pleasantry, stepped on the hose within sight of the 'Captain.' Some roguish fireman told the latter there was a fellow on the leaders. He turned around, exclaiming, 'Get off the leaders, you sir.' 'I won't,' was the prompt reply. 'Then I'll knock you down,' he rejoined. 'Don't you see that I am the Chief Engineer?' said Mr. F. 'I don't care for that; I am the Captain, and you sha'n't stand there. You ain't fit for Chief Engineer if you do so. Come off there.' Our good Chief replied, 'Thee is right, Captain, and I'll obey thy orders. I charge thee to see hereafter that everybody is kept off.' 'There,' says Johnny, 'don't you see that the Chief obeys the Captain? Now, boys, give me some gin.'"

Mr. Eng adds his tribute to "the distinguished character" borne by "our venerated brother Thomas Franklin. There are many now [1858] living who knew that noble philanthropist, and who will remember him to have possessed an influence over the Fire Department, and to have commanded a respect from its members, which has been the lot of no man before or since his day."

Mr. Carlisle Norwood, formerly foreman of Hose Company No. 5, now Presi-

dent of the Lorillard Insurance Company, being asked, "Upon what part of your life as a fireman do you look back with the greatest pleasure?" replied: "Upon the whole of it. I thought there was nothing like being a fireman. I would sooner go to a fire than to a theatre or any other place of amusement. There was no pleasure that equalled that." During his time of service the families of the first citizens were represented in some of the companies. To No. 14 Engine, for example, were attached as volunteers Bishop Hobart's son William, Dr. Hosack's son Edward Pendleton, Mayor Paulding's son Frederick, and Frederick Gibert, now a prominent resident of Fifth Avenue. Many highly respectable Quaker families —the Macys, the Townsends, the Jenkinses, the Haydocks, and others—belonged to the Department, a chief motive for joining being the consequent exemption from the military duty to which they were conscientiously averse. Then, too, many leading merchants were glad to be rid of jury duty. A well-known merchant once served on a jury for fourteen consecutive days, though allowed to go home in the morning, in charge of a deputy-sheriff, to change his shirt and to shave. The sheriff in those times was wont to pick out solid and good men for that service, and such men liked to escape liability to it by entering the ranks of the firemen. Another merchant served three weeks. Apart from these motives were the native love of excitement, and the honorable instincts of loyalty to the city. In 1820, when only eight years old, Mr. Norwood was at the Park Theatre fire, which he remembers distinctly, after the lapse of sixty years.

He remembers also the little tripartite keg hung in front of the engine, marked, "Spirits—Rum—Gin," each word standing over its appropriate compartment. The steward of the company had charge of this keg, and dispensed its contents at fires. In the later days of the Department the intemperance was a crying evil, and as long ago as 1812 the trustees of the Fire Department Fund were moved to ask Company 13 how far, in the latter's judgment, "the important duties of a fireman ought to be committed to men addicted to habitual intoxication."

The famous "Gulick affair," he says, has never been correctly related in print. The Common Council, eight years previously, had caused many resignations of firemen on account of the way in which that legislative body had treated John P. Bailey, the treasurer of the Department, and the foreman of Twenty-three Engine. Bailey had been insulted by an alderman, had been drawn into an altercation with him, and had in consequence been dismissed the force without a hearing. The memory of that indignity was fresh in the minds of the firemen at a fire at Avenue C and Third Street in 1836, when the news was circulated that the Common Council had removed Chief Engineer Gulick. The fact was that at a caucus it had resolved to remove him, but the protests of his friends had induced it to reconsider its action. The fire was at its height, when one of the firemen, Mr. Hubbs, who had heard of the first action of the caucus of the Common Council, but was ignorant that they had reconsidered the matter, went up to the Chief, and exclaimed, "Boss, your throat is cut!"

"It isn't possible," replied Gulick.

"Yes, it is," persisted the first speaker; "the Common Council have deposed you."

Gulick at the time was wearing the broad back rim of his hat in front, so as to shield his face from the heat, as was often done at fires. He withdrew a few steps, and then walked down the line silently and gravely, without changing the reversed position of his hat. His demeanor drew the attention of the firemen, one of whom asked the Chief what was the matter.

"I am Chief no longer," responded Gulick; "the Common Council have removed me."

Instantly the news was passed up and down the line, and almost before the appropriate comments had begun, the firemen were taking up their hose and stopping the playing of their engines. Only one company—No. 8—continued throwing water upon the burning buildings, and its hose was cut several times in succession. Gulick meanwhile had retired to his office in Canal Street, and word was sent to Mayor Cornelius W. Lawrence that the conflagration was progressing without hinderance. The situation had become truly alarming, and the safety of the whole city was imperiled. A messenger was dispatched for Gulick, and in a few minutes the late Chief, as the firemen believed him to be, though in reality he had not yet been deposed from the office, was seen walking through the ranks, a fireman on each side of him grasping him by the arm.

At Gulick's solicitation, and upon his assurance that he had not been removed, the firemen resumed their labors, and by-and-by succeeded in extinguishing the

JOHN A. CREGIER.

flames. Soon afterward, however, Gulick was deposed in earnest, and a general resignation of firemen took place. John Ryker, Jun., who succeeded him as Chief, was a handsome, active officer of commanding personal appearance, and, next to Gulick, the most popular fireman in the city. If he had not accepted the appointment in the circumstances in which it was offered him, he would have been the firemen's choice for that office. But he became at once exceedingly distasteful to them, in spite of his great executive abilities and rare personal worth, and during the next year had a very hard row to hoe. He was succeeded by that admirable officer Cornelius V. Anderson. Gulick in the mean time had been put in nomination for the office of Register, the firemen having gone first to the Democrats, and then to the

Whigs, who acceded to their desires in the matter, and under whose banner he was triumphantly elected by a majority of 6050, although the Whig party was in a minority. The excitement had been almost unparalleled in intensity, and the electioneering wild. One Sunday morning, for example, the worshippers at St. Patrick's Cathedral, on returning home, were greeted with placards that read:

"Who saved the Cathedral?
James Gulick.
Vote for him for Register."

That gallant fireman John A. Cregier, whose distinguished services as foreman

GEORGE W. WHEELER.

and engineer in the old Volunteer Fire Department have told severely upon the vigor of his once most vigorous constitution, was asked the other day whether, if he could live his life over again, he would choose to repeat his experience as a fireman. "Yes, I would," he replied, emphatically; "I would go it all over again. I have often been asked that question—whether, with my present knowledge, I would choose to relive my life as a fireman. Yes, sir, I would. The sight of a fire—the first kindling of the flames in the distance—used to make me glad. I never stopped to think of the misery and destruction that it was causing. My father used to whip me enough to break any boy's heart, and his back too, because I would

run with the engine. But it was of no use. What part of my experience as a fireman do I remember with the greatest satisfaction? A great deal of it. Our engineers' meetings were always a source of great pleasure to me; our engineers' and foremen's meetings too, and our meetings of representatives at Firemen's Hall. After the regular business was disposed of there was invariably something lively to attend to; there was always some one to offer a resolution, and open an inspiriting discussion. There was old Harry Mansfield—'Resolution Mansfield' we used to call him, because he always had a resolution to introduce—how much fun he made for us! The representatives of the Department in those days—say thirty years ago—were high-toned men, men of standing, character, and ability, men like Major Wade, Carlisle Norwood, David Milliken, Zophar Mills, Peter H. Titus, John S. Giles, James Y. Watkins. Norwood used to make those walls ring with his eloquence whenever any matter came up affecting the reputation of the Department."

George W. Wheeler is the secretary of the Association of Exempt Firemen. He is as familiar with the history of the old Volunteer Fire Department as any other member, living or dead. As soon as he was big enough to run at all he ran with an engine, and on the 9th of February, 1836, joined Engine Company No. 41. After serving five months he resigned, together with nearly all the other firemen, on account of the removal of Chief Engineer Gulick by the Common Council. In May, 1837, he rejoined his company, upon the election of Cornelius V. Anderson to the position of Chief Engineer. The several companies, at the time of their resignation, had indignantly removed the ornaments from their engines, and in some instances scratched and otherwise injured the paint and pictures. No. 13 had repainted their machine a dull lead-color in order to indicate their indignation. No. 41 had disfigured their machine by frequent scrapings, so that, when the Gulick trouble was over, an entire repainting was necessary.

Mr. Wheeler had some serious accidents during his term of service as a fire-

HARRY HOWARD.—[FROM A PAINTING IN THE CITY HALL.]

man. On one occasion (in 1839) he slipped while about to take hold of the brakes of the engine, was caught under them, and severely struck on the shoulders and across the back. The blow laid him aside for some weeks. About two years afterward he was run over by a hook-and-ladder truck. In 1843, while holding the pipe at a fire at Attorney and Rivington streets, he was ordered to climb over a pile of mahogany logs. The logs tumbled over him, and so badly bruised him that he tried to resign from the company, but the company would not let him. Subsequently he joined the Exempt Engine Company, and was chairman of a committee to negotiate with the insurance companies in reference to receiving from them a steam-engine. The Exempts were the first to agree to try a steam-engine; but while they were making their arrangements, Company No. 8 pushed matters in a similar direction, and won the distinction of being the first New York fire company to use steam.

The last Chief Engineer but one of the old Volunteer Fire Department was Harry Howard, who still lives, his left arm paralyzed, and his health otherwise much impaired. He holds an office connected with the Department of Public Works, and is a familiar figure in the region of the City Hall. He was fifty-eight years old on the 20th of August, 1880. Harry Howard does not know who his father or mother was. A kind-hearted old woman adopted him in infancy, and the Legislature, at his request, gave him his name. While a Chief Engineer, and on his way to a fire in Grand Street, he was suddenly stricken down, in his thirty-fifth year, by an attack of paralysis, which left him permanently crippled, after twenty or more years of most active service as "runner," fireman, foreman, assistant engineer, and Chief, during which he had been the *beau ideal* of the "boys" in the lower wards of the city. His portrait is better known than that of any other old fireman in the city of New York, Tweed's excepted. Asked recently upon what part of his life as a fireman he looked back with the most satisfaction, he replied, quickly and emphatically: "Upon none of it. See this arm of mine [paralyzed and stiff]. That's all I can do with it [lifting his shoulder up and then dropping it]. That's what I got for being a fireman. What can compensate me for that? Nothing. And there was many a man who went to an early grave in Greenwood on account of overexertion as a fireman. Look at the paid firemen to-day. They ride to a fire, and they ride from it again, and they have horses to draw their engines. There's nothing to destroy their health. They are as likely to live long as any other men. But the old volunteers endured the most exhausting hardships in the snow, in the rain, the cold, and the heat, dragging their machines block after block, lifting the heavy hose, running themselves breathless—and all for what? They never got even thanks. All the reward they received was to be accused of joining the Department in order to steal and pillage at fires."

"There was some drinking in the Department, I confess," he continued, "although I never could see that the firemen drank more than the militia did or do now. Getting drunk was not more characteristic of a fireman than of a soldier, and it is a mistake to suppose that it was. But firemen were continually overexerting themselves: men who had wives and children would kill themselves by overwork, and leave their families helpless. Three years before the Paid Fire Department was organized I said that we ought to have it. I was tired of seeing so many good men throw their lives away."

"What did they do it for?"

"I never could understand it, and I don't understand it now. Nobody ever thanked them for their services. Look at my arm—that's all the return I got. There's John A. Cregier, the best man the Fire Department ever produced—the very best man, the finest specimen of a fireman —he's sick too. Overexerted himself, that's all, and now he's suffering for it. We were burying men all the time who died from the same cause. I said that it ought not to be. I was in favor of a paid Fire Department. A volunteer Fire Department is well enough in a village, but not in a city. Yet I notice that with all their facilities—with their telegraphs, their horses, their riding, and their steam—the paid firemen don't get to a fire as quickly as the old volunteers did."

Harry Howard was Chief Engineer for three years. He was an extremely dashing, athletic, and brave fireman. Nothing gave him keener pleasure during the seven years of his assistant engineership than to succeed in outstripping his Chief, the late Alfred Carson, while running to fires, in arriving there before him, and in reaping the consequent reward of being temporarily in supreme command.

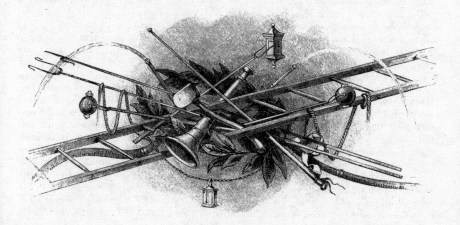

IN UP-TOWN NEW YORK

WHEN in the middle of the eighteenth century a man settled on the northern end of Manhattan Island, then gradually being reclaimed from the wilderness, he had every reason to be proud of the fact, even though this was Harlem. His neighbors, though not numerous, were distinguished; Harlem had become the rural retreat of the aristocratic New-Yorker, and the social significance of residing there caused a man to enter this rugged country in the same buoyant spirit which at a later date characterized his departure from it. This suburban life, however, had its inconveniences; access to the old Welvers Tavern in New York was not easy, and a glance at the rocky, uneven formation of Harlem to-day—its granite eminences and deep, unexpected embankments—would imply that the homeward journey of the jocose element was a particularly hazardous performance after nightfall. When once a man's midnight yodling has suddenly been interrupted by a twenty-foot drop down an embankment, it is apt to shake him up and make him sceptical. One may assume, then, that the old resident was good in spite of himself; made sacrifices and retired early.

But the chief charm of old Harlem—its well-bred seclusion—was destined to be transitory. Later, when New York's business centre moved steadily up-town, greatly increasing the value of real estate and the cost of living, a horde of New-Yorkers moved to the north, and Harlem soon became a haven for the clerks and small merchants, the family man and the newly married couple and the young professional man, who all flocked thither; and there came into existence in its logical sequence the Harlem flat: a frail, angular, overelaborated structure, which at the advent of spring occasionally showed strange crevices in its sides, preparatory to descending in a cataract of bricks.

With this influx of humanity a wise and humane administration caused railings or bumpers to be erected along the embankments and gullies, making access to one's home, at night, easy for the normal and possible for the abnormal. This was only a few years prior to the pre-digested breakfast-food era, and all were content and merry in Harlem—and might have continued so had not a certain individual with an undeveloped sense of propriety (whom many to-day denounce as a myth) thrown the bone of contention. It was at 125th Street—or was it at 120th Street? (opinions differ)—that this ostentatious person, who presumably had made money more rapidly and ingeniously than the law even to-day allows, drew an imaginary boundary-line for Harlem, with the unfortunate remark, " Thank the Lord, I'm out of it !" and forthwith moved to 115th Street. The seeds of discord had been sown. Our latent perversity makes us resent being told by a casual stranger just exactly where we are; it embarrasses a man and makes him feel cramped. Indeed, in this particular case it even went so far as to cast aspersions on one's social position, and has since been the means of much unnecessary bitterness in determining Harlem's exact boundary-line. Those who hitherto had been content—nay, even anxious—to live in Harlem soon began to speculate upon the possibility of there being a grain of wisdom in the stranger's exultation on leaving it. In short, a random remark had been the means of suddenly stimulating the Harlemite's critical sense at the expense of his happiness.

Thus, to-day, it is extremely difficult to get a Harlem resident with the correct mental attitude to answer you as to where New York ends and Harlem begins. He is rarely impersonal.

"Do you like Harlem?" you unwittingly ask your friend who resides at 120th Street.

HARLEM'S ARCADY
Etched on copper by C. H. White

"I'm not in Harlem," he replies, with considerable bitterness. "Oh no! Don't fool yourself . . . it's not as bad as *that!* Harlem begins at 125th Street!"

"Cheer up!" you say; "it's only temporary." And with this you leave him in Harlem, to grope about for a motive in this wilderness of asphalt and tomblike houses; to wander through interminable vistas of glaring white pavement and geometrical brick; to dodge trolley-cars and elevated structures; to pass beneath windows bulging with ill-assorted humanity in pink and blue undershirts, gazing vacantly across the street; or to tumble against a throng of perspiring rooters grouped about the corner baseball game—until his nerves reach a supreme crisis: he pauses deliberately to listen with a morbid interest to the hoarse metallic raspings of the distant phonograph in one of the local palaces of artificial merriment!

On such an occasion, after having formally cursed Harlem, should you catch a glimpse of a dim strip of silver fringed with green, with here and there a faint suggestion of distant shipping and still more distant hills, faintly outlined at the vanishing-point of some great brick and plaster vista,—follow it, and presently the obvious side of Harlem,

the appalling monotony of her streets, the tin mouldings and venomous rococo, are left behind. A gentle breeze laden with fern and earthy forest odors reaches you from somewhere beyond the lofty masses of patriarchal oak and elm, like a distant call from Vagabondia which must be answered. You press on; here scaling steep embankments and rocky promontories, scarred and weather-beaten, thickly carpeted with velvety green lichen; now wandering through drowsy vales of moss and fern, beneath a lofty canopy of soaring branch and leafy foliage, until confused murmurs—perhaps the distant whistle of some river tug signalling for the drawbridge, or the low muffled tremolo of a passing motor-boat—reach the ear faintly. You hurry along, expectant, emerging from the woods to find yourself in Harlem's Arcady.

At your feet stretches a shimmering sheet of water, winding its way placidly in long graceful curves about the distant points, or losing itself in a rare vista of sky and water spanned by a silver network of innumerable swinging bridges. A distant tug and its train of barges steal lazily down the river, looking not unlike some mammoth eel in the odd perspective; and in the valley far

IN THE LEE OF THE ONE-HUNDRED-AND-TWENTY-FIFTH STREET BULKHEAD
Etched on copper by C. H. White

below, seen through a veil of mist, the apartment-hotel, with its French towers and steep mansard roofs, rears itself defiantly in its girdle of heavy foliage, like some medieval stronghold. And this is Harlem! Not the barren, naked, obvious side with its strange anomalies, but unobtrusive Harlem, refined upon, jealously revealing itself in one of those rare moods when a monastic grayness steals imperceptibly over the river, lending to the most prosaic thing a new significance.

First blithe and debonair, mirroring in her depths great rocky highlands, this whimsical river drifts capriciously into a minor vein through the Harlem

Bad Lands — a barren tract hemmed in by raw, vacant tenements and the still remoter fringe of factories half veiled in smoke. The desolation here is so complete that it commands admiration. The stranded wreck of a canal-boat imbedded in the mud, its clawlike ribs overgrown with moss and barnacles, and perhaps a stray naked urchin besmirched with mud, alone in this city wilderness— knee-deep in the stagnant filth—only heighten the deserted, forbidding aspect of the place. This is a superannuated public dumping-ground. At the approach of night one may see here, on rare occasions, a few isolated black spots detaching themselves against the uniform grayness of the uneven ground; moving with painful uncertainty, and stopping from time to time to hover restlessly about the numerous pyramids of refuse. These are the local ragpickers — miserable, half-starved humanity — who occasionally haunt the scrap-heaps in a vain hope of sweating a few cents out of these thrice-sifted scavengerings.

To what extent Harlem is appreciated can only be fully realized after having seen the throngs of votaries in easy sprawl along her shores, who toil not, neither do they spin; or by a visit to Bill Conlin's—a derelict of a boat-house tucked away snugly in the lee of the 125th Street bulkhead, and dotted profusely by robust fellows in faded undershirts, contentedly watching the distant train of golden clouds roll past and tower into new formations; noting with unceasing interest the flood and ebb tide with its wake of stranded pleasure-craft, shaking with unfeigned good humor when the gasoline-launch runs foul of the sunken reef, or when the yachtsman, in immaculate white duck suit, slips with much throaty gurgling, amid a flood of bubbles, from the treacherous slime of the gangway into the river.

A fine old pensioner who fought with Farragut, an army veteran who went to Custer's relief, an ex-plumber and alleged gas-fitter, an involuntary tailor, a man of temperament who makes bromide enlargements that are never understood, and to this heterogeneous collection add Mike Dorlan, watchman of the dock, and "Fog Eye," an Italian junkman with a glass optic, and you have the little coterie of boat-house loungers that I stumbled upon by some happy accident one fine summer's day. They say little, these dreamers of the river, and when the spirit moves them to converse (which is seldom), it is usually a hoarse monosyllable spoken between clenched teeth —sideways through the corner of the mouth. Their infallible good humor and natural primitive buoyancy have been acquired in many cases by the liquidation of business interests; while others have sacrificed home and mother—at times even a wife and child—to answer the call of the river.

Bill Conlin calls this the "boat-house fever," and Bill is a close observer; but Cauliflower Jim's testimony, while hardly impersonal, is not without value. "It gits on me nerves," he explained, "to sit round the house with the wimmen, and hear talk o' feathers and the like, and the new shape o' corsets." Howbeit, year in and year out they are there, basking in the sunshine and ripening into a mature old age waiting for the final harvesting. Save for an involuntary trip or two to the Island, little, it seems, intrudes upon the even tenor of their existence. So secluded is this little niche that few outsiders ever gain access to it. Occasionally, it is true, a stray Italian laborer in quest of work may pass through the low doorway into the mysterious gloom within and timorously approach the ponderous carcass of Mike Dorlan, watchman and inspector of the dock, in easy sprawl on the narrow balcony.

"Gota job? . . . Gota work?" Mike will repeat after him in pidgin-English; and then the sunburnt face of the dock-inspector wrinkles in a philanthropic smile.

"See that bridge over there, and those hills 'way off 'n the east?" he will begin, softly. "Walk straight down the dock, turn to yer right and beat it acrost the bridge, and keep right on movin'," and, his simple duties accomplished, the felt hat descends once more over the broad good-natured face, and with a deep sigh he relapses into a blissful silence.

Bill Conlin tells me that with the exception of myself industry has only prompted one man to visit the boathouse. He was a newspaper reporter who appeared one day with elaborate photographic paraphernalia during the coal strike, three years ago, just after the boys had borrowed enough coal from the freight-yards across the river to last them the whole winter.

"He give us each fifty cents to git out on the float and have our pictures took sawin' wood," Bill explained, with a significant wink. "'It's just to show the people of New York what the poor is doin' durin' the coal famine,' sez the rayporter, winkin' and trainin' the camera on us." Bill chuckled softly. "We didn't say nawthin', but kept right on sawin'—see?"

In spite of the apparent lack of anything approaching industry in these river loungers, if the occasion seems to warrant it they can bestir themselves into feverish activity. When the Harlem River refuses to give up its dead, and the family of the deceased offers a handsome remuneration for the recovery of a suicide, the sporting element latent in the river's floating population comes to life.

Fishy-eyed, thick-necked dreamers, upon whose ponderous boots can be seen embryonic forms of vegetation, and who for months have lain by the river's edge in a state of alcoholic coma, promptly awake from their lethargy and seem to take a new lease on life, rising with the dawn, when the grotesque flotilla sets forth with its strange débris of dragging paraphernalia. Crowbars with hooks attached, drag-nets heavily weighted, lead pipes with newfangled wire attachments —anything with clawlike properties—are eagerly pressed into service. Men whose hands show everything but the signs of honest labor scour the wrecking-yards of the neighborhood for water-logged dories capable of floating, with vigorous bailing, one or two men; and Tony the barber and Angelo the peanut-vender, haunted by dreams of untold treasure and touched with the craze for speculation, draw out their hoard of pennies and strike for the river.

Meanwhile the cannons blaze away over the placid waters of the stream; here a boat-load of plumbers of an adventurous turn shout hoarse orders at one another as they pass in a derelict of a sloop, propelled at uncertain moments by the second-hand motor but lately rescued from the junk-yard; while behind them comes the pale, anæmic man who, after three sleepless days and nights, has just rescued a pair of archaic stays from the river-bed, and proffers, as he rows along, a string of foul and blasphemous oaths. Bill Conlin, too, laid aside his sandworm industry to search the river. "Every guy in the bunch was fer settin' himself up in business with the proceeds," he explained to me later, half-apologetically. "And late one afternoon when old man Duggan from Highbridge pulls him up, the crowd went ravin' mad. The cop was fer nailin' the stiff himself and fadin' away with the

proceeds; but, 'No,' says old man Duggan. 'I'll take care of *him* meself—see! Hands off!' sez he, with a wild look in his eye, 'or I'll have the law on ye,' sez he, tremblin' with excitement. 'It's my stiff and I seen him first,' and sez he, 'you can play with him all ye like after I've cashed in,' sez he. And with that he froze on to him like a lobster, and now he's retired entirely."

"What are the chances for floaters around this season?" I asked, after he had relapsed into silence again.

"*Nawthin'* doin'," he replied, derisively. "I tell you the river ain't what it was."

On a fine midsummer Sabbath afternoon all Harlem appears to have reunited along the river's edge in one great *fête champêtre*. Outing parties in their Sunday's best line the shores, and it would seem, in loitering along its banks, watching the innumerable pleasure-craft ply back and forth, and the distant train of restless tilted sails slowly beating their way across the treacherous channels of the "Kills," that along this stream pleasure surely plays as important a part as commerce. A warm, genial atmosphere envelops everything; and when this subtle influence takes hold of one, a strange metamorphosis takes place.

Jim the iceman, "Aulie" the plumber, and Fritz of the milk-wagon, resplendent in Third Avenue "Admiral Dewey" suits —a mass of gorgeous braid interlacing their ample bosoms, topped with white yachting-caps—issue forth and shape an uncertain course down the river in their improvised "power-boat"; power that comes when one least expects it—at half-minute intervals, preceded by violent explosions. Along the docks loiter the less fortunate—the workmen with their wives and children, a fluctuating mass of color relieved against the uniform gray and salmon of the houses. The throaty anthem of the perspiring Sängerbund, crowded together in the Casino, reaches the ear in fragments above the confused noises of the river; and in the hush which at times unexpectedly falls upon this Harlem Kermess the distant brassy strains of a band playing rag-time to the lunatics in the asylum on the Island steals softly across the river.

It takes the Harlemite to appreciate

A DERELICT OF A BOAT-HOUSE, WITH ITS HANGERS-ON
Etched on copper by C. H. White

THE "KILLS," SEEN FROM THE GOUVERNEUR MORRIS MANSION
Etched on copper by C. H. White

the real significance—the rare possibilities—of Sunday. Theirs is a Continental, a healthy German, Sabbath; a day
of leisure, evoking long, shimmering
stretches of water fringed with heather,
bathed in genial delight, and racing
clouds aloft, and untold wealth of beer
and pretzels.

Concerning Harlem's former history
little interest is manifested; crowds
daily ply back and forth across the
"Kills" almost in the shadow of "Morrisania," the romantic Morris mansion,
without so much as a glance at this
splendid Revolutionary relic, nor a
thought of the significance of its destruction. To wander through its spacious halls that once echoed to the tread
of a high-heeled Revolutionary pageant,
to loiter in the grand reception-room
where perhaps Washington and Lafayette
trod a measure, or to pause within the
sombre precincts of the library, panelled
with mahogany, where the first rough
draft of the Declaration of Independence
came to light, and then return to see
these panels rent asunder by the workmen engaged in demolishing it, is to

fully appreciate the capacities of a
miserable thin-skinned patriotism. As
the work of vandalism progressed, curious things came to light: a few old
French coins, an antiquated tea-chest inlaid with ivory, and a dainty eighteenth-
century flat-iron for the frills and ruffles
of former gallants—things of another
epoch—recalling the Reign of Terror
with its hasty departures, its deserted
palaces and deserted lawns run wild with
hyacinth and daisy.

If the down-town New-Yorker takes
but little interest in the significance of his
landmarks, his brother in Harlem cares
still less, for neither is imaginative. The
latter's temperament craves something
more vital, more tangible; and when the
conversation turns to local legend and
bizarre incidents, he shows an intense
appreciation. Late one cloudy afternoon
last summer Bill Conlin rowed me
through the "Kills" past Morrisania
and cheerfully dismissed it with, "It's
an old castle; they're goin' to tear it
down." But when we had entered the
treacherous currents that sweep in dangerous eddies past the almost unnavigable

channels in the rear of Blackwells Island, he showed signs of animation, the direct cause of which I perceived to be the long point stretching out before us, upon whose green turf were frequent ochre-colored furrows—the scars of recent excavating—and along whose shores walked sundry listless figures in blue overalls.

"Those are the dopes from the funny-house takin' an airin'," he observed, indicating the distant blue spots that moved aimlessly about the turf. Then he became visibly irritated.

"It's a pity the day ain't fine or they'd be out diggin' their canal," he mused.

I was somewhat in the dark, when he enlightened me.

"You see, it's this way," he went on. "Even a guy who's nutty gits tired o' talkin' it all over with himself. It's wearin' on him to have to give all the answers; so one o' the doctors over there hits on a new idea, and next day has all the dopes lined up—guys wot thought they was bank presidents side by side with others wot simply stood and picked at things—all looked alike to him; and that there doctor was chuck full o' brains, and could hand it out in a line o' talk with the best o' the lawyers.

"MORRISANIA," THE GOUVERNEUR MORRIS MANSION
Etched on copper by C. H. White

A BOAT CLUB ON THE HARLEM

Etched on copper by C. H. White

"'Friends,' sez he, after he had them all bunched together, 'we're goin' to dig a canal to cut off that there point,' sez he. 'Are ye on?' sez he, and some o' them waved at him and grinned and almost understood him. 'Fall to!' yells the doctor, 'and let's see how fast you can do it.' And when the warden give them spades and wheelbarrows you should have seen the dirt fly! They no sooner gits the canal dug, when the doctor comes down agin and steps behind a tree to wipe the smile off his face, and starts in again. 'Friends,' sez he, 'the administration has changed their minds,' sez he, 'and have decided to have the canal run through in the opposite direction; so you'll oblige me by fillin' this wan up and beginnin' th' other. It's a good job you've made, boys, and accept me compliments; it's a *very* nice little canal,' sez he, pattin' a couple o' them over the head. 'Ta, ta!' sez he, fadin' away.

"Year in and year out they keep on diggin' that there canal, and I only heard tell of one guy in the bunch who ever had the brains to see that somethin' must be wrong; and when the doctor begun givin' his little song and dance about the administration changin' their minds again and movin' the canal four points to the west, a lad named Leary, from County Cork, Ireland, who was out there on trial, butted in with, 'Say—will you tell me who the blazes voted fer this administration?' And they thrun him out of the funny-house next day . . . a sane man, fer fear he'd contaminate the rest."

THE STORY OF A STREET
(PART 4)

WITH the last exultant echo of Evacuation day Wall Street relapsed into the lethargy which had long pervaded the entire community. Many American cities had endured grievous hardships during the war; a few had been pillaged and partially burned; more than one had been practically obliterated; but for seven years New York had been remorselessly exploited to the point of exhaustion. Indeed, the city which the British abandoned in the fall of 1783 bore very little resemblance to the social and commercial centre they had wrested from Washington in the first year of the Revolution. Much of it was in an indescribable state of dilapidation and decay, part of it was in absolute ruins, and all of it was fairly reeking with dirt. In fact, the whole aspect of the place, with its empty houses and vacant streets patrolled by herds of prowling hogs, suggested a deserted village, and this is what it had virtually become. Of the twenty-five thousand inhabitants it had boasted in 1776 not more than twelve thousand remained at the end of the war, and those were by no means the flower of the population. Many of the best people had taken refuge in their country houses at the very first sign of trouble; all the patriots of ability and character had retired with Washington's retreating forces; most of the influential loyalists had anticipated the withdrawal of the royal troops, and between these various emigrations New York had lost all its leading citizens, many of whom had gone never to return. Certainly the remaining residents did not display any extraordinary energy or public spirit after the army of occupation departed, and for some months the wasted city made no effort to revive its commerce or set its dismantled house in order.

By February, 1784, however, a number of familiar faces began to reappear, and early in that month a small group of forceful men gathered in John Simmons' tavern, a little wooden building lying at the northwest corner of Wall and Nassau streets, to install James Duane as first American Mayor of New York. In view of the impoverished condition of the community this public-spirited citizen had requested that the inauguration ceremonies should be conducted without expense or display; but why Simmons' tavern should have been selected for such an occasion is not altogether certain. It is probable, however, that the City Hall, which had served for so many years as a prison, was not yet fit for civic duty, and that the inn was the nearest available meeting-place; but it may well be that the popularity of its proprietor deprived the Merchants' Coffee House of adding this event to its long list of historic honors, for John Simmons was something of a local celebrity.* Indeed, the fat, good-natured countenance of this rotund Boniface was for many years one of the familiar sights of Wall Street, over which he used to preside, squatting on his doorstep and exchanging salutations with all the passers-by, and the story that part of his tavern had to be torn down to remove his ponderous body when he died is a well authenticated tradition of the times.

James Duane, who was thus unceremoniously invested with the chief magistracy, was a man of wealth and refinement, whose long and efficient public service thoroughly qualified him for his task; and the other officials who were sworn in as his associates were energetic

* Washington attended a banquet at Simmons' Tavern on the evening of Evacuation day.

citizens whose achievements were already upon record. Marinus Willett, who became Sheriff, was the Revolutionary hero who had halted the British troops in Broad Street at the beginning of the war and prevented them from appropriating the arms of the local garrison. Richard Varick, who was appointed Recorder, had been one of Washington's junior secretaries, and had also served under General Schuyler; and Daniel Phoenix, who undertook the office of Chamberlain, was a merchant whose services as a member of the Sons of Liberty and the Committee of One Hundred entitled him to a high place in the public confidence. In fact the task of establishing order out of chaos could scarcely have been placed in stronger hands, and the whole town assumed a more cheerful air as soon as the new government entered upon the performance of its arduous duties.

Business was, of course, practically dead, but the Chamber of Commerce had been keeping up a flicker of life with its meetings at the Merchants' Coffee House, and on April 13, 1784, it was duly incorporated by the New York Legislature, and immediately began systematic work for a revival of trade. There was one field of activity in the prostrate city, however, which needed no encouragement, and that was litigation. Throughout the city the ownership of property was in serious dispute, and what with the conflicting colonial and State laws and the various confiscations, restorations, seizures, and claims under cover of military authority, no one knew what his rights or liabilities were, and confusion reigned supreme. Moreover, in the face of these legal tangles and complications all the Tory advocates had been disbarred, and for once at least in the history of New York the supply of lawyers did not equal the demand.

Into this land of promise two newly fledged lawyers hurried in the winter of 1783, and among the first shingles displayed on Wall Street was that of Alexander Hamilton, while almost around the corner Aaron Burr began his brilliant and eventful professional career.* Had the latter been less resourceful and energetic,

however, he would not have been numbered among the earliest arrivals, for the rules governing admission to the bar were strict, and he had served less than one of the required three years' legal apprenticeship. But no such obstacle could daunt a man of Burr's calibre, and he straightway journeyed to Albany and presented his case before the court in person. He could have completed his apprenticeship years ago, he argued, had he not been employed in the service of the army, and no rule could be intended to injure one whose only misfortune was having sacrificed his time, his constitution, and his fortune to his country. This appeal naturally won the court, and the rules having been suspended, the candidate easily passed the required examination and hastened to New York, where he speedily acquired an enormous practice. Indeed, for a time Burr and Hamilton had few rivals in the field, but in July, 1784, John Jay* returned from a successful mission to Europe, and with his advent, which was marked by a public reception in Wall Street and the presentation of the freedom of the city, a formidable competitor for legal honors was added to the rapidly growing list. But although the roll of the bar soon included over forty practising attorneys, Hamilton and Burr virtually had the pick and choice of business, and the judgment displayed by each man in exercising his preference was exceedingly characteristic, for Burr never took a case unless he felt sure of winning it, and Hamilton would advocate any cause in which he thoroughly believed. In fact, he had not been long in practice before he risked his popularity and even imperilled his life by defending a rich Tory sued by a poor woman under the terms of the Trespass Act.† This law had been passed for the express purpose of penalizing loyalists, and no better opportunity for aiding a needy citizen at the expense of the common enemy had yet occurred. Under such circumstances the defence was not only a forlorn hope, but a most ungrateful task. Yet Hamilton boldly attacked the law, declaring that it violated the provisions of the treaty of

* Hamilton's office was at No. 58 (now 33) Wall Street. Burr's was at No. 10 Little Queen (Cedar) Street.

* Jay's office was at No. 8 Broad Street.

† This case was known as Rutgers *vs.* Waddington.

Drawn by Harry Fenn

WALL STREET IN 1784

Based on records and prints in Lenox Library and New York Historical Society In foreground is the tavern at corner of Wall and Nassau streets; adjoining it the dismantled Presbyterian Church; at the intersection of Broadway the ruins of Trinity are indicated

peace guaranteeing protection to the Tories in the enjoyment of their property rights, and so ably did he present his case that he carried the day in spite of popular clamor. This notable legal triumph was achieved in the Mayor's Court, which was then held in a small building at the southwest corner of Wall and Broad streets, and here many of New York's most famous lawyers received their preliminary training. The men with whom Wall Street thus became acquainted, besides Burr, Jay, and Hamilton, were James Kent, Brockholst Livingston, Morgan Lewis, Robert Troup, Egbert Benson, Abraham de Peyster, Josiah Ogden Hoffman, and John Lawrence, some of whom were destined to become jurists of international fame, and many of them were soon engaged in re-establishing credit and promoting plans for civic betterment. Early in 1784 the Bank of New York was organized under Hamilton's guidance at the Merchants' Coffee House,* and that same historic building had the honor of witnessing the first practical movement against slavery; for there, close to the site of the old slave-market, were held the early meetings of the Society for the Manumission of Slaves, of which Jay subsequently became the president.

Meanwhile Wall Street had been gradually clearing away its seven years' accumulation of dirt and wreckage, and by June, 1784, the Presbyterian Church, which had been practically dismantled in transforming it into an army hospital, was sufficiently repaired to welcome its returning congregation. No immediate effort was made, however, to rebuild Trinity, and for some years its melancholy ruins stared down a sadly dilapidated highway. Of course the houses which had once been its pride were still standing, but they had been roughly handled, and their owners could not afford to put them in proper condition; so the street remained shabby and neglected, and such was its condition when the Continental Congress announced its intention of making its headquarters in New York. Here was a great oppor-

tunity for the struggling city, for the presence of Congress, impotent as that body had become, undoubtedly enhanced its importance and prestige, but the civic authorities were ill prepared to take advantage of the opportunity. Indeed, there were no suitable accommodations available for the visiting legislators, and the City Hall, which was finally placed at their disposal, was not much more than habitable. Nevertheless, the municipality offered the best it had, surrendering virtually the whole of the renovated City Hall and removing its own officials and records to the building on the southwest corner of Wall and Broad streets, which housed the Mayor's Court. Thus in 1785 all the representatives of the national as well as the municipal and State authority were concentrated in Wall Street,* and here daily congregated such men as John Hancock, Rufus King, Nathan Dane, Charles Pinckney, Richard Henry Lee, James Monroe, James Madison, and other distinguished statesmen of national repute, who with the lawyers and city officials in the building on the opposite corner constituted the Wall Street men of their day.

The presence of the Continental Congress and the steady influx of visitors soon brought about a sharp demand for accommodations in the residence section of the city, and while the price of almost everything else was falling, rents in Wall Street rose so that it was impossible to obtain even a very modest dwelling for less than £70 and taxes—an exorbitant figure in those days,—and this naturally affected the price of land. Not many sales occurred, however, for in 1786 the street experienced what was probably its first financial panic, and such was the stringency in the money market that cash practically disappeared from circulation. Indeed, credit throughout the whole country was almost suspended, and the conflicting laws of the various States discouraged business enterprise and threatened the complete extinction of trade.

---

* The bank was first housed in the Walton Mansion, 156 Queen (Pearl) Street; later at 11 Hanover Square, and later still at No. 48 Wall Street.

* Here on July 13, 1787, was passed the famous ordinance which dedicated the great Northwest to freedom, and virtually determined the slavery struggle which was even then beginning.

Such was the situation when the great struggle began for the formation of a permanent national government, and into this contest Hamilton plunged with the ardor of an enthusiast and all the unselfishness of a true patriot. There was much in the proposed Constitution which he did not approve, and his splendid legal practice could not be neglected without great personal sacrifice; but from the fall of 1786 to the summer of 1788 he worked unremittingly with voice and pen for the cause of the Union, and it was during this critical period that he wrote and published the famous Federalist papers which so profoundly affected the result. No less than sixty-three of those eighty-five brilliant essays were written by Hamilton in his office, No. 33 (then 58) Wall Street, and had the highway no other claim to historic interest its association with that epoch-making achievement would suffice to assure it national fame. Despite the stupendous efforts of the Federal leaders, however, and the strong support of almost the entire city, there seemed very little chance that the State of New York would ratify the Constitution, for the country districts were bitterly opposed to its adoption, and their representatives commanded a majority of the votes. Nevertheless, Hamilton continued to fight with unabated courage, and on the 26th of July, 1788, he succeeded in turning the hostile majority into a minority by a narrow margin of three votes, and returned triumphant to the city, where great crowds gathered in Wall Street and welcomed him with cheers, while all the bells in town were rung and a salute of eleven guns was fired in his honor.

Four weeks after this momentous vic-

tory Wall Street was alive with workmen removing the blackened ruins of Trinity Church and tearing down the City Hall, which was to be virtually transformed into a new structure dedicated to the use of the first Congress of the United States. The task of designing this building and superintending its erection was entrusted

OLD WATCH HOUSE

At the southwest corner of Wall and Broad streets, on the site of the famous Mayor's Court

to Major Pierre Charles l'Enfant, a French engineer who had served in the Revolution with great distinction under Baron Steuben, and was to win undying fame by planning the future capital of the nation.* The edifice which this distinguished architect located on the site now partially occupied by the Sub-Treasury Building and the southern end of Nassau Street, was fated to have a very short history, and the only mark it or its famous predecessors have left is the curious jog in the northwest corner of Wall and Nassau streets, which marks the turn of the lane or alley bounding their western foothold. But at its inception New York believed it was to be a monument for the ages, and this idea was fairly justified. Certainly no build-

* L'Enfant is also credited with having designed a portion of St. Paul's Church.

ing of such imposing proportions or such artistic design had ever been projected in any American city, and the sum expended on its construction was wholly unprecedented; but the speed with which it was erected and the quarrels between the architect and contractors undoubtedly resulted in bad workmanship and sealed its doom. At its completion, however, it not only realized but surpassed all expectations; for its exterior effect, with its stately arches and classic columns, was exceedingly dignified and imposing, and the interior decorations were the wonder and admiration of all beholders. Indeed, the marble pavement, the painted ceilings, the crimson damask canopies and hangings and handsome furniture, were considered altogether too magnificent by the anti-Federalist press, which saw in them new proofs of the aristocratic tendencies of the new government, and bitterly attacked the distinguished architect, who in the end received little glory and no pay for his services.*

It was the 3d of March, 1789, before the Recorder formally tendered the build-

* The Common Council offered L'Enfant $750 or a grant of city lots (which are to-day of great value) and the Freedom of the City. He deemed these provisions wholly inadequate, however, and refused to accept them. It is interesting to note that Washington

ing to Congress,† but very few of the Senators or Representatives had then himself evidently found L'Enfant rather difficult during the building of the Federal City, as the national capital was then called, for in one of his letters he writes: " It is much to be regretted, however common the case is, that men who possess talents that fit them for peculiar purposes should almost invariably be under the influence of an untoward disposition or are sottish, idle or possessed of some other disqualification by which they plague all with whom they are concerned. But I did not expect to have met with such perverseness in Major L'Enfant.

† Philadelphia was even then showing jealousy of New York, as appears from the following letter addressed to Recorder Richard Varick:

" DR. SIR,—It is in my opinion entirely necessary that the Common Council should be convened this day in order to pass an act for appropriating the City Hall to the use of Congress. The act should be published in the papers and notified by yourself, or if you are not well enough, by a committee or member of your board to the Senators and Representatives as they arrive. The Philadelphians are endeavoring to raise some cavils on this point. The thing must not pass the day. For propriety absolutely requires that the members should be offered a place by to-morrow which is the day for assembling.

Yrs   A. HAMILTON.
" March 3rd, 1789.
" To Richard Varick, Esqr."

From original (hitherto unpublished) MS. in collection of the Hon. John D. Crimmins.

WALL STREET IN 1789
Federal Hall is shown at the head of Broad Street

FEDERAL HALL

Erected on Wall Street in 1789 for the use of Congress.
On the balcony Washington took the Presidential oath

arrived in the city, and on the day appointed for the opening session there was no quorum in either House. Indeed, it was not until the 30th of March that the House of Representatives organized, with Frederick Augustus Muhlenberg, of Pennsylvania, in the Speaker's chair, and six more days elapsed before proceedings were initiated in the Senate. On that day, however, the Congress performed its first important duty, and the following morning a brief paragraph in the daily papers announced that a canvass of the electoral vote taken in Federal Hall on Wall Street April 6, 1789, had resulted in the unanimous election of Washington as first President of the United States, and that John Adams, as recipient of the next highest vote, had been declared Vice-President.

From that time forward the city was in a flutter of excitement and expectation, and the plans for Washington's reception were discussed on every side. Even the arrival of Adams on April 20th

and his formal installation on the 21st, though attended by highly dignified ceremonies, attracted scarcely any attention, and the news of the ovations which Washington was receiving on his journey from Virginia stimulated the citizens to make New York's welcome worthy of the greatest event in its history. Certainly Wall Street, which had completely recovered its prestige, rose to the occasion, and a brave sight it presented to the crowds which invaded it on the morning of April 23, 1789. From the East River to the rapidly rising Trinity Church flags and banners waved from every building, many of which were also decorated with wreaths of flowers and branches of evergreen; the stairs of Murray's Wharf were carpeted and the rails hung with crimson cloth, and on the pediment of Federal Hall appeared a colossal eagle grasping thirteen arrows and bearing the arms of the United States, which had been recently installed with imposing ceremonies as a finishing touch to the Congressional building.

Washington arrived at Elizabethtown Point, New Jersey, by nine o'clock on the morning of the 23d, but it was three o'clock in the afternoon before the roar of cannon and clashing of bells announced to the assembled throngs that his magnificent state barge, manned by thirteen pilots in white uniforms, had been sighted in the East River, and by that time the whole water front was black with humanity and every roof and window crowded to its utmost capacity. On swept the barge with an accompanying wave of cheers toward the Wall Street wharf, from which Captain Lockyer had made his ignominious exit fifteen years before, and as it swung alongside that historic landing-stage* the bands joined the bells and the cannon in tumultuous welcome. Then the man upon whom all eyes centred rose from his place in the stern of the barge, his plain uniform of buff and blue contrasting sharply with the crimson trappings of the stairs, and as his hand touched the rail the thunderous roar of cheers which greeted him silenced the music and the bells. Then on foot through that seething crowd, declining the carriage provided for his use, Washington passed, amid the acclamations of the assembled thousands, up Wall Street to Queen (Pearl), and thence through that thoroughfare, whose sidewalks were so wonderfully wide that "three persons could walk abreast," to the Franklin House, which had been prepared for his reception.

Thus ended this day of rejoicing, but during all the following week the city was agog with excitement, for from every direction and in all sorts of conveyances visitors kept arriving upon the scene, until every tavern and private dwelling was filled to overflowing, and even the meanest accommodations commanded extravagant premiums. Meanwhile more Senators and Representatives were making their appearance in Federal Hall, and such men as Oliver Ellsworth, Robert Morris, Samuel Otis, Roger Sher-

man, James Madison, Jonathan Trumbull, Richard Bland Lee, Elbridge Gerry, William Samuel Johnson, John Page, and others whose names were or were to become famous in the history of the nation, could be daily seen in Wall Street discussing questions of state etiquette and ceremonial and other details of the impending inauguration. Indeed, all the preparations for this great event had not been completed when the day arrived; and when church bells began summoning the people to their various places of worship for the special services ordained for the morning of April 30, 1789, the Congressional committees hastily convened to perfect their arrangements. Meanwhile part of the inaugural procession formed in front of Federal Hall, and by the time the congregation of the Presbyterian Church issued from their services they found Wall Street ablaze with bunting and festooned with evergreens, and densely packed with spectators who blocked every approach and crowded all the neighboring roofs and windows. It was twelve o'clock, however, before the procession started from the Presidential mansion, and even then the two Houses of Congress were still discussing with some heat and no little confusion the manner in which they should receive Washington and the form in which he should be addressed. Thus another hour slipped by, the dense crowds massed in Wall and Broad streets maintaining perfect order; and finally at one o'clock the head of the procession hove in sight, moving from Great Dock (Pearl) Street into Broad. Captain Stakes and his troopers easily parting the cheering multitude. Within a short distance of Federal Hall the Presidential carriage halted, and Washington, escorted by General Samuel Blatchley Webb (the Beau Brummel of the town), Colonel Nicholas Fish, Colonel William Smith, Colonel Franks, Major Leonard Bleecker, and John R. Livingston, passed through the double line of troopers to the Senate-chamber, followed by the other committees and guests of honor in dignified procession.

Then something very like a panic ensued among those in charge of the arrangements, for not until this critical moment was it discovered that an im-

---

* Among those waiting on the wharf were Governor Clinton, Colonel Morgan Lewis (subsequently Governor of New York), the Mayor and other civil officials, the French and Spanish Ambassadors, and many army officers.

WALL STREET FROM WATER STREET TO THE EAST RIVER ABOUT 1790

portant detail had been completely neglected and that there was no Bible in Federal Hall for the administration of the oath. Chancellor Livingston, however, rose to the occasion, and, hastily despatching a messenger to St. John's (Masonic) Lodge at 115 Broadway, procured the necessary volume, and in a few moments Washington stepped upon the balcony fronting on Wall Street. For an instant he stood in full sight of the assembled multitude, but the wild outburst of cheering which greeted his appearance drove him a step backward, visibly affected. He was dressed in a suit of dark brown cloth with metal buttons ornamented with eagles, his stockings were white silk, and his shoe buckles silver. At his side he carried a simple steel-hilted dress sword, his powdered hair was worn in the fashion of the times, and close beside him stood Chancellor Robert Livingston, wearing his official robe. Grouped about these two men stood John Adams, George Clinton, Roger Sherman, Baron Steuben, Samuel Otis, Richard Henry Lee, General Arthur St. Clair, and General Knox, and behind them, but not visible from the street, stood members of Congress and other distinguished witnesses.*

There was a moment's pause as the company took their positions, and then Samuel Otis, the Secretary of State, carrying a crimson cushion on which rested the hastily borrowed Bible, presented it to the Chancellor, who administered the oath; whereupon Washington kissed the book, and the official proclamation, "Long live George Washington, President of the United States," ended with a thunderous crash of artillery and a renewed burst of cheering.

Such was the day of glory which made New York the capital of the nation, in which for a brief but brilliant period Wall Street was to reign politically and socially supreme.

* Alexander Hamilton watched the scene from the window of his house on the opposite side of the street. Washington Irving, then six years of age, was also among the spectators.

THE NEW YORK CUSTOM-HOUSE

THREE things are perfectly clear to citizens of New York : first, the United States of America constitute the greatest country on earth; second, New York is the greatest city in the country; third, the Custom-house is the greatest institution in the city.

The Custom-house is a plain Doric building, of Quincy granite, with a portico of twelve front, four middle, and two rear granite columns, each thirty-eight feet high and four and a half feet in diameter. It has a frontage of 200 feet on Wall Street, a depth of about 160 feet on William and Hanover streets, and is 77 feet high. The rotunda has a height of 80 feet, and the dome is supported on eight pilasters of fine variegated Italian marble. Constructed for a Merchants' Exchange, at a cost of $1,800,000, it was purchased and occupied by the national government in 1862, and ought to be sold at the earliest opportunity. It is dark, damp, inconvenient, badly ventilated, and altogether inadequate for present uses. President Arthur, when Collector of the Port of New York, wisely advocated the erection of a suitable edifice on the block bounded by Whitehall and State streets, Bowling Green, and Whitehall Square. That would be a more eligible site. It is near to the Barge Office, which covers the water-front sold by the city to the government for $5000.

Plain as the Custom-house is, it is the commercial heart of the American people. What passes there is felt by every man, woman, and child in the land. There most of the duties are collected on the foreign woollens, silks, linens, cottons, and on the hats, bonnets, and furs they wear; on the carpets and mattings they tread; on the sugars, molasses, confectionery, spices, fruits, and breadstuffs they eat; on the spirits, wines, and malt liquors they drink; on the watches and jewelry they carry; on the earthenware, china, and glass that cover their tables; on the paintings that adorn their walls, the books that fill up their libraries, and the iron, steel, and other metallic instruments indispensable to their uses. All these articles cost the consumer more because of the work that is done at the Custom-house.

The total value of merchandise, free and dutiable, imported into the United States during the year ending June 30, 1883, was $723,180,914. The total value of dutiable merchandise entered for consumption, on arrival and after withdrawal from warehouse, in the United States during the same period, was $493,916,384. The entire value of dutiable merchandise imported into the United States, entered for consumption, and warehoused for payment of duties, in the fiscal year ending June 30, 1883, was $515,676,196. The total amount of duties collected thereon

was $214,706,496, or 43.49 per cent. of the whole value as officially stated.

This enormous revenue from duties on imported goods is the principal means wherewith the United States government maintains the army, the navy, and the civil service, pays the interest on the national debt, reduces the principal, and effects needed improvements.

In the fiscal year ending June 30, 1883, there were collected at the port of New York in duties on foreign merchandise no less than $146,483,964, or 68.5 per cent. of the aggregate amount collected in all the ports of the country. This fact shows the great national importance of the New York Custom-house. Another fact of similar bearing is that the foreign commerce of the United States, which has increased nearly one hundred per cent. since 1866, must in the future, as in the past, be mainly carried on through New York.

With the exception of Mexico and Canada, our commercial intercourse with other nations is conducted by means of steam and sailing vessels. By far the greater portion of these is owned by foreigners. The tonnage of foreign vessels entered at American ports increased from 3,117,034 tons in 1866 to 10,526,176 tons in 1883; whereas the American tonnage entered from foreign ports only increased from 1,891,453 tons in 1866 to 2,834,681 tons in 1883.

Great Britain, which, independently of her colonial and other possessions, is our largest commercial correspondent, and which imported from us goods valued at $425,424,174 in the year ending June 30,

EXHIBIT SHOWING THE IMPORTS FROM GREAT BRITAIN AND HER DEPENDENCIES INTO THE PORTS OF THE UNITED STATES DURING THE YEAR ENDING JUNE 30, 1883.

Country.	Number of Vessels.	Tonnage.	Steam Vessels.	Sailing Vessels.	Value of Imports.
England..........................	2,783	6,309,498	1,189	1,594	$161,960,672
Scotland	377	915,416	172	205	18,702,898
Ireland	39	30,328	....	39	7,959,049
Gibraltar.......................	97	160,184	48	49	4,573
Nova Scotia, New Brunswick, and Prince Edward Island	3,562	489,910	125	3,437	6,091,406
Newfoundland and Labrador	40	12,258	7	33	446,718
British West Indies.............	631	397,372	160	471	8,736,112
British Guiana	137	64,281	14	123	5,946,429
British Honduras	13	6,868	3	10	531,839
British East Indies.............	85	97,738	3	82	19,467,800
British Hong-Kong	77	159,007	36	41	1,918,894
British Possessions in Africa	27	26,551	7	20	1,840,020
British Possessions in Australasia ..	135	169,171	....	135	4,021,395
All other British Possessions	....	......	....	....	1,017,281
	8,003	8,838,582	1,764	6,239	$238,645,086

THE BARGE OFFICE.

1883, exporting to us within the same period goods amounting to $188,622,619, is, naturally enough, the principal owner of this shipping. She takes 51.6 per cent. of the total value of American exports, and sends to us 26 per cent. of all our imports.

In 1883 the total value of merchandise imported and exported at the port of New York was $857,430,637, or 55.43 per cent. of the whole value of our foreign commerce.

The tonnage of British vessels entering at United States ports in the last fiscal year amounted to 6,775,526 tons, a falling off in two years of 1,682,271 tons, but still constituting nearly two-thirds of the entire foreign tonnage entering at our ports.

EXHIBIT SHOWING NUMBER AND TONNAGE OF AMERICAN AND FOREIGN VESSELS WHICH ENTERED THE PORT OF NEW YORK FROM GREAT BRITAIN AND HER DEPENDENCIES IN THE YEAR ENDING JUNE 30, 1883; ALSO VALUE OF IMPORTS.

	American Vessels.		Foreign Vessels.		Aggregate.		Imports at New York.
	No.	Tons.	No.	Tons.	No.	Tons.	
England........................	64	86,679	756	1,838,438	820	1,925,117	$92,252,820
Scotland........................	..	....	128	326,290	128	326,290	16,082,713
Ireland.........................	5	5,558	28	17,557	33	23,115	7,487,061
Gibraltar.......................	..	....	44	75,776	44	75,776	4,573
Nova Scotia, New Brunswick, and Prince Edward Island	298	52,689	517	104,840	815	157,529	798,090
Quebec, Ontario, Manitoba, and Northwest Territory	..	....	1	118	1	118	1,873
Newfoundland and Labrador......	..	....	10	3,437	10	3,437	339,652
British West Indies	142	45,882	254	185,798	396	231,680	6,140,133
British Guiana.................	38	11,159	35	16,329	73	27,488	2,489,261
British Honduras	1	105	9	3,174	10	3,279	146,890
British East Indies.............	30	32,933	81	88,644	111	121,577	17,113,230
Hong-Kong	17	16,235	7	7,407	24	23,642	1,755,216
British Possessions in Africa and adjacent Islands	4	1,746	22	10,640	26	12,386	1,329,695
British Possessions in Australasia ..	3	1,372	8	2,791	11	4,163	1,803,334
All other British Possessions	..	....	1	287	1	287	1,005,964
	602	254,358	1,901	2,681,526	2,503	2,935,884	$148,750,505

Mr. George Hillier, superintendent of the Custom-house building, who entered the revenue service in 1841, keeps record of all the steam-ships entering New York from Europe. The average number of weekly arrivals is *forty*. This is a marvellous exhibit, in view of the fact that in 1845, only thirty-nine years ago, there cer, a Surveyor, and an Appraiser of the port of New York. Each is nominated for office by the President of the United States, confirmed therein by vote of the national Senate, and may retain his position for four years, unless removed for satisfactory reasons by joint Executive and Senatorial authority.

WILLIAM H. ROBERTSON, COLLECTOR OF THE PORT OF NEW YORK.

was only one steamer, the *Syria*, plying between New York and Liverpool.

The local administration of the national statutes regulating this vast and rapidly growing commerce, together with the collection of the differential duties imposed on imported merchandise, is intrusted to a Collector, assisted by a Naval Offi-

Collector William H. Robertson, a vigorous and robust gentleman of sixty years, was commissioned by President Garfield, June 29, 1881, and brought to his new office the experience acquired in a long and honorable legal, judicial, and legislative career. Whether as Congressman, State Senator, or judge, his reputation was of the highest character, and justified the expectations that have since been so abundantly realized. The discussions in the national Senate pertinent to his nomination, and the results to which they gave birth, will ever constitute one of the most memorable chapters in American political history.

The Collector's duty is to see that all vessels and the merchandise therein contained, coming within the jurisdiction of his district, are duly entered at the Customhouse; that legally responsible parties be held to their liabilities; that the other branches of the customs service be enabled to do their duty as by law required; that the duties be properly assessed and collected, and that the legal disposition be made of goods entered in bond, or otherwise, or which are unclaimed; that smuggling and other frauds be prevented; that claims for drawback or refund be paid upon due proof only; that just fines, penalties, and forfeitures be imposed and enforced; and to report fully, as by law required, on all that pertains to the customs revenue, to the Treasury Department at Washington.

It is the duty of the Naval Officer to verify the clerical work done in the Collector's office. The latter is performed under laws and regulations so complicated as to render independent revision, in order to insure perfect accuracy, indispensably necessary. The Naval Officer is sworn to correct errors, inadvertencies, and neglect; and to enforce strict compliance with the national statutes. His action is co-ordinate with that of the Collector "in all matters affecting the collection of customs revenue, so far as they involve the amount of money collectable and collected; the proper record, adjustment, correction, and certification of accounts, including those of drawbacks and refunds ; the enforcement of all laws and regulations for the safety of the revenue, and excluding any and all concern in the administration of the machinery of collection." General Charles K. Graham, formerly Surveyor of the Port, is now at the head of this department. The average cost per annum of the Naval Officer's department in New York for the past twelve or thirteen years does not exceed one-tenth of one per cent. of the duties collected at that port, and it certainly yields vastly more than that sum to the government in return.

The Surveyor is charged with the duty— subject in all cases to the Collector—of superintending and directing all inspectors, weighers, measurers, and gaugers within the port; of weekly reporting all neglect of duty to the Collector; of visiting, by proxy, all arriving vessels, and reporting in writing every morning to his superior all that have arrived from foreign ports on the preceding day; specifying the names and denominations of the vessels, the masters' names, whence arrived, whether laden or in ballast, to what nation belonging, and, if American vessels, whether the masters have or have not complied with the law requiring a definite number of manifests of the cargo on board. He may act in certain cases with the Collector and Naval Officer in allowing ships' manifests to be corrected. He must also put one or more inspectors on board each vessel immediately after its arrival in port; ascertain and rate, acording to law, the proof, quantities, and kinds of distilled spirits imported; examine into the correspondency between the goods imported in any vessel and the deliveries thereof, according to the inspectors' returns and the permits for landing the same, and report any error or discrepancy to the Collector and the Naval Officer; superintend the lading for exportation of all goods entered for the benefit of any drawback, bounty, or allowance, and report on the correspondency between the kind, quantity, and quality of the goods so laded with the entries and permits granted therefor; test the weights, measures, and other instruments used in ascertaining the duties on imports, with public standards; report disagreements, and execute directions for correcting them agreeably to the standard. The duties of this office devolve upon Mr. James L. Benedict, formerly Auditor of the department.

It is the duty of the Appraiser to ascertain and report to the Collector, under that official's orders, the quantity, description, and value of all imported merchandise, and to give his opinion as to what rate of duty such goods are liable to pay.

The duties of the Collector and his assistants not only include the collection of the tariff on goods entered for consumption, and the proper entry and clearance of vessels, but also the surveillance, appraisement, and forwarding of goods imported by citizens in other sections of the country, through the port of New York,

INSPECTION OF CABIN PASSENGERS' BAGGAGE ON THE DOCK.

and on which the imposts are collected at the places of destination. In the due discharge of these onerous, delicate, and often difficult duties, ability, faithfulness, and integrity in all the officials are essentially necessary. Added to these qualities, expert knowledge, careful training, judicial experience, and culture are also requisite in many instances. All these qualifications are sought — and should uniformly be sought — by subjecting applicants for office, and for promotion in

INSPECTION OF IMMIGRANTS' BAGGAGE.

office, to judicious competitive examinations, under regulations prescribed by the Civil Service Commission.

In February, 1884, there were 1538 public servants employed in the New York Custom-house, at salaries amounting to $1,988,237 per annum. Of these, 232, with salaries amounting to $311,513, in the Collector's special department, had been appointed under the Civil Service regulations. There were also 34, with salaries amounting to $50,800, in the Naval Office, and 126, with salaries amounting to $176,083, in the Appraiser's department, who had been appointed under the same regulations. Of the 1538 employés in the Custom-house, 470 were in the Collector's office, 95 in the Naval Office, 321 in the Appraiser's, 11 in the General Appraiser's, and 35 in the Surveyor's; while there were 322 inspectors, 9 inspectresses, 117 night inspectors, 94 weighers and gaugers, and 64 store-keepers.

Among the officials not subjected to competitive examinations are the Collector, Deputy Collectors, Naval Officer, Deputy Naval Officers, Surveyor, appraisers, engineers, ushers, laborers, etc.

The members of the large force belonging to the Collector's office are distributed into eight divisions, including the Auditor's, Cashier's, Warehouse, Navigation, Entry, Invoice and Order, Law, and Public Store departments. Besides these, there is a Customs Bureau at Castle Garden, with a superintendent in charge; and a Correspondence Bureau at the Custom-house, in charge of the Chief Clerk of Customs. Mr. Joseph Treloar, the latter official, enjoyed twenty-one years of training under the tutelage of Assistant-Collector Clinch; has been in office more than thirty years; is an encyclopædia of customs law and literature; holds all his knowledge at instantaneous command, and has the courage of his convictions. Each of the last six departments is in charge of a deputy collector, has a chief clerk, and a suitable number of subordinates. The Bureau of Statistics is included in the Auditor's department. There are also two deputy collectors for the current business of the office, an assistant collector at Jersey City, and a special deputy collector, Mr. Joseph Barrett, who is also the Collector's private secretary.

How the functionaries in these several departments come into active service is apparent as the progress of passengers and goods through the Custom-house is traced.

Armed with a pass from the Surveyor, the inquirer proceeds to the Barge Office, at the Battery. This is a granite and iron building of irregular shape, with rooms for the Surveyor's staff, day, night, and female inspectors, examiners, officials from the Collector's, Naval Officer's, and Appraiser's offices, and for the safe-keep-ing of public documents and records. A capacious shed, with 10,000 square feet of area, projects seaward from the building. Close by is the dock where he takes the revenue-cutter, in command of a uniformed officer of the revenue marine service, who is also a customs official, and subject to the Collector's orders. The sail down the bay on a bright, breezy May morning is a pleasurable experience not soon to be forgotten. The boarding in-

SEARCHING A FEMALE SMUGGLER.

spectors, as well as the revenue marine officer, willingly impart information.

The incoming steamer—the *Servia*, of the Cunard Line, will answer as an example for all—reported by telegraph from Fire Island, is soon met as she slowly enters port under the guidance of a skillful pilot. The breathing ocean monster, bearing still on her nostrils the salt of much tempestuous spray, is covered with eager Americans returning home, curious foreign tourists, and anxious immigrants gazing for the first time on the shores of the promised land that henceforth is to be their home.

The revenue marine officer assigned to boarding duty, and the inspectors of passengers' baggage, ascend the rope-ladder, as soon as the sanitary examination of the vessel has been completed by the Health Officer of the port. The revenue marine officer demands from the master the manifests of his cargo; and, if the vessel be American, he also demands the crew list, and has the crew mustered and compared with the list. He also identifies, by means of the consul's certificate, any destitute American seamen who may have been brought home in the vessel. Then he certifies the manifests, crew list, and consul's certificates, seals or secures the hatches and openings until the necessary permits for unlading are obtained, and hands over the charge of the vessel to the inspectors who have been temporarily assigned to her, or to superintend the delivery of cargo. At the Barge Office he subsequently makes report of his procedure, and delivers all duplicate manifests and other papers received from the master of the vessel to the boarding officer for transmission to the Collector at the Custom-house.

The examination of personal baggage belonging to returning Americans and to foreign visitors is a matter of great interest to the parties concerned. As soon as the staff officer in charge receives the passenger list from the purser, he and his fellow-officials take their seats at the end of one of the long tables in the saloon. Blanks containing declarations of the different trunks, valises, rugs, etc., and of the dutiable goods contained in them, are on hand, and are filled out consecutively as the passengers, in long lines, present themselves to the inspectors. When the blank is filled out, agreeably to the representations of each individual, or of the head of a family who acts for the whole, he solemnly swears that his statements are true, and signs the document. This is handed to another member of the staff, who numbers and retains it, and gives to the signer a ticket bearing a corresponding number. The signer's name is at the same time checked off on the passenger list by a third officer.

Under the inquiries propounded by the inspectors, the idiosyncrasies of the parties questioned not unfrequently become markedly apparent. Some are jolly, others sulky, and others nervous. Some promptly and others hesitantly respond to the query : "Have you any new or dutiable goods ?" Honest men at once blurt out : "Yes; twelve pairs of kid gloves for a friend;" "A piece of silk for my wife;" "A cloak for my daughter;" "A service of china — here are the bills." The answers are at once entered under the appropriate heading, together with the value of the articles specified, if known by the owner. A peculiar mark is also put on the back of the paper to indicate to the examining inspector that something "declared" is in the baggage of that individual. Experienced travellers pass the ordeal quietly ; others are occasionally restive under the pointed inquisition. While thus engaged, the inspectors answer a thousand and one questions, endlessly varied, about required forms, when the baggage will be examined, the rates of duty, and when the worrying querists will be able to leave the dock. Patience has, or ought to have, her perfect work in these pachydermatous gentlemen.

While this lively scene is in progress the steamer is proceeding up the bay, enters the North River, and slowly moves into her dock. There matters wear a still more exciting aspect. Crowds of expectant friends are in waiting. Eager salutations are exchanged. The voyagers are as willing to quit the luxurious steamer as was Dr. Johnson the ship that he defined as "a prison, with a chance of being drowned." The movable gangway is run from the dock to the deck. The cabin passengers pour down it in ceaseless streams, while the steerage passengers wait wistfully for later debarkation at Castle Garden. The staff officers, declarations in hand, follow. Baggage is landed and deposited in separate piles, according to the initials of the owners' names, the proper label having been affixed on the steamer.

LANDING IMMIGRANTS AT CASTLE GARDEN.

The places are designated by huge letters on the wall of the shed. If there are many Smiths aboard, for instance, there will be a crowded congregation of trunks and owners about S. The examining inspectors are already drawn up in line across the dock, and nothing passes them without due scrutiny. Wearied travellers, who can leave their matters in the hands of friends, are relieved of further waiting, and after quick search of wraps and valises are allowed to depart in peace. As each individual's baggage is brought together, he notifies the staff officer, and hands over his ticket. The officer selects the corresponding declaration, writes the name of an inspector—whom he calls from the line—upon it, and directs immediate examination. This is usually sufficiently thorough. Inspectors, through long practice, become involuntary disciples of Lavater, and such expert critics of human nature that they almost intuitively detect attempted fraud. Dutiable articles, not declared as such, are brought out, valued by the attendant appraiser, entered, with value attached on the declaration, and the owner is obliged to pay the requisite duty to a clerk in attendance for the purpose of receiving it. The inspector also signs his name to the declaration.

The efficiency and courtesy of the Dep-

THE SEIZURE-ROOM.

uty Surveyor, and also of the inspectors on the dock, together with the delicate discharge of their not particularly pleasing duties, are worthy of high praise. Exceptions are few and far between. The questions asked about dresses, laces, cloaks, etc., are not invariably met with precisely truthful rejoinders. To cheat Uncle Sam in revenue matters is regarded as a decidedly venial sin by most of his children, native or adopted. This notion is doubtless an unconscious remnant of the freebooting ethics of forgotten ancestors. It is slowly yielding to higher and better ideas. Even the wealthiest are not exempt from the smuggling mania. One gentleman, whose name is synonymous with almost fabulous wealth, returning from Europe in company with his wife, was compelled to pay about $1800 in duties on her enormous stock of wearing apparel, which he contended was not dutiable, whether it had or had not been worn. He appealed to the Secretary of the Treasury, who decided against him. He then brought suit within ninety days in the United States court. His wife swore that a portion of the whole had been worn in good faith. The duties paid on that portion were refunded, while those on the remainder were retained.

Smuggling is carried on in many ways, and will be carried on while human nature continues to be what it is. Foreign retail traders are adept instructors in the art of evading the payment of duties, as any one who has been in the lace establishment of Des Marets and other merchants at Brussels can testify. The ingenuity of inspectors is taxed to the uttermost to defeat their schemes. Female inspectors are employed to search persons of their own sex who are sent to them by the Deputy Surveyor for that purpose. Of these inspectresses there are nine. In 1866 there were only four. The inspectresses perform their duties, both at Castle Garden and on the docks, in rooms set apart for such searches. Recitals of their experiences are at once amusing and humiliating to believers in the natural goodness of men. German Jews are more addicted to smuggling than people of other nationalities, but none are altogether free from the vice. Modistes and dressmakers are naturally the most frequent and flagrant offenders. Extra gold watches; laces, silks, linens, wound around the body or limbs; human hair in toupees, wigs, and switches sewn into skirts; new dresses stitched to old ones; silks and laces made up into several voluminous skirts—are among ordinary discoveries. One unlucky wight, suspected of complicity in feminine designs, was found to have two sets of point lace in the crown of his hat.

By the 346 saloon passengers arriving at New York in the *Servia*, 230 entries of dutiable goods were made, and on them $946 85 in imposts were collected. The Collector's representative on the dock retains the declarations, makes the entries in his own name, and pays the duties received to the cashier, who receipts for them and checks his account. The revenue from this single source is quite considerable in the course of twelve months.

When all the work of the examining officers on the dock has been performed they return to the Barge Office, and the inspectors assigned to superintend the discharge of the cargo take charge of the vessel.

But what of the immigrants in the steerage? Their turn comes next. In the *Servia* their accommodations have been sumptuous compared with those provided in steamers of Continental lines, and especially in those sailing from Holland. All the oxygen of the Atlantic is needed to save them from the diseases that foul air, unaccustomed food, close contact, and unavoidable uncleanliness induce. But even this must be denied in stormy voyages, and many of them arrive in physical condition that imperatively calls for medical assistance. "Man's inhumanity to man" is often painfully visible on steamship and sailing vessel alike. Matters improve, it is true, but all too slowly. The dens in which many are cribbed, cabined, and confined are often unfit for the use of human beings. The smell of the ship is in the clothing of the unhappy occupants for long weeks after their escape. One vessel brought 1155 steerage passengers from Amsterdam in May, 1882. Spar deck and lower deck were crowded. An average of sixteen people occupied each room. The marvel is that the five deaths on the voyage had not been fifty.

These immigrants are a motley crowd. New York contains representatives of for-

SMUGGLING CIGARS ON THE JERSEY COAST.

ty-four different nationalities. Those Armenians in red fez and Oriental costume will swell the number to forty-five. Small steamers, under the control of a landing agent who contracts with the steam-ship companies, take off the Babel crowd in detachments from all steamers, and convey them to Castle Garden. There, at the inspectors' office, record is kept of the steamers arriving, the dates of

THE ROTUNDA OF THE CUSTOM-HOUSE.

steerage passengers, were thus recorded; 3791 packages were sent to the public store for appraisement, and somewhat less than $10,000 in duties collected upon them. In 1883 the number of immigrants recorded was 405,352.

arrival, the name of each vessel, the port from which she sailed, the number and names of the passengers, the births and deaths during the voyage, the number of packages sent to the public store at Castle Garden, and the names of the inspectors and inspectresses who examined each vessel. In 1881, 941 steamers, bringing 441,110 corded was 405,352. Smuggling among the steerage passengers is mainly confined to persons who have been visiting their friends in Europe. Minute examination occasionally detects pieces of silk and velvet, rings, watches, gold chains, and liquors. Discretion is wisely intrusted to the officials, and is sparingly exercised toward genuine immigrants. Here is one young Teuton whose trunk reveals, now that its false bottom has been knocked out, a formidable array of little phials containing *Magentropfen*, or stomach drops, and oils wherewith to lubricate rheumatic limbs. The value of the whole is about twelve shillings — certainly not an inordinate supply for a dyspeptic Dutchman, and hardly enough to last a hypochondriac Yankee for a single month. The value of the 710 seizures of goods of all classes smuggled by incoming passengers in the year ending June 30, 1883, was $125,519.

For each package sent in for appraisement a check is given to the owner, and also a receipt by the United States Public Store-keeper. This check is returned when the package is taken away. Immigrants being poorer now than formerly, only $9360 were collected in duties in 1883. Free baggage is sent into another department, and is duly checked. After the immigrants have been duly registered, their uncurrent funds exchanged for American currency, and their railroad tickets purchased, the baggage is forwarded, after presentation of tickets at the office, to their destinations in the West, or in other parts of the country. The Castle Garden Express delivers such as is addressed to New York, Newark, and other near cities.

Castle Garden is one of the most beneficent institutions in the world, and owes its present uses largely to Dr. Friedrich Kapp, now a member of the Imperial German Reichsrath, but formerly a resident of New York. It is under the control of nine Commissioners of Emigration, appointed for the term of six years by the Governor and confirmed by the Senate of the State of New York. Thither let us follow a portion of the 6730 immigrants who arrived by seven different steamers on the 15th of May, 1882. The name of each, the date of his arrival, place of departure, number of his family (if any), whither bound, his business, and other particulars, are all registered. This record, together with that of the cabin passengers, is compared with the manifest of each captain, which manifest ought to exhibit the names of all the persons he had on board. It thus becomes a check on the greed of some who have brought more passengers than the law permits, or than were named in the manifests.

Not only do the Commissioners of Emigration protect their often helpless charges against the extortions, robberies, and unspeakable villainies of the human harpies who formerly infested the docks, and preyed upon the luckless incomers—not only do they supply interpreters, maintain an employment bureau, assist in the exchange of funds, purchase of tickets, forwarding of immigrants and baggage—but they also license the boarding-house runners, and subject them to rigid supervision. They further provide for the sick and disabled, the lunatics, and the pregnant women whose husbands, if sick, are sent to the hospital on Ward's Island, furnish medicine to the ailing and trusses to the ruptured, and preserve recorded particulars of all thus coming under their special care by which they may be found and identified in the future.

Near the Information Bureau from 2000 to 2500 people waiting inquiringly for their friends have sometimes been congregated at one time.

The grandly beneficent work of the Emigration Commissioners deserves better medical facilities than the miserably inadequate hospital accommodations at their immediate command in Castle Garden. New York does the work and bears the expense connected with foreign immigration, but the whole country shares in its benefits. The railroads especially profit by it. The cash value of tickets purchased by inward-bound immigrants in 1881 was more than five million dollars. Moneys to the value of eleven millions were exchanged in Castle Garden, and the estimated amount of the drafts, bonds, and other representatives of specie value brought in during the same year was no less than one hundred million dollars. Castle Garden ought to be a national institution.

While all this busy, anxious work is going on at the dock and immigrant landing depot, the captain of the vessel repairs to the Custom-house and enters his vessel by delivering its register, together with his clearance and other papers, and particularly the original manifest of his cargo, to the Collector. He also affirms under oath that he sailed from the port of departure on a certain day, and that his manifest is truthful to the best of his knowledge and belief. He further signs this sworn affirmation, and attaches it to his manifest. Until this is done the bulk of his cargo can not be broken. The manifest is in writing, and contains the name of the vessel, where she is owned, master's name, tonnage, where built, whither bound, where cargo was shipped, the marks and numbers of the several packages, the contents of the packages, consignees' names and residences, and ports of destination, number of passengers, and the nature and amount of the vessel and cabin stores. The manifest is usually in the national language of the vessel, and is made up from the bills of lading, or copies of them, given to shippers of goods, and signed by the captain or his representative. It is an essential document, and copies of it are made to meet the several requisitions of the customs revenue. This statement of the captain or master is noted at once in the register of entries of vessels, and a copy of it is furnished next day to the appraisers.

Within forty-eight hours after arrival the master must also report in writing all necessary information about his vessel to the Surveyor, and particularly the quantities and kinds of spirits, wines, and teas he has on board, the number of packages in which they are contained, together with the marks and numbers, and also his sea stores of spirits, wines, and teas. If the vessel belong to the United States, the master must give to the Collector a true account of the number of persons employed on board since it was last in a United States port, and must pay forty cents per month, for every person so employed, into the Marine Hospital Fund before it can be admitted to entry. Fees and charges are about as numerous in New York as at Niagara. These paid, and legal demands all satisfied, the Collector issues a general order for the delivery of the cargo. This is effected under the supervision of the inspectors in care of the vessel. All cargoes must be unladed between sunrise and sunset. Special permits, however, may be granted by the Collector and Naval Officer to unlade between sunset and sunrise. In this and in many other cases indemnity bonds are required by the Collector.

The scene on the dock during the unlading and delivery of the cargo is one of great interest and suggestiveness. The two discharging inspectors in charge superintend the transfer of the goods from the vessel to the dock; see to it that all goods requiring to be weighed, gauged, measured, or proved are manipulated only by the prop-

er officers; send sample goods and goods ordered for appraisement to the Public Store, and other merchandise to warehouse or elsewhere as directed; allow no goods to leave the dock without due permits; deliver packages to authorized persons; and enter all permits, with specified particulars, to take away goods, and all goods taken away or sent to the Public Store, warehouse, or elsewhere, by marks, numbers, and descriptions, and what goods were apparently damaged on the voyage, in a discharging book. They also take charge of all the specie and valuables on board the vessel; compare the list of stores on board with those furnished by the master at the Collector's office; report dutiable goods and necessary stores to the Collector or Surveyor; seize all articles imported in violation of law, and close and lock the hatches of the vessel at night. They also, within three days after the delivery of the discharging book to the Surveyor, make another return of the discharge of the vessel, supported by permits, orders, and other vouchers, showing what goods were called for and not found, what did not agree with permit or order, what were damaged, what were not included in manifest, what sea stores were on board, and also the names of all officials who performed any duty in connection with the cargo. Discrepancies between ships' manifests and inspectors' returns are subsequently corrected by specific process in case no intention to defraud the government is apparent on the surface. Both manifests and inspectors' returns go through the Bureau of Liquidation and Closing of Vessels' Accounts, and ultimately find their way into that orderly cemetery of dead enterprises known as the Record Room.

When the discharging inspectors close their labors for the day, they are relieved as custodians of revenue interests by the night inspectors, who number 117 men, and are officered by Captain P. C. Bensel and three assistants. This force is composed of vigorous and active men, and includes medical and other students, who in this way acquire the funds necessary to complete their professional education. It is divided into two watches, which alternate in the discharge of duty from sunset to midnight, and from midnight to sunrise. Should any be detailed for all-night duty on vessels lying in the stream, they are excused from service on the following night. The sphere of these duties includes the waters and portions of the shores of New Jersey, Long Island, and New York city.

The night inspectors are appointed to prevent smuggling, are uniformed and armed, and are authorized to stop and search reasonably suspected persons who may go on board or come from the vessel. Their office is by no means a sinecure. It involves watching, exposure, and fatigue. The Cuban steamers have been wont to bring men who inclosed cigars in rubber bags and threw them into the waters of the lower bay. Confederates in boats then picked them up, placed them in express wagons waiting on the shore, and then drove rapidly away. There is something contagious in the glee of wide-awake officials as they relate how they had watched unseen the whole operation until the wagon was ready to start, when they seized the reins, and landed the spoils at the Seizure Room. One French steamer, notorious for smuggling by dribblets, when searched by this force, was found to contain thirteen hundred bottles of spirits, which it was intended to send ashore bottle by bottle. Tins about an inch deep, and fitted to the body under the armpits, have been taken from the bodies of men who were thus stealthily bringing in valuable bay oil. One dealer in human hair, who died in possession of about $200,000, was detected in illicit importations under the shirts of his agents. Another vivacious fellow, belonging to a French steamer, rejoiced in a profitable trade in kid gloves secreted by the dozen in his immense boots. Sailing vessels are watched by special agents, whose duties are irksome enough to render special supervision by superiors a matter of positive necessity. Dealers in contraband goods, scamps who live by their wits, and unscrupulous traders of many kinds tax the resources of human ingenuity and craft to the uttermost. Logs of foreign wood, cunningly excavated and packed with cigars or spirits; cases of boots and shoes, in the heels of which watches and jewelry are hidden; miraculous trunks, false as Machiavelli, being thinly hollow on side and end, top and bottom, concealing laces, hair, trinkets, etc., etc., are among the common devices of ingenious freebooters. Keen, honest, true men—such as may be seen on any tour of night inspection, like mastiffs at their posts, and especially if visitors be expected—are needed to baffle the plots of the rascals. Political affiliations constitute no guarantee of efficiency. The best attainable is through rigid adherence to the rules of the civil service reform.

All seizures of whatever value are sent to the Seizure Room at the Custom-house. This is under the authority of General G. W. Palmer, formerly Appraiser of the port, and now the learned and effective head of the Law Department. It embraces a singular collection. Here a jeweller's pack; there dresses, silks, shawls, laces, bundles of cigarettes, row-boats captured with contraband goods on board, cutlery, wines, liquors, cigars, and obscene literature. Contaminating articles are destroyed, unclaimed goods may be obtained by the owner in the course of twelve months if they are detained in the General Order Store, or within three years if warehoused, on payment of duty and order of the Secretary of the Treasury. Perishable articles are sold at auction as soon as possible. Other condemned and unclaimed goods are sold by auction at Collector's sale, after being kept in custody as just stated. Complete records of all transactions are carefully preserved.

A disappointed raiser of church debts said that he needed no evidence of total depravity additional to that of the unpaid subscription on his list. If he did, the Seizure Room would furnish it. Humanity, after all, is redeemable. Charles Reade maintains that it is "never too late to mend." The records of the Custom-house illustrate the theory of the novelist. In May, 1882, a check for $87 came to hand from a troubled individual who had imported silks, laces, and linens in 1873, and which he then believed to be free, but had since discovered to be dutiable to that amount; $50 to correct an undervaluation arrived the week before. Collector Schell once received $1500 from a burdened conscience, the owner of which requested him to acknowledge the receipt in a daily paper, which he did. Smaller sums appear in the list of the Conscience Fund, such as $36, $10, $7 27. Most commendable of all is an item of $10 transmitted to the Collector by an inspector, into whose pocket it had been thrust by a passenger. Tender conscience or something else would not allow it to stay there, and the bribe was "covered into the Treasury." With these facts before him, Collector Robertson may still hope to find out the author of the infamously celebrated "forged telegram," and more particularly since he himself received in the month of October, 1882, a check for $10,000 from a most excellent merchant whose clerk, unknown to him, had defrauded the government of about that sum by undervaluations. The fact of undervaluation had not been suspected at the Custom-house, and the length of time that had elapsed since it took place had placed the loss beyond the limits of legal recovery. New York has many such high-minded and sternly principled merchant princes.

Returning from the Seizure Room to the Rotunda, it is obvious that the concentrated activity on the dock receiving the cargo has many counterparts in that of the consignees and their agents. These are naturally anxious to obtain possession of their merchandise as quickly as possible. They therefore hasten to the Custom-house and make entry of their respective consignments. This is usually, but not always, done through the instrumentality of a class of men known as Custom-house brokers.

Custom-house brokers are principally pushing young men bent on the attainment of fortune. The fees charged for their assistance are matters of bargain between themselves and customers. If fraudulent and untrustworthy, they are sure to be extruded from the building. Some are men of high moral character and excellent business abilities. True policy would dictate their enrollment, and invest the Collector with power to exclude from practice all who are shown to be incapable or unjust. Self-interest would then hold the broker to the strictest honesty and probity.

At the Custom-house, the consignee or owner states under oath that he has certain merchandise on board the steamer, and verifies his statement by the production of an invoice, bill of lading, and consular certificate to the invoice given in the country whence the goods were exported. Invoices are made and certified in triplicate, the consul filing one in his office, sending a second to the Collector of the port whither the goods are shipped, and giving a third to the consignor. The last forwards his to the consignee. He also forwards the bill of lading, or copy of it, given by the steam-ship company for goods shipped. The consignee or owner attaches the bill of lading to the entry of the goods he wishes to take away from the dock. All entries are made in duplicate. Every entry must be of all goods coming by the same vessel to the same consignee, even if they come from ten, twenty, thirty, or more consignors. This requirement often makes it necessary for consumption entries to be made upon *pro forma* invoices, which practice has been used by dishonest men to further schemes for undervaluation and fraud.

The marks and numbers inserted in the entry must correspond with those in the bill of lading, and the description of contents of each package must tally with that found in the invoice. The invoice itself is also compared with that sent to the Collector by the consul. If the consignee wishes to have part of the dutiable goods claimed by him sent to a bonded warehouse, he makes a separate and specific entry of them. These papers are next examined as to their correctness by an entry clerk, and are then stamped with consecutive numbers. The entry clerk also indorses on the back of the invoice the value of the goods thus entered. In determining approximately this value, the consul's and commissioner's fees are deducted from the amount specified in the invoice, and the shipping charges, and proper commissions prescribed by law, are added to it. The rate of duty and the date of examination of entry are also inscribed on the invoice. The entry clerk then issues a consumption permit for the duty-free and duty-paid goods, and a bonded warehouse permit for those on which the consignee does not wish to pay the duty at once, each permit agreeing with the contents of the entry, the bill of lading, and the invoice. All these papers, except the original entry, which remains in the Collector's office, are then taken to the Naval Office, where the clerical work is verified. On their return a deputy collector compares the contents of the documents with each other, and ascertains whether the invoice is properly made, and the consular certificate duly attached. If the latter be not attached, the claimant is required to give bonds to produce a proper consular invoice. If all the papers be correct, the deputy collector then designates certain packages of dutiable goods—about 10 per cent. of the whole—and orders them to be sent to the Public Store for appraisement. Where this is inexpedient, as in the case of iron, marble, gypsum, soda-ash, soda crystals, live animals, grains, bones, building stones, etc., he orders an appraisement on the wharf; or in the case of glass-ware, etc., at the merchant's store. The number of the packages to be examined are described by indorsement on the invoice; which indorsement constitutes an order to the Appraiser to decide their dutiable character and value. A similar indorsement is written on the entry, and also on the permit. The last is an order to the discharging inspector to send the packages indicated to the Public Store for appraisement. The numbers written on invoice, entry, and permit must agree, inasmuch as they are designed to be safeguards against collusion and fraud, and guides to officers who act independently of each other.

The consignee, or his broker, papers in hand, next repairs to the cashier's office, and pays the estimated duty on the whole invoice of goods wanted for immediate consumption, together with the legal fees. The cashier affixes his check, in token of payment, to invoice and permit both. Then the merchant, compliant with law, gives what is termed a "return bond" that he will hold the packages intact for ten days after the Appraiser has passed upon the cases sent to his department, and that he will return to the custody of the Collector within that time any or all of the goods so received by him upon due notice so to do. All these preliminaries having been duly observed, the consignee leaves all his papers, except the permit, at the Custom-house. To the permit he procures the signature of the deputy collector, and the counter-signature of the Naval Officer, and at length presents it to the inspector in charge of the vessel, and receives his goods.

Record is kept of all invoices, of the kinds and numbers of the packages sent to the Public Store, and of the ship in which they came. The invoices, together with copies of record and entries, are sent to the Appraiser by the revenue cab running between the Custom-house and the Appraiser's office, so that by them he may identify the parcels sent to him for examination and appraisal. These are so numerous as to keep himself and the assistant appraisers in a state of decided activity during the spring and fall importations. In 1873 the number of packages appraised was 181,068; in 1881 it was

249,593; and in 1883 it was 267,202. The largest number of packages received in a single day was on the 16th of September, 1881, when it reached the total of 1542.

The United States Public Store occupies an entire block, owned by the heirs of a deceased New York merchant, and fronts on the Hudson River, between Hubert and Laight streets. The number of public servants employed therein is 349, of whom about 100 have held office for upward of ten years. Assistant Appraiser John A. Baush, who died in 1883, held office for forty-one years, and other officials have kept their places over twenty years. One hundred and seventy-seven other officers, watchmen, and laborers belonging to the Eighth Division of the Collector's office, and under the immediate orders of Deputy Collector Colonel William A. Jones, co-operate with them. The rules of the civil service are here applied with strict regularity. No temporary appointments have been made since the appointment of Colonel A. P. Ketchum to the office of Appraiser, except to positions of which the annual salary is under $900, and therefore below the grade to which civil service regulations apply. Papers different from those employed at the Collector's office are used in the examination of candidates. Goods and merchandise are assigned, on arrival for examination and appraisal, to one or more of the ten divisions in the office, each of which is under the supervision of an assistant appraiser, whose salary is $3000. Samples of textile and other fabrics sent to this country by foreign manufacturers for the inspection of merchants who order supplies, yet to be made, from them, are promptly examined and appraised in the sample office: 31,993 packages of samples were received in 1881, and 63,479 in 1883.

The tariff is an abstruse science. Heyl's work entitled *United States Import Duties*, or Morgan's *United States Tariff*, must be mastered to understand its application. Even then its principles are not readily comprehended. Some goods are subjected to specific, others to *ad valorem*, and still others to specific and *ad valorem* duties combined. The typical Philadelphia lawyer is needed to unravel all its mysteries. There are doubtless reasons of some sort why silk and wool dress goods should be charged a specific duty of eight cents per square yard, and forty per cent. *ad valorem;* why, if such goods weigh over four ounces to the square yard, they should pay fifty cents per pound, and thirty-five per cent. *ad valorem;* why one textile fabric with thirty-four warp and twenty-six woof threads to the quarter of a square inch, or 240 warp and woof threads to the square inch, should pay a specific duty of seven and a half cents per square yard, and fifteen per cent. of its value additionally; why, if there be less than 201 threads to a square inch, it should pay six and a half cents per square yard, and fifteen per cent. *ad valorem;* and why, if not exceeding 200 threads to the square inch (the difference of a single thread may and sometimes does determine the rate of duty), and costing over twenty-five cents per square yard, it should pay an *ad valorem* duty of thirty-five per cent.; but to the uninitiated these reasons appear to be inscrutable. As the laws of a nation are the crystallizations of its historical experiences, so the customs regulations of a people are the residual crystallization of its commercial relations with foreigners, its efforts at industrial development and self-preservation, and its bitter acquaintance with greed, guile, and guilt.

Passing through other departments of the Public Store we paused to criticise the costly, exquisitely beautiful, and marvellously constructed dresses imported from Worth and from Camus, in Paris; the paintings by Meissonier, son of the famous artist, whose "Charge des Cuirassiers" adorns the stately mansion of Mrs. A. T. Stewart, and other distinguished painters; the statuary, bronzes, watches, and jewelry; the carpets, rugs, and curtains; the cigars and tobacco, wines, spirits, and liqueurs; and specimens of all other articles proper and improper to high and wealthy civilization.

All packages are seemingly handled with skill and care. The contents of not a few are manifestly injured by injudicious nailing on the part of the consignor's employés; and from some, portions of the contents have been extracted *in transitu* by thievish hands.

When the invoices of imported goods arrive at the Public Store they are sent to the Invoice Bureau, and are there distributed to the appropriate divisions. The head of each division in turn distributes his allotment among the respective examiners, and charges each with the invoices assigned to him. Deft, cautious,

and expert examination of each and every parcel follows. The standard of value for each article in the foreign market where it was purchased is ascertained by correspondence with consular agents, by extensive comparison of invoices, and more especially from the invoices of the more prominent American merchants, whose reputation for integrity and square dealing is unimpeached and unassailable.

The most persistent attempts to defraud the government of its just dues take the forms of undermeasurement and undervaluation. Merchandise is frequently undervalued by foreign consignors. The consignees, aware of the fact, and instructed by previous failures, usually correct the fault by entering the goods at figures nearer to their true value. One case of merchandise exhibited an increased statement of value to the average extent of ten per cent. When the Appraiser raises the dutiable value of goods as much as ten per cent., the estimate carries with it an additional penalty to the importer of twenty per cent. The Chinese importers doing business in New York have not yet, in every instance, learned how business is done at the Custom-house. Their undervaluations are occasionally outrageous. Seven packages of silk fabrics had just been appraised at from 50 to 300 per cent. above the invoice price.

As soon as the examiners finish their inspection of the goods appraised, the quantity and quality thereof are noted on the invoice, and that document is sent to the Appraiser for his approval. Correct invoices are returned to the Entry and Invoice Department of the Collector's office on a black list, and corrected ones on a red list. No parcels are permitted to leave the Public Store without being corded and sealed and checked by the examiner. This is a precaution against possible theft. In the Entry Department the returned invoices are placed in the hands of the liquidating clerks, by whom the work of the Appraiser as to classification of goods and the true amount of duties to be paid is carefully revised. If either or both should be incorrect, the invoice is sent back to the Appraiser for reclassification and amendment. After this is done, and the exact amount of duty is ascertained, the amendment is revised by the amendment clerk in the Naval Office, and on his indorsement is again returned to the Bureau of Liquidation. If the importer have already paid the right sum on entering his goods, he is notified of the fact, applies for a delivery permit, and receives his goods. If a balance yet be due to the government, he is informed of the fact, and immediate payment is demanded. If he have paid more than the proper amount, he is notified of the fact, receives a refunding check from the Auditor, and payment thereof from the Assistant Treasurer of the United States.

The national government does business wisely, and always secures itself beforehand against possible loss. If the importer when apprised of the classification as to rate of duty made by the Collector be dissatisfied with it, he must make a written protest within ten days, appeal to the Secretary of the Treasury within thirty days, and if the Secretary's decision sustain the action of the Collector, must, within ninety days from said decision, bring suit in court in order to save any remedy to which he may be legally entitled. Or, if dissatisfied with the valuation noted and certified on the invoice, he may ask for a re-appraisement, or merchant appraisal. If he should do so, then the Collector selects one discreet and experienced merchant, a citizen of the United States, familiar with the character and value of the goods in question, and notifies him of his appointment. The General Appraiser is also notified of the appeal, and of the name of the merchant appraiser. A day is fixed for the appraisal, and the merchant selected is sworn to do his duty. Other merchants may be subpœnaed to act as mercantile experts at the examination. The importer or his agent presents his views of the case, and the decision of the General Appraiser and merchant appraiser is final. Ordinarily the judgment of the Appraiser of the port is sustained. Should they disagree, the Collector decides the matter. Only in the event of informality in the procedure can the importer institute further proceedings in the United States District or Circuit Court. The importer usually accepts the decision, pays the duty, and receives his goods. So accurately is the work of the General Appraiser's office done that not more than two per cent. of all its transactions is found to be incorrect by the Liquidating Bureau.

Damage appraisements are demanded where goods have been injured on the voyage of importation. When the damages claimed exceed $100 the percentage of damage to the goods is subtracted from the amount of duty assessed. Green fruit must be damaged in excess of twenty-five per cent. of the invoice value in order to admit of any reduction of duty, and then the reduction is only on the damage above twenty-five per cent. of injury.

A bulletin of correct entries, increased appraisements, and refunds to importers who paid more than the real duty at the time of entering their merchandise is hung up in the Rotunda for the inspection of interested parties. All invoices are stamped after final examination in the Liquidating Bureau, and are thence sent to the custody of a clerk, who records the date of reception, arranges them in packages according to the initial and terminal letters of importers' names, classifies them as miscellaneous, free, or duty-paid, and warehoused, and ties the several packages together with differently colored tapes. Invoices thus preserved are in constant demand for reference, re-appraisement, etc., and are always brought forward, on proper requisitions, by the heads or chief clerks of divisions. Responsible parties are also permitted to consult them on matters of business. After being retained for six months they are deposited in the Record Room.

The entry papers accompanying the invoices to the cashier's office are there separated from them, and sent to an official, who imposts them, or, in other words, classifies the articles therein described in separate columns according to the rate of duty that each is liable to pay. Articles paying duty by the yard are also classified in appropriate columns. The duties on the wholes are then calculated. The totals added together must correspond with the totals of the cashier's and Naval Officer's offices. This is another efficient safeguard against inadvertencies and inaccuracies. From the imposter the entries pass to other hands, which tabulate the contents for statistical purposes; from thence they pass to a third official, who therefrom prepares the statistics for publication in the newspapers. From him the Bureau of Liquidation receives them for examination and correction, reunites them with the corresponding invoices, sends them to the Naval Office, and receives them again after due revision by the amendment clerks. Again they pass into the hands of the imposting and statistical clerks, who correct their own work, in case any error should have been detected. The entry papers are then filed away.

Tedious and complicated as are the investigations connected with the appraisal of composite textile fabrics, and of wares whose dutiable value is based upon weighers' and gaugers' returns, still greater difficulties attach to the valuation of other articles, such as sugars, chemicals, etc., etc. Appeals from the decisions of the Collector and litigation in United States Courts often delay final settlement for some time. In these cases the aid of the United States Chemical Laboratory, situated in the Public Store, is invoked. This institution is conducted by Dr. Edward Sherer.

Not satisfied with all the precautions hitherto described in order to obtain a proximate approach to absolutely certain knowledge of the commerce of New York, the accounts of each vessel are put into the hands of a class of officials known as liquidators of vessels, about thirteen months after her arrival in port. The liquidators bring together all the papers connected with a single voyage of that vessel, compare and check off the officer's return and the ship's manifest, ascertain what disposition has been made of goods for which no entries or papers were filed, and, if such goods are still in general order stores, cause them to be put upon the sale list, and sold for the benefit of the government. They examine the accounts of the liquidators of entries, and inquire whether any refunds ought to be made or increase of duty assessed. All the entries of each vessel are tabulated upon a duty list, showing the original, additional, and liquidated duties, the increase and excess of duty, and the penalties exacted. All these are footed up, and referred to the Naval Officer for comparison. If found correct, the Naval Officer checks the duty list, which is then filed in the Record Room for statistical or other purposes.

To the same repository the documents associated with entries for warehousing, transportation, and exportation in bond, warehouse and immediate exportation, immediate transportation, and withdrawal for transportation and export to Canada or Mexico, ultimately find their way. Merchants entering imported goods, on which the duties are not paid, for warehousing, give bonds to the amount of twice the value of the goods with the duty added. Receipts for such goods, given by bonded warehouse proprietors, are negotiable, and available as collateral securities for the eventual liquidation of indebtedness. When importers wish to withdraw their merchandise, in part or in whole, from warehouse, withdrawal entries are made for that purpose, the estimated duties paid, and delivery permits obtained. A regular debtor and creditor account with them is kept by the warehouse department. It also keeps account of all goods received and delivered for transportation or export, including descriptions of marks, numbers, and contents of all packages.

Of bonded warehouses (most of which include from three to six buildings each) in New York, Brooklyn, Jersey City, and Hoboken, the number is fifty-nine. The United States government grants the privilege of private bonded warehouses to importers; but only one firm, that of Lanman and Kemp, the great drug importers, avail themselves of it. All the rest are for public use. Each is double locked every evening, the proprietors using one set of locks, and the United States storekeepers another. Any one may hire or erect a building for a bonded warehouse, and enter upon the business of conducting it, after having given a bond of $25,000 for each independent edifice, 25 by 100 feet in area, and an additional bond of from $10,000 to $15,000 for each building connected with the original structure by internal doors. Should the proprietor discontinue business, his books are compared with those of the warehouse department, and in case of correspondency his pecuniary liability ceases, but no bond is ever cancelled. All are preserved in anticipation of possible need. No suit, however, has as yet been brought against a proprietor on his bond. The store-keepers are United States officials, under the control and orders of the Collector, and number sixty-five persons.

On the 1st of February, 1884, there were 241 lighters and 1501 carts employed in the transfer of merchandise to and from the bonded warehouses. The owner of each lighter gives a bond for it by name. The 397 owners of the carts also give bonds that their vehicles shall be faithfully used for revenue purposes only while in government employ.

In the four bonded manufacturing warehouses—one in Brooklyn, and three in New York—merchandise such as Florida water, sarsaparilla, life syrup, and tricopherous is manufactured for export only. All dutiable goods imported for these purposes are sent into general storage warehouses, class 3, where the duties are ascertained, and are thence forwarded to manufacturing bonded warehouses, without payment of duties, but under the prescribed bonds. There they are manufactured, and are thence exported. None can be sold in the United States. The manufacturers file formulas specifying the nature of their manufactures with the Secretary of the Treasury. Government chemists detailed to test the quality and percentage of the alcohol used have free access to these establishments at all times, and on their favorable reports permits for exportation are issued to the proprietors. Each manufacturing bonded warehouse is under the charge of a United States store-keeper.

On many dutiable articles of commerce drawbacks of duties paid are allowed to exporters. Imported merchandise, exported within three years direct from the custody of the United States store-keepers, is entitled to drawback, less one per cent. to defray necessary expenses. Drawback of duties paid, less one per cent., is allowed on imported goods that have been withdrawn from warehouse to enter into the construction or repair of American vessels, or less ten per cent. if manufactured into articles for export to foreign countries. Rebate of internal revenue taxes is allowed on certain taxable articles of domestic production that are entered for export. The object of drawbacks is the encouragement of domestic manufactures, and the promotion of the influx of precious metals. The amount of drawback upon imported goods, afterward manufactured and exported from New York, in the fiscal year ending June 30, 1883, was $1,663,297; of drawback and remission of tax upon domestic and foreign goods, $4,816,659.

Bonds are required by the government in order to secure its rights and dues from individuals, corporations, and business firms who seek its protective aid and indorsement in the transaction of their business, to insure honesty and fair dealing, and to prevent frauds. Such bonds are never cancelled unless satisfactory proof be adduced that the legal conditions have been fulfilled. If the proof of fulfilled stipulations be not sufficient, then the importer often applies to the Secretary of the Treasury, who has discretionary power, to cancel the bonds. Should the Secretary decline to cancel them, the cases are then prepared in the law department of the Collector's office, and forwarded by him to the United States District Attorney for prosecution. The number of such suits instituted in the year ending June 30, 1883, was 280. The entire number of bonds of all kinds duly executed in connection with the public revenue at the port of New York in the same year was 140,963.

The Law Department of the Collector's office also reviews with critical legal eye the entire course of the revenue business and its results; interferes to correct irregularities; perfects it in a legal sense; prepares all the papers and evidence necessary to the defense of the Collector in the suits instituted against him by dissatisfied or fraudulent importers, or other persons whose business relations with him have not been agreeable to themselves; and prepares the documents and evidence needful to the prosecution of criminal offenders and the redress of irregularities. The number of suits instituted against Collector W. H. Robertson in the fiscal year ending June 30, 1883, was 586; and of suits brought by him against others for other causes than on bonds was 161.

Ship-building in the United States is one of the relatively decadent industries. Politico-economical reasons are readily adduced to account for it. But what vessels the country does possess in the locality of New York are cared for with minute fullness at the Custom-house. There United States vessels are documented, or registered, enrolled, and licensed. In the registry of each vessel the managing owner or president of the proprietary company deposes under oath to the names of the owners, to the share of each in the vessel, to the place of his residence, and to the fact that he is a citizen of the United States. The master of the vessel also makes oath that he is himself a citizen. No foreigner can own a recorded interest in a foreign-going American vessel, although he may own an interest in a steamer running on inland waters, rivers, or bays. The managing owner and master then unite in giving a bond, with sureties satisfactory to the Collector, that the certificate of register shall be used exclusively within the limits of the law.

The registers of all American vessels,

while in port, are deposited with the Collector at the registry desk. The owner's and master's oath and bond for registry are all included in a bound volume afterward preserved in the depository of records. Each foreign-bound vessel also deposits articles of agreement, signed by master and crew, and a copy thereof, which is certified by the Collector. A list of the persons composing the crew is also deposited with the Collector, and a certified copy thereof is given by him to the master. A crew bond is further executed by the master and sureties, binding them to produce the persons named as composing the crew to the first boarding officer at the first port of the United States at which the vessel shall arrive, unless the said persons shall have been discharged by consent of an American consul. If sailors are discharged, or desert in foreign countries, the fact is certified by the nearest American consul. Crew lists and articles of vessels are bound together in volumes. Returned crew lists are placed on file. If a vessel should discharge her crew at a port other than that from which she sailed, notification of the fact that the crew is accounted for is sent to the original port of departure, and the crew bond is thereupon cancelled. When a change of master of any vessel occurs, the new master makes oath that he is a citizen of the United States, and the certificate of this oath is attached to the certificate of the vessel's register. Particulars of all such changes are recorded. Abstracts of surrendered registers issued at other ports are also kept in book form, and monthly reports of them are sent to Washington.

Certificates of record are issued to vessels built in the United States and owned by foreigners, to enable such vessels, should they become the property of American citizens, to be documented and receive an American register. Bills of sale and mortgages of vessels are also received and recorded in books that describe the species and name of each vessel, names of grantors and mortgagors, parts owned, parts conveyed, species of conveyance (bill of sale, etc.), when made, amounts received for sale or mortgage, when received for record, dates of record, dates of cancellation, and names of parties who take the documents away from the office. Certificates of register, if lost, must be replaced by new ones; and new certificates must also be issued in correspondency with changes in the characteristics or occupation of vessels. Record is kept of all these registers, and of all issues and surrenders of documents, and copies of such records are sent quarterly to the Secretary of the Treasury.

Rebates of duties paid on imported goods are allowed by law to the extent in which these goods enter into the construction of American vessels. The rebate in one instance, in 1882, amounted to $3622. In the case of some Boston vessels it was still larger. In the registration of a new vessel, the production of the master carpenter's certificate, of the certificate of measurement, and of the inspector's certificate, as well as the oath of ownership, etc., are required in order to documentation. Application is then made to the Secretary of the Treasury at Washington for an official number, and for letters to be used in signaling at sea. Thus 130,052 is the official number, and *J. R. K. W.* the official letters, of the little schooner *Nettie Dobbins;* 10,456 the number, and *H. J. G. W.* the letters, of the barque *Gemsbok,* of New York. When any number and set of letters are exhibited by flags at sea, the officers of passing vessels who observe them can turn to the list of United States merchant vessels and learn what the name of the signaling vessel is.

The total registered tonnage of the port of New York, according to the latest report, is as follows:

VESSELS REGISTERED FOR FOREIGN TRADE.

Sailing vessels	540, with a tonnage of	346,485
Steam "	50,	82,490
Total	590, with a tonnage of	428,975

VESSELS OF FIVE TONS AND UPWARD ENGAGED IN THE COASTING TRADE AND UNDER ENROLLMENT AND LICENSE.

Sailing vessels	1452, with a tonnage of	132,260
Barges, etc.	375, "	68,246
Steamers	741, "	203,054
Total	2568, with a tonnage of	403,560

RECAPITULATION.

Registered vessels	590; tonnage,	428,975
Enrolled and licensed	2568; "	403,560
Total	3158; "	832,535

Eighty-six of the above-mentioned steamers are constructed wholly of iron.

American vessels engaged in domestic trade are enrolled and licensed. The process of enrollment and license is very similar to that of registration for foreign commerce. Records of steam vessels owned in New York and engaged in domestic trade are preserved in the Custom-house, whose officers enforce the execution of the navigation laws, including those relating to the inspection of vessels, the licensing of pilots, engineers, and masters, and the entrance and clearance of coastwise vessels. Particulars of all the wrecks and casualties of American vessels documented at New York are also preserved, and often prove to be of great service.

All receipts of duties, penalties, fees, etc., are revised and tabulated in the office of Colonel Charles Treichel, the Auditor. There all checks for refund of money paid in excess of the true amount of duty are drawn and furnished to the importers. Uncle Sam scarcely ever fails to assure himself against loss. In 1880 the sum of $2,256,487 73 was disbursed in refunds, $1,594,833 37 in 1881, and $3,313,159 73 in the first eleven months of 1882. The whole of the refunds made since 1870 is upward of $18,000,000. The average annual number of entries on which refunds are made is 28,512. Receipts for refunds are taken in duplicate; one copy is sent to Washington, and the other is preserved in the Collector's office for reference. All checks paid for refunds are reported to the Naval Officer, who compares the reports with his own books of record. Full particulars of all matters connected with each refund are also reported to Washington. All record books are kept in the Auditor's office for seven or eight years, and are then sent to the Record Room. Only lately a dispute as to which of two merchants a certain check had been paid was settled by appeal to the records. It was paid to the importer.

Prior to the advent of Mr. S. G. Ogden, who served in the Auditor's department for more than forty years, the Collectors were often placed in the position of defaulters by faulty book-keeping. But so thoroughly has the system of keeping accounts been revised and perfected that for many years they have balanced exactly at the end of every week. The system of checks and balances in use at the New York Custom-house, if not absolutely perfect, is at least a close approximate approach to perfection. Accounts of all receipts and disbursements by the Collector are rendered monthly to the Commissioner of Customs and to the First Auditor of the Treasury.

The multitudinous records and papers appertaining to the customs service in New York have been preserved from the commencement, and are now so classified and arranged that any of them can be readily found when sought, unless it be some very old papers packed away in the dark rooms. The record rooms occupy the entire upper story of the Custom-house, and a portion of the story immediately below it. The custody and care of all these papers and documents require a genius for classification and arrangement. Hundreds if not thousands of tons of account books, bond books, cargo and passenger manifests, entries, inspectors' returns, official certificates, withdrawals, invoices, consular certificates, permits, shipping articles, crew lists, pay rolls, check-book stubs, registers, etc., etc., are here stowed away in such order as to be almost immediately available when wanted.

Directly but independently related to the customs revenue in New York is a class of about twenty United States officials, three of whom are known as special agents. All are under the charge of an intelligent, active, and energetic head—Captain C. H. Brackett. The special agents keep vigilant watch over sailors, importers, and officials alike, and are, in fact, practical and practiced detectives. Suspicion of wrong may be awakened by personal observation, or by confidential information from different sources. Once on the track of offenders they are sure to run them down, unless the criminals be endowed with almost supernatural shrewdness and cunning.

Nothing that human ingenuity can devise appears to be left out of the machinery of this, the greatest revenue establishment in the United States. It is the most scientifically organized and economically administered of American national institutions. Under Collector W. H. Robertson's presidency the cost of collecting the public revenue at this point is 1.78½ per cent. of the whole sum—less than in the administration of any of his predecessors.

NOTE.—In the preparation of this article the writer has been indebted to the courtesy of several officials, and particularly of K. N. Prince, Esq., Chief of the Bureau of Statistics, for indispensable assistance. Whatever discrepancies may appear between the figures in this article and those in the Annual Report on the Foreign Commerce of the United States are due to the fact that the latter are largely made up from the duties estimated at the time of entry, whereas the former have been made up since the entries were finally liquidated and the due amount of duties paid.

The Artistic Young Lady.

THERE are, perhaps, no two words more frequently on the lips of the present generation than these two: "Internal Decoration." It seems like a poor and vapid plagiarism to talk of Renaissance nowadays, but we can not, as we stand in the full flood-tide of modern art improvement and beauty, as applied to household art, use any other word. We can not look through the tasteful and artistic interiors of New York without a pleasurable sense of having lived through a very dark night, to be rewarded with an exceedingly fresh and brilliant morning.

Those who have seen even three decades will remember the monstrous ugliness of the past—the floriated carpets, heavy frescoes, inartistic "reps," the crimson satin curtains against white walls, the staring papers, and the furnace holes in the floor. This dream is scarcely over. To Dante Rossetti, Burne-Jones, and William Morris do the lovers of artistic interiors owe an immortal debt, for they started in England an art crusade against the bad features of household furnishing, which was born of the reign of George the Fourth. His sense of fitness in architecture and household art is still present with us in the bombastic and ridiculous Pavilion at Brighton, and in the curved and crooked outlines of his showy but insincere chairs and tables. Even the silver-ware made for this selfish voluptuary is now considered in such bad taste that the collectors of old silver reject a George the Fourth piece as unworthy of standing by the side of the solid sugar bowl of good Queen Anne. But to the men whom we have just mentioned we owe our emancipation from George the Fourth. The artists began the reform, and an artist's studio was the first thing that was copied. Early attempts were made with tapestries, stuffs from the East, bits of old armor, brass pots, birds, and butterflies, the spoils of a European trip in the way of carvings from Switzerland and Venice, and with bronzes, plaster casts, easels, spinning-wheels, old clocks, and antique chairs: all these things were, by the ambitious young housekeeper, crowded into her small drawing-room, with the natural and innocent desire to make a pretty room. The artistic craze had seized her. She grieved over the ugly things which alone were to be bought in shops, but she had no light to guide her in her new departure.

The result was chaos. Witty callers declared that on entering a fashionable house they found a bric-à-brac shop; they stumbled on a Smyrna rug, and broke their necks over the Dying Gladiator. It was not a parlor, but a china shop, in which the "curled and perfumed Assyrian bull" of modern fashion overturned the table and smashed the Dresden darlings. The growing taste for pottery came in to confuse, and the piano, the writing-table, even the arm-chair, held cloisonné and majolica, Chinese crackle and Henri Deux. A calico cow from Liverpool elbowed early American, and Hispano-moresque stood cheek by jowl with Capo di Monte.

It was a jumble; it was the day of fantastic foolishness ; it was the " *Götterdämmerung*"—the twilight of the gods.

Still, it was better than the brilliant brocaded brocatelle, the rose-wood chair, all curves, the specious frescoes of the Goddess of Liberty holding a frying-pan, or the spotted carpet, which struck upon the sensitive optic like a stick.

It was about this time that the word "sincere" came into the furnishing world. Old mahogany, the square and straight-legged tables of our grandfathers, the finely finished old bureaus with their "sincere" brass handles, the plain papers, the plain carpets, began to crowd out floriated patterns. The classification of pottery became a study. Not every cracked tea-pot from the kitchen shelf was a treasure, only every other tea-pot.

Then came the great Philadelphia Exposition, with its pretty Eastlake house from England, with its stuffs of all nations, with its orderly cataloguing of the good things of past and present, picking out for us what had been worthy in the reign of the tasteful Stuarts, whatever was magnificent in the day of stately Elizabeth, whatever of good (and there was much) in the reign of Queen Anne, also what could be curiously sifted from the luxury of Louis XIV. and XV. The fine taste of Marie de Medicis was revived in jewelry ; the bookbinders revelled in the better past of Russia leather, and gilding through all the ages ; and workers in fine metals, in Russia and the East, in Italy and England, enriched the cabinets and filled the collections with models of "barbaric pearl and gold."

A great exposition is like the fairy's wand : it summons the genii, and then clears them away. The Philadelphia Exposition brought us all that the world could do in the way of household furnishing. With a wave of the wand the stuffs went into the shops, and the gentle housekeeper of to-day steps into a modern upholsterer's to find herself in the Hôtel Cluny as to the laces, mediæval tapestries, embroidered satins, and artistic cheap cretonnes which await her selection. If she wishes a Lucretia Borgia cabinet or a Caterina Cornaro chest, she has a hundred examples to choose from. Any tin and brass shop will give her a Roman lamp such as Beatrice Cenci may have used, and she goes to her bedroom with a candlestick in her hand which may have lighted an early Christian through the Catacombs.

Nothing can be more beautiful, more orderly, more harmonious, than a modern New York house which has blossomed out in this fine summer of perfected art. So universal and commanding is the necessity for an artistic house that our best artists are forsaking the canvas, and using their brushes on the plaster ceilings. It may be long before we have the great Buonarotti's inspired prophets and sibyls in our public buildings, or Correggio's boys on the walls of our dining-rooms; but the movement is in that direction, and the best and highest talent proclaims on every occasion the dignity and beauty of household art.

the house of Dr. W. A. Hammond in West Fifty-fourth Street. After giving his walls time to settle, he began a series of internal decorations, which it will be difficult for artists to surpass for some time to come. His dining-room is hung with a frieze copied from the Bayeux tapestry—patient Matilda's chronicle of the stirring times of William of Normandy. The

DINING-ROOM WINDOW WITH JAPANESE CARVING.

Music and sculpture, for some inscrutable reason, grew naturally in America. Painting and internal decoration came later. Although our landscape men are now amongst the best in the world, it was not an early development.

Perhaps one of the first conspicuously artistic interiors in New York was that of

ceiling is painted in the early Saxon ornamentation—ribbon winding through a conventionalized pattern. The room is decorated with choicest specimens of porcelain and china, and the windows are of stained glass. The portières are of Algerine stuffs, heavy and handsome.

The dining-room is a large room, thir-

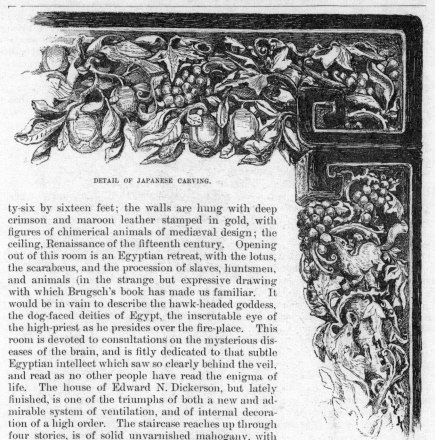

DETAIL OF JAPANESE CARVING.

ty-six by sixteen feet; the walls are hung with deep crimson and maroon leather stamped in gold, with figures of chimerical animals of mediæval design; the ceiling, Renaissance of the fifteenth century. Opening out of this room is an Egyptian retreat, with the lotus, the scarabæus, and the procession of slaves, huntsmen, and animals (in the strange but expressive drawing with which Brugsch's book has made us familiar. It would be in vain to describe the hawk-headed goddess, the dog-faced deities of Egypt, the inscrutable eye of the high-priest as he presides over the fire-place. This room is devoted to consultations on the mysterious diseases of the brain, and is fitly dedicated to that subtle Egyptian intellect which saw so clearly behind the veil, and read as no other people have read the enigma of life. The house of Edward N. Dickerson, but lately finished, is one of the triumphs of both a new and admirable system of ventilation, and of internal decoration of a high order. The staircase reaches up through four stories, is of solid unvarnished mahogany, with panelling of the same at the side. This is a superb feature of the modern house. The frequent landings, the broad low stairs, all are improvements on the old-fashioned narrow, ugly stairway of the immediate past. Mr. Dickerson has much beautiful stained glass; his drawing-room windows are made to repeat the delicate scarlet and dove-color of the paper and window curtains, while in a bedroom swallows fly through apple-blossoms, and are in more imperishable form represented in the glass window.

Here also we see that nothing is more effective than stamped leather for dining-room walls; and carved buffets with painting on leather, let in after the fashion of tiles, ably supplement this finish. Mr. Dickerson has a famous window in his dining-room, which is outlined by a fine bit of Japanese carving. This piece has given the key-note to the room, which has also a ceiling of painted plaques, very harmonious, curious, and ornamental. Brass sconces of cinque-cento and Henri Deux add much brilliancy to these darkly ornamented rooms. A boudoir in ebonized cherry, with tile fire-place, the tiles painted with bright flowers, and much ornamental brass-work about, is extremely pretty, as is the whole of this artistic dwelling.

In some of the fine interiors we see deep crimson hangings and carpets, with dead gold and bronze paper, chandeliers of silver and brass, and fire-place of burnished steel. This introduction of steel is one of the most beautiful of the modern improvements.

In others we see, as we enter, Algerine striped portières and rugs of Persia or Turkey, the furniture made in forms suggestive of lounging, and covered with Eastern stuffs. The sideboard has a severe simplicity, however. The lines are straight and formal, the outline definite. No shallow curves, no feeble-minded ornamentation. Perhaps shells cut out of hard wood, with some good brass-work to use for handles, key, and hinges. The richest brocaded Chinese silks, with the heavily carved teak-wood furniture of our Oriental brethren, fitly furnish forth the rooms where the pottery is collected. The Moorish vases, the Egyptian water bottles, Japanese cups, Thuringian porcelain, crackle-ware, cloisonné, Spanish faience, Palissy, Etruscan, Kioto, Dresden, Russian, biscuit, Nankin, majolica, and Hungarian porcelain can not be better lodged than in the Chinese room. It is a fitting tribute to China, which has given its name to every species of pottery. It is, however, now a reigning fancy to have rare plaques hung on the walls of every room.

A bronzed dining-room, brown leather lambrequins with gold monogram, a bay-window in which stands a white marble vase crowned with grapes, a finish of dark polished inlaid wood, inlaid arm-chairs, sideboard of such dimensions that it fills one end of the room, in the same dark wood; a spacious, hospitable, fine room, lighted up by the ceiling alone, which is pale buff, with broad cartouches of brown, with here and there a deep-toned picture on the walls. Such is one of the interiors, such is one dining-room.

People furnish their rooms now according to their caprices. The personal comes out. The rich literary young lady fits up her room with furniture of an antique pattern, with book-cases in dark wood or oak, with a tiled fire-place, and brass andirons, a Venetian mirror, and deep luxurious rugs. She has rare engravings, and a Sèvres writing-table. "Simple but choice," one says on entering. If she is a fashionable belle, her room will be festooned with pink or blue silk, covered with lace, or tufted satin let into the walls. Long mirrors will abound, and the furniture will be of ormolu. The spirit of Pompadour breathes from this interior; it is all roses and blue ribbons. The artistic young lady has three important caprices. A bunch of peacocks' feathers, a brass pot full of cat-tails, and a mediæval candlestick. These are the essentials. Japanese fans as a matter of detail; an easel, a few straight-backed chairs, a brown curtain embroidered with sunflowers, and a Persian cat. With all the stiffness, and the preference for a certain dirty yellow,

which has become the passion of the followers of Cimabue Brown, these modern æsthetes do sometimes make very pretty rooms. They are quaint and individual, but there is no doubt that the "high artistic craze" has produced some very ugly effects.

The severe stiffness of the cat-tail has entered much into modern embroidery. Every one feels for the stork which has stood so long on one leg.

> "The lilies lank and wan,
>   Each stork and sunflower spray,"

all are stiff and dismal. They are the pendants to the "lean disciples of Burne-Jones." The Postlethwaites and Bunthornes and their female adorers look like a stork on one leg. The hero of a modern æsthetic comedy says, as the highest synonym of despair, "I feel like a room without a dado."

It is one of the pleasantest caprices of modern luxury that women have their bedrooms and boudoirs furnished in colors which will set off their favorite dresses, and add china to match the bedroom.

The introduction of tapestry in the hangings of a room gives a touch of time-honored, delicate, silent, indescribable approval to the tastes of certain interiors. The heavy and freighted hangings bring back Florentine galleries, Venetian and Roman palaces and villas. Much of it is Gobelin tapestry, telling spiritualistic stories. Portières of tapestry in a large house are luxuries, but in a small one sometimes cumbersome. At Newport, for instance, they may seem too warm.

The decorative art school now produces a very good imitation tapestry, which has much of the charm of the old and time-stained heavy woollen stuff. In a city dining-room nothing can be finer than real old tapestry. If one is rich enough to command a tapestry from the Gobelins, with the "miraculous draught of fishes" of Raphael, what more appropriate hanging for a dining-room? Mr. Barlow's dining-room is especially rich in several of these rare luxuries.

Carved wood gilded, each square inch ornamental enough for a breastpin, in the style which we once thought stiff, but which we now find beautiful—the classic style of the First Empire (when the delicate Récamier in a Greek peplum stretched her gracious form on a severely simple spindle-legged sofa, and Josephine wore a robe embroidered in the rectangular fashion of the "Grecian pattern," and adorned herself with cameos held together with little chains)— such is now the favorite style of fitting for even a quiet salon. The chimney-piece of whitewood, carved formal vase, and festoon of vines, the early American wood-carving (done then with a jackknife probably, but done sincerely and well) — such is one of the latest and most pleasing of the fancies for internal decorating. For these architects of our early colonial period builded better than they knew. There were a few Frenchmen from Versailles and

CHIMNEY-PIECE IN EBONIZED WOOD.

Fontainebleau, men who had learned architecture from the best teachers, who came here after the wreck of that great storm-ship the Revolution, to find a home on the shores of the newer world. They have left the impress of their conscientious fingers on many a bridge, church, and old mansion. "No such work can be done now," sighs the modern architect, as he looks at an old staircase of the year 1804. The high wooden chimney-pieces of the old colonial style are eagerly bought up by the tasteful decorators of the present, and the *haute volée* at Newport buy gladly the disregarded carvings of the old town.

There is no greater mistake than to value a thing because it is old. But if

IN A DINING-ROOM IN FIFTY-SEVENTH STREET.

vantage in the house of Mr. D. O. Mills, lately finished by Herter. The library, panelled in carved mahogany to the frieze, is a superb room, which has cost sixty thousand dollars. The chimney-piece is much accentuated, as in all internal decoration. It is in three compartments, adorned with shelves and vases and clocks and plates, and the fire-place is filled with fine brass and tiles; mirrors are set in the frame-work of the chimney-piece. A fine bow-window, hung with gold-embroidered muslin, and also shaded with heavy plush curtains, commands the ever-varying gay panorama of Fifth Avenue. Large library tables, and superb lounges and chairs covered with Eastern stuffs, give this room the easy and inhabited look which its splendor might efface.

The grand salon of this superb house is in the white and gold and carved work of the days of Napoleon I. The chimney-piece, with its little Corinthian pillars and capitals heavily gilt, recalls that picture of the great Emperor nursing on his knee the sleeping King of Rome, as he looks at a map of the world that he has recently conquered. The ceiling of this gorgeous room is Venetian, in the style of the famous one in the Doge's palace.

Stones of deep red color, like glowing carbuncles, are let into the gilded wood-work, and Limoges enamels ornament the walls.

The chairs are white and gilt of the "Empire" shapes, covered with most exquisite pale satins, embroidered with here and there a rose, which looks as if Flora had just flung it down, and again with patterns in gold embroidery; all the colors are delicate and refined. The boudoir, or first drawing-room, is hung in velvet of most delicate crimson, embroidered where it meets the frieze with gold and colors, to imitate precious stones. The wood-work of this room is dark. The hangings are of crimson velvet—not

time has gone over it but to beautify it, if time can show that this thing had a reason for lasting, then it is good, and worthy of reproduction.

Many of the most conspicuous houses of New York are palaces in their way, and filled with most choice and rare pictures; but as they are not particularly in the modern style of internal decoration, we do not describe them. A fine staircase at Mr. J. J. Astor's, beneath which stands a piece of sculpture, the work of W. W. Astor, is most commanding in effect. The picture-gallery and dining-room of Mr. W. Astor are also most beautiful and artistic rooms. There are fine effects in the superb houses of Mr. Fish and of Miss Wolfe; but these houses are only possible to people of great wealth. The "new departure" in furnishing, combined with luxury, is seen to every possible ad-a high, but a pale crimson—and the ceiling is frescoed with the colors of spring flowers. Fine paintings ornament the walls.

The chief charm of this interior is that, in spite of its magnificence, it has a home look. The chairs are easy, the curtains are hospitably drawn, books and photographs and engravings lie around on so fashionable now in internal decoration, finds expression in a frieze at this magnificent house; it is the frieze in the gold drawing-room, which was painted in Paris by the best frieze-painter of to-day. This is simply several hundred feet of fine picture, with classical subjects, nymphs, fauns, and other dreamy creatures. A few feet of it would be gladly framed by

HALL WITH WHITEWOOD STAIRCASE.

tables; and although one is breathing the heavy air of luxury, there seems to be nothing too good for a human being, which is the perfection of art. This is perhaps the key-note of the modern school. The decorators strive to efface themselves, just as persons of the highest breeding possess the simplest manners. One is conscious of beauty, of the serenest loveliness, but it is toned down to one harmonizing chord.

The addition of valuable oil-paintings, ordinary mortals for an ordinary house as a fine picture.

A tasteful dwelling in Fifty-seventh Street has an artistic look from the very outside even of the door. Fitted with stained glass and iron, it opens with the seal of modern taste; the hall is in dark wood, curtained off by deep portières, and with its staircase is an object of beauty as well as of comfort. On one side are glimpses of carved wood and golden palm, with incised carvings, and ornaments of the Empire, whose mirrors might well reflect Josephine and Hortense—a beautiful little room.

On the opposite side opens the dining-room, fitted up with mahogany panelling, and a ceiling painted by John La Farge. The furniture is all of old mahogany, with brass mountings for sideboard and tables, which the owners have been fortunate enough to inherit from a long line of ancestry. When they desire privacy, the portières are drawn, and each room becomes separate. When they like, the curtains are pulled aside, and all the three rooms are one. The hall, however, with its wood fire, its brass andirons, sconces, clocks, chairs, rugs, and tables, is the gem of the house, and yet all this in twenty feet of width.

Another beautiful interior has the white-wood staircase of our early Revolutionary period, running up through a dark hall. The walls are wainscoted to the cornice with dado rails. The grand saloon is in white, with artistic carvings copied in hard plaster or papier-maché, and with Luca della Robbia fruits and flowers over the doorways. The bedrooms are shellacked, and some are stained of a deep tint; one, all in blue, is especially beautiful.

In the dining-room, which is of a deep dull red, the fire lights up bright brass surroundings, and the heavy mantel holds vases and French clocks. Everywhere warm and comfortable portières are drawn to exclude draughts, and a fine piece of Gobelin tapestry covers one side of the room. There are no glaring colors, no senseless and obtrusive frescoes, no crowd, no oppressive display of bric-à-brac in this house, yet bronzes and medals and gems lie about, and a fine picture stands in a good light on an easel. There is an overflowing beauty, but there is order and appropriateness. Books abound ; they stretch away in long low book-cases, which in their turn hold up the curious old silver, china, and delf of which the owner is fond.

There are large rich rugs in the centre of each parquet floor; there are massive chairs, no two of which are alike. Some of them have come from Venice, some from Japan, some from Morocco. One is an old Spanish chair with the seat of hide, the hair of the ox still left on the under side. Even the picture-frames have been made of oxidized silver, to meet the artistic demands of an eye sobered to cool tints.

The fine house of Mr. F. W. Stevens, at the corner of Fifty-seventh Street and Fifth Avenue, has long charmed the eye with its artistic outside. Within, it is well worthy of admiration. A room in ebonized cherry and scarlet proves the success of high-color decoration if in the hands of a master. The grand salon, in white and gold, is after the best spirit of the days of Louis XV., which was the age of salons. The dining-room, in old Spanish leather, collected piece by piece laboriously in Spain, and put together here, is a glorious room. The grand hall, with two or three flights of balcony, hung with rugs, tapestries, and rare embroideries, is a picture in itself. This house is thoroughly artistic, and in the modern style. There is a correctness about it which is satisfactory. It shows that all the study and talk about high art is not nonsense, but that it means harmony and perfection.

The lighting of the dining-rooms now receives very much attention. Gas is considered vulgar and low. Lamps of every degree are introduced, and are fearfully troublesome, but pretty. The candle is re-instated, but drips. There is no doubt that candle-light is very becoming; nor any doubt that the heat of a chandelier hanging immediately over the head is very great, almost heating a brain to fever. Side lights, brass sconces, and candles are used almost exclusively. The little red candles with colored shades are universal, sometimes assisted by lamps, which, however, are not yet quite certain enough to be altogether pleasing. These are the inconveniences now resorted to by housekeepers, displacing the neat and economical gas in order to get rid of the heat. But when the electric light can be managed for households, and tempered to a sufficient softness, no doubt the candles and lamps will be again banished to the garret and the country house. For in a town house they are vastly less convenient than that obedient slave which answers to the rubbing of a match with brilliant and certain light. Given, then, a luxurious dining-room, with its superbly carved buffet, which is loaded with glass, silver, and china, we come down to the chairs, which must be of carved oak, or of wood to agree with the wood-work of the room, with seats covered with stamped or tufted leather, or alligator-skin. These chairs should be high and straight, and, for large dinners, without arms.

Portières and curtains of Japanese or Chinese silks (gold storks on a dark ground are very handsome), or the laterally striped curtain stuffs, all hung by brass rings on a brass bar, are thoroughly in keeping with the room. The windows should be of stained glass, now so easily attainable.

Stained glass windows representing the Seasons, or the apotheosis of food in the shape of the goddesses Pomona and Ceres, the thousand fancies of genius and taste, are now very common in luxurious dining-rooms. They throw a "rose light o'er our russet cares," and are especially delightful in the morning. The carpet of the dining-room should be thick and soft, and thereby noiseless. Its colors may be rich, but should be unobtrusive. No one likes to hear a chair grate on a wooden floor, or to be annoyed by the footsteps of the servants at a seven-o'clock dinner. All should be quiet and serene.

We now come to the table, which in certain luxurious houses of New York has become a picture worthy of Rubens or Vibert. The favorite form is still the long extension-table, as better fitted to our rooms, but many hostesses for large dinners introduce the round table if their rooms permit of it. The table is covered first with a crimson cloth, over which is thrown the decorative lace-work table-cloth, divided into squares of solid damask and lace-work; this again is covered with a large mat of velvet, on which

STAIRCASE IN HOUSE AT FIFTY-SEVENTH STREET AND FIFTH AVENUE.

stands the silver salver lined with mirror, on which again elevates itself the silver épergne, or the basket of flowers. On the lake of mirror float Dresden swans, lilies, and aquatic plants. At the four corners of the crimson mat stand four high ruby-colored flagons mounted in gold, filled with claret. Other flagons of topaz or emerald glass, or plain white in silver mountings stand at convenient intervals. The covers are of silver, or of choice porcelain or china. Glasses of different color in Venetian and Bohemian crystal are grouped at each plate. Napkins of the same lace with embroidered damask or momie-cloth as the table-cover are laid at each plate. The colored embroideries of Russia for table linen have been much used during the last year. These naperies come from Moscow, and bear mottoes and devices in the strange Slavonic tongue. They are very expensive, and have not yet become common.

Mottoes painted on the walls of dining-rooms, being made a part of the ornamentation, are quite the thing. This is a German fashion (as every one will remember who has travelled on the Rhine), and has come down from Gothic times. It is mediæval in the design and in the execution, and is exceedingly charming, both in the spirit and in the letter, neither of which killeth in this elaborate connection.

We have now arrived in the nineteenth century at the splendor and magnificence, long forgotten, of the feasts which the chroniclers of the fourteenth century loved to dilate upon. At the feast of Lionel, Duke of Clarence, son of Edward III., thirty-two courses were included in the bill of fare. Silver dishes, platters, and cups, wrought in endless device and enriched with gems, glittered upon the board. To show how much these table ornaments were prized, Edmund, Earl of March, in 1380, left to his sons and daughters a silver salt in the shape of a dog. The halls were beautifully hung with crimson tapestry. Yet with all their tapestry, arras, stamped leather, their barbaric splendor of plate, their floors were strewn with rushes, and they had not the ordinary comforts of a chimney and a gas-light or a candle, but must have used flaming torches, unfragrant and uncertain. Yet we are glad now to get one of their great standing chests, carved and richly decorated, in which they kept the household linen; gladly would we inherit the laced napkins of that period, made probably by the nuns. The elegancies of the Italian Renaissance penetrated England, and blossomed into the Tudor Gothic, much of which we are copying in the dining-rooms of to-day.

It is curious, looking at the overflow of this Renaissance, to ask one's self why all this beauty has been pent up so long.

One goes back to contemplate the white marble mantel-piece of the immediate past as one looks at the bone of a megatherium; it is the type of a dead ugliness.

Yet the white marble mantel-piece surrounds a fire, which is better than the black hole in the wall or the floor which indicated the furnace; and modern taste can so well disguise the cold marble with tasteful lambrequin and curtain of serge or plush that it need not be altogether ugly.

The parquet floors, not altogether liked by people of uncertain foot-hold, are covered in winter with ingrain carpet of plain color. This is again broken into color and variety by rugs. The stairs are almost universally without carpet, and are rubbed down to a plain and slippery smoothness.

If there can be a word to be said against modern wood-work in internal decoration, it is that it sometimes looks a little crowded. To those who have enjoyed large rooms, high halls, and empty spaces there is, perhaps, a feeling of being shut up in a box in these exceedingly elaborate and artistic houses. Yet those who live in them get to love their carved wooden walls, their curiously quaint outlooks from staircase and balcony, their heavy and perfectly fitting doors.

Taine says that in every country which has stopped growing, and which begins to decay, there comes a moment of repose. Then, says the great art critic, "blossoms the consummate flower of art."

To that moment he relegates the construction of the superb palaces of Venice, and the masterpieces which fill them.

We need indulge no apprehensions that we have reached such a moment. The present achievement of American art, promising and full of interest as it is, is remote from that which should properly signalize the decay of a great nation. We may err in the direction of luxury in our large communities, but for the most part there has entered into the building and beautifying of American homes a most re-assuring and comforting amount of common-sense. The luxury that offends is the exception, and it is an agreeable characteristic of the public temperament that the exhibition of such luxury excites no sense of envy, but only affords amusement. If we are advancing toward decay, we are certainly barricading our fort against its insidious footsteps with many a strong mahogany plank, and much "heart of oak."

NEW YORK REVISITED
(PART 3)

IF the Bay had seemed to me, as I have noted, most to help the fond observer of New York aspects to a sense, through the eyes, of embracing possession, so the part played there for the outward view found its match for the inward in the portentous impression of one of the great caravansaries administered to me of a winter afternoon. I say with intention "administered": on so assiduous a guide, through the endless labyrinth of the Waldorf - Astoria was I happily to chance after turning out of the early dusk and the January sleet and slosh into permitted, into enlightened contemplation of a pandemonium not less admirably ordered, to all appearance, than rarely intermitted. The seer of great cities is liable to easy error, I know, when he finds this, that or the other caught glimpse the supremely significant one—and I am willing to preface with that remark my confession that New York told me more of her story at once, then and there, than she was again and elsewhere to tell. With this apprehension that she was in fact fairly shrieking it into one's ears came a curiosity, corresponding, as to its kind and its degree of interest; so that there was nought to do, as we picked our tortuous way, but to stare with all our eyes and miss as little as possible of the revelation. That harshness of the essential conditions, the outward, which almost any large attempt at the amenities, in New York, has to take account of and make the best of, has at least the effect of projecting the visitor with force upon the spectacle prepared for him at this particular point and of marking the more its sudden high pitch, the character of violence which all its warmth, its color and glitter so completely muffle. There is violence outside, mitigating sadly the frontal majesty of the monument, leaving it exposed to the vulgar assault of the street by the operation of those dire facts of absence of margin, of meagreness of site, of the brevity of the block, of the inveteracy of the near thoroughfare, which leave "style," in construction, at the mercy of the impertinent cross-streets, make detachment and independence, save in the rarest cases, an insoluble problem, preclude without pity any element of court or garden, and open to the builder in quest of distinction the one alternative, and the great adventure, of seeking his reward in the sky.

Of their license to pursue it there to any extent whatever New-Yorkers are, I think, a trifle too assertively proud; no court of approach, no interspace worth mention, ever forming meanwhile part of the ground-plan or helping to receive the force of the breaking public wave. New York pays at this rate the penalty of her primal topographic curse, her old inconceivably bourgeois scheme of composition and distribution, the uncorrected labor of minds with no imagination of the future and blind before the opportunity given them by their two magnificent water-fronts. This original sin of the longitudinal avenues perpetually, yet meanly intersected, and of the organized sacrifice of the indicated alternative, the great perspectives from East to West, might still have earned forgiveness by some occasional departure from its pettifogging consistency. But, thanks to this consistency, the city is, of all great cities, the least endowed with any blest item of stately square or goodly garden, with any happy accident or surprise, any fortunate nook or casual corner, any deviation, in fine, into the liberal or the charming. That way, however, for the regenerate filial mind, madness may be said to lie—the way of imagining what might have been and putting it all together in the light of what so helplessly is. One of the things that helplessly are, for instance, is just this assault of the street, as I have called it, upon any direct dealing with our caravansary. The electric cars, with their double track, are everywhere almost as tight a fit in the narrow channel of the roadway as the projectile in the bore of a gun; so that the Waldorf-Astoria, sitting by this absent margin for life with her open lap and arms, is reduced to confessing, with a strained smile, across the traffic and the danger, how little, outside her mere swing-door, she can do for you. She seems to admit that the attempt to get at her may cost you your safety, but reminds you at the same time that any good American, and even any good inquiring stranger, is supposed willing to risk that boon for her. "*Un bon mouvement,* therefore: you must make a dash for it, but you'll see I'm worth it." If such a claim as this last be ever justified, it would indubitably be justified here; the survivor scrambling out of the current and up the bank finds in the amplitude of the entertainment awaiting him an instant sense as of applied restoratives. The amazing hotel-world quickly closes round him; with the process of transition reduced to its minimum he is transported to conditions of extraordinary complexity and brilliancy, operating—and with proportionate perfection—by laws of their own and expressing after their fashion a complete scheme of life. The air swarms, to intensity, with the *characteristic,* the characteristic condensed and accumulated as he rarely elsewhere has had the luck to find it. It jumps out to meet his every glance, and this unanimity of its spring, of all its aspects and voices, is what I just now referred to as the essence of the loud New York story. That effect of violence, in the whole communication, at which I thus hint, results from the inordinate mass, the quantity of presence, as it were, of the testimony heaped together for emphasis of the wondrous moral.

The moral in question, the high interest of the tale, is that you are in presence of a revelation of the possibilities of the hotel—for which the American

spirit has found so unprecedented a use and a value; leading it on to express so a social, indeed positively an æsthetic ideal, and making it so, at this supreme pitch, a synonym for civilization, for the capture of conceived manners themselves, that one is verily tempted to ask if the hotel spirit may not just *be* the American spirit most seeking and most finding itself. That truth—the truth that the present is more and more the day of the hotel—had not waited to burst on the mind at the view of this particular establishment; we have all more or less been educated to it, the world over, by the fruit-bearing action of the American example: in consequence of which it has been opened to us to see still other societies moved by the same irresistible spring and trying, with whatever grace and ease they may bring to the business, to unlearn as many as possible of their old social canons, and in especial their old discrimination in favor of the private life. The business for them—for communities to which the American ease in such matters is not native—goes much less of itself and produces as yet a scantier show; the great difference with the American show being that, in the United States, every one is, for the lubrication of the general machinery, practically in everything, whereas, in Europe, mostly, it is only certain people who are in anything; so that the machinery, so much less generalized, works in a smaller, stiffer way. This one caravansary makes the American case vivid, gives it, you feel, that quantity of illustration which renders the place a new thing under the sun. It is an expression of the gregarious state breaking down every barrier but two—one of which, the barrier consisting of the high pecuniary tax, is the immediately obvious. The other, the rather more subtle, is the condition, for any member of the flock, that he or she—in other words especially she—be presumably "respectable," be, that is, not discoverably anything else. The rigor with which any appearance of pursued or desired adventure is kept down—adventure in the florid sense of the word, the sense in which it remains an euphemism—is not the least interesting note of the whole immense promiscuity. Protected at those two points the promiscuity carries, through the rest of the range, everything before it.

It sat there, it walked and talked, and ate and drank, and listened and danced to music, and otherwise revelled and roamed, and bought and sold, and came and went there, all on its own splendid terms and with an encompassing material splendor, a wealth and variety of constituted picture and background, that might well feed it with the finest illusions about itself. It paraded through halls and saloons in which art and history, in masquerading dress, muffled almost to suffocation as in the gold brocade of their pretended majesties and their conciliatory graces, stood smirking on its passage with the last cynicism of hypocrisy. The exhibition is wonderful for that, for the suggested sense of a promiscuity which manages to be at the same time an inordinate untempered monotony; manages to be so, on such ground as this, by an extraordinary trick of its own, wherever one finds it. The combination forms I think, largely, the very interest, such as it is, of these phases of the human scene in the United States—if only for the pleasant puzzle of our wondering how, when types, aspects, conditions, have so much in common, they should seem at all to make up a conscious miscellany. That question, however, the question of the play and range, the practical elasticity, of the social sameness, in America, will meet us elsewhere on our path, and I confess that all questions gave way, in my mind, to a single irresistible obsession. This was just the ache of envy of the spirit of a society which had found there, in its prodigious public setting, so exactly what it wanted. One was in presence, as never before, of a realized ideal and of that childlike rush of surrender to it and clutch at it which one was so repeatedly to recognize, in America, as the note of the supremely gregarious state. It made the whole vision unforgettable, and I am now carried back to it, I confess, in musing hours, as to one of my few glimpses of perfect human felicity. It had the admirable sign that it was, precisely, so comprehensively collective— that it made so vividly, in the old phrase, for the greatest happiness of the greatest number. Its rare beauty, one felt

with instant clarity of perception, was that it was, for a "mixed" social manifestation, blissfully exempt from any principle or possibility of disaccord with itself. It was absolutely a fit to its conditions, those conditions which were both its earth and its heaven, and every part of the picture, every item of the immense sum, every wheel of the wondrous complexity, was on the best terms with all the rest.

The sense of these things became for the hour as the golden glow in which one's envy burned, and through which, while the sleet and the slosh, and the clangorous charge of cars, and the hustling, hustled crowds held the outer world, one carried one's charmed attention from one chamber of the temple to another. For that is how the place speaks, as great constructed and achieved harmonies mostly speak—as a temple builded, with clustering chapels and shrines, to an idea. The hundreds and hundreds of people in circulation, the innumerable hugehatted ladies in especial, with their air of finding in the gilded and storied labyrinth the very firesides and pathways of home, became thus the serene faithful, whose rites one would no more have sceptically brushed than one would doff one's disguise in a Mohammedan mosque. The question of who they all might be, seated under palms and by fountains, or communing, to some inimitable New York tune, with the shade of Marie Antoinette in the queer recaptured actuality of an easy Versailles or an intimate Trianon—such questions as that, interesting in other societies and at other times, insisted on yielding here to the mere eloquence of the general truth. Here was a social order in positively stable equilibrium. Here was a world whose relation to its form and medium was practically imperturbable; here was a conception of publicity as the vital medium organized with the authority with which the American genius for organization, put on its mettle, alone could organize it. The whole thing remains for me, however, I repeat, a gorgeous golden blur, a paradise peopled with unmistakable American shapes, yet in which, the general and the particular, the organized and the extemporized, the element of ingenuous joy below and of consummate management above, melted together and left one uncertain which of them one was, at a given turn of the maze, most admiring. When I reflect indeed that without my clue I should not have even known the maze—should not have known, at the given turn, whether I was engulfed, for instance, in the *vente de charité* of the theatrical profession and the onset of persuasive peddling actresses, or in the annual tea-party of German lady-patronesses (of I know not what) filling with their Oriental opulence and their strange idiom a playhouse of the richest rococo, where some other expensive anniversary, the ball of a guild or the carouse of a club, was to tread on their heels and instantly mobilize away their paraphernalia— when I so reflect I see the sharpest dazzle of the eyes as precisely the play of the genius for organization.

There are a thousand forms of this ubiquitous American force, the most ubiquitous of all, that I was in no position to measure; but there was often no resisting a vivid view of the form it may take, on occasion, under pressure of the native conception of the hotel. Encountered embodiments of the gift, in this connection, master-spirits of management whose influence was as the very air, the very expensive air, one breathed, abide with me as the intensest examples of American character; indeed as the very interesting supreme examples of a type which has even on the American ground, doubtless, not said its last word, but which has at least treated itself there to a luxury of development. It gives the impression, when at all directly met, of having at its service something of that fine flame that makes up personal greatness; so that, again and again, as I found, one would have liked to see it more intimately at work. Such failures of opportunity and of penetration, however, are but the daily bread of the visionary tourist. Whenever I dip back, in fond memory, none the less, into the vision I have here attempted once more to call up, I see the whole thing overswept as by the colossal extended arms, waving the magical bâton, of some high-stationed orchestral leader, the absolute presiding power, conscious of every note of every instrument, controlling and commanding the whole

volume of sound, keeping the whole effect together and making it what it is. What may one say of such a spirit if not that he understands, so to speak, the forces he sways, understands his boundless American material and plays with it like a master indeed? One sees it thus, in its crude plasticity, almost in the likeness of an army of puppets whose strings the wealth of his technical imagination teaches him innumerable ways of pulling, and yet whose innocent, whose always ingenuous agitation of their members he has found means to make them think of themselves as delightfully free and easy. Such was my impression of the perfection of the concert that, for fear of its being spoiled by some chance false note, I never went into the place again.

It might meanwhile seem no great adventure merely to walk the streets; but (beside the fact that there is, in general, never a better way of taking in life,) this pursuit irresistibly solicited, on the least pretext, the observer whose impressions I note—accustomed as he had ever been conscientiously to yield to it: more particularly with the relenting year, when the breath of spring, mildness being really installed, appeared the one vague and disinterested presence in the place, the one presence not vociferous and clamorous. Any definite presence that doesn't bellow and bang takes on in New York by that simple fact a distinction practically exquisite; so that one goes forth to meet it as a guest of honor, and that, for my own experience, I remember certain aimless strolls as snatches of intimate communion with the spirit of May and June—as abounding, almost to enchantment, in the comparatively *still* condition. Two secrets, at this time, seemed to profit by that influence to tremble out; one of these to the effect that New York would really have been "meant" to be charming, and the other to the effect that the restless analyst, willing at the lightest persuasion to let so much of its ugliness edge away unscathed from his analysis, must have had for it, from far back, one of those loyalties that are beyond any reason. "It's all very well," the voice of the air seemed to say, if I may so take it up;

"it's all very well to 'criticise,' but you distinctly take an interest and are the victim of your interest, be the grounds of your perversity what they will. You can't escape from it, and don't you see that that, precisely, is what *makes* an adventure for you (an adventure, I admit, as with some strident, battered, questionable beauty, truly some 'bold bad' charmer,) of almost any odd stroll, or waste half-hour, or other promiscuous passage, that results for you in an impression? There is always your bad habit of receiving through almost any accident of vision more impressions than you know what to do with; but that, for common convenience, is your eternal handicap and may not be allowed to plead here against your special responsibility. You *care* for the terrible town, yea even for the 'horrible,' as I have overheard you call it, or at least think it, when you supposed no one would know; and you see now how, if you fly such fancies as that it was conceivably meant to be charming, you are tangled by that weakness in some underhand imagination of its possibly, one of these days, becoming a riper fruit of time, becoming so. To do that, you indeed sneakingly provide, it must get away from itself; but you are ready to follow its hypothetic dance even to the mainland and to the very end of its tether. What makes the general relation of your adventure with it is that, at bottom, you are all the while wondering, in presence of the aspects of its genius and its shame, what elements or parts, if any, would be worth its saving, worth carrying off for the fresh embodiment and the better life, and which of them would have, on the other hand, to face the notoriety of going *first* by the board. I have literally heard you qualify the monster as 'shameless' —though that was wrung from you, I admit, by the worst of the winter conditions, when circulation, in any fashion consistent with personal decency or dignity, was merely mocked at, when the stony-hearted 'trolleys,' cars of Juggernaut in their power to squash, triumphed all along the line, when the February blasts became as cyclones in the darkened gorges of masonry (which down-town, in particular, put on, at their mouths, the semblance of black rat-holes, holes of

gigantic rats, inhabited by whirlwinds); when all the pretences and impunities and infirmities, in fine, had massed themselves to be hurled at you in the fury of the elements, in the character of the traffic, in the unadapted state of the place to almost *any* dense movement, and, beyond everything, in that pitch of all the noises which acted on your nerves as so much wanton provocation, so much conscious cynicism. The fury of sound took the form of derision of the rest of your woe, and thus it *might*, I admit, have struck you as brazen that the horrible place should, in such confessed collapse, still be swaggering and shouting. It might have struck you that great cities, with the eyes of the world on them, as the phrase is, should be capable either of a proper form or (failing this) of a proper compunction; which tributes to propriety were, on the part of New York, equally wanting. This made you remark, precisely, that nothing was wanting, on the other hand, to that analogy with the character of the bad bold beauty, the creature the most blatant of whose pretensions is that she is one of those to whom everything is always forgiven. On what ground 'forgiven'? of course you ask; but note that you ask it while you're in the very act of forgiving. Oh yes, you are; you've as much as said so yourself. So there it all is; arrange it as you can. Poor dear bad bold beauty; there must indeed be something about her—!"

Let me grant then, to get on, that there *was* doubtless, in the better time, something about her; there was enough about her, at all events, to conduce to that distinct cultivation of her company for which the contemplative stroll, when there was time for it, was but another name. The analogy was in truth complete; since the repetition of such walks, and the admission of the beguiled state contained in them, resembled nothing so much as the visits so often still incorrigibly made to compromised charmers I defy even a master of morbid observation to perambulate New York unless he be interested; so that in a case of memories so gathered the interest must be taken as a final fact. Let me figure it, to this end, as lively in every connection —and so indeed no more lively at one mild crisis than at another. The crisis —even of observation at the morbid pitch—is inevitably mild in cities intensely new; and it was with the quite peculiarly insistent newness of the upper reaches of the town that the spirit of romantic inquiry had always, at the best, to reckon. There are new cities enough about the world, goodness knows, and there are new parts enough of old cities —for examples of which we need go no farther than London, Paris and Rome, all of late so mercilessly renovated. But the newness of New York—unlike even that of Boston, I seemed to discern— had this mark of its very own, that it affects one, in every case, as having treated itself as still more provisional, if possible, than any poor dear little interest of antiquity it may have annihilated. The very sign of its energy is that it doesn't believe in itself; it fails to succeed, even at a cost of millions, in persuading you that it does. Its mission would appear to be, exactly, to gild the temporary, with its gold, as many inches thick as may be, and then, with a fresh shrug, a shrug of its splendid cynicism for its freshly detected inability to convince, give up its actual work, however exorbitant, as the merest of stopgaps. The difficulty with the compromised charmer is just this constant inability to convince; to convince ever, I mean, that she is serious, serious about any form whatever, or about anything but that perpetual passionate pecuniary purpose which plays with all forms, which derides and devours them, though it may pile up the cost of them in order to rest a while, spent and haggard, in the illusion of their finality.

The perception of this truth grows for you by your simply walking up Fifth Avenue and pausing a little in presence of certain forms, certain exorbitant structures, in other words the elegant domiciliary, as to which the illusion of finality was within one's memory magnificent and complete, but as to which one feels to-day that their life wouldn't be, as against any whisper of a higher interest, worth an hour's purchase. They sit there in the florid majesty of the taste of their time—a light now, alas, generally clouded; and I pretend of course to speak, in alluding to them, of

no individual case of danger or doom. It is only a question of that unintending and unconvincing expression of New York everywhere, as yet, on the matter of the *maintenance* of a given effect— which comes back to the general insincerity of effects, and truly even (as I have already noted) to the insincerity of the effect of the sky-scrapers themselves. There results from all this—and as much where the place most smells of its millions as elsewhere—that unmistakable New York expression of unattempted, impossible maturity. The new Paris and the new Rome do at least propose, I think, to be old—one of these days; the new London even, erect as she is on leaseholds destitute of dignity, yet does, for the period, appear to believe in herself. The vice I glance at is, however, when showing, in our flagrant example, on the forehead of its victims, much more a cause for pitying than for decrying them. Again and again, in the upper reaches, you pause with that pity; you learn, on the occasion of a kindly glance up and down a quiet cross-street (there being objects and aspects in many of them appealing to kindness) that such and such a house, or a row, is " coming down "; and you gasp, in presence of the elements involved, at the strangeness of the moral so pointed. It rings out like the crack of that lash in the sky, the play of some mighty teamster's whip, which ends by affecting you as the poor New-Yorker's one association with the idea of " powers above." " No "—this is the tune to which the whip seems flourished—" there's no step at which you shall rest, no form, as I'm constantly showing you, to which, consistently with my interests, you *can*. I build you up but to tear you down, for if I were to let sentiment and sincerity once take root, were to let any tenderness of association once accumulate, or any ' love of the old ' once pass unsnubbed, what would become of *us*, who have our hands on the whipstock, please? Fortunately we've learned the secret for keeping association at bay. We've learned that the great thing is not to suffer it to so much as begin. Wherever it does begin we find we're lost; but as that takes some time we get in ahead. It's the reason, if you must know, why you shall ' run,' all, without exception, to the fifty floors. We defy you even to aspire to venerate shapes so grossly constructed as the arrangement in fifty floors. You may have a feeling for keeping on with an old staircase, consecrated by the tread of generations—especially when it's 'good,' and old staircases are often so lovely; but how can you have a feeling for keeping on with an old elevator, how can you have it any more than for keeping on with an old omnibus? You'd be ashamed to venerate the arrangement in fifty floors, accordingly, even if you could; whereby, saving you any moral trouble or struggle, they are conceived and constructed—and you must do us the justice of this care for your sensibility—in a manner to put the thing out of the question. In such a manner, moreover, as that there shall be immeasurably more of them, in quantity, to tear down than of the actual past that we are now sweeping away. Wherefore we shall be kept in precious practice. The word will perhaps be then—who knows?—for building from the earth-surface downwards; in which case it will be a question of tearing, so to speak, 'up.' It little matters, so long as we blight the superstition of rest."

Yet even in the midst of this vision of eternal waste, of conscious, sentient-looking houses and rows, full sections of streets, to which the rich taste of history is forbidden even while their fresh young lips are just touching the cup, something charmingly done, here and there, some bid for the ampler permanence, seems to say to you that the particular place only asks, as a human home, to lead the life it has begun, only asks to enfold generations and gather in traditions, to show itself capable of growing up to character and authority. Houses of the best taste are like clothes of the best tailors—it takes their age to show us how good they are; and I frequently recognized, in the region of the upper reaches, this direct appeal of the individual case of happy construction. Construction at large abounds in the upper reaches, construction indescribably precipitate and elaborate—the latter fact about it always so oddly hand in hand with the former; and we should exceed in saying that felicity is always its mark.

But some highly liberal, some extravagant intention almost always is, and we meet here even that happy accident, already encountered and acclaimed, in its few examples, down-town, of the object shining almost absurdly in the light of its merely comparative distinction. All but lost in the welter of instances of sham refinement, the shy little case of real refinement detaches itself ridiculously, as being (like the saved City Hall, or like the pleasant old garden-walled house on the northwest corner of Washington Square and Fifth Avenue) of so beneficent an admonition as to show, relatively speaking, for priceless. These things, which I may not take time to pick out, are the salt that saves, and it is enough to say for their delicacy that they are the direct counterpart of those other dreadful presences, looming round them, which embody the imagination of new kinds and new clustered, emphasized quantities of vulgarity. To recall these fine notes and these loud ones, the whole play of wealth and energy and untutored liberty, of the movement of a breathless civilization reflected, as brick and stone and marble may reflect, through all the contrasts of prodigious flight and portentous stumble, is to acknowledge, positively, that one's rambles were delightful, and that the district abutting on the east side of the Park, in particular, never engaged my attention without, by the same stroke, making the social question dance before it in a hundred interesting forms.

The social question quite fills the air, in New York, for any spectator whose impressions at all follow themselves up; it wears, at any rate, in what I have called the upper reaches, the perpetual strange appearance as of Property perched high aloft and yet itself looking about, all ruefully, in the wonder of what it is exactly doing there. We see it perched, assuredly, in other and older cities, other and older social orders; but it strikes us in those situations as knowing a little more where it is. It strikes us as knowing how it has got up and why it must, infallibly, stay up; it has not the frightened look, measuring the spaces around, of a small child set on a mantel-shelf and about to cry out. If old societies are interesting, however, I am far from thinking that young ones may not be more so—with their collective countenance so much more presented, precisely, to observation, as by their artless need to get themselves explained. The American world produces almost everywhere the impression of appealing to any attested interest for the word, the *fin mot,* of what it may mean; but I somehow see those parts of it most at a loss that are already explained not a little by the ample possession of money. This is the amiable side there of the large developments of private ease in general—the amiable side of those numerous groups that are rich enough and, in the happy vulgar phrase, bloated enough, to be candidates for the classic imputation of haughtiness. The amiability proceeds from an essential vagueness; whereas real haughtiness is never vague about itself—it is only vague about others. That is the human note in the huge American rattle of gold—so far as the "social" field is the scene of the rattle. The "business" field is a different matter—as to which the determination of the audibility in it of the human note (so interesting to try for if one had but the warrant) is a line of research closed to me, alas, by my fatally uninitiated state. My point is, at all events, that you cannot be "hard," really, with any society that affects you as ready to learn from you, and from this resource for it of your detachment combining with your proximity, what in the name of all its possessions and all its destitutions it would honestly be "at."

LISPENARD'S MEADOWS

HARRIET PRESCOTT SPOFFORD.

I.

 I N a little hill far out in the northwest-ern suburb of the city of New York stood a century and a half ago the farm-house of Leonard Lispenard. The farm to which this house related was a portion of the estate that was known to successive generations as the Duke's Farm, the King's Farm, the Queen's Farm, and finally—when it became the property of the Corporation of Trinity—as the Church Farm. Lispenard's holding, of which he was the lessee from Trinity, was styled specifically the Dominie's Bouerie or the Dominie's Hook, and was a con-siderable property lying between the North River and a bit of swamp where now is West Broadway. The southern line of the bouerie was close upon that of the present Reade Street; and thence it ex-tended to the southern edge of the wide valley through which discharged lazily into the Hudson the stream from the Col-lect or Fresh Water Pond.

Where that stream then was, now is Ca-nal Street. Of the swamp that once made the whole valley a dangerous quagmire, there does not remain a trace—save, possi-bly, in some of the cellars thereabouts; nor would any chance wayfarer along Canal Street be likely to identify this region with the meadows which came by luck and love into the possession of Leonard Lispenard.

The Council granted Anthony Rutgers (whose daughter Leonard Lispenard after-ward married) the fee of the swamp—being a parcel of seventy acres—on condition that he should pay for it "a moderate quit-rent," and that he should "clear it and drain it within a year." At his death the meadows passed into the hands of his daughter and her husband, and thence-forth were known as Lispenard's Mea-dows.

CANAL STREET AND ST. JOHN'S CHURCH.

II.

There were no brick walls in that vicinity in Lispenard's time. The upper end of Broadway, from about the Park onward, was a draggled bit of lane which came to a sudden ending (about where White Street now is) against a set of bars. Up this lane in the early mornings, and down it again in the late afternoons, went daily sleek and comfortable cows—going forth and back between their aristocratic stables in the court quarter of the city, over on Pearl and Nassau and Wall streets, and the meadows where (with the rating of bovine parlor boarders) they feasted in luxury upon Lispenard's rich grass.

After all, it is not so very long ago that the cows thus made their processional and recessional journeyings to open pastures which now are many miles away from even the smallest scrap of natural green. Several of the old gentlemen with whom of late I have talked about the days when all the world was young—that is to say, when they were young themselves—remember well those open meadows and those pampered cows; and one even has

told me that, by no more of a charm than closing his eyes and thinking about old times, he can hear again plainly the melancholy donging of the cow-bells—a dull, sad, droning sound—as the cows come slowly homeward down Broadway in the sunset glow of those vanished summer days.

It is only a lifetime ago, therefore, that Lispenard's Meadows were a conspicuous feature of what now is a far-down part of the town. Nowadays a New York boy cannot obtain a pleasure of that sort save by first taking a railway journey; but one of my blithe old gentlemen recalls with joy how time and again he put on his skates at the Stone Bridge—that is to say, where now is the intersection of Broadway and Canal Street—and skated away over the flooded meadows, and around the base of Richmond Hill, and up the Minetta Creek (across the marsh that later was transformed into Washington Square), and so, close upon the line of what in the fulness of time was to be the Fifth Avenue, clear to the north of the Fourteenth Street of the present day.

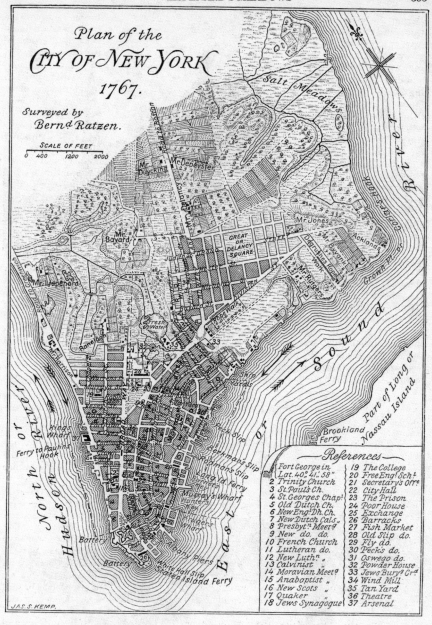

Plan of the
CITY OF NEW YORK
1767.

Surveyed by
Bernd Ratzen.

SCALE OF FEET
0   400   1200   2000

References

Fort George in Lat. 40°. 41'. 58"	19 The College
1 Trinity Church	20 Free Engl Schl
2 St. Paul's Ch.	21 Secretary's Offe
3 St. Georges Chapl	22 City Hall
4 Old Dutch Ch.	23 The Prison
5 New Engl Dh. Ch.	24 Poor House
6 New Dutch Cals	25 Exchange
7 Presbytn Meetg	26 Barracks
8 New do. do.	27 Fish Market
9 French Church	28 Old Slip do.
10 Lutheran do.	29 Fly do.
11 New Luthn	30 Peck's do.
12 Calvinist	31 Oswego do.
13 Moravian Meetg	32 Powder House
14 Anabaptist	33 Jews Buryg Grd
15 New Scots	34 Wind Mill
16 Quaker	35 Tan Yard
17 Jews Synagogue	36 Theatre
18	37 Arsenal

JAS. S. KEMP.

Richmond Hill—when my old gentleman thus came skating around it in winters more than seventy years gone by—really was a hill: the southwestern outjut of the low range called the Zandtberg (that is to say, sand hills), which swung away in a long curve from near the present Clinton Place and Broadway to where Varick and Van Dam streets now cross. The Minetta Water expanded into a large pond at the base of the hill, and—to quote the elegant language of an earlier day—

"from the crest of this small eminence was an enticing prospect: on the south, the woods and dells and winding road from the lands of Lispenard, through the valley where was Borrowson's Tavern; and on the north and west the plains of Greenwich Village made up a rich prospect to gaze on."

Yielding to the enticements of the prospect, Abraham Mortier, Esq., Commissary to His Majesty's forces, purchased Richmond Hill about the year 1760, and built there for himself a dwelling which was held in the taste of the period to be vastly fine. According to the description that has come down to us, Mr. Commissary Mortier's house was "a wooden building of massive architecture, with a lofty portico supported by

PUMP ON GREENWICH STREET BELOW CANAL: STILL IN USE.

Ionic columns, the front walls decorated with pilasters of the same order, and its whole appearance distinguished by a Palladian character of rich though sober ornament."

During Mortier's reign on Richmond Hill that agreeable country-seat gained a reputation for liberal hospitality that it long maintained. Its most distinguished guest of that period was Sir Jeffrey, afterward Lord, Amherst, who made the house his headquarters when he had ended those successful campaigns which broke the power of France in America, and which—it is well for New-Yorkers to remember—saved a good half of the State of New York from being now a part of Canada.

Later, Mr. Vice-President John Adams occupied Richmond Hill—keeping up the

PARK AT THE FOOT OF CANAL STREET.

establishment on a scale not quite so liberal as that of the Commissary, perhaps, but with a fitting state and dignity. A glimpse of the interior of this household is given by Gulian C. Verplanck, writing in *The Talisman* for 1829, in his description of a Vice-Presidential dinner party. "There, in the centre of the table," writes Mr. Verplanck, "sat Vice-President Adams in full dress, with his bag and *solitaire*, his hair frizzled out each side of his face as you see it in Stuart's older pictures of him. On his right sat Baron Steuben, our royalist republican disciplinarian general. On his left was Mr. Jefferson, who had just returned from France, conspicuous in his red waistcoat and breeches, the fashion of Versailles. Opposite sat Mrs. Adams, with her cheerful, intelligent face. She was placed between the Count du Mous-

THE LOCKSMITH'S SIGN.

tiers, the French embassador, in his red-heeled shoes and ear-rings, and the grave, polite, and formally bowing Mr. Van Birkel, the learned and able envoy of Holland. There too was Chancellor Livingston, then still in the prime of his life, so deaf as to make conversation with him difficult, yet so overflowing with wit, eloquence, and information that while listening to him the difficulty was forgotten. The rest were members of Congress, and of our Legislature, some of them no inconsiderable men."

The successor to Vice-President Adams in the tenancy of this estate, and the tenant with whom its name always is most closely associated, was Aaron Burr: to whom was executed a sixty-nine years' lease of the property on May 1, 1797; and who here, before and during his term as Vice-President, lived in the handsome fashion becoming to so accomplished a man of the world. It was from this house that he went forth, that July morning in the year 1804, to fight his duel with Hamilton over on the other side of the Hudson beneath the Weehawken Heights.

"The last considerable man to live at Richmond Hill," again to quote Mr. Verplanck, "was Counsellor Benzon; a man who had travelled in every part of the world, knew everything, and talked all languages." And Mr. Verplanck testifies that this gentleman maintained the hospitable traditions of the house by adding: "I recollect dining there in company with thirteen gentlemen, none of whom I ever saw before, but all pleasant fellows, all men of education and of some note—the Counsellor a Norwegian, I the only American, the rest of every different nation in Europe, and no two of the same, and all of us talking bad French together."

Not many years after this cosmopolitan dinner party, the cutting and slashing Commissioners by whom the existing City Plan was begotten doomed Richmond Hill, and all the rest of the Zandtberg range, to be levelled—to the end that the low lands thereabouts might be filled in. By ingenious methods, the old house was lowered gradually as the land was cut away from under it until it reached at last the present street level, and found itself on the north side of Charlton Street a little east of Varick—which streets, being opened, destroyed what remained to it of surrounding grounds. For a while it languished as a road tavern; and then, I fancy thankfully, disappeared entirely

OLD NEWEL-POST.

that in its place the row of smug little brick houses on Charlton Street might be reared. The garden which lay around this ancient residence was on the hill-top, a like sort: music, a hall for dancing, lamp-lit groves in which to wander between the dances, and "tables spread with various delicacies"—all for the benefit of

EMIGRANT HOUSE, NEAR THE DOCKS.

a hundred feet or so above the present level of the land; but there still remains, in the very open block between Charlton and King and Varick and Macdougal streets, a surviving fragment of the garden which lay westward of the house in its degenerate tavern days.

III.

Close upon the southern borders of Lispenard's Meadows were Vauxhall and Ranelagh gardens; two vastly agreeable places of genteel amusement to which resorted the gay gentlefolk of New York's frolic past. These gardens were in humble imitation of their famous prototypes in London, and provided entertainment of a "company gayly drest, looking satisfied," as Goldsmith phrased it when describing the older gardens in his *Citizen of the World*.

The New York Vauxhall was known originally as the Bowling Green Gardens, and as such—being shown on Lyne's map —certainly was in existence as far back as the year 1729. It received its more pretentious name about the middle of the last century, and continued to be a place of fashionable resort during the ensuing forty years. With the revival of the city's prosperity which came when the Revolutionary war was well ended, the land occupied by the gardens became too valuable to be used for such merely deco-

CAST NEWEL ON GREENWICH STREET.

of sleighs. The world went in a simpler and heartier way then, and the road-side taverns had a place in the social economy that was very far from low. I have quoted in another paper the appreciative comments of the Reverend Mr. Burnaby (an English traveller who surveyed this city about one hundred and forty years ago) upon the kissing-bridge—an institution which evidently struck him favorably—and his careful explanation of the conditions which made kissing-bridges possible also explains how such outlying resorts as Brannan's Garden were supported. "The amusements," writes his Reverence, "are balls and sleighing parties in the winter, and in the summer going in parties upon the water and fishing, or making excursions into the country. There are several houses pleasantly situated up the East River, near New York, where it is common to have turtle feasts. These happen once or twice a week. Thirty or forty gentlemen and ladies meet and dine together, drink tea in the afternoon, fish and amuse themselves till evening, and then return home in Italian chaises (the fashionable carriage in this and most parts of America, Virginia excepted, where they chiefly make use of coaches, and those commonly drawn by six horses), a gentleman and lady in each chaise."

Such a party as this, coming back about sunset from Turtle Bay, would be pretty certain to prolong the drive by switching off from the Post Road (now Broadway) at Love Lane (now Twenty-first Street), and so across to the Fitzroy Road (close on the line of the present Eighth Avenue) and down to Greenwich Village, and thence down the Greenwich Road toward home. And such a party also, even though it had stopped for a sup at the tavern which I am confident stood at the corner of Love Lane and the Southampton Road, and for another sup at "The Old Grapevine" in Greenwich, would find in these suppings only another reason for stopping at Brannan's for just one sup more.

And how brave a sight it must have been—the halt for refreshments being ended—when the long line of carriages got under way again and went dashing along the causeway over Lispenard's green meadows, while the silvered harness of the horses and the brilliant varnish of the Italian chaises gleamed and

rative purposes. Gradually the pleasure-grounds were diminished in size by encroaching buildings, and at last only the old Vauxhall House remained.

Ranelagh—in which pleasure-resort, presumably, Leonard Lispenard and his wife had a moneyed interest—had a handsomer beginning and a better end. It was the transformed homestead of Colonel Rutgers, Lispenard's father-in-law, and it remained respectable throughout the whole of its career.

About the year 1765 Brannan's Gardens were established over on the north side of the meadows, near the present crossing of Hudson and Spring streets. But this establishment, in the main, was a day-time resort, and made its account out of thirsty wayfarers—whereof there were many in that part of the island and in those cordial days. Close in front of it ran the Greenwich Road, the river-side drive along which went a gallant parade of fashionable New York in the bright summer and autumn weather, and which in winter was all ajingle with the bells

sparkled in the
rays of nearly level
sunshine from the
sun that was set-
ting there a hun-
dred years and
more ago!

IV.

For so long a
while did the cow-
bars across Broad-
way, a little north
of Warren Street,
check absolutely
the advance of the
city on the western
side of the island
that within the
present century
the ghosts of those
turtle - feasters, in
the ghosts of their
Italian chaises,
might have driven
across Lispenard's
Meadows without
perceiving any
change at all. Act-
ually, the levelling
undertaken at the
instance of the
Commissioners was
completed less than
sixty years ago;
and a still shorter
time has passed
since solid blocks
of houses were
erected on the land
which these radi-
cal reformers de-
spoiled of its natu-
ral beauty and then
proudly described
as "reclaimed."

AN OVAL WINDOW.

The secretary and engineer to these
devastating Commissioners, old Mr. John
Randel—who kept up a show of youthfulness to the last by signing his name
always John Randel Jr.—has left on
record a characteristically precise description of the region between the canal and
Greenwich Village as it was just before
the levelling process began; that is to say,
as it was a trifle over eighty years ago.

"In going from the city to our office
[in Greenwich] in 1808 and 1809," he
writes, under date of April 6, 1864, "I
generally crossed a ditch cut through
Lispenard's salt-meadow (now a culvert
under Canal Street) on a plank laid
across it for a crossing-place about midway between a stone bridge on Broadway
with a narrow embankment at each end
connecting it with the upland, and an
excavation then being made at, and said
to be for, the foundation of the present
St. John's Church on Varick Street.
From this crossing-place I followed a
well-beaten path leading from the city to
the then village of Greenwich, passing

AN OLD-TIME KNOCKER.

over open and partly fenced lots and fields, not at that time under cultivation, and remote from any dwelling - house now remembered by me except Colonel Aaron Burr's former country-seat, on elevated ground, called Richmond Hill, which was about 100 or 150 yards west of this path, and was then occupied as a place of refreshment for gentlemen taking a drive from the city. Its site is now in Charlton Street, between Varick and McDougal streets. I continued along this main path to a branch path diverging from it to the east, south of Minetta Water (now Minetta Street), which branch path I followed to Herring Street [now Bleecker Street], passing on my way there, from about 200 to 250 yards west, the country residence of Colonel Richard Varick, on elevated ground east of Minetta Water, called 'Tusculum,' the site of which is now on Varick Place, on Sullivan Street between Bleecker and Houston streets. On Broadway, north of Lispenard's salt-meadows, now Canal Street, to Sailor's Snug Harbor—a handsome brick building called by that name erected on elevated ground near the bend in Broadway near the present Tenth Street, and formerly the residence of Captain Randall—and from the Bowery Road westward to Minetta Water, there were only a few scattered buildings, except country residences, which were built back from Broadway with court-yards and lawns of trees and shrubs in front of them." All of which is quite in keeping with the statement of one of my old gentlemen that he remembers looking south from the stoop of his father's house on Leroy Street, in Greenwich, across a broad expanse of open country to the distant city; and east, also across open country, to the gallows which stood within the present limits of Washington Square.

V.

It is a fact illustrative of the high-pressure way in which this city of New York is run that the Canal Street region, whereof the youthfulness is proved by the foregoing testimony, already is old. In a fashion that would make a European city dizzy, it has dashed through all the phases which mark the progress from youth to age; and already, in no more than a man's lifetime, has passed on into decay.

Eighty years ago it was suburban and obscure. Twenty years later, Hudson Square having been laid out and St. John's Church built, it began to be fashionable. In another twenty years—the square being then surrounded by the wide-fronted houses of which many stately wrecks remain—it was one of the most gravely respectable parts of the town: and for more than a decade it remained at this aristocratical high-water mark. Then began its slow decline—which ended in a sudden and irrevocable plunge, in the year 1869, when the Hudson River Railroad Company crushed the region utterly, so far as its fitness to be an abiding-place of polite society was concerned, by clapping down four acres of freight station over the whole of the luckless park. Only one man of position staid by the wreck, and even may be said to have gone down with it. This was John Ericsson, the builder of the *Monitor*, who continued in his house for many years on St. John's Park, holding up in that frowsy and bustling region its traditional respectability, until he died there only a little while ago.

To-day, the dwellers upon St. John's Park are mainly foreigners: a few Germans, but more Italians—as even a blind man, possessing a travelled and intelligent nose, would know by the aggressive presence of several distinctively Neapolitan smells. The stately houses, swarming with this unwashed humanity, are sunk in such squalor that upon them rests ever an air of melancholy devoid of hope. They are tragedies in mellow-toned brick and carved wood-work that once was very beautiful.

By an odd twist of destiny it is mainly to the aristocratic houses on the square that an evil fate has come. The less-pretentious structures thereabouts have sunk only to the level of lodging or boarding houses; and many of them even—as is manifested by their superior air of self-respecting neatness — still are private dwellings.

THE STORY OF A STREET
(PART 5)

NEW YORK was flooded with visitors during the opening year of Washington's administration, and to many of them the cosmopolitan city of thirty thousand inhabitants must have been an astonishing and not altogether agreeable revelation. Certainly its accommodations for transients left something to be desired, for it had never recovered from the effects of the war; its houses and streets were in a lamentable condition, and sore discomfort was apt to be the portion of those who tarried within its gates. Indeed, the only quarter of the national capital which escaped the bitter complaints and scornful descriptions which are recorded at length in the diaries and correspondence of the day was Wall Street. For that well-ordered highway, however, even the most disgruntled strangers often had a word of praise, especially those who viewed it on fine afternoons from Daniel McCormick's doorstep. Of course only a favored few were privileged to join the charmed circle of that prince of bachelors, but the guests invited to view the passing throngs from the point of vantage of No. 39,* on the south side of the street, witnessed a uniquely interesting scene in the company of people who knew everybody and everything about everybody, and could appraise to a nicety the social standing of all the passers-by. In fact, McCormick's hospitable mansion was the news centre and clearing-house for gossip of the fashionable world of which Wall Street was the centre in the first year of the republic.

* This is the old numbering of the street. It is very difficult to locate the corresponding house numbers of the street as it exists to-day, as there was no regularity or sequence in the numbers until late in 1790. No. 5 was, however, apparently at the northwest corner of Wall and William; No. 20 was one of the corners of Wall and Water; No. 32 was near the Coffee House; No. 44 one door east of the northeast corner of Wall and William; and No. 81 one of the opposite corners.

Prior to the war the social prestige of the thoroughfare had been second only to Pearl Street,* but that famous highway, though it still boasted the finest houses in the city, had seen its best days, and politically, socially, and historically its rival now reigned supreme. Outwardly the appearance of Wall Street was not as attractive as it had been ten or fifteen years earlier, for few of its splendid shade trees remained, and that artistic feature had gone, never to return, for the local authorities had passed an ordinance imposing a penalty of five pounds for planting a tree anywhere below Catherine Street, except in front of a church or other public building, and no one seemed inclined to dispute the wisdom of this law.

From an architectural standpoint, however, its condition was vastly improved, for Federal Hall was far more imposing than the old City Hall, and Trinity, which had risen from the ashes of the former building, was altogether more dignified and impressive than its predecessor. Moreover, the whole aspect of the street was more settled, substantial, and uniformly residential than it had previously been, for, with the exception of Baker's Tavern, the headquarters of a club at the corner of New Street, a few shops like Adam Prior's, the fashionable caterer at No. 59, and Panton's, the leading jeweller, at No. 38, and the public buildings and churches, almost every house from Broadway to Pearl Street was a dignified private dwelling displaying the little oval tin plate which indicated that it had been duly insured in the Mutual Assurance Company against fire.

* At this time Pearl Street was only known as such from the present State Street to Broad. From Broad to Wall it was called Great Dock Street; from Wall to Chatham it was Queen Street. The finest houses were in the Great Dock Street section.

It was not the Wall Street of brick and stone, however, which fascinated those who viewed it on gala days from Daniel McCormick's high doorstep. What interested them was the panorama of life, the constantly changing figures, the gay colors, the quaint characters, the men of mark, the fashions and foibles—all the human elements of the miniature Vanity Fair that strutted and plumed itself on the fashionable promenade through which there swirls to-day a hurrying stream of life. Here approached a remarkable old gentleman gowned in a black clerical robe and bands, and wearing a white buzz wig, a three-cornered hat, and silver shoe-buckles, who threaded his way through the crowd, representing all the city could boast of worth, wit, and culture, with a masterful clumping of his gold-headed cane upon the pavement, and the most ceremonious of salutations to right and to left. Any one of McCormick's coterie could inform the uninitiated that this was the Rev. Dr. John Rodgers, of the Presbyterian Church, a patriot it well became one to know, and a gentleman of such majestic dignity that he seldom appeared in public without his official robes, and rumor had it that he and his wife exchanged a formal bow and a deep courtesy each night when they retired. Here, too, appeared another gentleman of the old school in a scarlet coat and cocked hat, enthroned on the cushions of a quaint pony phaeton, from which he surveyed the moving throng with a proprietary air, his hands resting proudly upon his massive cane, for Washington's physician, Dr. John Bard, was the fashionable doctor of his day, and he could count his patients by the dozen on Wall Street when society took the air. The handsome man whom both of these old gentlemen distinguished with particularly gracious bows was Sir John Temple, whose too great "inclination for the American cause" had lost him the Lieutenant-Governorship of New Hampshire, but won him the hand of Miss Bowdoin of Massachusetts, and made him the most popular of British consul-generals.* In-

deed, Sir John was New York's official host, for he invariably welcomed every distinguished arrival in the city with a call of ceremony, and no one in the community was more generally admired.

Logically it should have been the French and not the English representative who found favor with the public in those days, but the observer who noted the Marquis de Moustier's red-heeled shoes and gold earrings in the crowd and inquired concerning their owner would learn that His Highness was not in high favor with the elect, and that his sister, Madame la Marquise de Brienne, the lady greeting the passers-by from her sedan-chair, was courted for her entertainments and unmercifully ridiculed behind her back. It must be admitted, however, that the Marquis had been guilty of even worse manners than his sister's guests, for if the gossips at McCormick's could be believed he had once actually brought his own cook to Vice-President Adams's house and caused private dishes to be served to him at his host's table, coolly remarking that he had had some experience with bad dinners in New York and could not afford to repeat it.

Probably none of these distinguished gentlemen would have been recognized by a stranger, but there were faces in the moving throng which were familiar beyond the confines of New York. For instance, almost every Virginian would have been able to identify Cyrus Griffin, the President of Congress, and Lady Christiana, his wife, who were well known in that State; and Thomas Jefferson, lately returned from the court of Versailles, in his red waistcoat and breeches, was quite as familiar to his compatriots as he was to many of the leaders in the city's social whirl. Here, too, the observer could note John Hancock, whose name was writ large on the historic scroll, and Aaron Burr, the Attorney-General, conspicuous for the cordiality with which he was greeted upon every hand, particularly by the ladies, among whom he always found exceptionable favor; and Baron Steuben, the disciplinary genius of Valley Forge, now president of the Society of the Cincinnati; and Colonel John Trumbull, the portrait-painter, who

---

* Sir John Temple died in New York and was buried in St. Paul's churchyard, where the tablet erected to his memory can be seen to-day.

Drawn by Harry Fenn

WALL STREET THE CENTRE OF FASHION, 1789

Based on Old Prints and Documents in Lenox Library and New York Historical Society

had learned his art under Benjamin West; and Commodore Paul Jones, whom society preferred to call the Chevalier. There were many interesting rumors in circulation about the doughty little Commodore in those days, of which the story that he and Captain Landais had had an exciting encounter was on everybody's tongue. Landais was the naval officer who was credited with having displayed more discretion than valor, and more prudence than discretion, in the battle between the *Bon Homme Richard* and the *Serapis*. In fact, according to Jones's story, the Frenchman had remained safely out of range during most of that engagement, and when he had at last ventured near enough to be of service he had lost his head and raked the *Bon Homme Richard* instead of his adversary, after which masterly performance he had again sought and held the horizon line until the day was won. Landais denied these charges to his dying day, but a court of inquiry had found him guilty on other grounds, and from that moment the world was scarcely wide enough to hold him and his accuser. Therefore when it was rumored that he had confronted Jones on Water Street and spat upon the sidewalk, declaring, with great delicacy, that his defamer might regard the pavement as his face, there were those who thought the story characteristic of the Frenchman's histrionic instinct, but there were very few who believed that he could have roused his courage to the sticking-point and lived to tell the tale. Nevertheless, somebody must have credited the yarn, for Jones's spirited denial was printed over his own signature in a leading paper,* and the gossips continued to whisper it, glancing apprehensively over their shoulders, for many a long day after. There were others among the passing pedestrians, however, of whom the gossips had a less cautious word. For instance, Mrs. General Knox, decidedly plumper and altogether less romantic-looking than she was at the beginning of the war, when she eloped with Henry Knox (the Boston bookseller, turned artillerist), because her loyalist father would not countenance a rebel son-in-law. But it was not the stout-hearted young bride who accompanied her husband on

his perilous campaigns and lightened their hardships and won Washington's regard whom the gossips celebrated, but rather the stout-waisted matron who was the Mrs. Malaprop of their circle and at whose original remarks society twittered, not too politely, behind its well-drilled fans.

It was a fashionably attired company which filled the narrow sidewalks, the blue coats, variously colored waistcoats, and knee breeches of the men combining with the gay silks and satins affected by the women to lend brightness and an air of festivity to the scene. Indeed, some of the men arrayed themselves much more conspicuously than the women; for John Ramage, the Irish miniature-painter, whose studio was on William Street, not far from Wall, was accustomed to join the promenade attired in a scarlet coat with mother-of-pearl buttons, a white silk waistcoat embroidered with colored flowers, black satin breeches, with paste knee-buckles, white silk stockings, and a small cocked hat perched on his curled and powdered hair, and contrasted with this gorgeous display the description of the latest Parisian novelty in favor with the fair sex suggests extreme simplicity. This creation consisted of " a perriot and petticoat, both made of the same gray striped silk, trimmed all around with gauze cut in points, in the manner of Herrisons which were made of ribbons or Italian gauze. With this was worn a large gauze handkerchief with four satin stripes round its border, two very broad and the others less, the handkerchief itself being an ell and a half square, and for headdress a plain gauze cap made in the form of those worn by the elders or ancients in the nunneries."* Not all the ladies, however, exhibited such quiet tastes, for here and there were to be seen "celestial blues" and "caracos and petticoats of Indian taffaty" and "perriots with two collars, one yellow and one white"; and "blue satin shoes with rose-colored rosettes," and among the wearers of this brilliant raiment were numbered all the social leaders of their day. Here sauntered Mr. and Mrs. John Watts, the latter better known as Lady Mary (for the élite of the republican court still scrupulously accorded their titles to women

---

* New York *Packet*, October 29, 1787.

* New York *Gazette*, October 29, 1787.

of rank), and Assistant Secretary of the Treasury William Duer with his wife, the Lady Kitty of her day; and Colonel and Mrs. Alexander Hamilton, and Senator Ralph Izard and his lady, who was Miss de Lancey of New York, and many another couple whose names were widely known.

Indeed, Wall Street might have called the roll of the socially elect from Mrs. John Jay's famous list of guests almost any summer afternoon, and reported all present or accounted for; for many of the most prominent families, such as the Winthrops, the Jaunceys, the Verplancks, and the Ludlows, still lived on the highway, and several of the most distinguished members of Congress, such as Richard Basset, Benjamin Contee, Thomas Sumter, Elias Boudinot, Lambert Cadwallader, and Richard Bland Lee, dated from Mrs. Daubenay's (Dabney's) fashionable boarding-house. In fact, this exclusive establishment made almost every visitor of distinction a temporary resident of Wall Street, and fortunate indeed were those who secured its accommodations, for the Merchants' Coffee House* was no longer in its prime, and Fraunces' Tavern was not a desirable hostelry after its proprietor, Black Sam, assumed charge of the Presidential ménage. There was, however, another refuge for the wayfarer at No 81 (one of the southerly corners of Wall and William), and this private hostelry, which rejoiced in the plebeian

name of Huck's, sheltered Daniel Huger, Thomas Tudor Tucker, Edanus Burke, and other Congressional representatives from the South.

From McCormick's hospitable door-

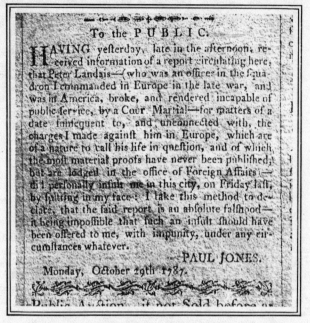

CARD FROM PAUL JONES PUBLISHED IN "NEW YORK PACKET"
From files of New York Historical Society

step the visitor could likewise descry the residences of most of the exponents of New York's official life. At the northwest corner of Wall and William streets lived Francis Van Berckel, the minister from Holland; at No. 5, Samuel Otis, the Secretary of State; at No. 8, the Postmaster, William Bedlow; at No. 13, John Lawrence, the first Congressman from New York city, who later became a judge and a United States Senator; at No. 44, General John Lamb, the first Collector of the Port; at No. 52, Richard Varick, the Mayor; at No. 58, Alexander Hamilton, the Secretary of the Treasury; at No. 60, William Irvin, the Commissioner of Accounts; at No. 64, James Culbertson, the High Constable; while at other points lived the Dennings, the Wilkes, the Pintards, the Edgars, and other prominent New-Yorkers of their day.

---

* Though this historic hostelry, then known as Bradford's, was passing, it was utilized by the Marine Society, the New York Hospital, the Order of Cincinnati, St. John's Masonic Lodge No. 2, and other notable organizations for their early meetings.

Such were some of the men and women who lived and moved and had their being in Wall Street, and the visitors who chanced to be present on one of the occasions when Washington attended Congress in his state coach saw the highway at its best. It was a wonderful creation, that canary-colored Presidential chariot,* with its ornamental crests and its decorations of gilded nymphs and cupids, but Washington doubtless often wished that it was a trifle less conspicuous as he rumbled over the stones of Wall Street to Federal Hall. Indeed, there was probably nothing in his many vexatious official duties which he so thoroughly disliked as making this public exhibition of himself, despite the anti-Federalist sneers at his aristocratic tastes and tendencies. But the general public unquestionably enjoyed the spectacle, and when the ceremonial carriage, with a gorgeous coachman on its thronelike box, and a footman standing behind, and its six horses with their gay trappings and "painted" hoofs, swung into view, pre-

ceded by uniformed outriders and followed by an accompanying cavalcade, all the local world was there to see.

As a matter of fact, Wall Street saw very little of the President during his official residence in New York. Of course he attended the inauguration ball, which was held on May 7, 1789, at the City Assembly Rooms on Broadway, just around the corner of Wall, where he danced two cotillons and perhaps a minuet, of which event Jefferson has left a description that would do credit to the most imaginative sensation-monger of the modern press. The Executive likewise honored the grand affair at the French Embassy, where those who took part in the quadrilles were attired in gorgeous costumes symbolical of America and France, and the festivities "were at their height at ten o'clock"; but there is very little evidence of his having been present at the other distinguished routs and entertainments of the day.* Nor did he grace the dinners for which Wall Street was famous in the years of its social glory, when many a distinguished company was gathered around its hospitable boards. This was partially due to the death of his mother, which occurred during the year, and his own ill health; but the difficulty of making distinctions was mainly responsible for his absence, and even then one of his letters shows that he and his wife never had an opportunity of dining alone. In fact, he had not been long in town before the necessity of adopting some general rules as to what invitations he would give or accept became apparent, and Hamilton drew a simple plan regulating the Presidential entertainments, re-

New-York, May 7, 1789.

The President's Houſhold.

WHEREAS all Servants and others employed to procure Provisions or Neceſſaries for the Houſhold of the PRESIDENT of the UNITED STATES, will be furniſhed with Monies for thoſe Purpoſes;——

NOTICE IS THEREFORE GIVEN, that no Accounts, for the Payment of which the Public might be conſidered as reſponſible, are to be opened with any of them.

SAMUEL FRAUNCES,
May 4, 1789. Steward of the Houſhold.

A Collection of Natural Curioſities.
From AFRICA and the Coaſt of BRAZIL,

A WARNING BY WASHINGTON'S STEWARD
From files of New York Historical Society

* Part of this historic vehicle was later cut into boxes and sold at a church fair, and the seat and steps turned into garden ornaments by the unimaginative individuals who obtained possession of it.

* There were no less than three dancing-schools in the immediate vicinity of Wall Street at this time.

ceptions, dinners, visits, etc., which, with very slight modifications, has governed every occupant of the White House to the present day. Thus the etiquette of the Executive Mansion may fairly be said to have originated in Wall Street, where Hamilton and his fair lady were famed for their hospitality.

At their table assembled such men as Jefferson, Knox, Adams, Jay, Madison, and other prominent statesmen, and the sentiments pledged on those occasions were eagerly awaited and variously interpreted, for more than one important event in the history of the nation had its inception at these little dinners in Wall Street.* Indeed, the political leaders usually divulged their policies and platforms through the medium of carefully worded toasts, and not all of them were as plain and pointed as that offered at the dinner of the General Society of Mechanics and Tradesmen, which suggested "*A cobweb pair of breeches, a porcupine saddle, a hard-trotting horse, and a long journey for all the enemies of liberty!*" But Hamilton was not the only official noted for entertainments of this sort, for Van Berckel, the minister from Holland, kept open house at the old Marston mansion on the northwest corner of Wall and William, and here all the members of the diplomatic corps with their wives and families were wined and dined informally and in state, and Daniel McCormick's bachelor banquets at No. 39 were justly the talk of the town. Of course there was nothing magnificent or luxurious in these entertainments. New York was still a provincial town of comparatively simple tastes, and there was nowhere any display of wealth. Society depended for its importance upon the personal qualities of its members, and in the heart of the capital there was gathered from all parts of the country a company which gave it a tone and distinction impossible under modern conditions.

Brilliant as its social record had become, Wall Street had not in the mean time lost anything of its former official dignity and had materially added to its historic laurels. On March 25, 1790, Trinity was duly consecrated, and, with

a canopied pew set apart for the President and another specially reserved for the Governor, it bade fair to continue its long tradition as the official place of worship.

Meanwhile within the halls of Congress business of vital importance to the nation had been transacted. On the 7th of April, 1789, a committee was appointed by the Senate to frame a bill for the judicial courts of the United States, and on June 12 of that year Richard Henry Lee reported the measures drawn by Oliver Ellsworth, of Connecticut, which brought into existence the most powerful tribunal known to the history of the law. Indeed, it was on September 24, 1789, in Federal Hall, at the corner of Wall and Nassau streets, that Washington performed the most important act of his administrative career, for on that day he signed the measure creating the Supreme Court of the United States. Certainly nothing ordained by Congress before or since that day has had so profound an effect upon American history as the creation of that mighty tribunal, and from the little court-house on the other side of Wall Street came two of its first judges—John Jay and Brockholst Livingston.

In February, 1790, another significant event occurred in Federal Hall, for a petition presented by the Quakers praying for the abolition of slavery led to a sharp debate, and the next day the last word of advice which Franklin was destined to offer his countrymen was received in the form of a memorial signed by him as President of the Pennsylvanian Society for Promoting the Abolition of Slavery. The discussion on this subject lasted for more than a month, and even at that early date there were muttered threats of secession in the air. It was not the slavery question, however, which then suggested the dissolution of the Union, but rather Hamilton's policy for the assumption of the State debts, which, to the State-rights men, seemed to foreshadow the extinction of all local sovereignty. So bitter was the feeling against the Federal plan that Hamilton was forced to offer great concessions to carry his point, and the compromise he negotiated disposed of New York as the permanent national capital.

---

* It was at a dinner at Jefferson's house that the bargain was struck whereby the national capital was located at Washington.

TRINITY CHURCH (CONSECRATED MARCH 25, 1790)
Taken from the northwest corner of Wall Street

Meanwhile the fates had long been combining to strip the city of its official honors, for an extraordinarily hot summer and a bitter winter had prejudiced all the visiting members of Congress and intensified the local jealousy and resentment of less favored communities, all of whom were vigorously contending for the possession of the prize. Such was the situation when Hamilton made his famous bargain with Jefferson by which the Potomac was selected as the site of the future capital, Philadelphia given a lease of power for ten years, and the national government authorized to assume the debts of the several States. The part of this compromise which divested New York of its official character took the form of an act of Congress which was signed by Washington on July 16, 1790, but Wall Street was privileged to witness one more interesting ceremony before it went into effect.

Late in that month Colonel Marinus

Willett, who had been in the South nego-
tiating a treaty of peace with the Creek
Indians, returned to New York, bringing
with him the chief and twenty-eight war-
riors of the tribe. At every stopping-
place on their journey Colonel Willett
and his party had been received with
great courtesy and hospitality, and on
their arrival in New York they were met
and welcomed by a new society whose
members donned bucktails and otherwise
arrayed themselves in full Indian costume,
and assuming entire charge of the proceedings, conducted the puzzled redskins
to Federal Hall.

Such was the first public appearance
of Tammany, organized in 1789 to spread
*" the smile of charity, the chain of friend-
ship, and the flame of liberty, and in
general whatever may tend to perpetuate
the love of freedom or the political advantage of this country."* None of those
worthy objects would seem to have called
the society into the field as the self-
appointed reception committee to the
visiting Creek Indians, but the occasion
undoubtedly served to bring the organization into prominence, and under its
auspices the proceedings, though smack-
ing somewhat of burlesque, were apparently conducted to every one's satisfaction. Indeed, the Society of the Cincinnati, whose aristocratic pretensions unquestionably called St. Tammany into
the field, fraternized with its rival on this
occasion, and on July 27, 1790, the President made his last official visit to Wall
Street in his ornate coach, with all the
trappings of dignity, to sign a treaty
with the Indians and pass the pipe
of peace.

It was August 12 when Congress adjourned, and on the 30th Washington
was conveyed across the North River in
the same magnificent barge that had
brought him to the city which he was
never to see again, and almost with his
departure changes were begun in Wall
Street which were to give it a new place
in a very different phase of history.

THE NEW YORK POLICE DEPARTMENT

NEW - YORKERS religiously believe that they have the best police system and the finest police force in existence. As represented by the Board of Aldermen — August 11, 1886 — they hold that "the Police Department has reached a standard of efficiency hitherto unattained, and superior to that of any force in the world." This opinion, expressed after the funeral of ex-President Grant, may only be that of a majority; but, nevertheless, exceptions prove the rule.

What is the number of the metropolitan police force? what are its duties? how is it organized? and in what manner are its duties performed? are questions whose answers determine the soundness or unsoundness of the popular faith.

The number of the police force, of all ranks and grades, on the last day of A.D. 1885, was 2933, including 35 probationers. The Legislature of the State of New York, on May 12, 1886, unanimously authorized the addition of 500, in deference to the general conviction that it was numerically too small to cope with the possible emergencies of the times. The city of New York, estimating its population at 1,650,000, then had, exclusive of the Central Park force, one police-officer to every 562 of the inhabitants. This, in view of the heterogeneous character of the people, and the peculiar relation of the city to the continent, was really an insufficient supply. In 1883 Philadelphia had one policeman to every 636 of its citizens; Baltimore, one to 525; Boston, one to 487; the metropolitan district of London, one to 342; and the ancient city of London, one to every 100.

The Police Department of New York, established and organized under the law of 1870, consists of the Board of Police — which is composed of four Commissioners, appointed by the Mayor — of the police force, and of officials appointed by the Commissioners. The term of each Commissioner extends over six years, during which his labors are lightened by the aid of a secretary. His salary is fixed at $5000 per annum. Stephen B. French, President of the Board of Police, is of French and Dutch ancestry, and is a native of Long Island. Fitness for his post was largely received through the early discipline of a sperm-whaler's adventurous experience, followed by nearly five years of changeful fortune in California. Mercantile life next sharpened his faculties, and prepared him for the conspicuous career in politics and public affairs upon which he entered in 1865. Appointed Police Commissioner in May, 1879, he was elected to the presidency of the Board in 1880, and still retains that office.

Fitz-John Porter, appointed October 28, 1884, is a native of New Hampshire, a graduate of West Point Military Academy, and a distinguished officer of the Mexican and civil wars.

John McClave, appointed November 24, 1884, was born in New York, graduated at the College of the City of New York, is a lumber merchant by occupation, and a successful politician.

John R. Voorhis, appointed May 9, 1885, was born in New Jersey, is a builder by trade, and is now serving for the third time as Commissioner of Police. Like all his colleagues, he is credited with rare intuition, quick perception, concentrated thought, remarkable tact, endurance, and executive ability. Courteous, prompt, positive, and efficient, the members of the Board of Police exemplify some of the best qualities of the American body-politic.

Each member of the Board of Police has specific duties. The President must examine and approve charges against officers of all grades before they are tried,

THE NEW YORK POLICE HEAD-QUARTERS, MULBERRY STREET.

ers. The office of Commissioner is not a sinecure, and when worthily filled absorbs most of the business time and energy of the incumbent.

Every Wednesday at 10 A.M. one of the number must preside at the trial of members of the force against whom written specific charges have been preferred. Pertinent testimony, sometimes given under subpœna, for or against the accused, is reduced to writing by an official stenographer, and must be examined by three at least of the Commissioners. Their proceedings are subject to review in the civil courts. All judgments must be in writing, entered in the department records, and notice thereof read to the force of the precinct to which the inculpated member belongs. During the year 1885 no less than 2570 charges were preferred against officers of all grades for violation of the rules. Some were accused of being off their posts, some of talking while on duty, and others of weightier offences. Sixteen dismissals, mainly for intoxication, followed, 1620 were fined to the amount of $9487 86, 317 reprimanded, and 517 exculpated. The remaining cases were still pending at the close of the year. All orders to the Superintendent of Police issue from the Board, and all expenditures of the Secret Service Fund for procuring useful information and for the arrest of criminals and suspects are at their discretion. Experience, observation, and inquiry combined have thus organized the Board of Police. They have also dictated the Superintendent's practice of frequently summoning each of the thirty-four cap-

and also answer communications on police subjects from all parts of the world. Commissioner Voorhis, as chairman of the Committee on Repairs and Supplies, is the purchaser of all required materials, and carefully scrutinizes the bills therefor rendered. He also visits all station-houses, and inspects their conditions and requirements. Commissioner Porter is chairman of the Board of Trustees of the Police Pension Fund, and as such spends much time in examining the applications of widows for pensions, petitions for retirement by old members of the force, and other matters of similar nature. Commissioner McClave is treasurer of the Police Board and also of the Pension Fund. In the first capacity he disbursed, during the year 1886, the sum of $3,853,272, appropriated by the Board of Estimate and Apportionment for the maintenance of the Police Department, and in the second, more than $250,000, collected from different sources, and paid over to pension-

tains to head-quarters, instructing them in the wishes of the Commissioners, and thus infusing fresh vigor and effectiveness into the entire force. The lax enforcement of excise laws, of the statutes in relation to gambling-houses and prostitutes, and the imminence of riot in labor strikes, are among the occasions of these personal interviews. Through this administration New York may justly claim that it affords as much of safety to life, liberty, and property as any city on the globe. Pugnacious ruffians, "sp'ilin' for a fight," can always be accommodated. The elements of violence and crime are never absent, but every outbreak is tolerably certain to leave the transgressor in the iron hands of justice. Political "pulls" have lost much of their ancient power, and should be totally paralyzed.

Under the instructions of the Board of Police, the members of the force exercise all the common-law and statutory powers of constables, except for the service of civil process; execute warrants for search or arrest issued by magistrates of the State in any part of it, and convey prisoners to the districts where they are made returnable; summarily arrest persons reasonably suspected of felony when found in the streets at night, or when visibly guilty of felony or misdemeanor; and may enter any house or building to suppress an affray or to execute plain duty. But they are prohibited from doing more than is necessary to the safe custody of prisoners in charge, from the use of pro-

STEPHEN B. FRENCH.

voking language, taking offence at harsh or abusive talk, or making arrests in personal quarrels, unless justified by the necessity of self-defence.

Ranking in the following order, 1, Superintendent, 2, Inspector, 3, Captain, 4, Sergeant, 5, Roundsman, 6, Patrolman, 7, Doorman, each division of the police force is charged with definite duties.

JOHN McCLAVE.

FITZ-JOHN PORTER.

JOHN R. VOORHIS.

watch-makers and jewellers, shows the estimation in which he is held by the mercantile community. The Socialists, whom he dispersed during the labor riots of 1877, respect his vigorous bravery. He divides with Inspector Byrnes the credit of unmasking more crime and convicting more criminals than any other man in the department. When raised from the rank of Inspector to that of Superintendent, he at once centralized the management, diminished the cost, and increased the efficiency of the force. He assigns the Inspectors in rotation to duty, issues orders received from the Board of Police, and supplements them with others in harmony with the originals and with the laws of the

WILLIAM MURRAY.

William Murray, appointed Superintendent of Police on the 9th of June, 1885, is the chief executive officer. For the occupancy of this arduous and responsible position he has been qualified by long years of excellent service. Born in New York, wounded at Bull Run while serving in the Ellsworth Zouaves, and joining the police force in 1866, he signalized himself by some very skilful arrests. To thieves, burglars, and gamblers his name is one of terror. A thousand-dollar watch and chain, presented by forty prominent

THOMAS BYRNES.

commonwealth. Exercising direct authority over detached companies, making and reporting details, inspecting prisons and station-houses, and the books and business of the latter; enforcing the laws against gambling-houses, lotteries, lewd resorts, and racing in the streets; assuming command at riots and great fires, reporting to the Board all diseases and nuisances that threaten the health or comfort of the citizens, providing for emergencies by suggestion, as in the establishment of the Bellevue Hospital ward for sick prisoners; keeping record of all orders, expenses, suspicious persons and places, reported crimes and misdemeanors for which no arrests have been made, houses of pros-

titution, assignation, and gambling—
his life is necessarily a busy one. Office-
work is abundant. The daily returns
from the various precincts must be examined and noted, grievances and complaints of visitors disposed of, Inspectors' reports scrutinized and the Inspectors instructed, the daily consolidated
report to the Board of Police prepared,
and the names of those arrested and
detained, and the reasons therefor, reported. Duty does not cease with daylight, but requires frequent nocturnal
visitation of precincts and station-
houses, in order to certainty that the
condition of all is agreeable to law.
The Superintendent is also obliged to
report quarterly upon the state of the
force, and to incorporate such statistics
and suggestions for its improvement as
to him may seem advisable. Besides
this, his duty is to forward all sworn
and formal charges against subordinates to the Committee on Rules and
Discipline for action. His salary of
$6000 appears to be well earned.

The four Inspectors are no less busily
employed. At present there are only
three, viz., Thomas Byrnes, George W.
Dilks, and Henry V. Steers. The last
joined the force in 1857, rose through all
the grades to his present position, while
patrolman saved seven persons from
drowning, and distinguished himself by
singly thrashing a desperate bully who
led a gang of desperadoes in their nightly
depredations. His knowledge of "crooks"
is exhaustive, and his respect for their
courage exceedingly small. Driven to
desperation, they often fight like cornered
rats, but will not add murder to lesser
crime unless certain of escape. To effect
the latter the most dangerous chances are
recklessly accepted. On the approach of
every storm Inspector Steers's barometric
ankle painfully recalls the memory of a
leap that nearly shook the teeth out of
his head, from the top of a high house to
that of one much lower, while in hot pursuit of a burglar, whom he triumphantly
captured.

George W. Dilks, who entered the force
as assistant captain in 1848, was made Inspector in 1860. In the tragic Astor Place
riot, incited by jealousy between the actors Forrest and Macready, he judiciously
commanded a body of police; and in the
terrible longshoremen's riots of 1857 conquered the disturbers, who fought with

GEORGE W. DILKS.

hay-sticks, cart-rungs, clubs, etc., after a
four days' conflict. In the draft riots of
1863 his gallantry was no less manifest.

Each Inspector is responsible for the
preservation of the peace and protection
of life and limb in his own district. His
daily and quarterly reports of duty, discipline, and police circumstance, together
with his books of record, contain much of
the matter on which the action of his official superiors is based. The long experience and excellent judgment of the three
Inspectors induced the Commissioners to

HENRY V. STEERS.

ALEXANDER S. WILLIAMS.

constitute them a Board of Examiners, whose duty it is to examine all applicants for promotion in the force before permitting them to appear before the Civil Service Examining Board.

The Board of Police Surgeons, which consists of eighteen professional men, including the president and secretary, is a constituent part of the force. Its members are not allowed to receive compensation for medical services to police-officers, nor to prefer private practice to the performance of official duty. It is also part of their task to take medical and surgical charge, gratuitously, of pensioners upon the Police Life-Insurance Fund and of their families whenever requested.

During the year 1885 the number of visits made by surgeons to police-officers was 22,863, and of visits to station-houses 816. More than 175 different diseases or injuries received treatment, and 2.48 per cent. of the corps were perpetually sick. Seven hundred and thirty-four applicants for appointment as patrolmen were examined, and 460 passed. Only three were found to be men of bad character and reputation.

Each of the thirty-four captains is vested with the power, subject to regulations, of posting the men under his command in such portions of his precinct, and of assigning to them such duties, as he may

think expedient. He must further make known the special merit or demerit of his inferiors, divide them into two platoons of two sections each, assign a sergeant to the command of each section, and one to the charge of the station-house.

The police captain is held strictly responsible for the preservation of the public peace in his own precinct, the safe custody of prisoners, the order and hygienic condition of his official quarters, and the due preservation of the library. Civility and due attention to all who call upon business affairs are to be exhibited, and all discussions of party politics by the men rigidly suppressed. He is required to journalize the times of his entering and leaving the building, to make requisitions for needful supplies, keep special record of all arrests and for what crimes, of the results of judicial proceedings, of the term of sentence and place of imprisonment of the convicted, and to report quarterly in detail. Every item of police duty, and of civil or criminal occurrence, is inscribed on the "blotter," which thus becomes a photographic exhibit of daily events affecting the peace and welfare of the city.

Many of the captains richly merit description of their services to the community. Space permits but the briefest allusions. Captain J. J. Mount and other officers of the same rank covered themselves with credit and renown by efficient gallantry in the draft and other riots. Captain Alexander S. Williams is one of the most prominent of his class. Perfectly fearless and resolute, he has made himself the dread and scourge of the worst criminals coming within reach of his arm. The Florence saloon and "Mulligan's Hell" were closed by his prowess. Very large amounts of property have been recovered by his ingenuity. His precinct is known as the "Tenderloin," because of its social characteristics. But none of its celebrities are allowed to infract the laws with impunity. One of the most eminent of newspaper proprietors is said to have been arrested and locked up on two different occasions for furious driving in the streets. Captain Williams's club enjoys the reputation among the roughs of being as hard, ready, and rough as themselves, and is certainly a notable instrument. Its owner is one of the most venomously hated, frequently tried, and most valuable of police-officers. Should any captaincy be vacant, or the incumbent be absent, a sergeant of the precinct is selected by the Superintendent or by the Board of Police to possess and exercise all his powers. Sergeants in rotation daily inspect the beds, bedding, clothes, and habits of policemen in their respective districts, and give to prisoners or lodgers memoranda of articles taken from them. One of the number goes on patrol with his section or platoon, vigilantly attends to duty throughout the tour, and returns with his men at its close. All of the 152 sergeants are required to have something of the military martinet in their composition, but not more than good taste and discipline justify. As such they report all derelictions from duty and all violations of order.

Sergeant T. V. Holbrow is keeper of the House of Detention, at 203 Mulberry Street, and returns daily to the Chief Clerk the number and names of committed and discharged witnesses who are unable to furnish security for appearance in criminal proceedings, and the number of those who remain in custody. He also reports weekly on the sanitary and dietary condition of his unique mansion. All letters addressed to the inmates must be open, submitted to his inspection, and also to delivery or retention as he may judge best. All conversations with the imprisoned are held in his presence, noted by him, and reported to the district Inspector. He himself is inhibited from converse with them, except in so far as their safe-keeping, comfort, or convenience is concerned.

Personal examination (April, 1886) of this dubious residence discovers that it consists of two buildings on the same lot, of which the one fronting on the street is allotted to women, who may go up and down its five stories at pleasure, but cannot leave it by front or rear. The back building is occupied by males, whose lavatory and bath-room are on the ground-floor; six bedrooms, with five beds in each, on the second, third, and fourth stories, and room for exercise in the fifth. The dining-room on the front lower floor displays the plain, wholesome food provided at so much per meal by the lady purveyor at the cost of the city. Six hundred volumes of light literature, history, biography, and travel beguile the tedium of captivity. Three women and fourteen men are held in durance questionable. One of the latter is deftly braiding horse-hair chains; the rest are vegetating in uncanny seclusion. All have been brought

PATROL WAGON.

hither since the 12th of the month. Unfortunates have occasionally been detained as long as four months, or even longer. Foreign residence, lack of fixed abode, probable purchasability, unwillingness to testify — as in the case of complainant strangers despoiled in houses of ill fame —and inability to give bail are held by many to warrant this forcible detention of witnesses to homicide or felonious assault. Here their board is free, remuneration by District Attorney or Judge probable, safety from bribery or intimidation assured, and presence, when needed to satisfy justice, secured. The Society for the Prevention of Cruelty to Children sometimes causes commitments to this establishment.

Opinions about the House of Detention are variant. It is a prison, and a gloomy one, although fare and lodging may be better than what the majority of miserable inmates ordinarily enjoy. Humanitarians, such as Mr. William Delamater, wish to see it abolished. The Police Report for 1885 regards it as "not only a blot upon the fair fame of this community, but a standing rebuke to the proper administration of justice in this great city." It is true that the wealthy criminal is often liberated on bail, while the poor friendless witness of his guilt is confined in jail. Here justice and liberty are at manifest odds. In 1885 the number of committals was 307; of discharges, 314; the average number of days' confinement to each prisoner, about 17; and the average price of meals for each person detained, $12 56. Add to the cost of food and maintenance the salaries of officers in charge, and the expenses of an institution "not demanded by justice or humanity" are seen to be considerable.

The duties of the 177 roundsmen—two to each platoon—include constant patrol, wise action in exigent cases, and exemplary conduct. Clerical offices and telegraphic operation when in-doors, behind the desk, are exacted of them.

The bulk of the police force, corresponding to the privates or enlisted men of the regular army, consisted on the 1st of January, 1886, of the 2396 patrolmen. On the 15th of June, according to the return of Deputy Chief Clerk Delamater, the native nationality of the 2936 men of all ranks and grades then constituting the police force was as follows: United States, 1745; Ireland, 974; Germany, 136; Austria, 4; Italy, 5; Switzerland, 1; Canada, 13; England, 30; Finland, 1; Scotland, 14; France, 6; Bavaria, 1; Nova Scotia, 2; Denmark, 1; Sweden, 2; West Indies, 1. Thus the United States have contributed 59.46, Ireland 33.17, and all other countries 7.37 per cent. of the whole. The Hibernian element, including those born in this country, is decidedly predominant. Naturally enough, those in whose constitution habits of subordination to authority have been ingrained by generations of servitude are most watchful and resolute when the enforcement of law is intrusted to their hands. Whatever their ancestral antecedents, the New York police have invariably illustrated the virtues of implicit obedience, self-control, manly courage, and intelligent fidelity. The club is at times quite freely used. The ideal policeman is only an ideal. The actual is but an approximation to the imaginary archetype, because he is only a man under all the limitations of the commonplace American citizen. Still, we are fain to believe he is a decided improvement upon the first uniformed policeman (July 8, 1693), who was invested by order of the Mayor with "a coat of ye citty livery, with a badge of ye citty arms, shoes, and stockings," charged to "ye account of the citty." He certainly is a vastly emended edition of the star-labelled functionary of 1850, whose favorite roosting-place was the barrels of a corner grocery, and who was commonly conspicuous for absence when his presence was most grievously needed. Out of the 700 or 800 more or less applicants for appointment every year, it is matter of congratulation that so few unfit men are successful.

Every candidate is duly examined as to his fitness for the service. This fitness must be of perfect physical health and superior muscular and physical development. Stature should not be under 5 feet $7\frac{1}{2}$ inches on the bare feet, avoirdupois, without clothing, of 138 pounds, and naked chest measurement of $33\frac{1}{2}$ inches. Any disease bars acceptance, and is ground of dismissal. He must also be neat and cleanly in person, and free from the use of private medicine at the epoch of appointment. Intellectual qualification must be equal to the due discharge of police duty. Besides the ability to read and write the English language understandingly, he must be sufficiently ac-

THE NEW YORK POLICEMAN OF 1693.

quainted with municipal, State, and national law to comprehend the nature and extent of his functions. This, together with expert professional knowledge, is acquired in the School of Instruction under the officer in charge and his assistants.

The School of Instruction has two departments, one for drill in the school of the soldier and of the company, and the other for instruction at Police Head-quarters. In the latter, Sergeant Henry O. Corbett instructs neophytes in about two hundred rules of patrol duty.

The undergraduates are further instructed as to the authority of policemen under the Code of Criminal Procedure. Police powers under the Sanitary Code are also made clear. No curriculum of instruction in pastoral theology, clinical surgery, or legal procedure is more exhaustive. Not one is so thorough. A surgeon sent by the Society on First Aid to the Injured adds the finishing touches by a course of five lectures. Examination follows, and if the examined pass the ordeal, each receives a certificate from the society. Familiarity with rules and duties is to be subsequently kept alive by comprehensive study of the Police Manual.

The moral character of every applicant must have the voucher of five petitioners for his appointment—all of whom certify from personal knowledge to his sobriety, industry, and good conduct—and also the corroborative testimony of independent official investigation. He must also endure the test of civil service examination by Inspector Byrnes, Hugh Bonner, the chief of the Fire Department, and the secretary of the Board. This puts his memory, knowledge of localities, and aptitude for business to the proof. Vacancies are filled by those who have passed highest in open competitive examinations, and have borne the athletic trials of Wood's Gymnasium and of preliminary drill. Promotions are regulated by the same standard. Preference in appointment is given to such as have been honorably discharged from the military or naval service of the United States in the civil war. One month of satisfactory probation is followed by certified appointment, but does not exempt from triennial inquiry into general fitness for continuance in service. Neither political nor religious opinion or affiliation can legally affect appointment or promotion. Both are professedly based upon positive merit. The Board of Police is equally divided between the two great political parties; a majority of the captains is said to belong to one, and a majority of the sergeants to the other; the inferior officers and men are equally divided between both. Religion and politics —the two things about which ordinary men care most—are supposedly ignored in presence of known and sworn duty. The persistence with which both intrude themselves into all human arrangements may, notwithstanding, lend some color of justification to the boastful assertion of power to "get a man on the police."

Investiture with all the rights and responsibilities of the baton is, according to the Police Manual, to be justified by the subsequent course of the appointee. He is required to be truthful and respectful, not meddlesome, prompt to quell disturbance, not to maltreat or use unnecessary violence toward citizen or criminal, to fill the measure of police regulations, not to drink nor to accept rewards, free passes, or tickets. He is expected to illustrate the golden virtue of silence, and to abstain from indulgence in some games, while permitted to play in others. The use of slang is forbidden to him; nevertheless, what he doesn't know of this peculiar form of language is not worth acquaintance. He is not allowed to borrow money of fellow-officers. On election days he must exercise due vigilance

in removing all ballot booths from within 150 feet of the polling-places. Fire-telegraph keys are to be faithfully kept, complaints and violations of city ordinances reported.

The privileges of police-officers are of such obvious value as to invest their position with the attribute of desirability. Unlike their brethren in the United Kingdom of Great Britain and Ireland, they may vote for all elective officers, but may not be active or offensive partisans. They may, with consent of the Board of Police, receive rewards for extraordinary and meritorious services. While actually on duty they are not liable to military or jury duty, nor to arrest on civil process, nor to service of subpœnas from civil courts. Each class of officers has a distinctive uniform; all are under impartial rules of transfer and promotion, and are paid monthly. Salaries range as follows: Doorman, $1000; Patrolman, $1000 for the first year, $1100 the second, and $1200 subsequently; Roundsman, $1200; Sergeant, $1600; Police Surgeon, $2200, Captain, $2750; and Inspector, $3500. After twenty years of service each member is entitled to retirement from active duty, and to an annual pension of $600. He may be in the full health and vigor of manhood, but the authorities have no power to refuse his legal rights. Steps that ought to be successful have been taken to remedy this defect in the pension laws.

Limitation is commensurate with privilege. The knights of the club are debarred from membership in fire or military organizations, from soliciting contributions for political purposes, asking any citizen to interfere in their relations to the force, conferring presents or testimonials upon other members, and from circulating subscriptions for charities without permission of the Board. All the time of every policeman must be bestowed on duty; his post is to be perpetually perambulated, his residence established in the city and known to his superior, his bed and bedding in the station-house, his presence at the roll-call, and his energies at command until his resignation—if he should resign—is accepted by the Board of Police.

Reprimand, delay or forfeiture of pay, or dismissal from further employment, follows upon intoxication, disrespect or insubordination to superiors, neglect of duty, disobedience to orders, incapacity, immoral or injurious behavior. The Corporation

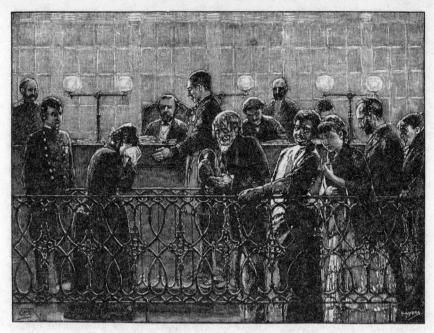

PRISONERS BROUGHT INTO ESSEX MARKET COURT.

Counsel is employed to defend them when charged as members of the force, if there be apparent grounds of defense. Dismissals are announced to the entire corps. Court squads, organized for the service of criminal processes and the execution of Police Court orders in criminal cases, are subject to the same disciplinary provisions. Appeal to the civil courts is allowed. Whether the proceedings in the trial before the Police Commissioners have been in harmony with the forms of law is then the subject of inquiry. If not, the dismissed officer is reinstated. Chancellor Howard Crosby, in the first number of *The Forum*, strongly objects to this, and says: "As it is at present, the Police Commissioners of New York know the abominable character of some men on the force, but cannot dismiss them, because the civil courts with their abounding technicalities will at once reinstate them. The thing has been tried, and with this result. Thus the police captain may defy the Board of Commissioners, for they dare not remove him. The Legislature should make the Board's power final." Men of large and long experience differ from the energetic reformer in respect of this matter, and maintain that the review of police trials by the civil courts is necessary to justice; that it preserves officers from the pique of politicians, imparts independence to police action, and strengthens fidelity by probability of redress from the higher constituted authorities. The Police Department prefers primary trial of an officer accused of felony or misdemeanor by a criminal court. If conviction follow, vacation of office is simultaneous, and clerical action alone is necessary. Superintendent Murray speaks of a policeman who on his "day off" left the station-house at 6.20 A.M., was convicted of drunkenness and disorderly conduct at 11, reported to the Superintendent and thence to the Police Board, and by 1 P.M. had ceased to be a member of the force. This course of action was certainly "short, sharp, decisive." In the Bureau of Records and Complaints, at the Central Office, the records of all complaints, civic or official, are preserved; papers are made out, subpœnas issued, and notes of procedure in all cases kept.

Doormen—77 in all—are the uniformed officers who exercise the functions of general house-keepers, maids-of-all-work, jailers, etc., at the several station-houses.

Changes in *personnel* of the police force in 1885 were such as indicate faithfulness, aspiration, efficiency, and healthy movement: 44 of the members died, and 77 were retired; only 2½ per cent. of all the days of service were those of sickness, and most of the sickness was clearly traceable to the unhealthiness, discomfort, and defective plumbing of barrack accommodation.

Clerks and employés belong to the Police Department, but not to the police force, although subject to many of the same regulations.

Each of the higher officers is held to the faithful performance of duty by a bond executed by himself and by two resident freeholders as sureties. That of the Property Clerk is for $25,000; of the Superintendent, for $20,000; of the Inspectors, for $15,000; and of the Captains, for $10,000.

How and to what extent the objects of the police system are accomplished by the metropolitan organization is of vital interest to the public. The *prevention of crime* is the most important object in view. To this end the patrolman devotes himself, or ought to devote himself. He acquires a sight acquaintance with residents, scrutinizes strangers, and suppresses criminal energies. The security of dwellings and other buildings, the surveillance of suspects and disorderly houses, the arrest of criminals, and the irregularities of servants, are within the scope of his action. In 1885 no less than 1190 buildings were found open, and were secured by the police. Among them were banks, churches, factories, 61 shops, and 765 stores. Suspicion of complicity with thieves is suggested by these figures. The patrolman is expected to search suspicious characters and parcels abroad at unseasonable hours, and thus to prevent the crime of housebreaking. Under section 1, chapter 747, Laws of 1872, he arrests sellers or possessors of obscene books, pictures, model casts, articles of indecent or immoral use, and thus prevents the corruption of society and the ruin of numerous lives. Repression, not cure, is the work of the police.

Gambling implements, lottery tickets, or lottery policies—all occasions of theft and embezzlement—the police aim to seize and destroy. In 1885, 122 persons were arrested for gambling, and 30 for keeping gambling-houses. Publicity of this vice has ceased, but those who wish to indulge in it will always find opportunity. Perverted ingenuity tasks its powers to create the means. Magisterial and judicial dignity is sometimes fascinated by "poker," and declares it to be a social and defensible amusement. Nevertheless the police have secured the conviction of some poker-players. "Pool-selling," "book-making," or the registration of bets on sporting events, is an annoying and pernicious form of gambling to many citizens, but not to all police-magistrates. Some of them have held that the gambler should see the event on which he stakes his money before he can be held for infraction of the law. Fortunately the opinion of the Counsel to the Corporation overruled that of these unwise Solons, and offenders were driven from the city to follow their nefarious trade in other localities. The number of arrests for all forms of gambling was 303; of these 152 were discharged, 115 convicted, and 36 left in suspense. The lottery and policy business is so nearly broken up that only 33 arrests were made, and these mainly of peripatetic venders who travel from one customer to another to book their ventures.

The sale and use of intoxicating liquors are well known to be the most prolific source of pauperism, intemperance, and crime. Public sentiment is not sufficiently educated to insist upon total prohibition. It consents to license, and the closure of saloons and bars on Sundays, prohibits sale to minors and drunkards, and endorses the Civil Damages Act. But it fails to speak with legislative precision. Legists and jurists, who may or may not love alcoholic stimulants, hamper and restrain the police by conflicting opinions as to their powers and duties. Failure to enforce the Sunday law is more frequently the fault of the police judiciary—whose trustworthiest supporters are liquor-sellers, —than of police-officers. The latter indignantly speak of notorious cases where the plainest evidence has been ignored by judicial Dogberries, and the flagrant offenders dismissed to prosecute their injurious business unpunished. Whatever of improvement is visible on Sundays is mainly due to the police, who in 1885 made 2144 arrests for violation of the Excise Law, of which 1715 were for transgressions of the Sunday clauses: 255 convictions, 735 discharges, and 1154 cases undecided do not afford too much encouragement to zealous fidelity in the future,

ONE OF THE BROADWAY SQUAD.

whatever their influence upon the official status of the eleven police justices—of whom three at a time are assigned to preside in the Court of Special Sessions—may be. Publicity should be given to the disposition of every case brought into court. If this were done through one or more reputable newspapers, it is not at all probable that so many as six thousand bailable cases would at any time in the future, as at one epoch in the past (Chancellor Crosby being the authority), be found pigeonholed in the District Attorney's office in New York. It is assuredly not the fault of the Police Department that judicial courts are taxed beyond their powers of administration, and that district attorneys are, as alleged, so occupied with the management of unbailable cases as to find no time for the prosecution of bailable ones. Many thousand cases of felony and misdemeanor are now pending in the criminal courts. Some of these have been waiting for trial for several years. The Grand Jury of the city has recommended the establishment of an additional criminal court for the special trial of excise cases.

On election days the office of the police is to protect the ballot-boxes. Much of the elective machinery is under the control of the Bureau of Elections, which consists of Chief J. J. O'Brien—who holds office for three years at an annual salary of $5000—aided by three patrolmen, who act as clerks. This Bureau endeavors to obtain unobstructed expression of the popular will by sending out in the months of July and August the requisite blanks on which applicants inscribe their own names for appointment as inspectors of election and poll-clerks. Captains of precincts inquire into the fitness of the candidates. Republicans are usually appointed first, then the Tammany, County, and Irving Hall Democrats, in proportions determined by the Board of Police, and are sworn into office by the Chief. Neglect of duty by those thus sworn in is a State-prison offence. Lists of voters in each house, maps of election districts, and posters are sent to inspectors on registration days. A copy of each register is filed with the Bureau of Elections within forty-eight hours of the close of registry, and the possible insertion of fictitious names hindered, if not prevented. The registry in possession of the Bureau becomes the final authority on voting qualification. On election days the in-

spectors again receive an ample supply of stationery, including statements of canvass, poll lists, and tallies. One statement of the canvass is sent to the Bureau of Elections, one to the County Clerk, and another to the Board of Supervisors; one of the tallies is forwarded to the Bureau and one to the Mayor within twenty-four hours of the close of the canvass, to prevent tampering with the returns. This has been attempted. In 1879 two men were sentenced to the State-prison for two and a half years in punishment of this offence, which was betrayed by the scratching on the bank-paper return. On the evening of election days statements certified by inspectors of votes cast for candidates are carried by police-officers to the station-houses as soon as the contents of each box have been counted. Thence they are sent by special messengers to the Bureau of Elections, where all returns are collated and filed away for reference. Election nights cause busy scenes in the bureaucratic office. All the police clerks lend a helping hand. The returns of Assembly districts, footed up by sergeants behind their desks, are reported in the room of the Police Board.

This Bureau also preserves record of the death of all males over twenty-one years of age, and of all convicted of felony, or sentenced to penitentiary or State-prison, in order to the correctness of the registry lists. Maps of Judicial, Assembly, Senate, and Congressional districts as arranged—really by the Bureau, but responsibly by the Board of Police—are drawn up in this office. Two large rooms, bursting with huge volumes and assorted documents, illustrate the painstaking care with which the elective franchise is guarded.

Situated as New York is, upon an island whose encircling waters are crowded by the shipping of all maritime peoples, it needs the energies of a special body of police to quell mutinies, arrest quarrelsome or insubordinate sailors, preserve order among the vessels, prevent smuggling, and check depredations upon marine property. This body it has in the Harbor Police, under the command of Captain E. O. Smith. Its duties are chiefly performed upon the water, and are invaluable to shipping interests. The steamboat *Patrol* is the dread of predaceous watermen, and is manned by a thoroughly efficient crew.

Special patrolmen are appointed to par-

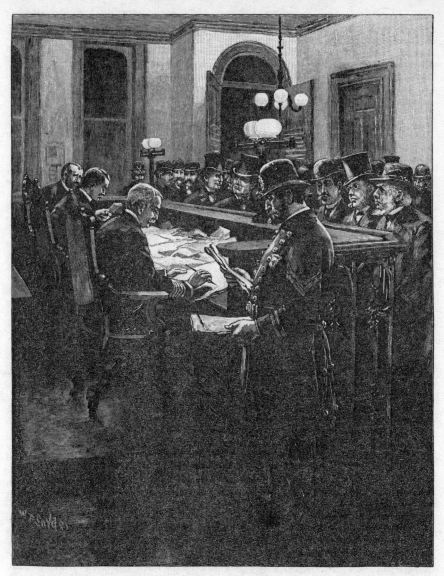

FOOTING UP ELECTION RETURNS.

ticular duties on the application of firms and corporations, and are paid by them. A system of raps with the club on the sidewalk calls up wanted policemen, brings the assistance of more than one officer at fires, riots, or other emergencies, and indicates the route of a policeman in pursuit of any person in the night-time.

Arrested persons are conducted to the station-house, and thence, after longer or shorter detention, to a District Police Court. Of these there are six, in different parts of the city. There the prisoners are charged with specified offences, and committed, bailed, or discharged by the sitting magistrate, according to the evidence adduced. The "Record of Arrests," kept by the Chief Clerk in the Central

Office, is alphabetically arranged, and contains the name, age, color, sex, nationality, occupation, state in life—whether married or single—of each person arrested; also the complaint, name of complainant, name of officer making the arrest, date of arrest, and disposal of the case. The number of apprehensions in 1885 was 74,315—an increase of 4061 over that of 1884; 54,898 were males, 19,417 females; 29.33 per cent. of the whole were arrested in the Fourth, Sixth, Tenth, and Fourteenth precincts, which adjoin each other, and contain as miscellaneous a population as can be found on any spot of equal size on the globe. Assault and battery, disorderly conduct, intoxication, larceny, vagrancy, violation of Corporation, Health, and Excise laws, constitute the majority of offences. 34,374 whites and 1897 blacks were natives of the United States, 20,115 of Ireland, 8288 of Germany, 2458 of England, 3151 of Italy, 791 of Poland, 88 of China, and the rest of many different countries. More than half were of foreign birth, and of the native-born very many were of foreign extraction; 8041 were under twenty years of age, 26,673 from twenty to thirty years, 18,483 from thirty to forty, 11,927 from forty to fifty, and 7191 over fifty years old; 24,172 were married, and 50,143 single. The percentage of single persons arrested was 67.47, against 61.60 in 1872 —an increase accounted for by general disinclination to marry. 71,120 were able to read and write; 3195 had not any literary education; 7 were, or professed to be, clergymen, 3 authors, 25 teachers, 16 students, 66 editors and reporters, 1457 bar-tenders, 2391 clerks, 3087 drivers, 1272 house-keepers, 3393 house-workers, 13,466 laborers, 1517 prostitutes, 1707 peddlers, 1065 printers, 1182 rag-pickers, and 20,108 of no occupation.

Conspicuous among the several divisions of the police force is that of the Nineteenth Sub-Precinct, with quarters under the Grand Central Depot. In addition to limited patrol duty, the members maintain creditable order among the pushing hackmen who crowd the entrances to that vast edifice. They also protect the incoming and outgoing passengers who, to the number of over five millions annually, patronize the New York Central, Harlem, and New Haven railroads, which terminate here. So effective is their activity and skill that no confidence man, sharper, or pickpocket cares to come within their

reach. Runaway boys are frequently apprehended on telegraphic notice from parents or guardians, and sent back to their friends. Telegraphic orders from police authorities and sheriffs in every part of the country to arrest fugitive criminals receive prompt attention. One of those gentry who had escaped from Adrian, Michigan, with $20,000 worth of sealskins, was caught at the window of the ticket office while demanding the rebate due on his ticket. The whole of the missing property was recovered.

The Broadway Squad, composed of 44 officers and men, is as famous in the police world as the gigantic grenadiers of Frederick the Great in the military. All are over six feet in height, and are far more commanding in presence and symmetrical in person than the unfortunate Prussians. From Thirty-fourth Street to the Battery they render highly appreciated assistance to pedestrians compelled to cross Broadway, and also regulate the endless procession of vehicles passing up and down that magnificent thoroughfare.

The Mounted Squad consists of 106 men, attached to five distinct precincts between One-hundred-and-tenth Street and the northern limit of police jurisdiction. The distances to be covered necessitate equestrian locomotion. On the several drives, such as St. Nicholas and other avenues north of the Central Park, nine policemen are specially assigned for duty during the day. Bestriding spirited steeds, trained to stop runaways by galloping alongside, the sturdy riders often incur great risks, but seldom fail to accomplish their object, or to save the lives and limbs of affrighted carriage occupants.

The *detection of crime* is a secondary function of the police force, but is one of such romantic and morbidly fascinating character that it possesses absorbing interest for the great majority of readers. The Detective Bureau, with apartments and records at Police Head-quarters, includes forty detective sergeants, under the orders of Inspector Thomas Byrnes. This officer, whose celebrity vies with that of Fouché and Vidocq, has been in command since 1880.

On May 25, 1882, the Detective Bureau as now constituted was created, at the urgent solicitation of Inspector Byrnes, by the State Legislature, and the salary of each detective sergeant raised to $1600.

ARRESTING A THIEF AT THE GRAND CENTRAL DEPOT.

Ward detectives serving under the captains of their respective precincts are not included in this particular branch of the force. Inspector Byrnes is a native of Ireland, but is of American training. Entering the force in 1863, he rose through its several grades to his present office. Weeding out all the worthless and inefficient, and supplying their places with young, active, and intelligent men, he instructed and organized the latter on his own plans. The Detective Bureau soon attained to national importance. Special attention was paid to Wall Street. Skilled thieves, the "best men" of their nefarious occupation, prized it as the richest of their hunting grounds. Fat purses were abstracted, tin boxes containing money, bonds, and valuable papers fell into their hands, and knavery was jubi-

lant. Now that district is to them as paradise to the lost spirit in Moslem legend. They may view afar, but may not enter. Any thief found below a line drawn across the city through Fulton Street is seized at once and compelled to account for himself. If the explanation be not satisfactory, the grip of the law tightens around the culprit, and the familiar jail again becomes his home. Ten or twelve detectives are always on duty at a room in the Stock-Exchange. On call, one or more can be sent to any place in the lower section of the city within two or three minutes. "From the 12th of March, 1880, until to-day, they have not lost a ten-cent stamp in Wall Street by a professional thief—not a penny, not a cent," is not an empty boast. It is sober truth. Somebody did steal President Simmons's over-

RELICS IN THE MUSEUM OF CRIME.

Exchange presentation of a splendid $500 Jorgensen gold watch to Inspector Byrnes in recognition of his signal usefulness. That fur-trimmed overcoat is still an estray from its legitimate owner, and whether the sinful appropriator be a professional thief or only an amateur is one of the unsolved mysteries of abnormal economic science. Infallibility is not a human attribute, but in the judgment of the criminal classes the Inspector and his subordinates come as near to it as is possible to policemen. They "size up a man for all he's worth" with really marvellous accuracy. Markedly individualized and independent, Inspector Byrnes in manner is very gentlemanly, insinuating, and invitive of confidence. He knows the thoughts, plans, ways, and characteristics of "crooks," and readily infers how any one of the category will proceed in the projection and execution of crime, and what he will do to cover his tracks. Charles Reade's advice to "put yourself in his place" he follows in practice of a profession to which pre-eminent fitness rather than choice has called him. Like every genuine "sleuth-hound" of just government, he exhibits rare coolness, self-possession, and bravery, persistence unwearying, sagacity almost unerring, and the fine scent that sniffs the slightest odor of the quarry. Kind as keen, and impartial as imperturbable, he has formed a class of police-officers equal to the needs of a municipality so free to ingress and regress that it is the most difficult of all to guard against criminals. "Honor among thieves" is one of the time-worn lies that

coat while that gentleman was busied with matters connected with the Stock-

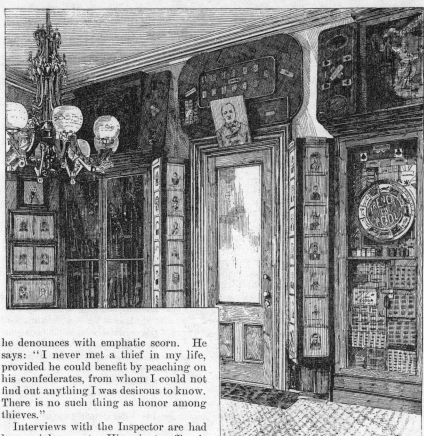

THE MUSEUM OF CRIME.

he denounces with emphatic scorn. He says: "I never met a thief in my life, provided he could benefit by peaching on his confederates, from whom I could not find out anything I was desirous to know. There is no such thing as honor among thieves."

Interviews with the Inspector are had by special request. His private office is adorned by photographs and crayon drawings, whose subjects are associated with police affairs. Some of the men reporting to him are said to be college-bred, and can pass muster in the best society. All are chosen in view of individual aptitude for certain kinds of work. The stamp of officialism is about the last of which there is any trace. Keeping *incognito* as much as possible, the chances of prompt detection are multiplied. "Crooks" are now afraid of their shadows; great robberies have ceased, and minor crime been reduced over eighty per cent. Detectives more or less closely imitate the example of their chief, who says: "Every evening I make it a point to meet some of these men in their resorts, and learn from them the whereabouts of their friends, and what they are doing. One crook of consequence generally knows what other good men are doing. In this way I keep posted, and know in what part of the country all the sharp men are. As experts are liberated from the State-prison I follow their tracks in this way." For the secret police of European countries, and for the private detectives in this, Inspector Byrnes entertains undisguised contempt. Crime, in his opinion, is a fine art, and criminal detection a science. "Set a thief to catch a thief" is a hoary mendacity. "In the long-run the honest officer is a match for the smartest thief." Detective opinion of the morality of American life, private or official, is not of roseate hue. The bribe-taking Aldermen of 1884 have not improved its complexion. Of Henry W. Jaehne, their former Vice-President, but now in Sing Sing through the Inspector's remarkable power of making rogues talk, he is represented as saying: "Jaehne thought I had more proof against him in regard to Mrs. Hamilton's stolen silver than I really did have, and I was careful not to undeceive him. As it was, I knew that he was a rascal, without having proof of the fact, until I had gained his confidence to such an extent that he admitted his guilt as to the bribery."

In the Photograph and Record Department, in charge of Sergeant Thomas H. Adams, are preserved about 60,000 portraits of between 6000 and 7000 criminals. Many of them have been received from other cities, and are not included in the Rogues' Gallery, which contains the busts of the "best people" arrested in New York. When a professional is photographed, fifty copies of the negative are taken, and the "pedigree" of the person printed on the back of each copy. One copy is then despatched to each precinct, where the pedigree is entered on the record-book, and the picture placed in the Rogues' Gallery, as at Head-quarters. The remainder are retained for the use of officers, and for exchange with the police authorities of other cities. Gallery and record-book are the patented inventions of Sergeant Adams. Portraits of deceased criminals are removed from their infamous companionship, as are those of the four per cent., more or less, of living ones who turn from their evil ways when young, and by years of well-doing entitle themselves to this favor, which is granted at their own request, seconded by that of reputable business men. Should they relapse, their portraits are returned to the case. The record of each of the 1700 originals in the Rogues' Gallery comprises full physical description and biography. One of them is, or pretends to be, a graduate of Corpus Christi College, in Cambridge, England. "Hungry Joe," ex-Governor Franklin J. Moses, of South Carolina, Bertha Heymann, "queen of the confidence women," "Whiskey" Short, who distilled whiskey from swill in Sing Sing State-prison, Annie Riley, who speaks five or six languages, "Ike" Vail, "king of the confidence men," bank burglars, forgers, and counterfeiters of strikingly intellectual countenance, are conspicuous among them. Basing his estimate on the reliable data at command, Sergeant Adams concludes that one-third of the "best people" are liberally educated, one-third fairly educated, and

the remaining third, with the exception of a very small number, so far educated as to be able to read and write. The youngest and most inexperienced are also the most reckless of criminals. These run all risks. Laziness is the cause of half the criminality in the land; temptation by successful thieves and by immoral reading, of the other half. Want has but little to do with it, except as it makes small thieves. These, by contact with hardened men in prisons, which are often schools of crime, develop into professionals.

The Museum of Crime, opposite the private office of Inspector Byrnes, is a shuddering horror; not so much from what is seen as from what is suggested. Speaking likenesses of shop-lifters, pickpockets, burglars, and eminent "crooks" glare from the walls upon visitors. Sledge-hammers whose heads are filled with lead, drags, drills, sectional jimmies, masks, powder-flasks, etc., that were used in the Manhattan Bank robbery of October 27, 1878, challenge inspection in their glass cases. The rascals made away with $2,749,400 in bonds and securities, and about $15,000 in money, on that occasion; but, thanks to our unequalled detective system, did not retain all their booty. Here are samples of the mechanical skill of Gustave Kindt, alias "French Gus," a professional burglar and maker of burglars' tools, which he let out to impecunious thieves on definite percentages of their robberies. The assortment of burglarious kits, tools, keys, wax impressions, etc., is complete. The genius of Kindt and Klein, so wofully perverted, ought to have made their fortunes in legitimate fields of operation. Nat White's bogus gold brick; Mike Shanahan's eighteen-chambered pistol; counterfeit Reading Railroad scrip; the lithographic stone on which ten or twenty thousand spurious tickets of the elevated railroad were printed; stones for printing fractional currency; bogus railroad bonds used by confidence operators; the black caps and ropes of murderers; the pistols wherewith various persons were slain; the lock curiosities of Langdon W. Moore, who knew how to open combination locks through studying their emitted sounds; the box in which the same thief, known as "Charley Adams," put $216,000 in government bonds, stolen from the Concord Bank, Massachusetts, in February, 1866, and which he first buried four feet below the surface of the Delaware River,

THE SANITARY SQUAD.

and then dug up and surrendered when under arrest; the pipes, pea-nut oil, lamps, liquid raw opium, and pills used for smoking in opium joints—are all here.

Instinct and experience unite to awaken profound dread of the Detective Bureau in the breasts of the criminal classes who understand police statistics. In 1885, Inspector Byrnes reported that 1080 males and females, including 7 detained as witnesses, were arrested for felonies and misdemeanors by his branch of the police force: 1 was hung, 98 were sent to State-prison, 88 to the Penitentiary, 12 to the City Prison, 23 to the Elmira Reformatory, 2 to the Workhouse, 4 to the House of Refuge, and 1 to the State Insane Asylum; judgment was suspended in 10 cases, 31 were fined (and $1612 collected), 103 delivered to other authorities, 318 discharged, 228 disposed of in other ways, and 161 left pending. The sentences involved 620 years' imprisonment, and the property recovered amounted to $121,202.

In the *prevention of calamities* the police force is not less efficient. To see that the street lamps are duly lighted and burning, that leakages or breaks of water pipes are quickly repaired, that rabid animals are killed, that diseases, noxious or inflammable substances, or explosives perilous to the public are reported, and that steam-boilers are legally inspected, is part of police duty. The presence of about six thousand steam-boilers—stationary, used for rock-drilling, pile-driving, barges, scows, elevators, etc.—in the city would be a constant element of danger were it not neutralized by the Steam-boiler Inspection Squad of 21 men under the Bureau of Steam-boiler Inspection and Engineers.

The *prevention of endemic diseases* is another important function of the Police Department. Disease frequently originates in and is propagated by the uncleanliness and filthy habits of ignorant and reckless people. Ashes, garbage, rubbish, dirt, and vile fluids, accumulating about the premises or in the streets, have bred the pestilences before which prayer has been powerless, and which have swept out the citizens with the besom of destruction. The Sanitary Code forbids all such practices, and police activity is employed to squelch them. Instruction is provided for the uninformed, and certain punishment for the wilful offender. Whatever malignant, infectious, contagious, or epidemic sickness may break out is reported forthwith. Pawn shops—so often the "fences" for concealing stolen goods—liquor and beer saloons, cheap lodging-houses or dormitories that are frequently mere fetid, crowded, human sties, abound most in the precincts infamous for poverty and crime, and cause plentiful toil for the Tenement-house Squad of the Sanitary Company. This includes thirty officers detailed by the Police Commissioners to assist the Board of Health, under whose orders they act, while reporting to and being paid by Sergeant Washington Mullen. They furnish protection, but not labor, when assisting the Sanitary Superintendent to vacate premises by order of the Board of Health. Sewerage, drainage, ventilation, and whatever pertains to the safety of life or health, is thus brought into relation to the Police Department. The 32,597 violations, including all grades of nastiness or negligence, of the Sanitary Code, reported by them in 1885, disclose the need of such a force, 125,045 inspections attest its activity, and 16,705 complaints its fidelity.

Charity and equity are elements of police duty, for the due observance of which the members of the force are held responsible. Lost children are necessarily numerous in tenement-house districts. Many of the small waifs know little of English, but all find favor in the eyes of the big, burly, warm-hearted protectors, who think of the cribs in their own homes. "I'd rather tackle a man twice my size than that chap," said a perspiring policeman as he deposited a dirty, tearful, kicking juvenile on the floor of Matron Webb's room at Police Head-quarters. The telegraph alarm sends description of person and clothing to all stations. Most of the estrays are soon reclaimed. Children rescued from inhuman parents or guardians by the Society for the Prevention of Cruelty to Children are also placed in care of Matron Webb until disposed of by the

courts. 4308 lost children were cared for in 1885, 4087 restored to friends in New York, 7 to friends in other cities, and 214 unclaimed or rescued ones committed to the care of the Commissioners of Charities and Correction, or to that of corporate or denominational institutions. The 112 foundlings received during the year met with care that should have been bestowed by despairing or unnatural parents, in homes, asylums, and private families. Many were adopted. All particulars that might lead to the discovery of parents are preserved. Truant children come under the supervision of the police; but the laws in connection with compulsory attendance at school are not rigidly enforced.

The Bureau of General Information, established in June, 1885, on the recommendation of Superintendent Murray, has charge of the records of all missing persons, lost children, foundlings, persons found dead in the streets, etc., etc. Letters, averaging about one hundred monthly, from all parts of the country and of the world, requesting information about relatives or friends not heard of for a long time, arrive at the Central Office. The utmost pains is taken to acquire the desired information, and due answer is returned to the anxious inquirers. One young man, inquired about by friends in Algiers, North Africa, was found at the Hotel Brunswick, and the questioning letter put into his hands. Of the 203 males and 59 females inquired about as missing in 1885, 196 males and 55 females were found and placed in communication with their friends; 11 only were unaccounted for. Very mysterious circumstances surround some of these cases. Of 154 runaways from home, 143 were returned; of 87 persons found dead, 43 were subsequently identified at the Morgue, and the 44 unidentified—homeless, friendless, alone—laid to rest in obscure graves.

Stranded strangers applying for help are assisted. Immigrants lost on arrival are sought and restored to acquaintances. Utter indigence is relieved by nocturnal lodging in clean cells at the station-houses, and that without too strict regard to the morals of the lodgers: 72,832 males and 61,513 females thus found shelter in 1885. Petty thieves, beggars, tramps, drones, and a small remnant of worthy folk eagerly seek these temporary refuges. 6803 persons who were sick and destitute, insane, or injured in various ways, were conveyed to station-houses and hospitals by ambulances, and 141 sent to their homes. Dead bodies of unknown persons, found in the waters and public places of the city, are conveyed to the Morgue, at the foot of Twenty-sixth Street, East River: 143 persons, committing suicide in one way or other, as well as the bodies of those who met with accidental death, afforded this repulsive employment to the police in 1885. Stray swine or cattle are delivered to the keeper of the public pound; beggars apprehended and sent to institutions or dealt with as vagrants; children dancing in the streets for gain arrested; and lost or stolen property restored to claimant owners. This last is ordinarily done through the Property Clerk, whose office at Police Head-quarters embraces the most miscellaneous variety of pistols, watches, jewelry, silver-ware, forged bonds, male and female clothing, horse-blankets, cigars, sides of beef, chests of tea, sacks of coffee, boots and shoes, etc., to be found on the continent. His store comprises everything except a piano—and Mr. John Harriott has had a piano lid—from a coffin to a diamond pin. Diamonds and jewelry valued at $200,000 have been in custody at one time. These articles are all held for evidence against prisoners, and are not handed over to claimants without regular orders from judicial courts. The unclaim-

ed and unawarded are sold every six months, and the proceeds paid into the Police Pension Fund. During the year 1885, 1711 different lots, valued at $755,356 73, came into the hands of the Property Clerk, and 650 lots, valued at $44,126 32, were delivered by him.

The *protection of interior communications* is an important part of police duty in the populous city of New York. The force is called upon to disperse crowds, to regulate processions and parades, to prevent racing in the streets, to supervise the driving of private and public vehicles, and to remove all obstacles to free locomotion to the Corporation Yard.

The Ordinance Squad, in command of Sergeant Joseph Stewart, investigates the facts and circumstances of applications for licenses issued under direction of the Mayor. Nearly 30,000 investigations were thus made by its 63 members in 1885.

The protection of interior marine communications is intrusted to the Steam-boat Squad and to the Harbor Police. The first, also called the Third Precinct, under Captain Gastlin, includes 109 men, among whom are six detectives. These guard the docks from Jackson Street, East River, to Fourteenth Street, North River.

The *supervision of public amusements*, under the provisions of State law, and the apprehension of all offenders, enter into society's requisitions upon its police pro-

PATROL BOAT.

RIVER AND HARBOR POLICE.

tectors. Masked balls, with their special opportunities of indecency, immorality, and crime, entail the obligation of alert vigilance. The $4465 for 263 masked ball permits, and the $1940 for 776 pistol permits, received in 1885, were paid over, as the law directs, to the Police Pension Fund. Prize-fights or slugging matches, under the hypocritical pretence of scientific play for "points," they are now instructed to prohibit.

In *the communication of recent intelligence and information* the metropolis lags behind some of her more enterprising Western sisters. Telegraphic boxes that responsible citizens might use ought to be judiciously scattered over the whole area of police jurisdiction.

The Police Telegraph system, under Superintendent James Crowley, is, so far as it goes, an admirably effective one. Notice of arrests, fires, lost children, riots, and multitudinous matters is promptly diffused. Inquiries or searches ordered through it are posted in the sitting-room of each station-house. Its record of transactions is perfect, and throbs with excitement. In 1885 the number of messages

sent over the wires of this bureau was 82,383. Of these, 57,334 related to coroners, sick cases, accidents, elections, etc.; 20,129 to dead animals; 1656 to general orders, arrests, and missing persons; 993 to property lost, stolen, or found; 648 to lost children; and 1713 to fire locations. At the Central Office the police lines are divided into five sections. By means of switching, two sections are connected, and general alarms sent to all stations. The office itself is connected, directly or indirectly, with the head-quarters of the Fire and other departments, with the police head-quarters of other cities, with railroad stations, prisons, banks, hospitals, asylums, factories, public schools, etc. The blotter, kept by three clerks, is a perfect diary of police experience since 1856.

The entire cost of the Police Department in 1885, as indicated by the report of the treasurer, was $3,679,421 78. The Police Pension Fund has an invested capital of $94,000; disbursed for pensions, etc., in 1885, the sum of $267,935 93; and received from various sources, $309,181 27. 662 men, women, and orphans are its beneficiaries.

RIDING IN NEW YORK

THE Central Park had been open for pleasure some years before it became evident that its bridle-path had not been made in vain. Even yet, astonishing as the progress of the last decade has been in the diffusion of knowledge about the uses of the bridle-path, there is no reason to believe that riding in New York has by any means reached its limit. Each new riding-school finds itself full of business without perceptibly diminishing the business of its older rivals. Fifteen years ago there was but one riding-school. Now there are four considerable, not to mention the Riding Club, which includes among its functions those of an academy.

There were horsemen in New York before the riding "fad" set in. One well known and now venerable physician has ridden in the suburban roads for fifty years, and may even yet be seen of sunny afternoons in the Park, or of stormy afternoons in the ring, taking his constitutional on a cob that is quite capable of throwing younger horsemen. He informs the present writer that when he began to ride in New York, during the remote thirties and under the consulate of Van Buren, at least one of his fellow-physicians made his professional rounds on horseback. It was a good many years after this, early in the fifties, in fact, that a riding-school was established "opposite the Hay Scales." How many of the readers of this paper know as much about the site of the Hay Scales as about the site of the choragic monument of Lysicrates? Yet the Hay Scales stood where the Cooper Institute now stands, and opposite, at the foot of Fourth Avenue, was "Disbrow's," which migrated twice afterward, and in its latest habitat subsisted until the war, when it was merged in another school that again migrated and still flourishes. The late William B. Astor was a rider in those days, and built a riding-hall on his own grounds for his use in bad weather. In good weather, though the Park was not, the unpaved roads were more accessible than now from the heart of the town, and along the Bloomingdale Road, now the dusty Boulevard, horsemen might have been seen as regularly, and in about the same numbers, as in the opening chapters of the then famous G. P. R. James.

Before the Park was fairly opened, and while its main lines were laying through a region of rocks and shanties, compounded of a goat pasture and a mining camp, the equestrian pioneers were exploring its untrimmed surfaces, and making the goal of their rides one of the road-houses to which the trotting men, then as now, resorted in much greater numbers. One little band of these was known to the keeper of the hostelry they frequented as the "literary cavalry." Mr. Charles A. Dana is, I think, the sole survivor of this informal club, which included, besides, Mr. Henry J. Raymond, whose white pacer was known to his companions as "The Little Villain," in allusion to an amenity of journalism current in those days, Mr. Frey, remembered as the stalwart and emphatic musical critic of the *Tribune*, and Edmond O'Flaherty, known then and long afterward in New York as William Stuart. There were already women who rode also, though for the most part they had learned to ride elsewhere, and there was the same scarcity of well-broken saddle-horses for ladies of which Fanny Kemble had complained years before, upon her first visit to these shores. Even after the Park was completed, the ordeal of riding to it attended by a company of grinning and hooting boys was very trying to the nerves of the weaker sex. Now the riding-schools have all been moved to the immediate neighborhood of the Park, and "a lady on horseback" is so familiar a sight that even the most excitable of the circumjacent small boys is not moved to make proclamation of it. Perhaps the strongest proof that riding had not become a fashionable amusement until a good many years after the facilities for it had been provided by the Park Commissioners is that the late Horace Greeley addicted himself to it during his latter years. Of course he rode in a sad sincerity, and because he thought it was good for him, but he submitted himself to a regular course of instruction, and he proved so plastic in the hands of his riding-master that those who have seen him ride declare that, if he did not precisely witch the world with noble horsemanship, he looked at all events considerably less irregular on horseback than he did on foot. Another candidate for the Presidency was an even earlier and a much more constant horseman. Twenty years ago, at least, Samuel J. Tilden used to disport himself in the Park on horseback, and he continued his riding until he was forced to abandon it by physical infirmity. Most of us remember among the cipher despatches the admonition, "Tell Russia saddle Blackstone," and this was in the crisis of November, 1876. When he was Governor of New York it was Mr. Tilden's habit to do his official reviewing on horseback, and once or twice this practice led him into perils from which it was a feat of horsemanship to extricate one's self. Nevertheless there are those who disparage his horsemanship, and not on political grounds. "He rode single-footers," says my informant, more in sorrow than in anger.

It is only fair to say that my informant is a German, and that in Germany, as for the matter of that in England, the walk, the trot, and the gallop (the latter subdivided in England into the canter and the gallop) are the only gaits permitted to a well-regulated saddle-horse. The single-foot and its variant, the rack, are cultivated only in regions, like our own Southern States, of which the horsemanship is ultimately derived from Spain. So that it is perhaps a piece of too Teutonic stringency to put a man out of court altogether as a rider because he prefers the languors of the single-foot to the strenuous joys of the German trot. For Germans there be who despise him who rises in the trot even as him who rides single-footers, and are prepared to maintain that he only rides who merely bobs and bumps. This view prevails chiefly, it is true, among those Germans who immigrated some years ago, and before rising in the trot had been enjoined upon the German cavalry as a proved preventive of sore backs. It is none the less held as an article of faith, and as it is well known that there is no other being on earth quite so uncompromising as a German professor of anything, it is inculcated by those who hold it in all its rigor.

This leads me to remark upon the vulgar error that riding in New York is mainly a phase of Anglomania, an error which appears in the scornful treatment of the equestrian dudes of the metropolis by a fearless Western press. In point of fact it is quite as much an importation from the land to which we owe our culture in beer and Beethoven, if not rather more. The proportion of Germans who ride for pleasure is at least as large as that of natives. Three of the four principal riding-schools are owned and managed by Germans, and at one of them German is the prevailing language. At another there is a Reitclubb, composed mainly of Germans, who pursue equitation with a German thoroughness, and have attained in it, perhaps, a greater proficiency than any other like body. Even in horseflesh German ideas have made their way, and horses imported from the great Prussian breeding establishment at Trakene, or their progeny, are preferred by many riders, Americans as well as Germans, for the work of an all-round saddle-horse, to the weight-carrying hunter or the half-bred Park hack which is the ideal of the Anglomaniac. In its effect upon horsemanship here the German influence is distinctly greater than the English. The German teachers outnumber the English probably three to one, and leave their impress upon their pupils, while the land of Baucher and the *haute école* is scarcely represented at all. Even at "the Club," which is commonly supposed to be the centre and citadel of Anglomania, the head riding-master is, or lately was, a German. Along with the vigor and rigor which, according to Mr. Matthew Arnold, characterize the German professorial mind in general, go the systematic and exact methods of German instruction. Apart altogether from the much-discussed question of the superiority for general purposes of the military seat or the hunting seat—a question not to be mooted here—the superiority, for the purposes of teaching, of the systematic instruction which the Germans have received, over the more or less happy-go-lucky way in which Englishmen learn to ride without knowing how they learned, is scarcely to be disputed. Inasmuch as almost all the German teachers "have served," and transmit the military seat which they have learned, it is not surprising that their pupils should sit rather like German cavalrymen than like cross-country riders, notwithstanding the English hunting man's sneer that the three men who cannot possibly ride horses are "a sailor, a tailor, and a cavalry officer." The Englishman who has learned to ride by riding, and not by being taught to ride, thus has his disadvantages in teaching and in training. It must be owned that he is apt to have his revenges also when there is "a downright nasty brute" to be mounted, or an obdurate refuser to be jumped. As for American riding, one

DER REITMEISTER.

may occasionally see in the Park the actual cow-boy in his deep saddle astride of his loping broncho, but he does not commend himself as a model for Park riding. The West Point seat, again, may be seen as exemplified not only by casual graduates of the Academy taking their pleasure, but also by the mounted policemen, many of whom are old troopers. Seats, however, as the excellent and entertaining Major Dwyer has shown, depend upon saddles, and as it is only with stirrups hung well forward that the characteristic hunting seat can be attained, so it is only in the McClellan saddles that are used by the mounted Metropolitans out in Seventh Avenue and the region beyond Macomb's Dam, but have been discarded for the Whitman by the Park police proper, that the fork seat and the straight leg with the toe rather down than up can be seen in perfection. The cross-country man and the *Reitmeister* agree in disapproving this seat, though they are both aware that men may ride horses well in many ways. Their disapproval rises to frantic intolerance when it is transmitted to their respective disciples, who are not aware of this important truth. The well greaved and buttoned Anglomaniac, whose own person makes a violent angle at the waist, whose feet lie out on his horse's shoulders, and between whose legs, when he trots, the following horseman gets really panoramic views of the landscape, declares that the policeman "cawn't ride." The vigorous and rigorous and procrustean German, who would rather fall off by bumping than stay on by rising, will tell you that no man with the policeman's seat "gan mannitch" a horse. Whoever has seen a mounted policeman in the act of catching a runaway, and noted the skill, the coolness, and the perfect command of his animal which the performance involves, could not help wishing to subject his critics to the same test of horsemanship, were it not that capital punishment is somewhat too severe for the offence of rash and incompetent criticism. It is not to risk committing this offence to say that, whether the hunting seat or the military seat be the better, the former lends itself the more readily to exaggeration, and that German riding cannot be so successfully caricatured as the riding even of an English groom is unconsciously caricatured by his complacent disciple when he takes a "kenter in the Pork."

These differences of horsemanship are very much softened when the question becomes of horsewomanship. They are not enforced by so widely different theories and practices of saddlery, and the male German who insists upon bumping for himself concedes to the weaker vessel the privilege of rising. The Kentuckian or Virginian equestrienne reveals her training mainly by holding her left hand with the reins in it level with the elbow and across the body, cavalry fashion, while the fair Anglomaniac can testify her devotion no otherwise than by exhibiting a crop instead of a whip, and by carrying both elbows as nearly as may be on a level with her shoulders—a posture which,

she will be pained to learn, is regarded by British horsemen as characteristic of the British cad. To Anglomania used to be imputed the banging of horses' tails, which has no longer anything distinctive, since a long-tailed saddle-horse has become an exceptional object, either on the road or in the ring. Where a long tail is seen, unless its beauty be its own excuse for being, it is commonly brandished as a patriotic protest against the manners and customs of the English.

It cannot be denied, however, that Anglomania has had its influence. The hunting in this country is, of course, English in its origin, and the humorists of the press hold it up to ridicule by pointing out that it is an anise-seed bag that is hunted—as if fox-hunting were anywhere a cheap and expeditious method of destroying foxes, or anything beyond a means, like "steeple-chasing," in its literal sense, of getting a gallop across country. The ridicule, however, is gradually ceasing as it is coming to be understood what riding across country involves. A man risking his neck for the sake of an exciting exercise may be reprehensible, but he is not properly ridiculous. Young men of the increasing class that is devoted to "high living and plain thinking" might make a much worse use of their abounding leisure, and be infected with much more injurious phases of Anglomania. In Boston the cross-country riders avowed Anglomania and anticipated ridicule by boldly calling themselves the Myopia Hunt Club, and possibly by glazing an eye each when they rode to the meet. There is no need of such an avowal on the part of the gilded youth who ride to hounds in Long Island and in New Jersey, and whose dock-tailed horses and pink coats and buckskin breeches and "hunt balls" to the neighboring yeomanry so excite the risibility of one class of patriots and the wrath of another. It is not quite true, by-the-way, that all fox-hunting, even in the Northern States, is imported. In Chester County, Pennsylvania, there is an indigenous hunt, with a pack of hounds and horses of native breed. The farmers ride after foxes as their fathers before them rode, and they would be as astonished to hear that they were imitating the English as was Molière's hero to learn that he conversed in prose. Nevertheless they have what to the scorners is one of the chief "notes" of

Drawn by T. de Thulstrup.

A TAILOR-MADE GIRL.

Engraved by Lindsay.

Anglomania, in that they do not pretend to hunt for the sake of the game, but only for the sake of the hunting. With them, as with the gilded youth of the suburban hunts, it is "not the conquest but the battle" that allures. "We cannot afford to kill foxes," said one of them to the present writer, implying, of course, that a fox that is hunted and runs away may live to be hunted another day, but explaining that early in the season it was customary to give one fox to the hounds in order to encourage them thereafter. But for our immediate purpose fox-hunting may be regarded as an importation, with all the modifications it has induced in horses, seats, and equipment, and these are many and considerable.

The seasons for riding in the Park are the spring and the autumn, and year by year the habitual rider notes the progress of riding by noting the increasing throng in the bridle-path. Mr. Olmsted, in his notes on the proposed suburban park of Boston, observes that by the opening of the Central Park, among other things, the number of saddle-horses kept in New York has increased a hundredfold. If we limit the statement to horses kept exclusively or mainly for the saddle, it is doubtless literally true. The Club alone houses 250 saddle-horses. The four principal riding-schools have together about 700 more. There is also another school, which is scarcely in the competition, being as yet but a small beginning, though it testifies in a powerful and pathetic way to the steady growth of the interest in riding, having a ring the size of a large drawing-room, in which sensitive persons may take secluded lessons and have their initiatory contortions veiled from the unfeeling and critical experts who lie in wait for them in the more frequented schools. Here we have a total of not far from a thousand horses, and to this is to be added the number of saddle-horses, not so easily ascertainable, kept in the private stables of their owners. In all, it seems safe to estimate that there are 1200 saddle-horses in New York, and it is not likely that there were a full dozen before the Park was opened. To help the reader realize how considerable this number is, it may be pointed out that the entertaining author of *Living Paris* cites as a proof of the luxuriousness of that city of luxury that there are at least 8000 private horses kept in Paris—meaning kept for pleasure.

Comparing the number of those who drive and those who ride in New York, rapidly as this latter number increases, it seems likely that in this article of luxury the American "metropolis" surpasses the capital of the world. The number of riders, at any rate, like the expenses of one of the departments in Washington, according to a memorable report of its chief, has "exceeded the most *sanguine anticipations." The projectors of the bridle-path were censured at the time of laying it out for allotting so much space to so little purpose. Since the Park was opened the bridle-path has been extended across the foot of it, and has already become in some respects inadequate. Experience has shown that some of the turns are dangerously sharp, and to avert the danger, so far as possible, signs are now put up to forbid "running or galloping" on the bridle-path, except around the reservoir, where the road has long straight stretches, and a horse approaching can be seen around the turns. Frightened horses, however, pay no heed to these warnings, and reckless horsemen, whether boys or "Sunday riders," pay little more, and there is an evident necessity that some of the sharper turns shall be straightened and made gradual against the increased chances of accident that increased numbers bring. The number of riders apt to be encountered at any point is not as yet so great as in Rotten Row during the London season, where the equestrians are often brought to a walk. If the suggestion made a short time since in the press for the establishment of a Rotten Row in Central Park were carried out, there might before long be danger of a like engorgement. This suggestion, it is not unfair to suspect, emanated from those equestrian visitors to the Park to whom their own visibility is an important consideration, but it is not likely to be carried out. In spite of the "Carriage Concourse" that was provided in the original plan of the Park, it is fortunate for the comfort of visitors in general that there is no one point in the circuit of it, as there is in Hyde Park, that is consecrated by usage to a general assembly. Both "carriage people" and equestrians can be conveniently observed from Mount St. Vincent, where the bridle-path joins the East Drive, which thence becomes the common highway to the upper end of the Park. The most eligible coigne of vantage for

THE HUNTING MAN.

seeing the riders alone is perhaps the east side of the reservoir, where fast riding is permitted, and where from five of a fine afternoon there is for nearly an hour a passage of horsemen and horsewomen so constant as to assume the character of a procession. The procession includes many men whose names are known throughout and beyond their own country—men eminent in all the professions and in nearly all the great industries. There are physicians, whose profession notoriously induces a fondness for horseflesh, and who here at least show a creditable willingness to take their own prescriptions; there are lawyers, men of letters, artists, "railroad men";

"Sometimes a troop of damsels glad,
An abbot on an ambling pad"—

for riding is so far from being regarded as an unclerical recreation that among many clergymen who ride there is at least one prelate, by no means recognizable from the poet's description, but apt to be seen bestriding an animal much less

episcopal of aspect and action and much less easily manageable than "an ambling pad," which I take to be mediæval for a single-footing cob.

It is no disparagement to these dignitaries to say that they do not compose the most attractive part of this daily procession. The "troop of damsels glad," under escort of a riding-master, or the family party of the same, personally conducted by paterfamilias, or the solitary horsewoman followed at a respectful distance by a belted groom, or accompanied by a more interesting male—these are the objects which the judicious spectator deems it worth while to retain his perch alongside the reservoir to see. The fashion in riding-habits abjures anything that suggests romance. The trailing robes and sweeping plumes of the last generation of horsewomen are banished to remote rural parts of the Southern States. A "silk hat" on man or woman seems the negation of romance, and nothing can be more prosaic and severely business-like than the habit which it surmounts, the absolutely plain garment in dark monochrome, of which the requirements are that it shall be without ornament, and that it shall fit and hang without a wrinkle. It is a fact as familiar as it is consolatory that no fashion can make a pretty girl look otherwise than pretty. The looker-on is inclined to believe, as Simplesse Munditiis passes him at a canter, that there was never any equestrian costume so exquisite, and that Queen Guinevere, with her gown of grass-green silk and her golden clasps and her light green tuft of plumes closed in a golden ring, was dressed very inappropriately for the sad-

dle compared with his tailor-made vision of loveliness. If of a romantic mind, he may drop again into Tennyson:

"As she fled fast through sun and shade
The happy wind upon her played,
Blowing the ringlet from the braid;
She looked so lovely as she swayed
The rein with dainty finger tips"—

we need not go on, though we may have every reason to suspect that the young man who escorts her has "gone on," under the friendly shade of the grove at the turn, where it is the custom of young couples of assorted sexes to pass at a walk before they come into the unsheltered straight stretch and break into a canter.

Around the Park, or twice around the reservoir if one keeps to the bridle-path, is the usual "promenade on horseback," and is about an hour in duration, if taken at a judicious alternation of gaits, and six or seven miles in extent. The more ambitious extend it out Seventh Avenue, along the broad road kept soft for the speeding of trotters, to the bridge two miles beyond the Park, or leave the Park at Seventy-second Street for the macadamized Riverside Drive, at

ANGLOMANIACS.

MOUNTED POLICEMAN.

the upper end of which there is half a mile or so of straight bridle-path. If the project is executed that was authorized by the last Legislature to connect the upper end of the Central Park with the upper end of Riverside Drive, by paving the connecting streets like the driveways in the Park for pleasure traffic, there will be a continuous driveway of some nine miles. To complete the felicity of the riders it will be necessary only to carry the bridle-path along the whole extent of the River-side, for which there is ample room.

When one has more time than the hour or hour and a half to which most riders of the male sex are restricted for their constitutionals, there is a choice of suburban excursions, though the choice is not so large as it should be, and as it is to be hoped it will be when it comes to be recognized that people who ride or drive for pleasure have rights as to the paving of a limited number of streets which drivers of drays are bound to re-spect. The bridging of the East River at Blackwell's Island, if it ever comes to pass, will make Long Island accessible, as it can scarcely be said to be now, with four miles of block pavement between the Brooklyn Bridge and the lower end of Central Park. The lower ferries to New Jersey are impracticable for a like reason, but the ferry to Fort Lee is at the upper end of the Riverside Drive, and a short climb brings you to a road through the woods at the top of the Palisades. Je-rome Park, too, at the end of another stretch of soft road which the riders owe to the trotting men, is the goal of a pleasant afternoon's ride.

In the summer, of course, the Park and the city are deserted by them that drive in chariots, although they sometimes leave their chariots behind in the keeping of their charioteers. In that case John Thomas drives Mary Jane daily in the Park, and excites the wonder of the midsummer pilgrim from the country concerning the manners and customs of rich New-Yorkers. It was one of the annual absentees who opposed the planting of a shrub that was fragrant and beautiful in midsummer upon the ground that in midsummer nobody ever went to the Park. Such of the horsemen as cannot get away take their constitutionals as usual—in the early morning, if they be of heroic mould and able to do things before breakfast, or otherwise in the late afternoon. For the most part the riding-schools are deserted, and some of them establish colonies at the watering-places as an alternative to turning their horses out to grass.

In winter the owner of a saddle-horse is the object of a commiseration of which he does not stand in the least need. Some horsemen, indeed, defy the season, and

A FAMILY GROUP.

THE CONSTITUTIONAL RIDER.

ride out-of-doors all winter long, although in midwinter it is to less hardy souls and bodies an abuse of language to call such riding riding for pleasure. At least one horsewoman there is who pursues the same courageous practice, and for whom no weather that a man can ride in is too severe. Most riders, after the winter has fairly set in, and until it has fairly broken, know the bridle-path only once or twice a month, when the weather relents for a day and the ice disappears from the roadway. But these enjoy their exercise little less for being compelled to take it under cover. This is the season for teaching, and the "rings"—the rectangles of riding-schools are always rings—are at their busiest. The timid and awkward girl who is hoisted upon a horse for the first time in December, and totters there in a state of highly unstable bodily equilibrium and of keen mental anguish—this

autumnal grub bursts the chrysalis of the ring in April, and appears upon the bridle-path as a fully developed horsewoman. All the morning is given over to lessons, but at the usual riding hour, between business and dinner, in the afternoon, the ring is shut against them, and opened for class riding. There are so many horses that some order has to be observed. At least everybody must ride in the same direction until a change is ordered by the ring-master. Even with this minimum of order riders going each his own gait are sure to obstruct one another, and it is for the general comfort that the riders shall form a line, and ride at the same gait by the word of command, the tedium of walking being relieved by the performance of such simple manœuvres as require only a moderate horsemanship. This is the daily practice during the winter in the larger schools. In addition to this daily

ride, there is once a week, or oftener, a
"music ride" in the evening, and last season one of the schools set the excellent
example of a daily music ride—an example that will no doubt be followed.

Those riders who are ambitious to carry
their horsemanship beyond the standard
required at the music rides associate themselves in clubs for that purpose, and one
of these clubs has for several years made
an excursion of a fortnight on horseback.
It is not defamatory to suggest that "The
First Hussars," an independent military
organization recently founded, with its
head-quarters at one of the riding-schools,
is in the nature of a riding club, and that
its objects are rather equestrian than warlike.

Of course these clubs are not to be confounded with *the* Club, the objects of
which may be said to be equestrian and
social, and which, though not yet five
years of age, has had a very powerful influence in developing the practice of riding and in giving it a status in "society."
The New York Riding Club was founded
by a few owners of saddle-horses who con-
stabulated, so to speak, at one of the riding-schools, and to whom it appeared desirable that there should be a school in
which they could select their own associates. No sooner was the project formed
than it became evident that it met that
long-felt want to which the projectors of
new enterprises invariably appeal. Already it has nearly five hundred members,
and one honorary member, I know not by
what merit raised to that lonely eminence.
Of the active members more than half are
actual horse owners and riders, and all of
them may be supposed to cherish more or
less definite aspirations toward horsemanship. The actual membership is much
larger than the figures indicate, since by
the constitution of the club the ladies of a
member's family and his minor sons are
entitled to its privileges, the daughters
forfeiting their privileges when they marry, unless they marry into the club, as it
were. There must thus be quite twice as
many virtual members of the club as appear upon the club list, and it is to these
unenrolled members that the club is most
nearly indispensable. Its male members
might find their own requirements very
nearly as well met in all essentials at one
of the public riding-schools. But a place
of instruction and exercise to which ladies

and children can resort unattended, and
about the associations of which they may
be quite secure, has the same advantage
over even the most carefully conducted
public school that an ordinary club has
over a restaurant. As has been hinted,
the club is regarded by outsiders as a citadel of Anglomania, nor is the charge
without some plausibility. The attendants
are habited in plush and small-clothes,
and exhibit those balustraded calves that
are the trade-mark of the British flunky.
When the visitor has got over his aversion
to this grewsome spectacle he will find
little else to offend his patriotic sensibili-
ties, unless he considers a high degree of
luxury in the living-rooms of the club, and
an absolutely flawless neatness in the stables, corrupting to the simplicity of republican manners. The club-house is within
a few hundred feet of the Fifth Avenue
entrance to the park. Its area is about
200 feet by 125. and gives room for a ring
in the centre 107 by 94, with a range of
rooms along the street front, and spacious
stables for some 300 horses in the rear.
The dimensions of the ring, when it was
built, were the largest in New York, though
they have since been exceeded by one or
two of the public schools, and of course by
such a monument of capricious extravagance as the famous subterranean riding-
hall of the Duke of Portland at Welbeck
Abbey. It is proposed to enlarge it still
further, but it is now ample for the music
rides, or, as they are called at the club,
the "drills," which occur during the winter twice a week in the afternoon, and
in which some sixty or seventy horsemen and horsewomen usually take part.
There are few prettier sights to lovers of
horseflesh and horsemanship than one of
these drills, exhibiting practised riders, on
the best and best-looking saddle-horses
that can be bred or bought, executing
more intricate evolutions than the schools
for the most part venture on, with admirable precision, and upon occasion at a
smart pace. There is not one of the riders
who is not deriving physical benefit from
an exercise for which very few of them
would find any substitute if this were not
at their command. If riding in New
York be, as with many of its votaries it
must be owned to be, a matter of fashion
mainly, the philanthropist may be well
satisfied if fashion inspires nothing less
useful or less delightful.

Drawn by T. de Thulstrup.

A MUSIC RIDE.

Engraved by Wolf.

THE CITY TO THE NORTH OF 'TOWN'

TO the average Englishman the word "town" means London; to the dweller therein the word "city" signifies only its business portion—Lombard Street and the busy district around about St. Paul's. To the New-Yorker, "town" for years meant that portion of the island of Manhattan extending from the Battery to Harlem. By a political movement the city charter has been extended to embrace a large territory far distant from the natural boundary of the metropolis. "The Greater New York" was created by legislation, but "town" itself will always be "Manhattan's dear isle"—as the old song hath it—and the wider country to the northward; for the city proper has but one direction in which to spread itself.

Greater New York includes all of New York, Kings, and Richmond counties, and parts of Queens and Westchester. It embraces some forty-odd small towns and villages threaded together by ferry and railroad, but as yet, to all intents, separate and distinct. Brooklyn and its many suburbs to the east and south, and Staten Island, separated by a wide stretch of navigable water, now can claim to be a part of the city itself; the pot-hunter of Goose Creek and the oysterman of Oceanus are now citizens, and it is expected of them to shoulder the responsibilities.

Of the history of the political struggle that resulted in the passage of the bill at Albany it is sufficient to say that the bill for the consolidation of the Greater New York was passed in 1896, and the charter in 1897. The charter will go into effect on the 1st of January, 1898. Not a few of the outlying towns were incorporated much against their will. A Long Island village, situated on a shallow inlet, moved to have itself declared out of the city limits, on the ground that the boundary-line, according to the charter, read " to the middle of the channel," and as the channel had shifted some distance (a way Long Island channels have of doing), according to the letter of the law the inhabitants declared themselves freed from the tremendous responsibility of belonging to the overreaching " Greater."

The new city will be the second in size and population in the world. In January next its inhabitants will number close to 3,500,000. London, the largest city, has a population in the neighborhood of 5,500,000. The area of the Greater New York will be little more than half that of England's capital, but it will be exactly twice that of the next largest city in America, Chicago. Including the waters of the bay, it will be thirty-five miles in length — that is, from Wards Point, the extreme southern limit of Staten Island, to the town of Mount St. Vincent, a little station on the Hudson. On Long Island, to the east, it takes in Little Neck Bay and extends to the limits of Garden City. Shelter Island is just outside the boundary-line to the south. All the Rockaway Beach summer-places are now part of the municipality, including the marshy islands of Jamaica Bay to the north of the long sandy strip which bounds it. The assessed value of all the property of the great city will reach the enormous sum of over two billions of dollars. Its water-front capacities are unexcelled, there being room for upwards of 550 miles of wharfage. The public-school system, the pride of American self-government, will be so extended as to embrace over 350 public schools,—which will carry upon their rolls, at their greatest limit, 450,000 pupils. Breathing-space aplenty

will be provided by the 6500 acres of public parks. Politically, Greater New York has been divided into five boroughs. The city of New York below the Harlem River comprises the Borough of Manhattan. The present city of Brooklyn, taking in the entire county of Kings, composes the Borough of Brooklyn. Queens is made up of the Long Island country to the east of it. Richmond, which comprises the whole of Staten Island, is the fourth; and the Borough of Bronx is the land above the Harlem, extending from a point just north of Hunters Island in the Sound, along the limits of Mount Vernon and Yonkers, to the Hudson. There will be but one Mayor and one Comptroller, elected every four years, but local self-government will be preserved in a measure, owing to the fact that each separate borough will have its own President. It cannot be said that the political scheme that has thus brought into close relations varied sections of a divergent territory is in a state of perfection. Probably

A NOOK IN GREATER NEW YORK.

many changes in the charter and in the proposed management of municipal affairs will take place. Nor is it just or proper to decry the means by which all this has been brought about. The results will show for themselves probably within the next decade. It is to be hoped that the ambitious views of the progenitors

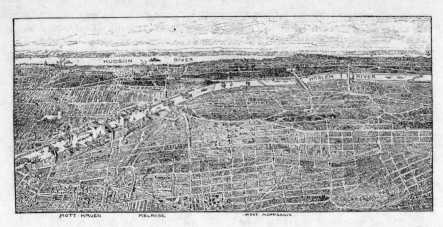

A BIRD'S-EYE VIEW OF UPPER NEW YORK FROM MOTT HAVEN TO MOUNT HOPE.

will meet with every success. Like all experiments in government, the development will be watched with interest. But Brooklyn will remain Brooklyn for some time to come. Staten Island is five miles and more from the South Ferry, and but a few hundred feet from the State of New Jersey. Neither will ever exactly enter into a New-Yorker's idea of "town."

But the absorption of the country-side to the north—the Borough of the Bronx—has been gradual and natural. Not long since Harlem merged into the city; it is "uptown" nowadays. The imaginary line that separated "up" from "down" has shifted northward. So it is New York in New York County, and that part of Westchester annexed in 1895, that is the subject of this article—the latter a tract of land extending northward to the boundary-line of the town of Mount Vernon, and embracing the large islands in the Sound to the east, and separated from Long Island by the East River and Flushing Bay, while the Hudson is the natural boundary on the west. It stretches for over seven miles to the north of 125th Street, and averages six and a quarter miles in width. The present population is not short of 200,000, who live, for the most part, along the lines of the railroads. The towns bear names well known in Revolutionary history; the majority of them were standing when it was three days and over to Boston by coach along the old post-road. And it is here that the proud city will be built. It will not be of mushroom growth, but, following

the plans that have been marked down for it, slowly it will rear itself. It will contain the finest parks in all the world, and people's play-grounds without number. Public institutions will have room for proper expansion, and there will be sites in plenty to encourage architectural ambitions.

There is no question that naturally beautiful country can be so "improved" that its only beauty will be entirely lost in artificial ruler-edged and compass-lined perfection. It is a satisfaction to be able to state that from the published plans of the Department of Street Improvements of the Twenty-third and Twenty-fourth wards of the city of New York in a great measure this has been avoided, and it is to be hoped that in furbishing and furnishing the new park system the commissioners and powers that be will to a certain extent let well enough alone. Nature herself has here provided pleasure-grounds without the aid of man.

To the wheelmen, and to those riders and drivers who really ride and drive for pleasure, this country is more or less familiar; but it would be safe to state that not one out of ten of the well-to-do citizens who take their airing along the Riverside or through Central Park knows anything of the charm of the region of hill and valley so near to hand. Harlem itself is a revelation to the average New-Yorker whose home is below the sixties. But a few years ago there was a distinct line of demarkation where the street names jumped into three figures, but now

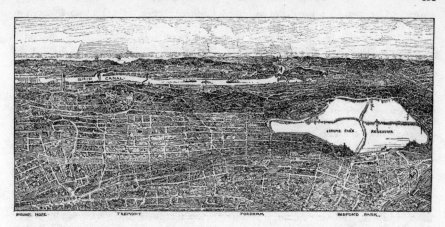

A BIRD'S-EYE VIEW OF UPPER NEW YORK FROM MOUNT HOPE TO BEDFORD PARK.

from the elevated railroads, to the east or west, except for the Park, and here and there a vacant lot or two, it is but an un-interrupted vista of house-tops, broken here and there by a spire or the tall chimney of some manufactory. The character of this portion of town is being influenced by the number of fine and dignified public and private structures that have recently been erected. The line of buildings to the west of Morningside Park and the location that they occupy cannot be excelled. When the Cathedral of St. John the Divine has reached completion, and all the dormitories of Columbia College are finished, taken with the great white hospital of St. Luke's, the sight will be one to give the New-Yorker a feeling of proper pride as he views it. It is all recent, and at this moment its newness is almost incongruously apparent. Within the shadow of one of the massive Columbia halls, and facing a glaring-windowed block of new dwelling-houses, nestles—no other word expresses it—a little country farm-house. The streets have been cut away surrounding it, and there it rests upon a little plateau of its own. For years it has stood there overlooking the valley of the Harlem, but now, with its old-fashioned grape-arbor and box-lined walk that tumbles off at the edge of the artificial divide, it seems as much out of place as would a hermit-thrush among the sparrows of City Hall Park. It appears to have swooped down from some New England hill-side and settled there overnight.

The location of the Columbia buildings is a most happy one. The buildings themselves lack nothing to be wished for, and with rare good judgment the architects and landscape-gardener have not lost sight of the natural adjuncts of the location. The hill-top in the neighborhood of what is now Amsterdam Avenue and 120th Street (in the old days called Vandewater Heights) was surmounted by a noble grove of trees, and as much as possible they have been left undisturbed. The buildings and the great iron fence rose about them, and at noon hour, when the workmen ceased their hammers and the derricks ceased swaying their heavy loads, the gray squirrels would come down from the branches to partake of the crumbs thrown to them by the laborers taking their rest there in the shade.

When the college is open the elms and oaks will give a homelike feeling to the place, will detract from the newness of appearance, and when the surrounding blocks shall be covered, every inch of them, and the little farm-house shall have been wiped out, Columbia will appear to have stood there for long years, and to lord it over the college precincts by the right of age and pre-emption.

At the foot of the Claremont Hill is the valley that divides the Harlem Heights (historic ground); here a ferry crosses the Hudson, and no finer view can be found within a half-day's travel of New York than that looking back toward the city across the river from the site of old Fort Lee on the Jersey shore. Although at a far distance, on a clear day it is visible its whole length; the shadowy hills of Staten Island are on the horizon, and against the sky-line the tall buildings on lower Broadway stand up like factory chimneys. Even the statue of Liberty, on her little domain, is plain to view. The spires of the various churches can be discerned, and the tall apartment-houses on the upper reaches of the avenues can be counted. Nearer, as the eye follows the line of the river, suddenly springs into view the glaringly white and, alas, not over-beautiful tomb on the Claremont Hill. The green trees mark the line of River-side Drive, a narrow line of green the Park, and over the gap in the hill-side, through the valley of the Harlem, is a view of the Sound and the blue shores of Long Island.

One can stand amid the ruins of the old fort that hangs upon the southernmost spur of the Palisades and imagine what it must have been like in the older days, when the British flag flew over the little town at the extreme end of the island, and the country above it was one great skirmish-ground. Yonder is Harlem Heights (130th Street); here Howe was checked. If only one of the old Continentals could stand here now where his clumsy iron cannon looked down upon the river, and gaze to the south! He would see what immediately strikes the eye of the latter-day observer—the tide of the city sweeping northward. It is as if one could feel the movement. Directly across the river are the advance-guards: a compact block of dwelling-houses stands opposite an old colonial mansion. The spires and roofs of great public institutions lift above the trees; and those hideous blots upon most suburban scenery, the huge brown drums of the gas-tanks, are grouped at the water's edge.

Occasional glimpses of the new park lands are to be seen through the car windows after one has passed the boundary-line of the city limits at Mount Vernon, but the tenements and dwellings have followed the line of travel, and the train rushes past stations whose only difference is in their names; it roars across the iron bridge over the Harlem, plunges through the smoke-laden tunnel, and discharges its passengers without ceremony into the midst of the cries and noises of the city. A person might travel in this fashion a hundred times, or a thousand, mayhap, and see nothing of what lies beyond. The traveller by steamboat, as he skirts this part of the new city, sees much more that is interesting; but even this trip has been taken by but a small percentage of those who rush in and out of town to their far-distant country places. The yachtsman alone is familiar with its many beauties. Where the money of the tax-payer goes is evident along the eastern shore; the great public institutions on the river islands, where the State and city gather their useless, their poverty-stricken, and their mentally twisted citizens, represent the expenditure of many millions, and account for much of the necessary drain upon the public purse. The shore from the entrance to Hell Gate through the East River is a beautiful sight. The numberless inlets are filled with small craft at anchor. Yachts and barges, coasting vessels and the great Sound steamers, follow the highway of the channel. Country clubs and old mansions throng the points. Numberless steamboat lines touch the towns on the Long Island and the New York shores, and when the entrance to the wide Sound has been gained, and the two fortresses that guard the city on the east—Fort Schuyler at the end of Throgs Neck, where the British suffered defeat at the hands of the Yankee riflemen, and Willets Point opposite—have been passed, there are still five miles to be spent before one is beyond the city limits to the north, for the charter has rightfully included the islands enclosing Pelham Bay, Rodmans Neck, and City Island (connected with the mainland by wide causeways), and Harts Island, and Hunters Island, which the city makes use of for public purposes.

But it is not of the water-front that this article treats. It is the inland country, away from the railway lines, the country into which "town" is pushing its streets and avenues and boulevards, that holds most interest. Perhaps it is for the reason that until lately there has been a sad lack of good roads that all this has been a *terra incognita* to the average New-Yorker. But the bicycle and the recent improvements have opened up this section, and there are many hundreds of riders and drivers who are now familiar with every foot of the beautiful country that will be preserved—good fortune—in the new parks and gardens. There will

WHERE THE BRIDGES LINK THE HEIGHTS.

be plenty of room outside their limits for thousands of homes and industries — a million people will not crowd it. It is all historic ground; battles and skirmishes between the British forces and the little army under Washington took place at almost every corner. Although progress is destroying landmarks, and a state of sudden transition is plainly visible everywhere, there is enough remaining to tempt the student of history to a tour of investigation.

The little towns and villages possess various individualities; incongruities of surroundings make somewhat startling effects. Juxtaposition of natural scenery and the result of man's handiwork abounds. Paved streets have pushed their way in advance of traffic; the grass grows lush among the cobble-stones. Stone sidewalks skirt miles of city lots — vacant except for a wooden shanty or a dingy roadside tavern. But here the city will be, and before ten years have passed the incongruities will have disappeared, the pasture bars and decaying farm-houses

will give place to iron gates and handsome residences, or blocks of dwellings.

For a time the Harlem River marked the apparent northern boundary of New York, but now, spanned by bridges, it is but a breach, an incident, although it yet has woody slopes and meadows where cattle feed at the water's edge and the small boy goes a-swimming.

At 155th Street, where the viaduct overlooks Manhattan Field and the Polo Grounds, familiarly known as "Deadhead Hill," the new Harlem Speedway begins. It will be one of the finest roads in all the world, as fine as lavish expenditure can make it. It stretches along the shore of the Harlem River, close under Washington Heights. At present it is in a very unfinished condition; hundreds of men and horses, scores of derricks and spile-drivers, are hard at work building the embankments and cutting out the right of way. Looking up or down the river, the view is fine. High Bridge, with its beautifully modelled arches, and, farther to the north, Washington

ACROSS THE RIVER TO FORT GEORGE.

Bridge, with its two great spans, link the two heights across the river. At the northern end of Fort Washington, where Amsterdam Avenue circles the edge of the cliff, there is a fine view of the lower meadows. From here to the northward can be counted the locations of six different little towns—High Bridge, Morris Heights, Fordham, Inwood, Spuyten Duyvil, and Kingsbridge; the beautiful Audubon Park is over to the southwest, looking down upon the Hudson.

One often finds in America evidences of the strong desire of our foreign-born citizens to hold fast to their national characteristics or peculiarities. They will adopt a certain locality, and make strenuous efforts to transform it into a semblance of what is to be found in their own fatherland. Here, where the Speedway will end, and where is now the terminus of the Washington Heights trolley system, the Germans of Harlem have full possession. A huge wooden caravansary crowns the hill (where stood the old Fort George in 1776). The avenue leading up to the curve is lined with tents and booths, merry-go-rounds, and catchpenny devices of all kinds. Beer-gardens are set back among the trees, and every-

thing is German—the signs, the waiters, and the language spoken. Like a famous excursion resort up the Sound, it has been nicknamed "Klein Deutschland." A battery of heavy wooden cannon frowns over an imitation parapet, a huge tun, almost as large as the famous one at Heidelberg, but empty and deceptive, looms above the garden wall. A German band plays popular airs, and in the great building, topped by its flags and streamers, there is room to seat five hundred people about the tables. On Saturday afternoons and evenings the place is crowded, and on Sunday throughout the whole twelve hours. Although the proprietors of the "Klein Deutschland" resorts do not depend so much upon the bicyclist as do the road-houses and inns across the river, they have not ignored his custom. Here are racks for two hundred bicycles, and a system of attendants to look after them.

Through the valley that divides the Inwood hills shows the top of the Palisades. Broad streets are being built through the meadows that stretch below, and lines of carts trail to and fro like caravans along the newly graded highways. It is in this meadow that the farmer-soldiers harvested their hay crop between the two armies, while the British rested at Kingsbridge and camped along the high ground of the Harlem River; and the Americans waited within the lines of Fort George and Fort Washington, which occupied high ground immediately across the Hudson from Fort Lee (Fort Constitution). The position of the old fort is plainly marked. It was well-nigh impregnable, and had it not been for the traitorous disclosure of the plans of its approaches, it might never have been taken.

Soon the Harlem River will be busy with ocean-going vessels, and the meadows and the shores on either bank will be filled with ship-yards and warehouses where now a few row-ing-clubs and some yacht-building establishments alone have place. The ship-canal has been cut through the steep hill-side at Kingsbridge, and slow-ly the work of widening it at Spuyten Duyvil has been pushed to a finish. The northern-most point of Manhat-tan is now a little island

Howe's advancing redcoats. A number of little country roads lead off to right and left, but they rejoice now in high-sounding names, Marcher Avenue, Nel-

NEAR FEATHERBED LANE.

by itself, less than a quarter of a mile in length and about the same in breadth. It is a famous boating-place, and rowing-clubs, whose number here will surely be increased, may transform it into a plea-sure-river like the upper Thames.

But to leave the Borough of Manhat-tan for the less well known country across the Harlem River: After crossing the broad driveway of Washington Bridge, a sharp turn to the north brings one to the entrance of the historic Featherbed Lane. But a few short years ago it was a lane indeed, but now it is a macadamized roadway full fifty feet in width. Up the old crooked lane the American forces retreated before they crossed the river, and in the woods yonder, at the crest of the hill, they made a brave stand against

son Avenue, Ogden Avenue, etc., soon to be opened, paved, and citified. That such a homely-sounding name as "Feather-bed" should have been allowed to survive is a gratifying concession to history and tradition. Further on, however, it be-comes plain East 174th Street.

In this neighborhood one is continually running against the vanguards of the municipality: a mounted policeman pa-trolling his beat along a shaded bypath that, so far as appearances go, might be in the Green Mountains of Vermont; while a steam-roller is puffing and snorting up and down a new-laid avenue, a bare-footed country boy is driving some brows-ing cows along the edge of a brook, just out of sight behind the bushes. A house with a well-sweep stands close by a block of wooden tenements. On the side hill, near McComb's Road and what will be Belmont Street when it is completed, is a little stone house covered with vines. It bears the date 17 hundred and something (the last two figures are hidden by the ivy), and it stood there when Washington and his raw troops came up out of the valley. Near the gateway a spring gushes into a wooden drinking-trough. Looking east toward Claremont Heights Park, a station near the New York and Harlem Railroad, everything is new—new houses, new roads, and, beyond all doubt, new people.

The broad Aqueduct Avenue cuts through the country by fine private places. It passes the Berkeley Oval, and ascending a slight grade on a graceful curve, it leads by the eastern edge of University Heights, where the University of the City of New York is building its new home, and a grand home it will be when the quadrangle and the campus

A FRENCH RESTAURANT IN BRONX PARK.

own. Along the road-sides enterprising individuals have erected neat little booths or canvas-covered stands, with insidious signs and drinks to tempt the thirsty wheelman. Some years ago a benevolent and philanthropic gentleman by the name of Webb, who had retired from ship-building in affluence, erected a large and, it must be confessed, a very homely building, as an asylum for aged and indigent members of the trade that had brought him wealth, and a place of instruction also for the aspiring builder. Its site is a commanding one; it overlooks Sedgwick Avenue, across the Harlem Valley, to the Palisades of the Hudson, and over the valley is a panorama of the upper hills of Manhattan. To the south rise the cliffs of Fort George. Below is the station of Fordham Landing, and where the landing-road crosses the avenue, almost hidden in a tangle of underbrush, is a small graveyard. The stones stand crookedly among the ferns. Some of them have fallen, and are covered up by the leaves and earth. A gnarled old willow-tree waves its sweeping branches over this forgotten resting-place. Wheelmen halt there and eat their luncheons, and the amateur photographer is tempted to stop and snap his camera. The writer asked an old man working by the roadside the name of the burial-ground. He replied, rather shortly, that he didn't know. "But they do say it's a good place for ghosts." Indeed it looks it.

But now to take across country in the direction of the new park lands. Although quite near together, the little towns, when distant from the railroad station, are distinctly separate. It is round a corner, over a hill, and you jump in less than a mile from one village to another. Each has its little centre of small stores, a restaurant, a barber's pole, and the omnipresent repair shop for bicy-

are finished. Between the grounds of this university and the river to the west is Sedgwick Avenue, a broad highway that runs from Morris Heights to Fordham Heights. It is now completed, and no better road could be found, search far or near. It overlooks the river, and the bicyclist has long claimed it for his

cles. Fordham, before one reaches the railroad station of the Kingsbridge Road, seems to be unchanged by the great avenues that have pierced through it. The projected Grand Boulevard, or Concourse, will run through the western portion of the little village. When completed, this grand driveway and pleasure path will be one hundred and eighty-two feet in width, and divided by four parallel lines of shade trees. It will stretch from Cedar Park at 161st Street to the entrance to Mosholu Parkway, where the streets number two hundred odd.

The construction of this Grand Boulevard was resolved upon after much thought on the part of the engineers and the Department of Public Improvements. It will have no equal anywhere in this country or in Europe. It follows the ridge carefully, and it would almost seem as if the latter had been prepared for its occupancy. Over one-half of the property has been acquired, and the Legislature has been generous in its appropriation. On the 24th of August, 1897, the entire right of way will be owned by New York city. The cost of finishing the Concourse will be, at a conservative estimate, at least $10,000,000. The cross streets, upon which surface roads are projected, will pass under it through spacious archways. All the approaches from the bridges of the Harlem will lead to it, joining near Cedar Park in a broad esplanade. Handsome residences and homes of the wealthy are bound to follow. To the east and west will lie the many thousands of homes of the well-to-do, following the line of the new systems of rapid transit soon to be developed. It will be a long time, however, before the boulevard will be finished, for a work of such magnitude grows slowly. Fordham Station will be but a stone's-throw from the Kingsbridge Road.

To the traveller by the railway the St. John's College grounds are a welcome re-lief to the eye. The buildings are just to the northeast of Fordham Station. They have a dignified appearance, and the wide stretch of campus is covered with the finest of green turf. To the southeast of the college are the towns of Belmont and

VAN CORTLANDT MANOR.

West Farms, both bordering upon the Bronx, the latter but two miles from where the little river debouches into the inlet enclosed between Hunts Point and Classons Point, on which stands the old manor, built before 1700. A road in very good condition leads eastward down a slight hill into one of the parks soon to be the pride of the borough. Before crossing the bridge over the stream, on the right-hand side, there is a little way-side inn. It has a most attractive look; its unpretentiousness gives to it a character that the dormer-windowed and cupola-crowned road-houses on the new avenues entirely lack. Over the next hill, less than a mile away, can be seen the flag-staffs and minarets of the Morris Park race-track, but the little village of Bronxdale is uncontaminated; it fits most naturally into the calm, delightful surroundings. To the traveller familiar with the smaller villages of rural Europe it has an Old World flavor, probably due to the fact that it has no railroad station; one might expect to see a rumbling mail-coach come bowling about the

THE SITE OF THE NEW RESERVOIR, JEROME PARK.

corner. Some of the little cottages have tiny windows with deep casements. They are built of stone, and whitewashed neatly; bachelor's-buttons and hollyhocks grow in the little front gardens. The appearance of the village makes one draw a breath of surprise at first sight. It is a place to fit into a book—it goes with the age of knee-buckles and cocked hats.

There is a good highway leading to the southeast that terminates at Fort Schuyler at the end of the peninsula, from which there is to be built a new boulevard along the shore leading in the direction of Baychester and Bartow. The Boston post-road crosses the village in a northeasterly direction, leading to Eastchester, Pelham Manor, and the towns along the Sound. The trolley (which it is to be hoped will penetrate no farther) stops within the precincts of West Farms, and the picnickers bound for Bronx Park come up on foot, following the Bear Swamp road, a name left over from a century or so ago, with the traditions that in the tangled marsh-land to the south a famous

Bruin lived, who preyed upon the Dutch farmers' piggeries and robbed their bee-hives. There is a cave in the woods near the river, on the west shore, that is known as Bear's Cave also, and not far away a curiously hollowed stone that collects the rainfall has been named the Indian's Bath Tub.

The stream itself is a step distant, and in those days it was probably more limpid. A winding road enters the woods to the north of the village; it leads directly to the old Lorillard mansion, to which estate all this property once belonged. The fine old house stands in a little park of its own, almost upon the edge of a deep gorge, through which the Bronx roars and tumbles, when the water is high, like a great trout-stream, just below the dam that held back the water that turned the wheels of the old snuff-mill, whose ruins are at the bottom of the steep path into the gorge. It is cool here in the shadows, for the trees are so thick that the sunlight filters through in flecks of light and color. The artist has found this place many times; it is a place to tempt the brush, and often a sketching class of young girls from the art-schools may be seen there trying to catch the reflections of the overhanging branches.

The great Botanical Gardens are to be in this section of the park, and it is to be hoped and prayed that in the construction of the buildings and their surroundings the greatest care will be employed. It would be a shame to destroy what nature has already done. In fact, the visitor is constantly struck with wonder that the woodman has spared his axe so long in the time-old forest, and has overlooked the hemlock grove on the west side of the Bronx. The manor-house is now occupied by the Department of Public Parks; the high-ceilinged dining-room is now the main office; and belowstairs the spacious kitchen has been turned into a restaurant for the visiting public. The Zoological Garden, which has been started under the best of auspices, and which promises to be in every way popular and successful, both from its location and from the fact that it is to be under good management, will border upon the Botanical Gardens, which occupy some three hundred acres, while the whole extent of the park system will not be less than four thousand, including Van Cortlandt, which is at some distance, and Pelham Bay Park, three miles away, which occupies the extreme northeastern portion of the borough and the neighboring islands in the Sound.

No expense will be spared to make the "Zoo" second to none in the world. There will be plenty of grazing-ground for herds of deer, and the supervision of the fauna and the management of the plans of park construction will be undertaken by Mr. Hornaday, late of the Smithsonian. This means much to those having a knowledge of zoological matters.

The New York Zoological Society was incorporated in 1895, and the grant of two hundred and sixty-six acres was received in March, 1897, the State appropriating $125,000 for the preliminary preparation of the park. Particular attention will be paid to American animals, and they will be shown amid natural surroundings. Life membership to the society costs $200, yearly membership, $10. It is intended that the gardens shall be opened free to the public, with the exception of two days in the week reserved for members, on

which days any one can obtain admission, however, by the payment of a small entrance-fee. The formal opening will not take place until the spring of 1899. It is the intention of the society to build and maintain a library of public instruction in connection with the garden. This will be a new, and it is to be hoped a successful venture. The grounds begin at the village of West Farms, thirty minutes by surface road from 129th Street and Third Avenue. They are bounded on the west by the Southern Boulevard, on the north by Pelham Avenue, and on the east by Bronx Lake and the pleasure-grounds.

Keeping onward through the park lands, and following the river to the north, the road passes an ancient orchard whose trees are so decrepit that few bear longer any fruit. Here the stream enters a tangle of alders and sumac from an open meadow, and above this meadow, from Williams Bridge to the city limits, the tracks of the Harlem branch of the Hudson River Railroad follow it closely. But before leaving the valley to cross in the direction of Van Cortlandt, it is necessary to pass that curious collection of little garden restaurants on the banks of the Bronx that have been so much written about because of their uniqueness in their surroundings. As the upper end of Amsterdam Avenue is essentially German, and altogether foreign in appearance and effect, these places are altogether French. The gardens are cut up into little vine-clad booths, each containing a table and some wooden chairs. The well-cooked meals are served in the open air.

If the visitor speaks French, the proprietor welcomes him effusively. "What will monsieur have? Une omelette aux fines herbes, un poulet sauté, or a salade romaine with mayonnaise?" One might imagine one's self but a few leagues from Paris. Here are the same games—the little cast-iron frog on the table, and the tiny quoits one tries to cast down his throat or into one of the numbered partitions; the ring at the end of the string, which one endeavors to catch on the numbered hooks; here is the jeu de quilles, and if you are fond of the game of dominoes you can play it as you sip your coffee. For a long time the proprietor depended upon the custom of the French colony of New York, whose members would come and spend a quiet Sunday with him; but now the wheelmen have found him out, which means, doubtless, larger crowds and more prosperity. When the railroad track is crossed at Williams Bridge, it is evident that it is America, after all. Climbing the old Gun Hill road, here is the work of the city improvements again; but the country is most promising. The Mosholu Parkway, a wide line of villa sites and woods that begins where the streets are in the two hundreds, sweeps up Gun Hill, connecting the Botanical Gardens with Van Cortlandt. The view here from the top to the northwest is the finest. It overlooks Van Cortlandt Park and the wide billowing country far beyond, and here the old Croton Aqueduct crosses. It has extended in a direct line from Featherbed Lane through the old colonial estates along the Fordham Heights.

Jerome Avenue will skirt the eastern shore of the Jerome Park reservoir when it is completed, but at present what will be a beautiful sheet of clear blue water is but an unsightly depression in the earth. Great derricks and steam-shovels are eating their way into the hill-side scenery. Busy little engines puff along their uneven tracks—to the unskilled observer, in a very aimless fashion. Jets of vapor mark innumerable steam-drills. Plunging horses tug at the heavy-laden carts. At evening squads of dark-visaged Italian laborers are to be met chattering along the road, lumbering homeward from their work.

Van Cortlandt Lake, famous for skating, is within a few feet of the station. In summer the water-lilies lie along the shores and the bull-frogs chorus lustily. The stream that drains it is known as "Tibbetts Brook"—what a delightfully bucolic name is Tibbetts Brook! The

public golf links extends up the eastern side of the little lake along the meadows at the foot of the sloping hill where runs the new aqueduct. The greens are kept in good order, and those players who are debating about joining some New Jersey golf club, or some distant Long Island links, had best look at that to whose use they are entitled gratis. The course is not an easy one, but it admits of long drives, and the turf is excellent.

The old Van Cortlandt mansion, built in 1748, is at the curve of the driveway leading from the bridge. It is now in charge of the Colonial Dames, and it contains an interesting little museum of relics and mementos well worth a visit. The sturdy old house has an unassuming beauty of proportion, plain and simple though it be. The Dames have surmounted the ridge-pole with three exceedingly high flag-staffs, which lend the effect of a military headquarters not altogether out of keeping with the character of the building, which is just north of the wide parade-ground. The Van Cortlandt parade-grounds are the nearest approach we have to an American Aldershot. It is within easy riding distance from town for the cavalry or artillery, and but a few minutes by train from the Grand Central Station. Broadway, the ancient post-road to Albany, skirts the edge of the park on the west, and it is but a mile south to the Harlem River, crossing which, one finds one's self again on the northern limit of the island of Manhattan. If it is evening, the reflection of the city's glare shows in the sky. But only a few twinkling lights on the wooded slopes to the north and east mark what soon will be the "town."

SEA ROBBERS OF NEW YORK

New York as it appeared about 1690

I.

SEA-STEALING, though they did not call it by so harsh a name, was a leading industry with the thrifty dwellers in this town two hundred years ago. That was a good time for sturdy adventure afloat; and our well-mettled New-Yorkers were not the kind then, any more than they are now, to let money-making chances slip away by default. Even in referring to what is styled (but very erroneously) the drowsy period of the Dutch domination the most romantic of our historians have not ventured the suggestion that anybody ever went to sleep when there was a bargain to be made; and in the period to which I now refer, when the English fairly were settled in possession of New York by twenty years of occupancy, exceeding wide-awakeness was the rule. Nor was anybody troubled with squeamishness. Therefore it was that our townsfolk, paltering no more with fortune than they did with moral scruples, set themselves briskly to collecting the revenues of the sea.

These revenues were raised by two different systems: which may be likened, for convenience' sake, to direct and to indirect taxation. In the first case, our robust towns-people put out to sea in private armed vessels ostentatiously carrying letters of marque entitling them to war against the King's enemies—which empowering documents they construed, as soon as they had made an offing from Sandy Hook, as entitling them to lay hands upon all desirable property that they found afloat under any flag.

The indirect method of taxation had in it less heroic quality than was involved in the direct levy; yet was it, being safer in a business way and almost as profitable, very extensively carried on. Euphemism was well thought of even then in New York: wherefore this more conservative class of sea-robbers posed squarely as honest merchants engaged in what they termed the Red Sea Trade. At the foot of the letter, as our French cousins say, their position was well taken. Their so-called merchant ships dropped down the harbor into the bay and thence out to the seaward, carrying, for merchantmen, oddly mixed ladings, whereof the main quantities were arms and gunpowder and cannon-balls and lead, and strong spirits, and provisions, and general sea-stores. Making a course to the southeastward, they would slide around the Cape to some convenient meeting-place in the Indian Ocean, usually Madagascar, where they would fall in with other ships— whereof the lading was Eastern stuffs, and spices, and precious stones, and a good deal of deep-toned yellow-red Arabian gold. No information was volunteered by their possessors, a rough-and-tumble dare-devil bushy-bearded set of men, as to where these pleasing commodities came from; nor did the New-Yorkers manifest an indiscreet curiosity—being content that they could exchange their New York lading for the Oriental lading on terms which made the transaction profitable (in Johnsonian phrase) beyond the dreams of avarice. When the exchange had been effected the parties to it separated amicably: the late venders of the Oriental goods betaking themselves, most gloriously drunk on their prodigal purchases of West India rum, to parts unknown, and the New-Yorkers deco-

rously returning with their rich freight-age to their home port.

Neither of these methods of acquiring wealth on the high seas, the direct or the indirect, seems to have received the unqualified endorsement of public opinion in New York in those days which came and went again two hundred years ago; yet both of them were more than tolerated, and the Red Sea Trade unquestionably was regarded as a business rather than as a crime. Because of which liberal views in regard to what might properly enough be done off soundings, or at out-of-the-way islands in the ocean sea, it is a fact that at the fag-end of the seventeenth century our enterprising townsfolk were sufficiently prominent in both lines of marine industry—as pirates pure and simple, and as keen traders driving hard bargains with pirates in the purchase of their stolen goods—to fix upon themselves the ill-tempered attention of pretty much the whole of the civilized world.

II.

That the New York of that period was as pluckily criminal a little town as there was to be encountered upon any coast of Christendom ('tis but fair to say that several worse were to be found on the coasts of heathen countries) was due as much to outward constraining circumstances as to inward natural disposition. Indeed, the coming of the pirates hither was less the result of their own volition than of a cruel necessity; and the hearty welcome here given them is to be credited as one of the earliest exhibitions of that heterogeneous hospitality for which our city still continues justly to be famed.

As everybody at all familiar with piratical matters knows, the pirates doing business in American waters in the latter part of the seventeenth century had a hard time of it. What with the increased vigilance of French and English warships in the Caribbean and off the West India Islands; the defection to the French service of many of their own number, and to the English service of Morgan— who was knighted for his misdeeds, and in the year 1680 was made Governor of Jamaica; and finally (this was the death-blow), after that infamous coalition of all Christendom against them, brought about by the Peace of Ryswick—it is not too much to say that even the most capable men in the profession were at their wits' end.

The prime necessity of these harried and bedeviled seafarers was a friendly port in which they could fit out their ships, and to which they could return with their stolen goods. Without these facilities for carrying on their work and for realizing upon their investment of courageous labor, they might as well— save for the fun of it—not be pirates at all; and such of them as were hanged by Sir Henry Morgan, their old comrade, or were turned over by him—as was a whole ship's company—to be racked and fagoted by the Spaniards of Hispaniola, did not even have any fun. Most fortunate, therefore, was it that at the very time that this dismal state of affairs was forward in Caribbean latitudes the possibility of relief for oppressed pirates was discovered here in our own hospitable and generous city of New York.

Like many other important discoveries, the revelation of the piratical possibilities of New York came about almost by accident: when one William Mason stumbled upon the simple plan of fitting out at this port a pirate ship in the guise of a patriot privateer. It was in the year 1689—during Leisler's short administration—that Mason was authorized to sail for Quebec and "to war as in his wisdom should seem meet" against the French. Several other ships similarly were commissioned at the same time, and as these engaged only in genuine privateering there is no reason for supposing that Mason's letter of marque was taken out in bad faith. What swung him from legal to illegal piracy appears to have been pure bad luck. He seems honestly to have tried to capture French ships off the Canadian coast; and then, worried and vexed beyond endurance by his ill fortune in not finding any French ships to capture, to have taken to piracy as a last resource. His shift turned out admirably well. In the course of his run across to the Indian Ocean all his bad luck was left behind; as a pirate he was as conspicuously successful as he had been unsuccessful as a privateer; and during the ensuing three years he mowed so wide a swath through East Indian commerce that at the end of that period the division of his spoils gave of the value of 1800 pieces-of-eight to every man before the mast.

Mason seems to have left his ship on the other side. Possibly his men murdered him. Pirates used to do that to their captains now and then—not necessarily for publication, but as an evidence of bad faith. At any rate, his ship came back to America in charge of one Edward Coats, and made the eastern end of Long Island in April, 1693. By this time Governor Fletcher—a weak brother morally —was in power; and with him negotiations presently were concluded by which, in consideration of the sum of £1800 to be divided between the Governor and his Council, Captain Coats and his men were assured against any harm coming to them, in New York at least, as the result of their piratical escapade. In the Governor's share was the pirate ship, on which—selling it to the respectable Caleb Heathcote—he realized £800.

III.

It was the deal between Coats and Fletcher which gave to piracy, under the genteel guise of privateering, its practical start in New York: as is made evident by the fact that as soon as the facilities offered for the transaction of piratical business by the obliging Governor were noised abroad there was a notable gathering in this town of well-seasoned adventurers under the black flag.

Quite the most prominent of these early arrivals was Captain Thomas Tew, a well-known practising pirate of that time; and an odd flavor of kindliness is given to this section of the chronicle by the fact that between him and the Governor— quite aside from the question of mutual interest—there was developed a friendship based upon mutual esteem. There was not the least doubt as to Tew's character, and his record was known. On the Indian Ocean he had cut and slashed into the East Indian Company's ships so brazenly, and so successfully, that his name was a terror in all that part of the world. To take a fresh start in his old business he had come to America, and before presenting himself in New York he had made an unsuccessful attempt to procure a so-called privateering outfit in Rhode Island. That he had failed in this attempt is an emphatic testimonial to his disreputability—for the man who was too bad for the Bristol of that period must have been very bad indeed.

Yet when Tew came down to New York, getting here in November, 1694, he and the Governor seem to have struck up a

"PIRATES USED TO DO THAT TO THEIR CAPTAINS NOW AND THEN."

friendship at the very start. Later, when Fletcher was hauled over the coals officially for his misdoings, he admitted his knowledge of the fact that Tew had been a pirate, but explained that the captain had promised to abandon piracy and to become an honest privateer. He added that he had found the captain "agreeable and companionable," and "possessed of good sense and a great memory"; for which reasons of good fellowship, and also to reclaim him to a better life, he had made the captain welcome to his home. The only serious defect in the captain's moral character, Fletcher declared, was his "vile habit of swearing"; which habit he, the Governor, seriously had set himself to cure, both by earnest counsel and by "lending him a book upon the subject"—and to these reformatory measures, he protested, the captain had been encouragingly responsive. Tew, on his side, had manifested his good-will toward the Governor by presenting him with a handsome watch (which presumably had come into the captain's possession as the result of a chance encounter with its lawful owner afloat); and also, according to rumor, had presented the Governor's lady and her daughter with some pleasing knickknacks in the way of jewels.

As I have said, Fletcher was but a weak-kneed brother morally; and no doubt —coming from a life in London to a life in this dull, coarse, raw little town—he must have been so insufferably bored that the arrival of the "agreeable and companionable" pirate must have seemed to him a veritable godsend. And so, partly from self-interest, partly from good-will, Fletcher gave Tew the privateering commission against the French for which he asked: whereafter the captain made sail to the eastward and resumed with great success his piracies on the Indian seas.

In the case of Tew—who came here with plenty of stolen money left over from his previous pickings afloat—New-Yorkers had no more interest than was involved in supplying him with stores and, probably, furnishing him with a crew. But this was not a typical case. I have cited it more because of its oddness, and because the name of Tew has a most dashing notoriety in pirate annals, than because it is exemplary.

A case truly typical is that of Captain John Hoar: who came up to New York from the s'uth'ard — where he had been engaged in buccaneering until driven out of that business by the stringency of the times—about the year 1695.

Captain Hoar was an Irishman, and he had an Irishman's handsome contempt for all petty subterfuge, as well as a birthright joy in the breaking of heads. He obtained from Fletcher letters of marque against the French—because that was the official way of transacting the business that he had in hand—but he scorned (he would have said "scarrn'd") to make a real secret of his intentions, and openly recruited his men for the Red Sea and on the account. His financial backing, as was proved later, came from an unostentatious syndicate of twenty-two merchants of New York: the members of which quietly directed the management of the venture in accordance with sound business principles, and left to their captain the congenial task of exploiting the joys and profits of a cruise with the jolly Roger at the fore. So well did the captain succeed with his part of the work that when he dropped down through the Narrows he carried with him as fine a crew of privateering pirates as ever sailed out of this port.

Something more than a year later the same syndicate quietly fitted out another ship — the *Fortune*, Captain Thomas Mostons — not as a privateer but as an ordinary slaver, and cleared her for Madagascar. Although professedly a slaver, the lading of the *Fortune* is described naïvely as consisting of "goods suitable for pirates." She made a good run to Madagascar, and there—by appointment, presumably — fell in with Hoar's ship, well laden with Oriental goods; whereupon an exchange of cargoes was effected; and the *Fortune*, bringing home also some of Hoar's crew, came safely back again to New York in the summer of 1698.

IV.

In this affair of Hoar's our enterprising merchants managed both ends of the business: they did their own piracy in one ship, and in another ship — as Red Sea traders — they brought home their piratical loot. It was an arrangement which obviously increased the profits; but it so greatly increased the risks that the odds were against it as a whole. Because of which prudent considerations the more steady-going of the merchants of

New York gave the go-by to direct piracy, and were content with the lesser profits arising from the more conservative methods of the Red Sea trade.

To be sure, these were not inconsiderable. For instance, in the record preserved of the venture made in the year 1698 by Mr. Stephen De Lancey and others in the ship *Nassau*, Captain Giles Shelley, the fact is noted that "rum which cost but two shillings a gallon was sold for fifty shillings and three pounds a gallon," and "pipes of Madeira wine which cost here about £19 for £300." With modest profits of this sort the mass of New York merchants was content; and it was only the dare-devil younger men who went in for the big returns to be won by piracy pure. These last, indeed, sometimes gave a taste of their quality to their own fellow-townsmen—as when the slaver *Prophet Daniel*, out of this port, was seized in Madagascar, and the supercargo (young Mr. John Cruger) noted among the captors "Thomas Collins and Robin Hunt from West Chester, New York." That was a case of dog eating dog.

As I have stated above, the Red Sea trade was not at first openly countenanced in New York, yet the fact remains that when the trade became too notorious to be ignored, it squarely was defended by those who were engaged in it; that is to say, by the most prominent merchants of this rascally little town. The matter being come to an open issue, the merchants "were high in their maintenance of the legitimacy of their trade....contending that they were right in purchasing goods wherever found, and were not put upon inquiry as to the source from which they were derived." In farther vindication of their methods they asserted that the vessels sent out by them to Madagascar "were engaged in the pursuit of regular commerce [*i.e.*, the slave trade] and that they accidentally came upon the ships in that region with which they trafficked for the East India goods brought into this port."

Certainly the profits arising from the trade were sufficiently great to dull the conscience of a better class of humanity than was found in the New York of that period. What these profits amounted to, and the conditions under which they were accumulated, may be shown by a more detailed statement of Mr. De Lancey's venture in the *Nassau*, to which reference has been made above.

The *Nassau* cleared hence for Madagascar in July, 1698, with a loading of "strong liquors and gunpowder," and in due course arrived at the port of St. Mary's. Here she disposed of her outward cargo at the handsome rates above given; took on board for the return voyage a cargo of "East Indian goods and slaves"; and received as passengers twenty-nine pirates homeward bound for New York. Off the coast of America she fell in with some vessel that gave news of the sea-change that had taken place in the New York government—with the arrival of Lord Bellomont as Fletcher's successor—and therefore "landed fourteen of her passengers at Cape May," while "the others were put aboard of a sloop from which they were put ashore on the east end of Long Island"—a region where pirates were most kindly entreated in those days. These latter, apparently, came well out of their scrape; but the luckless fourteen landed in New Jersey were harried and hounded across country by the authorities, and six of them were captured with their lading of stolen goods aboard. Probably they were hanged. Precedent to this dismal ending to their venture, under stress of some sort, they made a fairly full confession of their piracies in East Indian waters, and mentioned the interesting fact that the twenty-nine of them had paid for their homeward passage in the *Nassau* "almost £4000." With this item added to the sum of the returns, it is not surprising that the record of Mr. De Lancey's venture ends with the statement: "The voyage of the *Nassau* was an exceedingly prosperous one, netting her owners about £30,000."

Such great profits were had, of course, at the price of great risks. At the very time that the *Nassau* made her prosperous voyage three other ventures out of New York came to calamitous endings. Two of the vessels were captured by pirates, and the third, belonging to Frederick Phillipse, "was seized by an East India Company's frigate"—presumably for taking to piracy at first hand. This was before any effort was made by the New York government to check the Red Sea trade. After the institution of what was regarded as a policy of oppression, the New-Yorkers still more sharply were put to it to make their ventures come to a good end. Yet New York enterprise for a time was equal to the emergency, and in one way or another the trade went on.

As a typical instance of its spirited and intelligent conduct, Mr. Valentine makes the following statement: "About this time [1698] Frederick Phillipse, one of the Council of the Province, the richest man of that day in New York, expected a ship from Madagascar, and with a view to prevent her arrival in the port with contraband goods, subjecting her to forfeiture, he despatched his son Adolphus in a vessel ostensibly bound to Virginia. This vessel, however, cruised in the offing until the appearance of the expected ship, when she approached and discharged her of great quantities of East India goods, with which she sailed to the Delaware, leaving the Madagascar ship to enter New York with only negroes on board." Well conceived though this plan was, it ended badly. Mr. Valentine adds: "The East India goods were afterward sent to Hamburg, where the vessel in which they were carried was seized and the men brought to trial."

V.

It stood to reason that this sort of thing could not be permitted to continue. The New-Yorkers were too greedy. Had they been satisfied with their honest gains from the then legitimate slave trade, and with their winnings from the legitimated form of piracy then carried on in the guise of privateering, no fault would have been found with them, and they would have been left to their own money-making devices in peace. But the Red Sea trade, by which these impudent colonists preyed directly upon the commerce of the mother-country—to say nothing of the strokes of business done by New York pirates in the capture of English ships in West-Indian waters—was so flagrant an impropriety that the home government could not do otherwise than take strong measures for bringing them up with a round turn.

The obvious way to accomplish this necessary reform in New York business methods was to appoint in Fletcher's place a Governor who would have—what Fletcher certainly had not—a fair allowance of moral backbone. Such a person was found in Richard Coote, Earl of Bellomont, who, although he was appointed Governor in 1695, did not receive his commission until 1697, and he did not arrive in New York and assume the duties of his office until April 2, 1698—during which period, as will be observed by reference to the dates of the events above mentioned, the Red Sea traders were getting in their very best work.

But Lord Bellomont, during the time that he was hanging in the wind waiting for his commission to be made out, endeavored—under the tutelage of Robert Livingston, then temporarily resident in London—to make himself familiar with the affairs of the colony over which he eventually was to rule. What was more to the purpose—or less to the purpose, as the event proved—he even essayed to begin the reformation wherewith he was charged: a laudable effort that led directly, by one of those oddly perverse twists of misfortune to which this city ever unhappily has been subject, to setting afloat the most notable pirate who ever sailed from New York, and one of the most notorious pirates who ever sailed the seas—William Kidd.

According to Dunlop, "the English ministry were so deeply impressed with the necessity of suppressing piracy that Lord Bellomont was encouraged to solicit that a frigate might be fitted out for that purpose; but the war with France requiring all the naval force of Great Britain, the request was declined: however, a proposition to purchase and arm a private ship for this service met encouragement so far that the Duke of Shrewsbury, Lord Chancellor Somers, the Earls of Romney and Oxford, with others, became sharers in the enterprise with Livingston and Bellomont—the latter taking upon himself the equipment of the vessel." In other records of the transaction the King is credited with having suggested it, and with offering to contribute towards it from his private purse the sum of £3000; and his Majesty also is represented as having failed to pay up his promised subscription when it fell due. However the project may have started, its prime movers certainly were Livingston and Bellomont; of whom the former undoubtedly was responsible for the selection of Captain Kidd to command the armed vessel which presently went to sea.

Mr. Livingston's action was more than justified by the facts. Kidd's record was excellent. In New York, where he made his home, he was well known as the respectable commander of an honest merchantman, the *Antigua*, trading to England; while socially, as a well-to-do master-mariner, his position was good. He married in this city, in the year 1692, Sarah, widow of another ship-master, Jan Oort; and with the widow took over the late Captain Oort's establishment on Hanover Square. Shortly before his departure on the unlucky cruise that landed him eventually at Execution Dock, the captain had purchased a building site on the Damen farm, just then being sold off in lots, and had built for himself a comfortable house on what then was Teinhoven and now is Liberty Street, near Nassau: where, no doubt, the reorganized widow gave a handsome house-warming which drew heavily upon their store of "one pipe and one half-pipe of Madeira wine."

Livingston not only could, and presumably did, testify to the captain's good repute in their common home, but he also could testify—having but a little while previously made the eastward passage in the *Antigua*—to the captain's good seamanship. Another point in Kidd's favor was his knowledge of the Red Sea methods, picked up in friendly talk with the Red Sea men, his familiar acquaintances, in New York; which knowledge, it was supposed, would enable him to run them down promptly in their piratical haunts. And, finally, the captain's bravery had been proved, and his loyalty tested, by the gallant fashion in which, but a year or so earlier, while in command of a privateer, he had come to the rescue of a King's ship almost overmastered in a bout with the French.

Kidd received from the English authorities at first the regular privateer's commission of the period, giving him the right to war against the French; but this being judged insufficient, a special commission subsequently was made out for him, under date of January 26, 1696, which gave him "full authority to apprehend all pirates wherever he should encounter them, and to bring them to trial." The money side of the transaction provided that all the property wrested from the pirates should vest in the stockholders in this queer enterprise, save that one-tenth of the piratical profits should be reserved to the King: to clinch which arrangement Livingston joined with Kidd in giving a bond to Lord Bellomont to account for all prizes secured. These preliminaries being attended to, Kidd sailed on the *Adventure*, galley, in April, 1696,

for New York; lay at this port for a while perfecting his arrangements and strengthening his crew; and at last, in July, got fairly away to sea.

VI.

It is rather dreadful—looking at the matter from the romantic stand-point—to think what a picturesque figure would have failed to take its place in history had Captain Kidd remained an honest man. And a touch of melancholy is infused into the situation even as it stands by the painful certainty that Kidd was not nearly so desperate a character as the popular legends and ballads which chronicle his doings would lead one to suppose. Indeed, I am more than half inclined to believe—very much against my will—that he was a pirate in spite of himself; and that he was very sorry for it; and that he probably could have excused himself and got away scot-free had not his case become entangled with politics, and had not the need been urgent to make an example of some one pirate in the hand—for the good of those still in the bush—at that particular time. I feel that I owe an apology to the captain's memory for making these admissions, inasmuch as he paid fairly with a stretched neck for the glamour which ever since has loomed about his name.

What seems to have made him a pirate was the ill-advised contract under which he shipped his rapscallion crew. When he and Livingston were planning this pirate-hunting expedition together (as I believe that they did plan it) in the course of the long voyage over—talking it over night after night in the little cabin of the *Antigua* in the sanguine mood begotten of good-fellowship and stiff-mixed grog—there could have been no end to the fortune looming large before them in the bright future of their confident hopes. When their project actually materialized in London, with the fitting out of the ship to make it effective, their anticipations of a rich recovery of stolen goods must have put on a still more golden coloring—so that we almost can hear the captain (as the second bowl is getting low) vaporing away to Livingston and to the noble lords their partners in this enterprise about the prodigious profits certain to result from his cruise. Indeed, the terms of their joint agreement prove that they confidently expected to get out of it a relatively enormous return. The actual investment of capital was about £5000. The prizes taken, after deducting the King's tenth, were to be divided into four shares; of these, one share was to go to the crew, and the remaining three shares were to be divided again into five shares: of which Bellomont and his associates were to receive three, and Kidd and Livingston one; but these last were to receive the ship also in case Kidd delivered to Bellomont prize-goods to the value of or over £100,000. No doubt it was to emphasize his own confidence that the high hopes which this suggestion of £100,000 in prize-money held out to his partners would be fulfilled that induced the captain to ship his crew on the fatally unlucky basis of "no prize, no pay."

Kidd does not seem to have gone into his work with much energy. Reaching New York in the spring of 1696, he made several short cruises hence with the intent to head off and capture suspicious vessels returning from the African coast; but, in point of fact, he did not encounter any such vessels. His one small piece of luck was the capture of a French privateer — in recognition of which useful service the Provincial Assembly "voted him their thanks and a compliment of £250." Naturally, his no-prize-no-pay crew became impatient. A large proportion of his men had been recruited in New York, and the New-Yorkers of those days were not in the habit of going to sea merely for their health. Under Kidd's inert management they chafed until they were getting dangerously ripe for mutiny. It was in this strait—in order to retain his authority over his men; and also in order to justify himself to his backers, to whom he had been talking so glibly about prizes to the value of £100,000—that Kidd decided upon, and immediately put into execution, the dangerous plan of returning to New York and increasing his crew, and then making a course direct for the Madagascar region, and hunting for the pirates on what might be termed their native heath.

What actually happened, according to Kidd's own account of the matter, was precisely what the long-headed New-Yorkers prophesied would happen: the Adventure failed to find any pirate craft, or any merchantmen in obvious trade with pirates, and so made no prizes; the crew grew more and more clamorous for the promised booty; and Kidd had not what nowadays would be termed the "sand" to keep his men in order: out of which conditions came a mutiny that swung the Adventure into downright piracy, and replaced her ensign with the black flag. Of course Kidd's lack of backbone ceased to be weakness and became crime when he consented to act as commander to these new-made pirates; yet even here there is a little of saving grace in his assertion that he did not command them when they made their captures, and in his plea that he consented to be their commander betweenwhiles in the hope that he might swing them back again into the path of seafaring propriety.

After all, the actual amount of piracy committed by this half-hearted pirate is absurdly out of proportion to his piratical celebrity. Assuming him to be responsible for what was done by his crew, this is his record: he stole some provisions on the Malabar Coast; he captured three, possibly four, ships; and—here his bad luck came in again—he personally killed one mutinous seaman at whom, it would seem quite justifiably, he happened to shy a corrective bucket. Absolutely, this is the sum of Captain Kidd's piratical career. Presumably, his great notoriety at this late day — when pirates like Tew and Hoar, who really amounted to something, are almost forgotten—is due in part to the interesting fashion in which he fell from grace, and in part to the melodramatic legends which have arisen because of the burial of a portion of his pirate spoils.

VII.

News travelled slowly from Madagascar to England in those days. For more than a year the Adventure continued her mildly criminal career before any hint of her misdoings came westward from the Indian seas. But when the news did come, there was nothing slow in the action taken by the Admiralty for the abatement of this marine nuisance. Word of Kidd's piracies reached London in the autumn of 1698; and by the 23d of November of that same year a squadron of King's ships had started on their wallowing way to the Indian Ocean—charged particularly with the apprehension of Kidd and his fellows, and, generally, with the suppression of piracy in that sea. Farther notice of the doings of this squadron is unnecessary, inasmuch as Kidd was more than half-way across the Atlantic on his homeward voyage before the first of the pursuing tubby war-ships had her snub-nose fairly around the Cape.

In his thick-witted, luckless way the captain was at the pains to provide a part of the evidence which subsequently helped to hang him by coming home in his principal capture. This was the *Quidah Merchant*, a Moorish ship—but commanded by an Englishman—well laden with East India goods and treasure. Only a small part of his crew returned with him. Soon after his arrival on the African coast ninety of his men had revolted and had gone off with the *Mocha*, frigate; and when he shifted from the *Adventure* to the *Quidah Merchant* he was followed by only a portion of his crew.

Being aware, as Mr. Valentine gently puts it, "that under the best explanations he could give of his conduct he would be greatly censured," the captain had the prudence to lay his landfall upon the West Indies—to the end that he might investigate from a safe distance his chances for making his peace with the Governor of New York. Early in the spring of 1699 he made the island of St. Thomas; but the protection which he there sought was denied to him, and he was forced to put to sea again without victualling. Bearing northward until he was off Hispaniola, he fell in with a sloop commanded by one Henry Bolton; which vessel he first hired to run down to Curaçoa and purchase for him needed supplies, and then bought out and out in order that he might go in her upon a spying expedition to the northward before venturing openly to return to New York. Bolton—who seems to have been one of the most obliging souls in the world, ready to do anything for a consideration—agreed to remain in charge of the *Quidah Merchant*, out of which much of the treasure was transferred to the sloop, until the captain's return.

Kidd's first landing in the English colonies, in June, 1699, was made on the Jersey side of Delaware Bay—which fact probably lies at the root of the manifold legends of buried treasure all along shore from Salem Creek downward to Cape May. For a while he lay off the Horekills, picking up information in regard to Lord Bellomont's vigorous policy, which was so disheartening that several

of his men then and there deserted—yet for the most part were retaken again presently, some of them in the near-by town of Burlington, and others in Pennsylvania, and even in Maryland—and then sailed around to the eastern end of Long Island Sound, and from Gardiner's Island opened communication with Lord Bellomont, then in Boston, through the medium of their common friends.

Kidd's presentment of his case took the somewhat contradictory form of a denial of the charge that he had been a robber, coupled with what virtually was an offer to divide with the Governor stolen goods to the value of upwards of £40,000. He explicitly declared that, so far from sharing in the piracies of his crew, he had been locked fast in his cabin on each occasion when the *Adventure* had made a capture; and that in continuing in command of the galley in the intermediate peaceful periods—though swayed by the high moral motives already cited—he had but yielded to a constraining superior force. Under these conditions, he explained, he had come into possession of the Moorish ship *Quidah Merchant*, having on board goods to the value of £30,000; and he also had acquired, by purchase, the sloop in which he was come to make his terms, bringing with him "several bales of East India goods; 60 pounds weight of gold, in dust and ingots; about 100 pounds weight of silver, besides other things of the value of about £10,000"—all of which, seemingly, he intimated might be considered as a part of the profits of the voyage; and therefore divisible among its promoters, of whom Lord Bellomont was one.

In Kidd's favor, the fact is to be noted that his plea of superior force as the cause of his connivance at the piratical deeds of his crew carried on while he was fast under hatches was supported by various rumors which had drifted across seas to both England and America long in advance of his return, and in New York had been accepted as the fulfilment of the prophecies of his misfortunes which had been made before he sailed away. This strong point is proved by a letter of Lord Bellomont's, written in May, 1699, in which he refers to "the reports we have here of Captain Kidd's being forced by his men to plunder two Moorish ships," and to another report to the effect that "near one hundred of his men revolted from him at Madagascar, and were about to kill him because he absolutely refused to turn pirate."

VIII.

With this much to excuse him, and with the further mitigating circumstance that he had come home with full hands, the captain almost certainly would have been suffered to go free had there not been involved in his misdeeds far larger interests than his own. The manners and morals of the times were such that, when news came to England of the *Adventure's* piracies, the charge was made openly that Lord Bellomont and the other dignitaries who had promoted the undertaking were party to this perversion of its purpose; and there was more than a hint that the King himself was involved with them, and was to have a share of the piratical profits of the cruise. It was the bruiting of this scandal which sent the King's ships to sea for Kidd's arrest in such a tearing hurry; and because of this scandal—far more than because of his own crimes and misdemeanors—the unlucky captain eventually was hanged.

Lord Bellomont's answer to Kidd's message—possibly because he wanted to make sure of clapping hands upon this seafaring person whose misconduct had got his Lordship into such a pickle—was kindly and encouraging. He bade Kidd come to Boston, and promised him safety in case he made good his claim that he had been driven into piracy against his will. That the captain had his doubts as to the outcome of the matter was shown by his despatch of a part of his treasure to Stamford for safe-keeping, and by his burial of another part on Gardiner's Island; by his sending secretly to Lady Bellomont a rich present of jewelry—the receipt of which she immediately disclosed to her husband and to the Massachusetts Council; and, most of all, by his hesitant delay in going to Boston to plead his cause. Yet that he did go I take to be proof sufficient that he considered himself to be an innocent man.

The poor captain's misgivings were abundantly justified by the event. When at last in July, 1699, he presented himself to the Governor and Council for examination, his examiners made short work of him. On the ground that his explanations were trifling and frivolous, and because of his refusal to reveal the whereabouts of the *Quidah Merchant* unless Livingston's bond in his favor were discharged (which refusal was an evidence of very sturdy loyalty to his friend), a case was found against him, and he formally was committed to prison on the 6th of July.

Really, though, it was the Whig party that was under fire. So much political capital had been made in England out of the association of eminent Whigs with Kidd's so-called piracies that nothing short of hanging the captain could be counted upon to clear the Whig skirts. But while in America it was easy enough to make out a case against him upon which he could be committed, in England —when at last, in the summer of 1700, Admiral Benbow had fetched him over there—it was not found easy to make out a case against him upon which he could be tried. Actually, in the end, he was put upon trial for the murder of the mutinous sailor whom he had killed by whacking him with a bucket, one William Moore; and for this so-called murder a jury that evidently knew its business brought him in guilty. At the time, the theory was advanced noisily that the prosecution was afraid to press the piracy charge for fear of revelations of collusion with very eminent Whig noblemen, possibly even with the King, which certainly would ensue. Undoubtedly, the Whigs did want to get him out of the way: which effectually was accomplished by hanging him, in company with nine genuine pirates, on Execution Dock, in the city of London, May 12, 1701.

Before the unfortunate captain was carried away to England by Admiral Benbow he saw his wife and daughter in Boston for the last time; and was permitted to give his wife some trifling part of his fatal winnings for her support. It is known that for several years after he was hanged they continued to live modestly in their house in Teinhoven Street; and then—the mother probably dying, and the daughter probably marrying—all trace of them is lost. But, obviously, it is more than a possibility that lineal descendants of the ill-fated pirate-in-spite-of-himself, who in a way was a political martyr, are alive in America to-day.

As to the buried treasure that has had so much to do with keeping alive the captain's memory, it seems to be reasonably certain that the whole of his work in this line was performed at Gardiner's Island in June, 1699; and that the treasure then buried was dug up again and taken possession of by the colonial authorities within much less than a year. In Dunlop's time the Gardiner family preserved—and probably do still preserve —the receipt given by the commissioners appointed to remove the treasure from their premises; which treasure consisted, as Dunlop summarizes it, of "a box containing 738 ounces of gold, and 847 ounces of silver, besides jewels."

IX.

Long before Captain Kidd's execution, before even his return to America from his African voyage, the Red Sea trade from New York, and New York sea-robbing of all sorts, had been pretty much brought to an end. Lord Bellomont did the work that he had been sent to do, but at such a cost of strength wasted in overcoming needless obstacles, and with such travail due to unnecessary worry, that the victory won by this honest and gallant gentleman may be said fairly to have landed him in his grave. To make a modern (but most improbable) parallel, should a New York Mayor of our present enlightened period squarely set himself to breaking down the City Hall ring, he would be fighting practically the same fight that Lord Bellomont made against his own rascally Council, and against the rascally provincial officers generally, two hundred years ago; and Lord Bellomont's hands were tied by those whose sworn duty it was to aid him precisely as would be done in the case of this very imaginary reforming Mayor of the present day.

When his Lordship—who was turned of sixty, and who seems to have been a peppery gentleman—proclaimed his commission and assumed the duties of his office, the members of the Council received him with a commendable cordiality; and when he stated in set terms that he had been sent to New York to break up piracy and the Red Sea trade, and that he meant to do it, the affable Councillors – almost all of whom were engaged in these branches of marine industry—gave him at once to understand that in the accomplishment of his good work they were the very people who could be counted upon to uphold his hands. Actually, however, the members of the Council – being leading merchants of the city, and directly representing the very interest that Bellomont was to attack—uttered these fine words not with the intention of buttering parsnips, but to the end that they might retain their offices, and so weaken the effect of, perhaps even prevent wholly, the Governor's attempted reform.

The inevitable break in this factitious era of good feeling came before his Lordship had been two days Governor—upon his summary suspension from the Council of Colonel William Nicoll on the charge of being the go-between through whom Governor Fletcher had carried on business with the pirates, and who also had shared with Fletcher the pirate bribes. This was more than the Councillors had bargained for, and therefore—especially as there was no telling where the lightning would strike next—they resisted as far as they dared, and so forced a compromise. On the 8th of May the Governor wrote to the Lords of Trade: "Col. Nicoll ought to be sent with Col. Fletcher a criminal prisoner to England for trial; but the gentlemen of the Council are tender of him, as he is connected by marriage with several of them, and I am prevailed upon to accept £2000 for his appearance when demanded." Yet the case against Nicoll was admitted even by himself. According to Dunlop he "acknowledged the receipt of monies, but not"—this touch is quite inimitable— "from pirates known"!

As in the administrative so also in the executive department of his rotten little government, the Governor found at first covert and then violently overt opposition instead of support. The Earl's own kinsman, Chidley Brooke, Collector of Customs and Receiver-General of the Province, took the lead in traversing his Lordship's authority; and the example thus set naturally was followed, in the then state of public opinion, all down the executive line. In very bitterness of spirit this harried and tormented gentleman wrote to the King: "I am obliged to stand entirely upon my own legs: my assistants hinder me, the people oppose me, and the merchants threaten me. It is indeed uphill work"—and so most certainly it was.

The first clash came over the seizure of the ship *Fortune;* which vessel, as already has been stated, brought back from the African coast to the projectors of the

KIDD AT GARDINER'S ISLAND.

expedition the stealings of Captain John Hoar. As the object of the *Fortune's* voyage was a matter of common notoriety, the Governor ordered his Collector to seize her instantly in the King's name. Brooke's personal friends no doubt had money invested in this venture; very possibly he had money invested in it himself; certainly, as things then were going, he was to receive his share of the stolen goods as a return for permitting them to be landed by the thieves. Therefore Brooke at first objected that he had no boat at his command; then that it was not his business to make the seizure any way, and ended by interpreting the Governor's "instantly" as meaning the next morning—and in the night thus left available almost the whole of the *Fortune's* cargo was brought ashore.

Being, as I have said, a peppery gentleman, Lord Bellomont was in a fine temper over this evasion of his orders. He gave Brooke a practical lesson in the meaning of the word "instantly" by whisking him out of the Collectorship neck and heels; and in the same turn of the hand appointed in his place Stephanus Van Cortlandt, with one Mousay as Searcher, and sent the latter flying off to seize the pirate plunder of the *Fortune* in the house of Van Sweeten, a merchant, where, as word came to him, it had been stored. A constable was ordered to accompany Mousay; but each of three constables sent for, in turn, managed to be missing at the moment when his services were required. Finally, when Mousay, with one Everts, did at last go to make the seizure, a regular mutiny broke out among the merchants — who flocked to Van Sweeten's house and hustled the officers into an extemporized Black Hole, a close hot loft in which the goods to be seized had been concealed, and there locked them fast. For three hours they were thus imprisoned, and they "had like to died of it." Fortunately, before they were quite stifled, the Governor got wind of what had happened, and despatched the Lieutenant-Governor, backed by a file of soldiers, to relieve them and to enforce the seizure of the goods.

What seems to be another version of this same story gives the house of "the Sheriff" as the hiding-place to which the cargo of the *Fortune* was carried, and in which these racy liberties were taken with the persons of the officers of the

law. Color is given to this even stronger presentment of the impudent iniquity of the period by the fact that the then Sheriff was Ebenezer Wilson, a merchant (and therefore likely to have piratical interests), and that he was suspended from office during a part of his term. That he was thought none the worse of by his fellow-New-Yorkers because of his Red Sea dealings is shown by the facts that he was elected Mayor of this city in the years 1707-10, and that in the years 1709-10 he was a member of the Provincial Council. But fancy the height of the high-tempered Governor's rage at finding in one single morning the Collector of the Port, the Sheriff of the city, three constables, and a mutinous body of the principal merchants—that is, of the leading citizens—all joined in opposition to his authority and afloat together in the same piratical boat!

X.

In the nature of things an open issue between the Governor and his Council could not long be avoided. It came in the demand for clearances for the *Prophet Daniel*, the *Nassau*, and two other ships which sailed from New York in July 1698 for Madagascar. The Governor ordered that before receiving clearances these ships must be put under bonds not to trade with pirates. The Council—members of which had money up on the several ventures—decided that such bonds should not be required. The merchants of the city backed the Council, of course, and raised such a hubbub that the Governor—at that time but a little while in office—yielded to the general clamor, and suffered the ships to go unbonded to sea.

By this time the bitter feeling here was very strong against his Lordship; and it grew stronger as news came up from various points along the coast of more than half a dozen vessels, laden with piratical cargoes, which had turned about and put to sea again upon getting news of the hard times respectable traders were having under this devil of a Governor in New York. It was angrily—yet probably truly—declared that he had "hindered £100,000 from being brought into the city"; and to this was added the assertion that his continuance in office meant nothing less than the ruin of the commerce of the town. Wherefore a regular organization against him was effected among the merchants, and by these injured colonists an attorney was sent to England to present the record of his misdoings to, and to pray for his removal by, the King.

It was all the better for the Governor, probably, that the case against him was pressed with such brazen impudence. He was in a better position to defend himself than if he had been attacked in the dark. In short order he got rid of the most piratical of the members of his Council. Pinhorne was dismissed; Bayard, Willet, Mienville, and Lawrence were suspended; Phillipse resigned—and, in place of these frail brothers, Abraham Depeyster, Robert Livingston, Thomas Weaver, Samuel Staats, and Robert Walters were called to the board. With these honest allies it was possible for the Governor to do something at home; while over in England— where necessarily was to be had the final settlement of the whole matter—he gained his first point by securing the condemnation of Fletcher; and thereafter, in every point raised against him by the representative of the New York merchants, the charges made by his enemies were refuted and his own position was sustained.

It was in the very midst of Lord Bellomont's triumphal progress toward reforming the morals of this town that the news came from Africa that Kidd had turned pirate: which fact instantly was seized upon eagerly, both here and in England, as a proof that the Earl himself was as much a promoter of piracy as anybody, and

that his efforts to uproot the piratical commerce of New York were solely that he might himself secure the monopoly of its illicit gains. But the Governor, who was game all the way through, was only the more encouraged by this vilely slanderous outcry to hang on to his purpose with the more intense tenacity; and because he did so hang on—like the delightful old bull-dog that he was—he came out victorious in the end. .

He was a trifle over-old for such rough-and-tumble fighting, and he was of a gouty habit and choleric to a degree; wherefore, after being kept for near three years in a righteous rage, it is not surprising that his Lordship's overheated flesh could not longer contain his broiling spirit, and that, a martyr to his own high-tempered virtue, he incontinently died. His death occurred on March 5, 1701; and his body —after resting for some years in the chapel in the Fort—was laid at rest in St. Paul's church-yard: where still is his unmarked grave.

Very likely this sturdy old boy died not unwillingly, for his life here—save for the knowledge of the good that he was doing—most certainly could not have been a pleasant one. Moreover, he had the satisfaction of knowing that he had accomplished his purpose; that through his exertions New York piracy and sea-stealing at second-hand, rampant at the time of his coming, was as dead as he was about to be himself.

THE DUTCH FOUNDING OF
NEW YORK
(PART 3)

FOOT OF WALL STREET, AND FERRY-HOUSE, 1629

I

ON December 10, 1653, "the most important popular convention that had ever been assembled in New Netherland," to quote Mr. Brodhead's words, met in the Stadt Huys of New Amsterdam. That convention—being a gathering of representatives of the capital city, of the near-by Dutch towns, and of the English towns on Long Island—was in the way of being an impotent parliament: that came together not as a governing and law-making body, but to remonstrate against the existing government, and against the tangle of inequitable laws (still farther complicated by arbitrary edicts) in which the colonists were involved.

What gave that queer little parliament its chief significance was the presence, for the first time in Dutch councils, of English delegates; and the fact that those delegates came to the council rightfully, as representatives of their fellow-countrymen legally subject to the government of New Netherland, did not make them any the less representatives of the race that was crowding out the Dutch from their holding in the New World.

It was at the instance of the English, indeed, that the council was convened. Long Island had been filling up steadily with English settlers, and those settlers took even less kindly than did the Dutch to the eccentricities and the inefficiencies of the government under which they lived. Especially did they resent the failure of that government to protect them against the many little freebooters—of the Thomas Baxter stripe —who committed highly annoying robberies along the borders of the Sound; and against the many stray savages who, as occasion offered, engaged in little ravagings and murderings of a distasteful sort. Also, they had the characteristic English longing to be let alone in the management of their local affairs. Out of which conditions arose among them the not unreasonable desire either to be taken care of, or to be given a free hand in taking care of themselves.

In order to talk matters over with the Dutch authorities, representatives came up from Gravesend and Flushing and Newtown; and a conference was held in the Stadt Huys (November 26, 1653) to consider what could be done "for the welfare of the country and its inhabitants," and "to determine on some wise and salutary measures" which would bring up the Sound pirates with a round turn. The Dutch representatives who met them—members of the city government and of the Provincial Council—seeing their way to grinding some axes of their own, recommended that a general statement of grievances should be embodied, as usual, in a "remonstrance"; and that with the remonstrance, also as usual, should be coupled a prayer for relief. That method of procedure being agreed to, an adjournment of a fortnight was decided upon: to the end that the views of the colonists of Long Island and of Staten Island might be obtained more fully, and that a larger number of delegates might be got together; in effect, that the informal meeting might be raised to the dignity of a little Landtag. Stuyvesant had no relish for such doings. The action of the English, he declared, "smelt of rebellion" and of "contempt of his high authority and commission." But the popular will was too strong for him—or he was too weak to control it, which amounted to the same thing—and he "very reluctantly sanctioned the meeting that he could not prevent." Accordingly, on December 10, with an augmented membership, the council was reconvened. Four Dutch towns and four English towns were represented, and the delegates—apparently chosen on a basis of numerical representation—were ten of Dutch and nine of English nativity. And all of them, without regard to nationality, harmoniously were agreed to pool their grievances and to go for Director Stuyvesant horns down!

Considering how serious those grievances were, the "Remonstrance" which they formulated was couched in extraordinarily temperate terms. That document was drawn by one of the representatives from Gravesend, Ensign George Baxter—who is not to be confounded with the piratical Thomas—and as the work of an Englishman it is all the more remarkable for its tone of loyalty to the government of Holland. The preamble runs in these words: "Composed of various nations from different parts of the world, leaving at our own expense our country and countrymen, we voluntarily came under the protection of our sovereign High and Mighty Lords the States General, whom we acknowledge as our lieges; and being made members of one body, subjected ourselves, as in duty bound, to the general laws of the United Provinces, and all other new orders and ordinances which by virtue of the aforesaid authority may be published, agreeably to the customs freedoms grants and privileges of the Netherlands."

What the remonstrants did object to, and pointedly, was the publication of new orders and ordinances which distinctly were disagreeable to the customs, and still more disagreeable to the freedoms, of the home country. The first and the main charge of their remonstrance was that such orders and ordinances had been enacted by the Director and Council "without the knowledge or consent of the people," and that the same were "contrary to the granted privileges of the Netherland government, and odious to every free-born man, and especially so to those whom God has placed under a free state in newly settled lands, who are entitled to claim laws, not transcending, but resembling as nearly as possible those of the Netherlands."

Joined with this remonstrance in chief —which, in effect, was no more than an assertion of the fact that the colonists were denied common right and common justice—minor remonstrance was made against the failure of the provincial government to protect persons and property; against the obligation to obey "old orders and proclamations of the Director and Council, made without the knowledge or consent of the people" which "subject them to loss and punishment through ignorance"; against the "wrongful and suspicious delay" in confirming land patents; against land grants to favored individuals "to the great injury of the Province"; and against the appointment of officers and magistrates "without the consent or nomination of the people . . . contrary to the laws of the Netherlands." In conclusion, the authors of the appeal added: "As we have, for easier reference, reduced all our grievances to six heads, we renew our allegiance, in the hope that satisfaction will be granted to the country according to established justice, and all dissensions be settled and allayed."

There is a very marked difference between the verbose and mean complainings of the more famous Remonstrance of the year 1649 and the simple directness and dignity of this demand for obvious rights; and had there been any "established justice" for New Netherland—either in the provincial government or in the home government—it could not have been met, as it was met, by a flat refusal all around. Stuyvesant made answer to it by a general denial, that included a particular denial of the right of the delegates to assemble; and when the delegates replied, in turn, by an appeal to that natural law "which permits all men to assemble for the protection of their liberties and their property," he tersely ordered them to disperse "on pain of our highest displeasure": to which lordly mandate, by way of a cracker, he added: "We derive our authority from God and the Company, not from a few ignorant subjects; and we alone can call the inhabitants together." In Holland, when the Remonstrance got there, the answer was the same. The Directors of the Company wrote to Stuyvesant (May 18, 1654) in these terms: "We are unable to discover in the whole Remonstrance one single point to justify complaint. . . You ought to have acted with more vigor against the ringleaders of the gang. . . It is our express command that you punish what has occurred as it deserves, so that others may be deterred in future from following such examples." And at the same time the Directors wrote to the burgomasters and schepens of New Amsterdam commanding "that you conduct yourselves quietly and peaceably, submit yourselves to the government placed over you, and in no wise allow yourselves to hold particular convention with the English or others in matters of form and deliberation on affairs of state, which do not appertain to you; and, what is yet worse, attempt an alteration in the state and its government."

The answer from Holland sustained one-half of Stuyvesant's declaration that he derived his authority "from God and the Company"—so far as the Company went, his delegated authority was confirmed and sustained. But the other half of his declaration did not come out so well. A decade later his draft on divine power was returned dishonored; and only a turn of chance in his favor prevented

GOVERNOR STUYVESANT'S BOWERY RESIDENCE

that draft from going to protest within a year.

The twist of luck that saved him temporarily was the conclusion of peace (April, 1654) between England and Holland; and the consequent abandonment by Cromwell of his project for pacifying the colonial situation—in a breezily statesmanlike fashion—by annexing New Netherland out of hand. Actually, the Protector's annexation scheme came to the very edge of being realized. An effective naval force was despatched from England; the New England colonies—Massachusetts alone lagging a little—buzzed with eager preparations for the fight that they so longed for; and the English colonists on Long Island, delightedly bustling to the front, made a fair start toward the impending revolution by declaring their independence of Dutch authority and by setting up a microscopic government of their own. And then, just as everybody (with the exception of Director Stuyvesant) was ready for things to happen, the peace was concluded—and nothing happened at all! But it was only by a very narrow margin that the orders for the seizure of New Netherland were countermanded before New Netherland was seized.

While the war was imminent New Amsterdam was in a whirl. Stuyvesant's mental attitude in the premises seems to have bordered upon consternation. In regard to practical provision for defence he wrote: "We have no gunners, no musketeers, no sailors, and scarcely sixteen hundred pounds of powder"—a statement that exhibits in rather a startling fashion the physical unpreparedness of the colony for a long-threatened war. On its moral side the situation was worse. The Director declared that he did not expect "the people residing in the country, not even the Dutch," to back him in the fight that was coming on; and added: "The English, although they have sworn allegiance, would take up arms and join the enemy . . . to invite them to aid us would be bringing the Trojan horse within our walls."

By the Director's own showing, therefore, it appears that the spirit of loyalty in the colony—if such a spirit can be said ever to have existed — practically was dead, and that the spirit of revolt was very much alive. His English subjects— almost openly in New Amsterdam, quite openly on Long Island—were impatient for the coming of their countrymen. His Dutch subjects were in a state of sulky mutiny that made them more than half ready to welcome the coming of anybody who would give them a new government of any sort—because of their moody conviction that any change whatever must give them a better government than that under which they lived. And it was all quite logical. It was the natural and inevitable outcome of thirty years of consistent misrule.

II

For my present purpose, it is needless to treat at all in detail the last ten years of the Dutch domination of New Netherland. Little concessions continued to be made to the colonists; large wrongs continued to oppress them; there were more "remonstrances"; there was an Indian war. Fresh turns produced fresh figures in that small kaleidoscope, but the constituent elements of the figures remained unchanged. The essential change came from the outside; and even that was but the continued, yet always increasing, pressure of those forces which had begun to operate (as I have already written) before the unstable foundation of the Dutch colony was laid. With the steadfast persistence of fate inevitable the English grip tightened as the English cordon closed in.

By the year 1659 the eastern end of Long Island—surrendered by Stuyvesant under the terms of the Treaty of Hartford (1650)—was a vigorous English colony; and was manifesting its vigor in a characteristic English fashion by crowding down into the Dutch territory westward of the Oyster Bay line. That thrust at close quarters was not easy to deal with. Releases of land were obtained in due form by Englishmen from accommodating sachems in temporary financial difficulties—or in chronic thirst that such transactions in real estate would provide means for temporarily slaking—and on the land thus obtained modest settlements were made. Presently, becoming immodest, the settlers of those settlements asserted that they were under the jurisdiction of Connecticut; an assertion that produced awkward conflicts of authority, no matter how hotly it was denied.

Up in the north, in the back-country, Massachusetts was reaching out to tap the Dutch fur trade at its source: calmly ignoring the provisions of the Treaty of Hartford and claiming as her own all the territory between lines running westward from three miles south of the Charles and three miles north of the Merrimac straightaway across the continent to the Pacific. The southern line of that handsome claim of everything in sight down to sunset crossed the Hudson not far from Saugerties; and the kindly intention of the claimants was to relieve the Dutch of all care of the upper reaches of the river, and incidentally to divert from New Amsterdam to Boston the bulk of the trade in furs. In presenting the matter to Stuyvesant for consideration (September 17, 1659) the commissioners shyly urged "we conceive the agreement at Hartford, that the English should not come within ten miles of Hudson's river, doth not prejudice the rights of the Massachusetts in the upland country, nor give

BROAD STREET AND EXCHANGE PLACE ABOUT 1680

any rights to the Dutch there"; upon the strength of which ingenious conception they asked that free passage from the sea into and through the river should be given to the English settlers—"they demeaning themselves peaceably, and paying such moderate duties as may be expected in such cases"—resident upon its upper banks. And by way of justifying their modest request the commissioners drew an airy parallel in free international waterways between the Hudson on the one hand and on the other the Elbe and the Rhine. It is to Stuyvesant's credit that his reply (October 29, 1659) to those cheeky commissioners was a flat refusal; and that he immediately sent off to the Amsterdam Chamber—in order to be in a position to back his refusal practically —a demand for "a frigate of sixteen guns." That the frigate did not come was a mere administrative detail quite in the natural order of things.

By way of completing the English cordon, Lord Baltimore's people were pressing the Dutch from the south. The Dutch trading-post on the Delaware River—or the South River, as they called it—was a losing venture from first to last; and onward from the time (1638)

of the planting of the Swedish colony on the west shore of the Delaware, on what nominally was Dutch territory, the government of New Netherland was involved in snarling difficulties in its efforts to maintain its rights. Before the Swedes were reduced to approximate order—even after their official conquest they continued to give trouble—the much more serious complications with the English colonists of Maryland began.

Those complications were brought to a head by the formal demand (August 3, 1659) addressed by Governor Fendall, Lord Baltimore's representative, to "the pretended Governor of a people seated in Delaware Bay, within his Lordship's Province" to "depart forth of his Lordship's Province"—or to take the consequences. And Governor Fendall indicated what the consequences were likely to be by adding politely: "or otherwise I desire you to hold me excused if I use my utmost endeavour to reduce that part of his Lordship's Province unto its due obedience under him." The little ambassador who carried the Maryland governor's courteous but peremptory letter to the Dutch commandant on the Delaware delivered it in a "pretty harsh and bitter" manner; and emphasized its purport by remarking incidentally that, "as the tobacco is chiefly harvested," the people of Maryland were quite at leisure for a fight. "It now suits us," he concluded—in what no doubt was meant to be a persuasive spirit—"best in the whole year."

But the sporting offer of the Marylanders to fill in the close season for tobacco with a time-killing war did not materialize. Their ardor was a little cooled, perhaps, by the prompt despatch of reenforcements to the Delaware colony from New Amsterdam; and the assertion of possession was refuted so logically—on the ground that Lord Baltimore's patent gave him rights only to unseated lands, and therefore excluded him from a region colonized by the Dutch at least fifteen years before his patent was granted—that for the moment their claim was shelved. It was by no means quieted, however. Until the Dutch were squeezed out and done for, the pressure of the English upon New Netherland from the south was continued with the same persistence that characterized the pressure of the English upon that unlucky colony from the east and from the north. There was no escape from those advancing tentacles: behind which, resistless, was the power of England. It was a cuttlefish situation that could end in only one way.

The end would have come sooner, no doubt, had the Protector lived a little longer or had the Restoration followed more quickly upon his death. During the intermediate seven years (1653-1660) the domestic tribulations of the English gave them no time to bother about colonial extension: they had their hands full of matters requiring immediate attention at home. But when Charles II. resumed business as a king the would-be ousters of the Dutch in America instantly came to the front again.

Lord Baltimore was at the very head of the procession. "Charles had hardly reached Whitehall," as Mr. Brodhead puts it, "before Lord Baltimore instructed Captain James Neale, his agent in Holland, to require of the West India Company to yield up to him the lands on the south [west] side of Delaware Bay." Lord Stirling was a little less prompt; but he made up for his seemly delay by an unseemly insistence. In a petition to the King (May 31, 1661) he set forth that the "Councell for the affaires of New England . . . . in the eleaventh year of the raigne of your Ma^{ts} royall Father of blessed memory did graunt unto William Earle of Sterlyne, your petitioner's Grandfather, and his heires, part of New England and an Island adjacent called Long Island. . . That yor Peticôners Grandfather and father, and himselfe their heire, have respectively enjoyed the same and have at their greate costs planted many places on that Island; but of late divers Dutch have intruded on severall parts thereof, not · acknowledging themselves within your Ma^{ts} allegiance, to your Ma^{ts} disherison and your Peticôner's prejudice." Wherefore he prayed: "May yor Majestie be pleased to confirme unto your Peticôner his said inheritance to be held immediately of the Crowne of England, and that in any future treaty betweene your royall selfe and the Dutch such provision may be as that the Dutch there may submitt themselves to your Ma^{ts} governem^t or depart those parts." Considering that the Stirling grant covered what actually was Dutch territory, his lordship's neatest turn is his reference to the intruding "divers Dutch"; but there is an air of easy assurance about his whole petition that does credit to even a Scotch earl.

To Lord Baltimore's jaunty requirement, cited above, that the West India Company should "yield up to him" the lands on the west side of Delaware Bay, the Directors gave "a proud answer": to the effect that they "would use all the means which God and nature had given them to protect the inhabitants and preserve their possessions." But they manifested less pride, and more alarm, in a memorial that they promptly addressed to the States-General: praying that a protest should be presented by the Dutch ambassador in London against English aggression; and that a demand should be made for the restoration to New Netherland of the territory that the English had "usurped." Under instructions from their High Mightinesses, the ambassador protested and demanded accordingly: and with precisely the same practical result that would have followed had he protested against the flowing of the tides, and had he demanded the cause of tidal eccentricities—the moon!

The Connecticut people, being keen to assert what they were pleased to call their rights, followed close at Lord Stirling's aggressive heels. Governor Winthrop, on behalf of the General Court at Hartford, drew up (June 17, 1661) for the King's consideration a "loyal address": that wandered on lightly from expressions of loyalty to a specific request for a new charter by which his Majesty would assure them in possession of their territory against the Dutch—whom they affably described as "noxious neighbours," having "not so much as the copy of a patent" to the lands which they held. That there might be no room for a doubt as to what they wanted, they asked in set terms for a charter—calmly inclusive of the unpatented lands of their "noxious neighbours"—that should cover all the country "eastward of Plymouth line, northward to the limits of the Massachusetts colony, and westward to the Bay of Delaware, if it may be"; and that their modest petition might be presented properly and urged effectively they commissioned Governor Winthrop as their agent to carry it to England and to lay it before the King.

In those days passages across the Atlantic were taken where they offered. Actually, Winthrop went down to New Amsterdam—where he was given an "honourable and kind reception"—and sailed for England in the Dutch ship *De Trouw*. The Governor was not a dull man, and I think that he must have enjoyed, in the strict privacy of his inner consciousness, the subtle irony of the situation: as he courteously accepted his "honourable and kind reception" and then went sailing eastward under Dutch colors —and all the while having in his pocket that document which was meant to be a knife in the neck of his hosts at New Amsterdam and in the neck of the friendly power under whose flag he sailed. Had there been a Colonial Office in those days, and had Mr. Chamberlain been at the head of it, how he would have relished the story which that first colonial agent would have had to tell him when he got to land!

III

In a way, the state of affairs in North America in the year 1661 was very like the state of affairs in South Africa just before "Captain Jim" made his raid. It all was on a smaller scale, of course, but the facts and the conditions were much the same. The Dutch were loosely seated in a valuable holding; their rule, arbitrary and corrupt, was resented mutinously by incrowding greedy English settlers who nominally were Dutch subjects; a belt of English colonies—more complete than in South Africa — was tightening about them; and at the back of all the forces working for their destruction was the English government: moved by the normal human desire to take possession of other people's valuable property; and more deeply moved by the instinctive feeling (which had no parallel in South Africa) that only by crushing the commerce of Holland could England become the leading commercial nation of the world.

It was against Dutch commerce that the blow was struck which led on quickly —and I think fortunately—to the extinction of the Dutch ownership of New Netherland. That blow was the revision, very soon after the Restoration, of the Navigation Act of 1651. As originally framed, the act had forbidden the importation of goods into England save in English ships or in ships belonging to the country in which the goods were produced. As amended, the act forbade, after December 1, 1660, the importation or the exportation of goods into or from any of his Majesty's plantations or territories in Asia, Africa, or America save in English ships of which "the master and three-fourths of the mariners at least are English."

This direct thrust at the commercial life of Holland was not lessened in force by the Convention agreed upon (September 14, 1662) between England and the United Provinces; rather, indeed, did the friction over that Convention tend to make matters worse. Mr. Brodhead, in his kindly way, asserts that "the Dutch fulfilled their stipulations with promptness and honor"; but, with all due deference to Mr. Brodhead, the Dutch did nothing of the sort—as the minutes of the Council for Foreign Plantations abundantly prove. On August 25, 1662, the Council ordered that "some heads of remedies" should be drawn up to correct

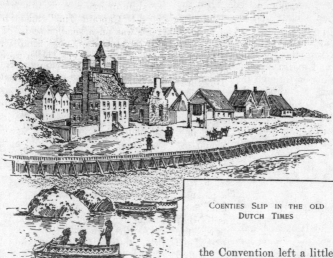

COENTIES SLIP IN THE OLD
DUTCH TIMES

the abuses incident to "a secret trade driven by and with the Dutch for Tobacco of the growth of the English Plantations, to the defrauding His Matie of his Customs and contrary to the intent of the Act of Navigation." On June 24, 1663, the Council issued a circular letter to the governors of Virginia, Maryland, New England, and the West Indian Islands, drawing their attention to the "many neglects, or rather contempts, of his Maties commands for ye true observance" of the Navigation Act "through the dayly practices and designes sett on foote by trading into forrain parts . . . both by land and sea as well as unto ye Monadoes and other Plantations of ye Hollanders"; and in an undated document (Trade Papers lvii., 90) giving "certaine reasons to prove if the Duch bee admitted trade in Virginia it wilbe greate loss to the Kings Matie and prejudice to the Plantacôn," the fact is stated that "there is now two shippes going from Zeland to trade there wch if they be admitted it wilbe losse to his Matie at least 4000^{11}, wch by your Lordshipps wisdome may be prevented."

All this, and more like it, goes to show that the "promptness and honor" of the Dutch in living up to the stipulations of the Convention left a little to be desired on the side of practicality; but it also goes to show — since two traders are necessary to a trade— that the English colonies took an active part in whistling the laws of their mother-country down the wind. This secondary fact is brought out with clearness in a report (March 10, 1663) upon the South, or Delaware, river colony, which contains the pregnant assertion: "Trade will come not only from the city's colony but from the English; who offer, if we will trade with them, to make a little slit in the door, whereby we can reach them overland without having recourse to the passage by sea, lest trade with them may be forbidden by the Kingdom of England, which will not allow us that in their colony." In this same report is the statement: "The English afford us an instance of the worthiness of New Netherland, which from their Colony alone already sends 200 vessels, both large and small, to the Islands"— an involved presentment of fact that Mr. Brodhead misunderstands, and in his restatement of it perverts into meaning that the trade of New Netherland "with the West Indies and the neighboring English colonies now [1663] employed two hundred vessels annually." Obviously, the two hundred vessels referred to in the report hailed from English colonial ports; and they are cited to show the "worthiness"—that is to say, the fitness —of New Netherland to take a larger share in the intercolonial trade. But the essential fact is clear that the many busy little ships then plying in American waters, Dutch and English alike, were snapping their topsails at the Navigation Act, and that a deal of illegal trading was going on through that " little slit in the door." Mr. Brodhead—in this case with absolute correctness — summarizes the situation: " The possession of New Netherland by the Dutch was, in truth, the main obstacle to the enforcement of the restrictive colonial policy of England." And the obstacles which stood in the way of England's colonial policy in those days — there is no very marked change in these days—had to go down.

The final diplomatic round between England and Holland began in January, 1664, when the Dutch ambassador in London was directed to insist upon a ratification by the British government of the long-pending Hartford Treaty; and so, by a definite settlement of the boundary question, clear the air. The answer to the Dutch demand certainly did settle the boundary question, and certainly did clear the air. It came two months later (March 12-22) in the shape of that epoch-making royal patent by which the King granted Long Island (released by Lord Stirling) and all the lands and rivers from the west side of the Connecticut to the east side of Delaware Bay to his brother, the Duke of York.

The actual conquest of New Netherland by the force sent out by the Duke of York to take possession of his newly acquired property, as I have written elsewhere, was " a mere bit of bellicose etiquette: a polite changing of garrisons, of fealty, and of flags "; and by way of comment upon that easy shifting of allegiance I farther have written in these general terms: " Under the government of the Dutch West India Company, the New Netherland had been managed not as a national dependency, but as a commercial venture which was expected to bring in a handsome return. Much more than the revenue necessary to maintain a government was required of the colonists; and at the same time the restrictions imposed upon private trade—to the end that the trade of the Company might be increased—were so onerous as materially to diminish the earning power of

the individual, and correspondingly to make the burden of taxation the heavier to bear. Nor could there be between the colonists and the Company—as there could have been between the colonists and even a severe home government—a tie of loyalty. Indeed, the situation had become so strained under this commercial despotism that the inhabitants of New Amsterdam almost openly sided with the English when the formal demand for a surrender was made—and the town passed into British possession, and became New York, without the striking of a single blow."

IV

On the side of ethics, the taking over of New Netherland by the English admits of differing opinions. Mr. Brodhead flat-footedly calls it " bold robbery." Mr. Asher, himself a Dutchman, regards it as the occupation by the English of territory that was theirs by right of discovery, of settlement, and of specific grant. For my own part—lacking the temerity to pass judgment upon so vexed a question—I am content to ignore the ethical side of that easy conquest and to ground my approval of it on the fact that, as things then stood in Europe and in America, it was the only practicable treatment of an impossible problem; to which, with submission, I add my conviction that for all the parties in interest it was the best substitute for a solution possible under the conditions which obtained.

The gain to England was so obvious that it need not be discussed. The gain to Holland was getting rid of a nettle of a colony which—by involving her in an outlay of more than a million guilders above returns, and by most dangerously complicating her relations with her most powerful rival—from first to last did little but sting her hands. The gain to the English colonies in America was an immediate enlargement of intercolonial trade: with a resultant solidarity of interests which strongly helped—a little more than a century later—to bring about their formal union and their definite independence. The gain to New Netherland—the essential matter here to be considered—was escape from a harsh and incompetent government, that crushed trade and that did much to make life unendurable, to the fostering care of a government that developed trade in every direction and that in its treatment of individuals erred on the side of laxness.

Out of that laxness came ill results. That the morals of New Amsterdam did

MAP OF NEW YORK, 1642
The upper cross-road is the present Maiden Lane, then called "T' Maagde Paatje"

A. The City Tavern.
B. The Fort.
C. The Wharf.
D. Burial Place.
E. The Strand, or Shore.

not improve under English rule is not surprising—because New Amsterdam had no morals. On the other hand, its immorals—of which its supply was excessive—developed vigorously, in sympathy with its vigorously developing commercial life. In the last decade of the seventeenth century—what with our pirates and our slavers and the general disposition on the part of our leading citizens to ride a hurdle-race over all known laws, including the Ten Commandments—New York certainly was as vicious a little seafaring city as was to be found just then in all Christendom. But the fact is to be borne in mind that the evil state of affairs which developed under English government was put an end to by an English governor. And the farther fact is to be borne in mind that onward from the time of that first reform governor there has been in this town—as there conspicuously was not in this town during the Dutch period of its history—at least an avowed outward respect for decency and for law. I do not assert, of course, that this admirable sentiment has shone brilliantly or steadfastly, or that it is not badly snowed - under at times even now; but I do assert that until we came under English rule such sentiment practically did not exist at all. Lord Bellomont was the first of our governors— and this is not to cast a slight upon the excellent reorganizing work of Colonel Nicolls— who forced us to put some of our worst sins behind us, and so set us in the way (along which we still are floundering) to achieve that civic rectitude which was an unknown virtue in the Dutch times.

Having thus, for truth's sake, set forth the development and the curbing of our immorals which followed our taking on of a new nationality, I am free to make my final point—the enormous gain in material prosperity—in favor of that shifting of ownership which changed New Amsterdam into New York. When the English took over the city (September 8, 1664) the number of houses in it —as shown by Cortelyou's survey of the year 1660—was about 350, and the population was about 1500 souls. An authoritative record has been preserved—in the petition of the New York millers and merchants against the repeal of the Bolting Act—of exactly what this city gained in its first thirty years of English rule. The petition states that in the year 1678, when the Bolting Act became operative, the total number of houses in New York was 384; the total number of beef cattle slaughtered was 400; the total number of sailing-craft (3 ships, 7 boats, 8 sloops) was 18; and the total revenues of the city were less than £2000. The petition farther states that in the year 1694 (there is a secondary interest here, in that we see what two hundred more years have done for us) the number of houses had increased to 983; the number of beef cattle slaughtered (largely for profitable export to the West Indies) to 4000; the number of sailing-craft (60 ships, 40 boats, 25 sloops) to 125; and the city's revenues to £5000.

That statement of fact I conceive to be the most striking commentary that can be made upon the relative material merits of Dutch and of English rule. The sudden prodigious increase of the population and of the commerce of this city equally were due to a general easement of political and of commercial conditions: the first impossible while the Dutch domination continued; and the second rigorously withheld (of set purpose or of set stupidity) during the half-century that the West India Company betrayed all the interests of New Netherland in order to gain—yet failed to gain —its own selfish ends. I hope that we may be able to make as good a showing in the Philippines at the end of our first thirty years.

But argument for or against that bold robbery, or that resumption of vested rights—as our two most authoritative historians, with a somewhat confusing divergence of opinion, respectively describe the English acquisition of New Netherland—no longer is necessary. As I have written, that once burning question became a dead issue in a time long past. Whatever were the equities of the conflicting Dutch and English claims to the most valuable slice of the continent of North America, they were quieted legally by the Treaty of Breda. And they have been quieted ethically—in the flowing of the years since that remote diplomatic agreement was executed—by the passage of the property in dispute away from both claimant races into the possession of their descendants: who have coalesced into a new race, and who take their title from themselves.

THE ICE AGE ABOUT NEW YORK

GLACIAL GROOVES, CENTRAL PARK.

A GREAT many years ago—exactly how many I never could find out, because the men who have told me piecemeal the story which I am now rehearsing were never very certain themselves whether it was ten or fifty or a hundred thousand years ago, and were withal so pleasantly liberal with their centuries that it somehow seemed mean to urge the matter, but at any rate a great many years ago—one might have visited unattended the far northern regions toward which Peary and Nansen are struggling, and thought no more of it than as a somewhat long and toilsome summer journey.

The way northward would have led through forests much the same as those which grace New England and the Middle States to-day, or with an aspect even more tropical than these, and many smaller plants, suggesting those familiar to us now, would have brightened his path.

Even over distant Greenland and into those desolate regions where so many brave and hardy explorers have perished he might have wandered, finding all as warm and bright and teeming with life as are our own latitudes to-day.

One thing, however, would have made such an undertaking adventurous, if not dangerous, and that is the hideous and gigantic animals which roamed over the country in those times. Great flying beasts, huge hulks of flesh like overgrown elephants, colossal lizards, and all manner of uncanny breathing things would have relieved the stroll northward of too tame and pastoral a tendency. In a word, a long time ago the temperate regions of our earth, with plants whose families at least still flourish, and monstrous, uncouth animals now happily extinct, extended over the arctic regions.

But for some reason or other, or for a number of reasons together, reasons which it would lead us too far afield to consider now, this warm, sunny, plant-clad region about the north pole began to grow colder. And, as century after century passed, gradually, but relentlessly, the snow began to accumulate. At first it didn't melt away as early in the spring as it was wont to do, and there seemed to be more of it, and it got packed into solid masses of ice in the valleys and the cooler places. By-and-by there was snow all the year round, and more and more ice formed. The animals were driven southward and the plants died off. Finally ice and snow covered everything and formed great masses hundreds of feet thick.

The worst of it was that this was not confined to the far-away regions about the north pole. The ice sheet crept slowly southward like a white shadow; over Greenland, over British America, over northern Europe. Great bodies of water, lakes, rivers. and inland seas, were frozen solid, and still the white terror crept slowly on: down over New England, over New York State, over the region of the Great Lakes, over Ohio and into Pennsylvania and New Jersey, and over many of the Northwestern States.

This ice mantle was hundreds, in places thousands, of feet thick. Our great hills, the White Mountains, the Adirondacks, and the Catskills, were either altogether covered up, or just showed their tips, like tiny islands in the great white solid sea.

Now it was so cold over all the northern part of North America that this ice mantle once formed staid there for thousands of years. But it wasn't still by any means. When ice and snow collect in great masses, filling up valleys and covering the land, it has an enormous weight, and although ice seems so solid and firm and brittle, it actually does, when on slopes or when pressed upon from behind, flow like thick molasses or asphalt, only very slowly. But its motion, when in such huge masses, is irresistible, so that great

rocks are torn away from the cliffs and carried off, sometimes on top of the ice rivers, sometimes at the bottom, sometimes buried deep out of sight. Often rocks are broken and ground to fine powder as they are held fast at the bottom of the ice mass and pushed along the solid rock surfaces beneath. Furthermore, these rock surfaces over which the great moving ice masses slide, no matter how rough and jagged they may be, are rounded off and ground smooth, or, by the stones which the ice mass holds and grinds against them, they are deeply grooved and scratched.

Such great slowly flowing ice masses are, as everybody knows, called glaciers, some moving a few inches, some many feet in a day. The lines of the grooves and scratches which glaciers leave in the surfaces over which they have passed indicate the direction in which, at the time they were made, the ice and its stone graving tools were moving.

Although glaciers flow downward through the valleys, they do not advance much, as a rule, at the bottom, because here it is usually so warm that the ice melts and the glacier becomes a stream or river and flows away to sea. The Swiss glaciers and those of our great Northwest are, for the most part, only forlorn remnants of the greater ice masses of long ago, and year by year are dwindling away.

At one place in the Selkirk Mountains, on the Canadian Pacific Railroad, in a series of valleys once filled to their brims with ice, one may count from a favorable outlook scores of glaciers, unnamed and mostly untrod. Some, like the great Illecillewaet, are still large and imposing, and still grinding away at the earth's crust, tearing off great rocks, rolling and crushing them along the top and sides and bottom, and sending daily tons of powdered rock wreckage down the turbid stream to join the Fraser River. But most of the glaciers here have, like frightened ani-

Map of NORTH AMERICA in THE ICE AGE.

Scale—0 100 250   500 Miles.

mals, taken to the hills, and hang as great snow banks among the crags, or stretch their feet timidly down into the tops of the desolate valleys which erst they themselves have sculptured.

To one, even not very venturesome, who would like to learn the ways and haunts of these remnants of the old ice age, a few days spent in the environs of the comfortable hotel at Glacier will be found abounding in interest.

The rocks and detritus which glaciers carry and heap up in ridges along their sides or at their feet are called moraines. Those along their sides form the lateral, those at their feet the terminal, moraines.

When the foot of a glacier stays for a long time at about the same place, the melting ice, dropping year by year its store of shattered rock brought down from the back country, may make very large terminal moraines. Or, if it melts and retreats rapidly, the old glacier valley may be left scantily rock-strewn.

For many miles a great glacier may carry rocks which it has ravished from the cliffs, and when at last it melts and leaves them, rounded and scratched, far from their kindred rocks, scattered over the desolate surfaces or piled in the moraines, they tally well with the names which geologists have given them—"erratic bowlders," or "erratics," waifs, and aliens.

The masses of transported rock which the larger glaciers still are piling up along their sides and at their ends in some parts of Switzerland or on our Alaskan seaboard are sufficiently imposing under any circumstances, and make in a measure comprehensible the gigantic forces in the ice, silent, persistent, and relentless, which have sculptured the mountains.

But if the reader should chance, as was once the writer's hap, to spend a night astray among the towering masses of rock ruins which the Zmutt Glacier in the Alps carries on its back in witness of its prowess as a world-sculptor, and in the

A GLACIER-PLANED ROCK SURFACE WITH GROOVES AND SCRATCHES, CENTRAL PARK.

lulls of the great glacier's groans, as it yields to the pressure of the greater snow and ice masses far up the valleys, should be brought now and again, body and heart, to a sudden halt by the crashing and booming of enormous avalanches, seemingly just above him on the high slopes of the Matterhorn, he will be more vividly impressed with the power wielded by great masses of ice and snow than by any array of figures with which the physicist may juggle in the lecture-room by daylight.

Still, if one be endowed with a soul craving for figures, he may find solace in the knowledge that the old glaciers which once covered our northern North America with a layer in places at least 5000 feet thick would press downward, bowldershod and moving irresistibly southward, with a weight not far from 150,000 pounds to a square foot. With such a graving tool did the old ice age carve its records on the rocks.

But now a change has come upon the forces, terrestrial or celestial, which have wrought such havoc on our globe, and the long winter is drawing to a close. At first the snow and ice melt a little faster than they form, and the forbidding rock-clad edges of the great white mantle draw slowly backward. The retreat of the ice is not continuous nor steady, and for how many hundreds or thousands of years the fierce struggle between heat and

A SCARRED AND SCRATCHED "ERRATIC" IN A GLACIAL GRAVEL-
BED NEAR MORNINGSIDE PARK.

cold for the mastery of the continent may have lasted no man can say.

At last, however, in the region of North America which we now inhabit the sun was victor. But he looked down upon a desolation which language can but feebly describe. Gone are the forests which through earlier ages had struggled for a foothold on the hills; swept away southward or destroyed are the forbidding monsters which wandered here. No green or growing thing has outlived those frigid centuries, or withstood the scraping and scarring of the rocks. Sharp crags and ragged peaks upon the hills are worn and ground away, and old landmarks forever effaced. Some of the great inland lakes are deepened, some are gone, while new ones here and there are formed by the damming up or obliteration of the old watercourses by the vast masses of débris which the vanishing glacier has left.

And now the life forces must begin their work anew over this scene of desolation. The ice mantle has left not only loose rocks and bowlders scattered and piled in masses over the land, but great gravel and clay beds here and there witness the thoroughness of the work. But the manufacture of soil suited to higher plant life must be slowly accomplished under the influence of lower forms.

And so the plants crept slowly back over the bare scarred rocks; at first the lichens and their lowly brethren, then the hardier plants which had clung desperately to life along the borders of the ice mantle for so many weary shivering years; and at last, as the longer summer claimed its own, the full tide of green and blossoming forms poured up over the reconquered realm, bringing with them insects, birds, and beasts.

But Greenland, save for its scant verdant fringes, still shivers in the grasp of its age of ice not vanished yet. And if one would know how the regions which we have just described, and now inhabit, once looked, he has but to read the thrilling stories of the hardy seekers for the north pole, and especially the tale of Nansen's wanderings over the great ice plateau of Greenland, whose mountain-tips are even now but just beginning to peer out over the dreary wastes of ice and snow. The plants and the animals have come back to our region because they or their descendants had only to return by land over easy paths to the home from which they were driven. But the warmer, inhabitable, sea-girt borders of Greenland are still only scantily endowed with living forms of animals and plants after all these centuries, because there has been no way open to them to travel home again, after their long exile, save through the perilous chances of the sea.

But we must hasten to fulfil the promise which the title of this paper bears, and seek for the traces of this old ice age about New York.

The rocks which underlie New York were not the very first to peer above the nearly universal sea ages ago when the world was slowly forming, but they followed on so soon that even for rocks they may be regarded as patriarchal. And any observant wanderer about the unbuilt regions of upper New York, or stroller in the parks, will see, where the rocks are exposed in masses, that their layers are curled and twisted and folded into such fantastic shapes that there must have been some wild and boisterous periods hereabouts while the world was building, or slowly working its way toward stability. He will further see that the rock surfaces must once have been tossed up into sharp and jagged peaks and crags. But now all their surfaces are smoothed down and rounded off as if some titanic scraper had been dragged over them. Rounded knolls, projecting bosses, smooth sloping surfaces—such greet the eye everywhere. Even the great looming summit of the Palisades across the river shows upon the top no ruggedness or roughness, but rounded smooth surfaces. All this has been accomplished by the great moving ice mantle which for so many centuries swept across the land.

If the stroller in Central Park, or in the parks and unbuilt regions farther inland, or over the Palisades, will examine attentively the exposed rounded rocks where they swell upward in large sloping masses, or here and there peep through the sod, he will find nearly everywhere the grooves and scratches made by the old glaciers' graving tools so many centuries ago. Where the old rocks have been long exposed these grooves and scratches are usually somewhat obscure, but where the rocks have been more recently laid bare, in park or street or house making, they are still distinct and unmistakable.

The great ice mass hereabouts was moving in a general southeast direction, and so in general run the grooves and scratches in the rocks. Notwithstanding the hardness and firmness of the granitelike rock on which New York rests, glacial grooves twelve inches deep may in places readily be found, witness to the enormous pressure and propulsive force of the old ice mass. The children have long since discovered that some of these grooves in Central Park are fine places for sliding and ball-rolling.

But many of the glacial traces about New York are buried up by the soil which has been slowly forming over them since the end of the great ice age. If, however, one lingers in his wanderings hereabouts where the ground is being cleared for building, he will observe, almost everywhere, where much soil and earth and gravel are being dug out and carted off to clear the rock surfaces in preparation for blasting, that larger and smaller rounded rocks are found embedded in the gravel. They are usually too round and awkward in shape to be useful in the masonry even of the foundations of buildings. Many of them are too large to be shovelled into the carts and carried away with the dirt and gravel. And so one usually sees them rolled off on one side, out of the way, on the bared rock surfaces, until these are freed from soil, when they too

FOLDED ROCK LAYERS IN CENTRAL PARK.

are hoisted up and dragged off to some convenient dumping-ground where land, as they say, is being "made."

If one looks a little closely at these despised bowlders he will find that many of them are of entirely different character from any of our native rocks. Sometimes they are rock called trap, like that which makes the Palisades; sometimes rock like that which is at home in regions many miles to the north and west of New York. And they are rounded and smoothed in a way which indicates an enormous amount of wear and rubbing sometime somewhere.

It is curious, turning back in the books to the record of a time only a few decades ago, to read the speculations of the learned as to the origin and nature of these erratic bowlders, which, from their noteworthy shape and their structure, often so different from that of the rocks over which they lie scattered, early attracted attention. Some thought that they must have been cast up out of a distant volcano in an earlier time, and fell scattered here. For some they were rounded by the wash of Noah's flood, and swept by its fierce torrents into alien regions. Others sank — in theory — the earth's crust hereabouts for many feet, and — in theory still — let enormous icebergs from some distant arctic region drift over here, and melting, drop their ice-borne freight of rocks. Some would have it that the earth was once surrounded by a separate rocky shell which somehow came to grief, and left its shattered remnants sown broadcast. Others, still more dramatic, worked up their facts and fancies to the point of assuming collision with a comet. The record graven on the rocks told the true story at last, however, when the people got ready to read it.

These rounded rocks or bowlders—these erratics, waifs, and aliens—are, as we well know to-day, the torn-off and transported fragments of rock masses which the great ice mantle brought down here from the back country during the cold weather so long ago, and incontinently dropped when the climate changed and the sun swept its borders back toward Greenland and the pole. Many of these erratics still bear bruises and scratches testifying to their fierce encounters with the old bed-rock along which the relentless ice mass ground them in their journey toward the coast.

Here they have lain, these stony aliens, through all the long ages, buried up with other glacial wreckage, covered in by soil later formed, sharing their secrets with the rootlets of vanished generations of plants and trees—until at last another alien, Italian or Celt mayhap, breaks in upon their seclusion with pick and shovel, and rolls them ignominiously away. Then at the scarred rock surfaces the steam-drill pecks viciously, puny successor to the gigantic sculptor of the old ice age, whose records it and its explosive allies soon erase.

Many of the rounded rocks which the thrifty farmer has piled together about the borders of his fields throughout New England to form fences are waifs of the old ice age, stranded with the other wreckage as the ice mantle stole backward to the north.

In some parts of our Northern States it has been possible, in journeying backward over the path of the old ice mantle, to find the very hills and crags from which the erratic bowlders were torn so long ago.

Some of the bowlders which the ice brought down from the hills were very large, and though weighing hundreds of tons were dragged from their places in the earth's foundations and carried away for miles. While many of these larger bowlders are partly or wholly buried up by sand and gravel—the smaller grist of the great ice mill—many were stranded high upon the bare rock, where they stand perched to-day like patient sentinels watching the centuries.

In some places these great ice-borne stones were left, as the ice vanished, so delicately poised on their narrow edges, or on some projecting knob or ridge of the underlying rock, that, though weighing many tons, they may be swayed or tilted by the pressure of a hand. These so-called "rocking-stones" are not at all uncommon over the path of the great ice mantle, and New York city has its own example in the Bronx Park, so nicely poised on a flat rock surface, still faintly glacier-grooved, that, though weighing several tons, it may be easily rocked back and forth.

But the old ice age left a monument near New York more striking than its scattered bowlders, more readily seen than its graven records. An enormous ridge of broken rock fragments, mostly covered now with soil, marks the line of one of the terminal moraines of the great ice mantle. Eastward it is seen in the hills of Cape Cod, of Nantucket, and of Martha's Vineyard. From Montauk Point at the seaward to the great city at its western end the high land of Long Island is an ice-built ridge of jumbled rock fragments stolen from the northern hills.

Its curious subsidiary spurs, its symmetrical knolls and hummocks, its scattered hollows in which here and there a lakelet nestles—all tell the story of a great glacier's long presence and slow retreat.

The geologists tell us that the great inland region about and beyond our Great Lakes before the ice age sent its waters largely down the Hudson River. When the ice retreated and the water from this inland region began in its more impetuous way to seek the sea, it found its old channel blocked by glacial débris, and sought a new outlet, now the Niagara River and the St. Lawrence.

The Hudson River, as we call it, along the western shore of the island of Manhattan, is now a majestic estuary rather

A GROUP OF ALIENS ON HARLEM HEIGHTS.

This colossal ridge of shattered rock is broken through at the Narrows, giving access to the sea to the great streams which pour into New York Bay; crosses Staten Island, forming imposing highlands there; and then bears away in a sinuous line across New Jersey and on to the west. Along this line for century after century the old ice mass made its terminal dumping-ground, and as it wore and tore down the distant mountains and scooped out the great valleys to the north and west, it brought the wreckage down upon its back, or in its depths, and "made ground" for the future Empire State.

than a river, and is deep enough for all the uses of great ships. But its present bottom is formed of the rock wreckage of an earlier day, which has largely filled up a chasm once several hundred feet deep, through which the old river ran.

So colossal was the sheet of ice which came sweeping down from the northwest over the top of the Palisades in the ice age that this ancient chasm of the Hudson River—a veritable cañon once—changed its course no whit. For the direction of the grooves and scratches seen everywhere on the exposed surface of the Palisades, and pointing obliquely across the river's course, run in the same direction as do those on the rocks over which the city stands.

It not infrequently happens that steamers and ships bound for New York, when not quite certain of their whereabouts as they approach the coast, are compelled to seek what help they can by consulting the nearest land, which, under these conditions, is the sea-bottom. The sea-bottom along our coast has been so often and so carefully "felt" that we know a great plateau extends out beyond the coast-line for some eighty or ninety miles, where it suddenly falls off into the great depths of the Atlantic. The place on which New York stands was, it is believed, once much higher than it is now, and was separated from the North Atlantic border by some eighty or ninety miles of low sea-coast land, now submerged, and forming this great continental plateau. Indeed, the New Jersey and adjacent coast is still sinking at the rate of a few inches in a century.

For us to-day the Hudson River ends southward where it enters New York Harbor. But a channel, starting ten miles southeast of Sandy Hook, and in a general way continuing the line of the Hudson, runs across the submerged continental plateau, where finally, after widening and deepening to form a tremendous submarine chasm, it abruptly ends where the plateau falls off into the deep sea.

This chasm near the end of the submerged channel is, if we may believe the story of the plummet, twenty-five miles long, a mile and a quarter wide, and in places two thousand feet in vertical depth below its submerged edges, themselves far beneath the ocean's surface.

This "drowned river" is probably the old channel of what we call the Hudson River, along which a part of the melting glacier sent its flood during and at the close of the Age of Ice.

And so at last—rounded and smoothed rock surfaces, where once sharp crags towered aloft; glacial grooves and scratches on every hand; erratic bowlders, great and small, cumbering the ground; a typical rocking-stone delicately poised by vanished forces long ago; a terminal moraine so great that it forms picturesque landscape features visible many miles away—these are some of the records of the great Ice Age which one may spell out in a holiday stroll about New York.

THE ROCKING-STONE, BRONX PARK.

THE STORY OF A STREET
(PART 6)

DOWN by the Battery the building designed for the Executive Mansion was nearing completion, and, up on Wall Street, Federal Hall, dedicated to the use of Congress, was almost paid for; but the President had gone never to return, and Philadelphia had become the national capital. The situation was disappointing, humiliating, and, in view of the futile preparations, even ludicrous, but New York wasted no time in idle lamentation. Socially and politically its year and a half of glory as the seat of the national government had given it a pleasant prestige, but the thoughts and ambitions of its people were concerned with more material advantages. Moreover, it still remained the capital of the State, and with the Legislature and the municipal authorities quartered in the City Hall, Wall Street was not wholly divested of political importance. Indeed, within six months after Congress abandoned it, the highway witnessed an event profoundly affecting the history of the nation, for in the building still commonly known as Federal Hall, on January 3, 1791, Aaron Burr was elected to a seat in the United States Senate, and from that moment a new and decidedly disturbing factor was injected into all political calculations.

The exact causes of Burr's sudden elevation to power have never been satisfactorily determined, but it is possible that he was, even then, cultivating the friendship of Tammany, over which he subsequently exerted a commanding influence, and it may well be that the approval of some of its prominent members contributed to his success. Officially the society had not as yet evinced any direct interest in politics, but there is evidence that its leaders were already manœuvring for a political opening, and

the advice of its patron saint to the children of "the second tribe" was deeply significant of coming events. "*The tiger affords a useful lesson for you,*" observed that legendary sage. "*The exceeding agility of this creature, the extraordinary quickness of his sight, and, above all, his discriminating power in the dark, teach you to be stirring and active in your respective callings; to look sharp to every engagement you enter into, and to let neither misty days nor stormy nights make you lose sight of the worthy object of your pursuit.*"*

Probably this admonition had no controlling influence upon the founders of the organization, but its activities had already brought it into prominence, and it early obtained a foothold in the City Hall for the public-spirited purpose of establishing a Museum of American History.† Thus Wall Street, which had housed the first public library known to the city, became the repository of one of the earliest collections of historic relics assembled in the country, and not many years later it witnessed the founding of the New York Historical Society, whose early meetings were held in the picture-room of the City Hall. Meanwhile other societies secured accommodations under the same roof, which thus became the headquarters of the Medical Society, the St. Cæcilia, the Uranium, and similar organizations, while toward the other end

* Chief Tammany is supposed to have divided his people into thirteen tribes, each of which had a totem or symbol of clanship in the form of some animal whose virtues the chief recommended to their notice. The New York institution claims identification with the second tribe.—*History of the Tammany Society.* (Drake.)

† This collection was later moved to a house on the south side of the street, and was subsequently scattered, part of it passing into the possession of P. T. Barnum, of circus fame.

of the historic highway a group of auctioneering firms were quietly moulding its future. As a matter of fact, however, Wall Street's destiny had been determined at that little dinner at Jefferson's house, where Hamilton had sold New York's political birthright to insure the assumption of the State debts, for most of the public stock which the Treasury issued to finance its plan was marketed through the auctioneering establishments located at the eastern end of the still fashionable thoroughfare. Indeed, the first "stock exchange" known to the city, opened at No. 22* about the first of March, 1792, was a direct effort on the part of the auctioneers to control this business, and it is a curious fact that two of the men associated in this enterprise, McEvers and Pintard, represented families closely identified with Wall Street's previous history.

No marked alteration had yet occurred in the appearance of the street, but under one of the few shade trees† which had escaped destruction during the Revolution there now gathered daily a small group of men who acted as brokers in the purchase and sale of the public stock, and their presence gradually effected a change in the character of the quiet residential neighborhood. Moreover, it was soon apparent that these men had determined to maintain the foothold they had acquired, for they were quick to resent the combination of the auctioneers which threatened to drive them from the field, and lost no time in declaring war against all the allied firms. At a meeting held in Corre's Hotel on March 21, 1792, they resolved to have no dealings with the monopolists, and on March 17 of the same year they subscribed to a written memorandum agreeing upon a definite commission and undertaking to give each other preference in all brokerage transactions.

Such was the origin of the New York Stock Exchange, but there was no immediate attempt to effect a permanent organization, and for some years the trading conducted under the old buttonwood tree

was almost entirely confined to the marketing of the public stock.

Meanwhile the first notable break from its ancient traditions was occurring at the eastern end of the highway, for the Merchants' Coffee House was nearing the close of its distinguished career, and in 1793 it was practically eclipsed by a rival establishment housed in a modern structure erected by subscription* on the Tontine plan at the northwest corner of Wall and Water streets. This building, known as the Tontine Coffee House, was conducted not only as an inn, but also as a Merchants' Exchange, and is fairly entitled to rank among the first office buildings known to the city, which then numbered thirty-five thousand inhabitants. Here in 1793 the associated brokers established their first official headquarters, and before long it became the storm centre of the absurd political agitation which then convulsed the entire city. In default of a better issue at that time the community ranged itself on either side of the impending struggle between France and England, and the local elections were fiercely contested by the partisans of those countries, without the slightest regard to any other question. Provincial and undignified as such a contest was, party feeling ran high in 1793, and it was at this juncture that Wall Street was drawn into the inglorious fray. The trouble began at the Tontine Coffee House, where the zealous champions of France raised a liberty cap, which the English contingent immediately threatened to remove. The French party thereupon set a guard over the building and defied their opponents, the supporters of each side rushed to the rescue, and Wall Street was soon thronged with hundreds of angry men. Neither faction, however, seemed inclined to take the initiative, and after daring and double-daring each other with puerile provocations to the point of exhaustion, the farcical contest ended.

About this time Citizen Bompard, a French naval officer, commanding the warship *L'Ambuscade,* arrived in the port, and taunts and defiances were soon flying thick and fast over the glasses of the mettlesome sons of the sea who fre-

---

* The street numbers used at this period practically correspond to those of the present day.

† A buttonwood standing in front of Nos. 68–70 Wall Street.

* Two hundred and three persons contributed $200 apiece to this enterprise.

quented the Tontine. Finally the Master
of a United States revenue-cutter arrived on the scene bearing a message
from Captain Courtney, of his Majesty's
frigate *Boston,* challenging the French
commander to a naval duel. This extraordinary communication was actually
spread upon the books of the Coffee
House, and when Courtney appeared in
the town, Citizen Bompard and he soon ran
foul of each other. Thereupon the preliminaries were quickly arranged, and sailing
out of the harbor, the two valiant gentlemen pummelled each other with cannon
for several hours, within hearing but just
out of sight of the cheering throngs gathered on the neighboring hills.*

A year later the Franco-British controversy was still raging, and had it then been
known that Jay had negotiated his famous treaty with England, his candidacy
for the Governorship would have been
seriously affected. He was, however,
safely inaugurated in the City Hall, July
1, 1795, and the contents of the treaty
did not become public until later in that
year. Then the partisans of France
raised a howl of indignation, and shrieking every charge against the statesman
which ignorance and malice could invent,
called mass meetings to demand his re-
pudiation at the hands of the Senate. One
of these meetings was scheduled for Wall
Street, and in front of the City Hall a
turbulent throng assembled. There was,
however, a strong anti-French contingent
represented in the crowd, and when efforts
were made to adjourn the proceedings
there was a scene of wild confusion.
Richard Varick and Brockholst Livingston attempted to address the mob, but
were howled down, and then Alexander
Hamilton, mounting the steps of his
house on the corner of Wall and Broad
streets, tried to gain a hearing. The
mob, however, was in no mood to listen
to a man whom it regarded as a notorious
champion of England, and stones were
soon flying through the air. "*If you employ such striking arguments, I must
retire,*" announced the orator, and in a
few moments the rabble swept by him
toward the Government House on Bowling Green, where Jay was violently de-

nounced, the rejection of his treaty demanded, and a copy of it burned in front
of the official residence. Neither Washington nor the Senate, however, paid the
slightest attention to these noisy demonstrations, and the ratification of Jay's
negotiation which followed was soon justified by the event. Indeed, within a few
years some of the very men whose wild-
eyed enthusiasm for France suggested a
religious frenzy were shrieking maledic-
tions against that country and urging
the administration to make an immediate
declaration of war against her. In the
mean time, however, Jay did not add
to his popularity, for in 1796 he incurred
the displeasure of Tammany by declining
to honor the anniversary of the society
by ordering a display of flags—a precedent which has not protected other in-
cumbents of the City Hall from similar
outbursts of wrath.

The volume of business transacted by
the brokers during these turbulent years
was not very great, and the dealings
were still limited to a few stocks, but certain memoranda contained in the note-
book of one of the small group who continued to assemble under the buttonwood
tree in 1795 show that some phases of
the brokerage business were much the
same in the eighteenth century as they
are in the twentieth. For instance, in
the note-book above mentioned, under
date of February 13, 1795, this entry has
survived: "*I bet G. McEvers 10 Dollars
to 5 Dollars that there would not be
3000 votes taken at the ensuing election
for Governor in the City and County
of New York.*" And again: "*Feby. 17,
1795, I bet Robert Cocks, Sr., a pair of
satin breeches that Jay would be elected
Governor by a majority of 500 or more.*"

The writer of these engagements was
evidently doing a brisk business in the
winter of 1795, but Jay was almost the
last Federalist upon whose success at the
polls it would have been safe to count
for a pair of silk breeches or any other
advantage, for Burr's political star was
in the ascendant, and Tammany was preparing to supply him with what Hamilton termed his "myrmidons" and Theo-
dosia Burr called "recruits for the
Tenth Legion."

The Federalists were, however, still
sufficiently entrenched in power to pre-

* This remarkable contest took place near
Sandy Hook. The English commander was
killed.

WALL STREET DURING THE BANKING PERIOD—1847

vent their opponents from obtaining a charter for any rival to the Bank of New York, which had been organized with Hamilton's assistance, and was, in 1798, located in a building erected on the site of the McEvers mansion at the northwest corner of Wall and William streets.* During its existence of fourteen years this corporation had acquired virtual monopoly of the local banking business, and as New York was rapidly increasing in population, the advantage of the facilities afforded by the Federal institution became a valuable political asset. Indeed, it was openly charged that none but Federalist sympathizers could obtain accommodations at its hands, and in the Legislature every effort to place a competitor in the field was summarily blocked. In 1799, however, Burr appeared

* See inscription on present building No. 48 Wall Street.

upon the scene as the sponsor for a company whose ostensible business was the improvement of New York's water-supply. In view of the recent epidemics, which were generally attributed to bad water, the projectors of this public-spirited enterprise were promptly accorded the necessary charter, authorizing a capital of two million dollars, and providing that any surplus not needed for the immediate prosecution of the business *" might be employed in any way not inconsistent with the laws and Constitution of the United States, or of the State of New York."*

It must have been difficult for Burr and his adherents to conceal their joy when they perceived the ease with which they were to accomplish their ends, but their secret was well kept, and not until the Manhattan Company was safely established at No. 23 Wall Street, employing its "surplus capital" in the banking business, did the Federalists discover that their enemies had stolen a march on them, and were in a position from which they could not be dislodged. From this time forward the business of chartering banks played an important part in the sessions of the Legislature, and methods were employed to obtain the coveted privileges which would scandalize the most hardened of modern corruptionists, but within a few years the Merchants',* the Mechanics', and the United States Bank were incorporated, and all of them made their headquarters on Wall Street.

Less than ten years elapsed between the retirement of Congress and the establishment of the Manhattan Company, but during that time the population of the city had increased from thirty-five to sixty thousand people, and the character of its historic highway was being gradually transformed. Indeed, the advance guard of fashion had already begun to move up to Park Row at the opening of the nineteenth century, and the gaps caused by this migration were quickly occupied by the pioneers of finance. Business was still conducted on a very modest scale, however, and for some years the thoroughfare maintained a residential aspect. Fashion had never favored the neighborhood of the Tontine Coffee House, and such private houses as there were in that vicinity fell an easy prey to the commercial invasion, but between Pearl Street and Broadway every foot of territory was contested, the private dwellings surrendering only one by one. Even then those that capitulated often managed to conceal the fact until long after the event, for the days of conspicuous advertising had not yet arrived, and the new tenants frequently preferred to make no alteration in the premises. Here and there a sign was displayed, and at a few points the oldest houses were replaced by modern structures, such as that of the Bank of New York, but save in these particulars there was as yet little evidence of the coming transformation.

Such was the aspect of the street on the morning of July 11, 1804, when a bulletin displayed on the Tontine Coffee House attracted the attention of the earliest arrivals, and in a few moments messengers were speeding through the city carrying the startling news that Hamilton and Burr had met in a duel, and that the former lay at the point of death. From that moment business was practically suspended, and all day long great throngs gathered before the Coffee House, watching the bulletins which reported the famous statesman's brief struggle for life. The end was announced on the afternoon of the 12th, and on Saturday, the 14th, Wall Street witnessed the most impressive funeral pageant known to the history of the city. Every window and roof was crowded with mourners as the body was borne to Trinity, and the junction of Wall Street and Broadway was lined with troops, the soldiers leaning their cheeks against the butts of their inverted rifles in an attitude of grief. Between their ranks passed the procession, which included the Governor, the Mayor, the judges, members of Congress, foreign ministers, representatives of Tammany, the Cincinnati, St. Andrews, Columbia College, the Chamber of Commerce, members of the bar, delegations of law students, and scores of distinguished citizens.* In front of the entrance of Trinity a platform had been erected, and here Gouverneur Morris delivered an oration, at the conclusion of which Hamilton's body was consigned with full military honors to the ground where Sir Henry Moore, Sir Danvers Osborn, James De Lancey, and others closely associated with Wall Street's history already slept, and where Robert Livingston, Marinus Willetts, Morgan Lewis, and Robert Fulton were to find their final rest.

With this event the political history of the street may fairly be said to close, and during the next twenty-five years the new era, which had already dawned, slowly but surely developed. Close in the wake of the banks and insurance companies came the lawyers, and among the numerous representatives of the legal profession who established their offices on

---

* The Merchants' was located at No. 25, the United States at No. 38, and the Mechanics' at No. 16 Wall Street. The first two were incorporated in 1805, and the last in 1810.

* The New York *Evening Post* and the New York *Commercial* of July 15, 1804.

the highway about 1809 was a young attorney whose work was destined to give it a new and unique distinction. Washington Irving had originally studied law in the offices of Brockholst Livingston and Josiah Ogden Hoffman, two of the early practitioners in the famous Mayor's Court at the corner of Wall and Broad streets. In 1809, however, he was associated in practice with his brother, John T. Irving, at No. 3 Wall Street, and another brother, Dr. Peter Irving, had an office in the same building, and here it was that Washington Irving began the *Knickerbocker History of New York* which was to make him known to the whole English - speaking world.*

Meanwhile New York had scored another astonishing gain in population, for in 1810 the census showed no less than ninety-six thousand inhabitants, an increase of over fifty per cent. in the preceding ten years, and by 1820 the city included fully one hundred and twenty - three thousand souls.† Three

* Washington Irving and Dr. Peter Irving were jointly responsible for the original idea, and they collaborated on the opening chapters, which were subsequently rewritten by Washington Irving alone.

† By 1830 population was approximately 202,000; by 1840, 312,000; by 1850, 515,000; by 1860, 805,000; by 1870, 942,000; by 1880, 1,200,000; by 1890, 1,500,000 (U. S. Census Reports).

New-York City Lottery.

SCHEME of a LOTTERY, for the purpose of raising Seven Thousand Five Hundred Pounds, agreeable to an Act of the Legislature of the State of NEW-YORK, passed 8th February, 1790.

SCHEME.

	Prize of	£.		£.
1		3000	-	3000
2	-	1000	-	2000
3	-	500	-	1500
10	-	200	-	2000
30	-	100	-	3000
50	-	50	-	2500
120	-	20	-	2400
180	-	10	-	1800
7950	-	4	-	31800

8346 Prizes. 16654 Blanks. } 25,000 Tickets, at 40s. each, - - - - £. 50000

Subject to a deduction of 15 per Cent.

THE object of this LOTTERY being to raise a part of the sum advanced by the Corporation for repairing and enlarging the CITY-HALL, for the accommodation of CONGRESS, which does so much honor to the Architect, as well as credit to the City. The Managers presume, that their Fellow-Citizens will cheerfully concur in promoting the sale of Tickets, especially, as the success of this Lottery will relieve them from a Tax, which must otherwise be laid to reimburse the Corporation.

The above SCHEME is calculated in a manner very beneficial to Adventurers, there not being two Blanks to a Prize.

The Lottery is intended to commence drawing on the first Monday in August next, or sooner if filled, of which timely notice will be given. A list of the fortunate numbers will be published at the expiration of the drawing.

Tickets are to be sold by the subscribers, who are appointed Managers by the Corporation.

ISAAC STOUTENBURGH,
PETER T. CURTENIUS,
ABRAHAM HERRING,
JOHN PINTARD.

New-York, March 6, 1790.

LOTTERY SCHEME TO PAY FOR FEDERAL HALL
From original in possession of the New York Historical Society

years before this amazing result was achieved the brokers, who continued to assemble in steadily increasing numbers in Wall Street, organized under the name of the New York Stock and Exchange Board and adopted a written constitution, but they were soon driven from their customary haunt by an outbreak of yellow fever, taking refuge for a time in Washington Hall, corner of Broadway and Reade Street, but eventually finding their way back to the *Courier and Enquirer* office at No. 70 Wall Street, which sheltered them for a part of the decade closing in 1830.

By this time the street which had once been the centre of government and the resort of fashion had become completely transformed. Federal Hall, the wonder and admiration of the city, had disappeared, the buildings erected on its site had gone up in smoke and flames; the Bank of the United States occupied the present Assay Building; the great Merchants' Exchange, covering the block lately abandoned by the Custom House, had been constructed, numbering among its many tenants the New York Stock and Exchange Board, and on all sides the hum of business was deepening into a roar. Old buildings were still giving way to new, however, and other changes were being effected, when the great fire of 1835 swept through the thoroughfare, levelling the monumental Merchants' Exchange and scores of other buildings to the ground; but almost before the ruins had cooled, the work of tearing down and building up was resumed—and it has never ceased. *"It is as difficult to wend one's way through Wall Street as it ever was,"* wrote the chronicler of the New York *Gazette* in 1839. *"Physically as well as financially there is peril in perambulating that street. Stocks may rise, but stones are falling prodigiously in all directions. The Manhattan and the City Bank are being torn down, and there are other edifices in old Wall Street under the besom. New York, ever since we knew it, has been a city of modern ruins—a perfect Balbeck of a day's growth and a day's dilapidation. The builder is abroad one day, and is relieved of his labors by the destroyer the day after. We never expect to see the city finished, but we have the greatest anxiety to see it fairly commenced."**

Almost threescore years and ten have passed since those lines were printed, but they fairly depict the modern conditions. Moreover, three years before the writer in the old *Gazette* described the physical aspect of the street, another contributor to the same periodical recorded some impressions of its life, which reflect the conditions of to-day.

"Between ten and three o'clock," re-

* New York *Gazette*, Vol. XVI., p. 375.

ports this observer of 1836, *"Wall Street is crowded with speculators, money-changers, merchants, bank directors, cashiers, and a whole menagerie of bulls, bears, and lame ducks, and all is anxiety, worry, fretfulness, hurrying to and fro, wrinkled brows, eager eyes, calculating looks, restless gestures, and every indication which follows in the train of grim-visaged care. Wall Street is a place to study character, and the moralist would find material there to rewrite the 'Spectator,' the 'Tattler,' the 'Rambler,' and the 'Guardian' with scenes, incidents, personages, and manners peculiar to New York, and to no other city under heaven."**

Such was the highway twelve months before its first great panic in 1837, and for the next three years the brokerage business languished to such an extent that the Stock and Exchange Board distributed its surplus among its members and virtually dissolved, though maintaining at least a nominal headquarters at one of the Jauncey buildings, No. 43 Wall Street. By 1842, however, the financial storm was over, and for the next twelve years the Board occupied a large hall over the reading-room of the new Merchants' Exchange, erected on the site of the building destroyed by the great fire, and so prosperous did it become during the interval that rivals† were induced to enter the field. During all this time the outdoor market or place of public assembly for the brokers was on the corner of Wall and Hanover streets, but in 1854 the Board moved to the Corn Exchange Bank Building on the corner of William and Beaver streets, and from that day to this the Stock Exchange has never had its headquarters on Wall Street. It would almost seem as though its desertion of the thoroughfare carried ill luck, for one of the most notorious scandals associated with the history of banking and railroads in New York—the Schuyler frauds of 1854—occurred about the time of its departure, and shortly after it moved again to Lord's Court at William Street, Beaver Street, and Exchange Place, the great

* New York *Gazette*, Vol. XIV., p. 135.

† It had at least one formidable rival prior to 1837, which the panic of that year virtually eliminated.

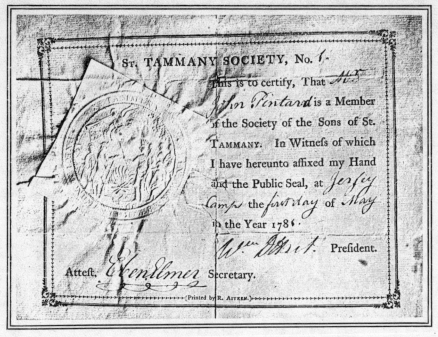

St. TAMMANY SOCIETY, No. 1.

This is to certify, That *Mr.*
John Pintard is a Member
of the Society of the Sons of St.
TAMMANY. In Witness of which
I have hereunto affixed my Hand
and the Public Seal, at *Jersey*
Camps the *first day* of *May*
in the Year 1786.

Wm. Malcom President.

Attest. *Eben Elmer* Secretary.

[Printed by R. AITKEN.]

ONE OF THE EARLIEST CERTIFICATES OF MEMBERSHIP IN TAMMANY

From original in possession of the New York Historical Society

panic of 1857 caused wide-spread disaster and alarm. The full force of this financial convulsion was felt in Wall Street, for by 1850 the highway had become the banking centre of the metropolis, whose population had risen to over half a million. Indeed, in that year there were no less than fourteen banks and sixty-nine insurance companies quartered on the thoroughfare,* and as the day of the modern office buildings with their thousands of tenants was still far distant, these concerns almost monopolized the limited territory. Every vestige of residential ownership had long since disappeared; the Presbyterian Church had been torn down and removed brick by brick to Jersey City; the Custom House, occupying the former site of the City Hall at the Nassau Street corner, had been erected at an enormous cost; the street had been somewhat widened; the Trinity of 1790

had been demolished and the present structure erected, and other changes were occurring every year.

It was not until 1863, however, that the old Stock and Exchange Board became known as the New York Stock Exchange,* and six more years elapsed before it merged its interests with those of its rival, the Open Board of Stock Brokers. Then came that Black Friday of September 24, 1869, well within the memory of many of its present denizens, when the street swarmed with demoralized victims and half-crazed captains of finance, while a little group of conspiring speculators dealt out ruin to thousands before they were themselves engulfed in the pit which they had digged.

From this time forward the history of the highway cannot be distinguished from that of the neighboring thoroughfares. Indeed, much which it is accused of and much that it is credited with is not properly associated with it

* From a rare publication of that year in possession of the New York Historical Society called " New York Pictorial Directory of Wall Street."

* It moved into its present quarters, Nos. 10 and 12 Broad Street, December 9, 1865.

at all, for the wide field of operations now conducted in its name is by no means limited to its own narrow confines, and "the street" no longer means the canyon down which Trinity gazes.

But though its story has lost in color and picturesqueness during the last hundred years, its fame within this period has almost reached the uttermost ends of the earth, and it would seem as though its latest phase, as the financial centre, was destined to endure. Yet who can tell? The strip of land that has seen Stuyvesant's wooden palisade rise to the gigantic walls of brick and stone which now enclose and shadow it—the spot where Zenger's words were burned and the Declaration of Independence read—

the route along which royal pageants passed and the ragged Continentals made their triumphal march—the forum of the Revolution and the birthplace of the nation—the haunt of fashion and the heart of business — the home of Hamilton—the school of statesmen—the firing - line of commerce — the battle-ground of politics and of money—the scene of financial master - strokes and speculative orgies—of loud-tongued victories and wild-eyed panics — the lair of the money spiders and the workshop of a Washington Irving and a Stedman—this is no mere street or thoroughfare. It is historic ground, of whose final destiny none dare prophesy.

THE CITY OF BROOKLYN

JUST as a summer rain begins with
big drops out of a half-clear sky, so
the rush to Brooklyn sets in around the
New York end of the East River bridge
on every work-day evening. The gaping
maw of the bridge has been at work lazily during the afternoon sucking in a
few stragglers and throwing out little
squads of folk from the trains that run
behind it. But when five o'clock comes
the drops of the approaching tempest of
humanity that is to storm the place like
a revolutionary mob around a Bastille
begin to appear in Printing-house Square.
They come faster, and run together in
little rivulets up Park Row, down Chatham Street, along Centre Street, and
across the City Hall Park—all turned one
way, all streaming toward the bridge.
Even then they give no warning of what
is to come, except to those who know that
the torrent is as certain to develop and
as sure to become tremendous as that
tidal bore which daily swells the Sague-
nay with its overwhelming flood.

The black drops come faster and thick-
er. They splash in sudden numbers from
the near-by office buildings and the
horse-cars. The little streams now length-
en out, and form far up and down the
streets and across the park in Broadway.
It is five o'clock, and the offices in the
buildings that hold villagefuls are closing. It is no longer a sprinkle. It is a
shower. Farther and farther away the
human drops mingle; bigger grow the
converging streams. At half past five
the wholesale stores and the warehouses
are closing. It is a torrent now. At six
the factories and the workshops thrust a
myriad toilers upon the streets. The very
clouds of the city's humanity appear to
have gathered over one spot. The streams
have become swollen rivers. The usual

confines no longer hold the two-legged
drops which now jostle one another off
the sidewalks, into the gutters, out upon
the roadways, all over the park's asphal-
tum. The outlook from the upper stories
of the neighborhood is upon a sea of people, in droves like wild cattle, coming up
as if out of the earth from every direction, pushing, hurrying, covering every
open place like locusts. Now it is a pelting rain. Half an hour passes, and the
elevated trains, which come like breathing, absorb half the crowd so fast that the
station stairs become as the beds of inverted cataracts up which the dark torrent
climbs resistlessly. The horse-cars from
both directions stop and discharge people
as guns are wheeled up, fired, and dragged
away on a battle-field. It is a cloud-
burst, and it has made a mill-race—something far bigger than that—the swollen
drain of a human freshet.

Thirty thousand men, women, and children are in the torrent, thirty thousand
pedestrians in a ninety-minute downpour;
for though the rush is between five o'clock
and seven, it is thinned at both ends, and
the bulk of it is compressed in a period
of between sixty and ninety minutes.
This is not counting the almost equal
numbers that seek the elevated cars.
The surging black waves, white-capped
with human faces, hurl themselves against
the granite steps that lead to the yawning
iron throat of the bridge and spread over
them. There is no more sign of individual motion than there is in the herds of
sheep one looks down upon from the Col-
orado mountains when the droves are
moving along the valleys like floating
brown islands, as clouds move against
the sky. Overhead, on a trestle that
crosses from the City Hall Park, another
black current, from the steam-cars, keeps

pace with the tide below. In that way the exodus to Brooklyn moves over everything ahead of it, as if, were the bridge to fall, the people would still keep straight on, filling the river, and pressing forward upon the undermost bodies.

We read about the European capitals, treated with the skill of artists, clothed with the glamour of tradition, and colored by the fancy that grows richer with the distance of its subject. But what has London to show like that daily congestion at the Brooklyn bridge? What crowds in Paris are to be measured with this? What European city has even one of the many strange conditions that produce this scene? Here come the elevated railways that carry three-quarters of a million souls a day, the surface vehicles of the million and six hundred thousand people of Manhattan, the streets leading from the densest population in America, all meeting in one little square, all pouring out people, and all the people streaming into a great trumpetlike mouth of iron in order to be shot across a hanging cobweb of metal threads into a city that has not its mate or counterpart on earth— Brooklyn! It is like a city in some things. It is a vast aggregation of homes and streets and shops, with a government of its own. Yet many things it has not got — things with which many a little town could put it to the blush. And every other city earns its own way, while Brooklyn works for New York, and is paid off like a shop-girl on Saturday nights.

"Stop shoving so!" "Look out who you're pushing!" "Don't try to run over me, I say." These are notes from the chorus of the solid mass of persons that crowd up the stairs to the bridge cars. On the upper platform the trains sweep away regiments at a time. Burly bridge policemen are there, urging every one forward, and at times — until the newspapers cry out, periodically — putting their hands on their betters and wedging them into the cars, through three doors at once, as revolvers are charged. There are fourteen other ways to Brooklyn, all by ferry-boats, and at the time of which I write all these are crowded. They are not mobbed, like the bridge, to be sure, but they are packed with people so that you can only see the rims of the decks as you see the edge of a grocer's measure that has been filled with pease. At first the big bridge hurt the business of the ferry companies, but after a while it built up a surplus and paid them back, just as our elevated roads in time increased the traffic of the horse-cars. In a word, then, everything that is going to Brooklyn at nightfall is crowded. That is even true of the drays which start empty for the bridge that carries forty-one millions of passengers in a year, and for the ferries, one company of which collects thirty-six millions of fares annually.

What is Brooklyn, to which all these persons go? It would be a quarter of New York, like the east side or Harlem, if it were not for the East River, and the political division of the soil into two counties. It is the home of the married middle people of New York, Manhattan Island being the seat of the very rich, the very poor, and the unmarried. It has been called the sleeping-room of the metropolis. It is far more and far better than that. It will become a proud part of the Greater New York of the time to come. And that will be before the realization of the rest of the boast of the fatalists, that "whatever is is."

Nine hundred thousand persons call Brooklyn "home," though, as a rule, they write New York opposite their names on the hotel registers when they travel. All the people of the Greater New York do that. The Brooklyn people inhabit a great fan-shaped city whose handle is out by Jamaica, Long Island, while the sticks of the fan reach to the edge of New York Harbor and the East River from near the Narrows to Newtown Creek on the way to the Sound. In this great area are several tenement districts and three considerable shopping centres, but, in the main, Brooklyn is made up of hundreds of miles of avenues and streets lined with little dwellings. These are the homes of men who work in New York, and earn between $1500 and $3000 a year. Speaking generally, these men are far more interested in New York than in Brooklyn. They do not know in which ward of Brooklyn they live, they cannot name the sheriff or their members of Assembly, and in politics the only local episodes that stir them are the contests for the mayoralty.

As New York is recruited from the country, so is Brooklyn. Many a countryman who comes to New York and prospers never masters the metropolis, or feels at ease or safe in it. Sooner or

THE HEIGHTS, FROM WALL STREET FERRY.

later such ones move to Brooklyn, where there is elbow-room and a hush at night, and where they see trees and can have growing flowers. Those who are married when they come, and the great self-respecting majority of the poor who marry afterward, are certain to settle in Brooklyn, or, in far fewer numbers, in the other suburban towns. They must choose between cozy homes and crowded tenements. There lies the secret of the suburb, whose growth is only matched by a few cities, which are all in the West. It is customary to say that we New-Yorkers move to Brooklyn, or settle there, to save money. That is true, but comfort and self-respect are in the same dish of the scale with the saving for all whose incomes are small. It is possible for a clerk to own a house in Brooklyn; it is easier for a clerk to fly than to own one in New York. But the people go to Brooklyn to rent houses, not to buy them. They pay the landlords one-fifth of their incomes, or $25 to $50 a month, and that is about half what they would pay to live relatively well in New York — in tenements and flats, mind you, whereas they have houses across the river. Once in Brooklyn, in the evening, these men stay there. They do not go to New York for their dissipation. They do not maintain great social clubs. Few patronize the Brooklyn theatres. The fun these men have is what their wives provide for them.

The women are very different. Just as the few old rich families on the Heights (in Brooklyn) used to despise New York as a "shoddy" town and a Babel, so the great mass of wives in the miles of dwellings look down upon the metropolis. It must clothe and feed them, but it may not have their love. They regard it as a cold and monstrous place, where people live for years next door to other people without getting acquainted, where the un-American rich have set up social boundaries, where nice children may not play out-of-doors without maids to watch them, where the morals of growing boys and girls are in danger, and where young wives sit cooped up in barracklike tenements, without society—unless their country cousins come to town to see them. On the other hand, these women are intensely interested in Brooklyn. Their husbands buy the *Eagle, Times, Standard-Union,* or *Citizen* (Brooklyn newspapers), and find them Greek, but the wives digest their paragraphs with gusto. It is a woman's town. By day there are no men in those endless miles of dwellings. They have gone to New York to make six trips in as many days, and to bring back millions of money in pay envelopes on the sixth day. The women have the city to themselves, and rule over the children, maids, nurses, shade trees, flowers, and pretty door-yards. Thus encouraged, each studies her own neighborhood. Each remembers how the others called on her when she moved to Brooklyn, and each calls on those who come after her.

The wives cut a great figure there—a lovely figure, of course—and one that reveals wholesome and normal conditions. Everything tends to widen their freedom —the quiet city, the saving in rents, the absence of the men, and the fatigue or the desire for entertainment, either or both, of the men at night. Therefore the women have had the opportunity to build up a very pretty rivalry for self-improvement. They get the latest books from the libraries. They go to cooking-school in order to shine at dinners of their own preparing. They flock to dancing-school that they may triumph at their own parties. They prepare papers to read in other houses so that the others may read papers at theirs. There is no whim of feminine fashion that is set spinning in New York but whirls when it gets over to Brooklyn —always provided that it does not cost

too much or require going to the theatre. The women are the very backbone of the churches, in which they sing and hold fairs, and by means of which they figure in circles that are proud of them. Is it any wonder that they cannot tolerate New York, where the shopkeepers won't send a purchase around the corner without pay in advance, where the pews are private property in the best churches, and where a lady feels herself of no account in the hurly-burly? In Brooklyn the police understand who owns the town, and the car-drivers pull up in the middle of a block. Besides, if my lady has no carriage, she observes that her neighbors also use the horse-cars.

I have said that the women provide dissipation for their husbands at night. That is a curious feature of Brooklyn life. It has no Ward McAllister, no Four Hundred—nothing that those names imply. It is true that there used to be a smart set on the Heights, and there are others in Clinton Avenue, in New York and Brooklyn avenues, and on the Park Slope, but then no one has ever decided that one is any better than another. Instead of one crowning triumph of caste, society there is divided into church coteries as a basis, and out of these grow many sorts of little circles, each combination being reproduced over and over again, beyond calculation, in the same district, and in the many districts which in Brooklyn are quite as distinct as if they were separate cities. The lesser circles of which I speak are bowling clubs, whist clubs, euchre clubs, poker clubs, literary guilds, musical coteries, amateur dramatic companies, and dancing classes. Poker is played for small stakes in many circles in Brooklyn—solely, I trust, because it has charms to keep the men at home; but bowling is a passion with the Brooklyn folk. Investigate what set you will, and it is almost sure to include a bowling club in its ramifications and adjuncts. A page of the Brooklyn *Eagle* almanac is devoted to the bowling matches of seventy clubs, but those are the clubs of skilful, earnest players, and do not form a drop in the bucket of the clubs formed by neighborhood coteries all over the town.

Brooklyn was a string of villages before the great bridge was built. The Heights, overlooking New York, where a row of house gardens has been built on the roofs of the river-side storehouses,

ST. MARK'S PLACE, NEAR BROOKLYN AVENUE.

was settled by the Dutch in the old days. They used to pull away from the bustle of town in rowboats after business hours. They called the place variously—Breucklen, Broucklyn, Breuckelen, and Brucklyn. Such shipping firms as the Lows and others followed the Dutch to the tree-clad Long Island shore from time to time. In 1790 there was talk of building the national capital there, and very much later Plymouth Church and Henry Ward Beecher made the Heights world-famous. The Hill district, northeast and far back of the original ferry, grew up on its own account; and so did Williamsburg, which was incorporated as a village in 1827, and swallowed up by Brooklyn in 1855. Greenpoint, beyond Williamsburg, grew into a town; ancient Flatbush, straight back from the ferry, was a Dutch farming village; Bushwick was another; East New York was a suburban outgrowth; and South Brooklyn, a seat of heavy population, maintained its distinct individuality. The growth over the seams between these places began in anticipation of the building of the bridge, and to-day not only are all these towns joined, but the fan-handle is pushing into Jamaica, which ancient burgh of the Dutch will soon be nominally what it already is in fact—a part of Brooklyn.

This is very like the history of Manhattan Island, with its villages of Chelsea, Greenwich, Bloomingdale, Harlem, and the rest, that, like drops of quicksilver, ran into and lost one another. But the parallel goes little further. The Manhattan Dutch were traders and had money; the Long Island Dutch were farmers. One looks in vain for Brooklyn Knickerbocker families of great wealth in land and houses. They are not there. During many decades in Brooklyn, now nearly 270 years old, farms have been changing into city blocks, but the prevailing rule of the place, marked by littleness in financial operations, affected the transformation. The process was slow. The farmers sold a little now and a little later, to middle-men, ahead of the actual demands of the inrushing tide of humanity. Some of the old families, like the Bergens, Brevoorts, Bensons, and others, are still there, and are well-to-do; but, as a rule, the old families were large, and not one parallels the fortunes across the East River. Many new and old families who have got rich in various ways have

gone to New York. The same centripetal force which the metropolis exerts as far away as San Francisco to pull millionaires into its brilliant vortex is felt in Brooklyn, whence, for a century or more, those who have amassed riches or an identity have come to New York to enjoy the fruits thereof. Cases like those of Seth Low, Roger A. Pryor, Demas Barnes, and a certain wealthy brewer, who have but just come to New York, form a long list as one looks back over the years that reach at least as far as present memory goes.

Some of these had as fine houses as any in Brooklyn, and were distinguished in the social, commercial, professional, or intellectual life of the town. And that brings me to speak of the houses of the place. The old city, and what is even yet the greater part of it, was solidly built up, like New York, Boston, Philadelphia, and St. Louis, of brick and frame houses, set close against one another. It was one of the cities that seem to have been turned out by a quarry company and a sawmill. We think now that the stage of our civilization which was thus marked was the natural result of the beginning of large towns when America was almost wholly agricultural, and men who came to the cities sought a complete, diametric change from country life. To-day a later generation has a different taste. Tired of the monotone of brick and mortar, spending months of every year in the country, the people delight in detached houses, trees, flowers, and elbow-room. Even the newer parts of New York demonstrate the hold this new longing has upon all our people in every section of the country. In oldest Brooklyn there are not even door-yards; but the chief beauty and charm of that city was that it always had long and pretty gardens or rear yards. It has never been fortunate in gaining fine houses, if we accept the New-Yorker's or the Londoner's interpretation of that term; but I am not competent to reflect the general New York sentiment on that subject, though Manhattan Island is my birthplace, for I have always admired the villalike homes of the modestly rich in Brooklyn more than the fortified castles of my millionaire neighbors in New York.

The oldest fine Brooklyn houses on the Heights are of brick and brownstone, like our own on Manhattan. They are becoming boarding-houses now, for the Heights district is not what it was in days of yore. It is not this district that I would have praised at its best. But out on Clinton and Washington avenues, on the Hill, there grew up a fine array of frame and brick villas, set in spacious grounds, with carriage drives and trees, conservatories, flower beds, croquet and tennis grounds, and a combined effect of semi-rusticity, which I made many a trip to enjoy when such spots were few and I was younger. This Hill splendor and comfort is still maintained, and is the seat of a comfortable circle of those rich who typify the spirit of Brooklyn in their love for their homes, for quiet, and for the charms of nature. They no longer monopolize this quintessence of the Brooklyn spirit, for other and newer districts share in such display. There is a beautiful part of the Twenty-fourth Ward, where New York, Brooklyn, and St. Mark's avenues pursue their ways between noble houses, decorating ample grounds. This is more modern, more beautiful, and is, perhaps, supported by greater wealth than the older beauty-spot of the town. Another among the new and attractive residence districts is the Park Slope section, where, on Eighth and Ninth avenues, are many houses of considerable showiness, more closely built, but revealing the varied individual tastes of the owners.

This new region is close to Prospect Park, which is one of those great triumphs of civic enterprise whose class includes Central, Forest, Fairmount, and Druid Hill parks, in four of our older cities. Prospect Park is not one of the largest of these. It comprises only 516 acres,

STATUE OF HENRY WARD BEECHER.—J. Q. A. WARD, SCULPTOR.

but every rod of it is the subject of taste and care, and its drives, ponds, playgrounds, and various other ornaments are all of the finest. The people have been adding to its attractions in notable ways quite recently. At its entrance they have erected a great soldiers' and sailors' monument that has the form of a memorial arch of granite, the design of Mr. John H. Duncan, of New York. It is of great size and massive appearance, but the piers are hollow, and stairs within them lead to a hall at the top, where it is proposed to maintain a museum of war relics. Another new and interesting ornament in the Park is the statue of James S. T. Stranahan, by Frederick Macmonnies, the sculptor and artist, whom Brooklyn claims as one of her sons. This is a bronze statue of a man who is yet living among those who have paid this high and singular compliment to him as the creator of their park and boulevard system. He also earned the public gratitude for lending the force of his earnestness and influence to quicken the building of the bridge across to the metropolis. He is aged now, though sound in limb and mind, and is closing a life that shines with many and striking virtues. He has been the chief constructive character of the city, an apostle of annexation, a member of the Greater New York commission, was for many years the president of the Park Board, and was once a member of Congress. Active as is his record, his single aim seems ever to have been to enrich the public, and self-interest never marred his work or weakened the love of his neighbors. Prospect Park has other statues, of Lincoln, J. Howard Payne, Moore, and Washington Irving. But perhaps the sculptured figure which attracts the most attention from visitors is that of Henry Ward Beecher, which rises above the flagging in front of the City Hall. Brooklyn has six other parks and three noble boulevards. These parks are all small, but one of them is, in my opinion, the most beautiful of all the small parks of the United States; at least, it ranks next to Battery Park, whose beauty is solely that of its situation at the point of Manhattan Island. This beautiful Brooklyn pleasure-place is Washington Park, best known by its old name of Fort Greene. It contains only thirty acres, but they are high upon the Hill, and overlook the first and fourth cities of America, the first of our harbors, the local navy-yard, and many other notable sights. By day the view is majestic; by night it is gorgeous.

But I have strayed from the pretty residence districts of the city before I had my last word about them. There is a fine district of pretty residences of a much more modest character in what is called East New York. There is promise of a noble residence district in Flatbush; and along the shore of the harbor, between Brooklyn and Fort Hamilton, are several suburban towns that are made up of picturesque homes. These places are not in Brooklyn, but they are of it. In one of the pretty dwelling districts within the

STATUE OF JAMES S. T. STRANAHAN, IN PROSPECT PARK. FREDERICK MACMONNIES, SCULPTOR.

THE SOLDIERS' AND SAILORS' ARCH.—JOHN H. DUNCAN, ARCHITECT.

city a Du Maurier might find new grist for his pencil, because those who enjoy the fruits of generations of refinement find as neighbors such *nouveaux riches* as a millionaire chewing-gum manufacturer, the leading jockey of America, his most ambitious rival on the turf, a pawnbroker, and a milliner. In administering this touch of color let it not be supposed that I reflect upon the old and dignified circles of the town. I do not need to tell any American reader that in the ornamental quarters of Brooklyn are as refined and progressive folk as any old city in the country boasts.

Brooklyn is a city of residences. From a balloon it would look like a sea of them, only broken here and there by parks and factory districts, but so largely made up of so vast an area of dwellings as to have earned for the city the nickname of "the bedroom of New York." In one place this great level of low dwellings is broken by a clutter of tall structures, such as we see in the more complete cities that serve as trading centres for the regions of country around them. That is at the lower

end of Fulton Street (the Broadway of Brooklyn). Here the main ferry, the great bridge, the Post-office, and the City Hall have centralized trade and the travel of the people. The huge piles of iron and masonry at this point are used for offices, banks, insurance companies, and the great mercantile establishments of the town. From beside many of these buildings run the streets which lead, at many odd angles, to every part of the spreading city. It is a queer spot—a miniature mountain range of tall roofs rising above an otherwise unbroken level of low ones. It is still more queer in that half of it is for the men, and the other half for the women. The men's half would seem familiar to every resident of a city. The women's half is the extraordinary yet natural result of an assemblage of nearly half a million women and girls in a city of dwellings.

Here is a long double row of shopping stores, many of which are palatial and enormous. They compare favorably with the best and largest of the department stores of New York; and since they are new, and stand almost side by side, the district impresses the visitor more than our less compact shopping region in New York. Along the double line, beside the giant stores, are restaurants and small shops by the score. This centralization at this point is a new thing, and the bar-rooms, cigar shops, and various places that offered goods for masculine needs and tastes have all been bought out and moved away, so that lovely woman may be un-interfered with in her opportunities for "shopping" over the whole area. In place of the former traders are now seen those who deal in candy, soda-water, flowers, bric-à-brac, pictures, boots and shoes, millinery, children's clothing, mu-sic, medicines, patterns, and stationery. The number of women who crowd there to buy is remarkable. It is not always easy to pass along the streets in the neigh-borhood of the more showy windows. The music of their voices beats upon an atmosphere in which the odor of cologne is perceptible, and the scene is rendered gaudy by the flowers and gay colors that are woven to and fro past the splendor of the window decorations. It is said of a great shopping store in another suburb that its business languishes because it has no other place of the kind near by in which the women may compare prices; but if that is a fault, here must be per-fection, since such emporiums are massed as they are nowhere else that I have been in the world. Carriages are few, men are in a ridiculous minority, and the police gain the appearance of giants among so many women. Indeed, the crowds of ladies pouring in and out of the great doorways set the fanciful spectator to imagining what Eden might have been were Adam and his part in life dispensed with.

Atlantic Avenue has a minor shopping district at one end of town, and Williams-burg has its own quite pretentious trad-ing quarter at the other end. Here, by-the-way, in Williamsburg, is a peculiar German district, known politically as the Sixteenth Ward. There are many per-sons in it who never saw the Brooklyn City Hall, or even the bridge. They put signs in the shop windows reading, "Eng-lish spoken here." They employ petty neighborhood lawyers and agents to pay their taxes and deal with the great Eng-lish-speaking world beyond them. They maintain their own target and singing

clubs, their dance halls, their delicatessen shops and pork-butchers, their beer sa-loons and summer gardens. It is said of them that when a financial crash, like the failure of the Barings, palsies capital ev-erywhere, and gilt-edged bonds beg pur-chasers, a man may sell a house or a piece of land in that strangely foreign quarter.

The city has no hotels worthy of its size, and needs none. It has not one morning newspaper. It has no vicious section or houses of evil savor, no gam-bling-dens, no speculative exchanges. New York supplies all these things for it. But it has several evening newspapers, of which the leading ones are the *Eagle* (Democratic) and the *Times* (Republican), the last-named journal being published in the Eastern (or Williamsburg) Dis-trict. The *Eagle* is admired by journal-ists all over the country as the best ex-ample of a purely local newspaper. It publishes all the news of the world; but its first aim is to record the affairs of Brooklyn, and this it does with remark-able thoroughness, and with such fairness that even in political contests it publishes full reports upon both sides. It is clean and dignified, and has prospered to the point of owning a model building which is one of the "sights" of the town. The *Times* is such another journal, deserving of praise for the same characteristics.

I have said that the men of Brooklyn do not support great social clubs. I was referring to the average and typical citi-zen who works in New York, and whose kind inhabit the long reaches of quiet and shady streets. The other class, whose professional and mercantile careers keep them in Brooklyn, as well as the well-to-do men of all sorts who possess the lei-sure, are supporting several clubs, such as the Brooklyn and the Hamilton, in old Brooklyn; the Lincoln, Oxford, and Union League, on the Hill; the Montauk, of the Park Slope; the Hanover, in the East-ern District; the Algonquin, of South Brooklyn; and the Crescent, an organi-zation of a large number of young men with country quarters and a fondness for out-of-door life. The old club of the old residents is the Brooklyn, and the Hamil-ton is of the same class, but is more youth-ful and alert. There are twenty-five less-er clubs which I have not mentioned, but of the above it may be said that all are admirable and important, though not one is decidedly prosperous in the degree

SHOPPING ON FULTON STREET.

which marks the prosperity of clubs in the more masculine great cities. A peculiarity of some of these clubs—which they borrow from the character of the city—is the manner in which the members refer to their wives, and, in the old Brooklyn Club, to their personal servants, with the knowledge that these personages are known to the other members. The ladies share the club life to a slight extent, four of the leading clubs having restaurants and rooms for ladies, after a well-established fashion which obtains in New Orleans and Chicago, and which has crowded the toe of one boot into New

York club life as I write. "Interest your wife, and she will let you join," is the principle upon which this evolution is working.

Brooklyn has always had a sharp taste for music, and feasts itself upon a varied programme of good quality during every winter. The Brooklyn Philharmonic is an organization of citizens, but not of musicians, which for many years has employed one orchestra or another to give concerts over there. For many years Theodore Thomas played for it; but since his orchestra could no longer be had, the plan of the Philharmonic has

THE NEW TABERNACLE.

slightly changed, and in inducing the Boston Symphony Orchestra to play in Brooklyn, it gives only its moral support to the venture. The more active musical society now is the Seidl Society. One purpose of this society is to bring Anton Seidl and his orchestra over there for a course of concerts, but the society is unselfishly working to cultivate the musical taste of the people beyond its clientèle and their friends. The Brooklyn Choral Society of three hundred voices gives winter concerts after the manner of the Handel - Haydn Society of Boston, the famous oratorios being excellently rendered by them. The Apollo Club, of three or four score voices, forming a male chorus, and led by Mr. Dudley Buck as conductor, gives several concerts a year before fine assemblages that fill the Academy of Music. The Amphion Society, in the Eastern District, is such another organization. The Euterpe Society, under the direction of C. Mortimer Wiske, is a society of musicians maintaining an orchestra of gentlemen and ladies, some of whom are professionals. A male chorus is also formed of this membership, and the concerts of the society are admirable. The conductor, Mr. Wiske, is also the director of the work of the Choral Society. Brooklyn has two dozen other musical clubs. The Arion Society and the Saengerbund are leading German organiza-

tions, of which there are many. Their concerts and masquerade balls are great events, in the estimation of the large German element in the city. The Germania is their social club.

Brooklyn is famous for its amateur dramatic and operatic clubs, of which it has more than twenty. Some of these are composed of cultivated persons, some have seen members win distinction on the stage, and all contribute greatly to the winter pleasures of the town. Strangely enough, where this is true the theatres are second-rate at the best, and the legitimate drama is but slightly successful. Lawrence Barrett liked Brooklyn, and used to say that he meant to build up a clientèle there. In time he had a following, but not a great one. The city is too close to New York, and its play-goers prefer the fresher plays and greater variety of the metropolitan stage. In Brooklyn the preparation of the average citizen for a night at the theatre is the donning of a hat and overcoat or a bonnet and wrap. There is no display of fashion or of beauty much adorned. Musical farces and opéras comiques draw best there. The place has half a dozen theatres, the finest being the Academy of Music, and the Amphion Academy in the Eastern District; but the greatest success there has been that of a firm who built a variety theatre upon the site of that old forgotten market-house to which the bodies of the dead were taken from the ruins of the ill-fated Brooklyn Theatre.

On the other hand, Brooklyn has always been distinguished for the number of its churches (now 352), and its good fortune in attracting brilliant and able preachers to preside over their congregations. Of the galaxy of talented men of the last great era of Brooklyn's church work, the Rev. Richard S. Storrs remains, and is no less greatly beloved and admired than before. The Rev. Dr. A. J. F. Behrends, of the Central Congregational

Church, has risen far above the firmament, with a following that considers him the most eloquent preacher in the town. The Rev. Dr. Charles H. Hall, of Holy Trinity Episcopal Church, is another leading figure there. The Rev. Dr. T. D. Talmage is, of course, the preacher whose popularity is widest. A new personage of note in church circles is the young Catholic bishop, Dr. McDonnell, an engaging man

zation, and appears at no political meetings or councils, yet he is the absolute ruler of the Democratic "machine," and has been for a longer period than any active Democratic politician of to-day can remember. It seems to be a superstition over there that he is to be consulted about all party matters, and that his dictum shall be final. He sits all day in an auction shop in which he has no interest, a

A SCENE IN "KLEIN DEUTSCHLAND," SIXTEENTH WARD.

of brilliant parts, who has already brought to the front, around himself, the brainy, cultivated Catholics of the city.

But a character who cannot be left out of any description of the strong forces which make Brooklyn peculiar is Mr. Hugh McLaughlin, the most remarkable and the oldest Democratic boss in America. He is now sixty-four or sixty-five years of age, with a Scotch face, though of Irish blood. He holds no office in the government or in the Democratic organi-

gentle, soft-spoken, undemonstrative man, who finds enjoyment in smoking, but none in drink or profanity. He acts as the political clearing-house of his party. His plan seems to be to listen to everybody on all sides of every disturbing question, and at the end to let fall a word or a sentence that shall settle each question in its turn. "I wouldn't if I were you," or "I don't think so," becomes a command against a proposed course of action. "All right" or "Go ahead" serves as an order to move. He never dictates or speaks imperatively. He is secretive and tactful, and listens rather than talks. He is often able to manage so that troublesome matters settle themselves without his interference. When there are several men who want a nomination that can go to but one, he says to each, "Go out and make your case." Of course they stir the town and the Democracy, and, before the "boss" decides, the applicants themselves perceive which is the strongest, if not the best, among them. Thus, year in and year out, this strangest of these strange products of our political methods pursues his course. He is given to announcing at times that "the people want a young man for Mayor," or "the people want a soldier for sheriff," and intelligent men actually insist that he thinks himself the agent of the people and the interpreter of their wishes. He was a fish-dealer in his youth, and he made money then and afterward. He lives well, and plays the part of an amiable father to a large family.

There is a view of Brooklyn which gives it the appearance of a smoky seat of manufactures. It is obtained from the east side of New York, looking over at the great sugar-refineries which tower like Rhenish castles beside the swift East River. Brooklyn really has great manufacturing interests, and many of the goods that the people of the country buy as of New York make are really made in Brooklyn. The census reports 10,560 manufacturing establishments in 229 different lines of industry. These employ nearly 104,000 hands. Very large hat-works, chemical-works, foundries and iron-works, candy factories, coffee and spice mills, and boot and shoe factories are notable among the industrial establishments of the place. It will be news to most persons, I think, that thirty lines of steamships (all but two or three of them transatlantic) dock at Brooklyn wharves, and

ALONG THE DRY DOCKS.

THE SUGAR-REFINERIES AT NIGHT.

use 231 steamers in their regular service. The city has fourteen dry docks, upon which 2000 vessels are docked every year, and thirteen grain-elevators are upon its water-front. So will it also surprise those who have not yet reflected upon the size of the town to know that it has thirty-nine more miles of paved streets than New York city, or 380 miles in all. It is in advance of New York in the use of the trolley electric system for surface cars, and its principal street railways are adopting that power rapidly. It has had elevated railways for years.

The growth of Brooklyn in population has been very remarkable. It is only twenty years ago that the city was smaller than Boston is now, having less than 400,000 souls. In 1880 her people numbered 566,689. In 1890 the census-takers estimated the number of residents at 806,-343; and to-day no one who is familiar with the strides the town has been making, and the number of new houses that have been built and occupied, questions that the place contains more than 900,000 inhabitants. This growth is a loss to New York, to be sure. It is mainly made up of those who draw support from Manhattan Island, but find Brooklyn more

convenient, and in other ways preferable to our annexed district. New York regards this with complacency, knowing full well that no city except London compares with her in size if the truth is acknowledged. This truth is that her dependents and subjects should be counted without regard to political boundaries, that interfere in law and on the map but not in copartnership of interests with those who live on Manhattan Island.

In no city that I have yet studied is there such an enthusiasm for education as in Brooklyn. From that, again, one sees how thoroughly it is a city of homes, and how closely allied to the hearth-stone are all the interests which prosper, while all that languish are certain to be those which are apart from or antagonistic to home influences. Whatever a mother would concern herself about is what thrives in Brooklyn, and everything else is poor or despairing. The schools are wonderful: the effort toward the polish of pretty and refining accomplishments is epidemic; the churches have made the town famous; the shopping stores are second only to those of New York's; the parks are all that they should be. But the clubs and theatres are second rate; the bar-rooms

JOSEPH C. HENDRIX.

appeal to the pride and affection of the town. There are nearly 100 of these schools. They are housed in modern buildings, some of which are beautiful, and cost $70,000 to $100,000 each. They are features of a very rich, commodious system enjoyed by 100,000 pupils, and officered by teachers of whom it is said that they exhibit more intellectual activity than one finds among the teachers in any other of the older cities. Under President Hendrix's administration, the Department of Public Instruction took up the question of secondary or higher education, and elaborated its development to a point that required the expenditure of a million dollars and more. The largest girls' high-school under one roof in America and the most beautiful of all the boys' high-schools have resulted from this. Both schools are thoroughly equipped, and so ordered that in the girls' school, for example, three courses of study are provided, requiring two, three, and four years. Knowing that I question whether the people should be taxed for a system more elaborate than the poorest are able to take advantage of, Mr. Hendrix spoke boldly for his policy.

"A people with a highly developed common-school system," said he, "is better than a dull, degraded, despairing peasantry. The schools give to the people a share in the government, in actual benefits that they feel. They are more interested in their government, and more anxious to support and defend it in consequence. For the children, a perfect common-school system offers grand opportunities. A poor boy in Brooklyn has the chance to gain the education that the sons of the rich obtain. He may start in our primary grade and go through Cornell University without the payment of a cent for tuition."

But in Brooklyn these public opportunities for education are swelled by private philanthropy and popular combination.

are mere kennels; the hotels and restaurants are few and poor, and the wholly vicious resorts are none at all. Brooklyn is the only female among our cities—the sister city to New York. Like a good woman, she offers little to the chance visitor, impelled to come by idle curiosity, and nothing to the *roué*. But if you live in her house, as one of her family, you are well off indeed.

First among the schools, in point of a celebrity that has grown out of long and good standing, are the Packer Collegiate Institute for girls, and the Polytechnic Institute for boys. Both are thoroughly modern schools, with a large attendance. A certificate from the Packer secures admission to Smith, Vassar, or Wellesley, and the four courses of instruction at the Polytechnic lead to collegiate degrees. The Adelphi Academy is another fine school; and then come the public schools, which, under six years of management by the Hon. Joseph C. Hendrix, have reached a high degree of development, and now

SALUTING THE FLAG.
FRIDAY MORNING SERVICE AT
PACKER INSTITUTE.

The Pratt Institute is a noble monument of Brooklyn's progress, and of such love as many of her people bear for their city. Among the most enlightened citizens the admiration for this educational establishment is remarkable. It is a new benefaction, but one that has met with a great success, which, after all, is but proportioned to the advantages it almost gives away to whosoever wishes them. Mr. Charles Pratt, a wealthy business man of New York, whose great fortune had come through connection with a modern gigantic commercial combination, established the institute which bears his name.

He did so after years of study of the question how he could do the most good with the money he was able to devote to the people. He was a resident of Brooklyn and a lover of it. Manual training, as an adjunct to the schools, for the training of the eye and hand, he concluded to be as important as any need which he was able to assist in supplying. We often hear it urged that the elaborate superficiality of our inflated public-school system — as it is called by its critics — turns the heads of the young, and causes them to regard themselves as superior to those who earn their livelihoods with their hands. If that is even in a measure true, such institutions as this, which is a veritable six-story hive of busy and willing young artisans, are of priceless value as offsets to such a tendency among the masses of public pupils. Mr. Pratt, who has now passed away, dealt with this offspring of his philanthropy in a spirit of royal liberality. Apart from its buildings, their equipment, and those adjuncts which yield a part of its revenue, he endowed it with two millions of dollars. The following extract from a report for last year (1892) shows how much he bestowed upon it:

Endowment fund	$2,000,000 00
Real estate, building and equipment fund, to be used as required	835,000 00
Cost of present Institute buildings, equipment, and grounds	523,337 61
Cost of Astral, Inwood, and Studio buildings	332,437 07
	$3,690.774 68
Income from endowment fund, rents, leases, etc.	$182,136 23
Less deficit (expenses and receipts of the Institute)	120,462 90
	$61,673 33

The Institute was founded in 1887, "to make the way open to as many young people as possible to intelligently enter upon the technical high-school course of instruction, and to establish for other schools a type of what kindergarten and primary education should be"; in a word, to make a school which should be complete, from the primary to the graduating courses, and for fitting the youth of both sexes to gain their livelihoods at skilled manual labor. It has courses in many trades, but its best teaching is toward thrift, self-reliance, and an appreciation of the dignity of intelligent toil.

The Institute buildings are models of their kind, as well as types of what the future school-houses are to become, now that elevators increase the height of buildings and render the higher floors even more desirable than the bottom ones. These houses, of which the Institute has several, are built of brick and stone, and are notable for their strength, simplicity, plentiful illumination by windows, and the neatness and cleanliness that distinguish all parts — even the engine-room, foundry, and machine and plumbing shops. In the rooms of the department of science and technology a visitor sees the boys and young men at work as carpenters, as wood-workers, at moulding and forge-work, at painting, sign-writing, frescoing, and wall-papering, and in the

studies that are pursued in a well-equipped machine-shop. He also sees boys and girls and men and women studying in complete chemical laboratories and at wood-carving. Classes of girls learn dress-making, millinery, plain sewing, art needle-work, biology, cookery, laundry-work, and what is called "home nursing," which is a science including and going beyond what is known as "first aid to the injured." Other classes study drawing (including mechanical and architectural drawing), clay-modelling, designing, and painting. There are music classes, and classes in phonography, type-writing, and book-keeping, and the foundation includes a kindergarten, a large circulating library, a very excellent technical museum with a wide range of exhibits, a class in agriculture studying in a country district on Long Island, a play-ground for ball and tennis, and a class in "thrift," taught by the practical means of a savings-bank managed upon the profitable system of a building and loan association.

In the high-school department, which includes physics, chemistry, and the technical courses, further instruction is given in English literature and our language, mathematics, natural science, political economy, French, Spanish, Latin, elocution, and physical culture, forming all together a three years' course for both sexes. The circulating library has a branch in the Astral model tenements in Greenpoint, the rents from which are part of the Institute's revenue, as is the income from the Studio building, which is separate from the Institute and at a distance, and in which some artist graduates have already taken work-rooms.

Perhaps I have given more space to this great school than the room for my article warrants, and yet I have but skimmed the surface of what I would like to tell about it. To me it is one of the most interesting products of the remarkably quick intellectual spirit of the town, and the time that it takes to go through the buildings is as enjoyably spent as if the workers there were actors in another sort of theatre. The milliners' work, made of Canton flannel and farmer's satin, is often as stylish as if it was seen on Broadway. The home-nursing practice attracts gentlemen to study it beside their wives, and to experiment upon a most amiable boy, whom they bandage as if he had not a sound limb, and lift in and out of bed as if he was at death's door. The cooking classes are attended by well-to-do housewives by day, and their servant-girls at night. The gymnasium is well equipped, and both boys and girls practise in separate classes there—the girls in picturesque short-skirted costumes, which I had described to me, but was not permitted to admire except upon hearsay. The plumbers' class and its neat products in solder-work, the paper-hangers' street of open cabins that are papered as nothing short of a Browning Society was ever "papered" before, the class of art seamstresses turning out needle-work that ranks with jewelry, the sewing class with a little boy interested and skilful in its work, the bevy of girls in coarse smocks carving beauty into wood, and the chemistry room packed with young men and women, and decorated with blackboards bearing appalling triumphs in chemical formulæ—these are but fragments from the memory of what I saw while I was in this busy and attractive temple of learning and education. Though some of the trades are taught, it is not "a trade school." In some of the courses of study it is purely professional, such as the training of teachers in the arts, domestic science, and kindergarten departments. In these lines no higher grade is reached in the country. In the departments of science and technology it resembles the English technical schools, and assumes a place between the public schools and the higher universities, or schools of engineering. In the high-school, with which is allied the Froebel Academy of Brooklyn, it carries on a complete course from the kindergarten to the college. In the library the books have a circulation surpassing that of any library in Brooklyn, and this is not of a common character. The percentage of works of fiction is much lower than in any other library in town; and the Institute is carrying on, in this branch, classes in library training and economy for the instruction of library assistants and others. The Institute is unique, and reflects only the intelligent thought of its founder and directors.

But "if all signs come true," as the old saying is, there is in Brooklyn an institution that will yet become a rival of our Metropolitan Museum of Art and our Museum of Natural History, while performing a more extensive work than both. I refer to the Brooklyn Institute of Arts and Sciences. Its president is General John B. Woodward, its vice-presidents are the Rev. Richard S. Storrs and the Hon. James S. T. Stranahan, and Professor Robert Foster is its secretary. This is so old an ornament of the town as to date from "a meeting of several gentlemen at Stevenson's tavern in 1823," for the purpose of establishing a free library for the apprentices of Brooklyn. As a result, in 1825 General Lafayette laid the corner-stone of the library building. In 1843 the charter of the library association was amended to enlarge its scope, and it then became the Brooklyn Institute. "For many years the Institute was a most important factor in the social, literary, scientific, and educational life of Brooklyn. Its library had a large circulation; its public hall was the scene of many social and historic gatherings; and from its platform were heard such eminent scientific men as Agassiz, Dana, Gray, Henry, Morse, Mitchell, Torrey, Guyot, and Cooke; such learned divines as Drs. McCosh, Hitchcock, Storrs, and Buddington; and such defenders of the liberties of the people as Phillips, Sumner, Garrison, Emerson, Everett, Curtis, King, Bellows, Chapin, and Beecher."

A Mr. Augustus Graham, one of the founders, gave to the Institute the building it occupied on Washington Street, and bequeathed to it $27,000 for lectures, collections, and apparatus illustrating the sciences, toward a school of design and a gallery of fine arts, and for maintaining Sunday evening religious lectures. In time the Institute weakened in vitality, and it was not until 1887-8 that its new scope was formulated. The building was improved in readiness for what was to follow, and what followed reads like the magical growth of a venture in Chicago or St. Louis, where all the people take hold with a will in every improving public enterprise.

During a little more than a year after the reorganization a membership of 350 was recorded. The Brooklyn Microscopical Society became the department of microscopy; the American Astronomical Society, of which Garrett P. Serviss is president, became the department of astronomy; and the Linden Camera Club and Brooklyn Entomological Society were merged into the Institute as special departments. Some of these associations which then, or since then, allied themselves with the great body were proud organizations. They were not wholly composed of Brooklyn people, and their standing was acknowledged abroad. Nothing shows the popular and forceful nature of the new interest in the Brooklyn Institute more than this magnetism that it exerted upon the other scientific and educational foundations around it. Seven other departments were added, and next year the growth was even more remarkable. The citizens supported a movement to secure museums in connection with the Institute, and the new name "Brooklyn Institute of Arts and Sciences" was adopted. In 1890 the headquarters building was burned, and the members accepted shelter for their classes from many educational and religious societies. But the wonderful growth did not stop. The geographical department, under President Cyrus C. Adams, exhibited in this year the collection of maps, charts, globes, and kindred objects, which has since been shown in many cities, and is unrivalled by any such collection on the continent. In the same year the citizens' movement bore fruit in legislation at Albany, authorizing the city to expend $300,000 in the erection of museum buildings for the Institute whenever the association should become possessed of $200,000 with which to maintain them.

In 1891-2, six hundred and thirty-two new members came in, one-third of the number being teachers in the public and private schools. The architectural department established a school for junior architects and draughtsmen; the department of painting established the Brooklyn School of Fine Arts; departments of music and pedagogy were formed; the photographic section housed itself advantageously; one summer school of painting, under Mr. William M. Chase, was established by the sea on Long Island, and another was started in the Adirondacks. The lectures and meetings numbered 405, and more than 100,000 persons attended them. Exhibitions of collections were given by several departments. In the mean time the Institute sold its old building, and from that and other sources the new association has raised more than the needed $200,000. The city is about to begin building the museum on a conspicuous site beside Prospect Park, and

when it is finished only "a nominal rental" is to be charged for it. No one doubts that it will be handsome and complete, or that the edifice will be extended and added to from time to time as the collections grow.

There are now twenty-five departments in the Institute. In addition to the earlier ones already mentioned are the departments of architecture, anthropology, electricity, engineering, fine arts, geography, music, painting, pedagogy, philology, political and economic science, psychology, and sculpture. Each of these sections holds meetings, maintains a lecture course, and is making collections. The initiation fee is five dollars, and the yearly dues are five dollars. For that sum an associate member, so called, may attend forty-five lecture courses, including hundreds of lectures, may take advantage of the collections, may enjoy the library of 15,000 volumes, and may attend a wide variety of receptions, addresses, and the other entertainments of the general body. It is a great and wonderful work, and has been the result, or else the creator, of a revolution in the city of Brooklyn. From having few monuments of art, and, at best, an inharmonious interest in intellectual progress, Brooklyn is now possessed of this extraordinary organization, already operating like a powerful dynamo to stir thousands of households, to gather the citizens at meetings that take place every day, and to embellish the place with a museum whose beginning is thought to be but as a seed from which a tree may grow.

I close this study of Brooklyn with the reflection that whether it might have been better done or not, it will still attract the interest that attaches to news for most of my readers in my own town. It has been said of us New-Yorkers that if we travel at all, it is only to go to Europe. And it is certainly true, and of my life-long knowledge, that most New-Yorkers see Brooklyn only when a funeral takes them to the cemeteries in and beyond it. They will find it well worth an occasional visit for its own sake. Its peculiarities are not all even hinted at here. It has no transient population, and nothing, therefore, to amuse a floating crowd. Its drives are fine, notably that by way of Prospect Park and the Ocean Parkway to Coney Island. It is a grand place for fast horses and the sport of driving. It is soon to have a new road,

A CORNER IN THE PHYSICAL LABORATORY, PRATT INSTITUTE.

to be called the "Shore Drive," and to follow the edge of our Upper Bay—a road not equalled in scenic attractiveness by any that we now have in New York. The city has no promenade for the display of fashion, and its people are fond of boasting that whatever electrical force it is that makes us metropolitan, that keeps all New-Yorkers under a strain, and that charges even the night air like a magnificent essence of strong coffee, is lacking in beautiful Brooklyn. Rest, comfort, and cozy homes, that bring independence even to the poor, are the richest offerings of this lovely sister of the metropolis. She has grown almost as old in years as New York has—if that should be spoken —but she has never kept evil company or late hours, or indulged in any dissipation. The consequence is that to-day she is more green and coquettish and attractive to all whose tastes are not vitiated by the artifices of a metropolis than New York has been in the last half-century.

THE NEW YORK
COMMON SCHOOLS

I.

THE town meeting in a rural community is perhaps the only contrivance for local government of the people by the people which has ever proved completely successful.

The things to be done for the general good are the same that each man does for himself. The men who manage their own farms and enforce order in their own families are able, by like methods, to repair the roads and keep the public peace and direct the district school.

But as population becomes varied, and towns and cities grow up, the work of providing for the common needs becomes complicated, and requires special training and aptitude. Very soon the citizen, occupied in his own affairs, is unable to criticise the processes by which the public work is done, and he is left to judge only of the results. This is usually not difficult. When we observe that the streets are ill paved and dirty, that property is unsafe, and that disorder is prevalent, we try to put in power officials who will remedy these evils according to methods which have been tested and have proved effective. In this way public opinion has been brought to bear upon all the branches of our municipal administration, and they have been from time to time reorganized and suited to the needs of the community.

But the system of common schools has seemed to be almost beyond the reach of such reformation. From the first the process of teaching cannot be supervised by untrained critics, and as the community grows, the results of teaching become difficult to follow. It is not easy to decide whether one child is well taught. It is quite impossible for most of us to have any personal opinion as to the teaching of three hundred thousand children. The work goes on in many hundred classrooms. If it is ill done, the teacher will not tell us, if she can, and the children cannot tell because they do not know.

It is clearly impossible that the community should have the kind of knowledge about the matter that it has in regard to the working of other branches of local government.

Not only the vastness of our system of education, but its undoubted merits and its immeasurable service to the community protect it from criticism. A great majority of our citizens have been taught in the common schools, and cherish for them the affection due to the foster-mother, the *alma mater* of Commencement speeches. These men and women are not eager to learn that the teaching which fitted them for their life-work was inefficient and unsatisfactory. Then there are the five thousand teachers, whose *esprit de corps* is aroused by attacks (and criticism seems to be attack) on the great army in which they serve; and there are the men who have filled the numerous school offices. Some of them have spent years in the performance of arduous and unrequited duty, and they have a natural pride in the result of their labors, and a natural reluctance to have their success brought in question. So, quite apart from the motives which we term unworthy, there are powerful influences perpetually tending to prevent the community from learning the real value of the school system.

If fault is found with particular schools, we are told that the defects are exceptional, and due to the incompetence of some principal or school officer. It is impossible to determine whether inefficiency is the rule or the exception without an examination more thorough than any ordinary citizen can give; and so criticism is ineffectual, and the great organization goes on in its own way with constantly increasing momentum.

It must be said, however, that the pride of the community in its schools is less general and less confident than it used to be. Formerly they were shown to every traveller as models of organization and discipline. It was possible for the City Superintendent in 1857 to say, "There can be little doubt that in respect to all the essential elements which go to make up a practical and efficient system of popular education and public instruction, the ward and primary schools of the city of New York, with their appendages, are fully equal, if not superior, to any in the world."

The recent reports of the Board of Education contain no such assertion of the excellence of our schools. On the contrary, they are very largely concerned with pointing out that the best results cannot be obtained without larger expenditure than the board is allowed to make. From time to time some Commissioner of Education has publicly and sharply criticised the schools. To the looker-on these criticisms have sometimes seemed serious and important, and sometimes trivial, insincere, and unreasonable. But, serious or trivial, they seem to share the same fate. They pass away, and the schools go on as before.

If we turn for instruction to competent advisers not connected with the system, we hear little praise of it. Dr. Rice, after a methodical inspection of the schools of several cities, says:

"The typical New York primary school is a hard, unsympathetic, mechanical-drudgery school—a school which the light of science has not entered."

"In many cities the children read better at the end of the second year than they do in New York at the end of the third."

"I have not yet found a single primary school conducted on modern educational principles."

Other volunteers have looked into the accommodation given to the scholars. Their story is no sadder than Dr. Rice's, but it touches and arouses the people as his criticisms never could. Most of us know very little about methods of teaching, but we can in some degree imagine what it means to crowd little children into ill-ventilated rooms, and keep them for hours at work by the light of flaring gas. About such facts as these there can be no dispute. Any observer is competent to prove their existence. The Board of Education admits that the schools are not all housed as they should be, and pleads as an excuse a want of sufficient appropriations. Of course this answer is open to the reply that one of the duties of the Board of Education is to obtain from the tax-payers the money necessary for its work. If the school moneys, managed carefully and to the satisfaction of the people, are not sufficient, they are likely to be increased, and when school appropriations are too small there is a question whether the Board of Education has done its full duty in making known its needs. A school board which obtains the public confidence and informs the public conscience can usually find a way of reaching the public purse.

There is another shortcoming of which we can all form an idea, though we can-

not measure nor even imagine its unhappy consequences. Full to overflowing, our schools yearly turn thousands from their doors. The board says ten thousand. Other people say more than one hundred thousand. Until there is some census of school-children no one can tell what the number actually is. More than thirty years ago it was computed that the children unable to attend school numbered sixty thousand. Then, as now, the authorities thought the estimate far too high. Then, as now, everybody said that it would be desirable to have a census; and there the matter has rested for a generation.

The advocates of particular kinds of instruction given in kindergartens and manual-training schools are dissatisfied with the experiments in these directions, and their dissatisfaction affects many people who cannot tell whether it is just.

On the whole, it may be said that there is a widespread feeling that New York has fallen behind other cities in the development of its public education, and that the teaching of its children is not well done when judged by modern standards. With some of us this feeling amounts to belief, with others it is only a doubt. It is clearly our duty to arrive at certainty if in any way it can be done.

A tree can be judged by its fruits, but it is equally reasonable to judge of fruit by the tree which bears it. Whatever fruit it may be, it is not fig nor grape if we gather it from thorn or thistle. Just as invariable is the connection between the machine and its product. If this great engine of ours was built on an ill-chosen pattern, if it has been unskilfully patched to keep it going, if the motive force is wasted in overcoming the friction of useless parts, if its power is applied obscurely and at a score of different points, if some parts are overloaded and others do no work at all, if it is antiquated and lumbering, and is constructed in ignorance of modern invention and in disregard of settled mechanical law, we can safely believe those who tell us that its operation is inefficient and wasteful.

II.

There were free schools in New Amsterdam, and there were charity schools in the city of New York before and shortly after the Revolution, but the history of public education on the island of Manhattan really begins in 1805, when DeWitt Clinton founded the Free-School Society.

No one then understood the work to be done nor the methods of doing it, and the progress of the society was neither rapid nor constant. An insufficient income was with difficulty obtained from several sources—State and city aid, private benevolence, a share in the excise moneys, and a half-interest in lottery licenses. At one time an unsuccessful effort was made to supplement these revenues by charging the scholars a tuition fee. The methods of teaching were of course experimental, and very dreary experiments some of them must have been. There was the Lancasterian system, with hardly any teachers, and a Pestalozzian system, with hardly any books, and combinations of the two. Most of the churches maintained parochial schools, which sought and obtained a share of the public money. Very bitter controversies arose, and in 1842 the Legislature attempted to settle them by establishing in the city the common-school system, which for thirty years had prevailed throughout the State.

A Board of Education was created consisting of forty-four members elected from the several wards, but its powers were very limited. In disregard of the obvious unity of the city, each ward was considered as a separate town, and having received its proportionate share of the school moneys, the school officers, of whom nine were elected by each ward, proceeded to expend them as they pleased, to put schools on their ward boundaries to attract the children of their neighbors, to establish their own courses of study and systems of teaching. The report of the County Superintendent for 1843 described the beginnings of the new plan:

"Unhappily the Board of Education has been left without power. It can recommend, but, no matter how wisely, it has no power to enforce. Hence in the reorganization of the new schools its recommendations have been disregarded."

He enumerates some of the misdoings of the trustees, and goes on: "Thus, instead of system, we have incongruity, and chaos has usurped the seat of harmony and good order."

And he concludes: "My own experience has abundantly proved that the exploded country system, which the recent laws have imposed upon the city, will prove a failure equally signal."

For some years the ward schools and the public schools existed side by side, but the new system was popular, and was favored in the division of public moneys. In spite of skill and prudence, rigid economy and superior organization, the society found its revenues unequal to its growing needs. It could neither repair its buildings nor construct or hire new ones, and in 1848 it was forbidden by law to open new schools without the consent of the Board of Education. In 1853 the society gave up the unequal contest, transferred its schools to the city, and ended its useful and honorable career.

The field of education was now divided between twenty-two independent democracies. The need was seen for providing a more perfect union, and some steps were taken to strengthen the central authority. A Chief Superintendent was appointed with considerable powers, including the licensing of teachers. The purchase of books and supplies for all the schools was committed to the Board of Education, and the salaries of teachers throughout the city were fixed by general rules.

In 1858 Governor King transmitted to the Legislature the report of a commission appointed to examine the schools of New York city. It was painstaking and elaborate. At that time two commissioners, two inspectors, and eight trustees, in all twelve school officers, were elected by the people of each ward. The legislative commission noted that:

"The various wards of the city are very unequal in population and superficial extent."

They reported that: "The school-houses are various in capacity, comfort, and accommodation."

"Some schools are overflowing, others diminish in numbers."

"The want of simplicity in the system is one of the chief difficulties."

"The multitude of officers and functionaries, the peculiar distribution of power, the power exercised by ward officers over the scholastic department.... present a system of complexity unjust and uncalled-for."

"It is one thing to designate existing evils in such a complex system; it is another to suggest an adequate remedy."

And the commission asked for an extension of its powers that it might frame the needed measure of reform. Unhappily the request was not granted. The

Board of Education declined to be reformed. Its president, Mr. Andrew H. Green, defended the existing system in a vigorous address. He saw clearly that if the schools were to succeed they must be popular, and he thought that no system could be popular which was not administered by officers chosen directly by the people.

"The introduction of twelve men into the management of the schools in each ward, selected from those by whom they were elected, supplies a feature necessary to their success by commanding the confidence of the electors and their families."

"If it be true that the centralization of management in the hands of an association not elected by the people, but appointed, and having the power of a close corporation to perpetuate itself, will secure more system and economy, while you reduce expenses you will reduce the number of scholars, and the jealousies and dissatisfaction which have characterized the schools under other management will spring up."

"I see no occasion for legislation to perfect the theory of the system."

He called upon the Board of Education to overcome the evils, which he saw plainly enough, by an energetic use of its authority, till then untried.

Mr. Randall, the City Superintendent, followed this masterful leadership. In 1856 he had said that the organization needed modification and improvement. In December, 1857, he reported that things were not so bad, after all.

"A system which, however defective and imperfect it may be in some or even many of its provisions, is found upon the whole.... satisfactorily to accomplish the substantial object of its creation, and to fulfil the public expectation, should not lightly be subjected to the dangerous process of revision and reconstruction."

So was established the New York city system of administering common schools —a system whose several faults may perhaps be equalled in other cities, but which in its combination of disadvantages is without a peer.

For many years no school officer has been elected by the people, and yet the schools are crowded and the system is popular. Mr. Green's apprehensions, baseless as they now seem, enable us to understand how rapidly political thought has changed in a generation. It has come to be fairly well understood that the people of a great city can administer its affairs, as a great nation can govern itself, only by devising a representative system which will put all the power of the people into the hands of responsible public servants for reasonable periods. We are not yet agreed as to whether an autocratic mayor or an absolute council is best, but nobody would now propose that the voters of the city should elect two hundred and sixty-four officers to administer the affairs of one department.

In 1864 a law provided for the election of twenty-one commissioners from seven large districts, and for the appointment of inspectors by the Mayor. In 1869 the number of commissioners was reduced to twelve, chosen from the city at large. In 1871 it was provided that the Mayor should appoint commissioners and trustees. In 1873 the number of commissioners was restored to twenty-one, and the Board of Education was empowered to appoint the trustees. In 1893 the Legislature created a commission to revise the New York city school law. Its report shows the same essential defects of organization which Governor King's commission exposed nearly forty years ago.

"A system so complicated of necessity results in inefficient action and protracted delays.... and renders it almost impossible to fix responsibility where it justly belongs."

Since 1857 all the administrative branches of the city government, the departments concerned with the police and firemen, the docks, the parks, the charities, the public works, the public health, and the cleaning of the streets, have been successively remodelled and rationally organized. In good hands they all work well. Even in bad hands they continue to perform their functions, and whenever anything goes wrong the responsibility for it can be fixed. It is discreditable that the essential vices of the school system should have been left undisturbed for forty years. It is true that the machinery has been from time to time improved in details of operation, but, on the other hand, the work to be done has enormously increased, and the education of three hundred thousand children is now mismanaged on the same clumsy plan which was shown to be inadequate to the requirements of fifty thousand.

III.

It is not possible within the limits of this article to do more than refer to some of the conspicuous defects of the system.

The fundamental vice is the division of power, and consequent destruction of responsibility.

The Board of Education is the central authority, but in each of the twenty-four wards there is a board of five trustees. These appoint and remove teachers and janitors, nominate and virtually appoint principals; they conduct and manage the schools, and furnish supplies therefor; they procure sites, and erect new schoolhouses, and repair and alter the old ones. With the exercise of some of these powers the Board of Education may interfere, as may the District Inspectors, and the City Superintendent, and the State Superintendent of Public Instruction; and out of the conflict of authority grow constant controversies, which occasionally blossom into scandal. When the construction of a much-needed school is delayed for years because two boards cannot agree upon a site, or when one board gives an order to principals, and another board with equal authority forbids them to obey it, we are disgusted even while we are diverted. But the evils which flow from conflicting authority are probably less than those which come from misplaced authority.

The Commissioners of Education are prominent in the community; they meet publicly and keep full records, and thus are accountable for their actions. But how can we follow the doings of these twenty-four ward committees of five? They have nearly all the patronage and substantial power, and they act obscurely and without responsibility.

It is to be noted that the principle of local self-government is not involved. It would not be easy to show that the principle could be applied. There are regions of the city where the American common school will not thrive if left to local influences. But, however this may be, the Boards of Trustees are at present appointed by the Board of Education, and so are not springs of popular force, but only scattered tanks into which authority is drawn away from the central reservoir.

The wards are divisions of the city long disused for most governmental purposes, and now known only to school officers and conveyancers. The inequalities noted by Governor King's commission have increased with the growth and movement of the population. In the Third Ward nothing remains of the school system but the Board of Trustees. In the Second Ward there is one primary school, with an average attendance of forty-six. In the Twelfth Ward are twenty schools. The expenditure controlled by the trustees is over $630,000 a year; the number of children enrolled is over 56,000 — a school population about equal to that of Albany, Troy, Rochester, and Syracuse combined. Is there any other city where such great powers as those of the Twelfth Ward trustees are exercised with so few of the guarantees which publicity furnishes? It is a striking instance of the moderation of Tammany Hall that the list of its General Committee contains the names of only four of these five oligarchs. It may also be noted, though with less surprise, that not one of the schoolless trustees of the Third Ward appears to belong to the General Committee.

A grave defect in the school system is the weakness of the professional element in its general management.

There is an accepted formula used in making scientific skill and knowledge available for the good of the community. In pursuance of it public buildings and aqueducts and bridges are constructed, and hospitals and colleges are maintained. Laymen control the expenditure, and prescribe the scope and purpose of the undertaking, but they commit the work itself to the hands of an expert architect, engineer, physician, teacher, as the case may be. From this rule our school system widely departs. There is a City Superintendent, but his tenure is too insecure, his powers too limited, and the number of his assistants too small. In this last respect we are not so well off as formerly, for there are but eight assistants for 300,000 scholars, or about one to each 37,000, whereas in 1857 there were three assistants and 50,000 scholars, or one superintendent to less than 17,000 scholars. An increase in the number of superintendents does not necessarily involve increased expense. The supervision of our schools is now very costly, but it is almost all local supervision. Three hundred and twenty-four principals and vice-principals, sometimes several under one roof, are engaged in it. Competent authorities say that proper reorganization and redistribution of duties will give us better supervision at less cost. It should be made possible for the Board of Education to consider this question. It results from the present plan that a great deal of work strictly professional, such as the planning of courses of study, the choice of text-books, and the like, is done by the commissioners. This was natural enough when the New York schools were found-ed, for there were then no experts in pub-lic education. Now, however, pedagogy has become a science, and the managing of public schools is an art. To practise it requires special training, as does sur-gery or engineering. It is an unsatisfac-tory arrangement which makes it the duty of a board of laymen to provide the clas-sification of studies and scholars, while twenty-four boards of laymen are choos-ing the teachers, and eight other boards of laymen are inspecting their work.

The Inspectors of Common Schools were, in 1842, introduced into our city organization as a part of the "exploded country system," and it may be remarked that the office in the rural districts was long ago abolished. At first there were forty-four of them here, elected by the people; now there are twenty-four, ap-pointed from eight districts by the Mayor. Their powers are also exercised by other officials, but the inspectors are endowed with functions of interruption and an-noyance which enable them to retard the transaction of business, and sometimes to prevent the licensing or removal of a teacher. For fifty years they have con-tributed to the confusion of our educa-tional system. I cannot learn that any one thinks it desirable that they should continue.

IV.

Mayor Gilroy's commission, in 1893, un-like Governor King's commission, in 1857, suggested what it considered an adequate remedy for these chronic ills.

In the intervening years the problem had been greatly simplified. The general principles on which a system of public instruction should be based have become as well understood as the method of or-ganizing a ship's crew, and Dr. Rice and other observers have pointed out how great cities can adapt to their use sys-tems which in smaller communities have proved successful.

It is the opinion of most people compe-tent to judge that the bill framed by the commission accords with recognized prin-ciples, and takes due account of existing circumstances, and that under it a good Board of Education can do good work. That, after all, is as much as can be hoped from human institutions. The Commis-sioners of Education, after making some amendments suggested by their experi-ence, unanimously recommended the bill to the Legislature, so that the proposed reform has the official approval which was lacking in 1857. It has also received much support from the newspapers, and from the clubs and societies, which at once indicate and help to form public opinion, and it has been approved by the Committee of Seventy. I have seen but one published dissent from the plan of the commission. It has been suggested that the Board of Education should con-sist of only a small number of com-missioners, who should receive a salary. At first sight such a plan seems to have advantages. In some respects the busi-ness efficiency of the board would be increased, but it would become sooner or later a home for professional politi-cians. More than this, paid commission-ers would undoubtedly exercise a constant and excessive control over the profession-al work; and instead of the management of experts we should have the rule of sciolists. It would be as if a board of college trustees should be constantly in attendance directing the college work.

The payment of commissioners would also seem to be unwise because the estab-lished American practice is to leave the work of education to unpaid boards. So great a city is not the place to try exper-iments in such matters. Ordinary pru-dence would thus dictate. But a higher motive than prudence prompts us not to break away from the general custom. The American citizen is not usually generous in his dealings with the State. The Eng-lish institution of unpaid legislators and magistrates has never flourished here, and we have the habit of exacting compensa-tion from the community for all that we do for it. But in regard to public educa-tion this is not so. From the district school to the university all its branches are controlled by unpaid officers. The instruction of youth is thus kept apart from other public labors, because men feel that when serving these little ones in an especial and solemn sense they serve their country and their God. From so noble a tradition it is not wise lightly to depart.

THE METROPOLITAN OPERA HOUSE

APOLLO CROWNED BY THE MUSES—FOR CENTRAL PANEL ABOVE CURTAIN.

"FROM a psalm of Asaph," remarked the late Mr. Carlyle, in one of his most bilious seasons of reflection, "to a seat at the London opera in the Haymarket, what a road have men travelled!" The distempered sage had himself, upon one occasion, been induced to take a seat in the London opera, which he abandoned during the ballet, upon the ground, as he subsequently explained, that he "hadn't the heart to stay and watch a woman with an immortal soul making a Manx penny of herself." The outcome of all the cost and of the various art that had been lavished upon the performance he declared to be "an hour's amusement, not amusing either, but wearisome and dreary, to a high-dizened, select populace of male and female persons, who seemed to me not much worth amusing."

These are extremely bilious remarks; but it must be owned that to many persons the Italian opera in its present estate makes no more appeal as a serious form of art than it did to Carlyle or to Wagner. The high-dizened, select populace is very apt to wear a bored aspect except when a Patti or a Nilsson or a Schalchi or a Campanini breaks in for moments upon its apathy at the crisis of an aria. The interest in opera is at least three parts social to one part musical. To recur to our Jeremiad: "Euterpe and Melpomene, sent for regardless of expense, were but the vehicles of a kind of service which I judged to be Paphian rather." The more, or possibly the less, wonderful the heroic and unexampled sacrifices which are laid upon the operatic shrine! An impresario was long ago defined as a person who paid all his money for the pleasure of being blackguarded by everybody, and the definition remains so far true that the successful managers of Italian opera who have escaped its perils with their lives and fortunes are scattered columns in a waste of ruins. And yet the seed of the martyrs of Italian opera continues to fructify. From the lean and primitive opera seasons which Mr. Richard Grant White not long ago commemorated in a very interesting series of magazine papers until now the "cause" has never lacked a forlorn hope. A whole procession of Curtiuses, each girded with an orchestra and a chorus, and brandishing his poetical prospectus in his good right hand, have followed each other into the gulf of insolvency, which obstinately declines to close over them. Managers who have amassed competences in the more prosaic departments of their calling do not consider their careers rounded until they have embraced the opportunity to beggar themselves in behalf of the lyric drama.

Nor is it only these altruistic servants of "society" who burn the lamp of sacrifice before this modern shrine. In what other cause of charity or of culture would it be possible so to enlist the men of business who have for years carried the New York Academy of Music, and cheerfully threw what, from a commercial point of view, was the good money of assessment after the bad of hopeless investment? In what other cause would it have been found

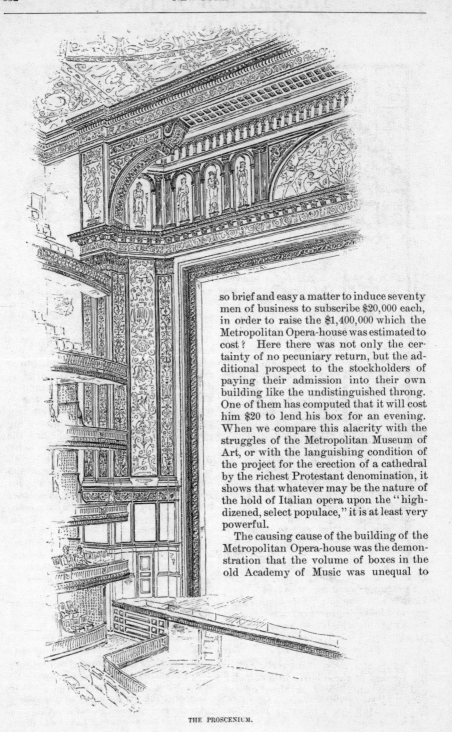

so brief and easy a matter to induce seventy men of business to subscribe $20,000 each, in order to raise the $1,400,000 which the Metropolitan Opera-house was estimated to cost? Here there was not only the certainty of no pecuniary return, but the additional prospect to the stockholders of paying their admission into their own building like the undistinguished throng. One of them has computed that it will cost him $20 to lend his box for an evening. When we compare this alacrity with the struggles of the Metropolitan Museum of Art, or with the languishing condition of the project for the erection of a cathedral by the richest Protestant denomination, it shows that whatever may be the nature of the hold of Italian opera upon the "high-dizened, select populace," it is at least very powerful.

The causing cause of the building of the Metropolitan Opera-house was the demonstration that the volume of boxes in the old Academy of Music was unequal to

THE PROSCENIUM.

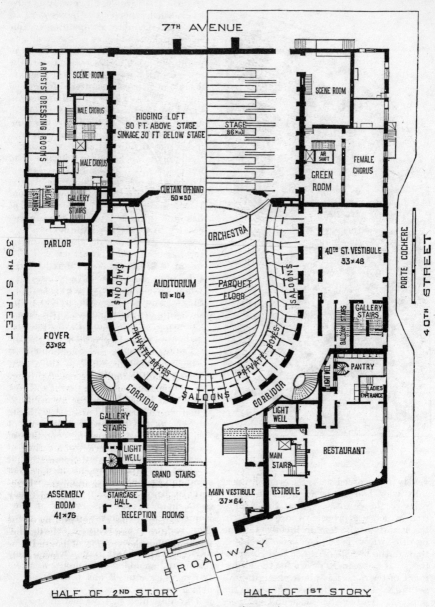

Labels within the plan:

7TH AVENUE

39TH STREET

40TH STREET

ARTISTS' DRESSING ROOMS

SCENE ROOM

MALE CHORUS

MALE CHORUS

BALCONY STAIRS

GALLERY STAIRS

RIGGING LOFT 90 FT. ABOVE STAGE SINKAGE 30 FT BELOW STAGE

STAGE 86×101

CURTAIN OPENING 50×50

SCENE ROOM

AIR SHAFT

GREEN ROOM

FEMALE CHORUS

ORCHESTRA

PARLOR

AUDITORIUM 101×104

PARQUET FLOOR

SALOONS

40TH ST. VESTIBULE 33×48

SALOONS

PORTE COCHERE

FOYER 83×82

PRIVATE BOXES

PRIVATE BOXES

GALLERY STAIRS

BALCONY STAIRS

PANTRY

LIGHT WELL

LADIES ENTRANCE

CORRIDOR

SALOONS

CORRIDOR

GALLERY STAIRS

LIGHT WELL

LIGHT WELL

RESTAURANT

LIGHT WELL

MAIN STAIRS

GRAND STAIRS

STAIRCASE HALL

RECEPTION ROOMS

MAIN VESTIBULE 37×64

VESTIBULE

ASSEMBLY ROOM 41×76

BROADWAY

HALF OF 2ND STORY

HALF OF 1ST STORY

PLAN OF OPERA-HOUSE (INTERIOR).

the wants of society. Beggarly as was the account of these boxes in a commercial sense, and freely as their owners grumbled about their possessions to the reporters with the advent of each suc-cessive season, they showed no willing-ness to part with them to any of the in-creasing number of New-Yorkers who were entitled to aspire to the financial and social distinction of an opera-box,

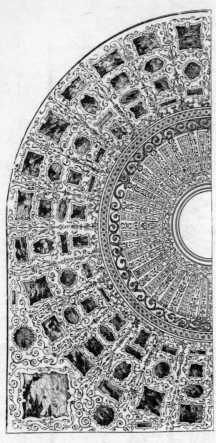

DESIGN OF CEILING.

boxes. The parquet, however, was rarely crowded, whereas the boxes were always taken, and the competition became so keen that the boxes of the Academy of Music quite lost their character of unprofitable investments. Just before the project of the new opera-house was undertaken, $30,000 was offered for one of them. This condition of affairs culminated during the operatic season of 1880, and in the course of the following summer sundry gentlemen who had been unable to obtain suitable accommodations in the old building determined to build an opera-house for themselves. The stately structure we are describing was the result of that determination. It was a very short and easy matter, as has been intimated, to raise the sum necessary to secure the building of a new opera-house. Indeed, while the building has been under construction, a premium of $5000 has been offered for the title of a box. Seventy subscribers, whose investment at present is between $15,000 and $20,000 each, united themselves in the Metropolitan Opera-house Company. The name itself indicates rather a long stride away from the "Psalm of Asaph." The opera-house in Fourteenth Street, which is rather less than a generation old, would have failed of subscriptions if it had not been presented to the public under the guise of an "Academy of Music." The opera-house in Brooklyn — as interesting a piece of architecture as the Fourteenth Street building is uninteresting — has been described by a satirist as an edifice which the subscribers intended to look as much like a church as it could without actually being a church, in which "they could hold a religious revival if they wanted to, and a Shakspearean revival if they had to." It is quite certain that when these edifices were built, it would have been as difficult to obtain the money for an undissembled opera-house as twenty-five years later it has proved easy to obtain ten times as much.

The site which then seemed most available for the purposes of an opera-house was the plot near the Grand Central Station, bounded by Madison and Vanderbilt avenues, Forty-third and Forty-fourth streets, nearly a square of 200 feet. It was for this site that the preliminary drawings were made which the committee in charge invited from four well-known architects.

yearly re-enforced as these were by persons who had made fortunes in other parts of the country. That this aspiration, which was probably more fervent in the breasts of the female members of the families whose heads competed for boxes than in the breasts of the actual competitors, was not a mere desire for the enjoyment of opera, seems plain enough. No actual hardship is attached to a seat in the parquet. In fact the music and the spectacle are at least as available from that humble station as from the coigne of vantage in the box tier, and the philosopher who occasionally goes to the opera, even if his liver be in much more tolerable order than that of Mr. Carlyle, can not have failed to remark that the most attentive looking and listening is not done from the

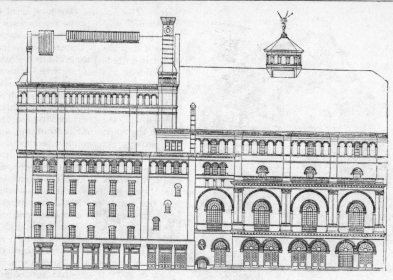

SIDE VIEW ON THIRTY-NINTH STREET.

The design submitted by Mr. J. Cleaveland Cady was accepted, and he was appointed architect of the work. But it was soon after discovered that the adjoining owners held under a guarantee that the plot in question should not be occupied for certain specified uses, among which prohibited uses was the erection of any place of public amusement, and that satisfactory waivers could not in all cases be obtained, even in the cause of Italian opera. This seeming obstacle was an excellent thing for the project, since a square of 200 feet does not afford space for the satisfaction of the complicated and conflicting requirements of modern opera. The competing architects had recognized this fact, some of them by stinting the stage and its accessories, some by diminishing the auditorium, and some by cramping the space devoted to the foyer and the lobbies. A glance at the ground-plan of a typical modern opera-house, say that of the New Opera in Paris, shows how small a part of the whole is devoted to the audience, or is even brought to the notice of the ordinary attendant upon opera, in comparison with the space devoted to the acces-

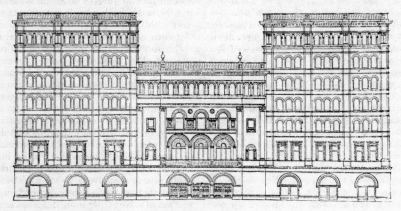

FRONT VIEW, ON BROADWAY.

BACK VIEW, ON SEVENTH AVENUE.

sories of the entertainment. The removal to a site which gave sixty feet of additional length not only enabled the architect to give a more liberal treatment to all the parts, but left two corners on the Broadway front of which the opera will require only the two lower stories, while the upper stories are to be devoted to apartments for bachelors.

It is not to be supposed, however, that there were no longer any sacrifices to be made. The design of an opera-house is at every point a compromise between conflicting claims. Fortunately there was no question between the two great divisions of the house, the stage and the auditorium. On the larger site, which by advancing the entrance and the main staircase left almost, if not quite, the area of the original site to be divided between them, there was no need of a sacrifice of either to the other. The auditorium is quite the largest in the world, exceeding its closest rivals, San Carlo, at Naples, and La Scala, at Milan, by some feet in every dimension. The stage is exceeded in area only by two, that of the Imperial Opera in St. Petersburg and that of the New Opera in Paris. But it is evident from the plan that the dependencies of the auditorium have been in some degree sacrificed to the auditorium itself. This sacrifice is not of the stairways, by any means,

but simply of the corridors, which are in some places narrowed beyond what an architect entirely untrammelled as to space would probably think desirable for the free circulation of an audience between the acts. The number of occupants in each tier of the boxes is so small, 222 being the maximum, and only the male half of these being liable to engagements between the acts, that the narrowing of the corridors does not threaten any physical inconvenience, but only some impairment of the character of dignity and spaciousness which it is desirable to give to the corridors.

The entrances and exits, indeed, are entirely ample, almost beyond example elsewhere. It has often been pointed out how far inferior modern public buildings are in means of access and departure to those of the Romans. It would not occur to anybody to call the doorways of a modern building *vomitoria*, even if modern notions of verbal propriety did not restrain him. Here, however, with the rare good fortune in New York of a building standing free on all four sides, it was comparatively easy to contrive ample and separate entrances to all parts of the house, at no greater inconvenience than that of an increase in the number of ticket takers. The great double staircase, which is gained from the Broadway entrance, through a vestibule 63 × 37, in two flights, each of twelve feet in width, gives access to all parts of the house except the gallery, that is to say, to the three tiers of boxes and the balcony of which the auditorium consists, the parquet being practically on the level of the entrance floor. There are also large vestibules midway down each side, that on Thirty-ninth Street 70 × 33, that on Fortieth Street 50 × 33. To each of these entrances carriages may drive un-

der cover of a permanent veranda of metal, and from each a
winding staircase, contrived in the space between the curve of
the amphitheatre and the rectangle in which it is inscribed,
gives access to the boxes; while from each of these side entrances a staircase rises to the balcony, and two to the gallery,
these latter four stairways giving the only access to the galleries,
and being shut off from the rest of the house throughout their
whole course by stout brick walls. It is estimated that the
house can be emptied by these multiplied and abundant means
in three minutes, and even after making a liberal allowance for
the difference between theory and practice which may arise
from the unfamiliarity of many of the audience with the readi-
est exit, it seems clear that the house, which can be emptied in
three minutes, will be emptied in a surprisingly brief space for
its great size, and in this respect will come nearer than most
modern buildings to the Roman standard.

The interior form of an opera-house is distinctly established
by experience as the amphitheatrical, and very few innovations
upon this typical form are possible. The amphitheatre in this
case seems elongated beyond what is usual, and then widens at
the stage end so as to give it more nearly the form of a lyre
than of "the glittering horseshoe's ample round," which belongs
to the conventional temple of the lyric drama. The modification of the curve which produces this result is, however, slight.
There is a more important departure from the conventional
opera-house,

> "Where flame on flame the immense proscenium glows,
>   With magic counterchange of gold and rose,"

for the proscenium is altogether omitted. In the Fourteenth
Street Academy the proscenium boxes have been objects of
desire to achieve which there have been given whole seasons
of intrigue and social politics. Inasmuch as the proscenium
could not be extended so as to include the amphitheatre, it was
resolved to cut the Gordian knot of preference by abolishing
the occasion of rivalry, and converting the stockholders into an
oligarchy, indeed, but not into a graded hierarchy — into a
republic of oligarchs with no precedence among themselves,
nodding on equal terms all round Olympus. A widely splayed
opening of a very few feet in depth, decorated with large
pilasters at the re-entrant angle, and still for convenience called
the proscenium, is the only representative of the abolished
feature.

The purpose of making any box as desirable as any other box
has by no means been attained, however, when the proscenium
has been abolished; and the study of "sight lines" and acoustics,
so as in some measure to bring this about, is one of the chief of
the many problems which beset the architect of an opera-house.
In the present case sight lines were drawn from every part of
the house in each tier to the sides and the rear of the stage, to
ascertain how much of the view of the stage would be lost from
that point, and the contour of the auditorium and the pitch of
each tier were modified in conformity with the results of these
studies to the arrangement actually adopted. The result has
been so satisfactory that it is safe to say that there is no theatre
in which there are fewer bad seats in proportion to its size, nor
any opera-house in which the difference between the best and
the worst boxes is so small.

There are three tiers and a half of boxes—122 altogether.

DESIGN OF PILASTER.

The half-tier utilizes, in "baignoir" boxes, the side walls of the parquet, or rather of that half of the parquet nearest the stage, where the pitch of the floor makes room for them. Over this, in succession, are the parterre, the first and second tiers, and then the balcony and the gallery. These last two are simply seated with chairs, like an ordinary theatre. The parterre and the so-called "first" tier are distributed among the stockholders, with four boxes over, since there are only seventy subscribers to thirty-seven boxes in each of these tiers. The twelve baignoirs and the thirty-six boxes of the second tier are left at the disposal of the manager. For some mysterious reason—possibly the facility of escape between the acts—the baignoirs are expected to be especially attractive to clubs. The three full tiers are counterparts of each other, except that the uppermost is one box the shorter. The boxes themselves are all of the same dimensions, seven feet front by thirteen deep, divided nearly midway of their depth by an upholstered partition into a salon so called and a box proper, and they are intended for six persons each. They are screened from each other by panels set in iron frames against the partitions. It is plain that the intention has prevailed to make them as nearly of equal value as may be, and the same accommodations of smoking-rooms, dressing-rooms, and the like dependencies are given to each tier.

The seating capacity of the house seems arranged with a liberality almost extravagant. The total number of seats is 3045, divided as follows: parquette, 600; baignoir, 72; parterre, 216; first tier, 222; second tier, 222; balcony, 735; gallery, 978. And yet the New Opera in Paris, which occupies nearly if not quite as great an area, has only 2156 seats.

In its foyer and assembly-rooms the Metropolitan Opera-house is very amply provided. The foyer proper, which will be ample for all but the largest public balls and assemblies for which the opera-house may be required, is a great room on the south side of the building, 85 × 43 in area, and very lofty. When the southern corner building is completed, the second story of this building, constituting a single apartment of 33 × 67, will connect the foyer with the large room over the main entrance, making a suite of 214 feet in length. This great advantage has not

been gained without some loss. The main staircase has been sacrificed—not as a practical staircase at all, but as an architectural feature of the interior—to the desire to make the most out of the room over the vestibule.

The facilities for emptying the opera-house, while they are beyond those of almost any other theatre, are less needed than in almost any other theatre. Their amplitude is a matter of convenience, not a matter of safety. The destiny of a theatre almost proverbially is to die by fire, and there is scarcely a famous theatre in the world which has not been rebuilt more than once. Here it has been attempted to construct not merely a slow-burning but a really fire-proof theatre. The only combustible material it contains, outside of the stage, is the wood used in the floors and their furrings, and in the fittings of the galleries. The stairways throughout are of iron in brick wells; the partitions, apart from the main walls of brick, are of fire-proof material, the construction of the floors of fire-proof arches turned between iron beams, the flooring of the corridors of tiles. The ceiling is a great sheet of metal hung from metal bars, and its dome a great saucer of the same material hung from the roof. The partition which runs from the floor of the parquette to the floor of the gallery is of fire-proof blocks stiffened by a system of iron studs. The roof rests upon the elliptical walls of the auditorium, which are the main constructional walls of the building, and the roof construction is of iron trusses. The supports of the gallery are iron beams anchored in the walls of the auditorium. Many difficulties arose in applying this construction to the ever-varying lines and forms required in an opera-house, and many interesting expedients were adopted to overcome them. In order to gain an easy descent from the corridors to the front of the boxes, for example, it was found necessary to interpolate two steps, and this necessitated a double bending of the rolled beams which were to carry the galleries. Moreover, as both the pitch and the slope were continually changing, no beams would require exactly the same bending, except the pairs opposite each other in the same tier. The contractor found it necessary to erect a mill of his own in which the beams could be bent as well as rolled. The proscenium wall is continued twenty-five feet above the au-

THE BALLET.   THE CHORUS.

DESIGNS FOR PANELS ABOVE CURTAIN.

ditorium, and required to be supported from the walls on either side of the curtain opening. A brick arch was not practicable from lack of abutment. The expedient adopted was a truss some eighty feet in length by fifteen in depth, upon which the gable wall of the stage stands, and to which it is additionally secured by rods built in the brick-work. A smaller truss spans the curtain opening.

The stage is required to be an open space from top to bottom and from side to side. The end wall of the building, corresponding to that carried by the truss over the proscenium, thus becomes an isolated piece of brick-work, unstiffened by floors,

125 feet high from the street, and 106 feet wide. It is an unbroken surface within, but on the outside is re-enforced by two massive buttresses five feet deep. The roofing of the stage is also an interesting piece of construction, for it is not often that a roof of 106 feet clear span is required to be set upon walls 101 feet high. This is effected here by an iron truss, set upon rollers to provide for the expansion and contraction of the metal throughout so great a span.

As the stage is the point of any theatre especially vulnerable to fire, it is of prime importance to confine to the stage any fire that may originate there. This is accomplished not only by making the rest of the house incombustible, but by converting the stage itself into a flue, inclosed in the brick walls which rise above the rest of

TERRA-COTTA PANEL ON FACADE.

the house. A large skylight in the roof of the stage is weighted so as to fall open when its fastenings are removed, and these fastenings are arranged to give way at a comparatively low temperature, and thus open the top of the chimney of which the walls are the sides and the proscenium opening the hearth. To put out fires

which may arise on the stage, reliance is placed, beyond the ordinary precautions, upon a novel automatic appliance. A network of small pipes is hung above the stage, filled with water from a tank in the roof, and pierced at frequent intervals with holes stopped with soft solder, which melts readily, and drenches the stage as from a great shower-bath.

Among the novelties the arrangement of the orchestra deserves mention. It is placed, not in Wagner's "Mystic Gulf," but in a brick bowl sunk below the parquet, and floored at a level which will leave the musicians visible only from the upper tiers. The sonority of this reservoir is expected materially to re-enforce the volume of tone.

Another novelty is the system of supporting the stage. The supports of the stage must be readily removable, so that any point underneath may be utilized as it may be called for by the varying exigencies of the drama. Ordinarily this requirement is fulfilled by the use of a wilderness of timber supports, any section of which may be knocked away as the space it occupies is needed. This arrangement is hardly compatible with a fire-proof building. Here a light iron construction has been devised, containing some 4000 members, which has all the facility of removal and reconstruction of the carpentry. The cellar of the stage is thirty feet deep from the floor, and this depth is divided into three stories, of which any one, or any section of all three, can be made available at once.

The main elements of the architectural effect of the interior, apart from color, are of course its great size and the grace of its lines. Treatment of detail is of comparatively little importance in the general view, except as it re-enforces these, as we may see in theatres which have not a respectable detail, but which when they are filled present a spectacle of undeniable brilliancy. We have had occasion already to deplore the economy of space which prevented the staircase from asserting itself as an architectural feature, and this is especially to be regretted, since a clever and original treatment would be both more feasible and more effective there, as being better seen, than in the auditorium. The most obvious criticism upon the detail generally is that the architect has not attempted to treat the interesting construction which he has adopted. Occasionally an iron post shows for what it is, and the gallery fronts are unmistakably of metal. But with these exceptions the structure is one thing and its envelope quite another. It is treated, that is to say, in the conventional manner, in which the differences are differences only in refinement of detail. No doubt a more expressive treatment would have been desirable. But it is almost too much to require of a single architect that he should develop a decorative construction suitable to an opera-house from the modern construction of clay and metal which has been employed here. There are almost no precedents in point. M. Viollet-le-Duc, indeed, made some essays—on paper—toward the solution of this problem, but they were not so felicitous as to allure his successors to follow them. At all events, if a single architect could be called upon to develop the architecture of an opera-house out of this construction, he could not be called upon to do it in three years, while also meeting all the practical exigencies of so great a work. Moreover, it may well be doubted whether a really serious architectural treatment of an opera-house, such, for example, as would befit a real "Academy of Music," would not strike the operagoer, that is to say, the citizen in an opera hat and an opera frame of mind, with a certain sense of incongruity. He does not go to the opera, he would say, or feel, to study, nor even to have things explained to him; he goes to be lapped against eating cares in soft Lydian airs, and he prefers the Lydian mode also in the appointments of the place. A treatment *mezzo serio*, as Rossini said of his own music to the "Stabat Mater," is all that he will willingly endure. The architectural treatment of the interior is concentrated upon the proscenium wall. The truss already spoken of above the curtain opening is relieved at the ends by vigorously projected brackets, and the re-entrant angles of the splay are re-enforced, after the manner of the Italian Renaissance, with panelled pilasters. The wall above the opening is modelled into niches with a large panel in the centre, upon which Mr. Lathrop's allegory of "Apollo crowned by the Muses" is to be painted. On the piers flanking the opening at the level of the gallery are Mr. Maynard's figures "The Chorus" and "The Ballet." The panels of the large pilasters at the opening are filled with delicate ornaments in cast metal.

Color, however, is the chief element in the decoration, and the attainment of "tone" the test of its success. A mellow golden tint is the resultant tone aimed at

TERRA-COTTA PANEL ON FACADE.

from the combination of colors employed in this interior. The necessity of a red background for an audience in full dress is almost as well settled as the amphitheatrical form itself. This convention has been recognized here in the upholstery of the boxes, which is of a silk specially

TERRA-COTTA PANEL ON FACADE.

manufactured for the purpose, having a ground of red interspersed with threads of gold-color. The field of the vast ceiling is of a deep ivory yellow, overlaid with a design in deeper colors. A modification of the same tint is the color of the walls, in the comparatively unimportant spaces of these which are visible from the body of the house. The pilasters and brackets of the proscenium arch are to be of gold, oxidized to mellow its glare. For the effect of this scheme of decoration, which has been carried out, under the supervision of the architect, by Mr. Treadwell, we must await the "first night," which is destined to become so memorable in the annals of opera in New York.

The exterior of the building is considerably less like the stereotyped treatment of an opera-house than the interior. Costly as the building is, it is so very large as to limit the expenditure upon its external architecture. And this limitation seems to have determined the architect, together with other considerations, to seek for the effect of the great building through simplicity and expressiveness of general composition, and the utmost delicacy of such decorative detail as he must somewhat sparingly employ. The main divisions, the stage, the auditorium, and the portico, are distinctly marked. No architect has yet ventured to exhibit upon a large scale the sweep of the auditorium as part of the external architecture of a theatre, although upon a small scale this has been done, and done with striking success, in the north front of the Casino, just opposite

TERRA-COTTA PANEL ON FACADE.

the new opera-house. The style, in deference, possibly, to the purpose of the building, is Italian, and in the Broadway entrance, which is more copiously decorated than any other part, is a correct and academic Italian Renaissance. This style has more elegance than vigor.

The portico on Broadway is noteworthy not only for the refinement of the detail, which never fails Mr. Cady in whatever style he is working, but for the breadth of the composition. This is secured by strong horizontal belts, and the vertical lines of the large order which runs through two stories, and by the simplicity of the main divisions. The breadth and simplicity of the composition will be enhanced by the more varied masses and broken lines of the flanking structures which are yet to be built. All of the detail has plainly been studied with great care, and all of it is marked by much elegance. The reliefs in the panels, which are unfortunately too small in scale to have, when seen from the street, the effect to which they are really entitled, have the same naïve and child-like grace which belongs to the exquisitely executed imitative modelling introduced in the capitals of the porches. It is noteworthy that this character, which we recognize as that of the early Italian Renaissance before it had stiffened into Vitruvian formula, was the character of the Italian Romanesque, and is as visible in the work of Nicholas Pisano in the thirteenth century as in the work of Luca della Robbia in the fifteenth. Where the architecture escapes from academic trammels, this naïveté may be said to be its note also.